VOLUME 2

STORY BY
YONG-SU HWANG

ART BY
KYUNG-IL YANG

Hammond Public Library
Hammond, IN

🐾 TOKYOPOP®

HAMBURG // LONDON // LOS ANGELES // TOKYO

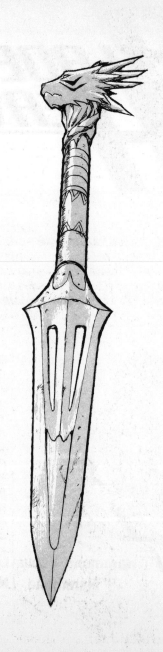

PREVIOUSLY IN

BLADE OF HEAVEN

AFTER BEING CAUGHT IN HEAVEN AND ACCUSED OF STEALING THE LEGENDARY BLADE OF HEAVEN, SOMA WAS FREED BY THE BEAUTIFUL PRINCESS AROOMEE. BEFORE THEY COULD MAKE GOOD THEIR ESCAPE, THEY WERE CONFRONTED BY GENERAL WINTER AND THE KING OF HEAVEN. THE KING ALLOWED SOMA TO RETURN TO EARTH IN ORDER TO SHOW HIS DAUGHTER AROUND THE MORTAL REALM. HOWEVER, THEY WOULD BE ACCOMPANIED BY A CHAPERONE, GEN. WINTER. ON EARTH THE

GROUP ENCOUNTERS THE DIMINUTIVE FAT NINJA, AS WELL AS THE IMPISH BABY DEMON. MEANWHILE, REALIZING THAT THE BLADE OF HEAVEN IS MISSING, THE DEMON BARURUGO LAUNCHES HIS EVIL PLAN TO CONQUER THE KINGDOM OF HEAVEN. BUT THE MYSTERIOUS WARRIOR MAKUMRANG AND HIS UNLIKELY COMPANIONS – SOMA, WINTER AND AROOMEE – WILL HAVE TO BE DEALT WITH FIRST.

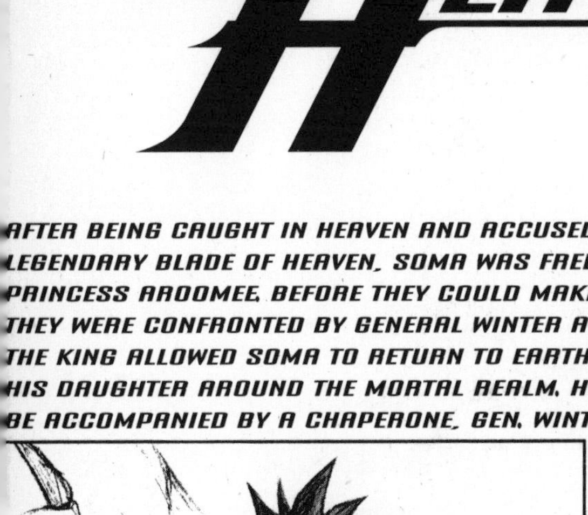

Blade Of Heaven Vol. 2
written by Yong-Su Hwang
illustrated by Kyung-Il Yang

Translation - Lauren Na
English Adaptation - Troy Lewter
Copy Editors - Suzanne Waldman and Peter Ahlstrom
Retouch and Lettering - Abelardo Bigting
Production Artist - Eric Pineda
Cover Design - Anne Marie Horn and Thea Willis

Editor - Bryce P. Coleman
Digital Imaging Manager - Chris Buford
Pre-Press Manager - Antonio DePietro
Production Managers - Jennifer Miller and Mutsumi Miyazaki
Art Director - Matt Alford
Managing Editor - Jill Freshney
VP of Production - Ron Klamert
Editor-in-Chief - Mike Kiley
President and C.O.O. - John Parker
Publisher and C.E.O. - Stuart Levy

A  Manga

TOKYOPOP Inc.
5900 Wilshire Blvd. Suite 2000
Los Angeles, CA 90036

E-mail: info@TOKYOPOP.com
Come visit us online at www.TOKYOPOP.com

ISBN: 1-59532-328-7

First TOKYOPOP printing: May 2005
10 9 8 7 6 5 4 3 2
Printed in the USA

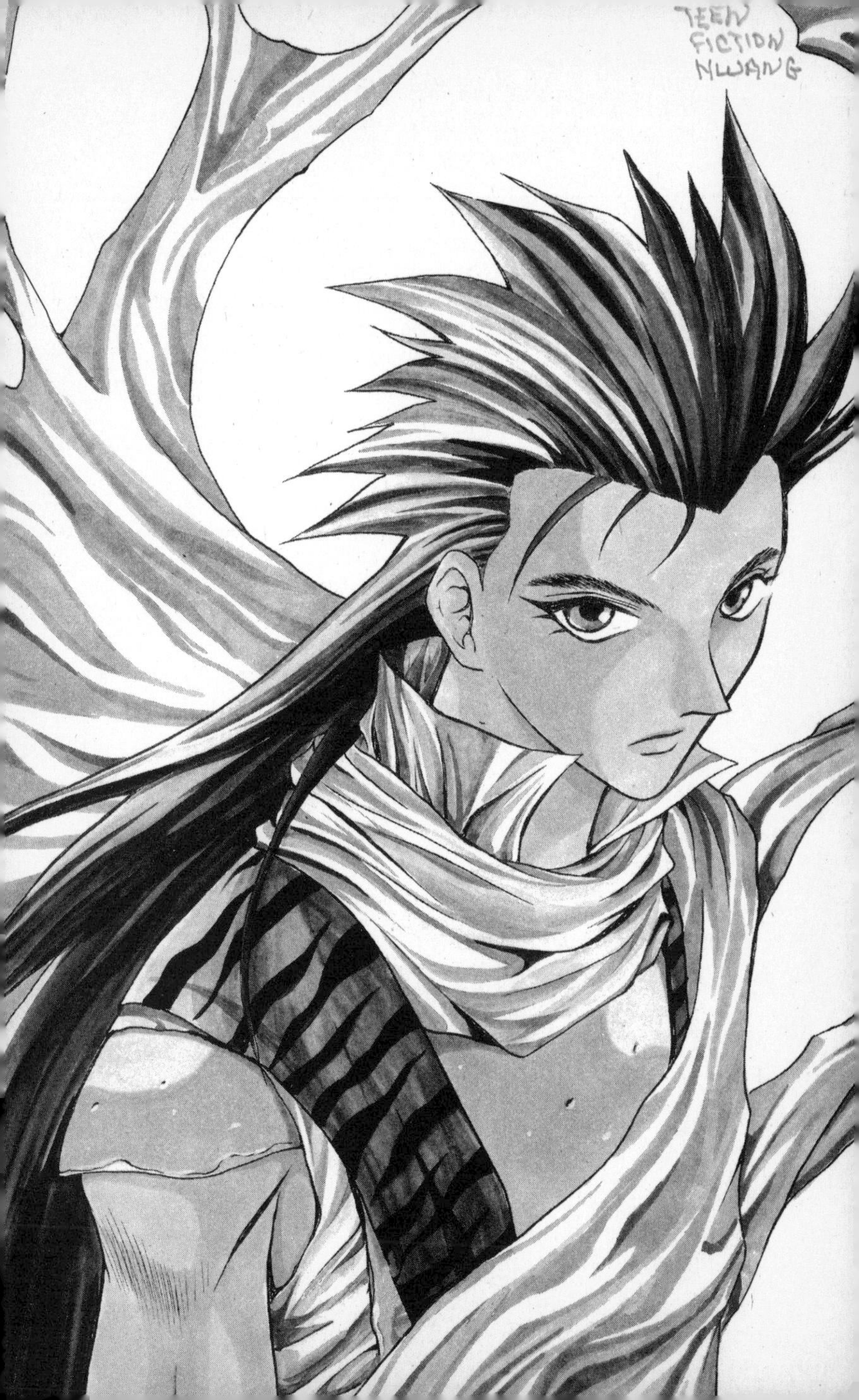

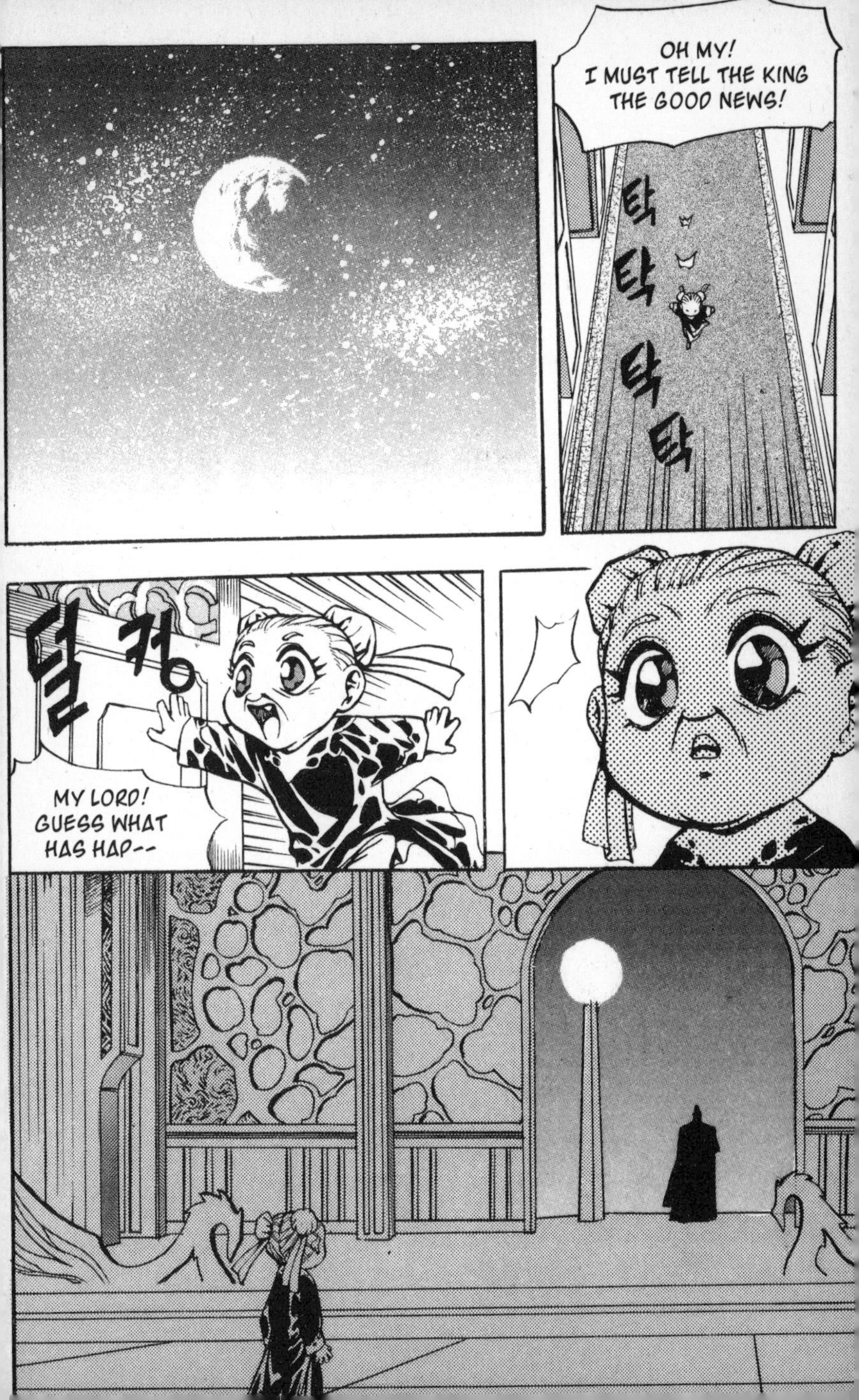
OH MY!
I MUST TELL THE KING
THE GOOD NEWS!
탁탁탁탁
덜컹
MY LORD!
GUESS WHAT
HAS HAP--

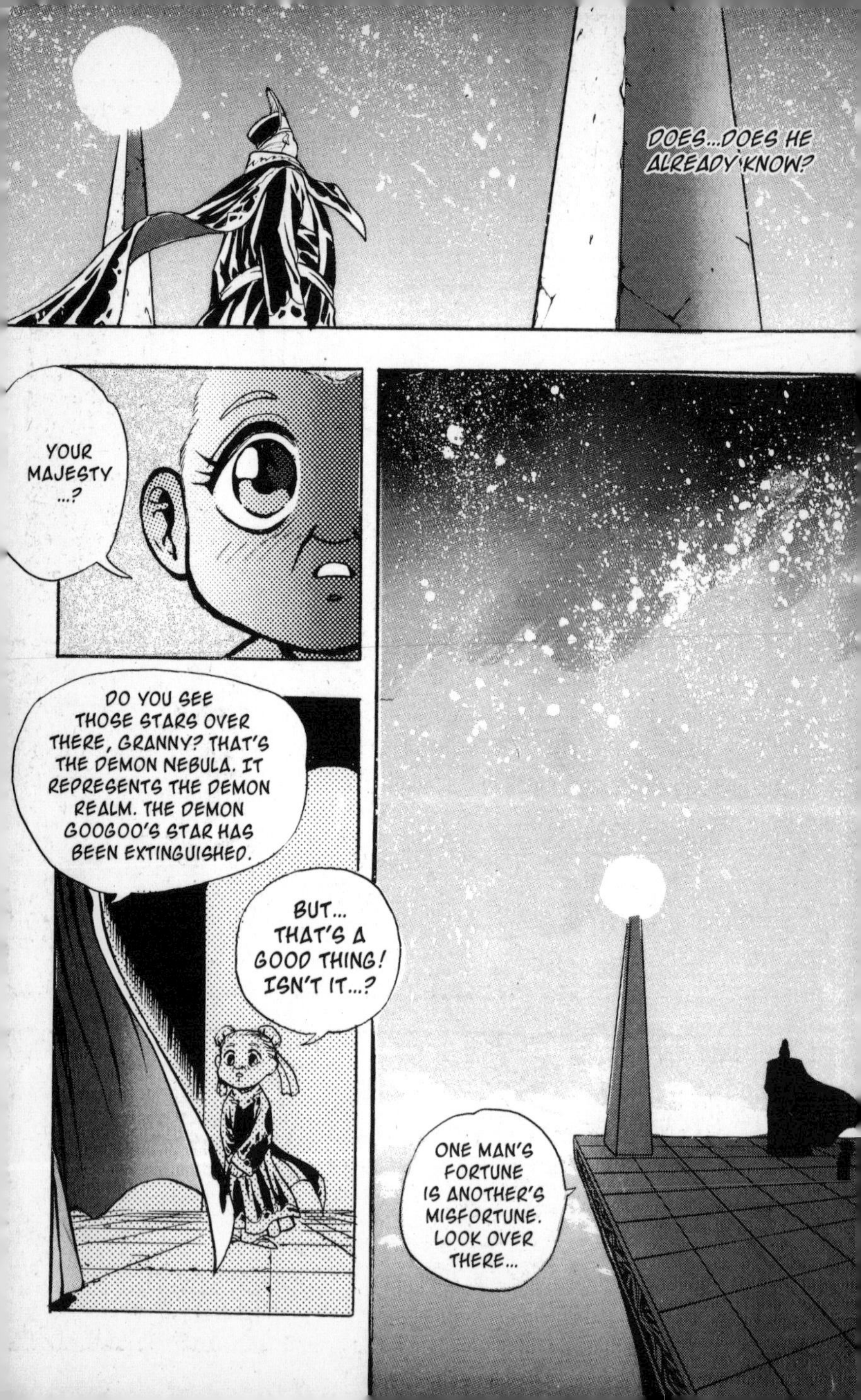
DOES...DOES HE ALREADY KNOW?
YOUR MAJESTY ...?
DO YOU SEE THOSE STARS OVER THERE, GRANNY? THAT'S THE DEMON NEBULA. IT REPRESENTS THE DEMON REALM. THE DEMON GOOGOO'S STAR HAS BEEN EXTINGUISHED.
BUT... THAT'S A GOOD THING! ISN'T IT...?
ONE MAN'S FORTUNE IS ANOTHER'S MISFORTUNE. LOOK OVER THERE...

OH...!
THERE'S A RED
AURA SURROUNDING
THE PHOENIX NEBULA!

Editor: The Phoenix Nebula is the celestial representation of Heaven.

I'VE SEEN THIS
BEFORE...DURING
THE GREAT BATTLE
OF HEAVEN...

BUT...THAT'S
AN OMEN OF
DESTRUCTION!!

THE WAR ISN'T OVER...
THE EVENTS SET IN MOTION THEN
WERE MERELY A PRELUDE
TO A MORE DIABOLICAL PLOT!

SOON, A
MIGHTY WAVE OF
DESTRUCTION WILL
WASH OVER US!

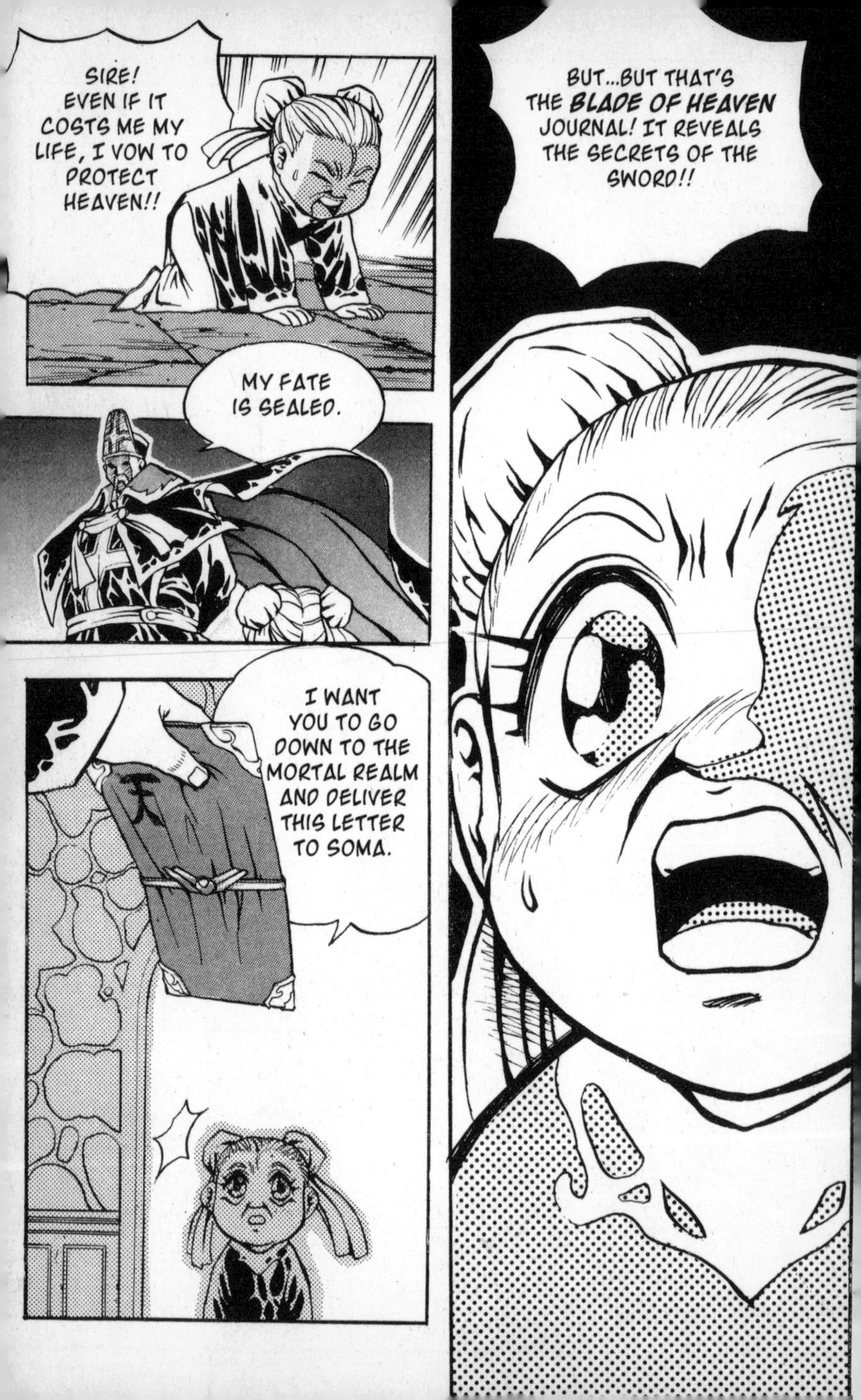
SIRE! EVEN IF IT COSTS ME MY LIFE, I VOW TO PROTECT HEAVEN!!
MY FATE IS SEALED.
I WANT YOU TO GO DOWN TO THE MORTAL REALM AND DELIVER THIS LETTER TO SOMA.
BUT...BUT THAT'S THE BLADE OF HEAVEN JOURNAL! IT REVEALS THE SECRETS OF THE SWORD!!

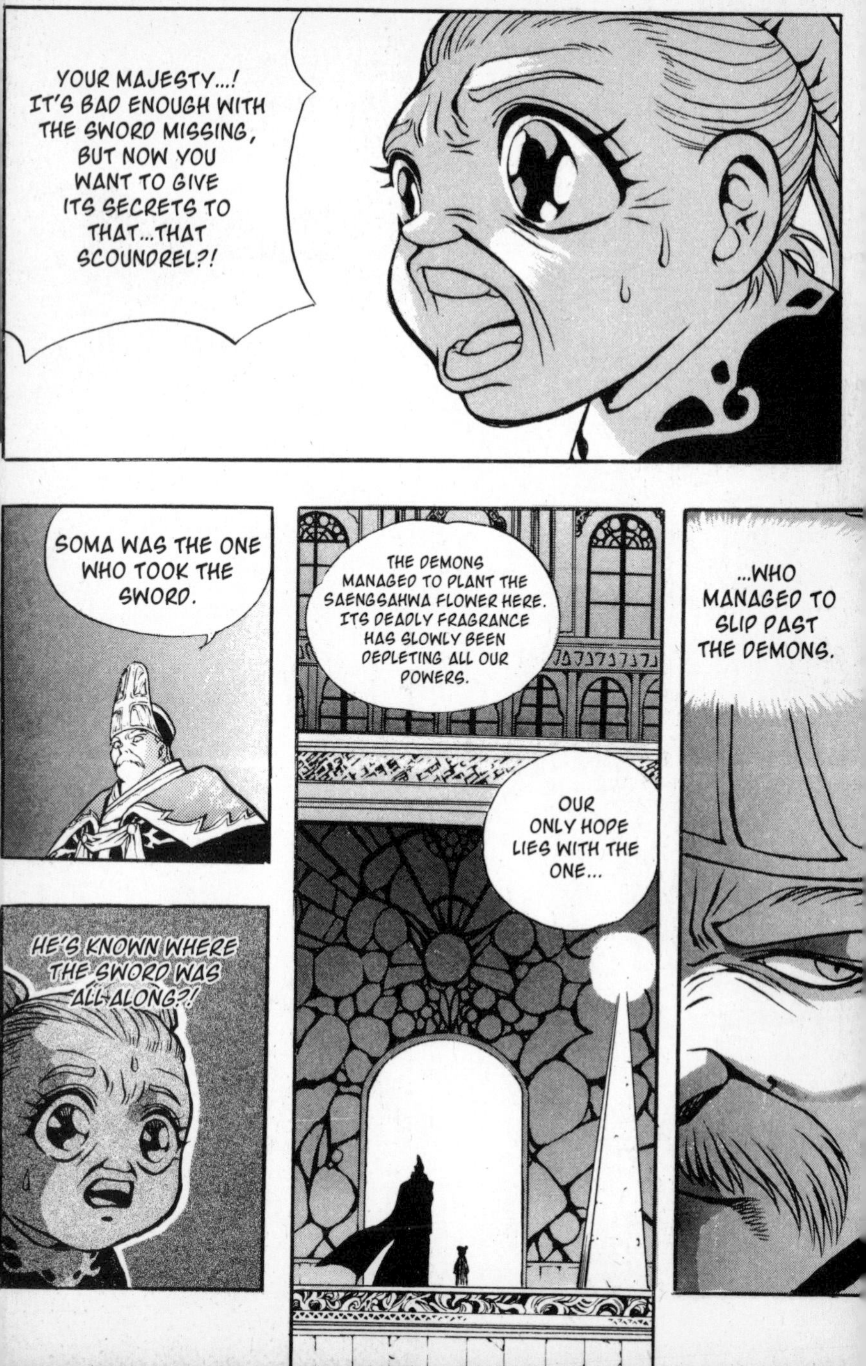
YOUR MAJESTY...! IT'S BAD ENOUGH WITH THE SWORD MISSING, BUT NOW YOU WANT TO GIVE ITS SECRETS TO THAT...THAT SCOUNDREL?!
SOMA WAS THE ONE WHO TOOK THE SWORD.
HE'S KNOWN WHERE THE SWORD WAS ALL ALONG?!
THE DEMONS MANAGED TO PLANT THE SAENGSAHWA FLOWER HERE. ITS DEADLY FRAGRANCE HAS SLOWLY BEEN DEPLETING ALL OUR POWERS.
OUR ONLY HOPE LIES WITH THE ONE...
...WHO MANAGED TO SLIP PAST THE DEMONS.

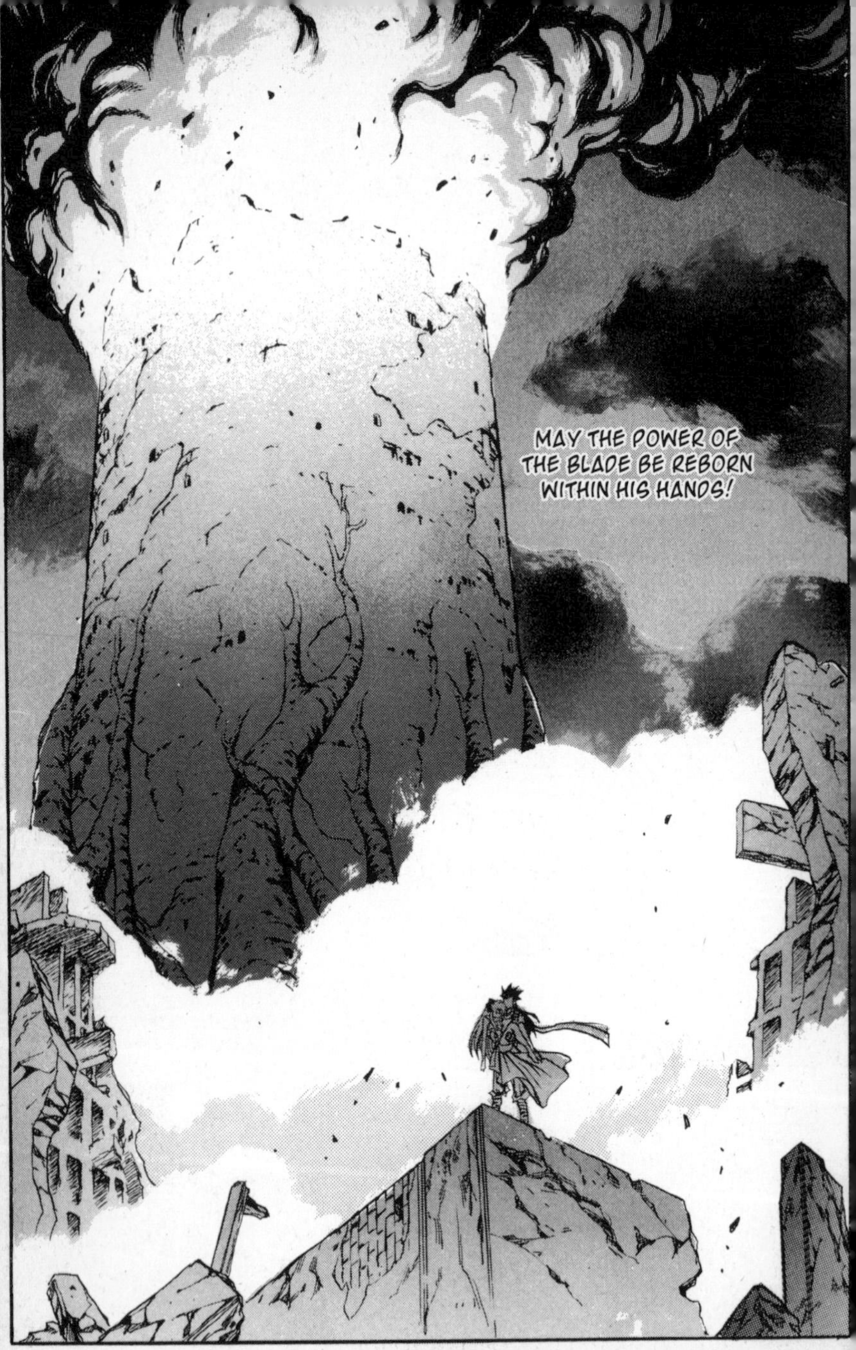
MAY THE POWER OF THE BLADE BE REBORN WITHIN HIS HANDS!

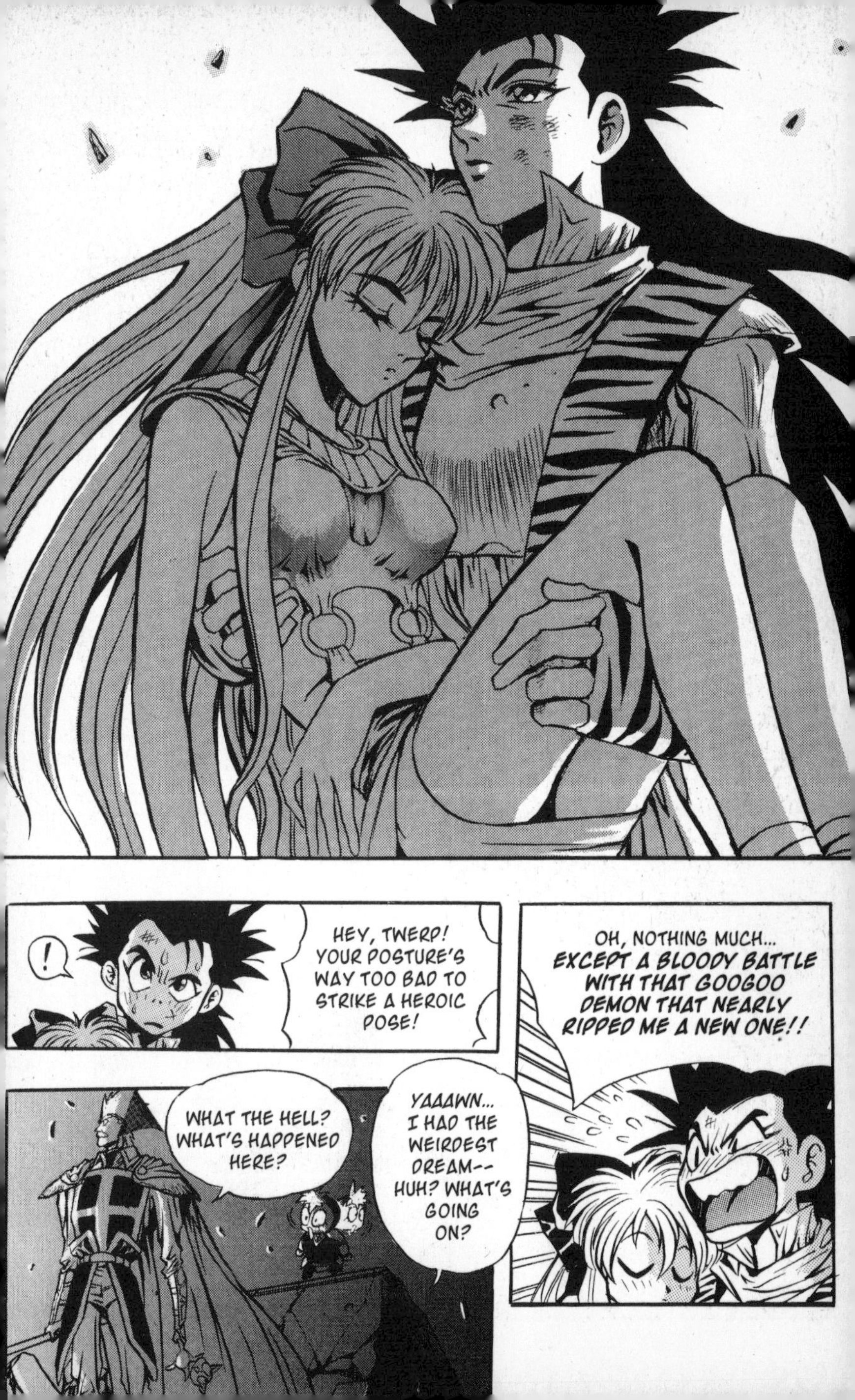
!
HEY, TWERP! YOUR POSTURE'S WAY TOO BAD TO STRIKE A HEROIC POSE!
WHAT THE HELL? WHAT'S HAPPENED HERE?
YAAAWN... I HAD THE WEIRDEST DREAM-- HUH? WHAT'S GOING ON?
OH, NOTHING MUCH... EXCEPT A BLOODY BATTLE WITH THAT GOOGOO DEMON THAT NEARLY RIPPED ME A NEW ONE!!

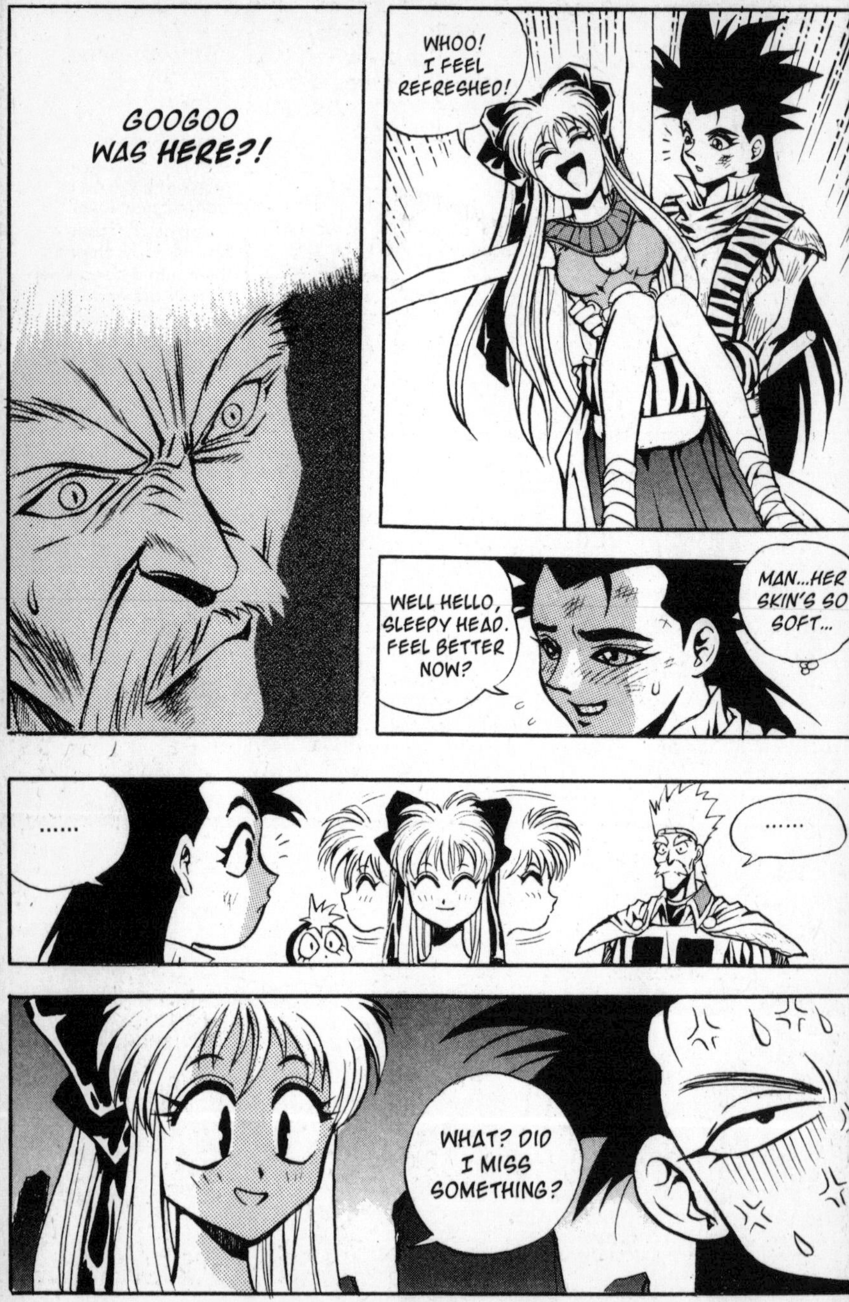
GOOGOO WAS HERE?!
WHOO! I FEEL REFRESHED!
WELL HELLO, SLEEPY HEAD. FEEL BETTER NOW?
MAN...HER SKIN'S SO SOFT...
......
......
WHAT? DID I MISS SOMETHING?

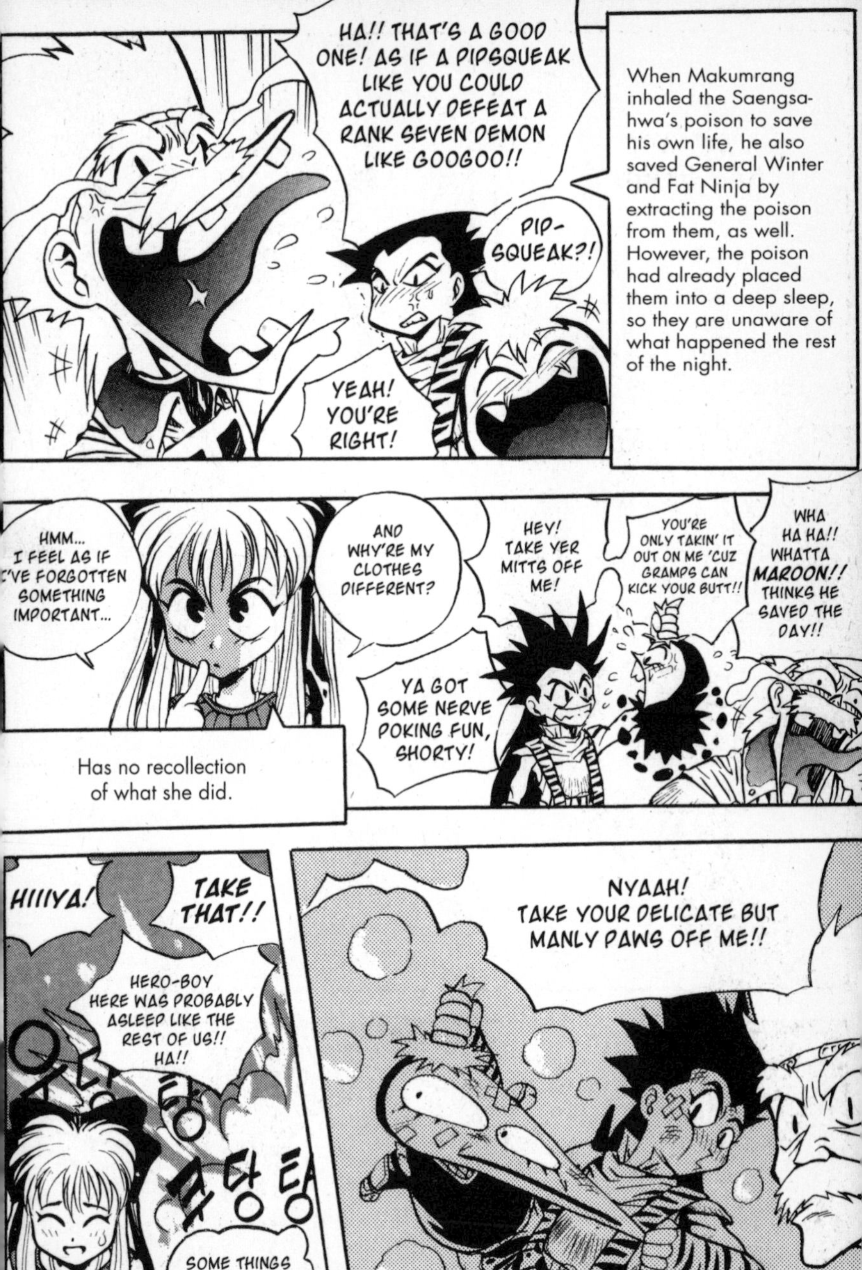
HA!! THAT'S A GOOD ONE! AS IF A PIPSQUEAK LIKE YOU COULD ACTUALLY DEFEAT A RANK SEVEN DEMON LIKE GOOGOO!!
PIP-SQUEAK?!
YEAH! YOU'RE RIGHT!
When Makumrang inhaled the Saengsa-hwa's poison to save his own life, he also saved General Winter and Fat Ninja by extracting the poison from them, as well. However, the poison had already placed them into a deep sleep, so they are unaware of what happened the rest of the night.
HMM... I FEEL AS IF I'VE FORGOTTEN SOMETHING IMPORTANT...
AND WHY'RE MY CLOTHES DIFFERENT?
Has no recollection of what she did.
HEY! TAKE YER MITTS OFF ME!
YOU'RE ONLY TAKIN' IT OUT ON ME 'CUZ GRAMPS CAN KICK YOUR BUTT!!
WHA HA HA!! WHATTA MAROON!! THINKS HE SAVED THE DAY!!
YA GOT SOME NERVE POKING FUN, SHORTY!
HIIIYA!
TAKE THAT!!
HERO-BOY HERE WAS PROBABLY ASLEEP LIKE THE REST OF US!! HA!!
SOME THINGS NEVER CHANGE...
NYAAH! TAKE YOUR DELICATE BUT MANLY PAWS OFF ME!!

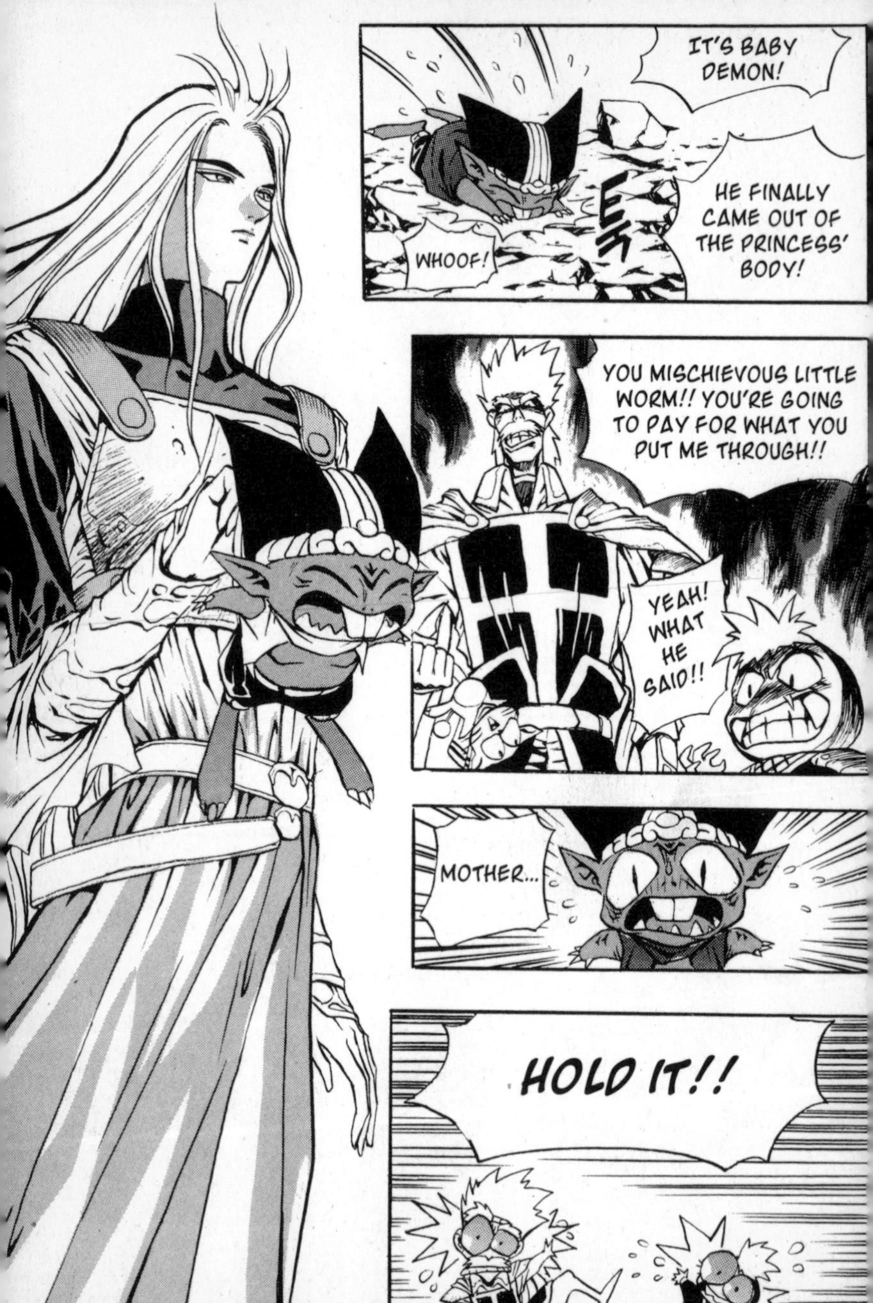

IT'S BABY DEMON!
HE FINALLY CAME OUT OF THE PRINCESS' BODY!
WHOOF!
YOU MISCHIEVOUS LITTLE WORM!! YOU'RE GOING TO PAY FOR WHAT YOU PUT ME THROUGH!!
YEAH! WHAT HE SAID!!
MOTHER...
HOLD IT!!

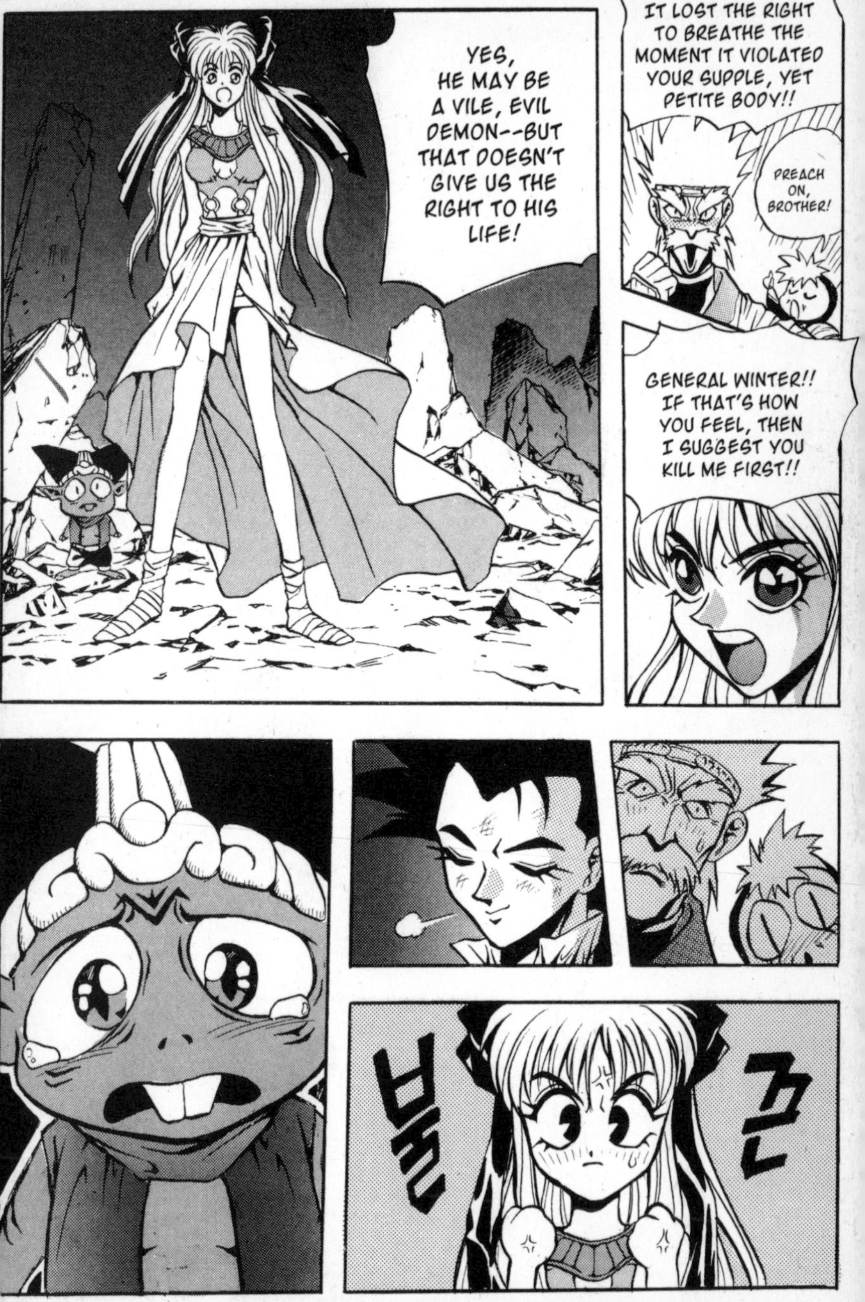
YES, HE MAY BE A VILE, EVIL DEMON--BUT THAT DOESN'T GIVE US THE RIGHT TO HIS LIFE!
IT LOST THE RIGHT TO BREATHE THE MOMENT IT VIOLATED YOUR SUPPLE, YET PETITE BODY!!
PREACH ON, BROTHER!
GENERAL WINTER!! IF THAT'S HOW YOU FEEL, THEN I SUGGEST YOU KILL ME FIRST!!

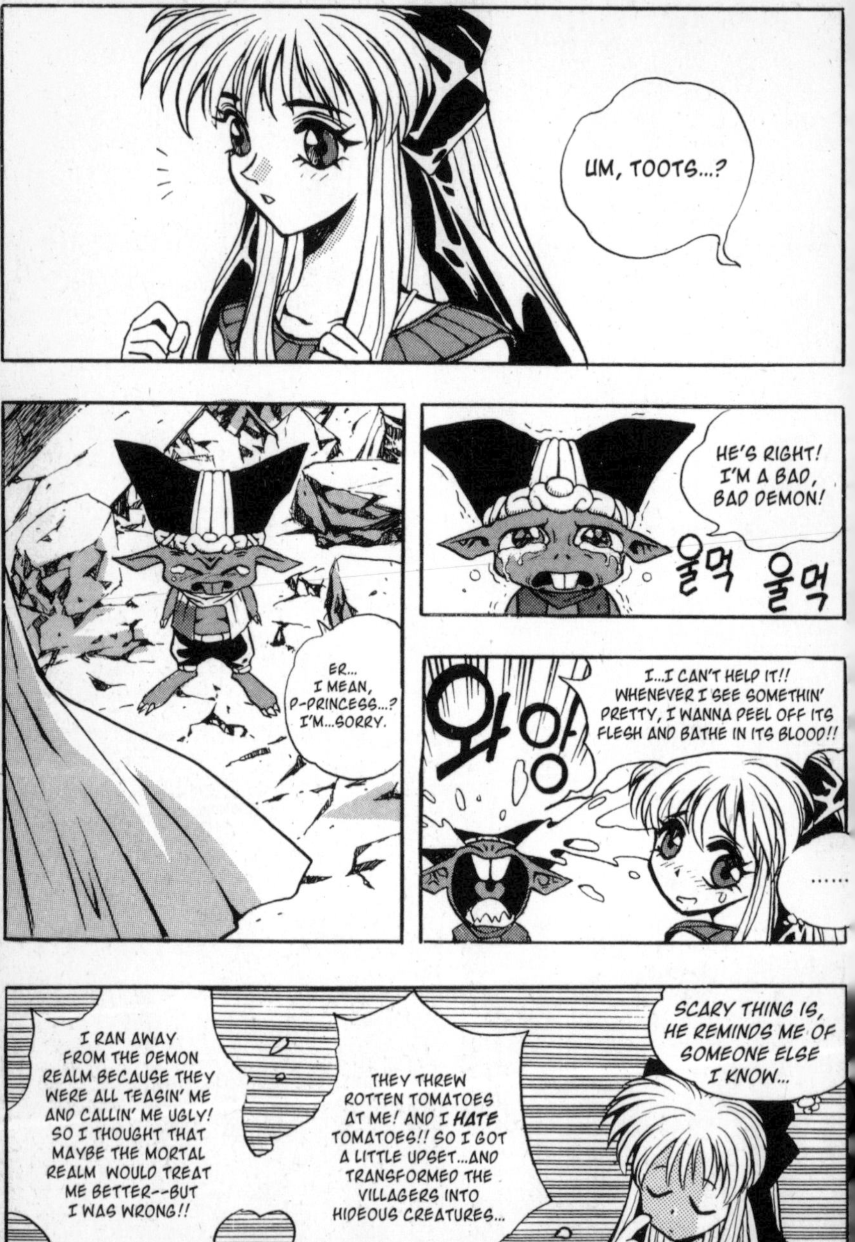
UM, TOOTS...?
ER... I MEAN, P-PRINCESS...? I'M...SORRY.
HE'S RIGHT! I'M A BAD, BAD DEMON!
울먹 울먹
와앙
I...I CAN'T HELP IT!! WHENEVER I SEE SOMETHIN' PRETTY, I WANNA PEEL OFF ITS FLESH AND BATHE IN ITS BLOOD!!
......
I RAN AWAY FROM THE DEMON REALM BECAUSE THEY WERE ALL TEASIN' ME AND CALLIN' ME UGLY! SO I THOUGHT THAT MAYBE THE MORTAL REALM WOULD TREAT ME BETTER--BUT I WAS WRONG!!
THEY THREW ROTTEN TOMATOES AT ME! AND I HATE TOMATOES!! SO I GOT A LITTLE UPSET...AND TRANSFORMED THE VILLAGERS INTO HIDEOUS CREATURES...
SCARY THING IS, HE REMINDS ME OF SOMEONE ELSE I KNOW...

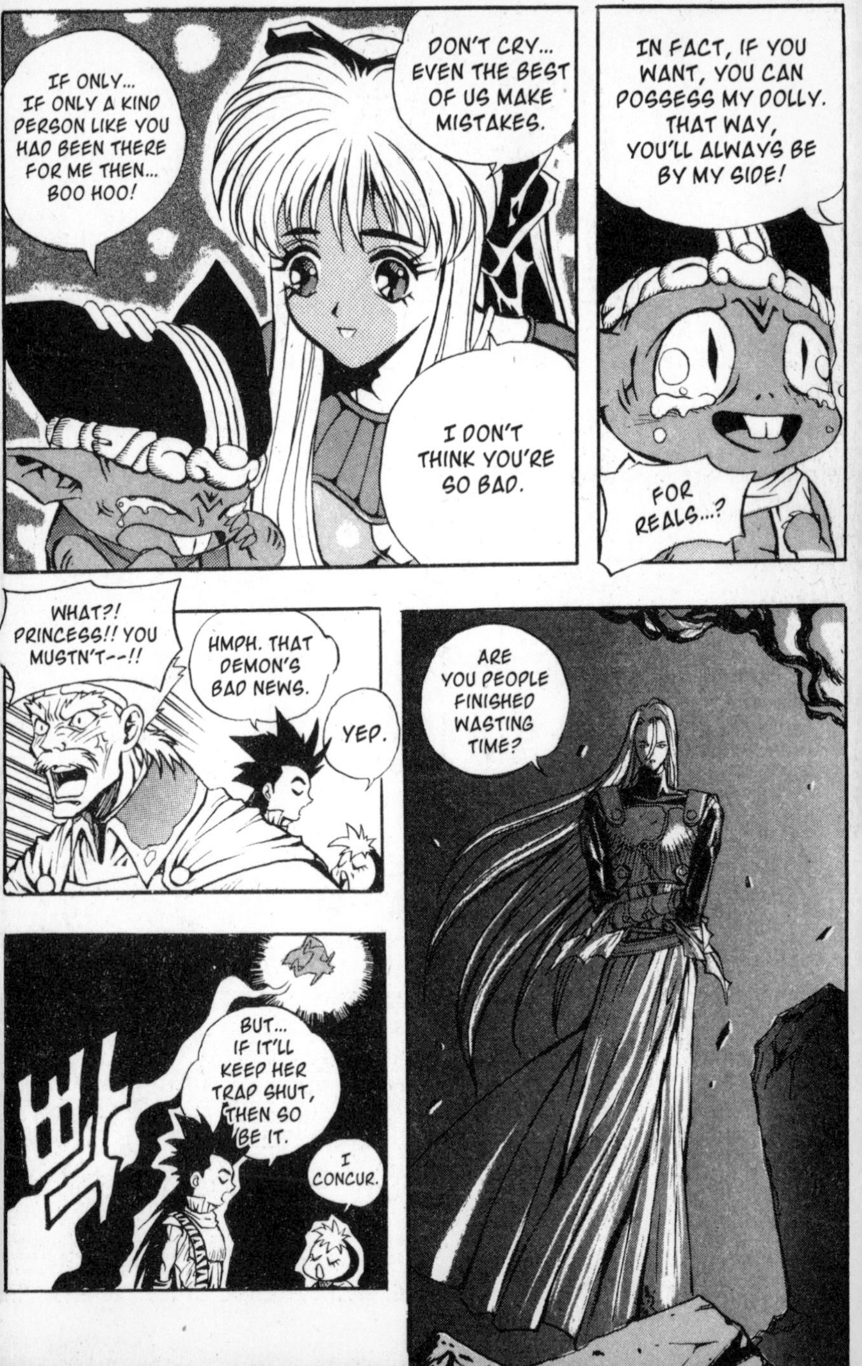
IF ONLY... IF ONLY A KIND PERSON LIKE YOU HAD BEEN THERE FOR ME THEN... BOO HOO!
DON'T CRY... EVEN THE BEST OF US MAKE MISTAKES.
I DON'T THINK YOU'RE SO BAD.
IN FACT, IF YOU WANT, YOU CAN POSSESS MY DOLLY. THAT WAY, YOU'LL ALWAYS BE BY MY SIDE!
FOR REALS...?
WHAT?! PRINCESS!! YOU MUSTN'T--!!
HMPH. THAT DEMON'S BAD NEWS.
YEP.
빡
BUT... IF IT'LL KEEP HER TRAP SHUT, THEN SO BE IT.
I CONCUR.
ARE YOU PEOPLE FINISHED WASTING TIME?

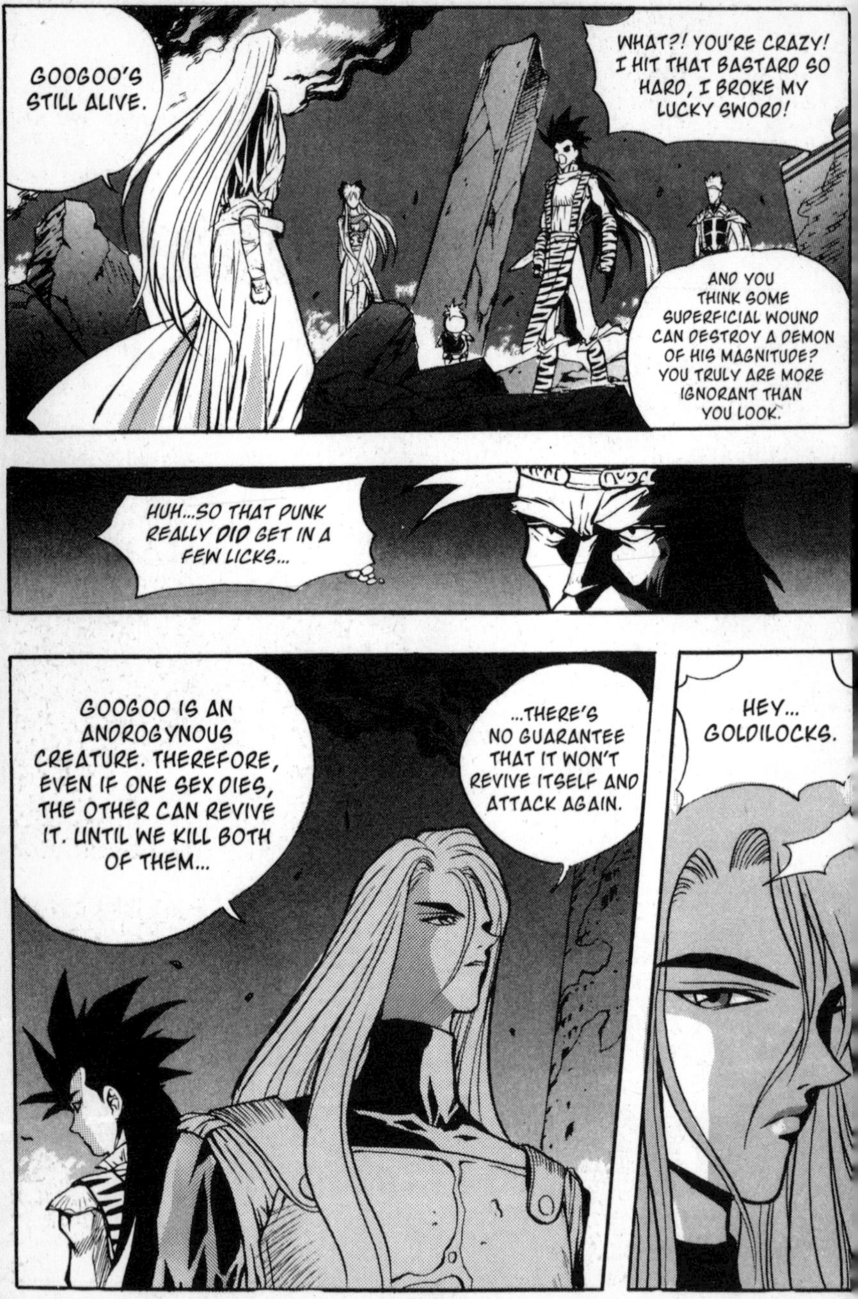
GOOGOO'S STILL ALIVE.
WHAT?! YOU'RE CRAZY! I HIT THAT BASTARD SO HARD, I BROKE MY LUCKY SWORD!
AND YOU THINK SOME SUPERFICIAL WOUND CAN DESTROY A DEMON OF HIS MAGNITUDE? YOU TRULY ARE MORE IGNORANT THAN YOU LOOK.
HUH...SO THAT PUNK REALLY DID GET IN A FEW LICKS...
GOOGOO IS AN ANDROGYNOUS CREATURE. THEREFORE, EVEN IF ONE SEX DIES, THE OTHER CAN REVIVE IT. UNTIL WE KILL BOTH OF THEM...
...THERE'S NO GUARANTEE THAT IT WON'T REVIVE ITSELF AND ATTACK AGAIN.
HEY... GOLDILOCKS.

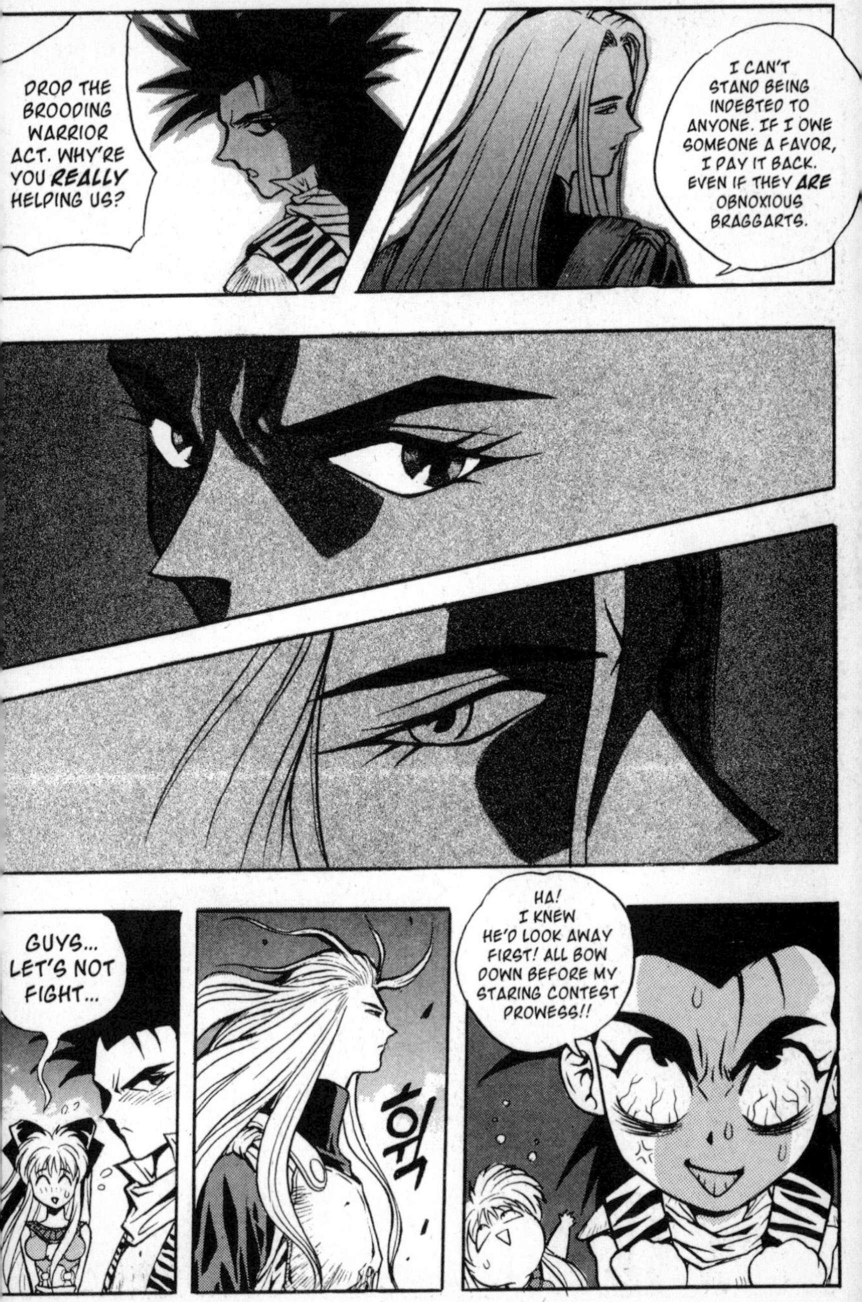
DROP THE BROODING WARRIOR ACT. WHY'RE YOU ***REALLY*** HELPING US?
I CAN'T STAND BEING INDEBTED TO ANYONE. IF I OWE SOMEONE A FAVOR, I PAY IT BACK. EVEN IF THEY ***ARE*** OBNOXIOUS BRAGGARTS.
GUYS... LET'S NOT FIGHT...
HA! I KNEW HE'D LOOK AWAY FIRST! ALL BOW DOWN BEFORE MY STARING CONTEST PROWESS!!

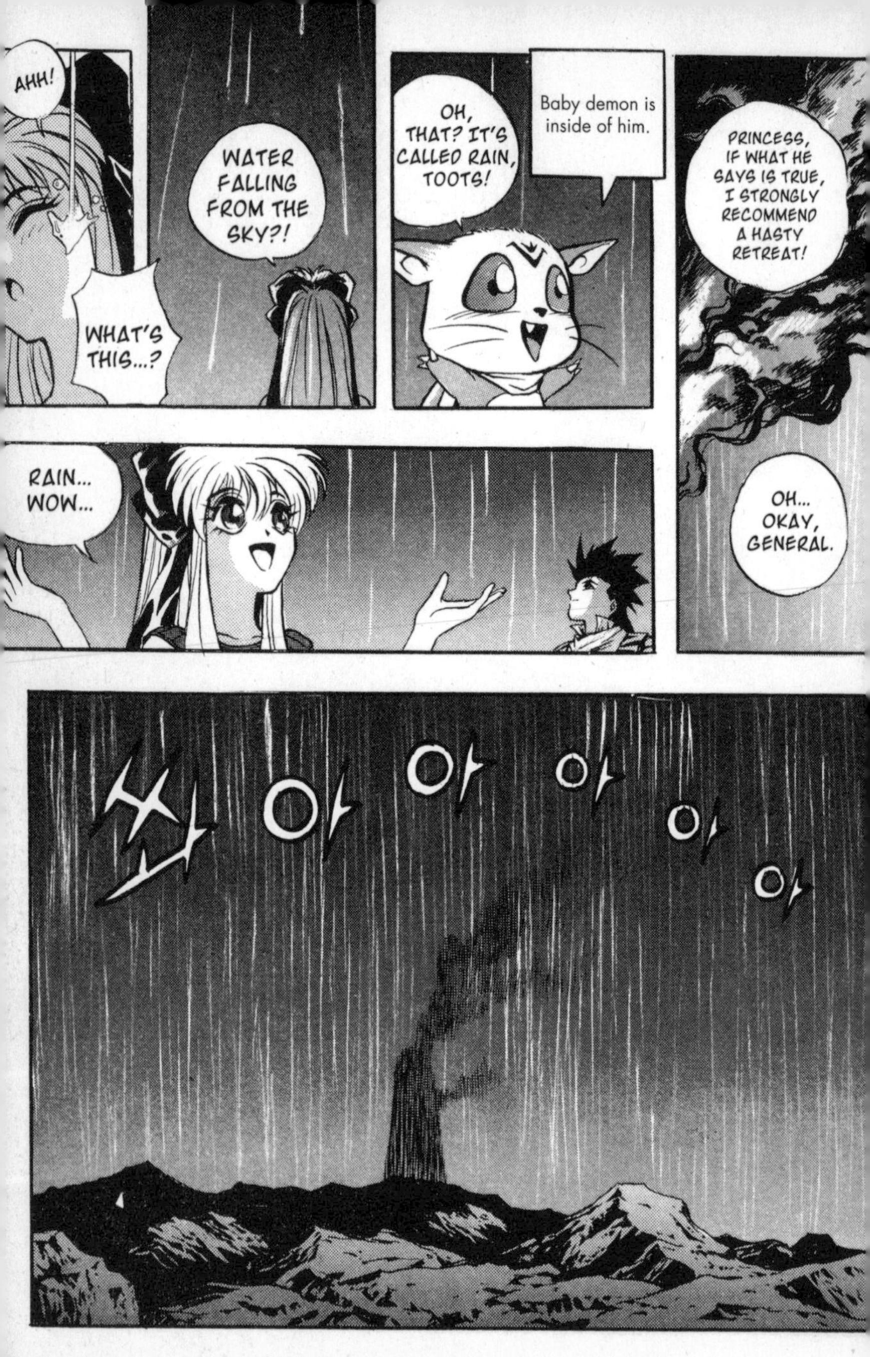
AHH!
WHAT'S THIS...?
WATER FALLING FROM THE SKY?!
OH, THAT? IT'S CALLED RAIN, TOOTS!
Baby demon is inside of him.
RAIN... WOW...
PRINCESS, IF WHAT HE SAYS IS TRUE, I STRONGLY RECOMMEND A HASTY RETREAT!
OH... OKAY, GENERAL.
쏴아아아아아

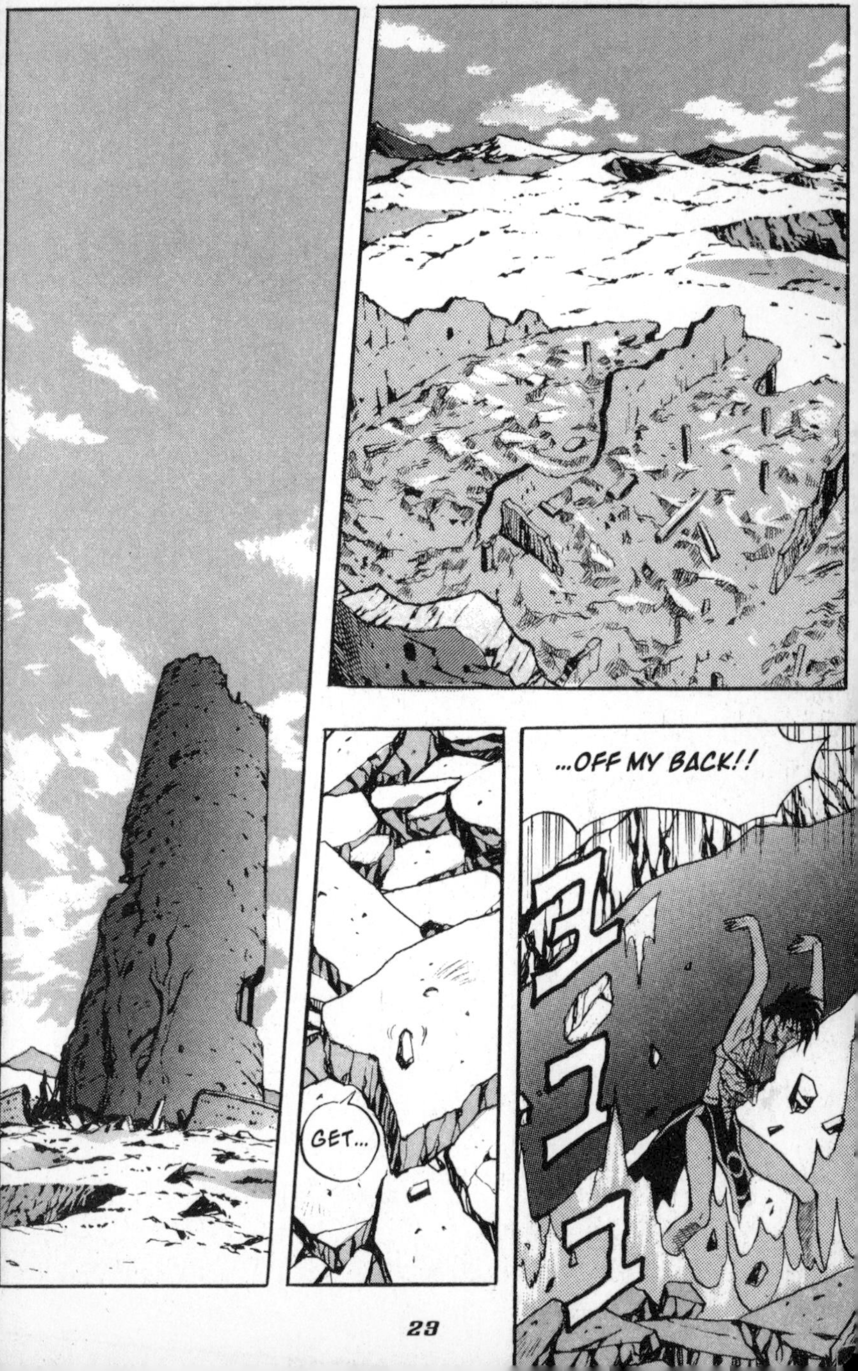
GET...
...OFF MY BACK!!

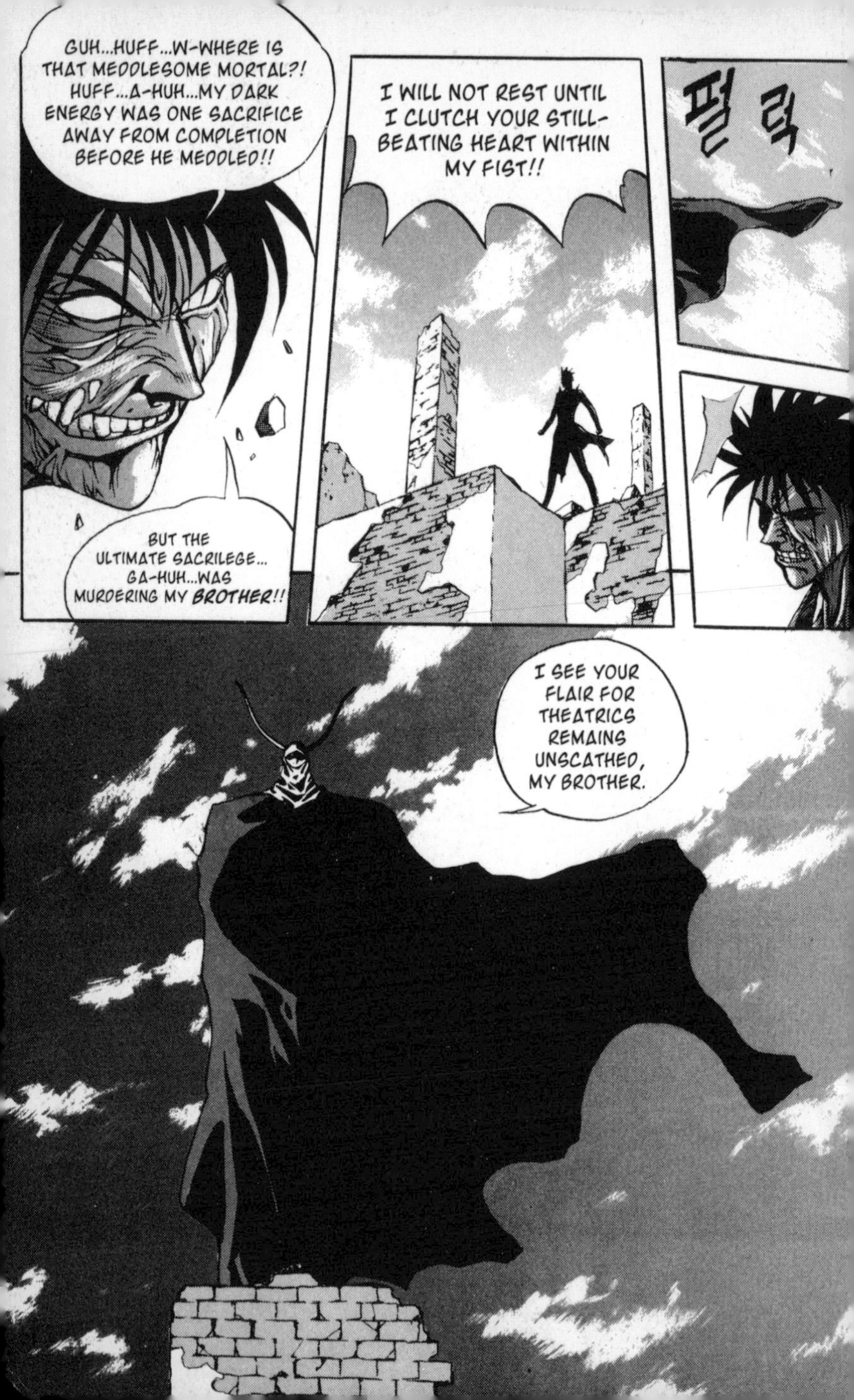
GUH...HUFF...W-WHERE IS THAT MEDDLESOME MORTAL?! HUFF...A-HUH...MY DARK ENERGY WAS ONE SACRIFICE AWAY FROM COMPLETION BEFORE HE MEDDLED!!
BUT THE ULTIMATE SACRILEGE... GA-HUH...WAS MURDERING MY BROTHER!!
I WILL NOT REST UNTIL I CLUTCH YOUR STILL-BEATING HEART WITHIN MY FIST!!
펄럭
I SEE YOUR FLAIR FOR THEATRICS REMAINS UNSCATHED, MY BROTHER.

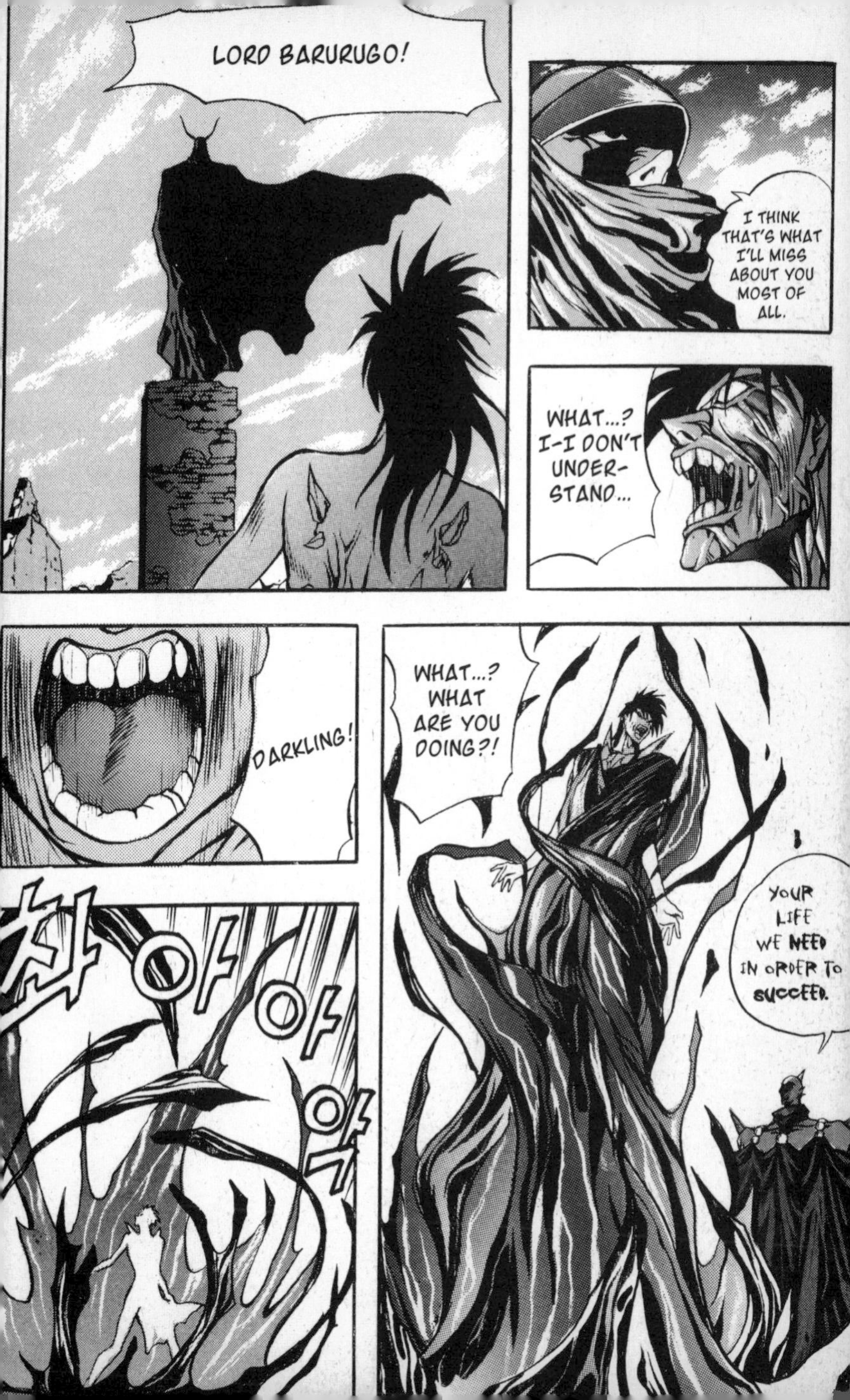
LORD BARURUGO!
I THINK THAT'S WHAT I'LL MISS ABOUT YOU MOST OF ALL.
WHAT...? I-I DON'T UNDER-STAND...
DARKLING!
차아아악
WHAT...? WHAT ARE YOU DOING?!
YOUR LIFE WE NEED IN ORDER TO SUCCEED.

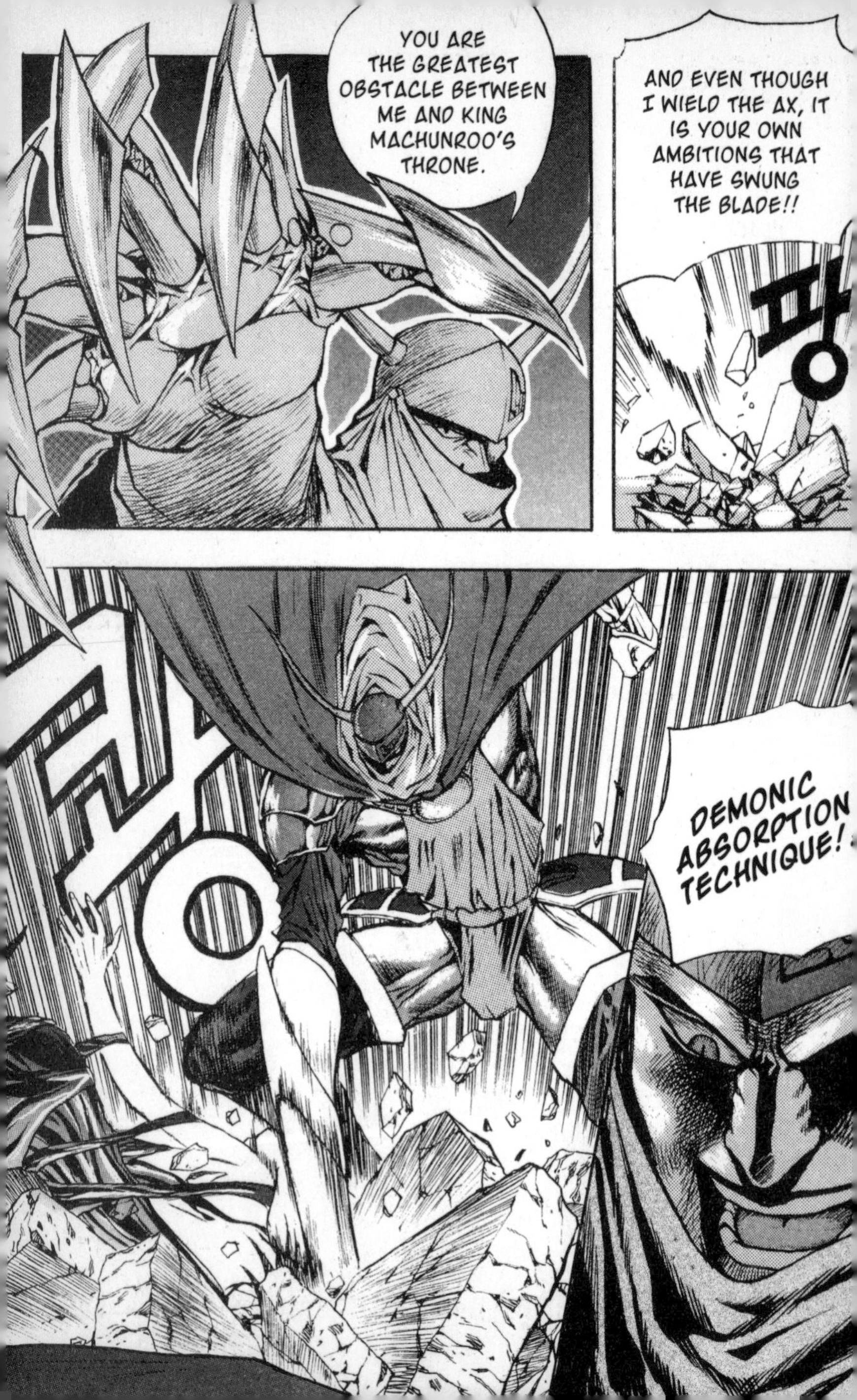
YOU ARE THE GREATEST OBSTACLE BETWEEN ME AND KING MACHUNROO'S THRONE.
AND EVEN THOUGH I WIELD THE AX, IT IS YOUR OWN AMBITIONS THAT HAVE SWUNG THE BLADE!!
DEMONIC ABSORPTION TECHNIQUE!

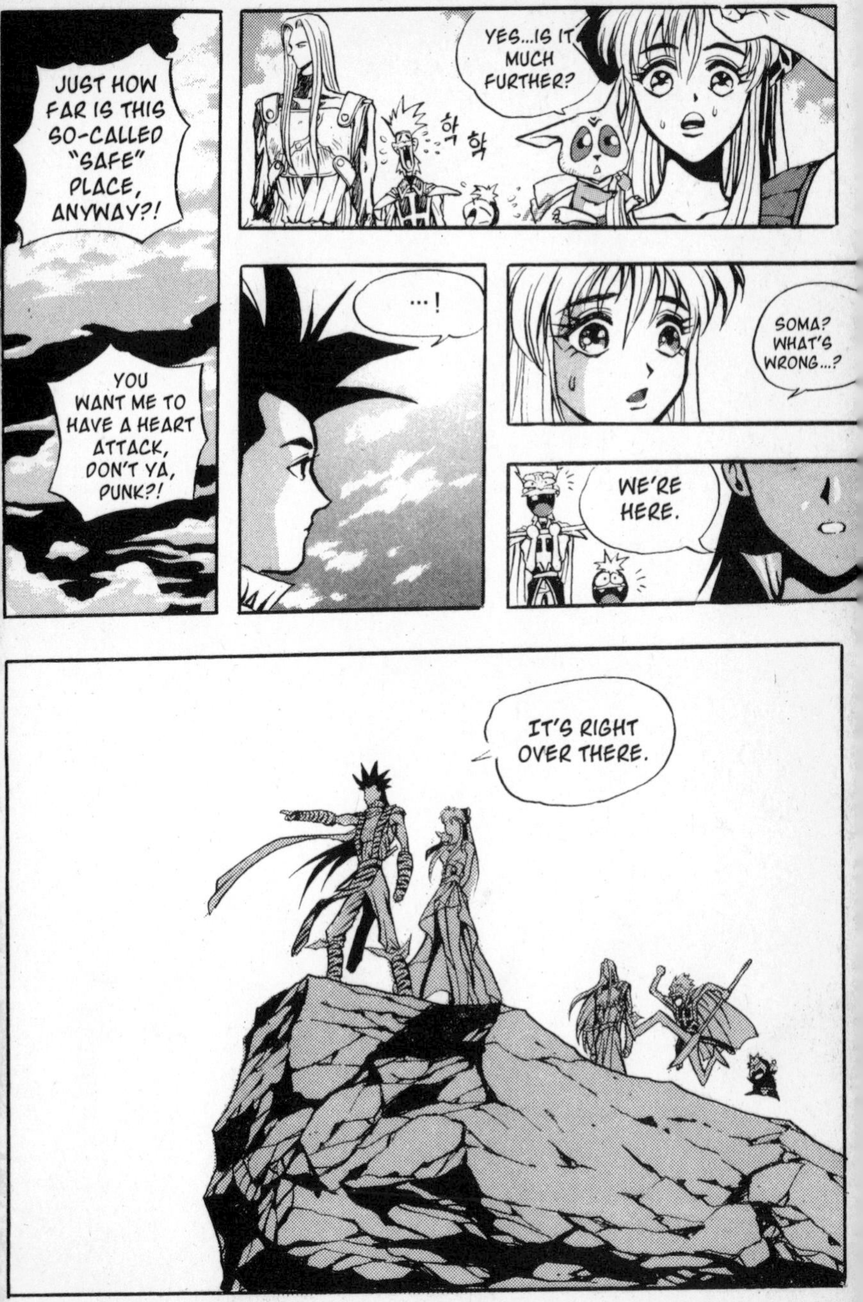

JUST HOW FAR IS THIS SO-CALLED "SAFE" PLACE, ANYWAY?!
YOU WANT ME TO HAVE A HEART ATTACK, DON'T YA, PUNK?!
학 학
YES...IS IT MUCH FURTHER?
...!
SOMA? WHAT'S WRONG...?
WE'RE HERE.
IT'S RIGHT OVER THERE.

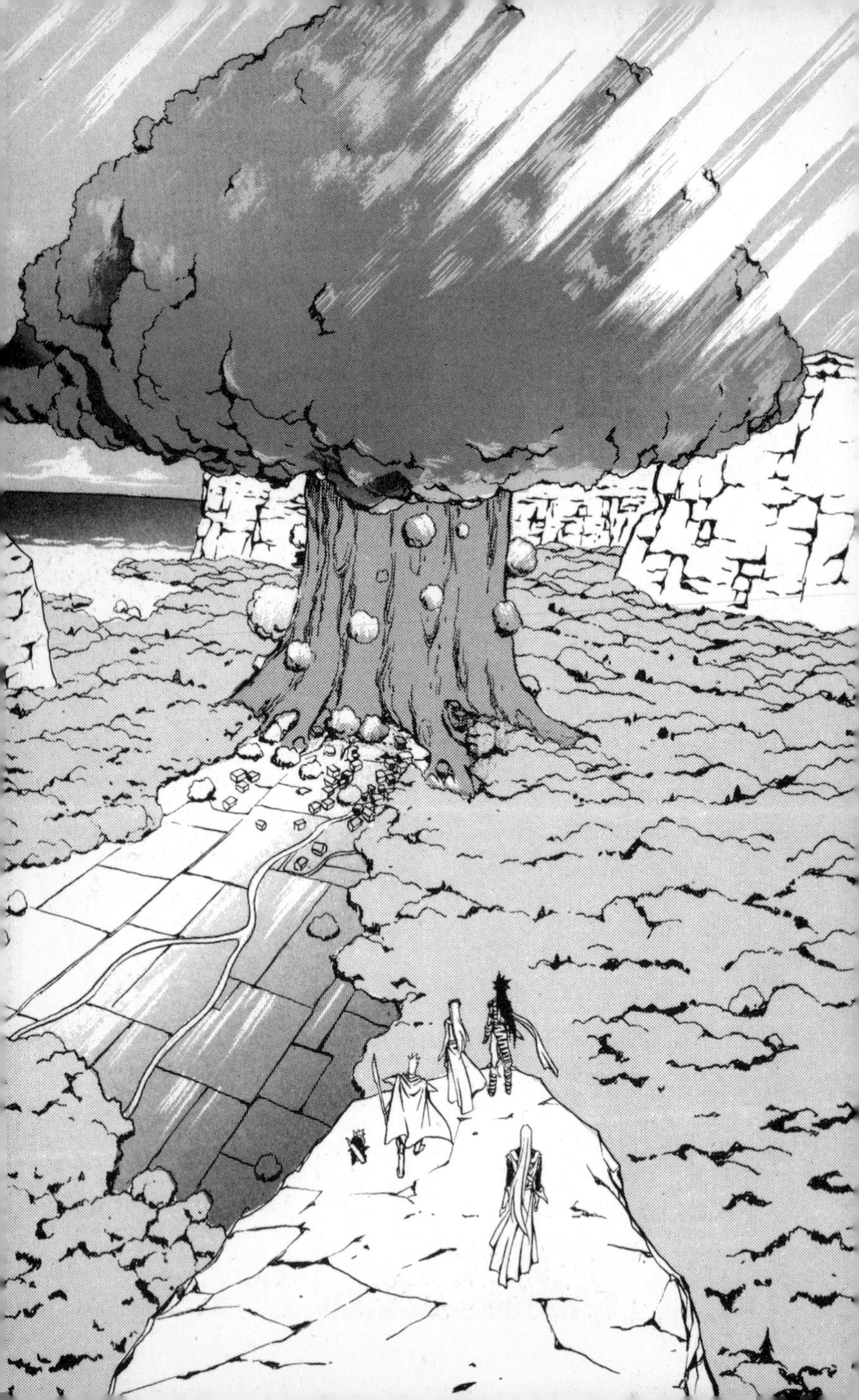

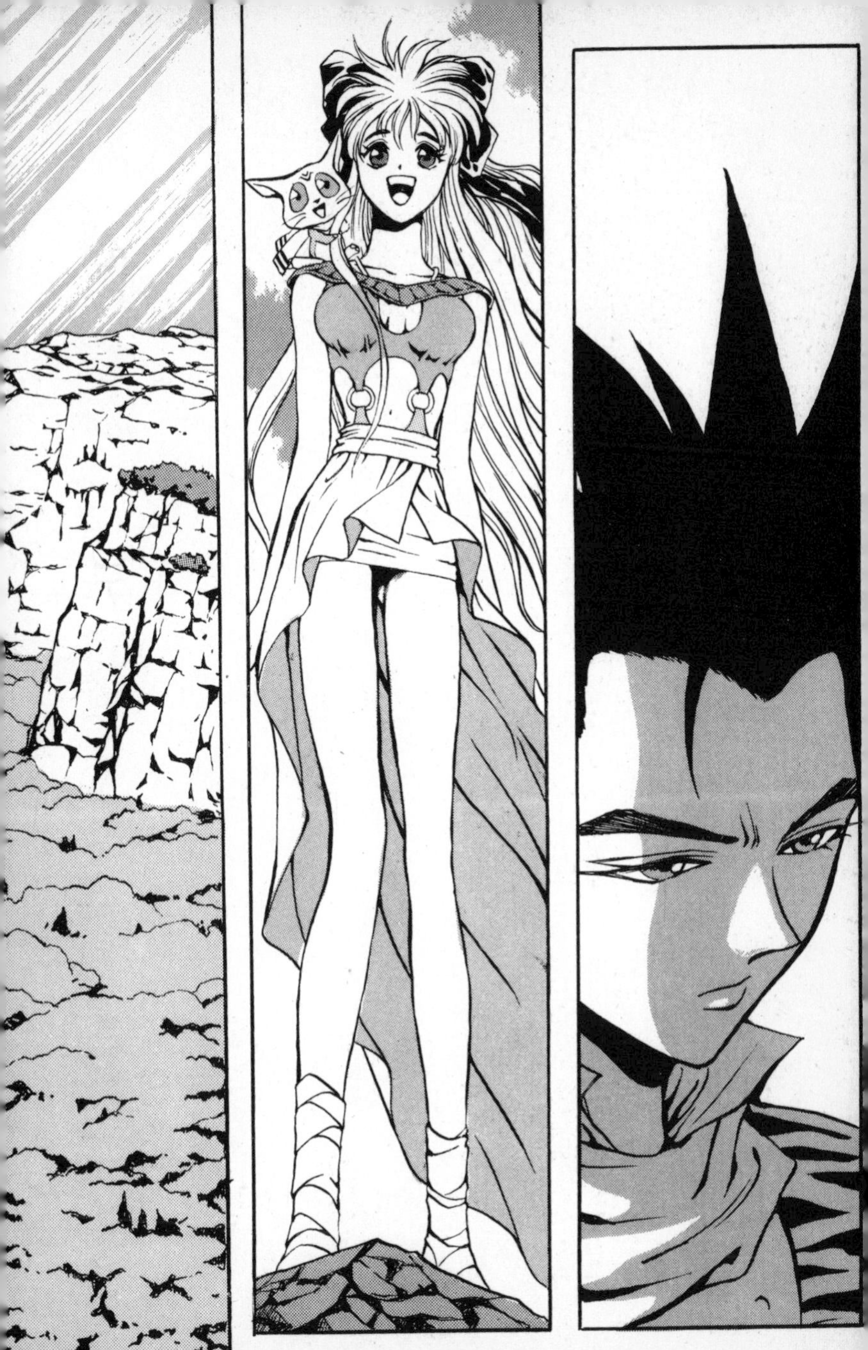

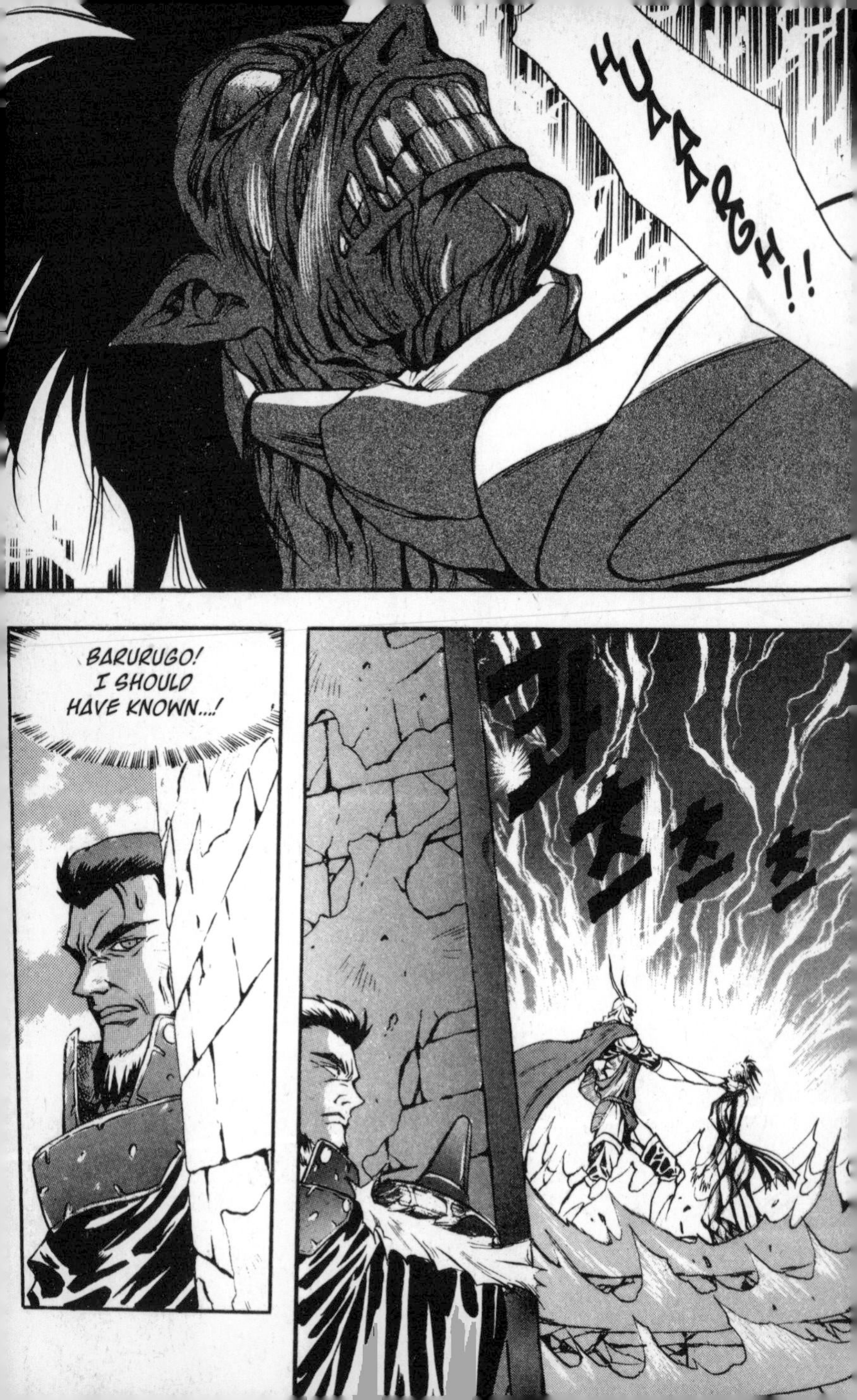
HUAAARGH!!
BARURUGO! I SHOULD HAVE KNOWN...!

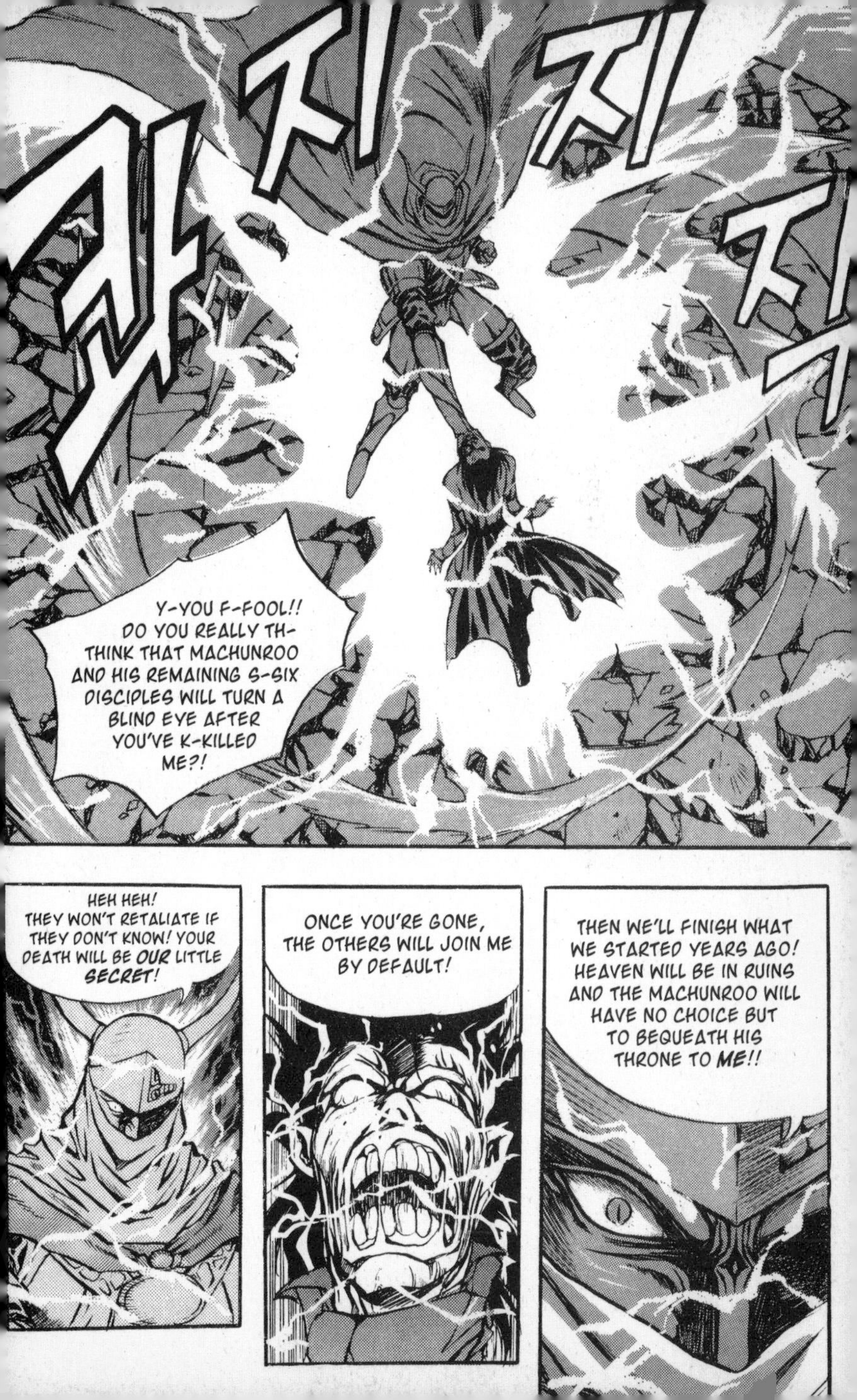
Y-YOU F-FOOL!! DO YOU REALLY TH-THINK THAT MACHUNROO AND HIS REMAINING S-SIX DISCIPLES WILL TURN A BLIND EYE AFTER YOU'VE K-KILLED ME?!
HEH HEH! THEY WON'T RETALIATE IF THEY DON'T KNOW! YOUR DEATH WILL BE OUR LITTLE SECRET!
ONCE YOU'RE GONE, THE OTHERS WILL JOIN ME BY DEFAULT!
THEN WE'LL FINISH WHAT WE STARTED YEARS AGO! HEAVEN WILL BE IN RUINS AND THE MACHUNROO WILL HAVE NO CHOICE BUT TO BEQUEATH HIS THRONE TO ME!!

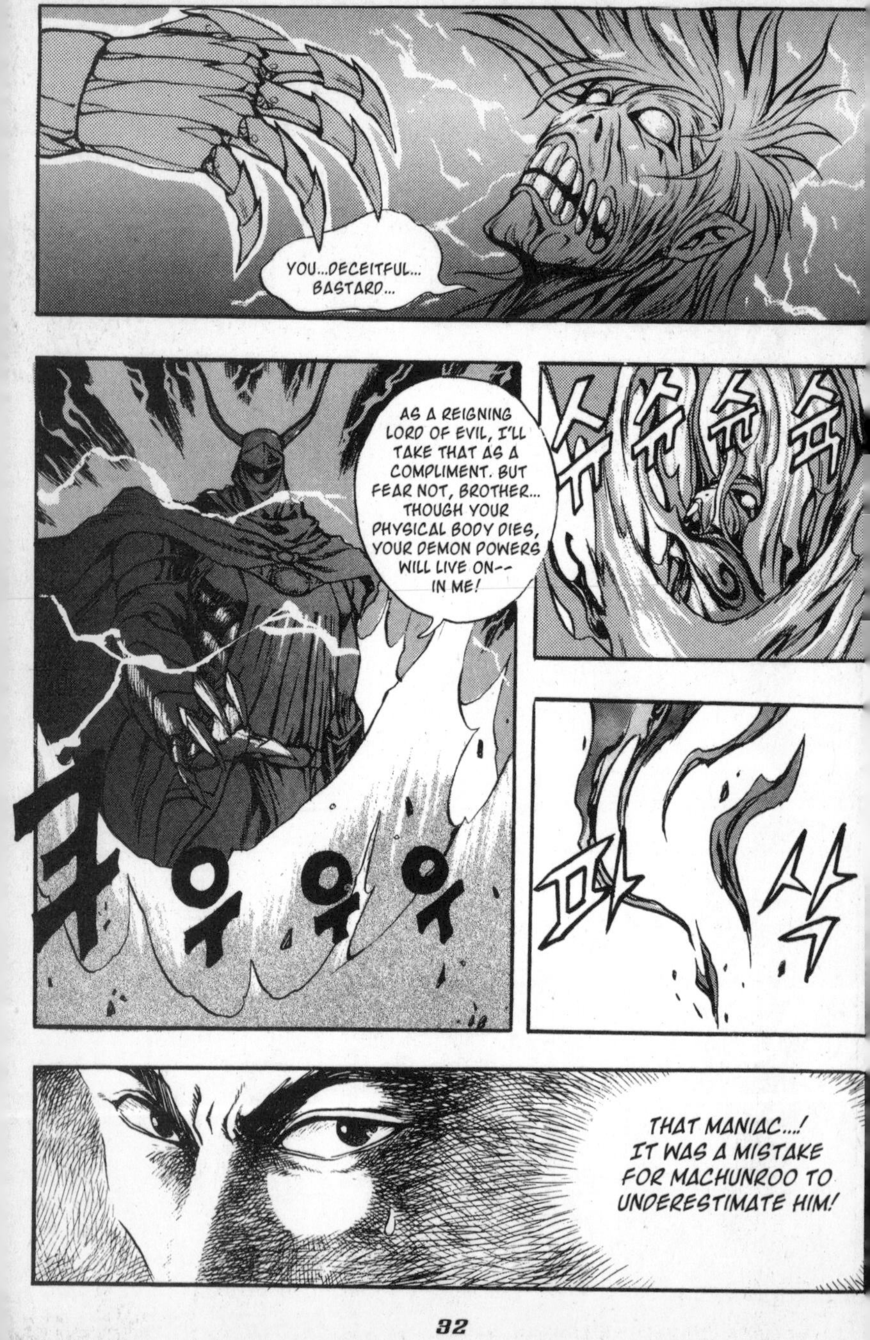
YOU...DECEITFUL... BASTARD...
AS A REIGNING LORD OF EVIL, I'LL TAKE THAT AS A COMPLIMENT. BUT FEAR NOT, BROTHER... THOUGH YOUR PHYSICAL BODY DIES, YOUR DEMON POWERS WILL LIVE ON-- IN ME!
THAT MANIAC...! IT WAS A MISTAKE FOR MACHUNROO TO UNDERESTIMATE HIM!

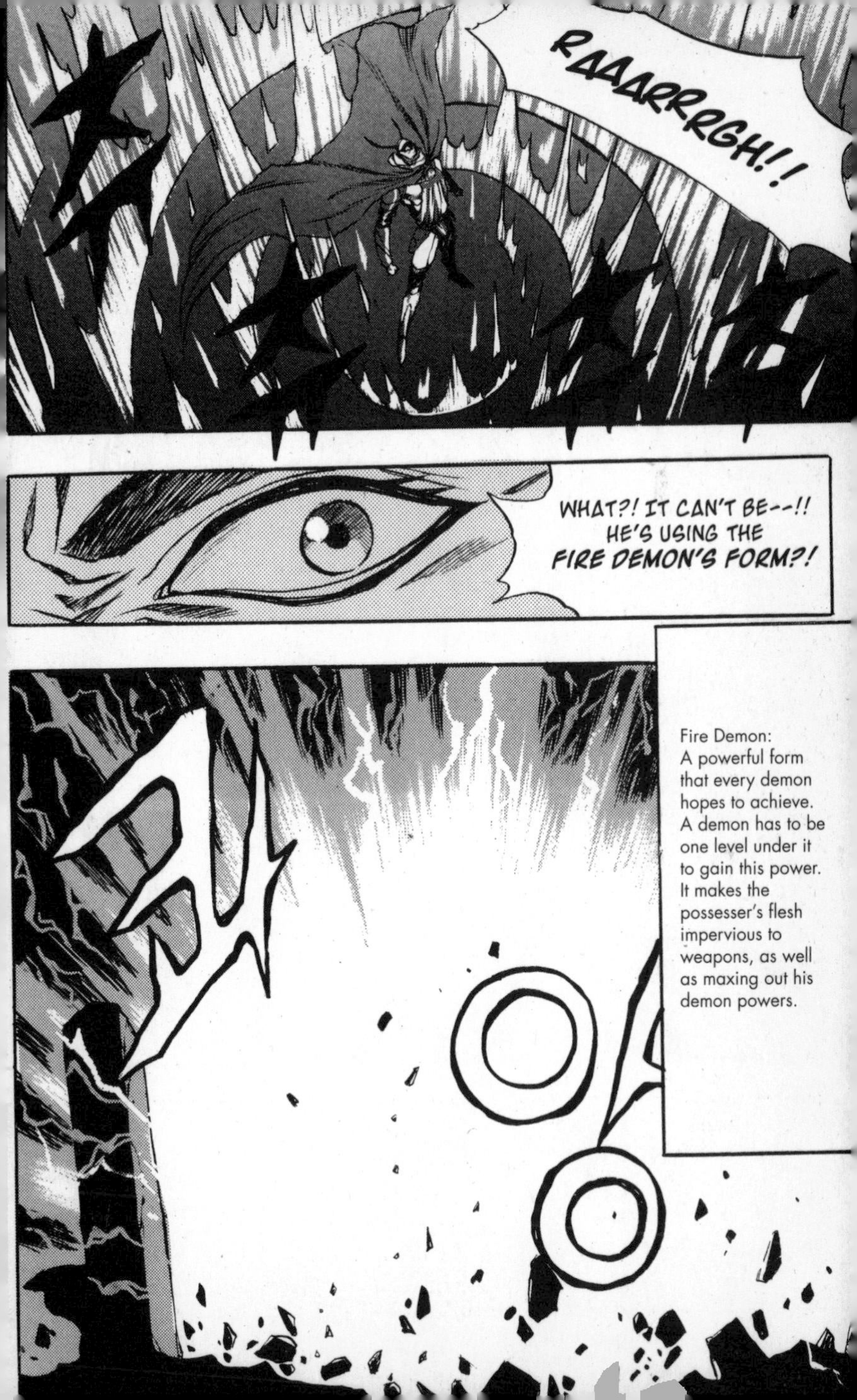
RAAARRRGH!!
WHAT?! IT CAN'T BE--!! HE'S USING THE FIRE DEMON'S FORM?!
Fire Demon: A powerful form that every demon hopes to achieve. A demon has to be one level under it to gain this power. It makes the possesser's flesh impervious to weapons, as well as maxing out his demon powers.

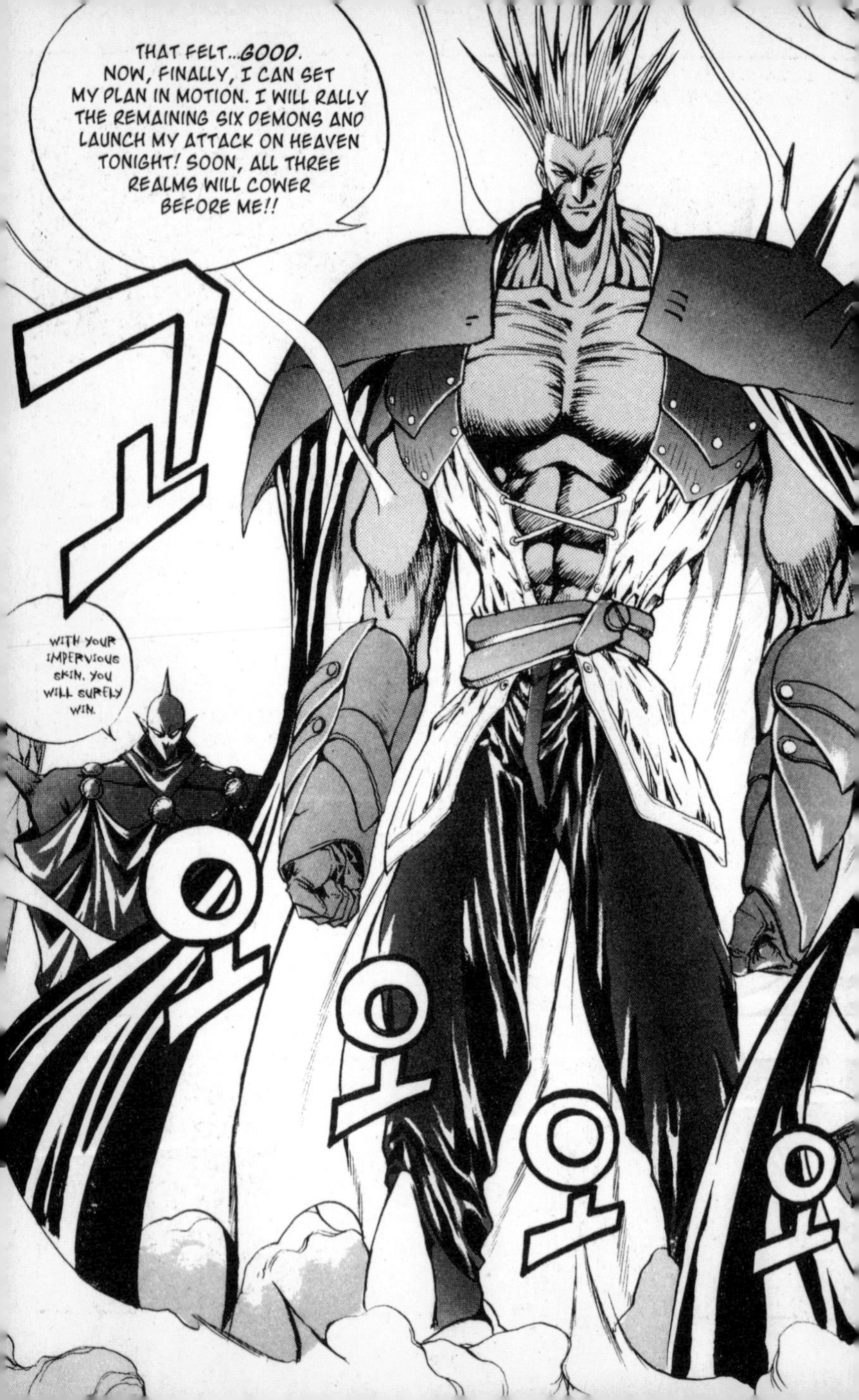
THAT FELT...*GOOD.* NOW, FINALLY, I CAN SET MY PLAN IN MOTION. I WILL RALLY THE REMAINING SIX DEMONS AND LAUNCH MY ATTACK ON HEAVEN TONIGHT! SOON, ALL THREE REALMS WILL COWER BEFORE ME!!
WITH YOUR IMPERVIOUS SKIN, YOU WILL SURELY WIN.

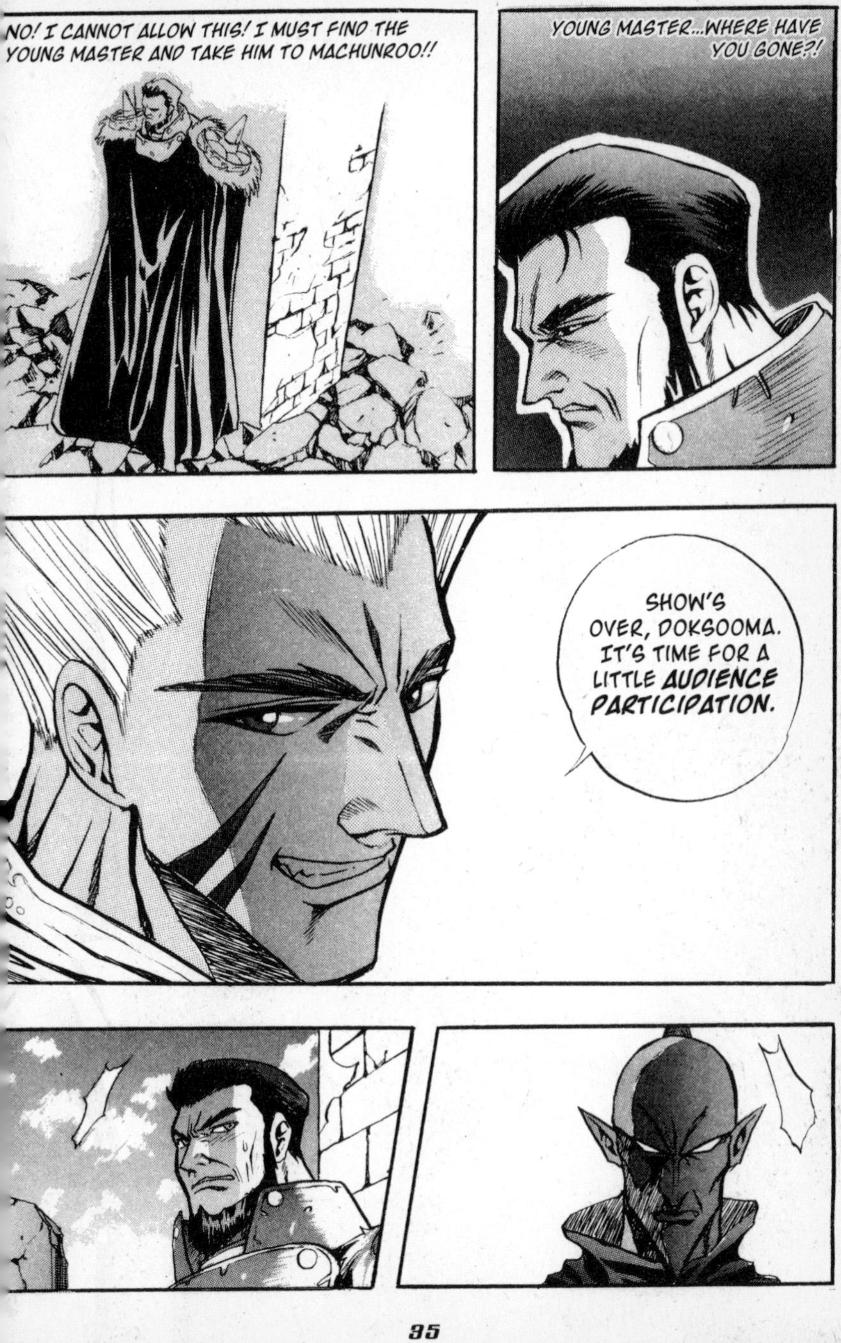
NO! I CANNOT ALLOW THIS! I MUST FIND THE YOUNG MASTER AND TAKE HIM TO MACHUNROO!!
YOUNG MASTER...WHERE HAVE YOU GONE?!
SHOW'S OVER, DOKSOOMA. IT'S TIME FOR A LITTLE AUDIENCE PARTICIPATION.

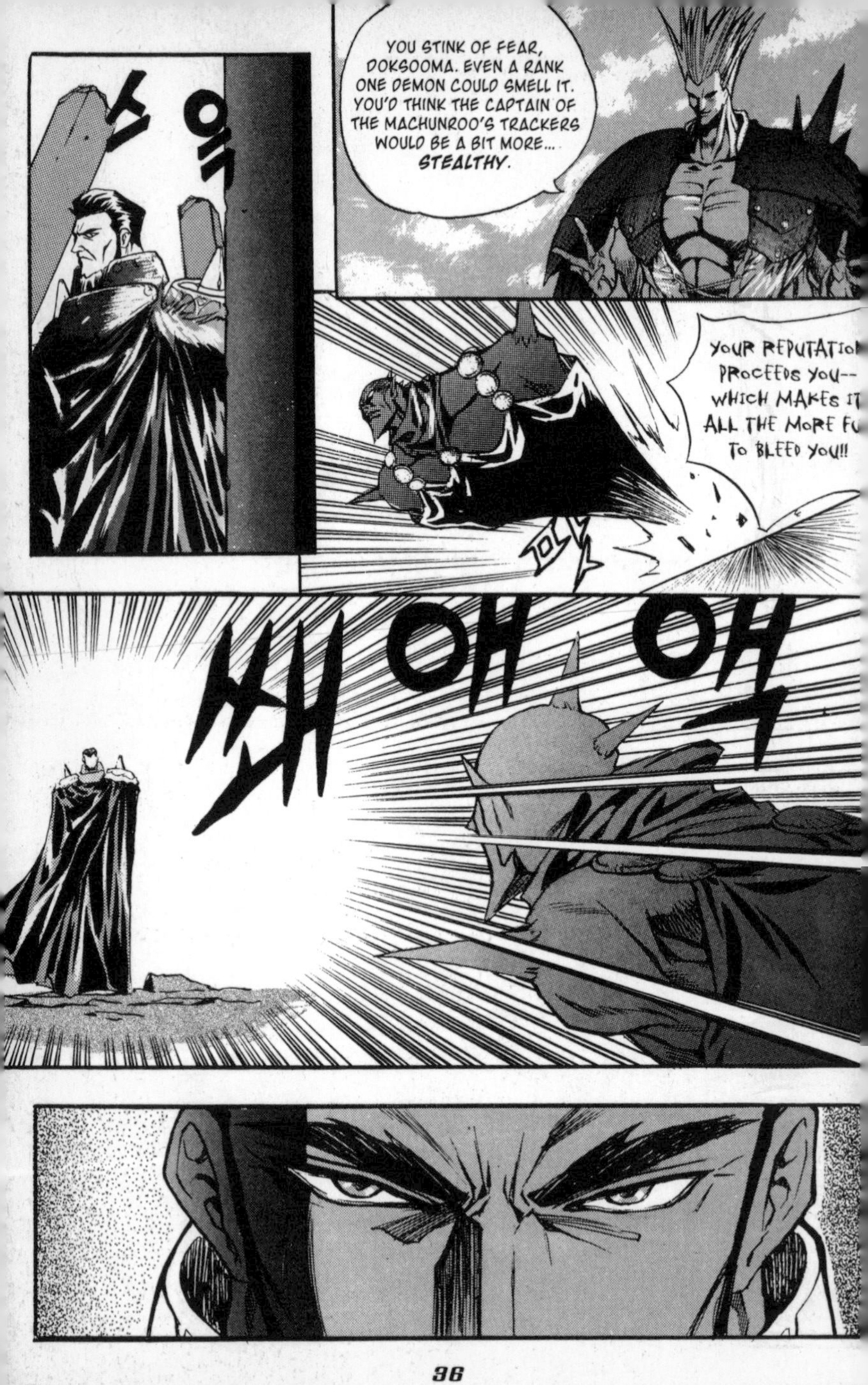
YOU STINK OF FEAR, DOKSOOMA. EVEN A RANK ONE DEMON COULD SMELL IT. YOU'D THINK THE CAPTAIN OF THE MACHUNROO'S TRACKERS WOULD BE A BIT MORE... STEALTHY.
YOUR REPUTATIO PROCEEDS YOU-- WHICH MAKES IT ALL THE MORE F TO BLEED YOU!!
HWOH OH

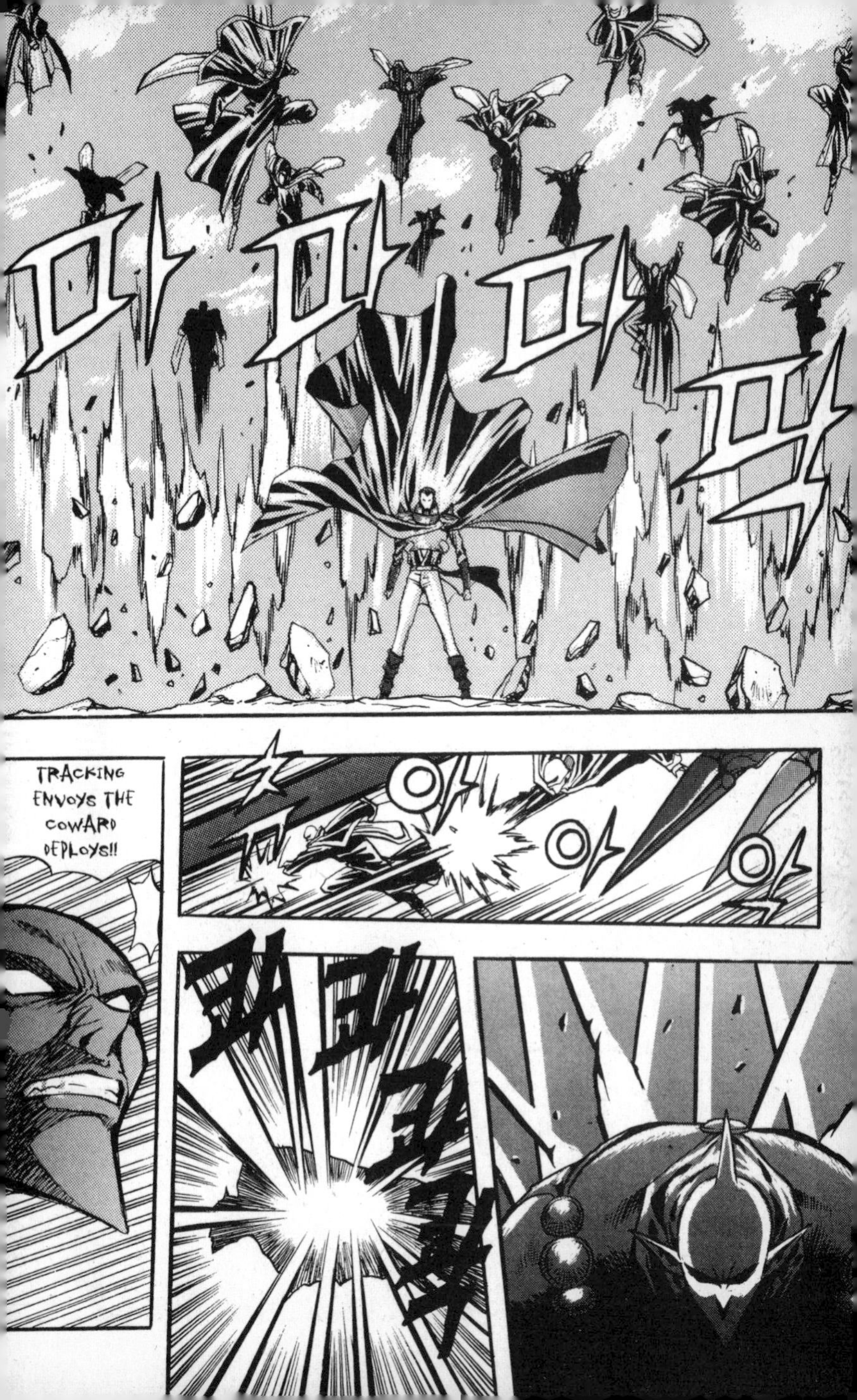
TRACKING ENVOYS THE COWARD DEPLOYS!!

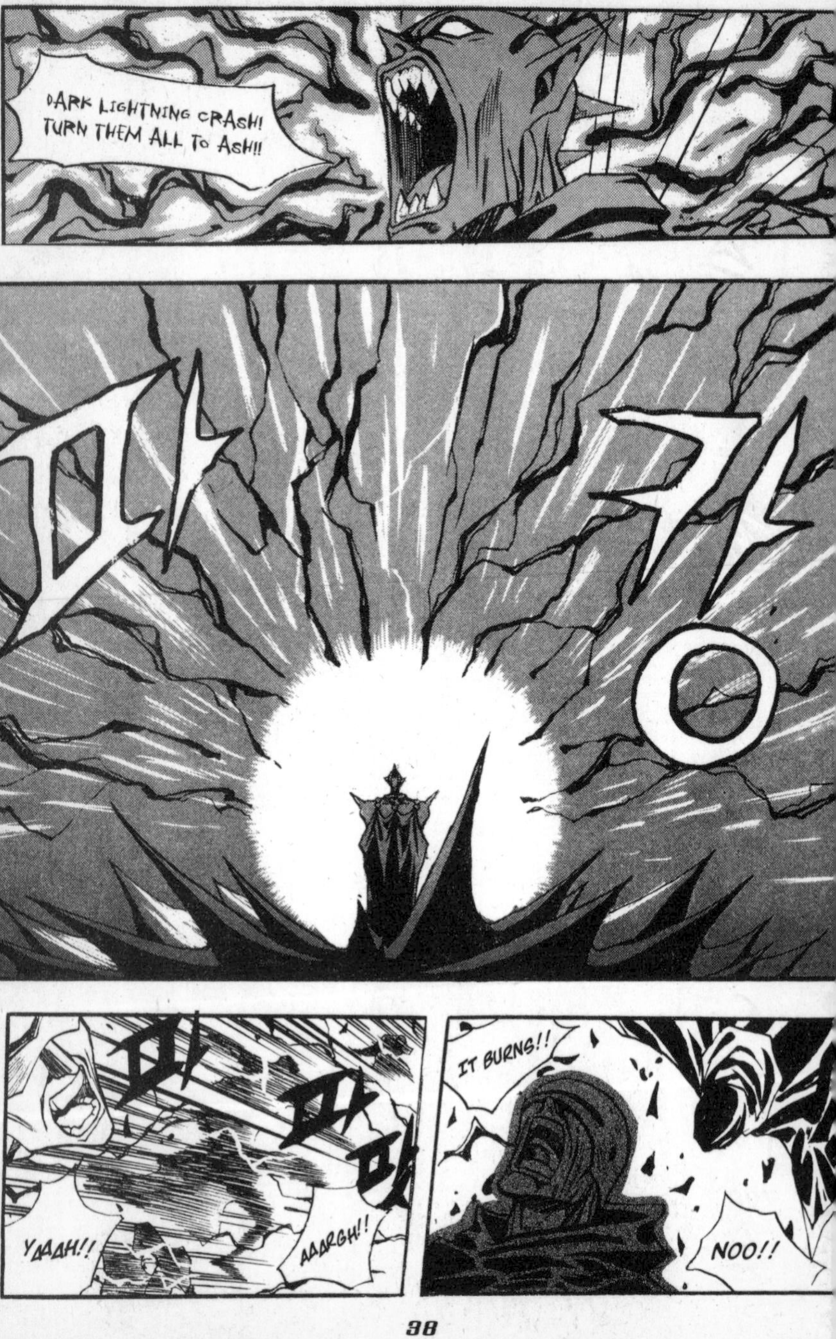
DARK LIGHTNING CRASH! TURN THEM ALL TO ASH!!
YAAAH!!
AAARGH!!
IT BURNS!!
NOO!!

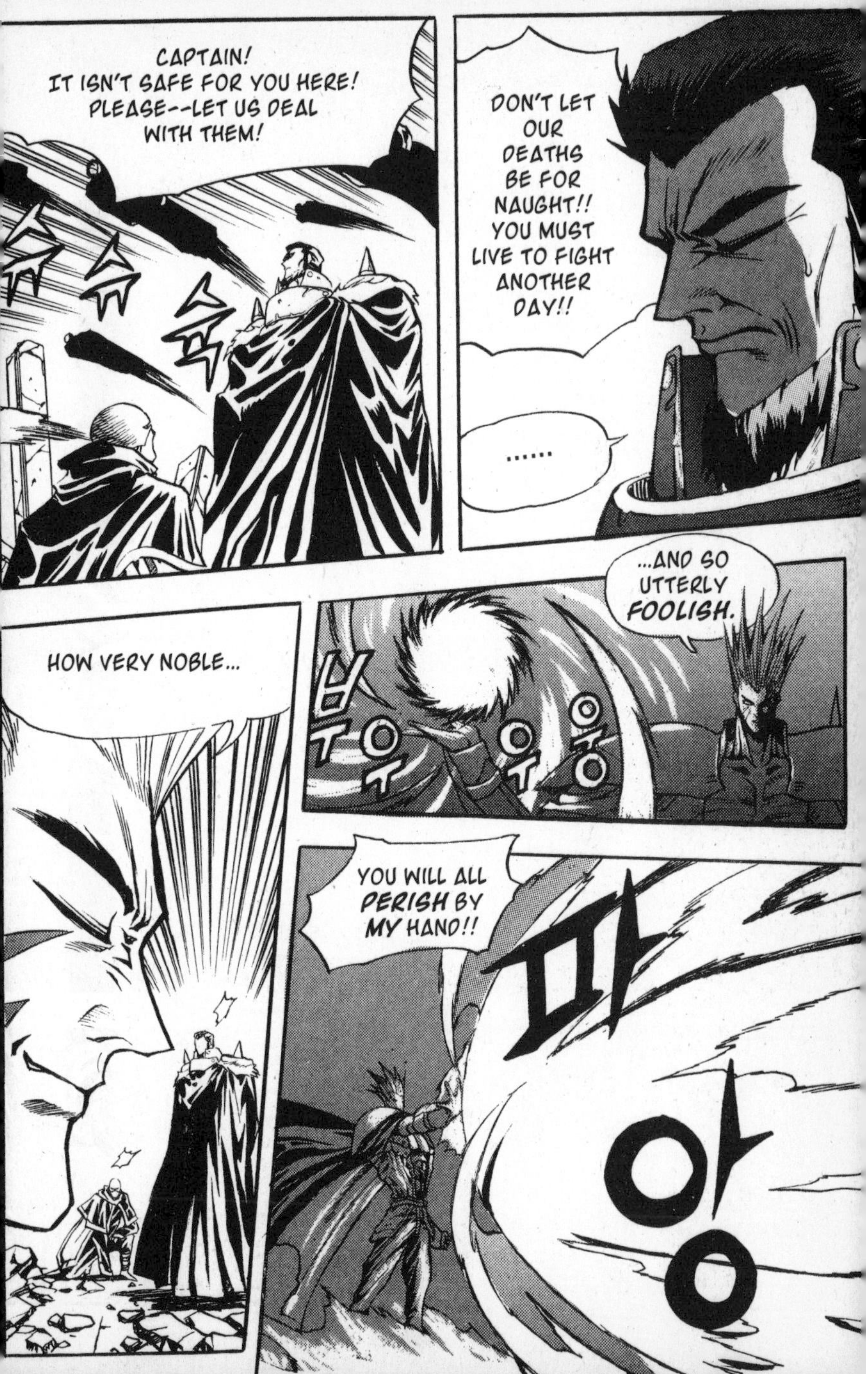
CAPTAIN!
IT ISN'T SAFE FOR YOU HERE! PLEASE--LET US DEAL WITH THEM!
DON'T LET OUR DEATHS BE FOR NAUGHT!! YOU MUST LIVE TO FIGHT ANOTHER DAY!!
......
HOW VERY NOBLE...
...AND SO UTTERLY FOOLISH.
YOU WILL ALL PERISH BY MY HAND!!

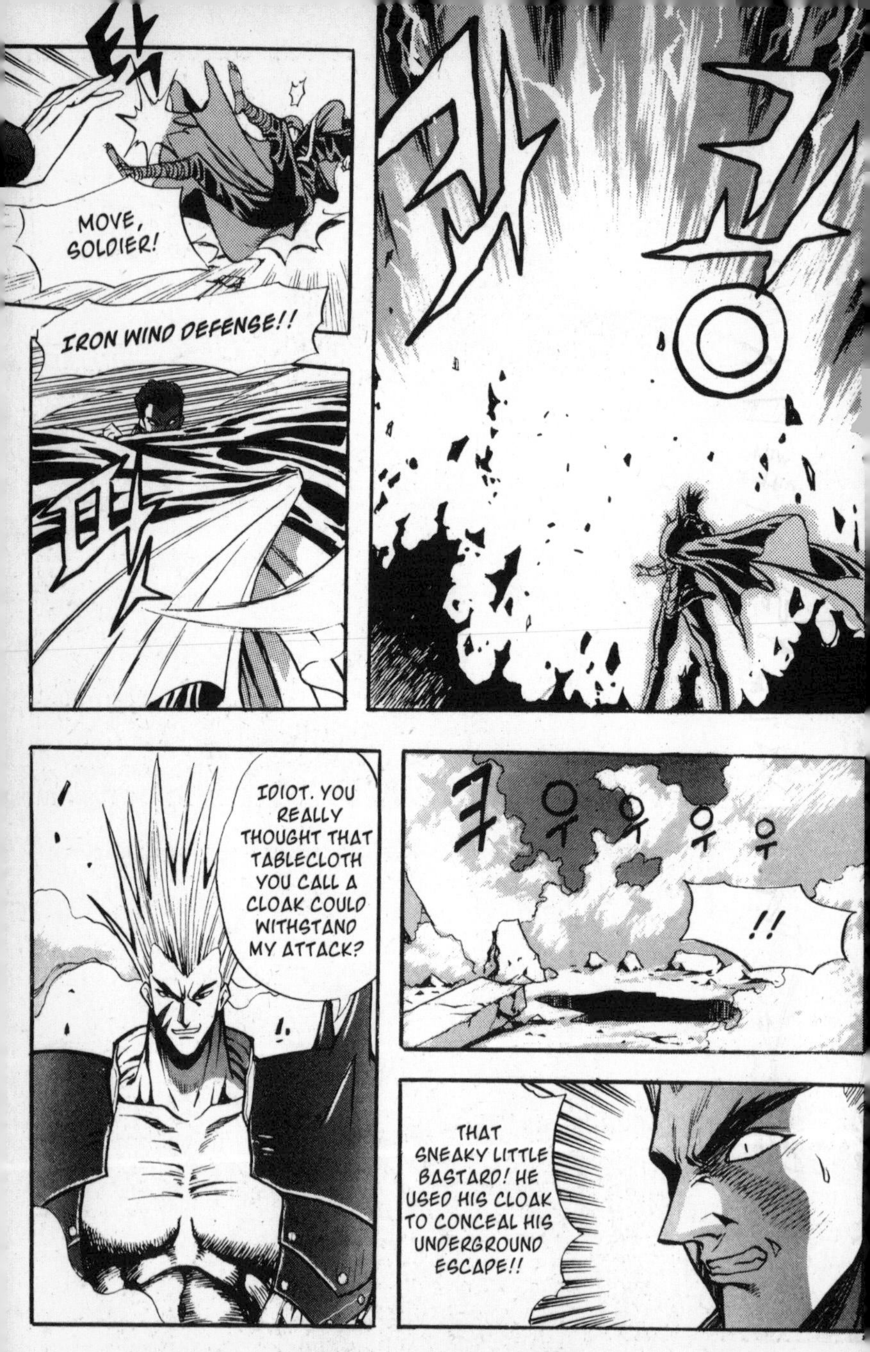
MOVE, SOLDIER!
IRON WIND DEFENSE!!
IDIOT. YOU REALLY THOUGHT THAT TABLECLOTH YOU CALL A CLOAK COULD WITHSTAND MY ATTACK?
!!
THAT SNEAKY LITTLE BASTARD! HE USED HIS CLOAK TO CONCEAL HIS UNDERGROUND ESCAPE!!

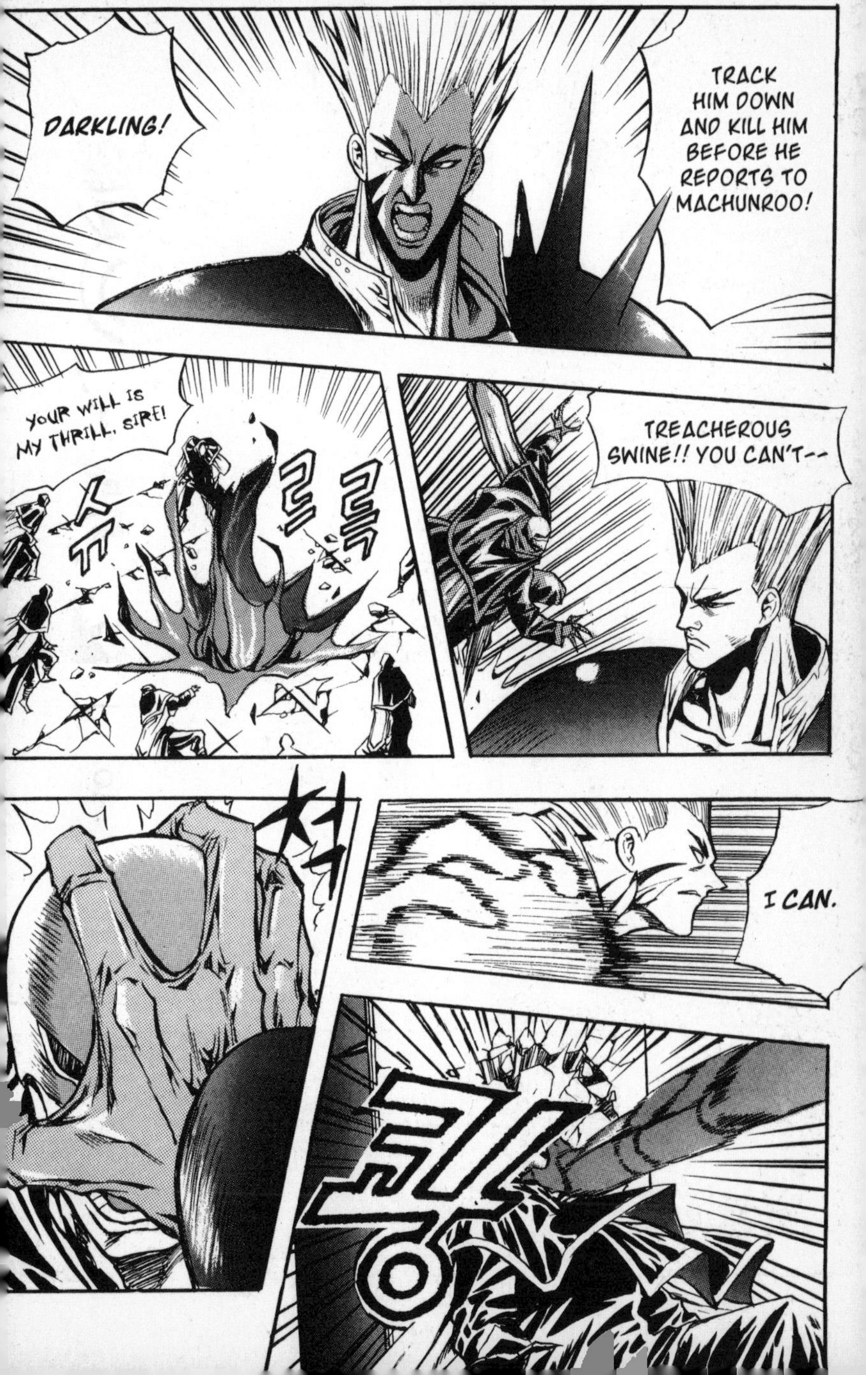
DARKLING!
TRACK HIM DOWN AND KILL HIM BEFORE HE REPORTS TO MACHUNROO!
YOUR WILL IS MY THRILL, SIRE!
TREACHEROUS SWINE!! YOU CAN'T--
I CAN.

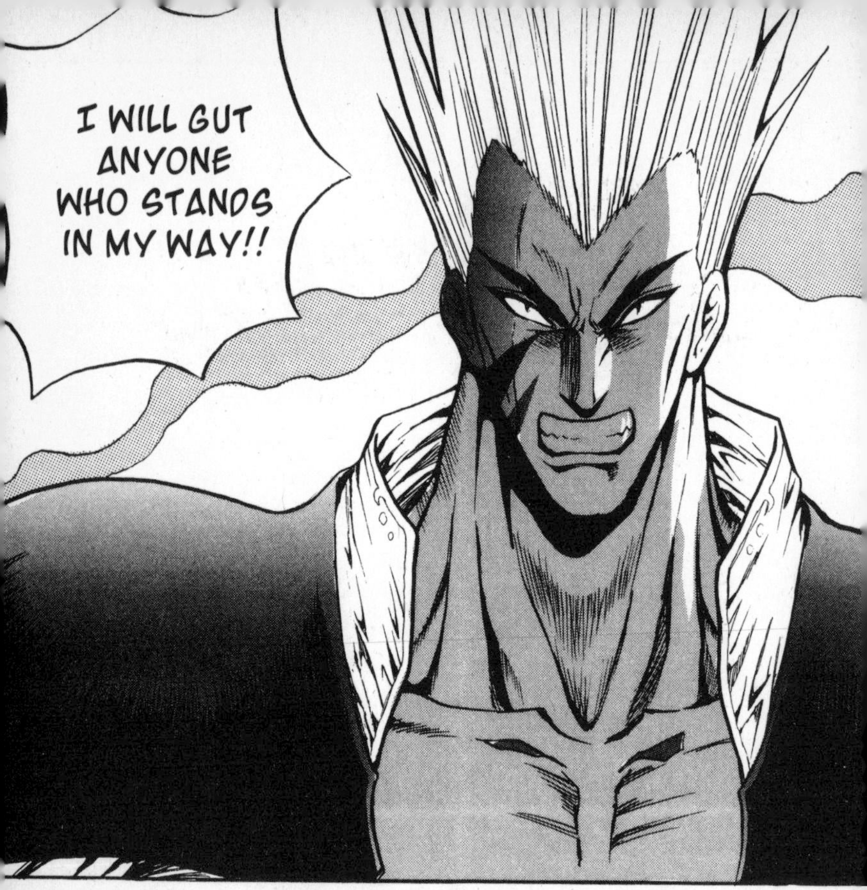
I WILL GUT ANYONE WHO STANDS IN MY WAY!!
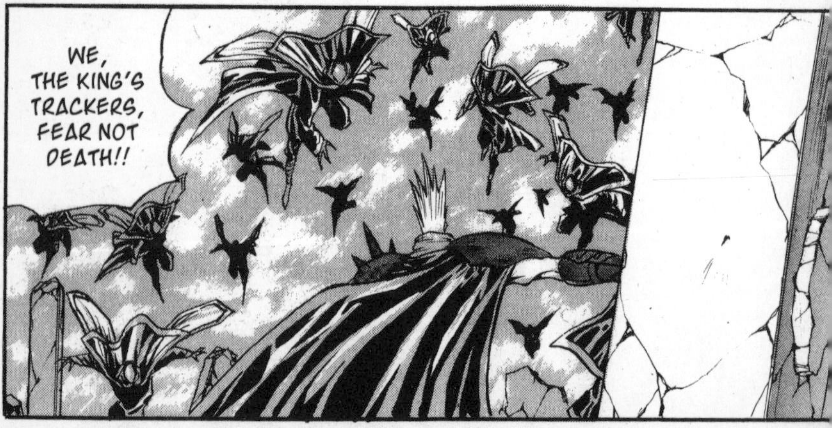
WE, THE KING'S TRACKERS, FEAR NOT DEATH!!

BLADE OF HEAVEN

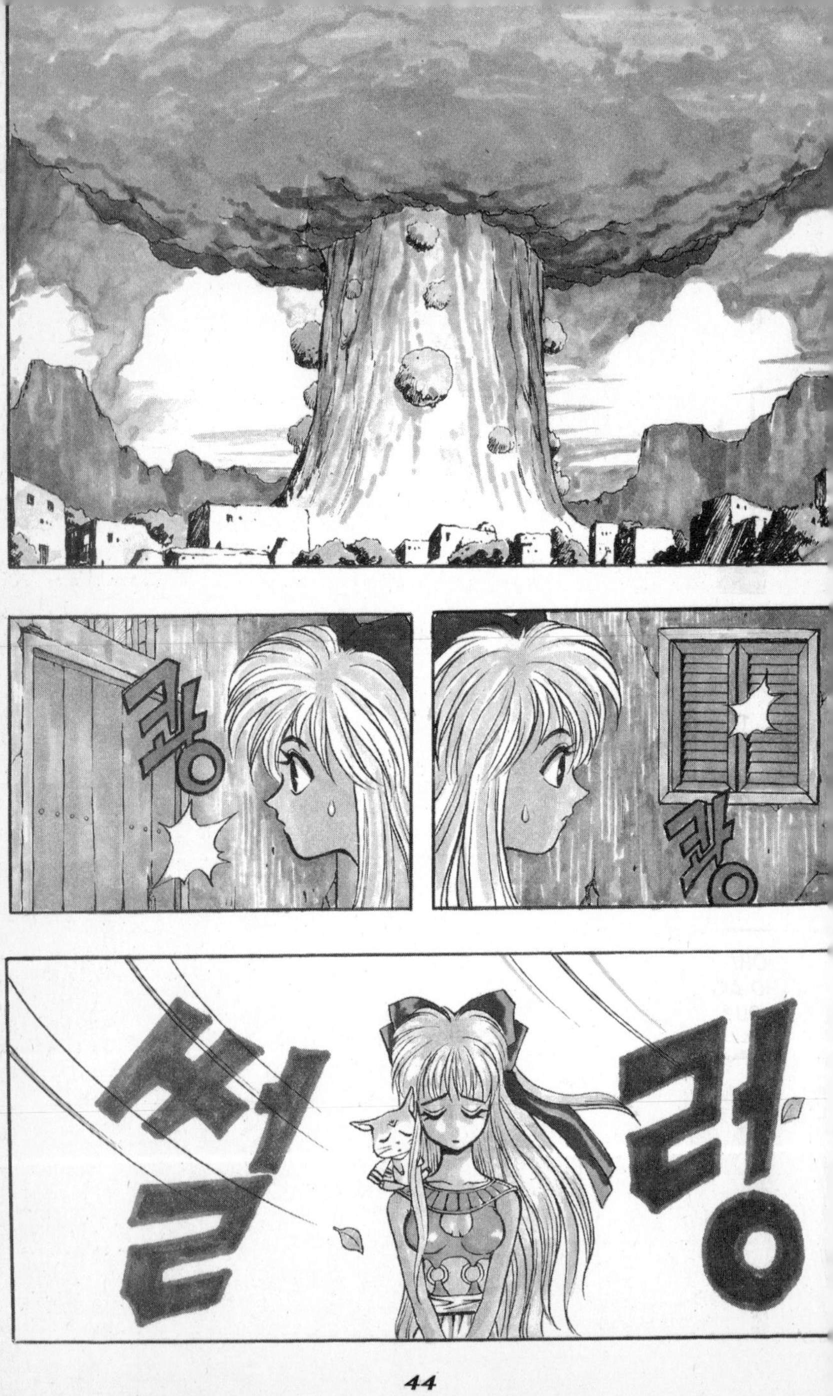
쾅
쾅
철렁

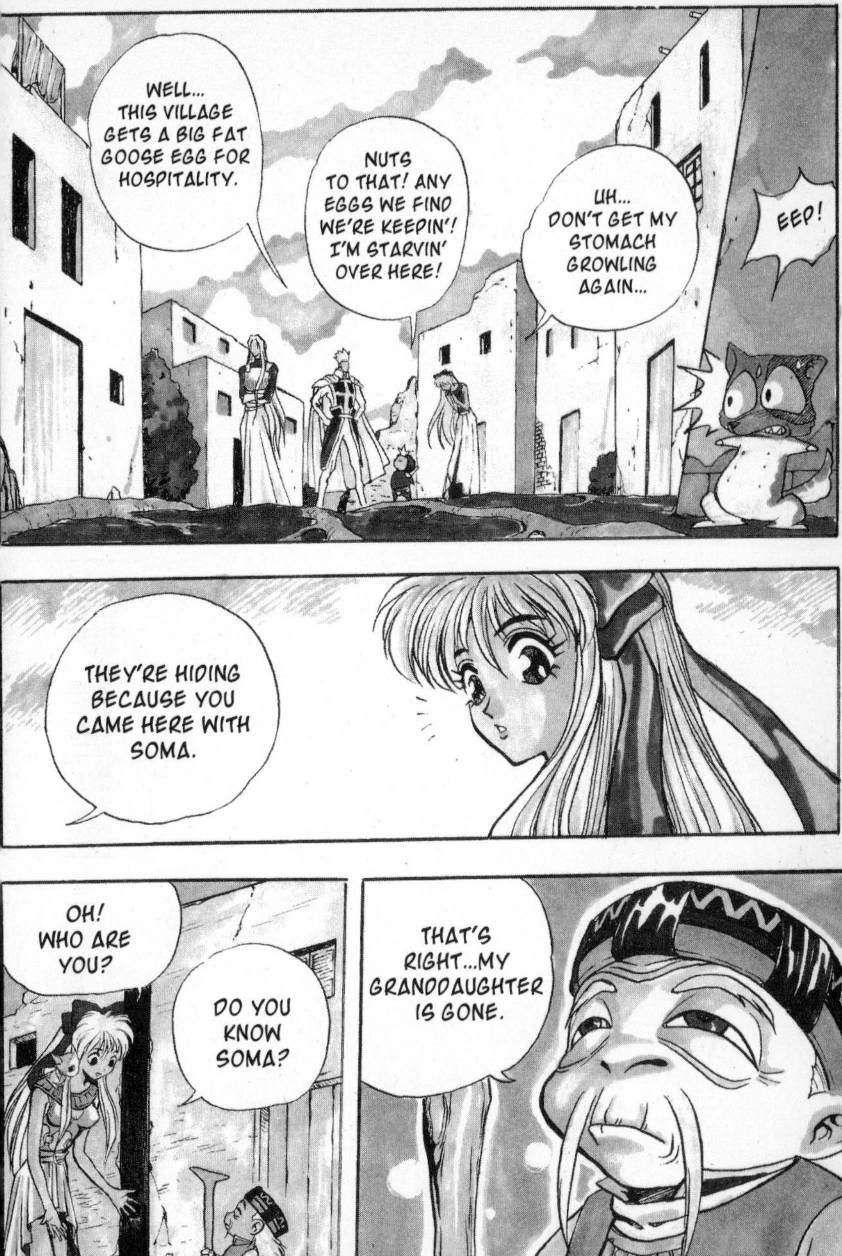
WELL... THIS VILLAGE GETS A BIG FAT GOOSE EGG FOR HOSPITALITY.
NUTS TO THAT! ANY EGGS WE FIND WE'RE KEEPIN'! I'M STARVIN' OVER HERE!
UH... DON'T GET MY STOMACH GROWLING AGAIN...
EEP!
THEY'RE HIDING BECAUSE YOU CAME HERE WITH SOMA.
OH! WHO ARE YOU?
DO YOU KNOW SOMA?
THAT'S RIGHT...MY GRANDDAUGHTER IS GONE.

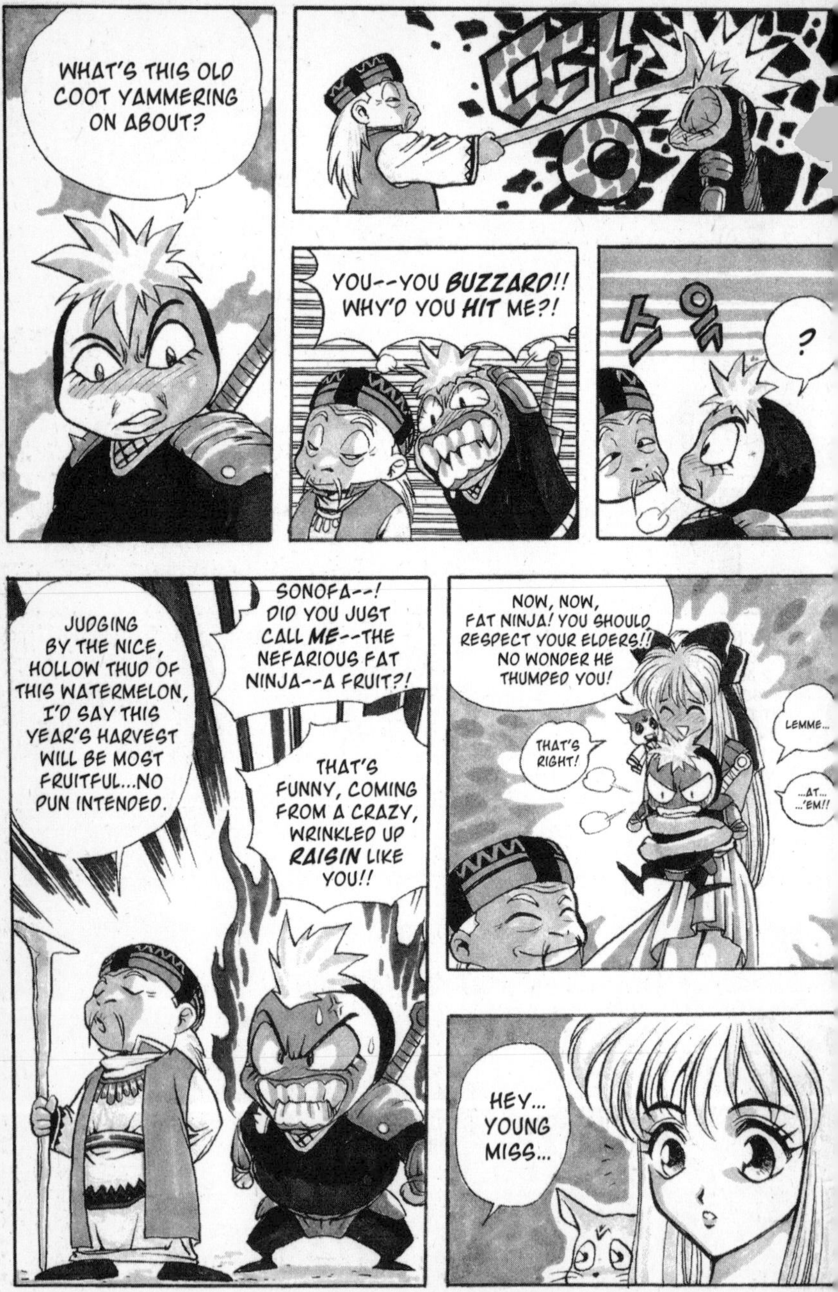
WHAT'S THIS OLD COOT YAMMERING ON ABOUT?
YOU--YOU BUZZARD!! WHY'D YOU HIT ME?!
?
JUDGING BY THE NICE, HOLLOW THUD OF THIS WATERMELON, I'D SAY THIS YEAR'S HARVEST WILL BE MOST FRUITFUL...NO PUN INTENDED.
SONOFA--! DID YOU JUST CALL ME--THE NEFARIOUS FAT NINJA--A FRUIT?!
THAT'S FUNNY, COMING FROM A CRAZY, WRINKLED UP RAISIN LIKE YOU!!
NOW, NOW, FAT NINJA! YOU SHOULD RESPECT YOUR ELDERS!! NO WONDER HE THUMPED YOU!
THAT'S RIGHT!
LEMME...
...AT... ...'EM!!
HEY... YOUNG MISS...

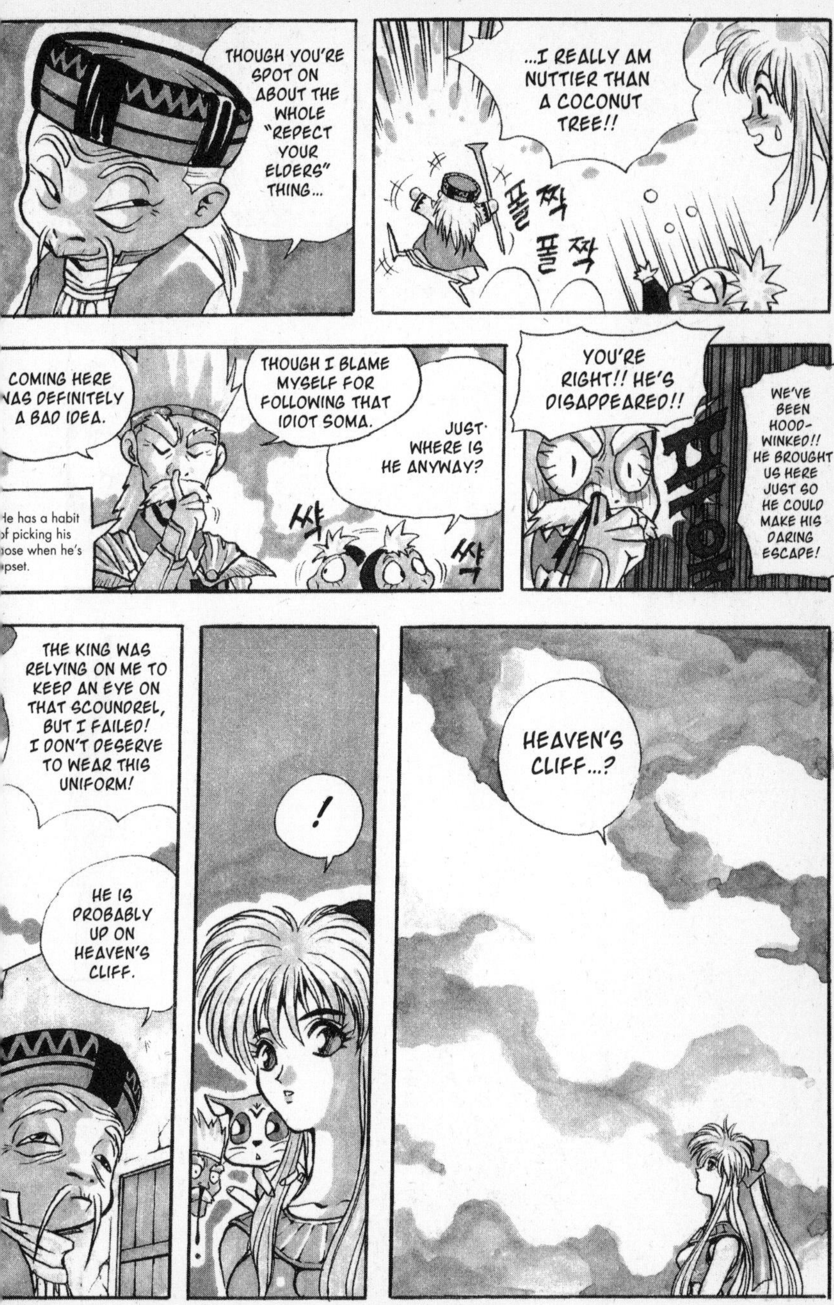
THOUGH YOU'RE SPOT ON ABOUT THE WHOLE "REPECT YOUR ELDERS" THING...
...I REALLY AM NUTTIER THAN A COCONUT TREE!!
폴짝
폴짝
COMING HERE WAS DEFINITELY A BAD IDEA.
THOUGH I BLAME MYSELF FOR FOLLOWING THAT IDIOT SOMA.
He has a habit of picking his nose when he's upset.
JUST WHERE IS HE ANYWAY?
쌱
쌱
YOU'RE RIGHT!! HE'S DISAPPEARED!!
WE'VE BEEN HOOD-WINKED!! HE BROUGHT US HERE JUST SO HE COULD MAKE HIS DARING ESCAPE!
THE KING WAS RELYING ON ME TO KEEP AN EYE ON THAT SCOUNDREL, BUT I FAILED! I DON'T DESERVE TO WEAR THIS UNIFORM!
HE IS PROBABLY UP ON HEAVEN'S CLIFF.
!
HEAVEN'S CLIFF...?

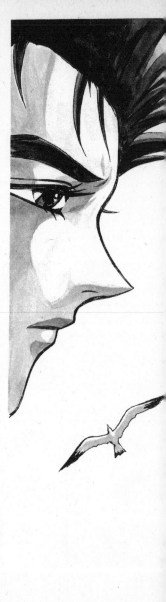

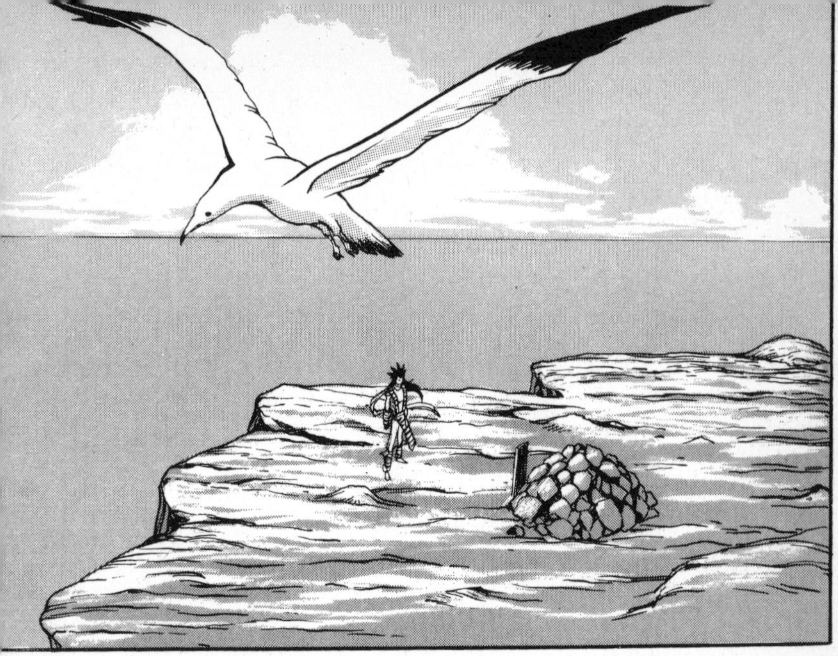

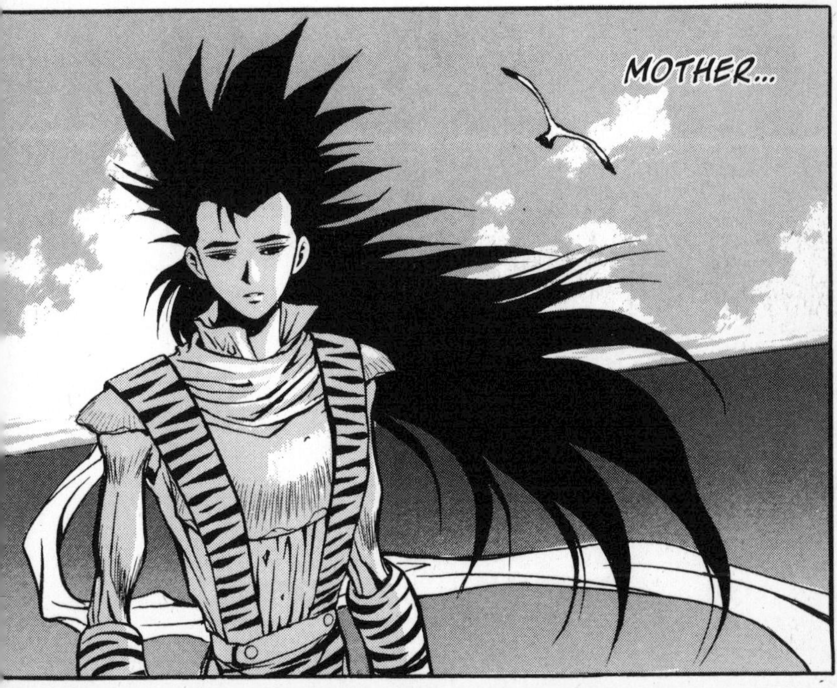
MOTHER...

우아아우웅

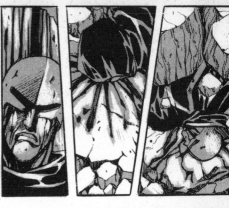

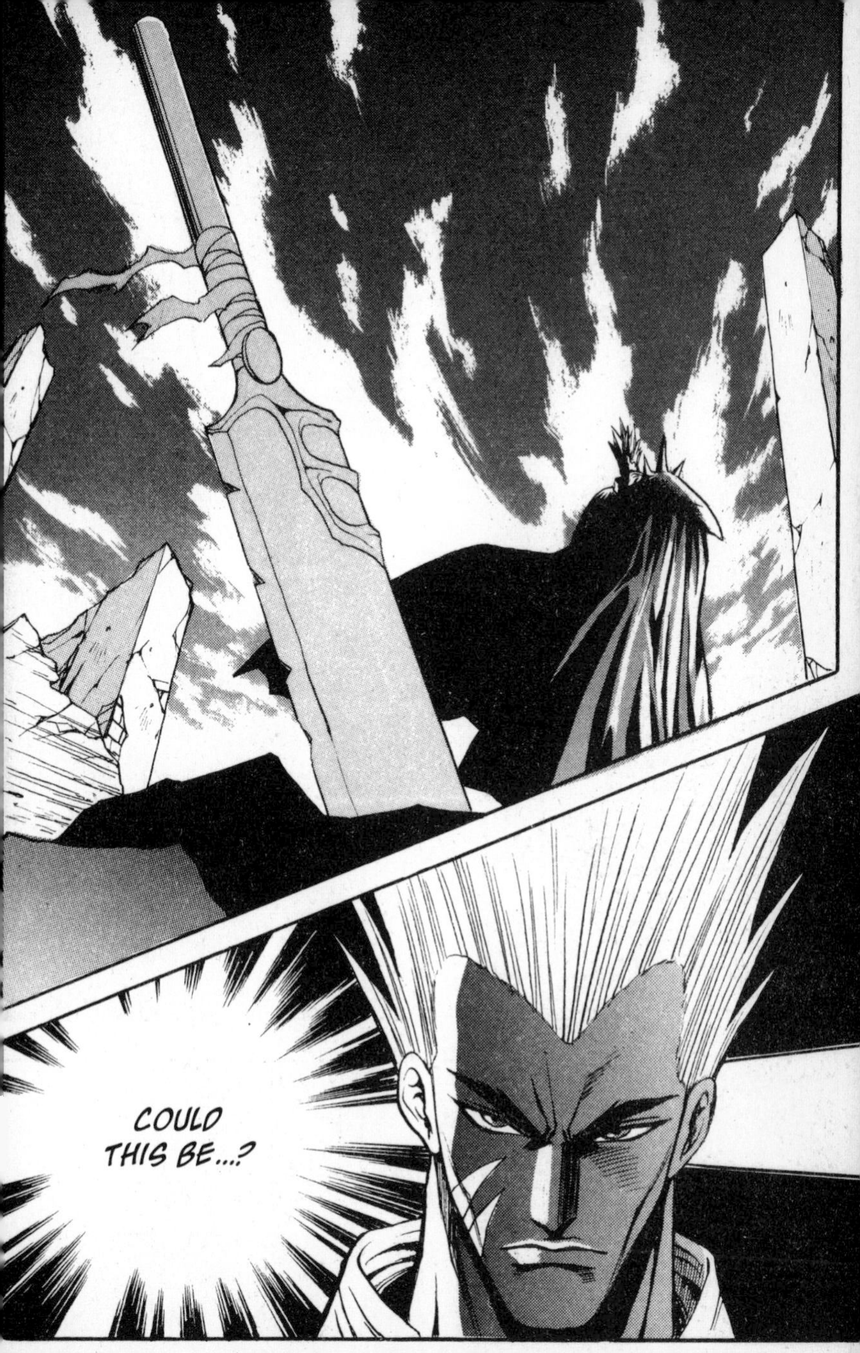
COULD THIS BE...?

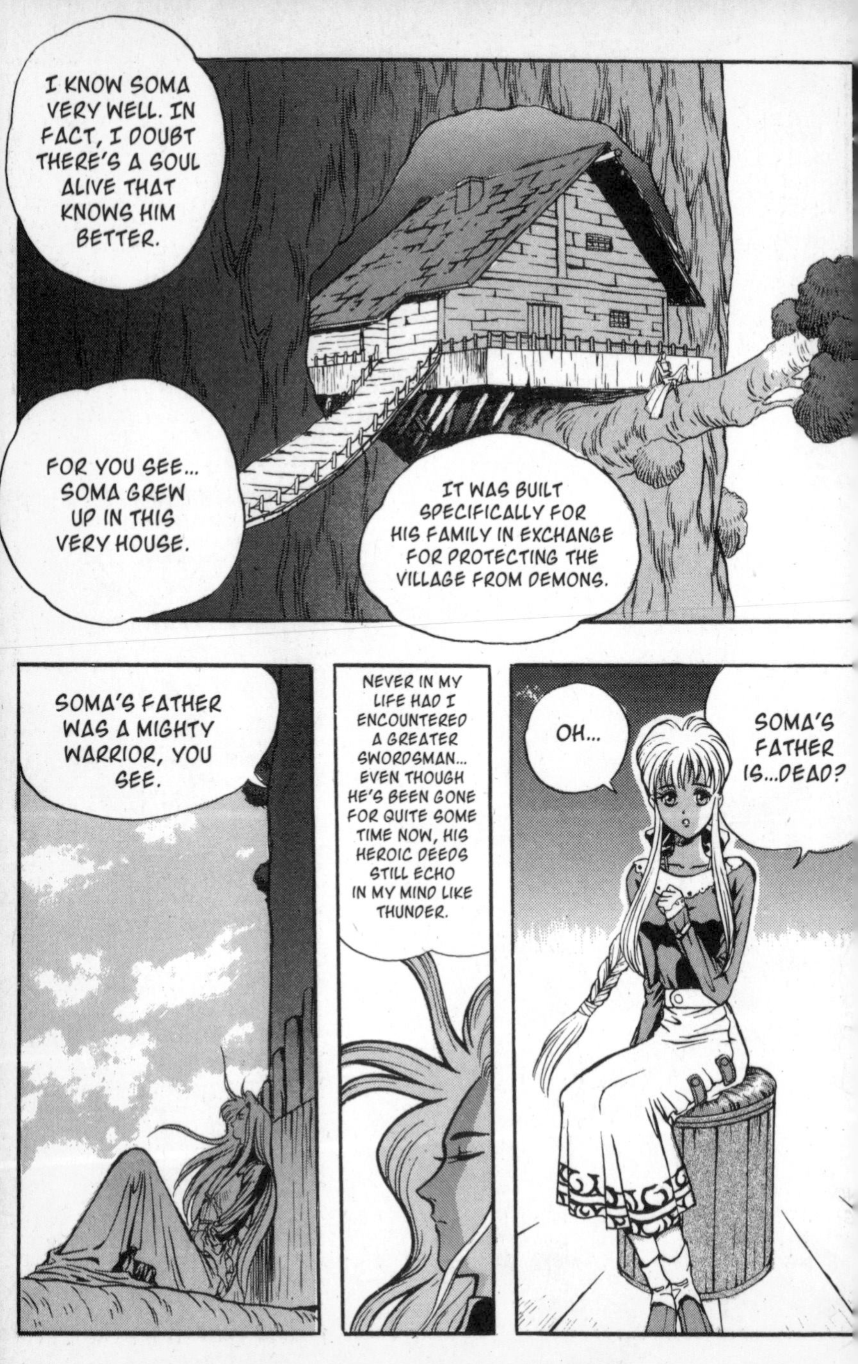

I KNOW SOMA VERY WELL. IN FACT, I DOUBT THERE'S A SOUL ALIVE THAT KNOWS HIM BETTER.
FOR YOU SEE... SOMA GREW UP IN THIS VERY HOUSE.
IT WAS BUILT SPECIFICALLY FOR HIS FAMILY IN EXCHANGE FOR PROTECTING THE VILLAGE FROM DEMONS.
SOMA'S FATHER WAS A MIGHTY WARRIOR, YOU SEE.
NEVER IN MY LIFE HAD I ENCOUNTERED A GREATER SWORDSMAN... EVEN THOUGH HE'S BEEN GONE FOR QUITE SOME TIME NOW, HIS HEROIC DEEDS STILL ECHO IN MY MIND LIKE THUNDER.
OH...
SOMA'S FATHER IS...DEAD?

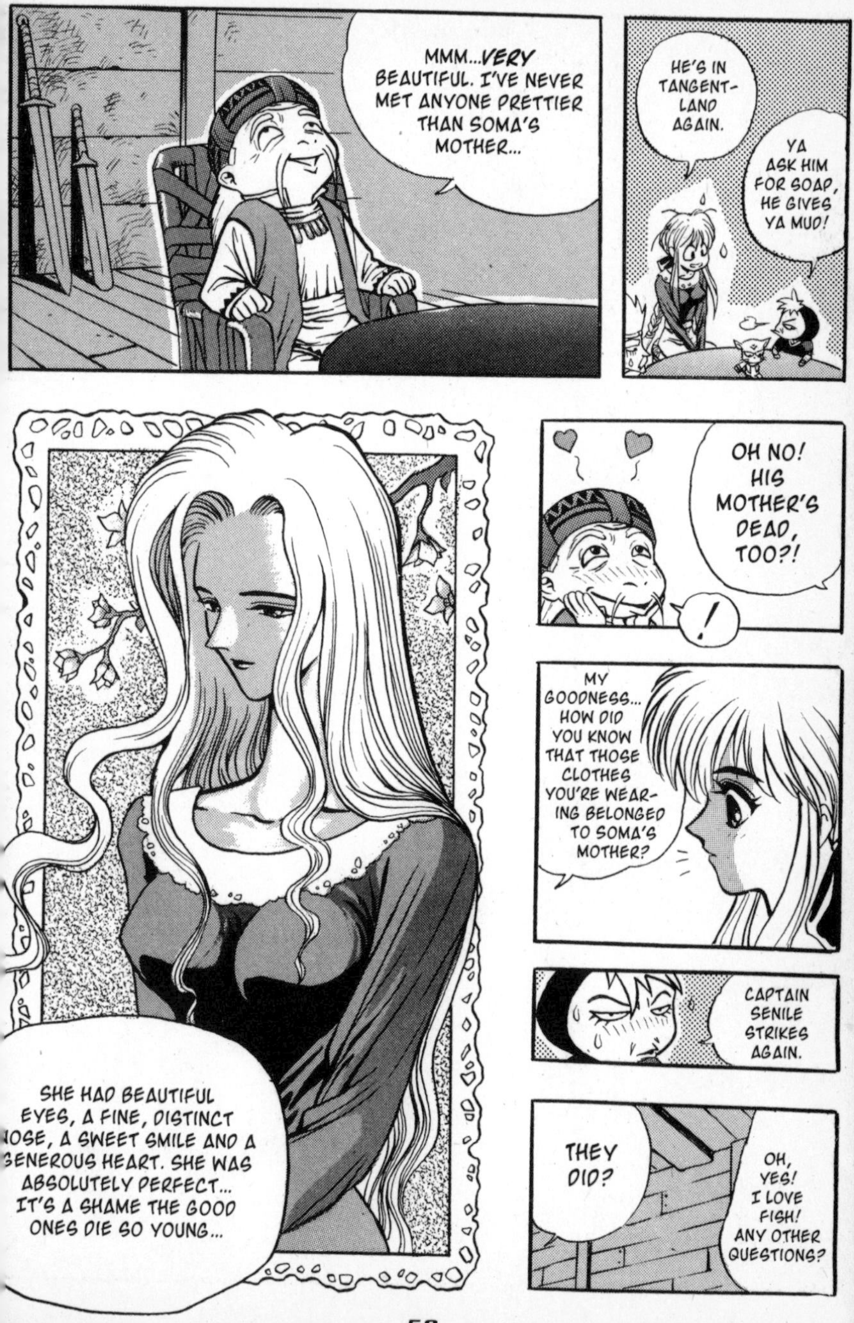

MMM...*VERY* BEAUTIFUL. I'VE NEVER MET ANYONE PRETTIER THAN SOMA'S MOTHER...
HE'S IN TANGENT-LAND AGAIN.
YA ASK HIM FOR SOAP, HE GIVES YA MUD!
SHE HAD BEAUTIFUL EYES, A FINE, DISTINCT NOSE, A SWEET SMILE AND A GENEROUS HEART. SHE WAS ABSOLUTELY PERFECT... IT'S A SHAME THE GOOD ONES DIE SO YOUNG...
OH NO! HIS MOTHER'S DEAD, TOO?!
!
MY GOODNESS... HOW DID YOU KNOW THAT THOSE CLOTHES YOU'RE WEARING BELONGED TO SOMA'S MOTHER?
CAPTAIN SENILE STRIKES AGAIN.
THEY DID?
OH, YES! I LOVE FISH! ANY OTHER QUESTIONS?

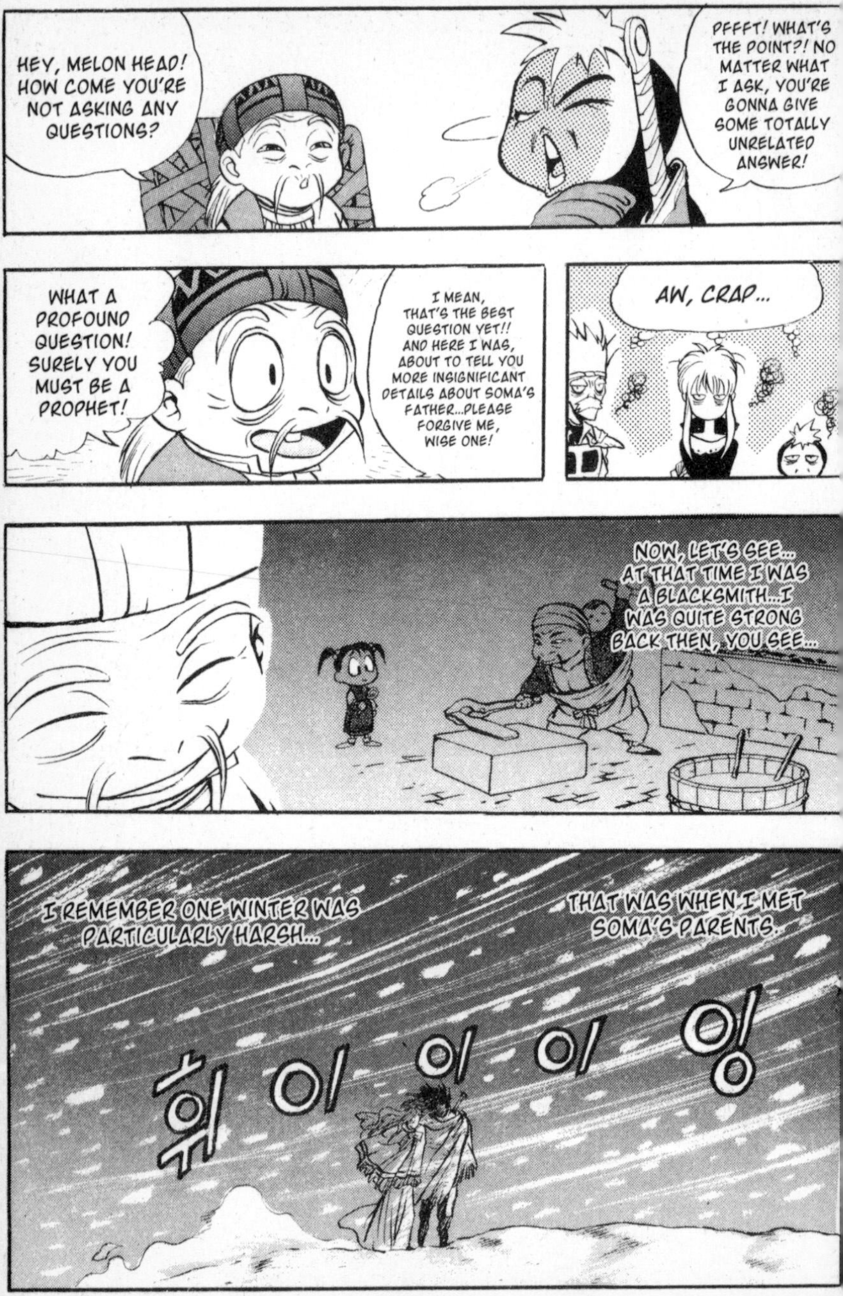
HEY, MELON HEAD! HOW COME YOU'RE NOT ASKING ANY QUESTIONS?
PFFFT! WHAT'S THE POINT?! NO MATTER WHAT I ASK, YOU'RE GONNA GIVE SOME TOTALLY UNRELATED ANSWER!
WHAT A PROFOUND QUESTION! SURELY YOU MUST BE A PROPHET!
I MEAN, THAT'S THE BEST QUESTION YET!! AND HERE I WAS, ABOUT TO TELL YOU MORE INSIGNIFICANT DETAILS ABOUT SOMA'S FATHER...PLEASE FORGIVE ME, WISE ONE!
AW, CRAP...
NOW, LET'S SEE... AT THAT TIME I WAS A BLACKSMITH...I WAS QUITE STRONG BACK THEN, YOU SEE...
I REMEMBER ONE WINTER WAS PARTICULARLY HARSH...
THAT WAS WHEN I MET SOMA'S PARENTS.
휘이이이잉

IN THOSE DAYS, DEMONS WOULD PLUNDER AND PILLAGE THE MORTAL VILLAGES AT WILL, KILLING ANYONE IN SIGHT. SO WHEN DARKNESS FELL, DOORS WERE PROMPTLY LOCKED AND WINDOWS BARRED.

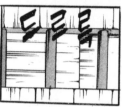

W-WHO'S THERE...?

PLEASE, MY LORD...I'M SORRY FOR DISTURBING YOU, BUT COULD YOU PUT US UP FOR THE NIGHT? MY WIFE IS SICK AND MY CHILD COLD...

I-I'M SORRY...BUT I CAN'T HELP YOU!

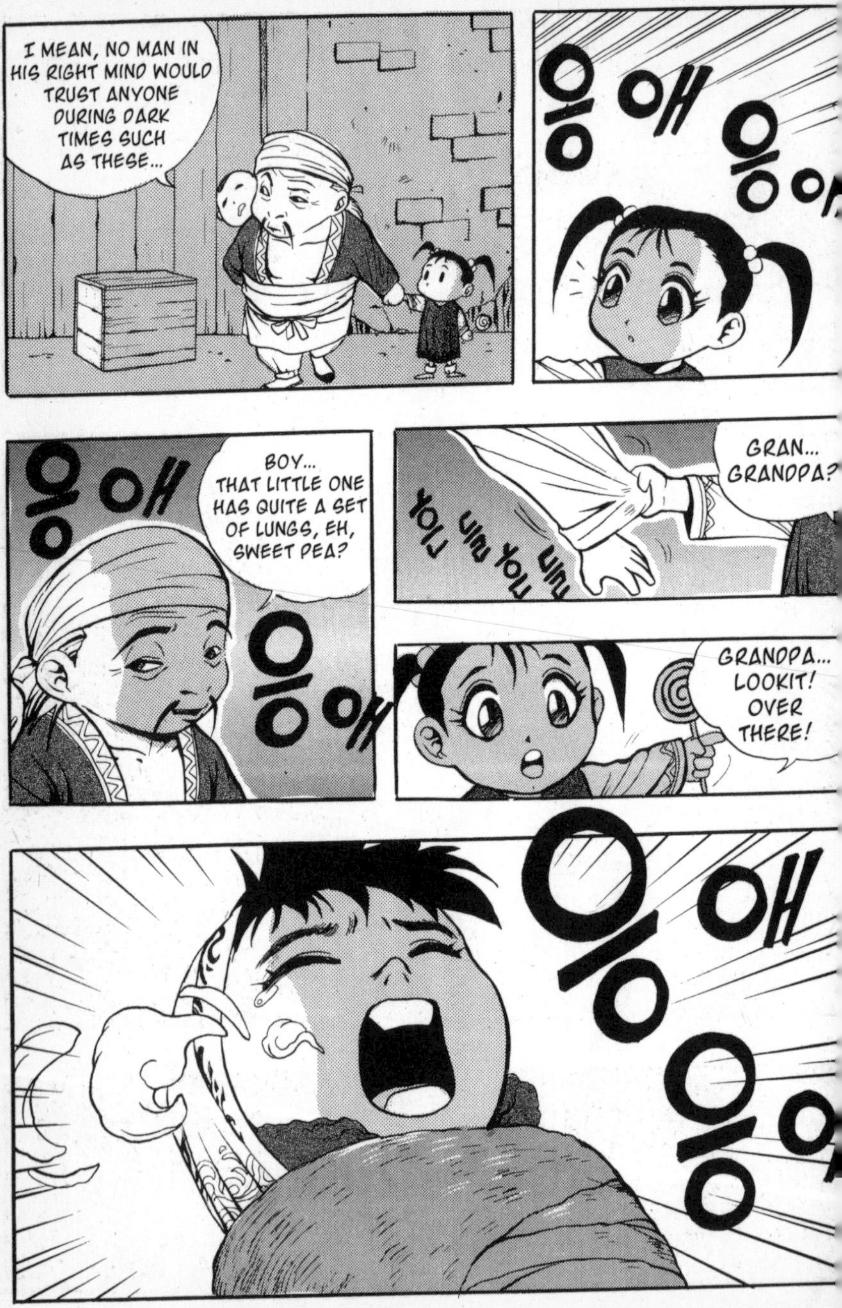

I MEAN, NO MAN IN HIS RIGHT MIND WOULD TRUST ANYONE DURING DARK TIMES SUCH AS THESE...
응애 응애
응애
BOY... THAT LITTLE ONE HAS QUITE A SET OF LUNGS, EH, SWEET PEA?
응애
GRAN... GRANDPA?
GRANDPA... LOOKIT! OVER THERE!
응애 응애 응애

IT'S ALL RIGHT.

NO...IT'S **NOT.** I'M...SORRY.

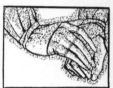

I'M FINE, MY LOVE. AS LONG AS I HAVE MY FAMILY, THAT'S ALL THE WARMTH I DESIRE.

DARLING...I'M SORRY I FAILED YOU.

LOOK...IF YOU WANT...YOU CAN SLEEP IN THE STORAGE SHED. IT ISN'T WARM, BUT AT LEAST YOU'LL BE SHELTERED FROM THE WIND.

IT WAS THE INNOCENCE OF MY GRANDDAUGHTER THAT OPENED THAT DOOR. AFTER LOOKING INTO HER EYES, I COULD NO LONGER IGNORE THE INFANT'S CRYING.

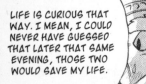

LIFE IS CURIOUS THAT WAY. I MEAN, I COULD NEVER HAVE GUESSED THAT LATER THAT SAME EVENING, THOSE TWO WOULD SAVE MY LIFE.

BLADE OF HEAVEN

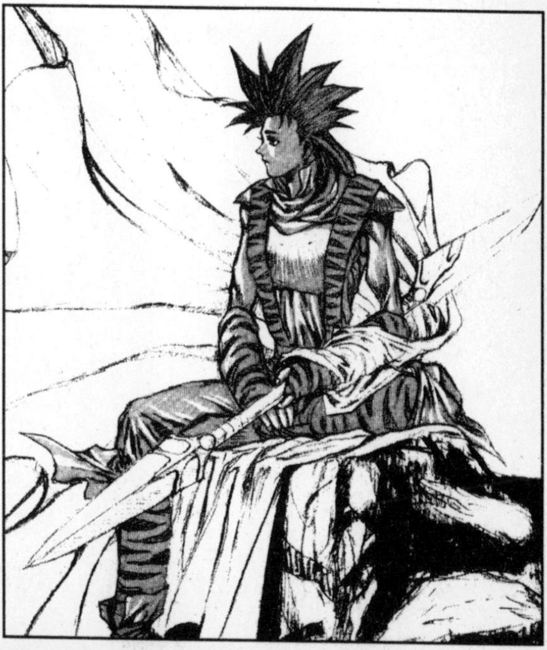

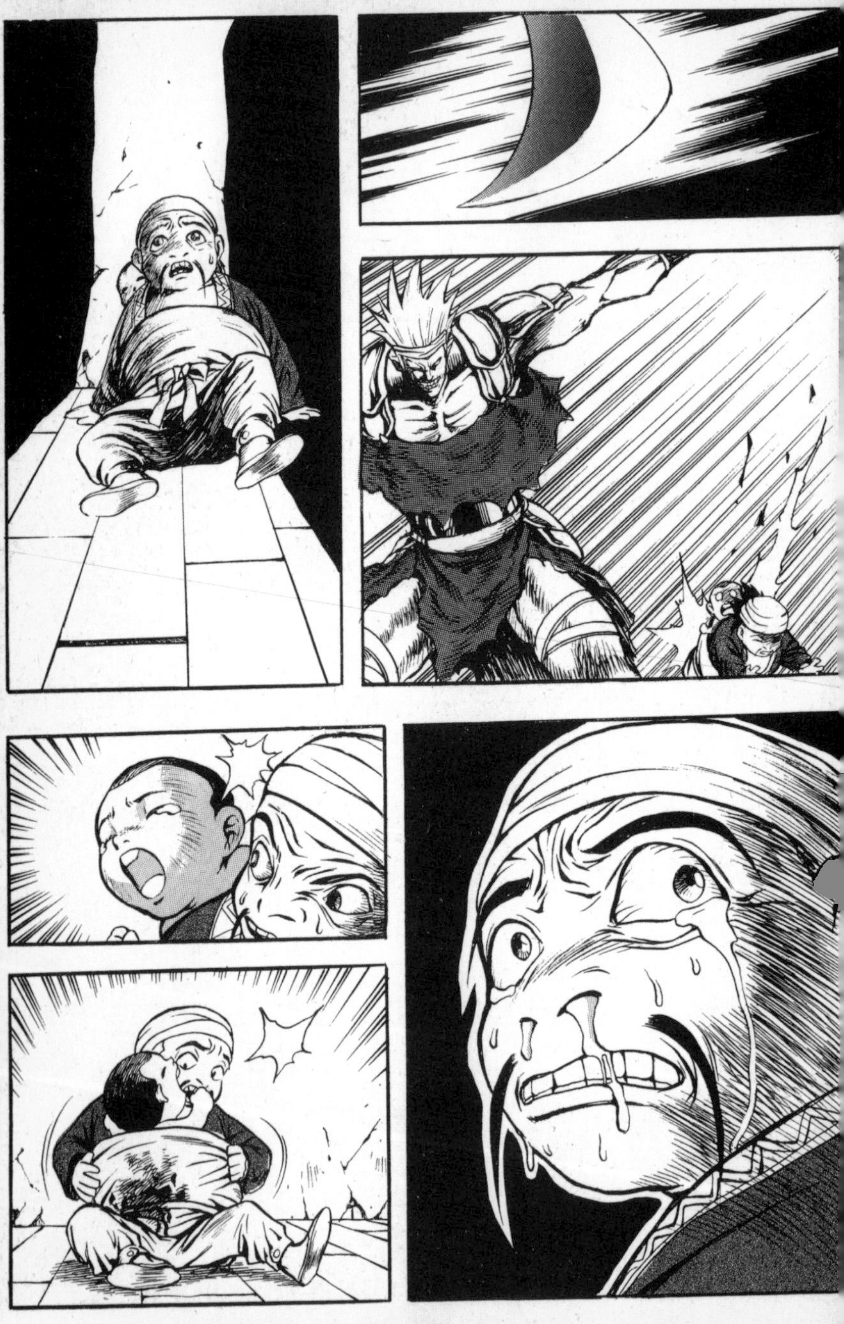

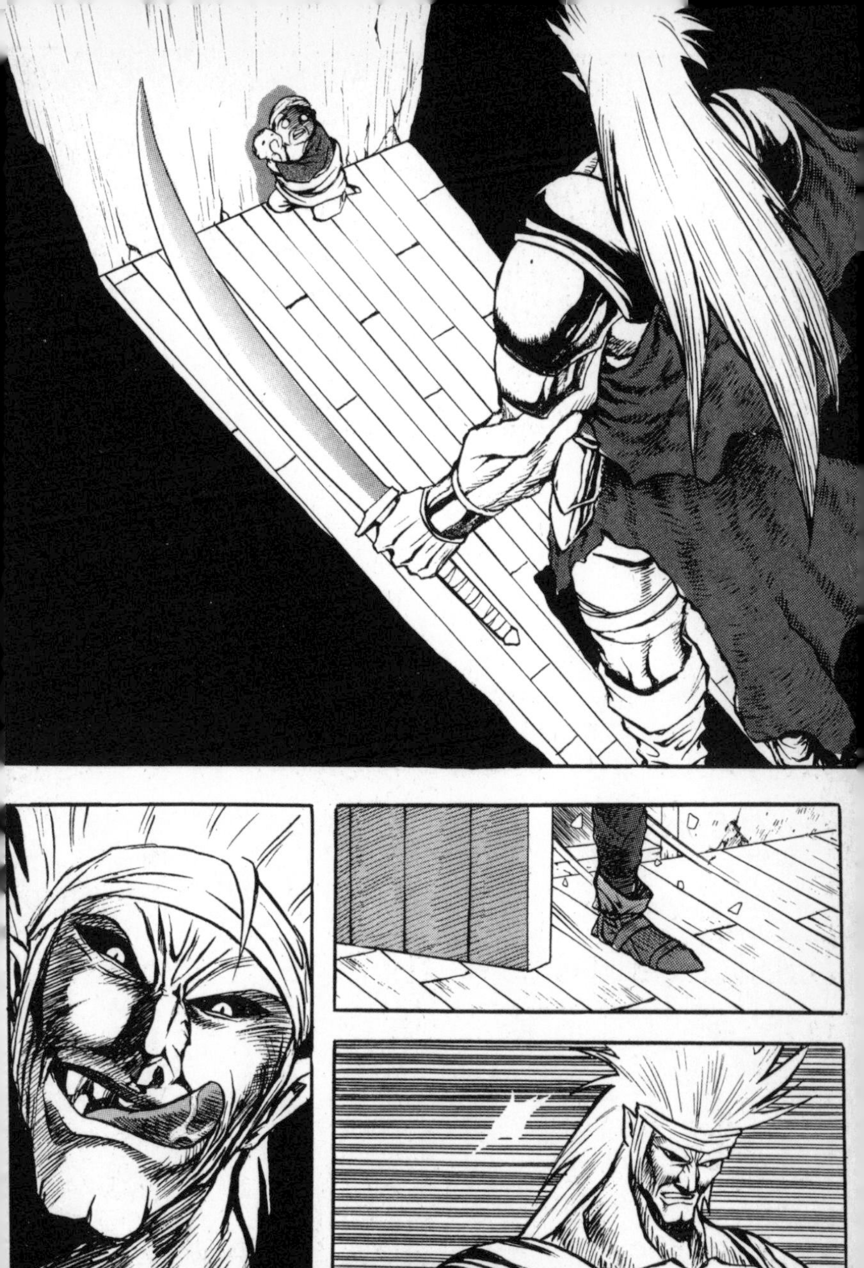

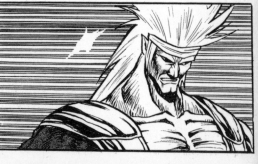

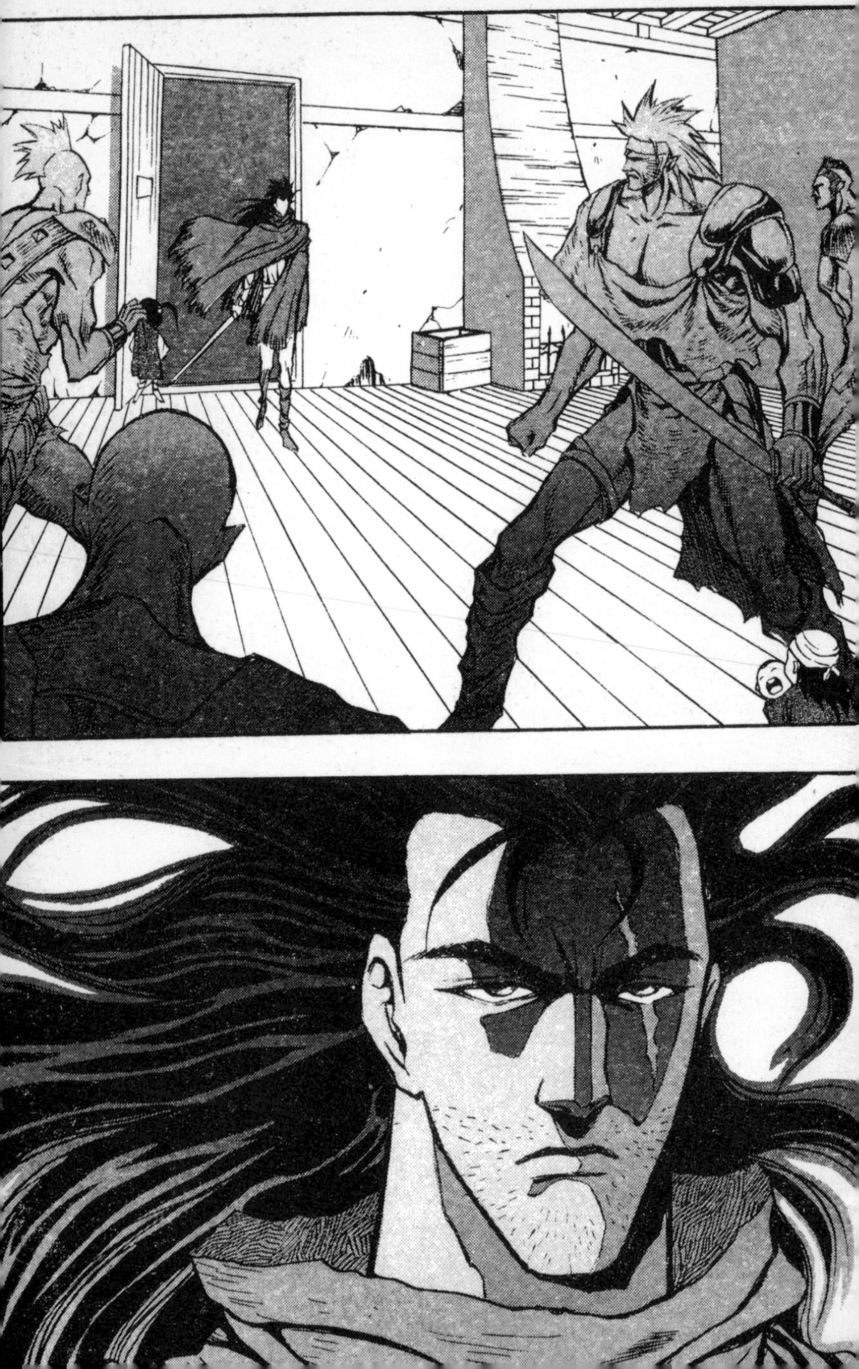

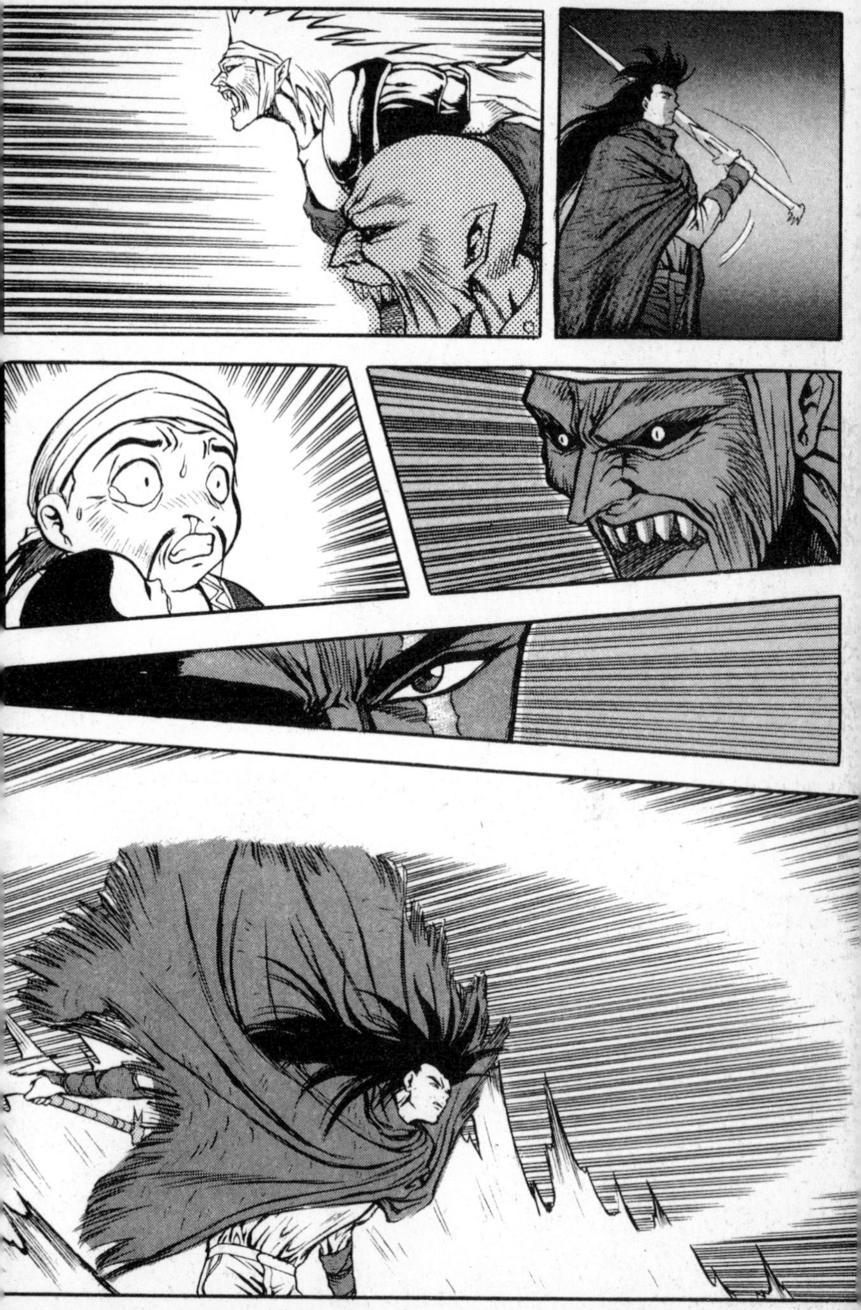

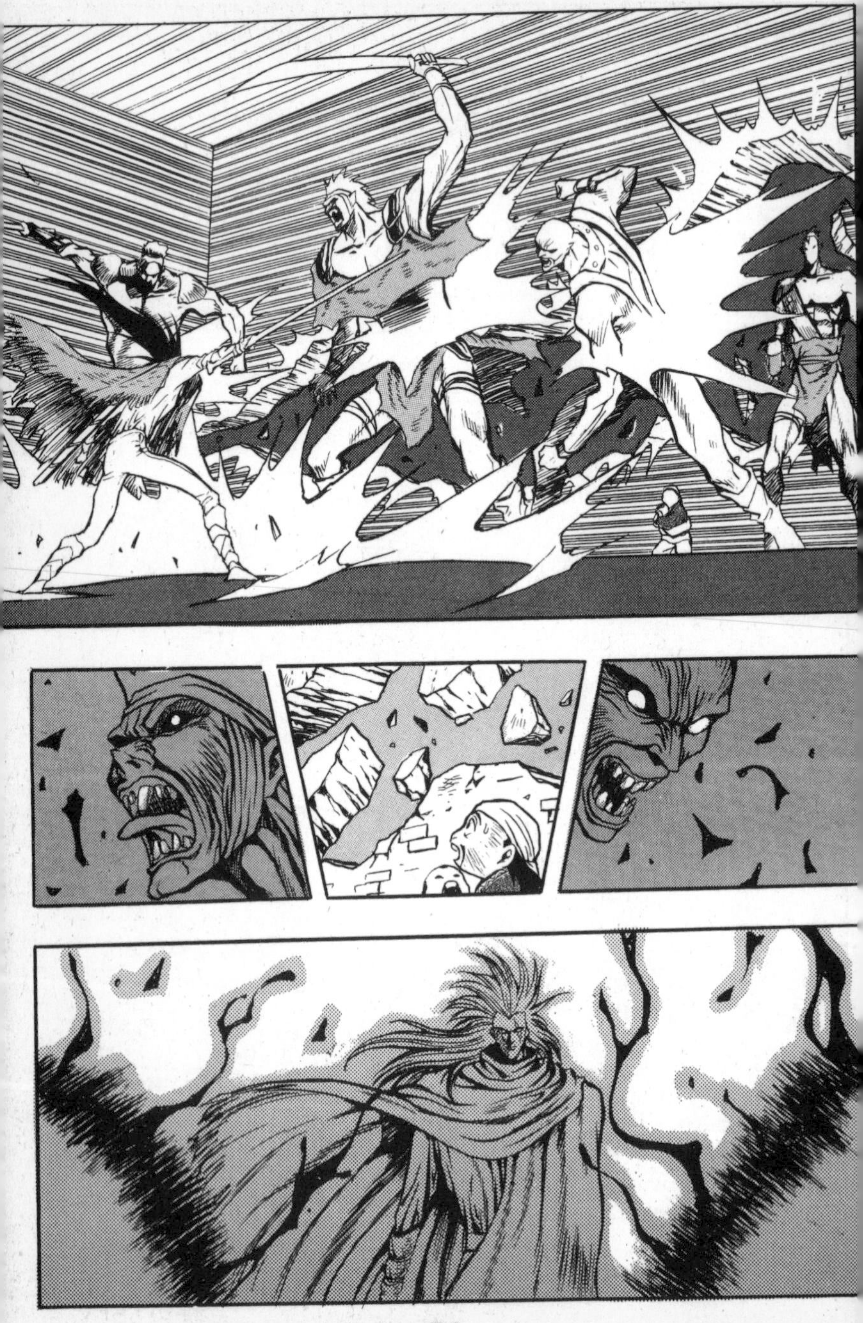

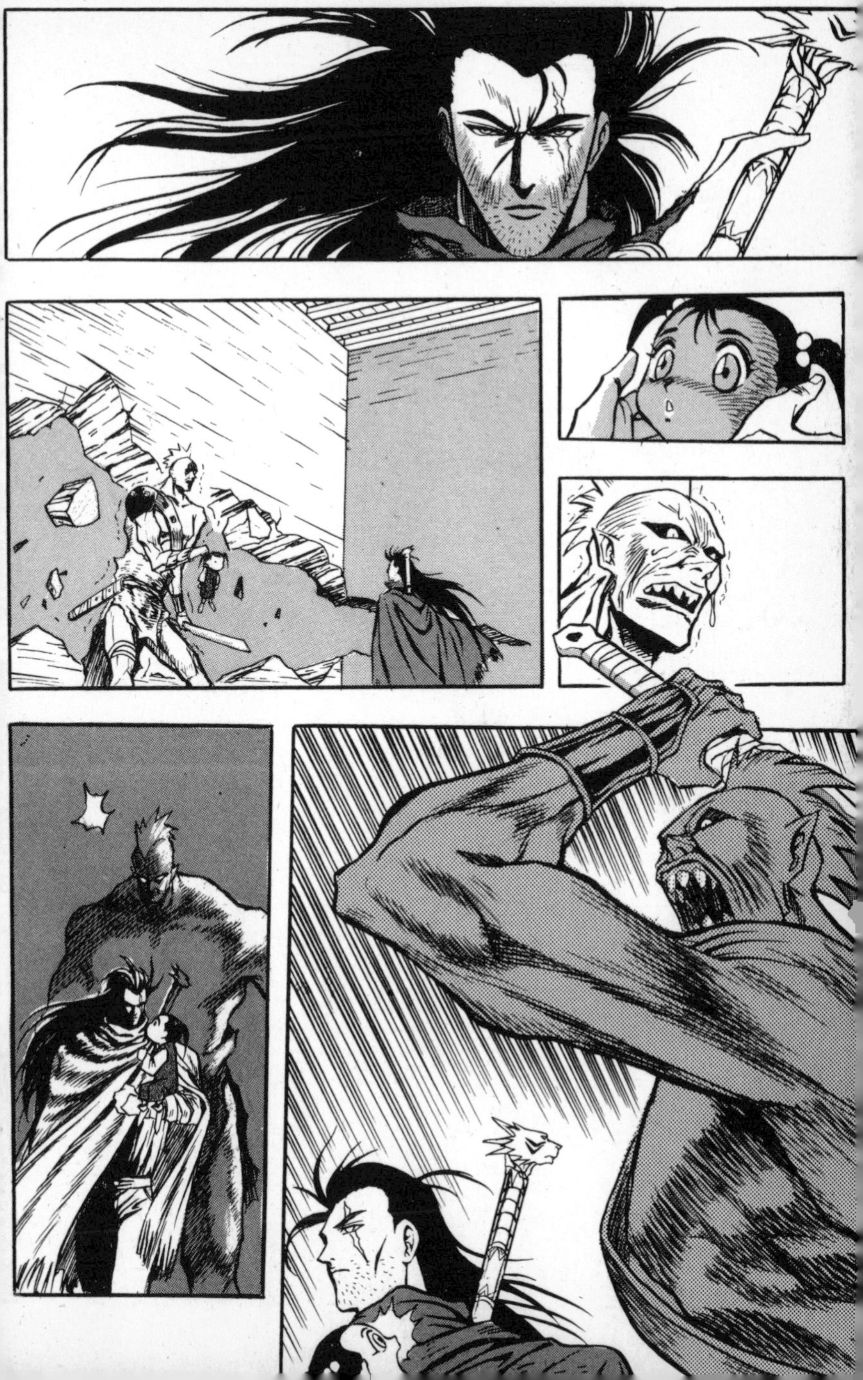

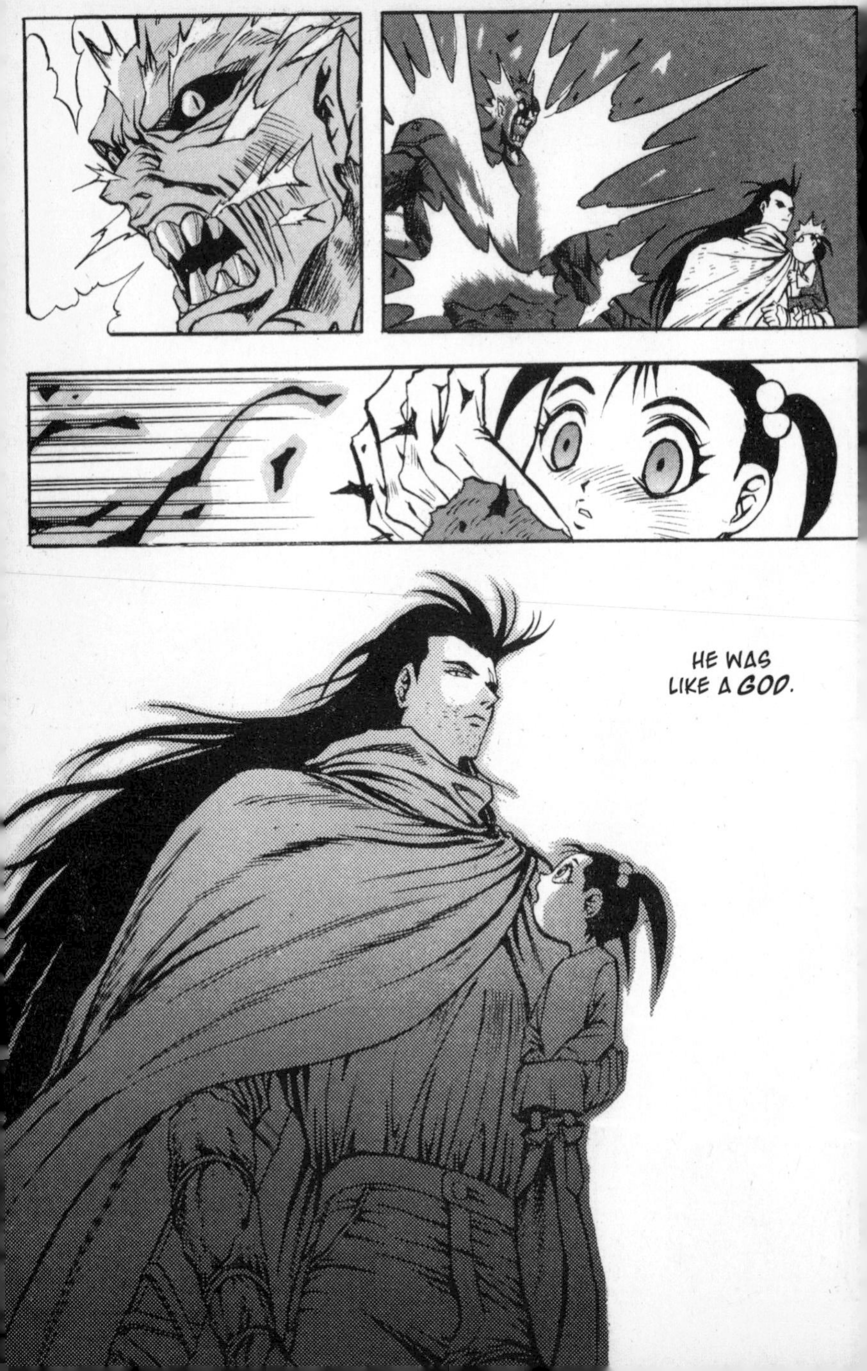
HE WAS
LIKE A GOD.

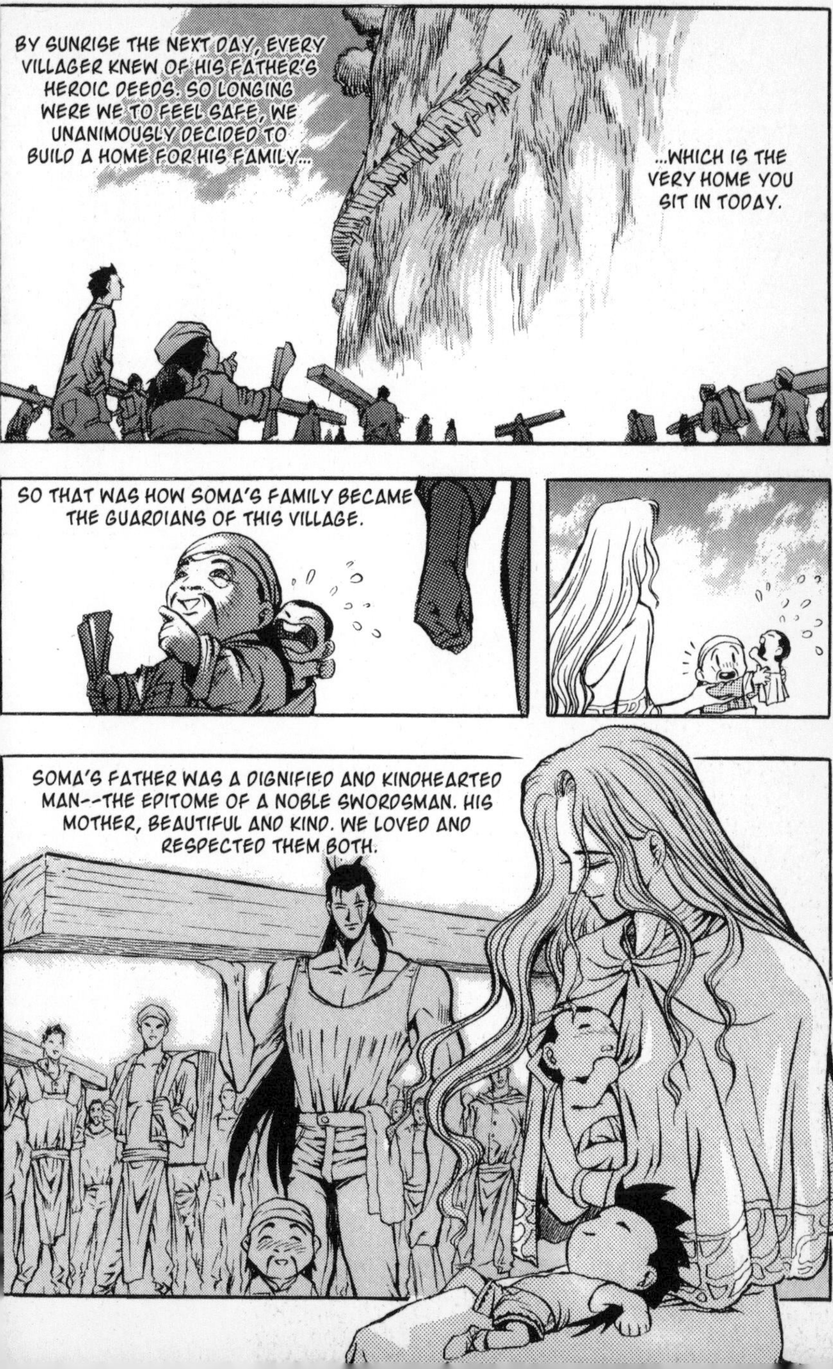

BY SUNRISE THE NEXT DAY, EVERY VILLAGER KNEW OF HIS FATHER'S HEROIC DEEDS. SO LONGING WERE WE TO FEEL SAFE, WE UNANIMOUSLY DECIDED TO BUILD A HOME FOR HIS FAMILY...
...WHICH IS THE VERY HOME YOU SIT IN TODAY.
SO THAT WAS HOW SOMA'S FAMILY BECAME THE GUARDIANS OF THIS VILLAGE.
SOMA'S FATHER WAS A DIGNIFIED AND KINDHEARTED MAN--THE EPITOME OF A NOBLE SWORDSMAN. HIS MOTHER, BEAUTIFUL AND KIND. WE LOVED AND RESPECTED THEM BOTH.

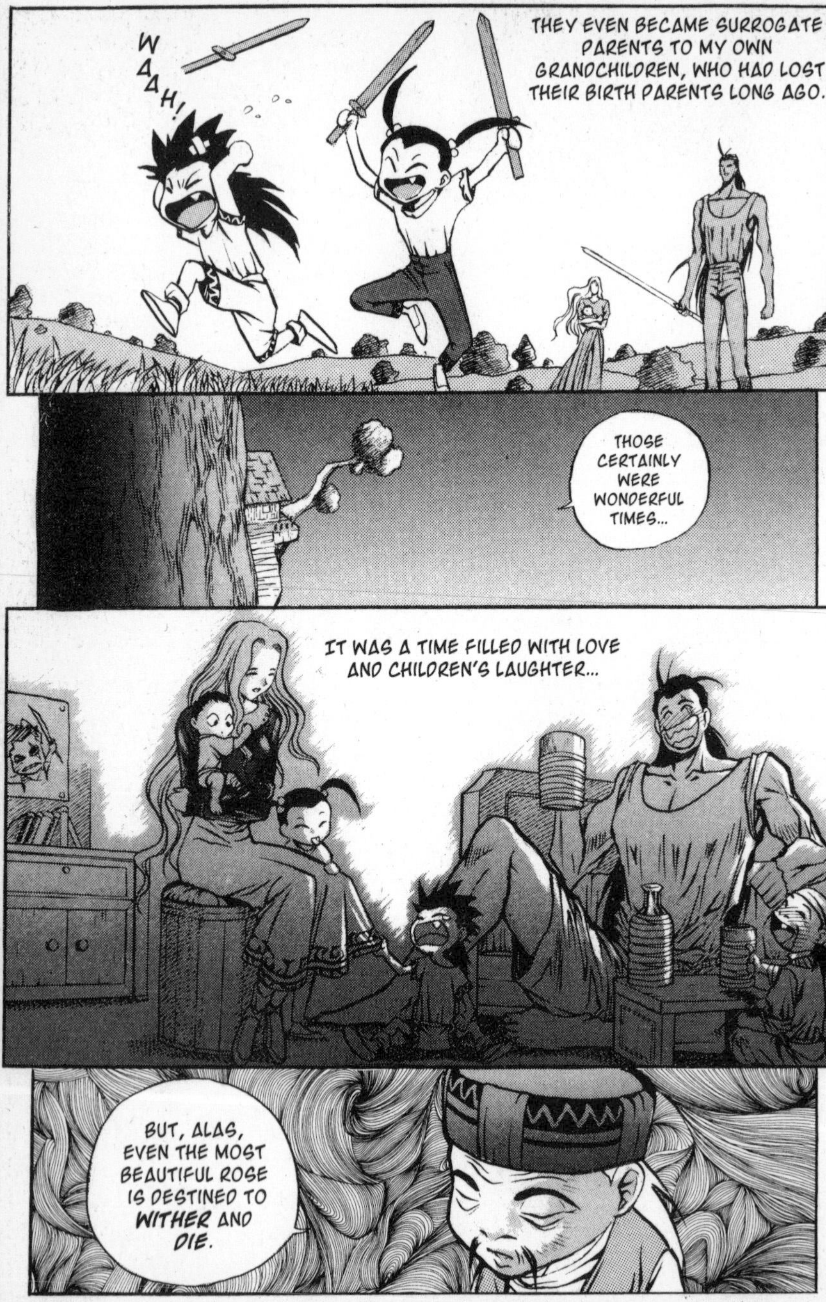
WAAH!
THEY EVEN BECAME SURROGATE PARENTS TO MY OWN GRANDCHILDREN, WHO HAD LOST THEIR BIRTH PARENTS LONG AGO.
THOSE CERTAINLY WERE WONDERFUL TIMES...
IT WAS A TIME FILLED WITH LOVE AND CHILDREN'S LAUGHTER...
BUT, ALAS, EVEN THE MOST BEAUTIFUL ROSE IS DESTINED TO *WITHER* AND *DIE*.

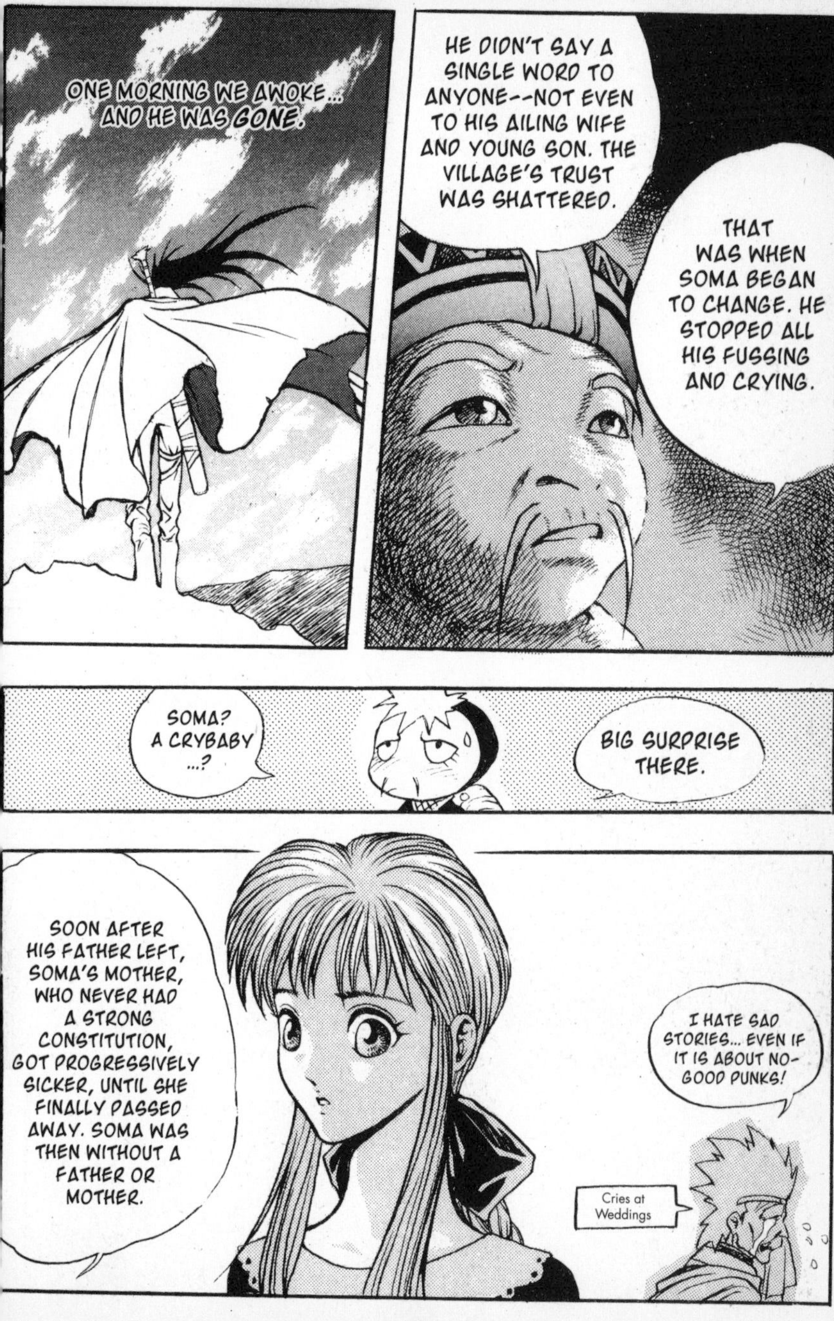
ONE MORNING WE AWOKE... AND HE WAS GONE.
HE DIDN'T SAY A SINGLE WORD TO ANYONE--NOT EVEN TO HIS AILING WIFE AND YOUNG SON. THE VILLAGE'S TRUST WAS SHATTERED.
THAT WAS WHEN SOMA BEGAN TO CHANGE. HE STOPPED ALL HIS FUSSING AND CRYING.
SOMA? A CRYBABY ...?
BIG SURPRISE THERE.
SOON AFTER HIS FATHER LEFT, SOMA'S MOTHER, WHO NEVER HAD A STRONG CONSTITUTION, GOT PROGRESSIVELY SICKER, UNTIL SHE FINALLY PASSED AWAY. SOMA WAS THEN WITHOUT A FATHER OR MOTHER.
I HATE SAD STORIES... EVEN IF IT IS ABOUT NO-GOOD PUNKS!
Cries at Weddings

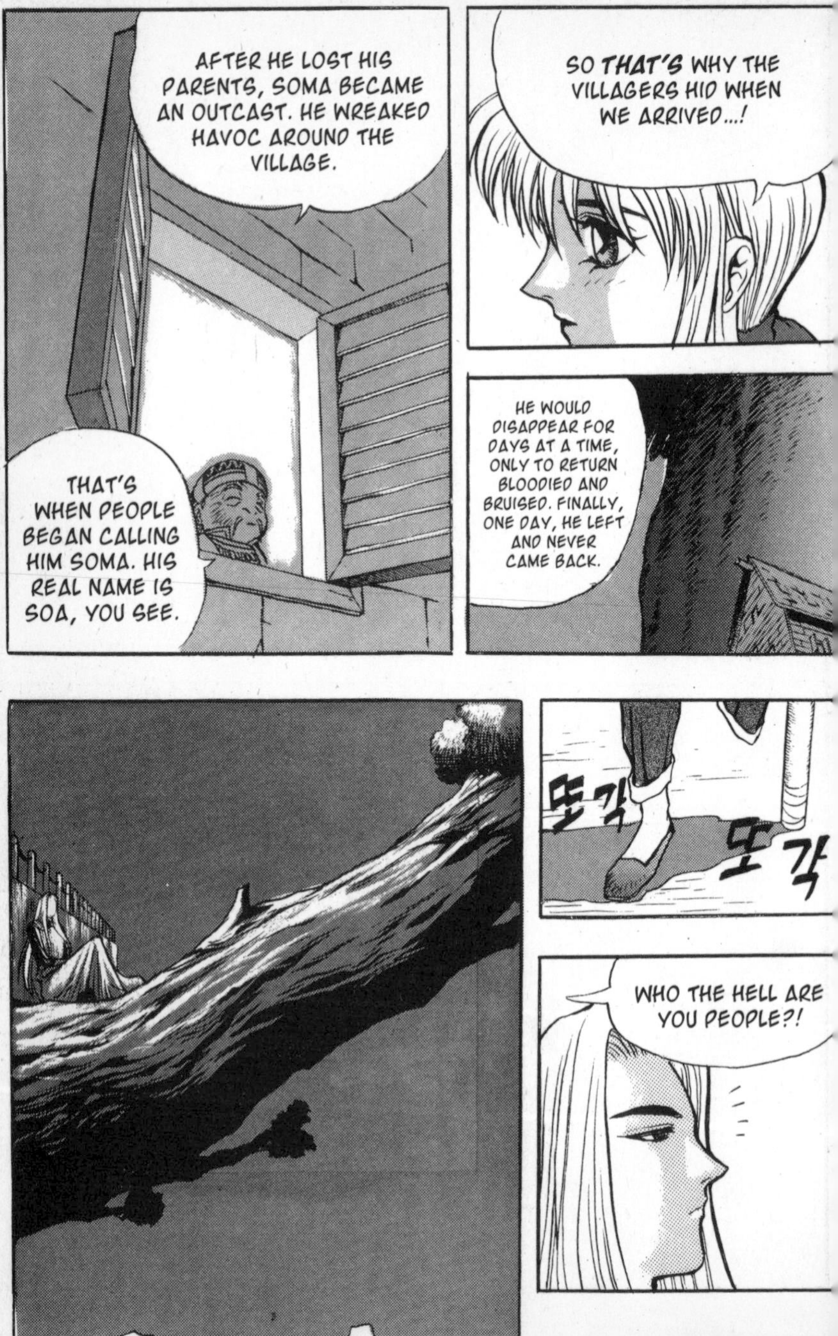
AFTER HE LOST HIS PARENTS, SOMA BECAME AN OUTCAST. HE WREAKED HAVOC AROUND THE VILLAGE.
THAT'S WHEN PEOPLE BEGAN CALLING HIM SOMA. HIS REAL NAME IS SOA, YOU SEE.
SO *THAT'S* WHY THE VILLAGERS HID WHEN WE ARRIVED...!
HE WOULD DISAPPEAR FOR DAYS AT A TIME, ONLY TO RETURN BLOODIED AND BRUISED. FINALLY, ONE DAY, HE LEFT AND NEVER CAME BACK.
또각
또각
WHO THE HELL ARE YOU PEOPLE?!

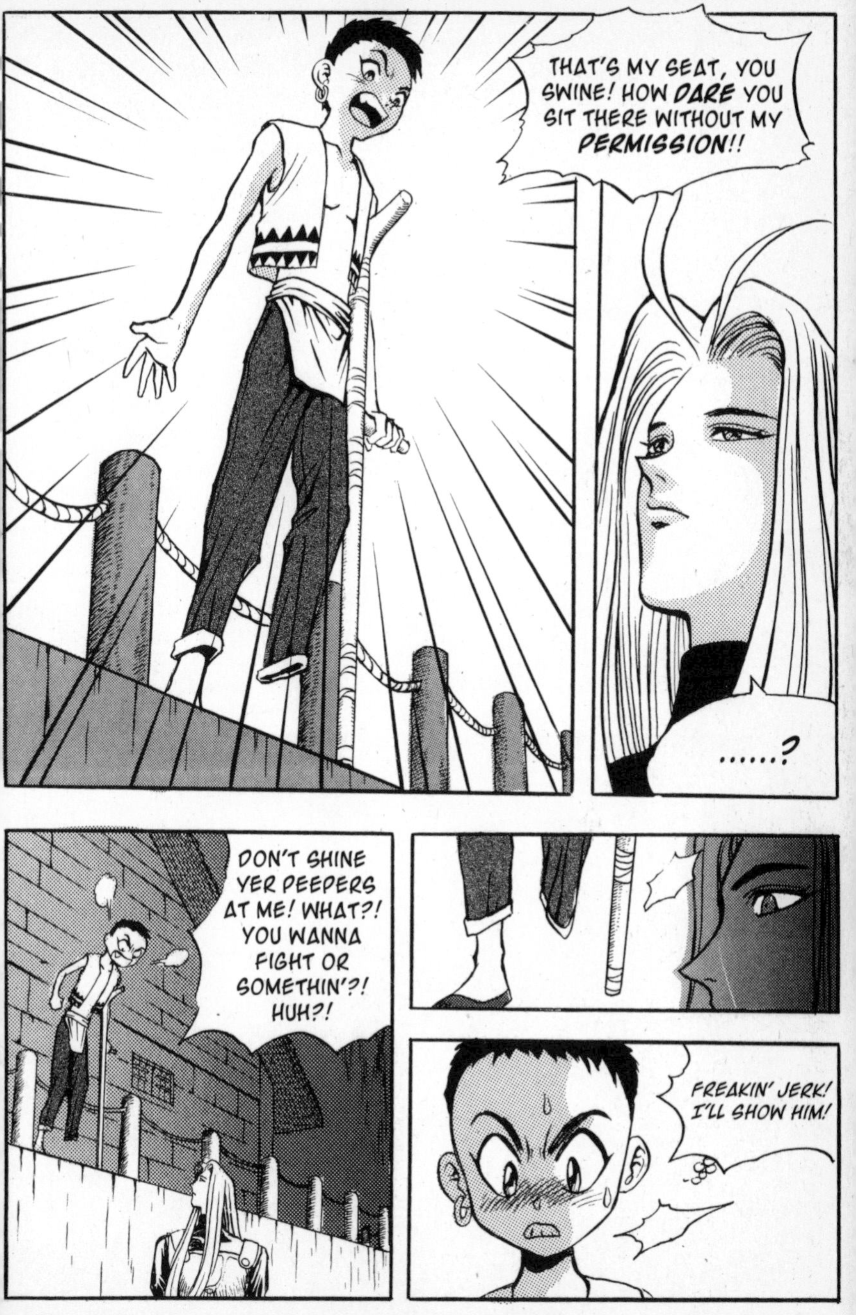
THAT'S MY SEAT, YOU SWINE! HOW DARE YOU SIT THERE WITHOUT MY PERMISSION!!
......?
DON'T SHINE YER PEEPERS AT ME! WHAT?! YOU WANNA FIGHT OR SOMETHIN'?! HUH?!
FREAKIN' JERK! I'LL SHOW HIM!

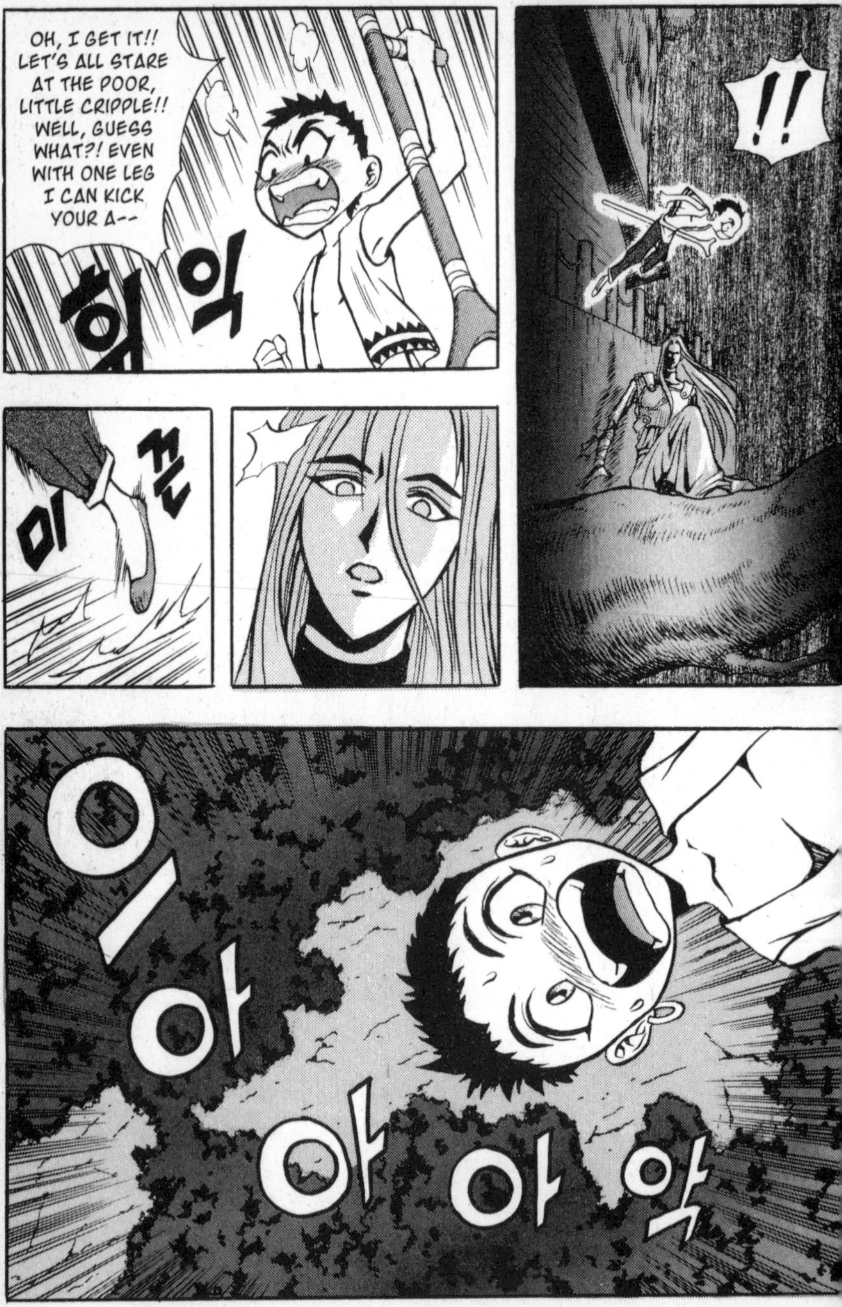

OH, I GET IT!! LET'S ALL STARE AT THE POOR, LITTLE CRIPPLE!! WELL, GUESS WHAT?! EVEN WITH ONE LEG I CAN KICK YOUR A--
!!

...LIVE?

I...

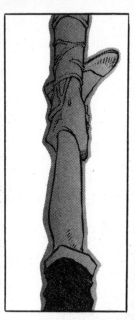

CHAEHA!!

덜컹

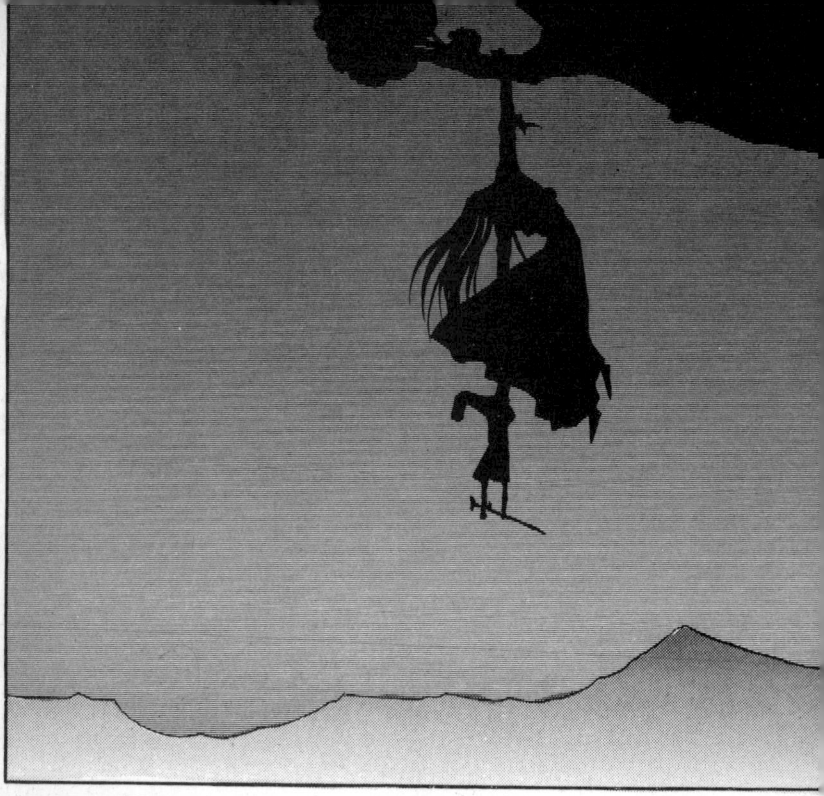
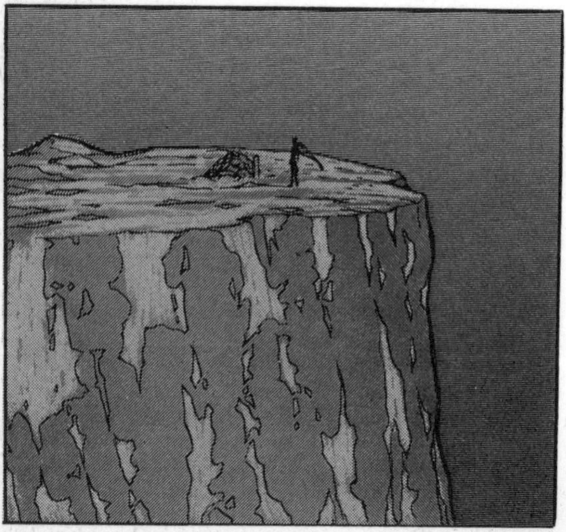
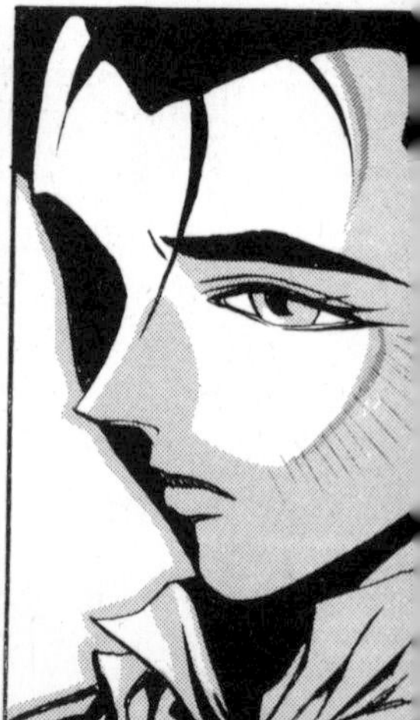

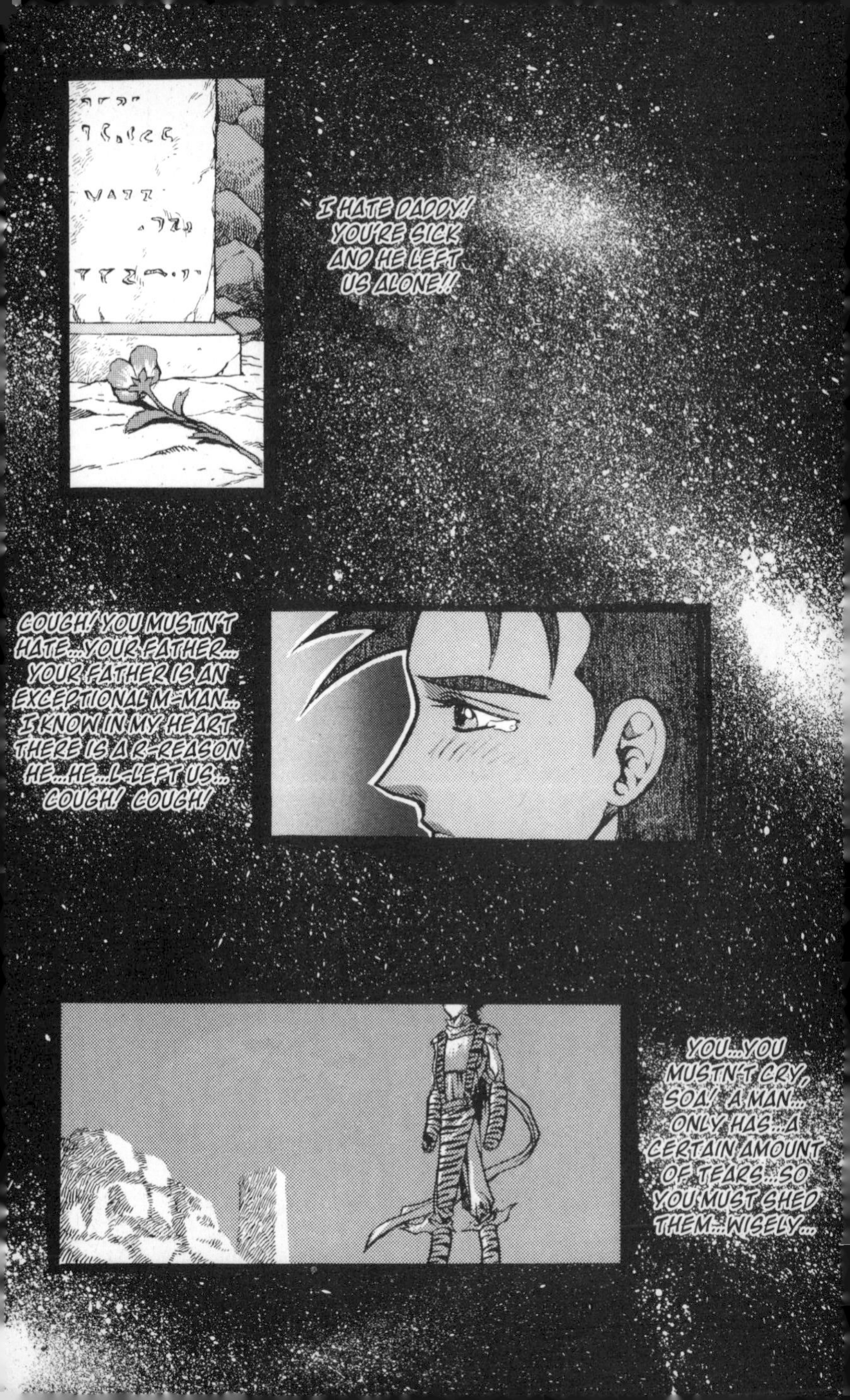
I HATE DADDY! YOU'RE SICK AND HE LEFT US ALONE!!
COUGH! YOU MUSTN'T HATE...YOUR FATHER... YOUR FATHER IS AN EXCEPTIONAL M-MAN... I KNOW IN MY HEART THERE IS A R-REASON HE...HE...L-LEFT US... COUGH! COUGH!
YOU...YOU MUSTN'T CRY, SOA! A MAN... ONLY HAS...A CERTAIN AMOUNT OF TEARS...SO YOU MUST SHED THEM...WISELY...

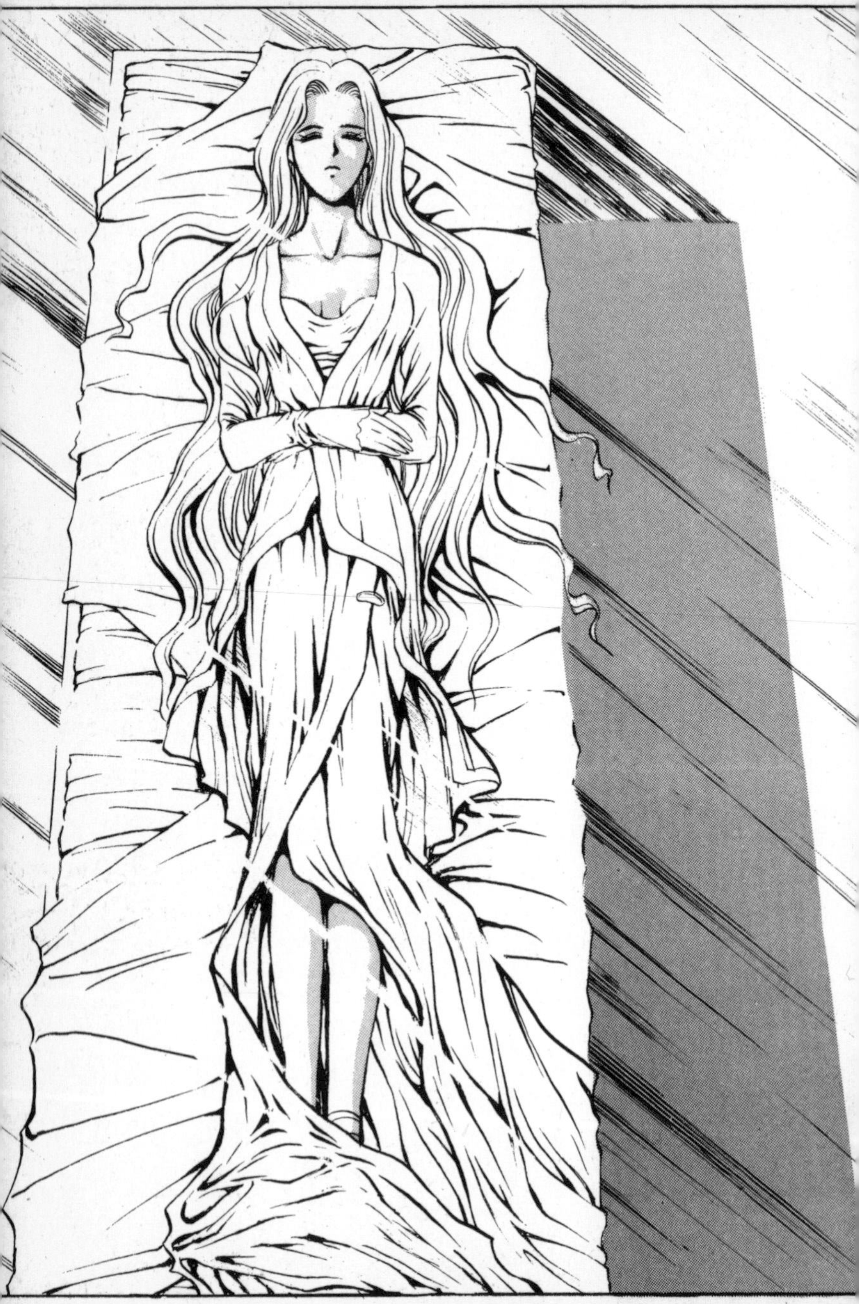

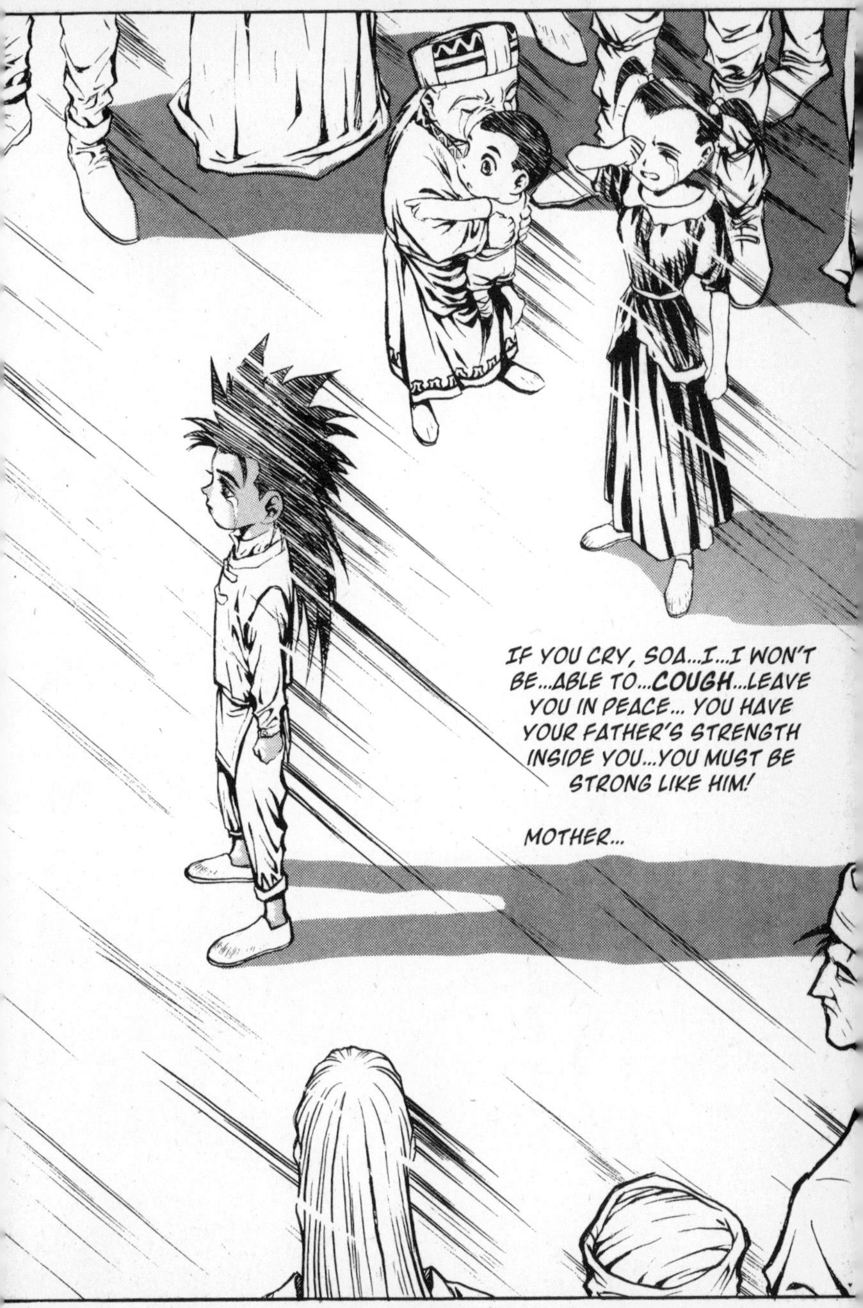
IF YOU CRY, SOA...I...I WON'T BE...ABLE TO...COUGH...LEAVE YOU IN PEACE... YOU HAVE YOUR FATHER'S STRENGTH INSIDE YOU...YOU MUST BE STRONG LIKE HIM!
MOTHER...

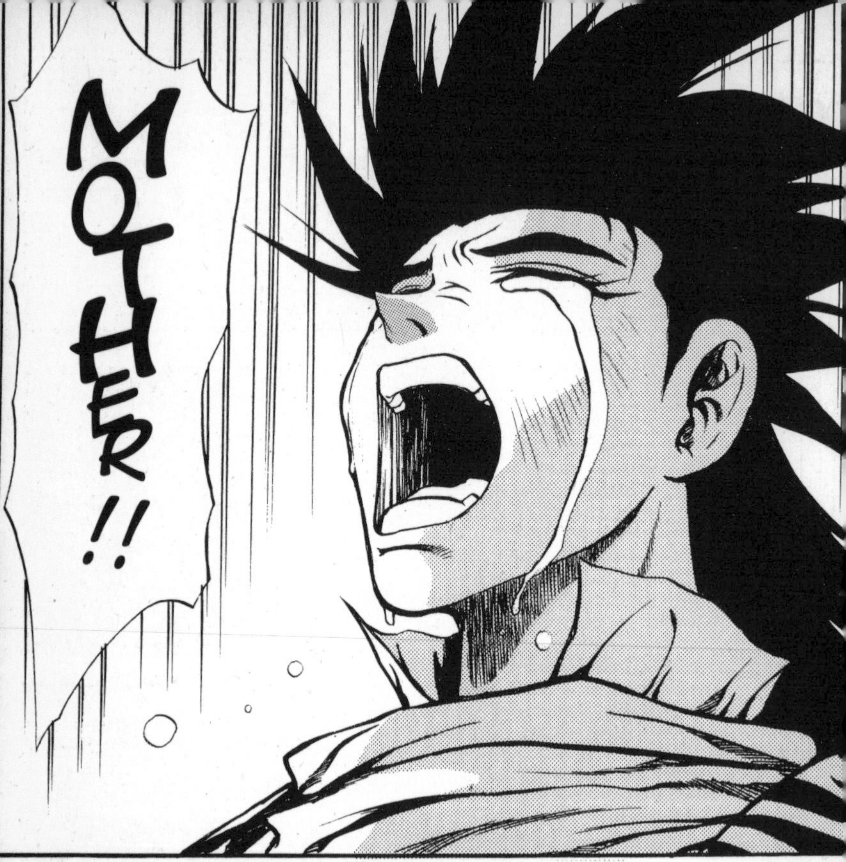
MOTHER!!
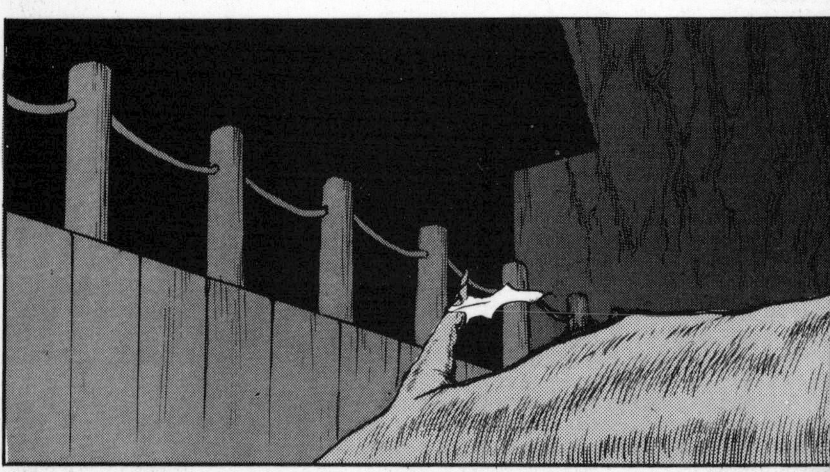

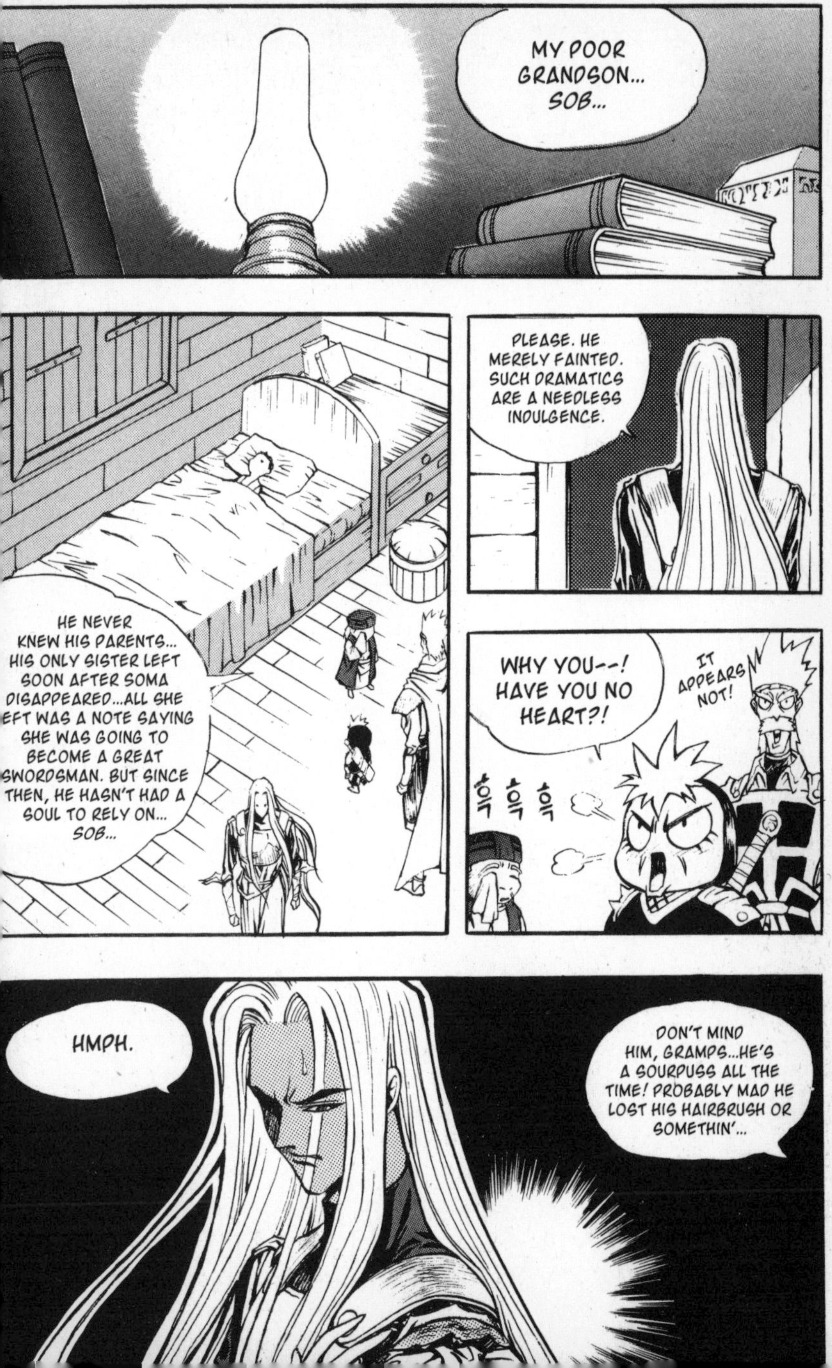
MY POOR GRANDSON... SOB...
HE NEVER KNEW HIS PARENTS... HIS ONLY SISTER LEFT SOON AFTER SOMA DISAPPEARED...ALL SHE LEFT WAS A NOTE SAYING SHE WAS GOING TO BECOME A GREAT SWORDSMAN. BUT SINCE THEN, HE HASN'T HAD A SOUL TO RELY ON... SOB...
PLEASE. HE MERELY FAINTED. SUCH DRAMATICS ARE A NEEDLESS INDULGENCE.
WHY YOU--! HAVE YOU NO HEART?!
IT APPEARS NOT!
흑 흑 흑
HMPH.
DON'T MIND HIM, GRAMPS...HE'S A SOURPUSS ALL THE TIME! PROBABLY MAD HE LOST HIS HAIRBRUSH OR SOMETHIN'...

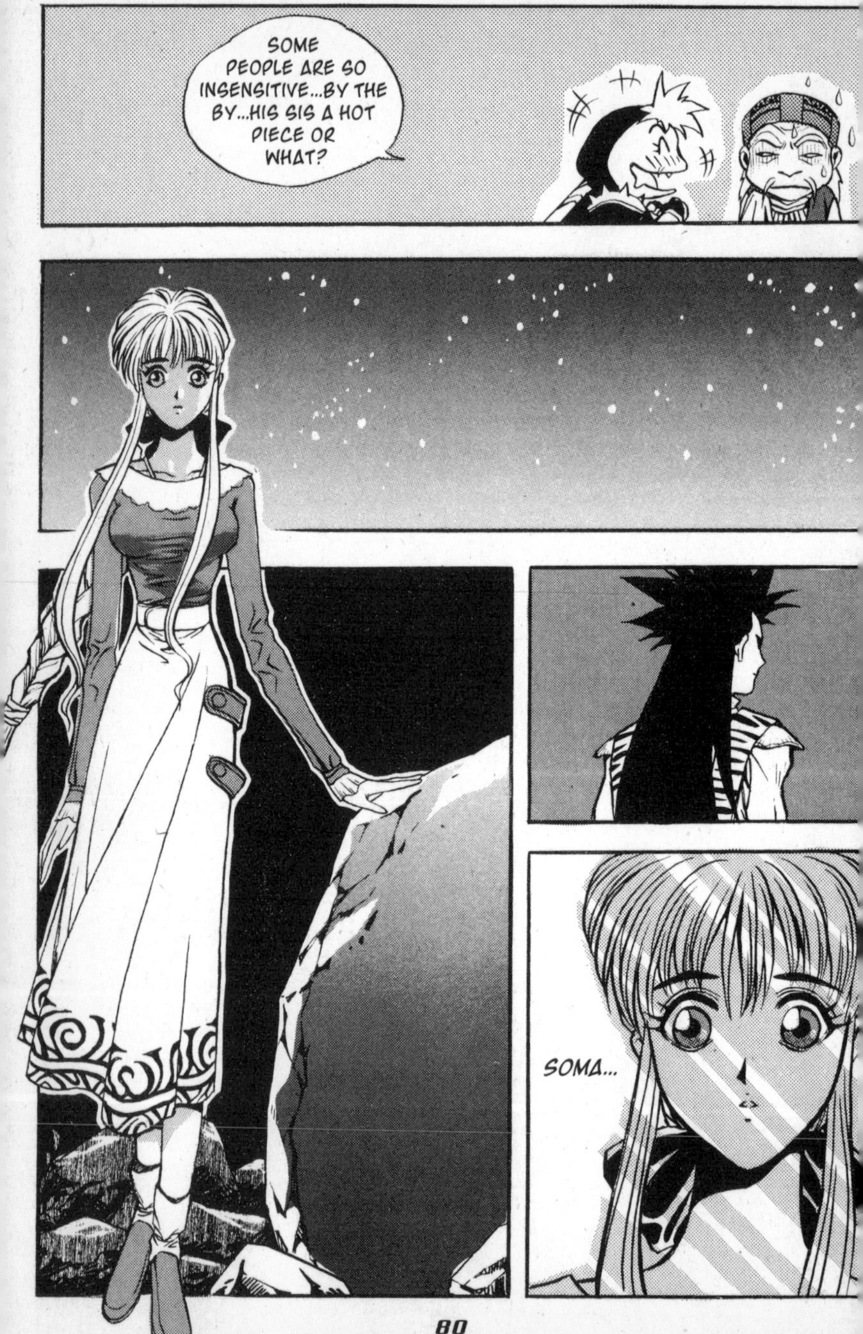
SOME PEOPLE ARE SO INSENSITIVE...BY THE BY...HIS SIS A HOT PIECE OR WHAT?
SOMA...

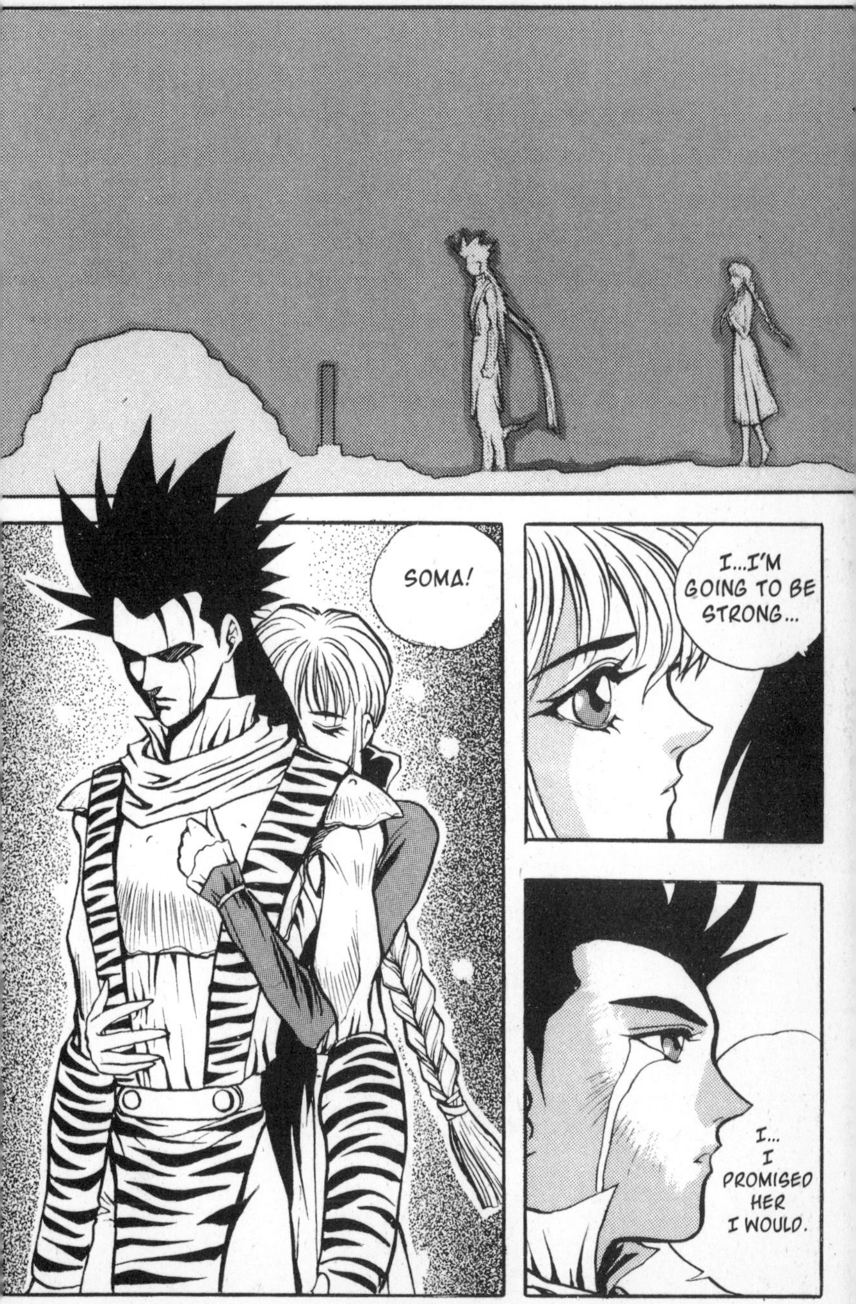
SOMA!
I...I'M GOING TO BE STRONG...
I... I PROMISED HER I WOULD.

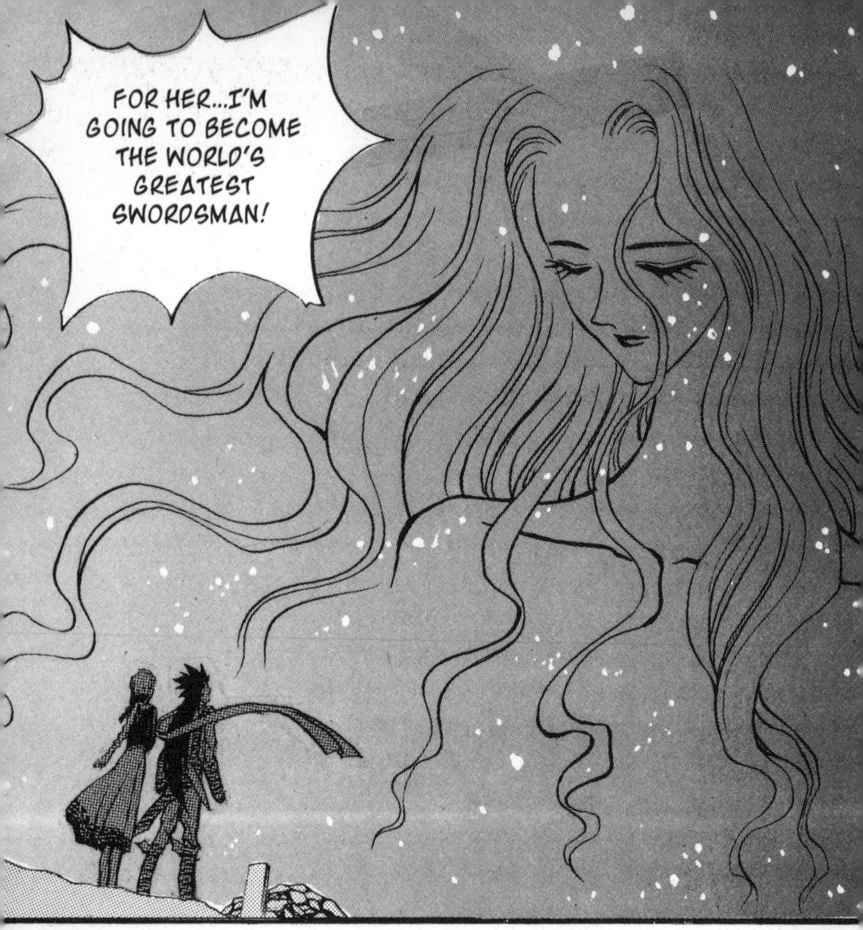
FOR HER...I'M GOING TO BECOME THE WORLD'S GREATEST SWORDSMAN!

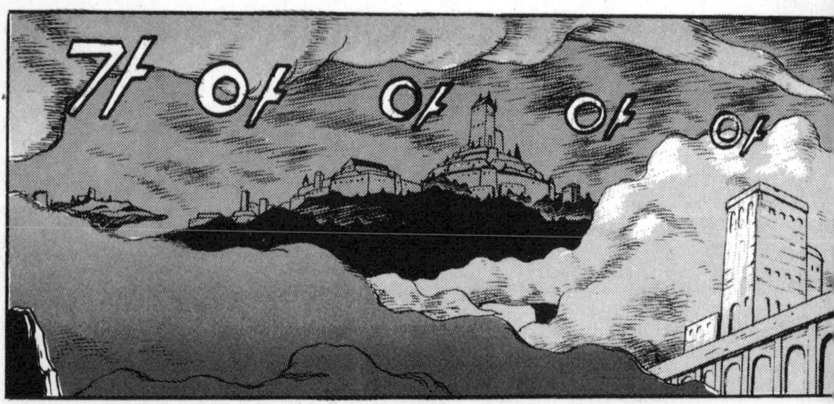
가 아 아 아 아

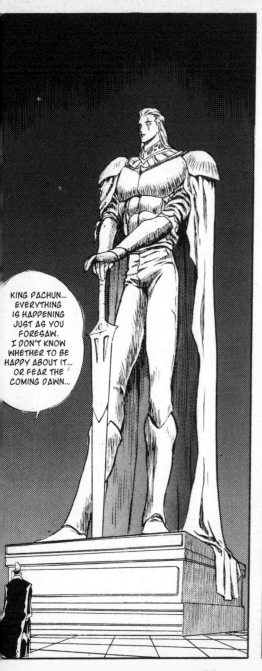

KING PACHUN... EVERYTHING IS HAPPENING JUST AS YOU FORESAW. I DON'T KNOW WHETHER TO BE HAPPY ABOUT IT... OR FEAR THE COMING DAWN...

I FEEL SO ASHAMED... IN MY MIND'S EYE, I CAN STILL SEE YOU SHATTERING HEAVEN AND EARTH WITH YOUR SWORD...

...BUT THE ONLY THING I CAN DO IS PASS ON THE BURDEN OF DESTINY TO THE NEXT GENER-ATION!

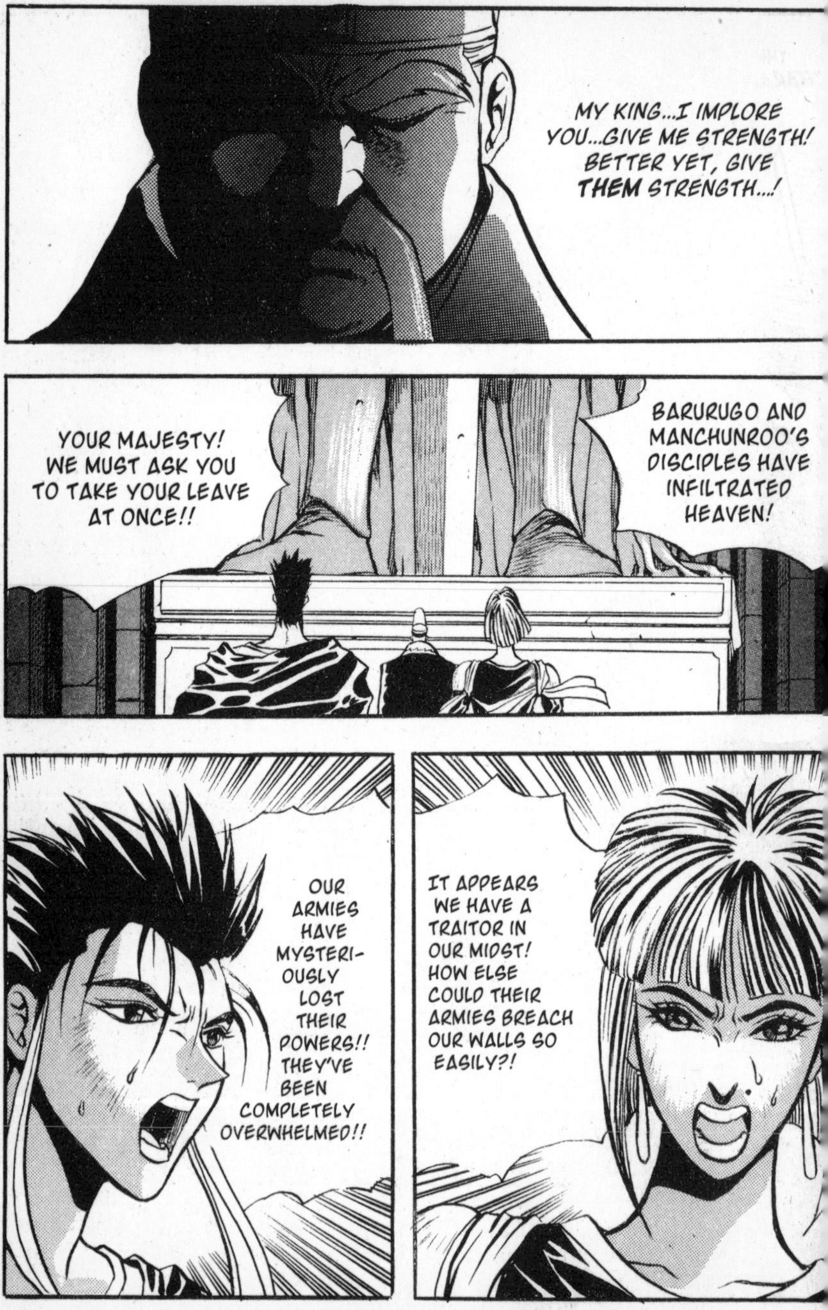
MY KING...I IMPLORE YOU...GIVE ME STRENGTH! BETTER YET, GIVE **THEM** STRENGTH...!
YOUR MAJESTY! WE MUST ASK YOU TO TAKE YOUR LEAVE AT ONCE!!
BARURUGO AND MANCHUNROO'S DISCIPLES HAVE INFILTRATED HEAVEN!
OUR ARMIES HAVE MYSTERIOUSLY LOST THEIR POWERS!! THEY'VE BEEN COMPLETELY OVERWHELMED!!
IT APPEARS WE HAVE A TRAITOR IN OUR MIDST! HOW ELSE COULD THEIR ARMIES BREACH OUR WALLS SO EASILY?!

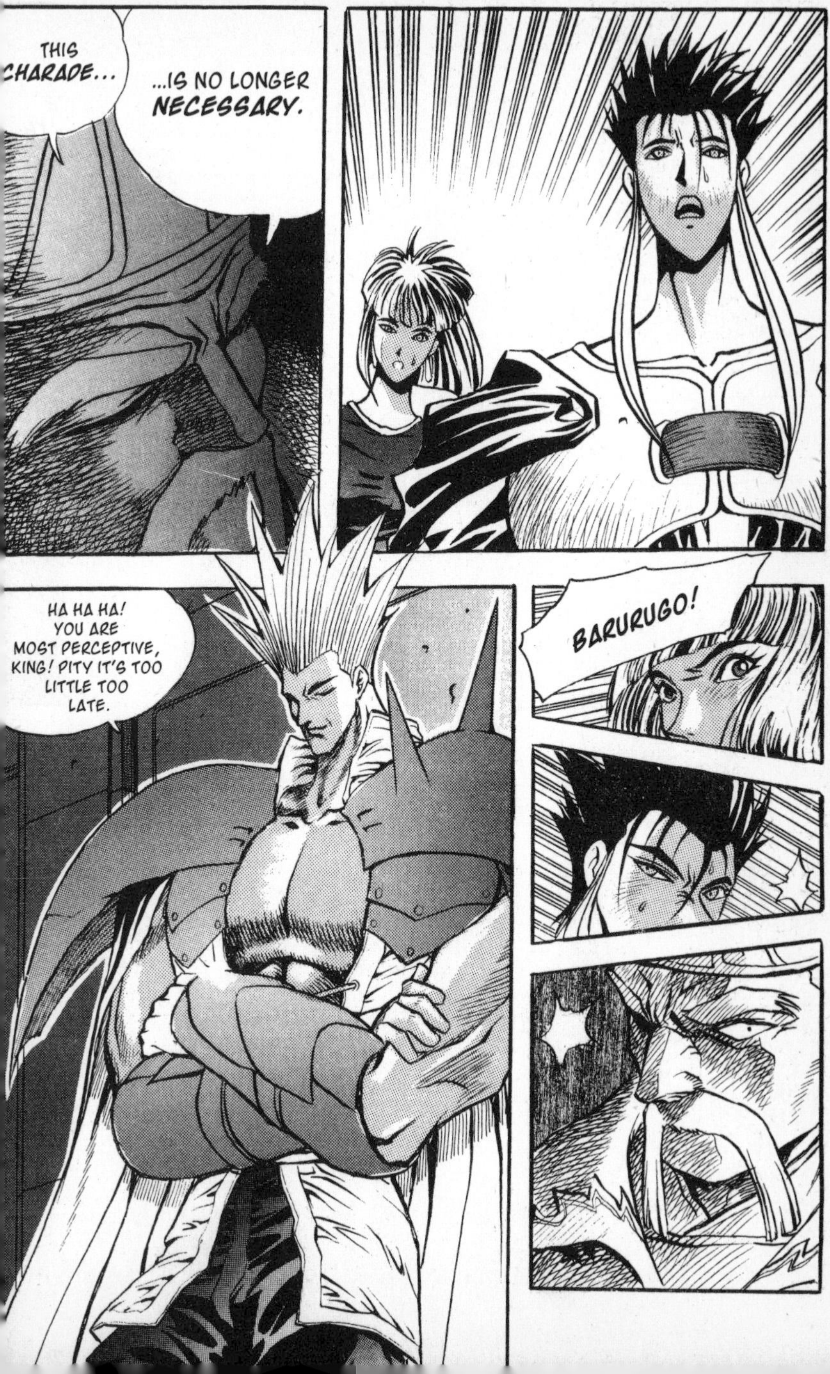
THIS CHARADE...
...IS NO LONGER NECESSARY.
HA HA HA! YOU ARE MOST PERCEPTIVE, KING! PITY IT'S TOO LITTLE TOO LATE.
BARURUGO!

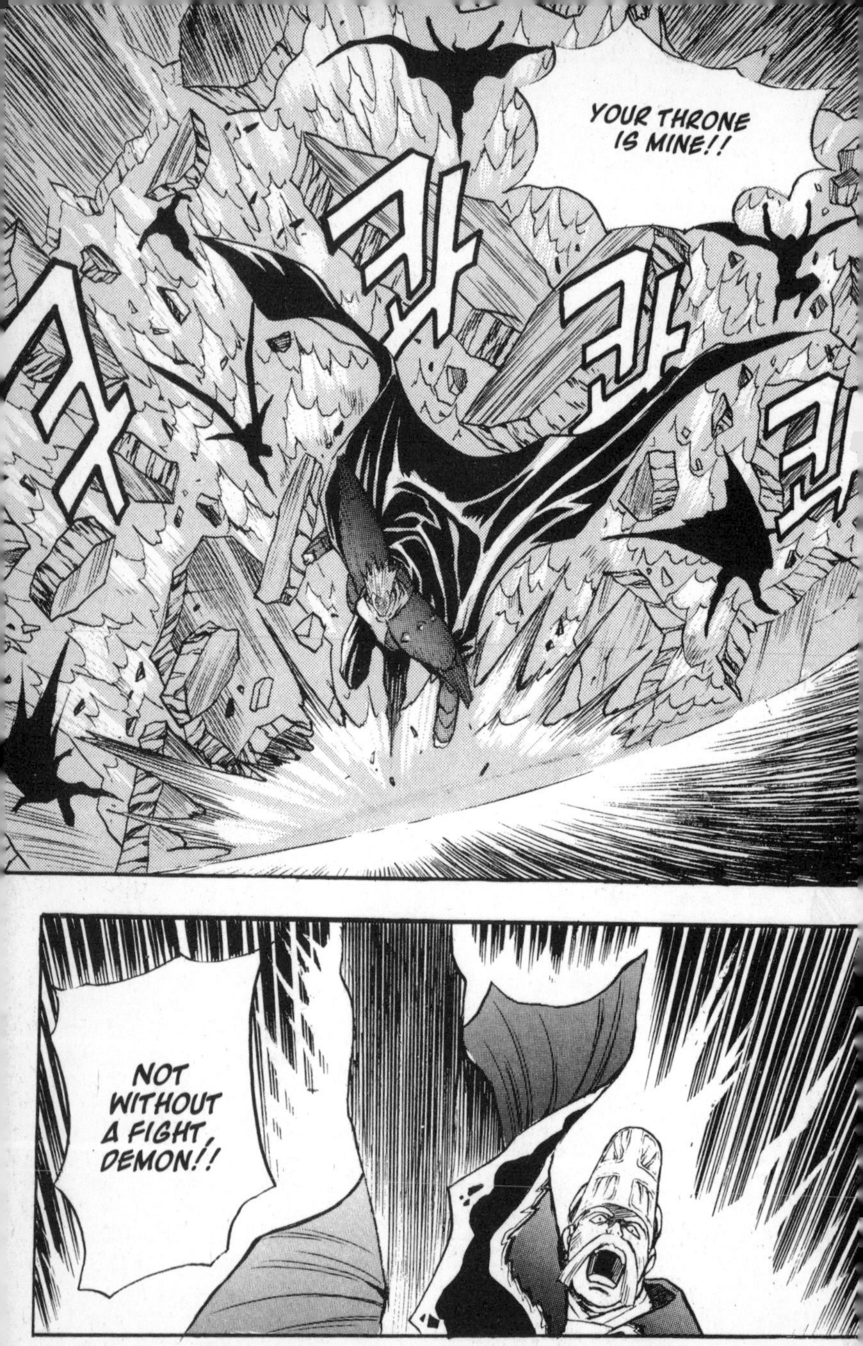
YOUR THRONE IS MINE!!
NOT WITHOUT A FIGHT, DEMON!!

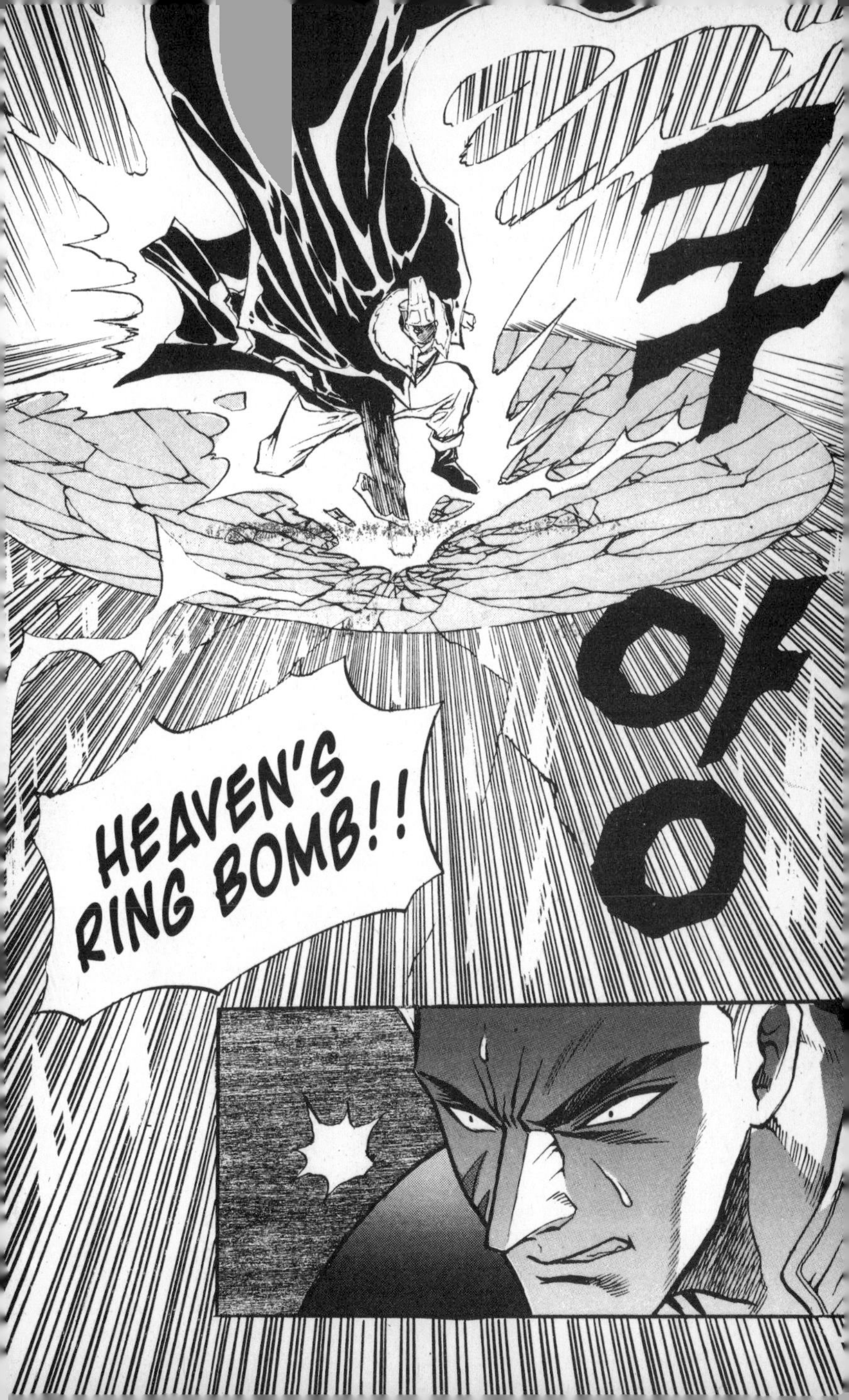
HEAVEN'S RING BOMB!!

IT'S WARM...

THIS SMELL...I HAD FORGOTTEN...

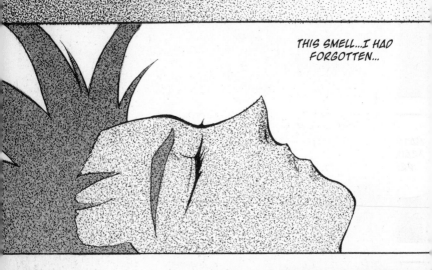

THIS IS MY MOTHER'S SMELL...! NO! IT CAN'T BE! MY MOTHER'S DEAD!

SO THEN... WHOSE FRAGRANCE IS THIS...?

plip!

HUH?

IS THAT...?

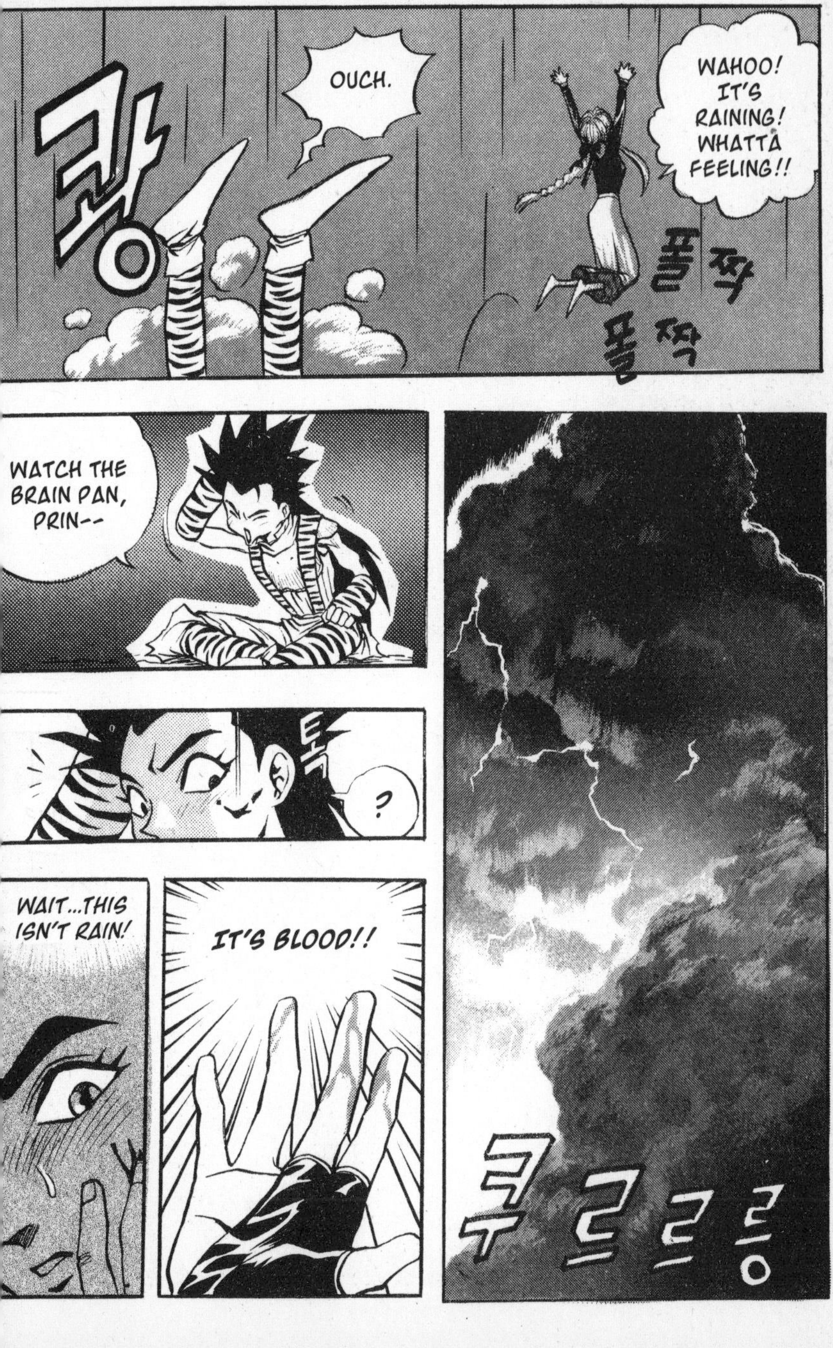

쾅
OUCH.
WAHOO! IT'S RAINING! WHATTA FEELING!!
폴짝 폴짝
WATCH THE BRAIN PAN, PRIN--
톡
?
WAIT...THIS ISN'T RAIN!
IT'S BLOOD!!
쿠르르릉

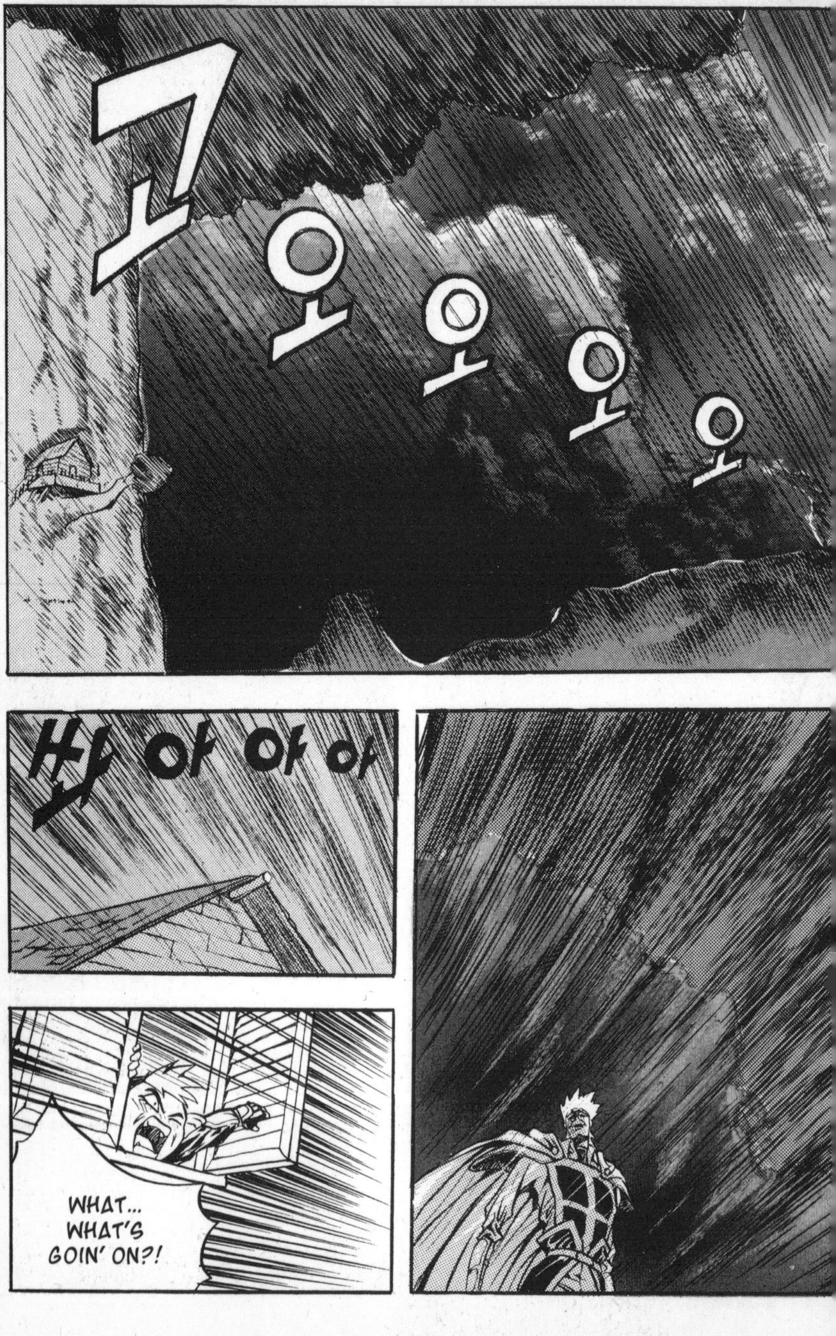
WHAT...
WHAT'S
GOIN' ON?!

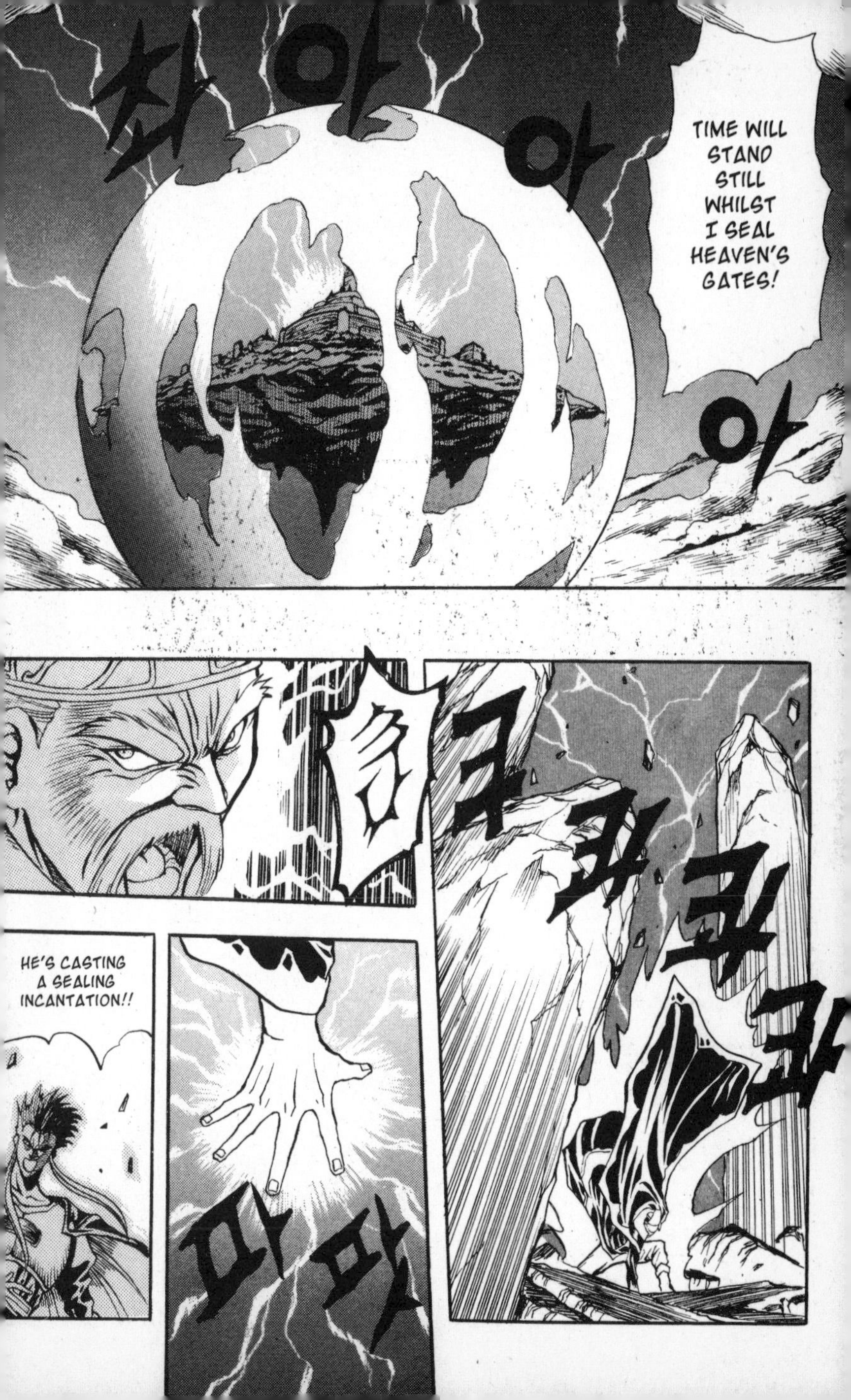
촤아아아
TIME WILL STAND STILL WHILST I SEAL HEAVEN'S GATES!
HE'S CASTING A SEALING INCANTATION!!
파앗

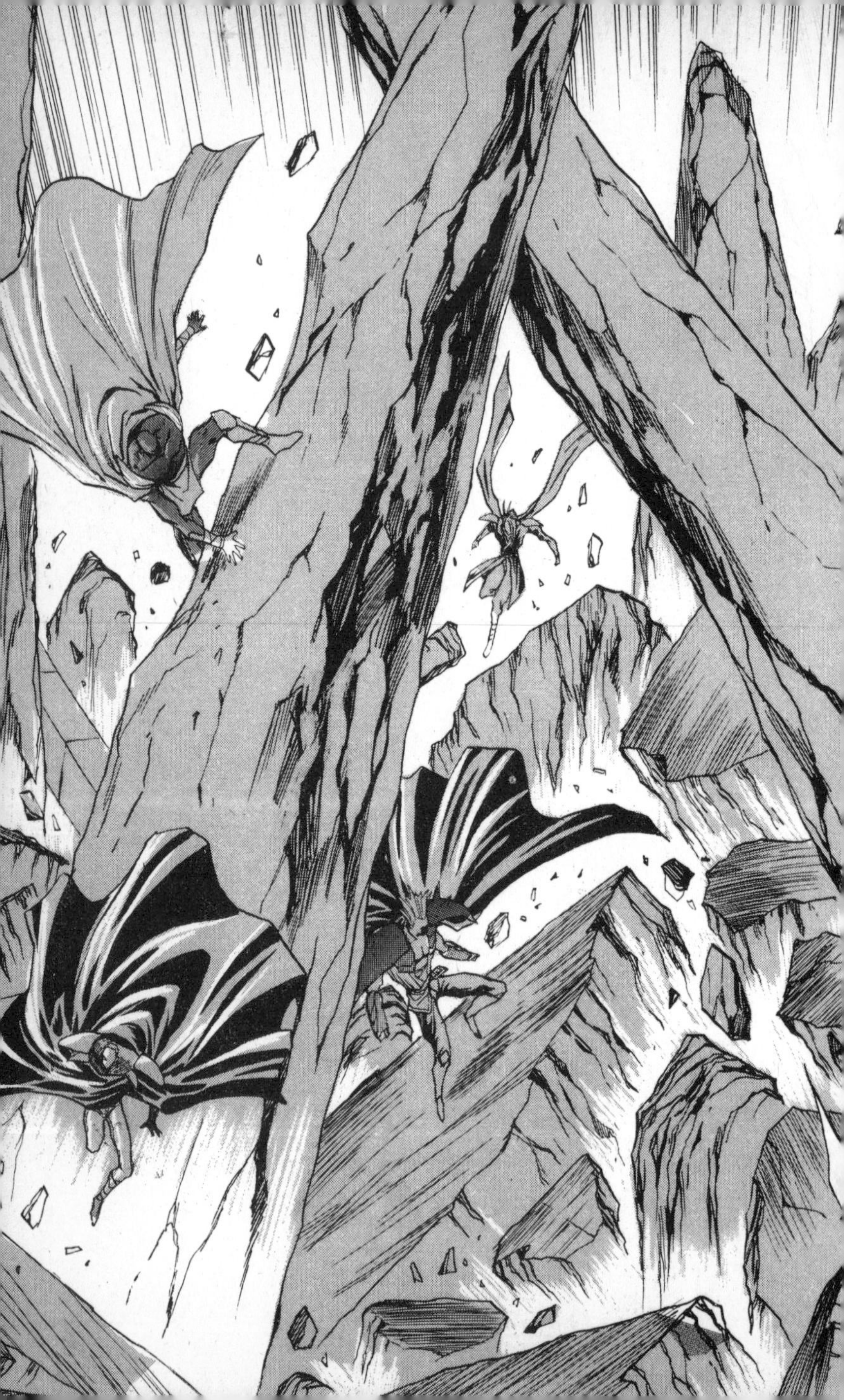

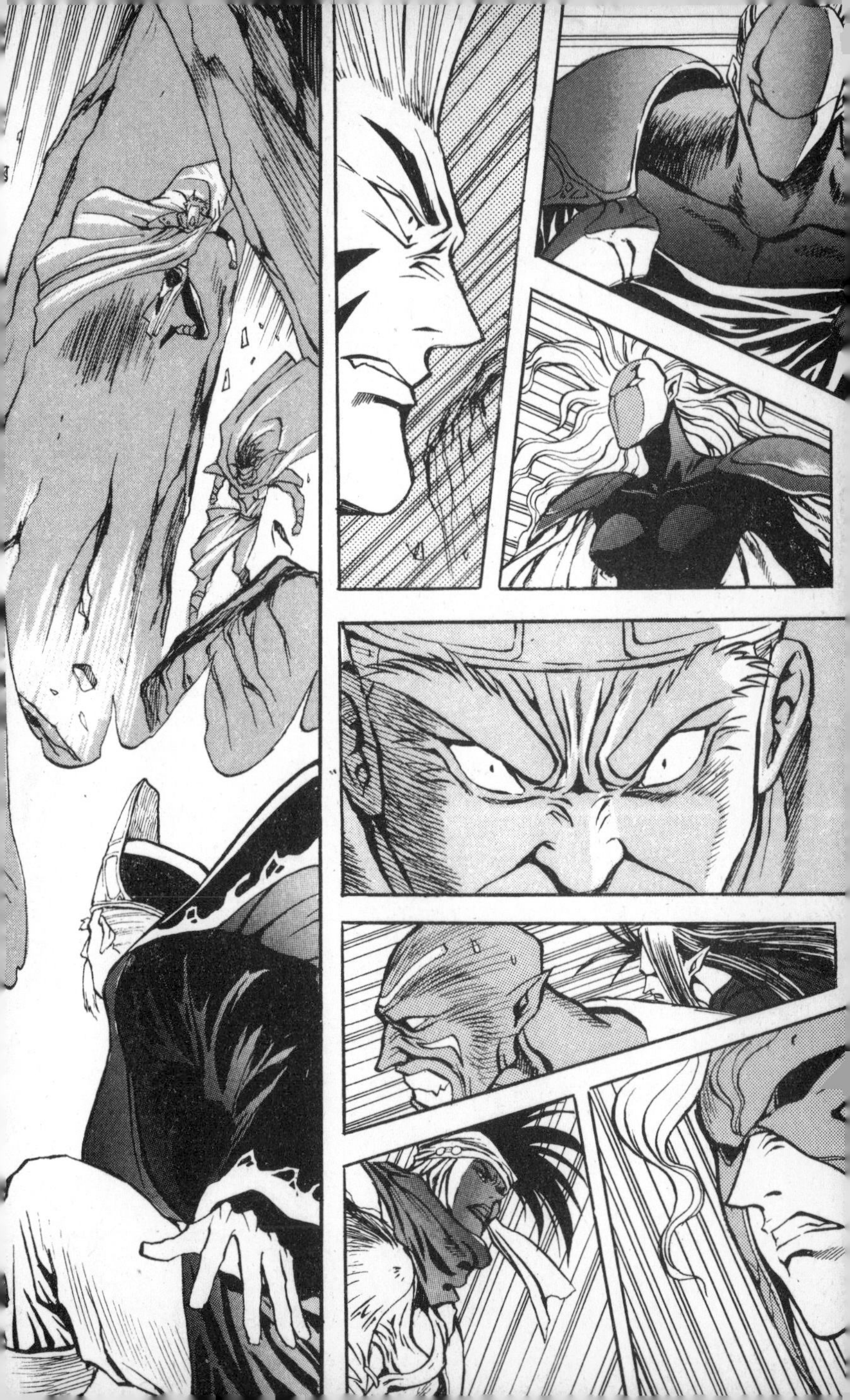

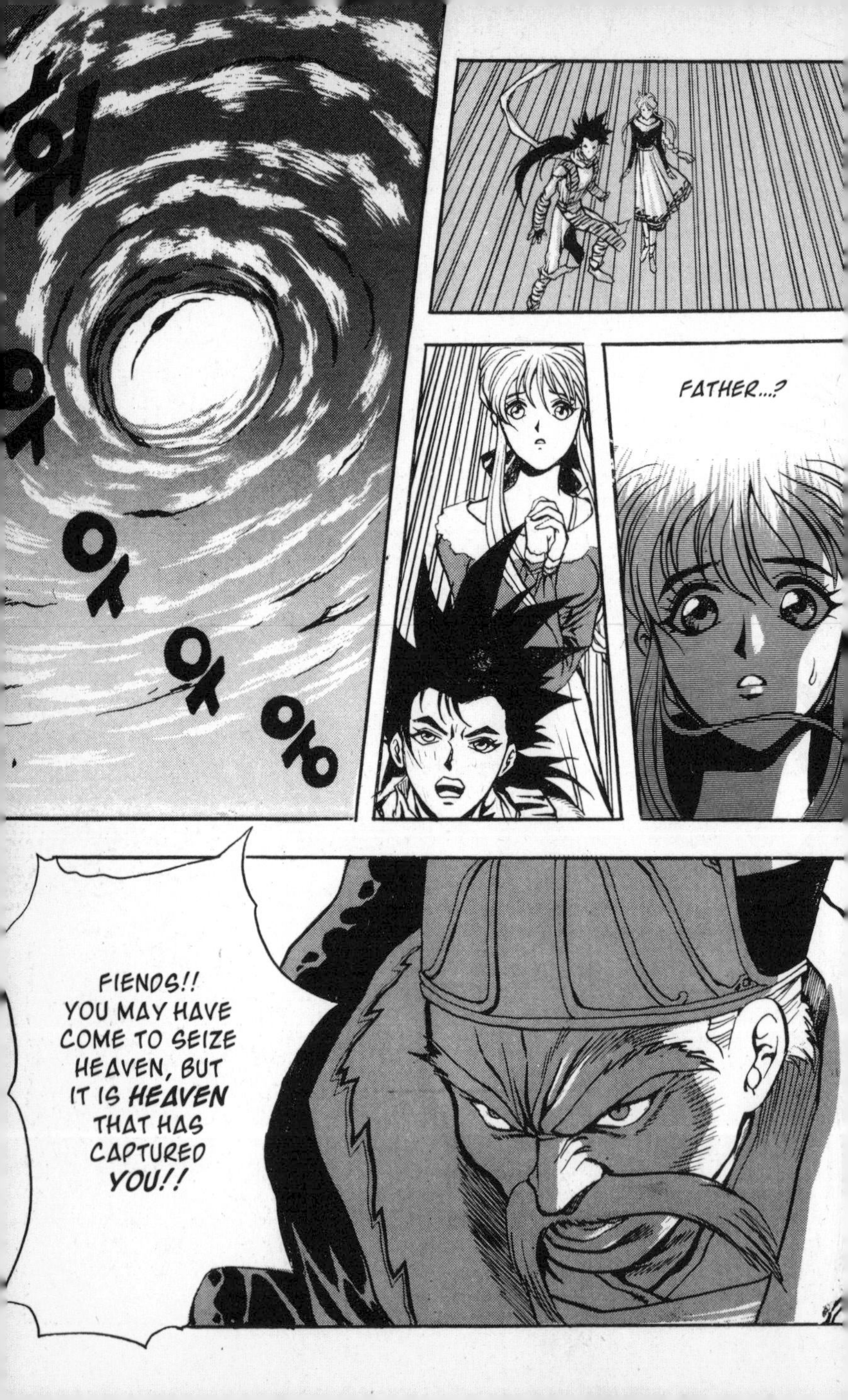
FATHER...?
FIENDS!! YOU MAY HAVE COME TO SEIZE HEAVEN, BUT IT IS **HEAVEN** THAT HAS CAPTURED **YOU!!**

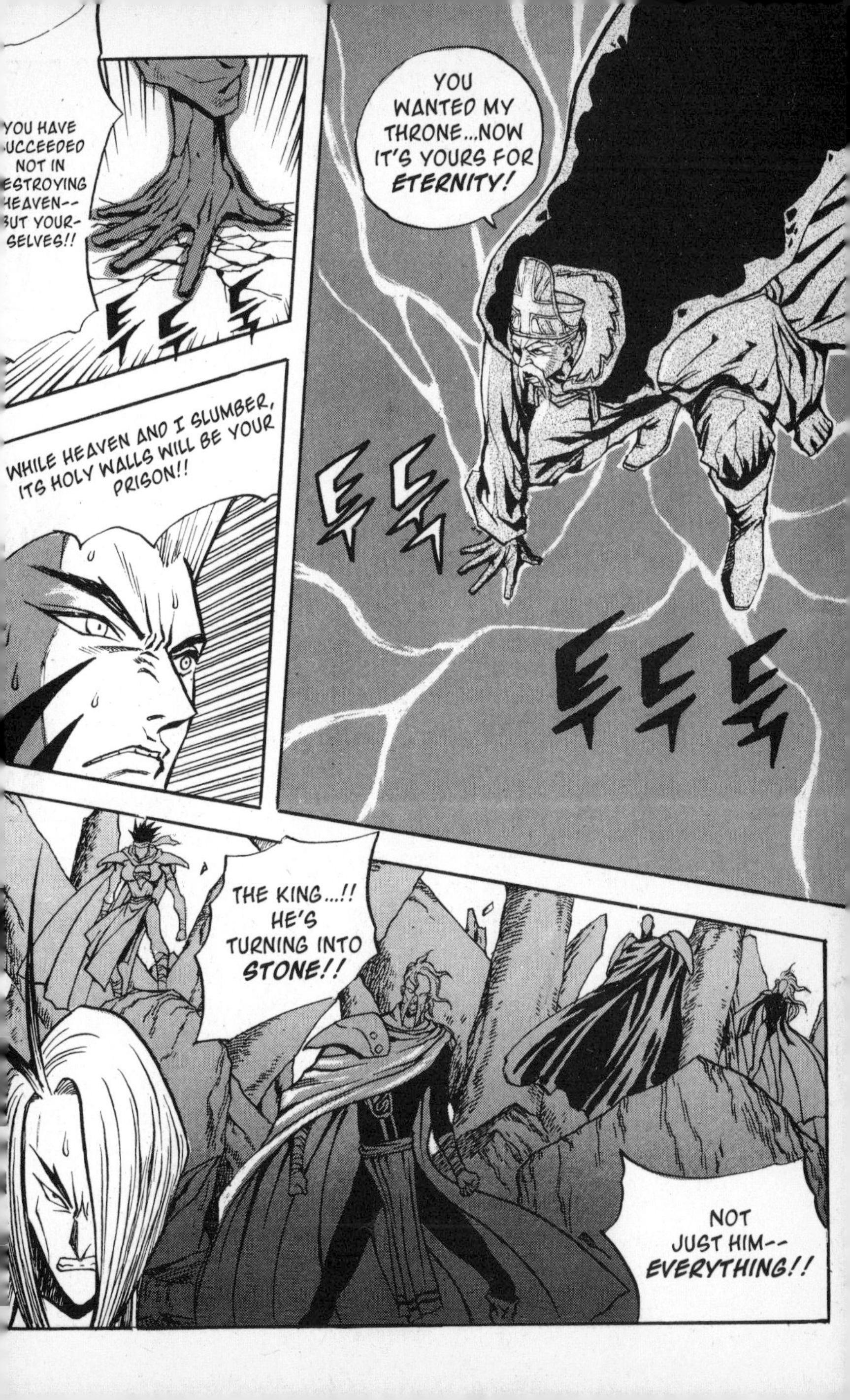
YOU HAVE UCCEEDED NOT IN ESTROYING HEAVEN-- BUT YOURSELVES!!
WHILE HEAVEN AND I SLUMBER, ITS HOLY WALLS WILL BE YOUR PRISON!!
YOU WANTED MY THRONE...NOW IT'S YOURS FOR ETERNITY!
THE KING...!! HE'S TURNING INTO STONE!!
NOT JUST HIM-- EVERYTHING!!

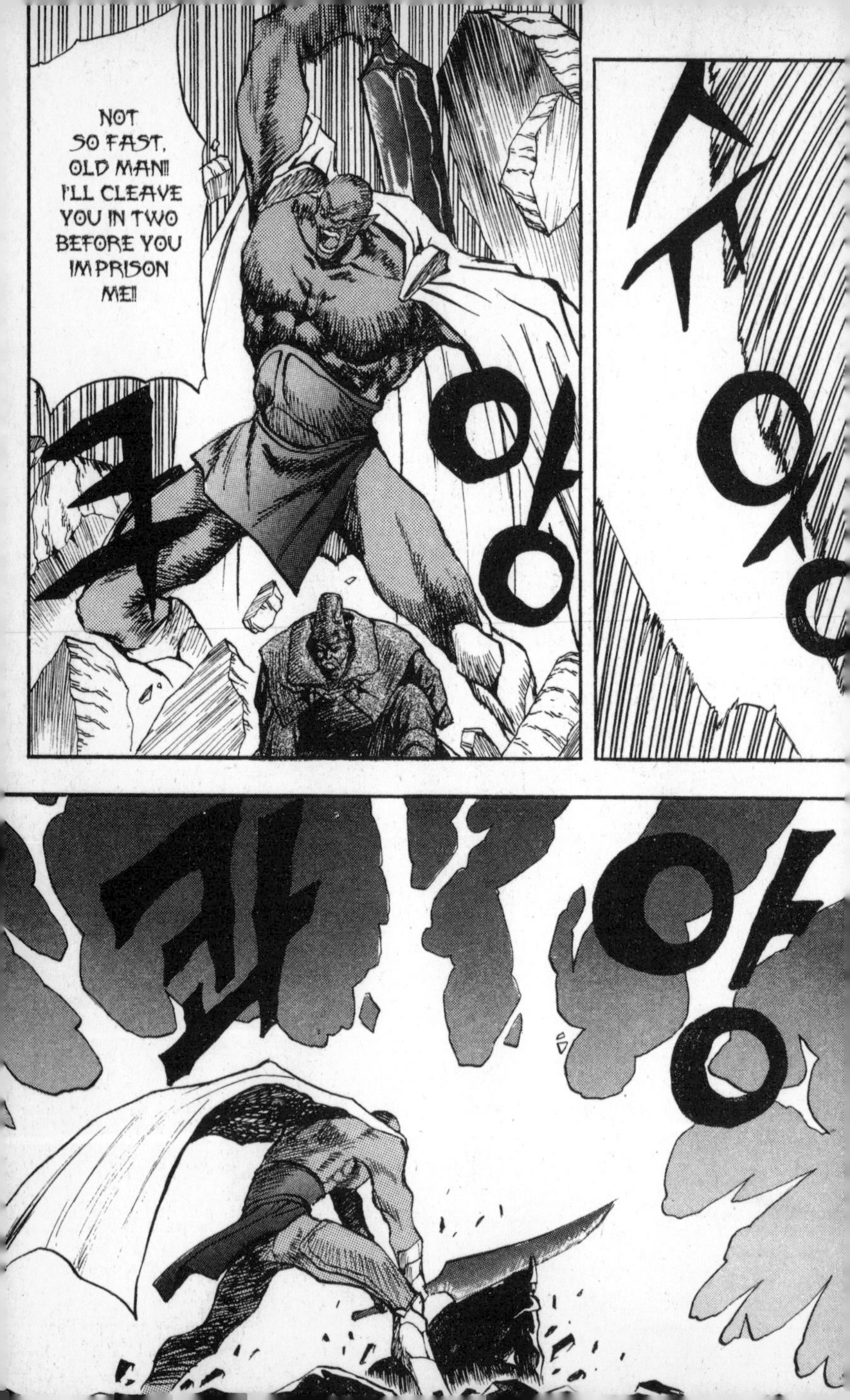
NOT SO FAST, OLD MAN!! I'LL CLEAVE YOU IN TWO BEFORE YOU IMPRISON ME!!

IT'S...I CAN'T...!

I... CAN'T... LET... GO...!

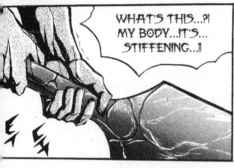

WHAT'S THIS...?! MY BODY...IT'S... STIFFENING...!!

NOOOOO!!

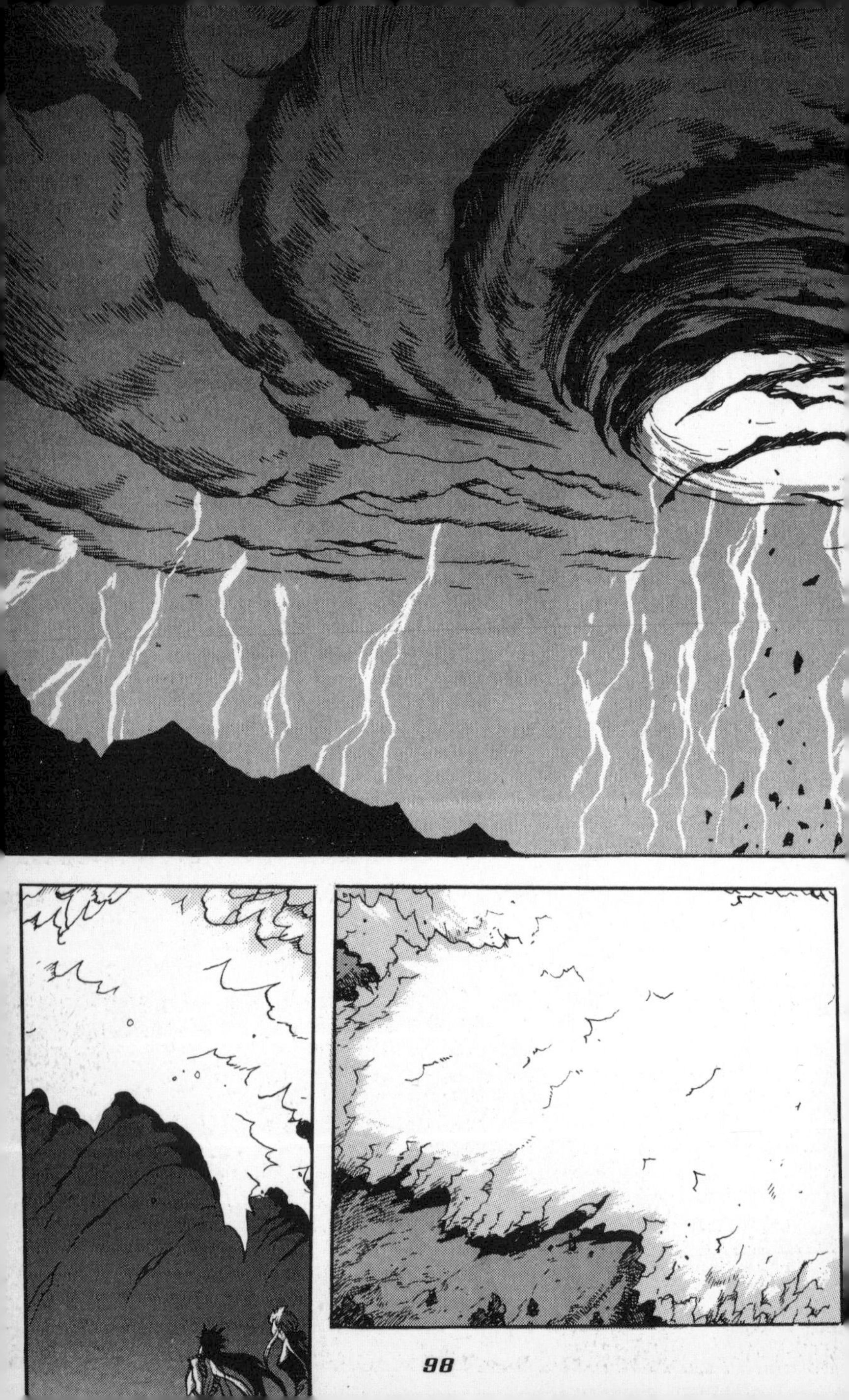

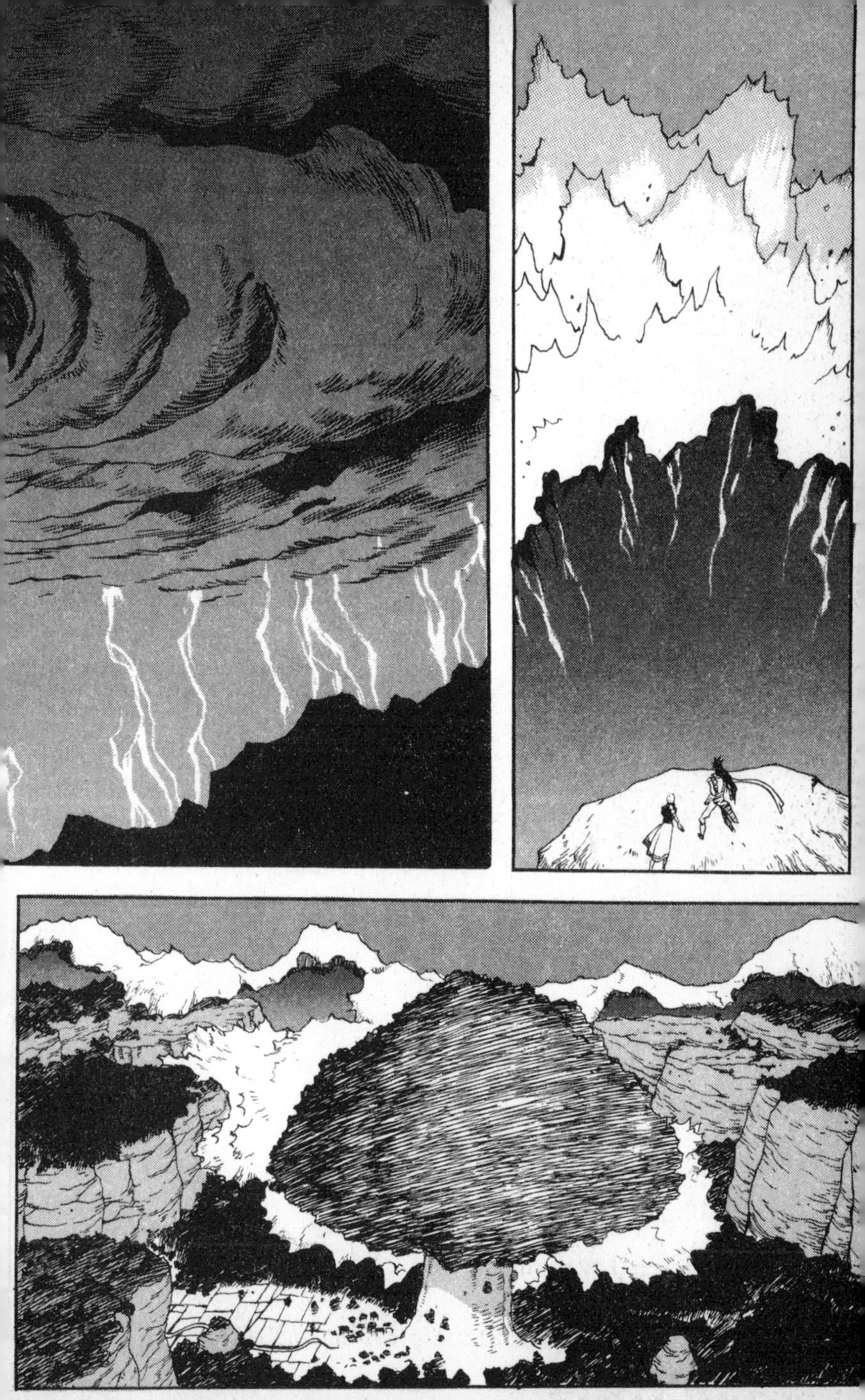

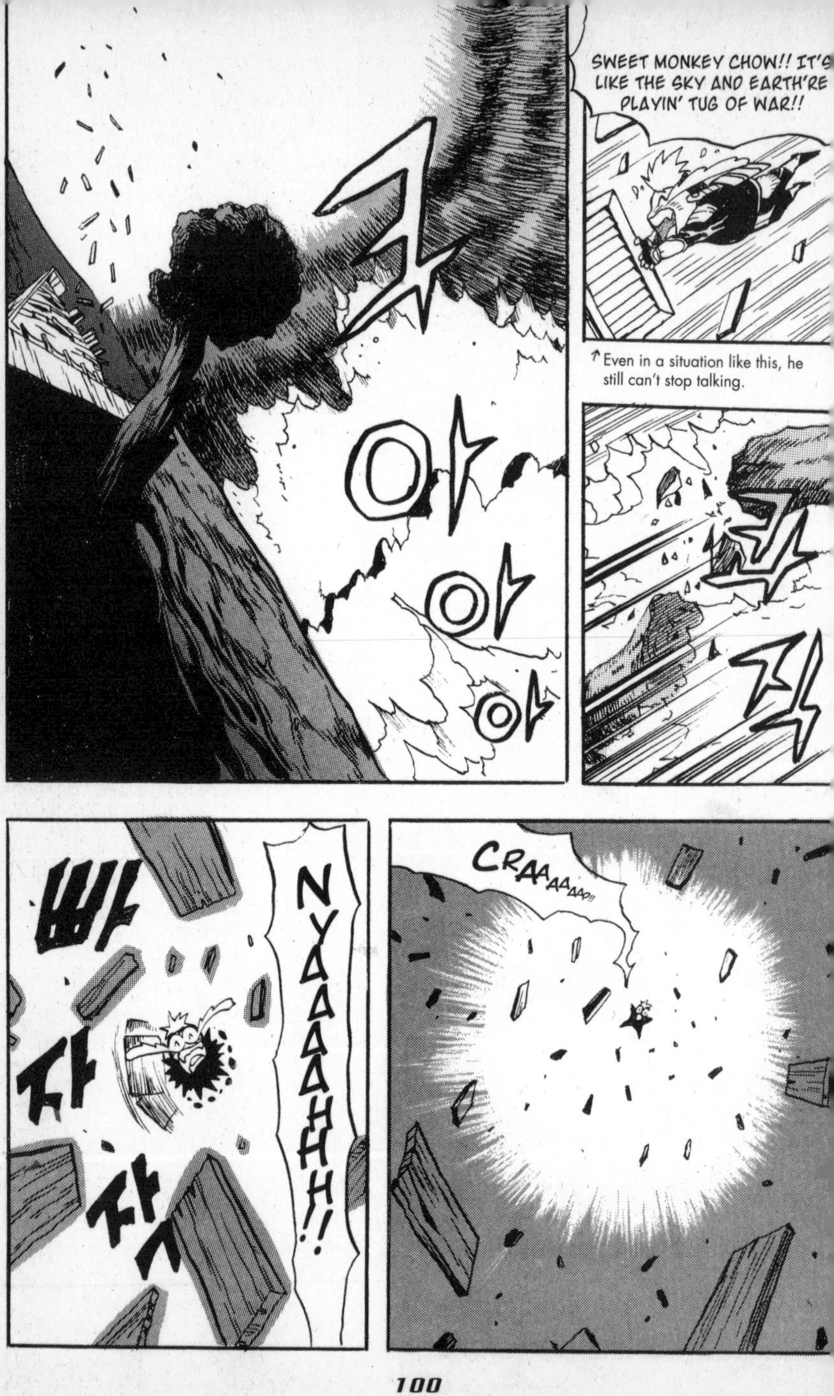
SWEET MONKEY CHOW!! IT'S LIKE THE SKY AND EARTH'RE PLAYIN' TUG OF WAR!!
↑ Even in a situation like this, he still can't stop talking.
NYAAAAAHHH!!
CRAAAAAP!!

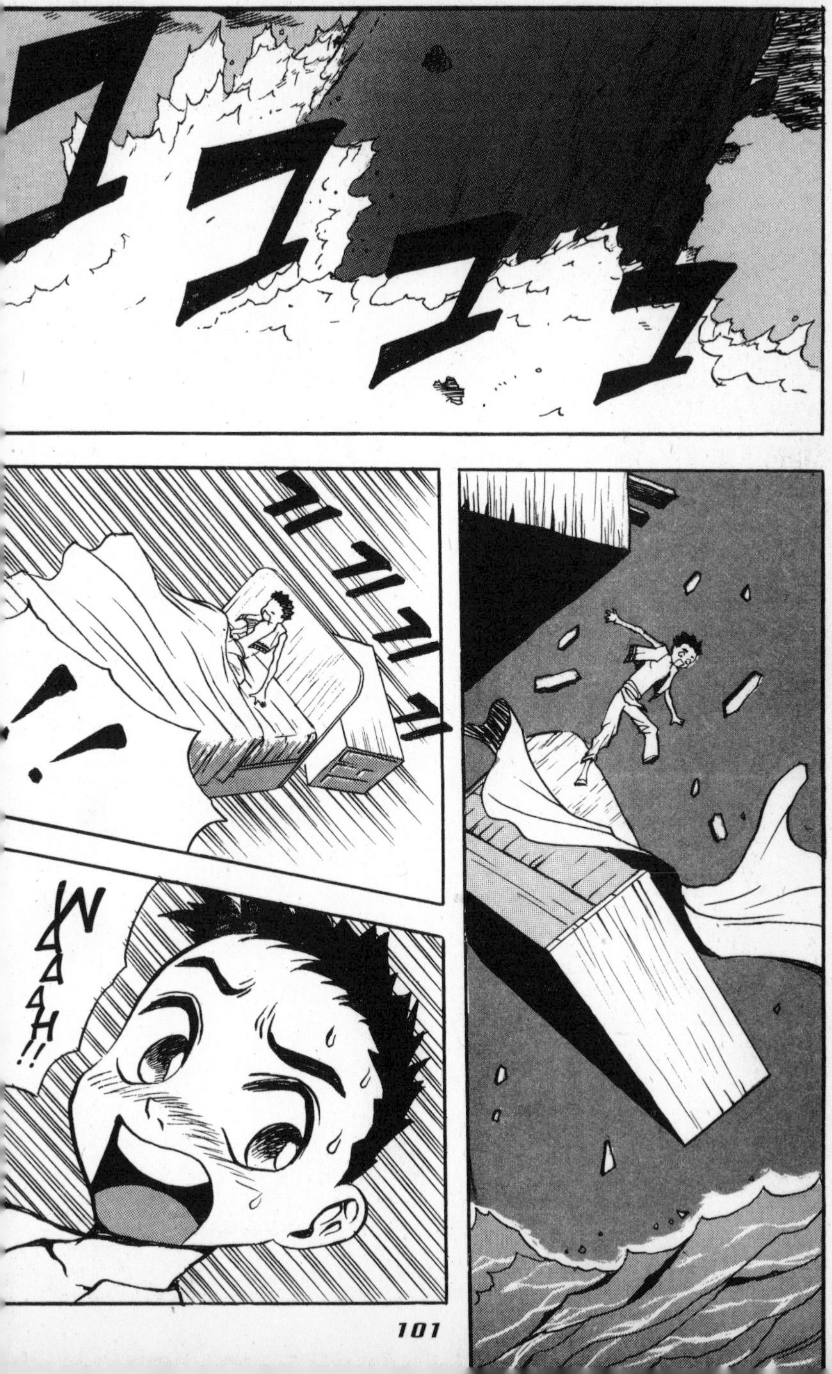
!!
WAAAH!!

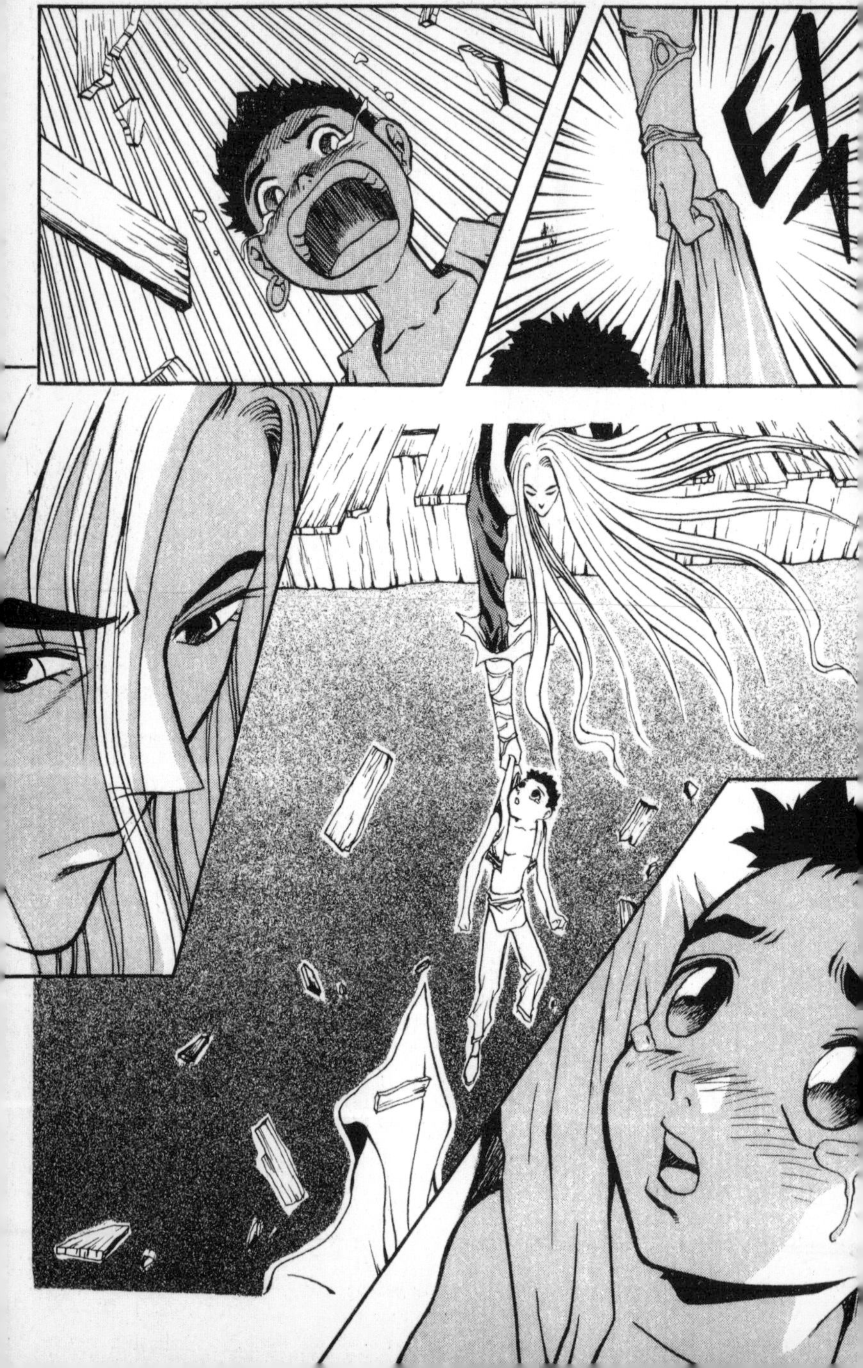

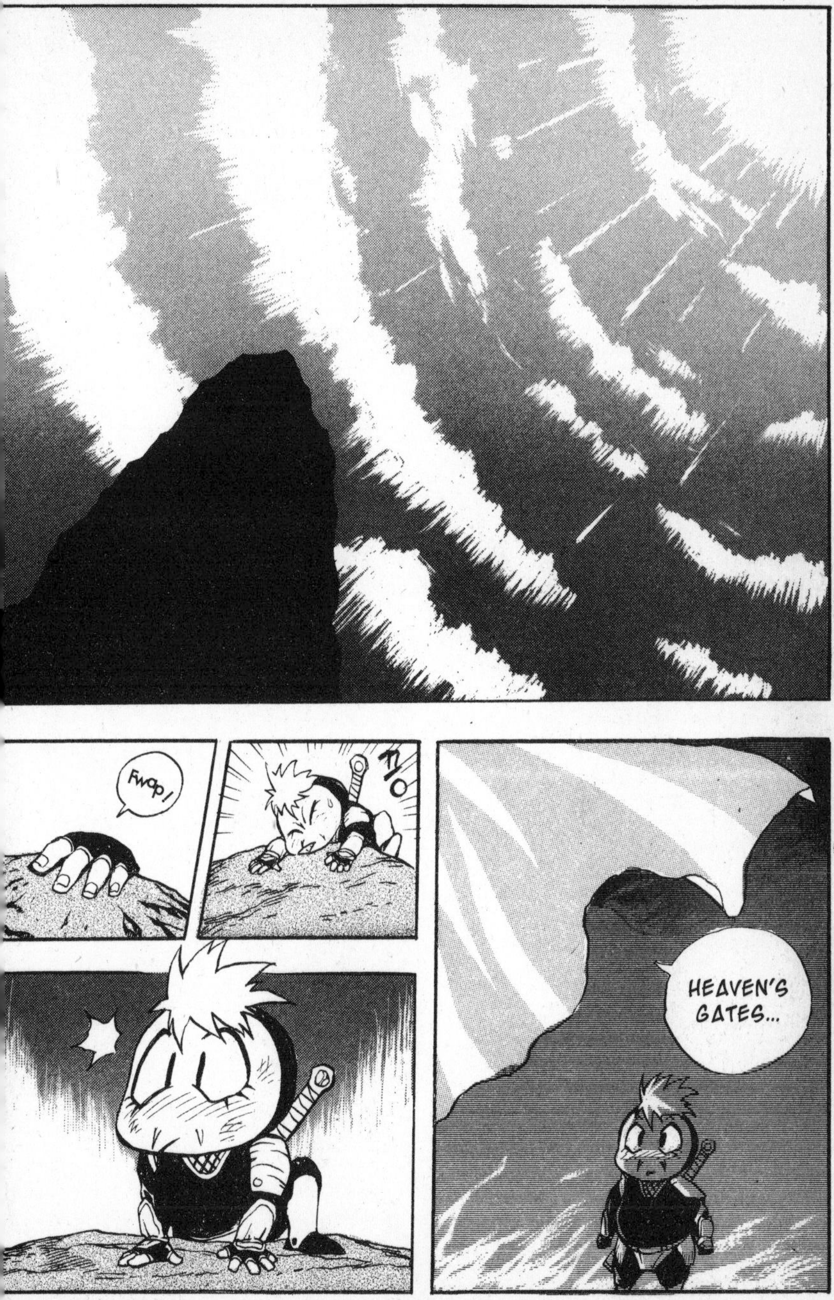
Fwap!
HEAVEN'S GATES...

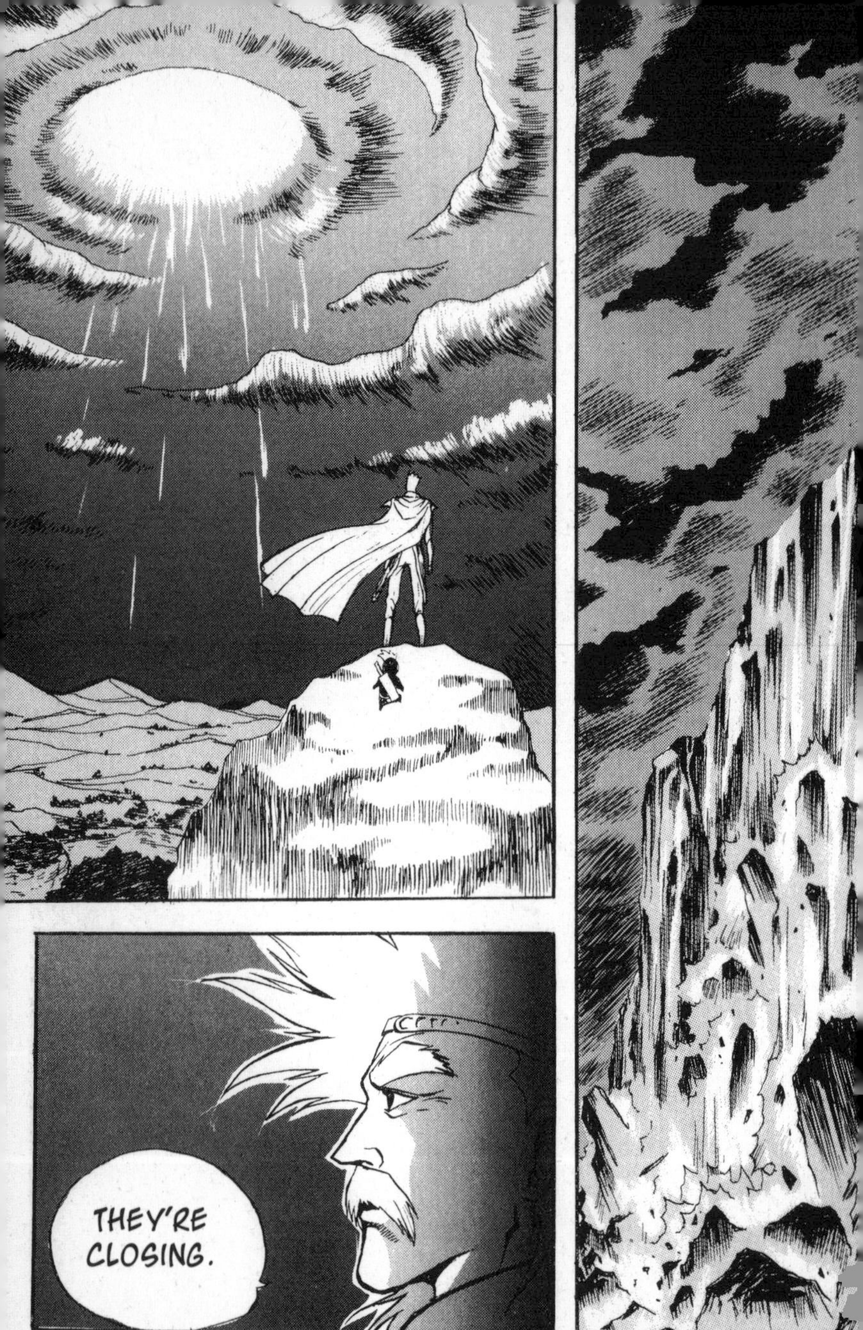
THEY'RE CLOSING.

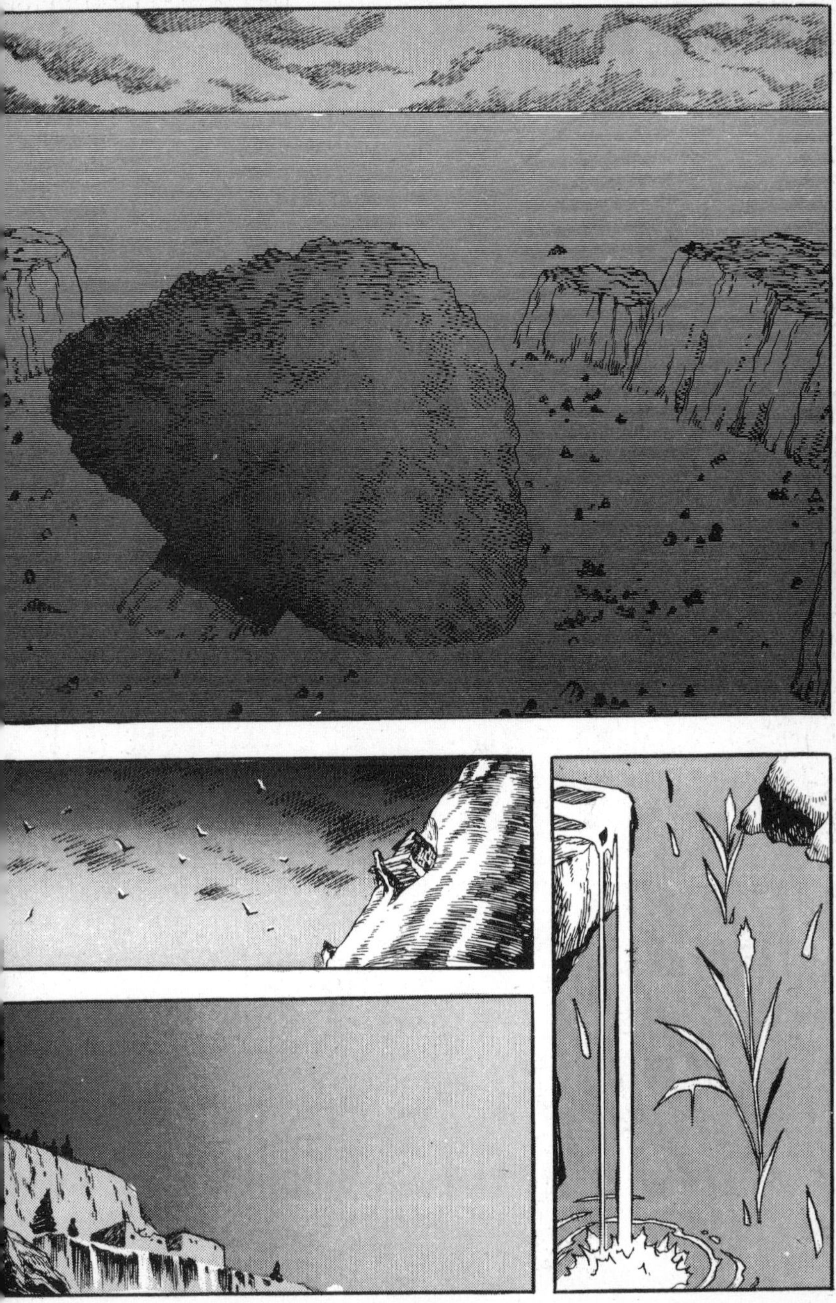

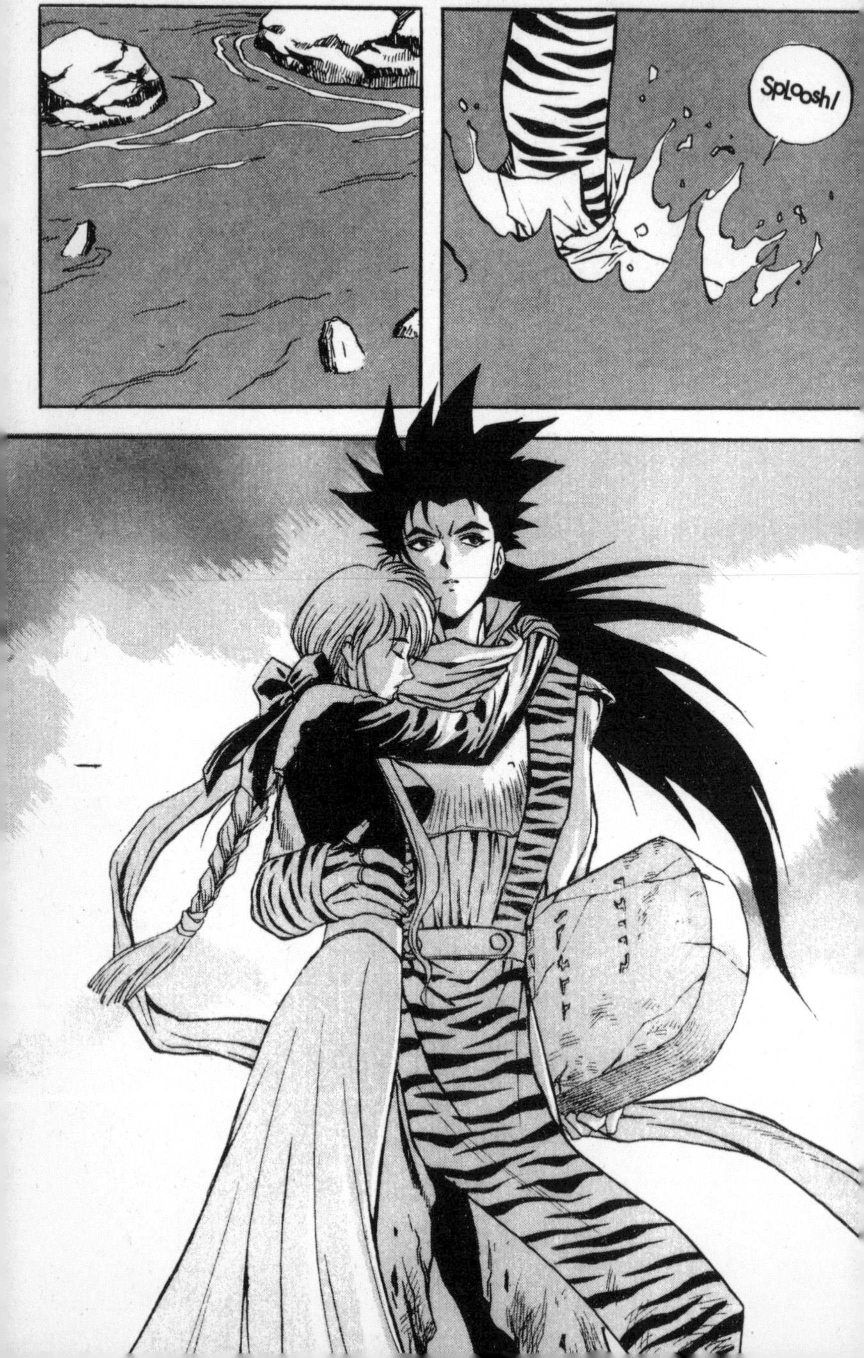
SPLOOSH!

BLADE OF HEAVEN

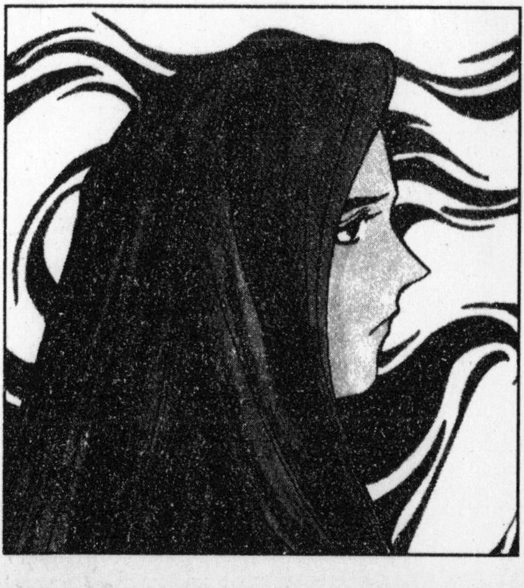

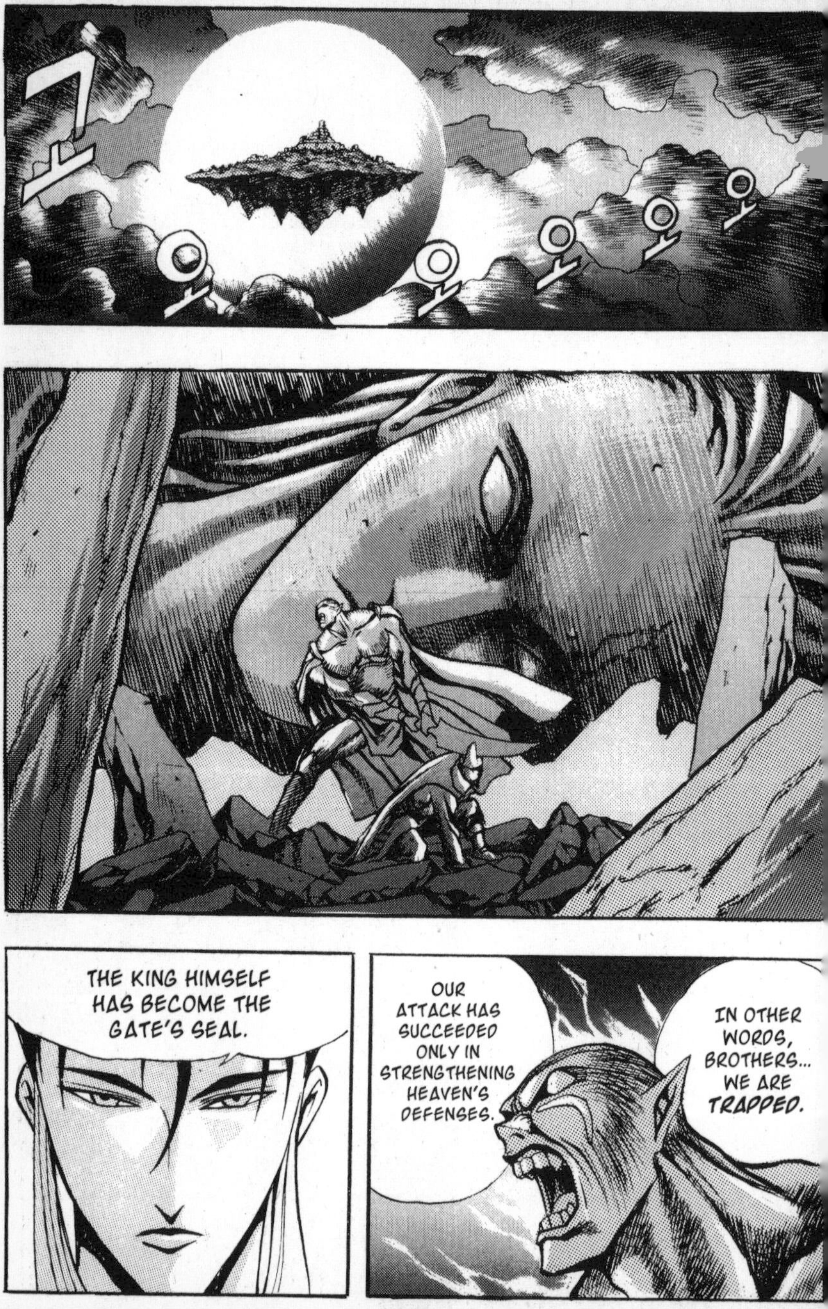
THE KING HIMSELF HAS BECOME THE GATE'S SEAL.
OUR ATTACK HAS SUCCEEDED ONLY IN STRENGTHENING HEAVEN'S DEFENSES.
IN OTHER WORDS, BROTHERS... WE ARE **TRAPPED**.

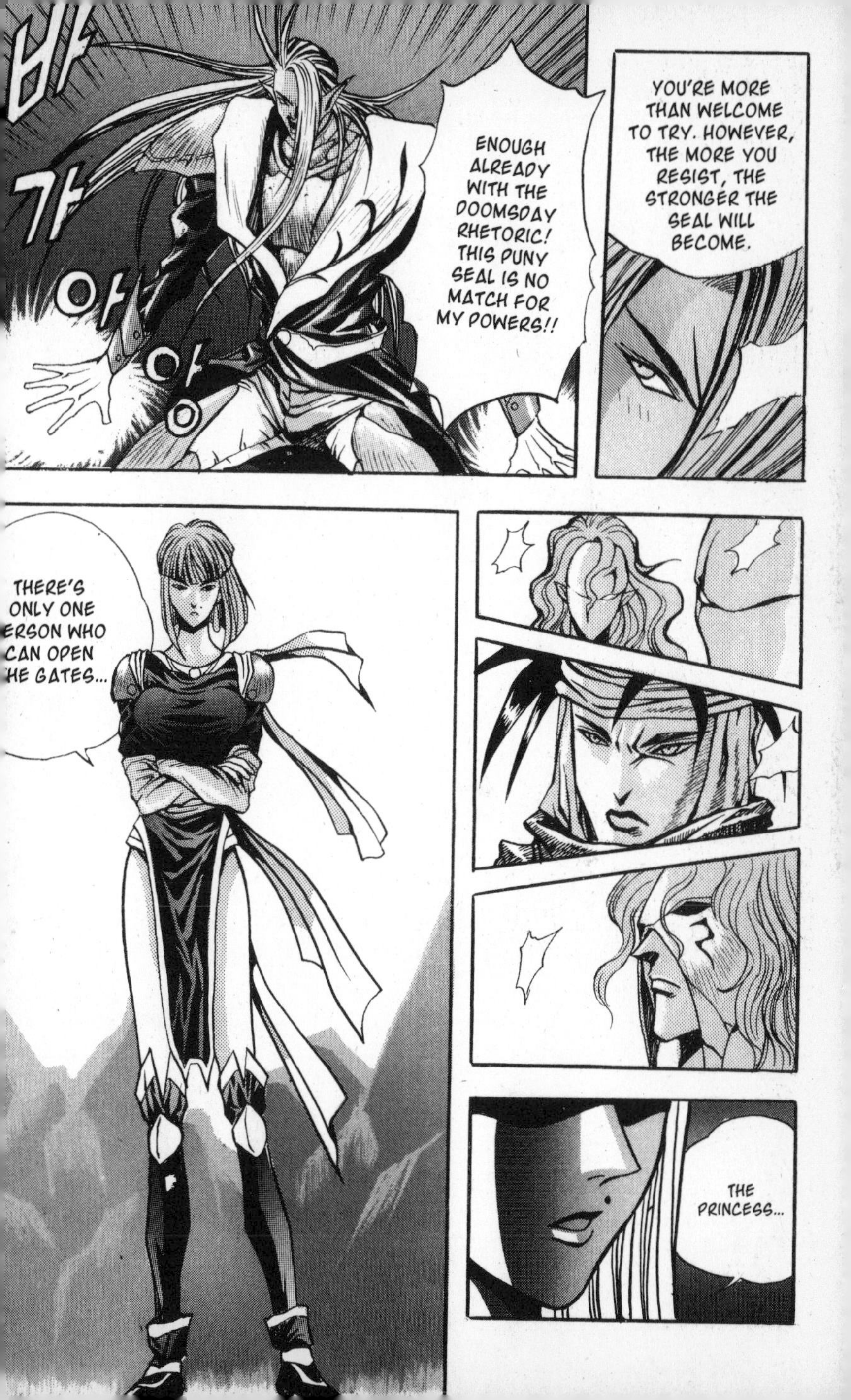
ENOUGH ALREADY WITH THE DOOMSDAY RHETORIC! THIS PUNY SEAL IS NO MATCH FOR MY POWERS!!
YOU'RE MORE THAN WELCOME TO TRY. HOWEVER, THE MORE YOU RESIST, THE STRONGER THE SEAL WILL BECOME.
THERE'S ONLY ONE ERSON WHO CAN OPEN HE GATES...
THE PRINCESS...

...OF HEAVEN!

INTERESTING...

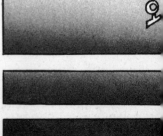

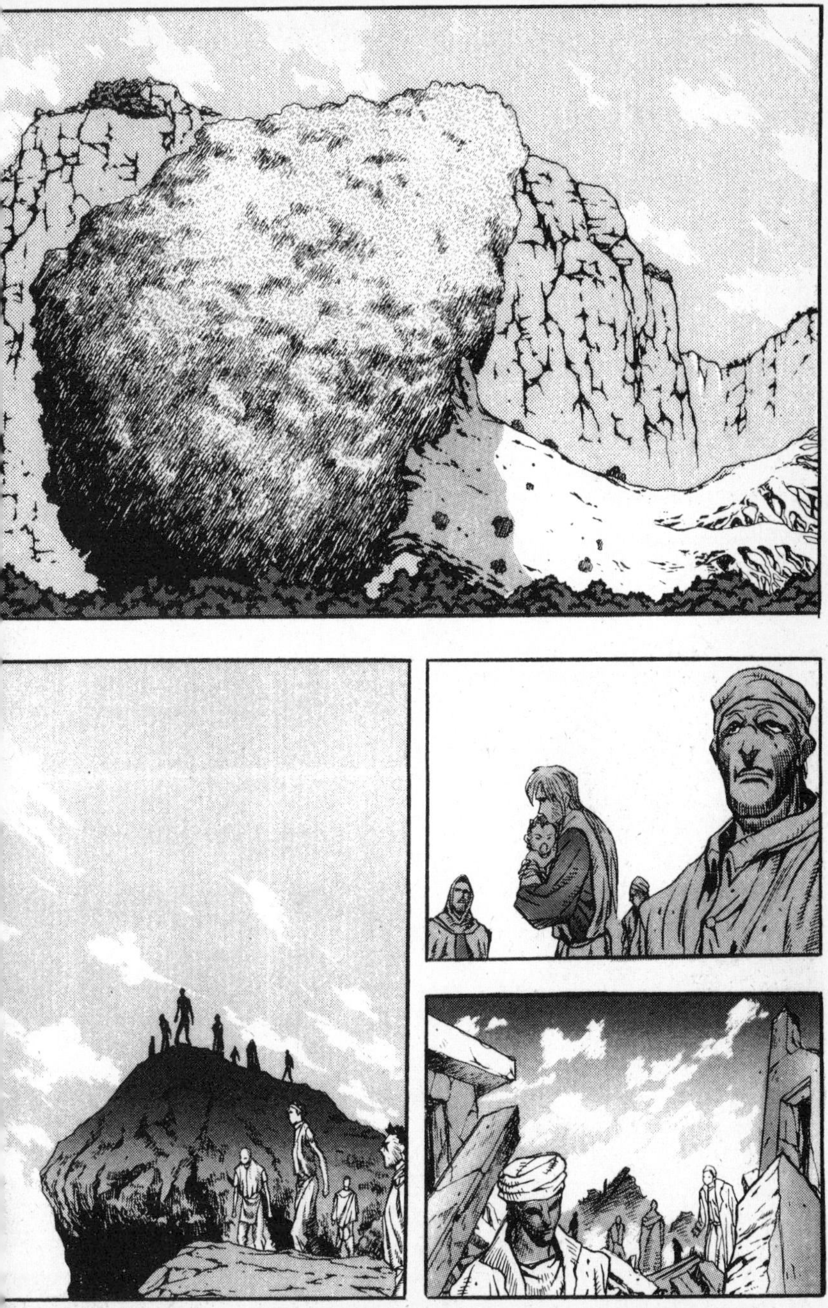

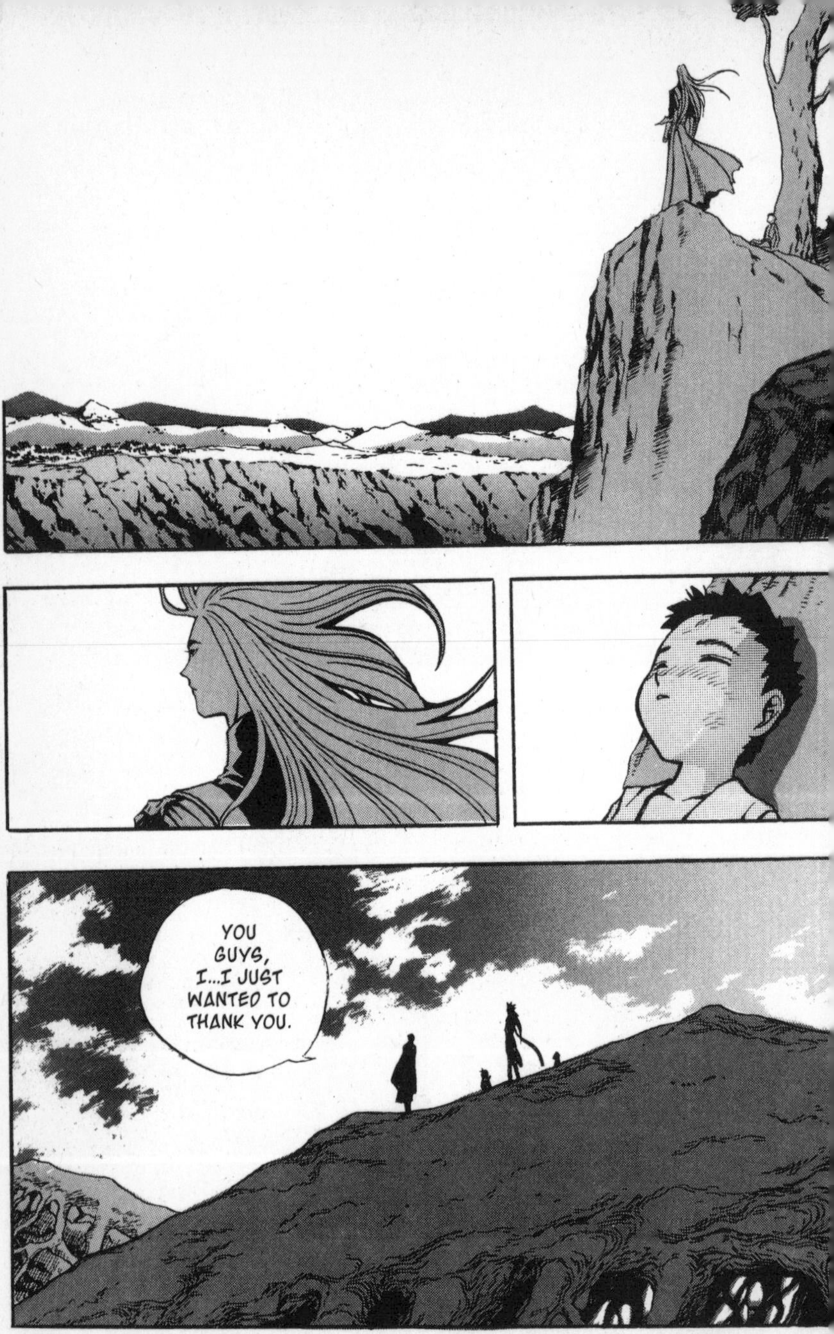
YOU GUYS, I...I JUST WANTED TO THANK YOU.

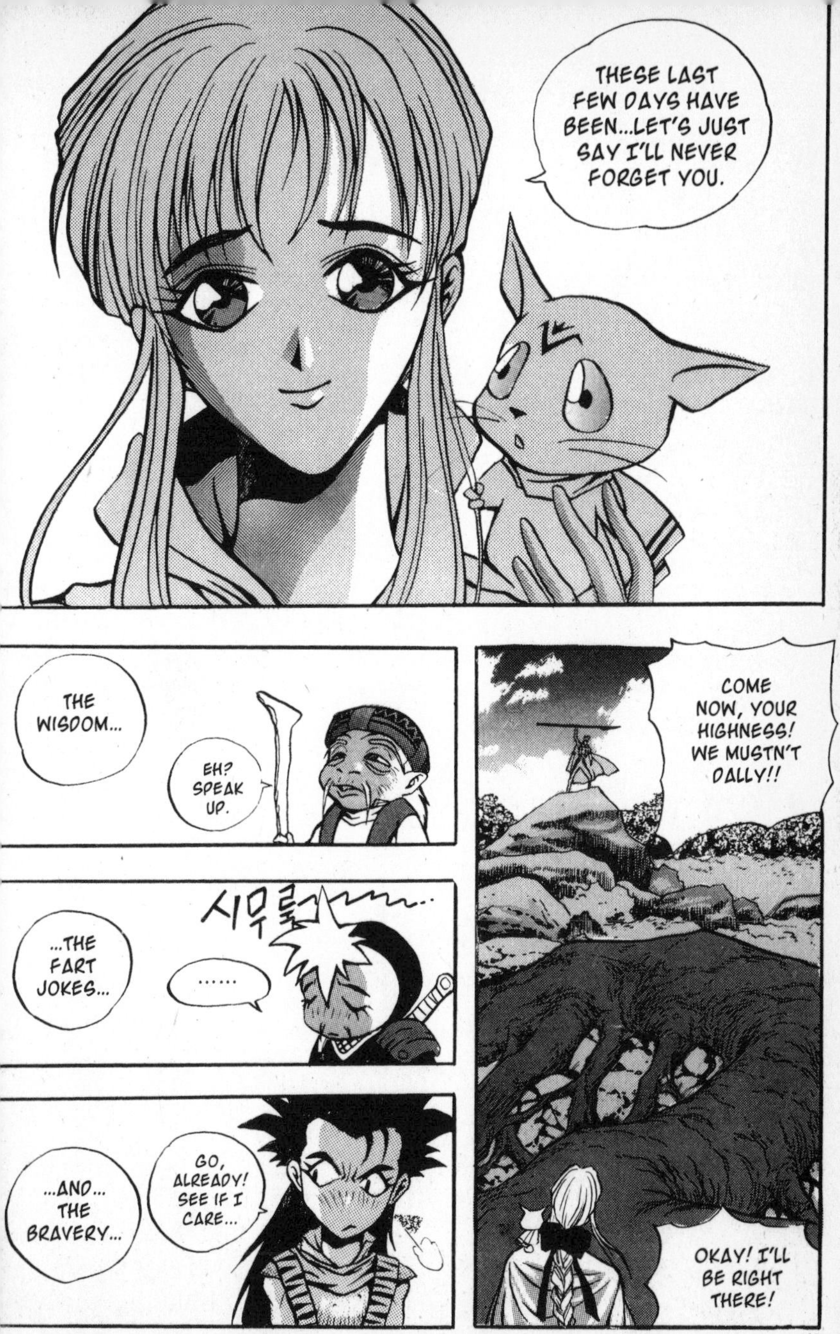
THESE LAST FEW DAYS HAVE BEEN...LET'S JUST SAY I'LL NEVER FORGET YOU.
THE WISDOM...
EH? SPEAK UP.
...THE FART JOKES...
......
시무룩
...AND... THE BRAVERY...
GO, ALREADY! SEE IF I CARE...
COME NOW, YOUR HIGHNESS! WE MUSTN'T DALLY!!
OKAY! I'LL BE RIGHT THERE!

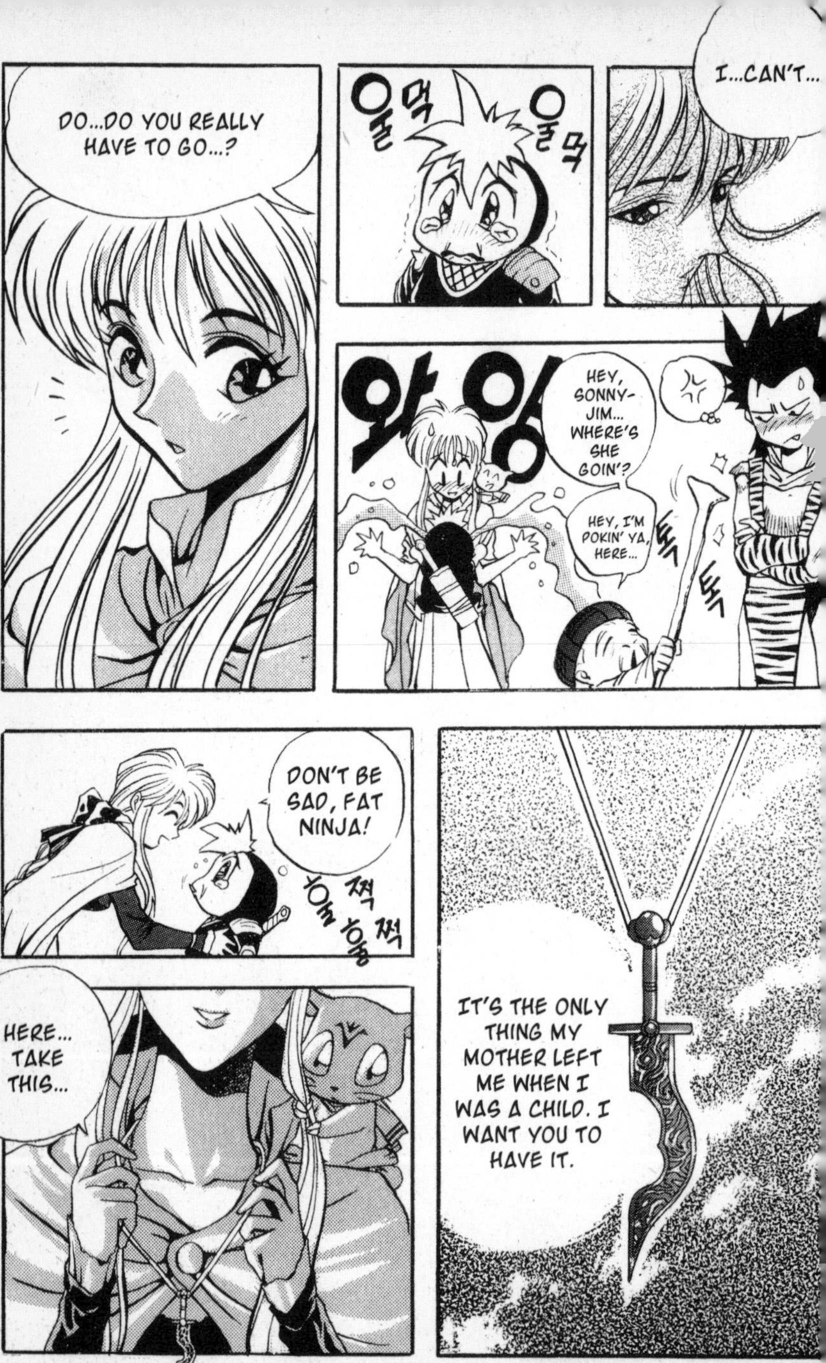
DO...DO YOU REALLY HAVE TO GO...?
울먹
울먹
I...CAN'T...
와앙
HEY, SONNY-JIM... WHERE'S SHE GOIN'?
HEY, I'M POKIN' YA, HERE...
톡
톡
DON'T BE SAD, FAT NINJA!
훌쩍
훌쩍
HERE... TAKE THIS...
IT'S THE ONLY THING MY MOTHER LEFT ME WHEN I WAS A CHILD. I WANT YOU TO HAVE IT.

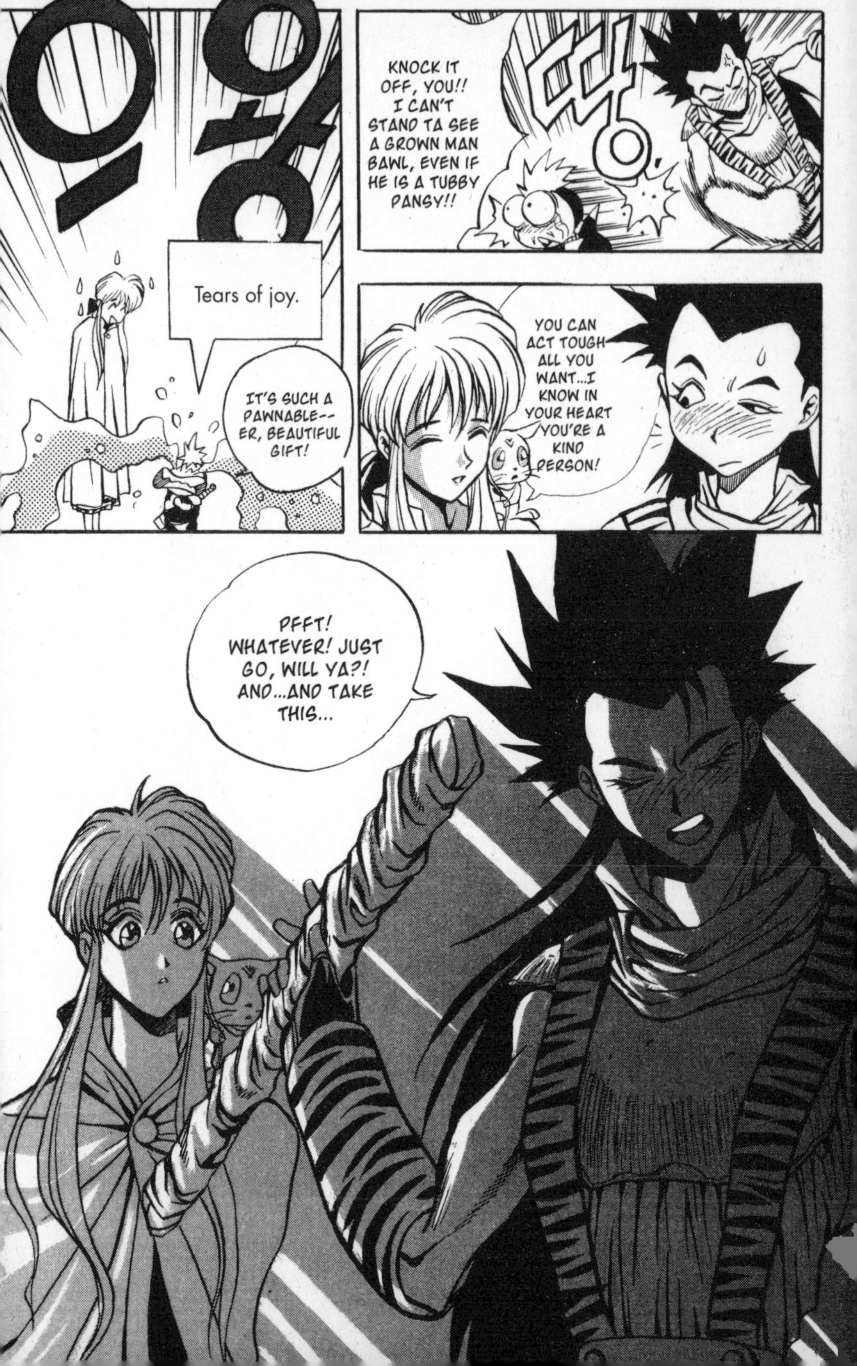
Tears of joy.
IT'S SUCH A PAWNABLE--ER, BEAUTIFUL GIFT!
KNOCK IT OFF, YOU!! I CAN'T STAND TA SEE A GROWN MAN BAWL, EVEN IF HE IS A TUBBY PANSY!!
YOU CAN ACT TOUGH ALL YOU WANT...I KNOW IN YOUR HEART YOU'RE A KIND PERSON!
PFFT! WHATEVER! JUST GO, WILL YA?! AND...AND TAKE THIS...

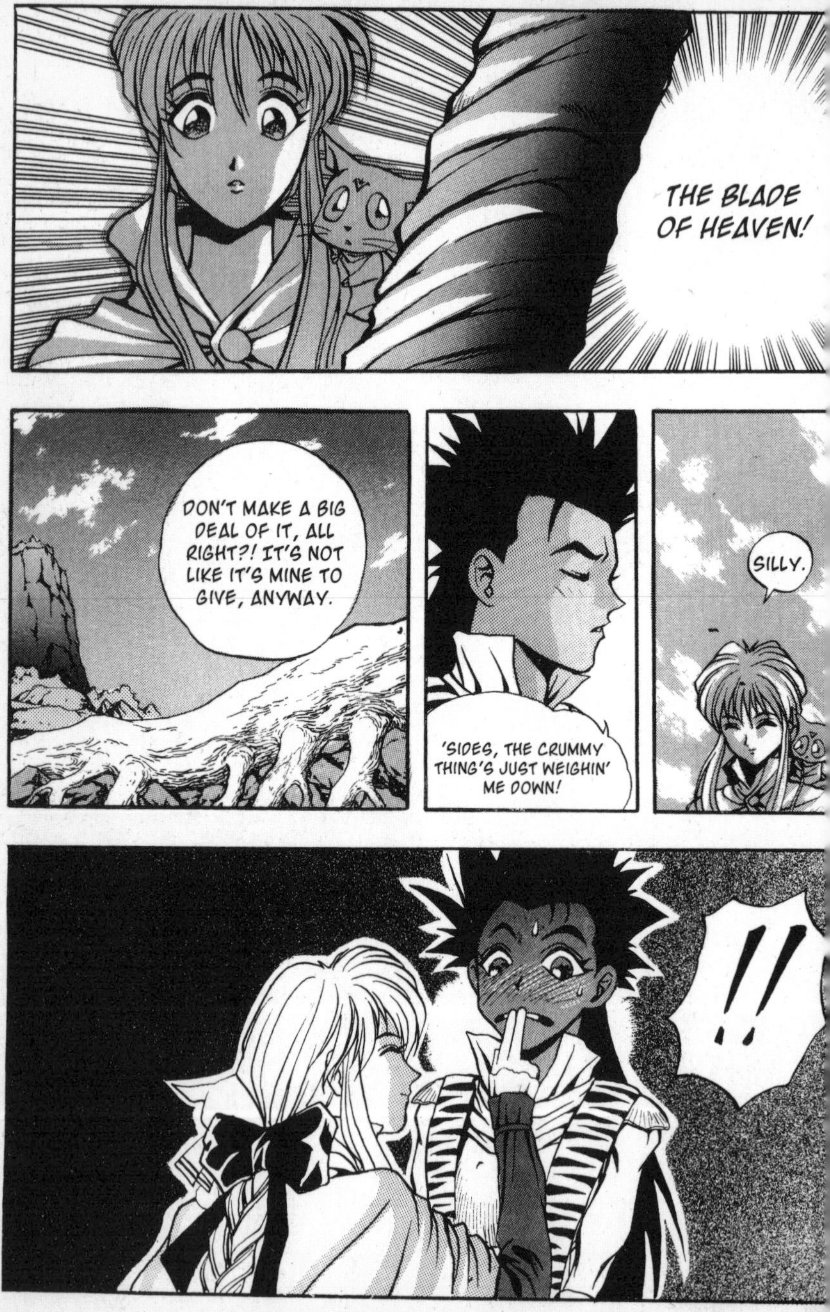
THE BLADE OF HEAVEN!
DON'T MAKE A BIG DEAL OF IT, ALL RIGHT?! IT'S NOT LIKE IT'S MINE TO GIVE, ANYWAY.
'SIDES, THE CRUMMY THING'S JUST WEIGHIN' ME DOWN!
SILLY.
!!

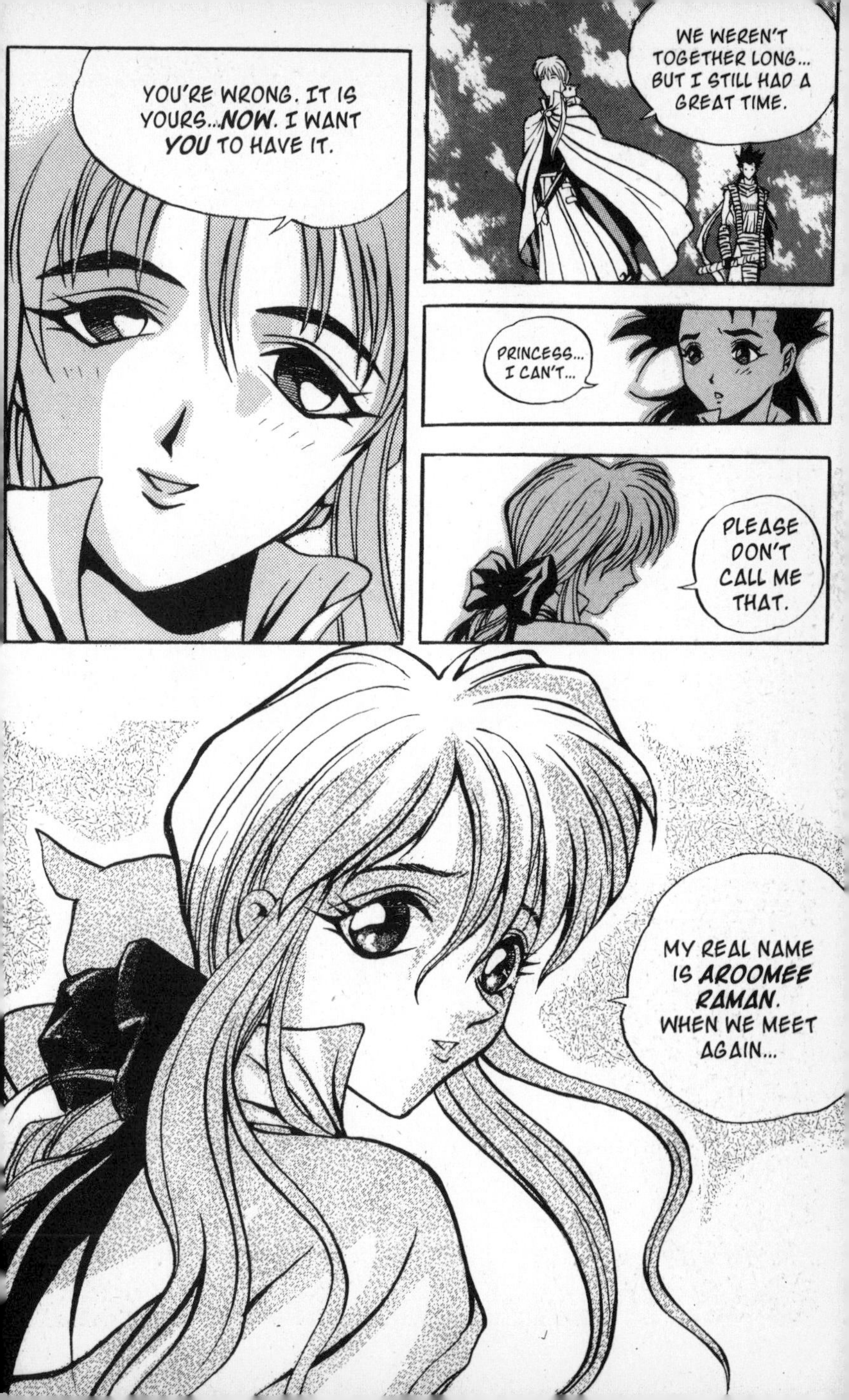
YOU'RE WRONG. IT IS YOURS...**NOW**. I WANT ***YOU*** TO HAVE IT.
WE WEREN'T TOGETHER LONG... BUT I STILL HAD A GREAT TIME.
PRINCESS... I CAN'T...
PLEASE DON'T CALL ME THAT.
MY REAL NAME IS ***AROOMEE RAMAN***. WHEN WE MEET AGAIN...

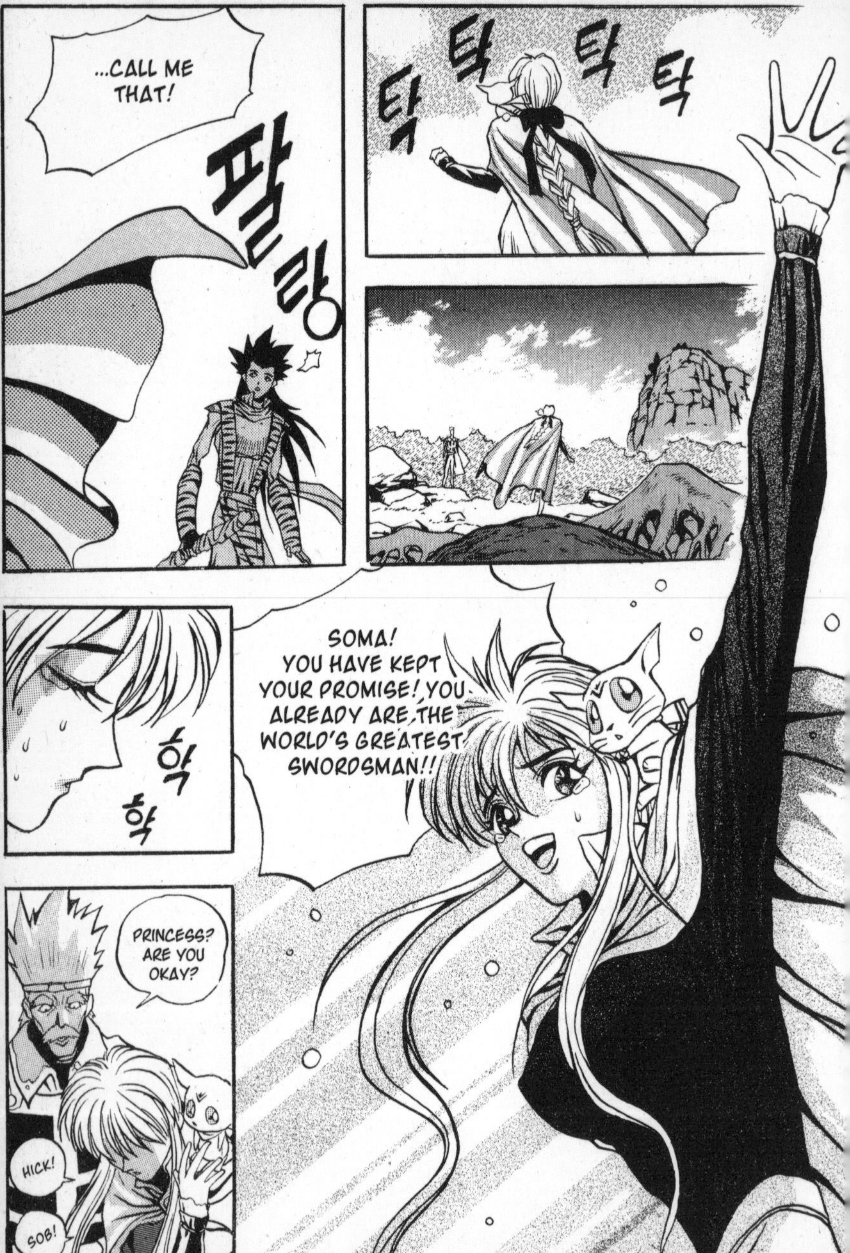
...CALL ME THAT!
팔랑
탁 탁 탁 탁
헉 헉
PRINCESS? ARE YOU OKAY?
HICK!
SOB!
SOMA! YOU HAVE KEPT YOUR PROMISE! YOU ALREADY ARE THE WORLD'S GREATEST SWORDSMAN!!

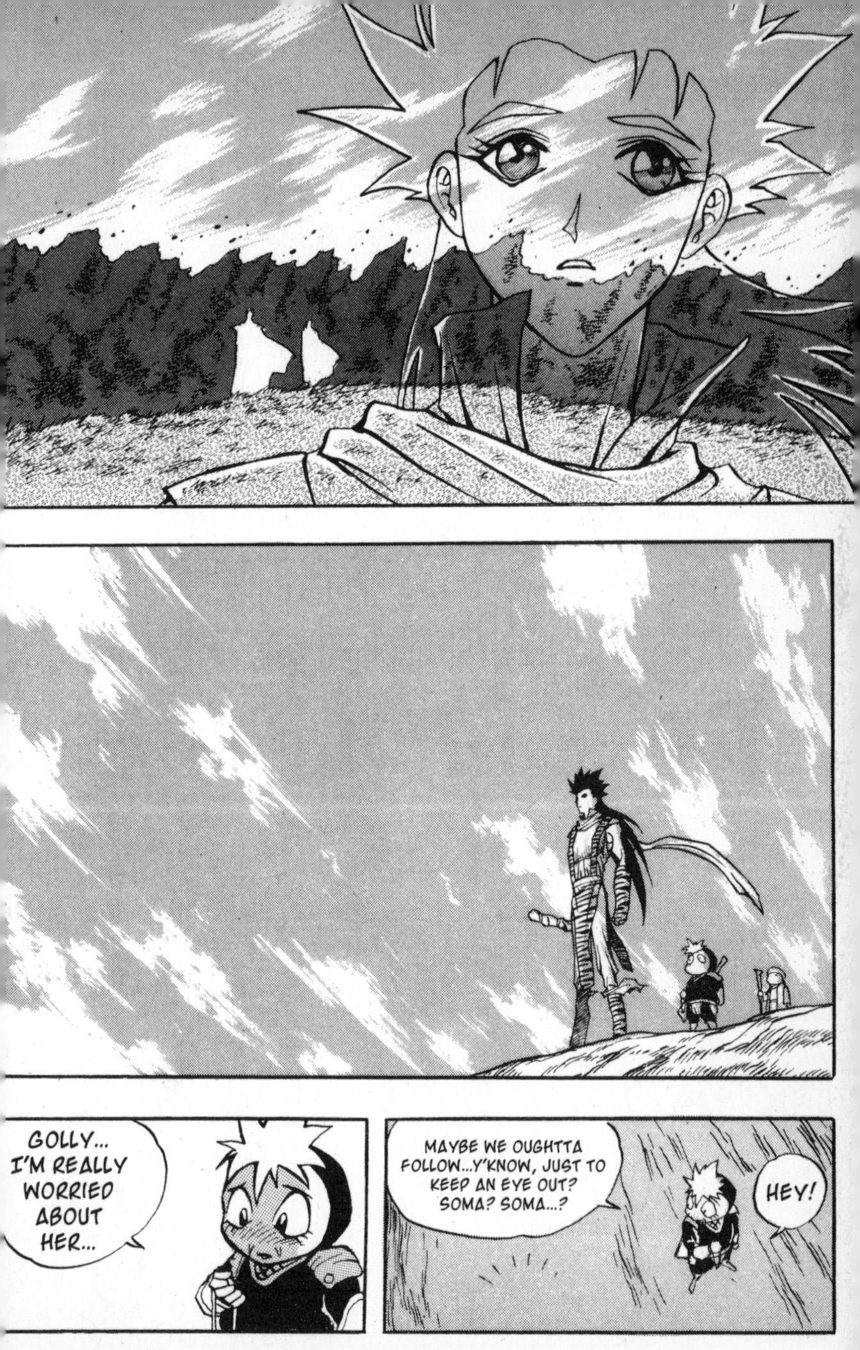
GOLLY... I'M REALLY WORRIED ABOUT HER...
MAYBE WE OUGHTTA FOLLOW...Y'KNOW, JUST TO KEEP AN EYE OUT? SOMA? SOMA...?
HEY!

WHERE'RE YOU GOIN'?! DON'T YOU THINK WE OUGHTTA HELP THEM?!

RELATION-SHIPS... ARE MADE AND BROKEN.

EVERYONE WALKS THEIR OWN PATH.

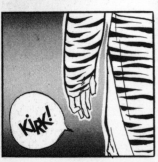

KIRK!

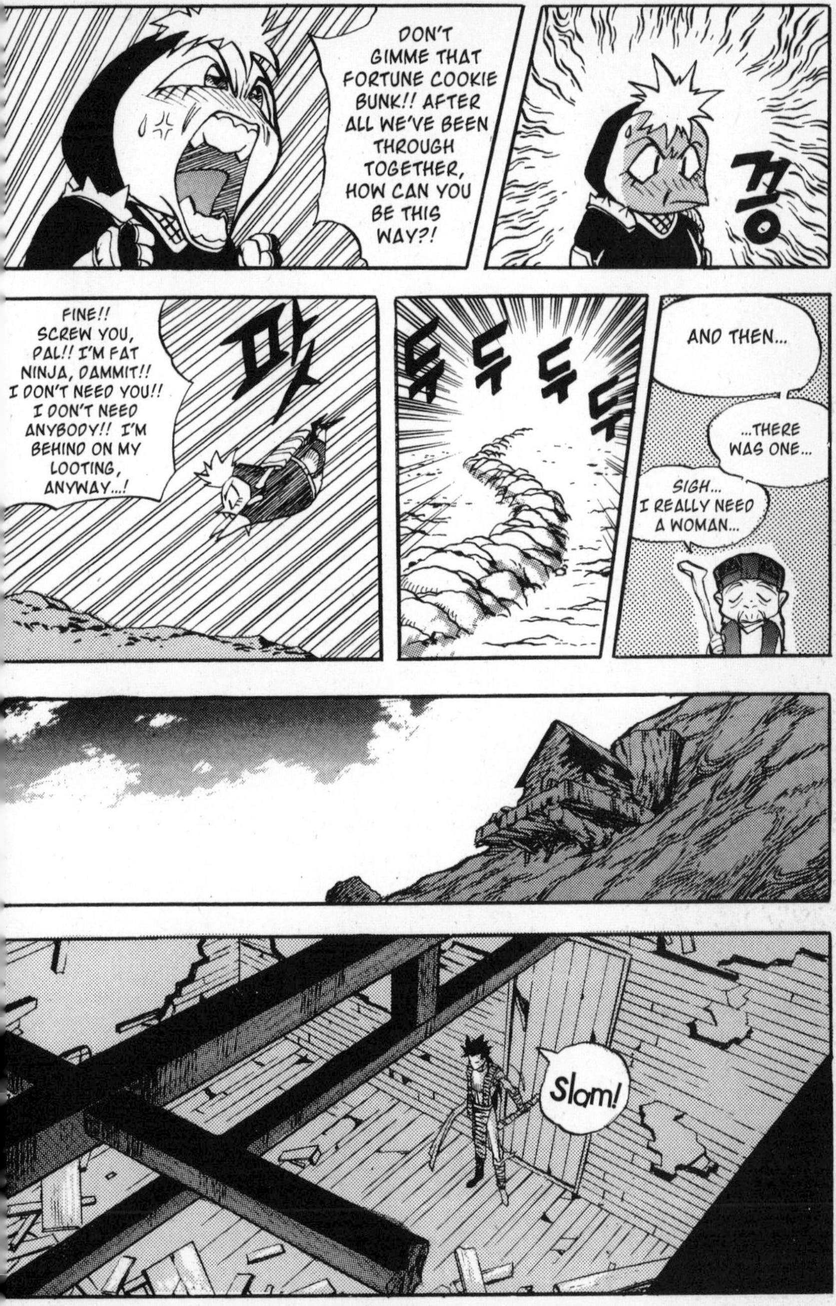
DON'T GIMME THAT FORTUNE COOKIE BUNK!! AFTER ALL WE'VE BEEN THROUGH TOGETHER, HOW CAN YOU BE THIS WAY?!
FINE!! SCREW YOU, PAL!! I'M FAT NINJA, DAMMIT!! I DON'T NEED YOU!! I DON'T NEED ANYBODY!! I'M BEHIND ON MY LOOTING, ANYWAY...!
AND THEN...
...THERE WAS ONE...
SIGH... I REALLY NEED A WOMAN...
Slam!

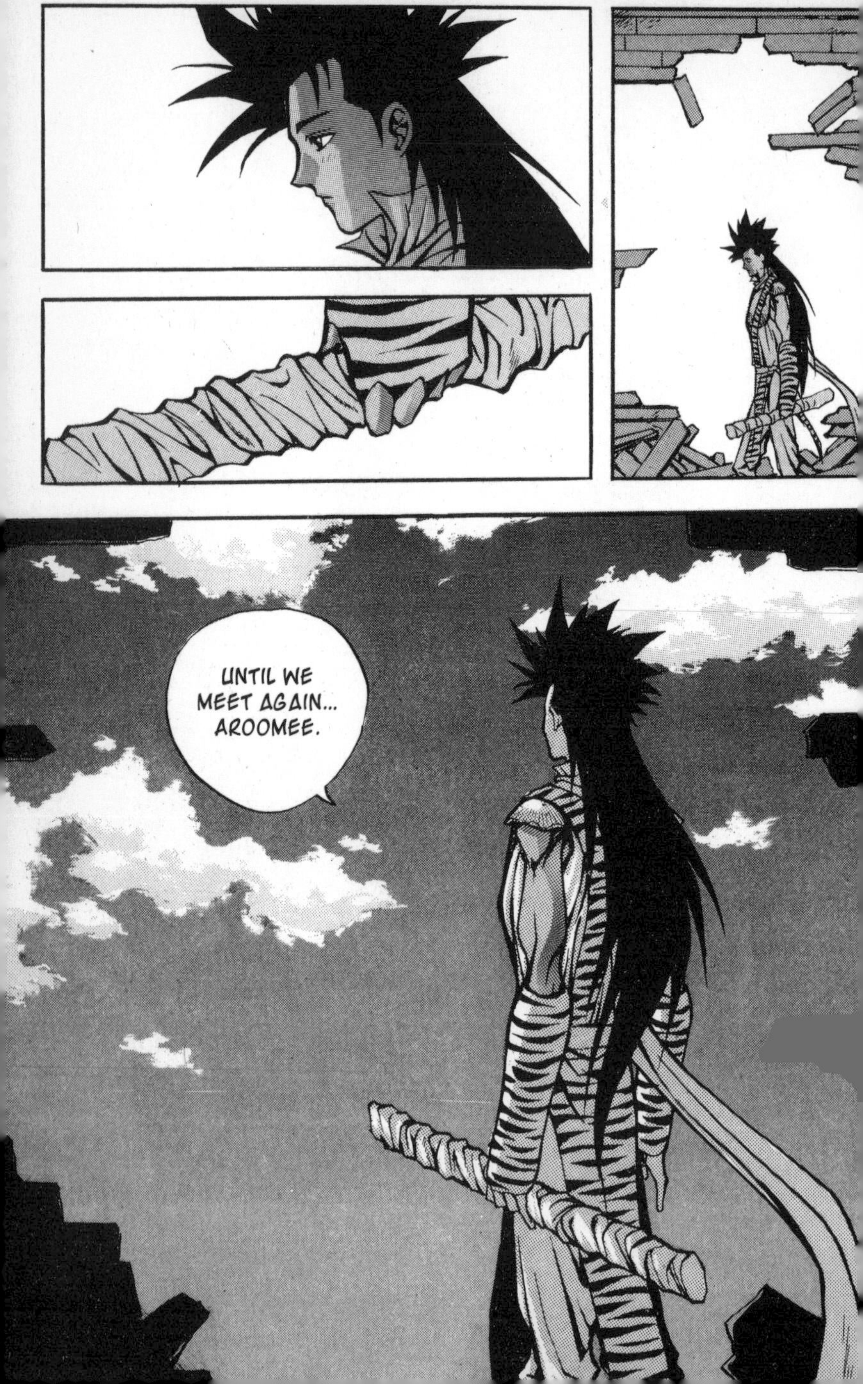
UNTIL WE MEET AGAIN... AROOMEE.

BLADE OF HEAVEN

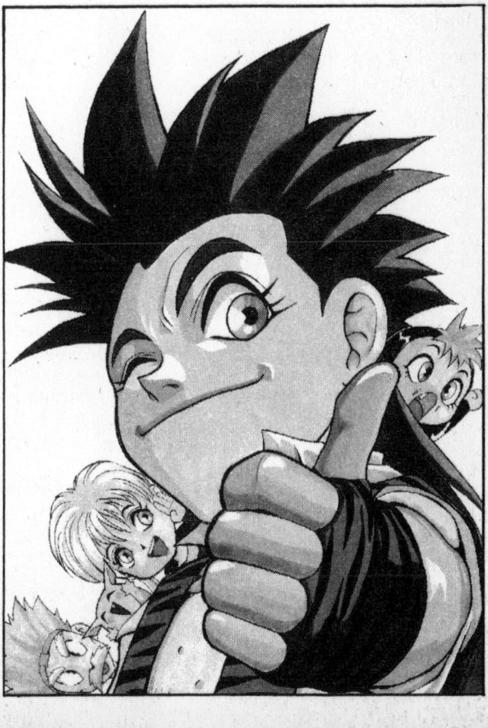

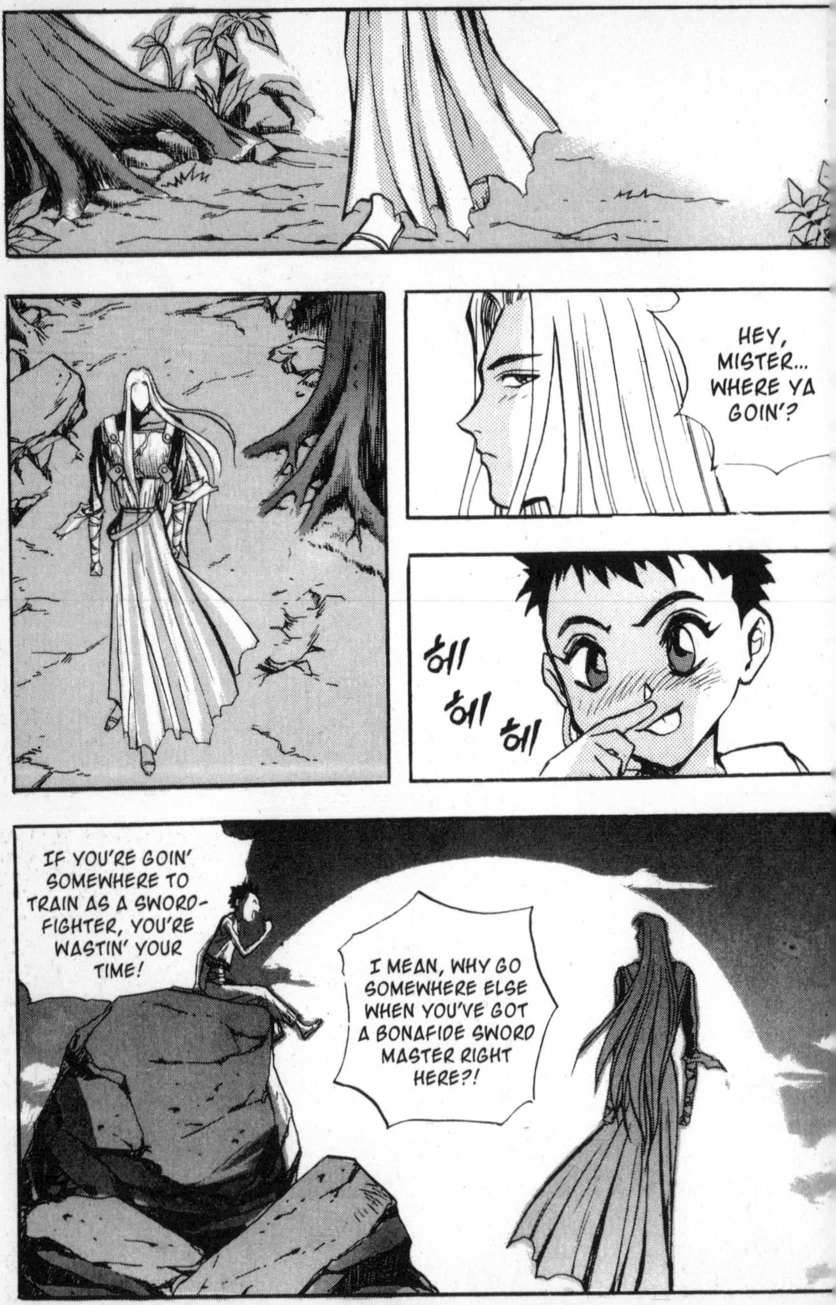
HEY, MISTER... WHERE YA GOIN'?
헤
헤
헤
IF YOU'RE GOIN' SOMEWHERE TO TRAIN AS A SWORD-FIGHTER, YOU'RE WASTIN' YOUR TIME!
I MEAN, WHY GO SOMEWHERE ELSE WHEN YOU'VE GOT A BONAFIDE SWORD MASTER RIGHT HERE?!

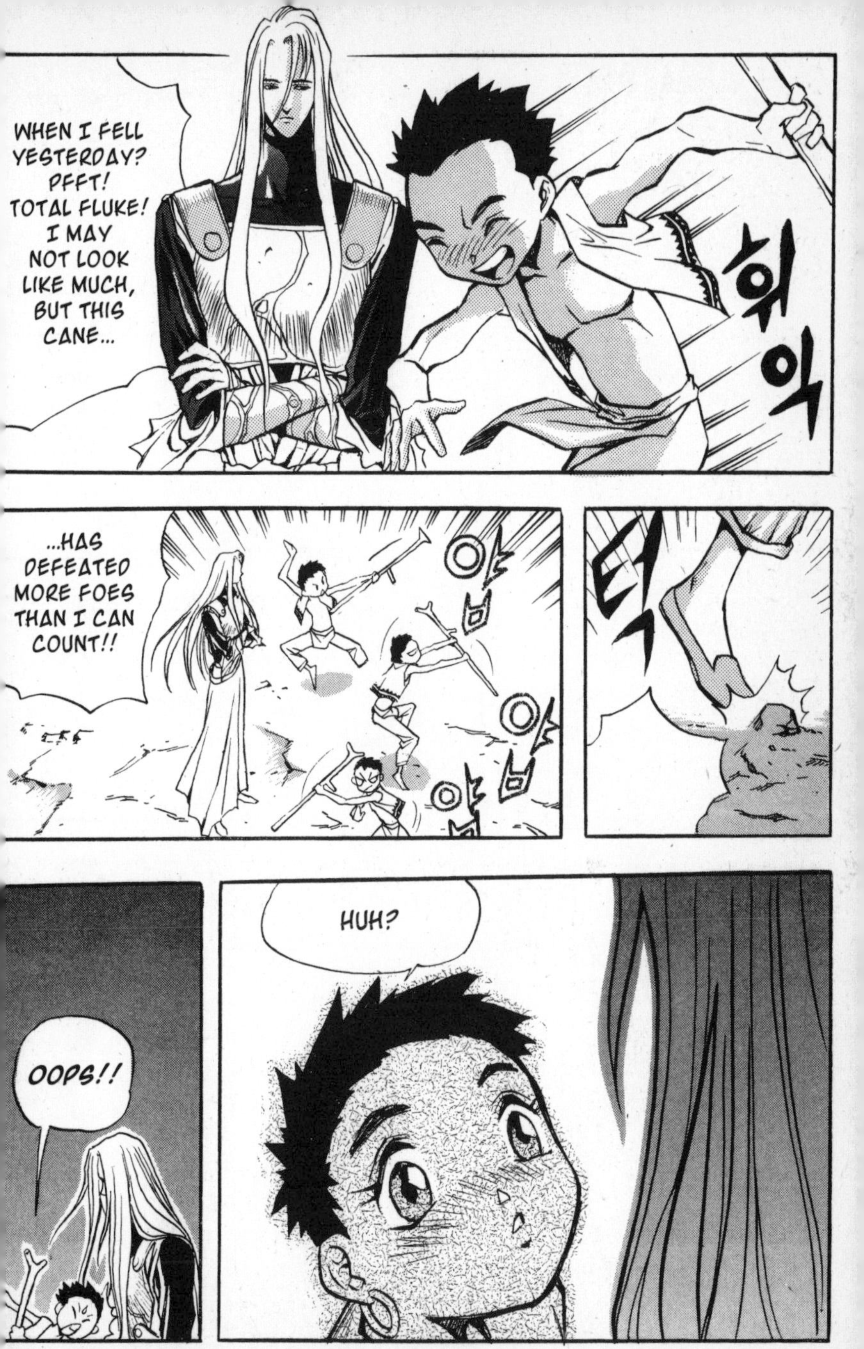
WHEN I FELL YESTERDAY? PFFT! TOTAL FLUKE! I MAY NOT LOOK LIKE MUCH, BUT THIS CANE...
휘익
...HAS DEFEATED MORE FOES THAN I CAN COUNT!!
얍
얍
얍
턱
OOPS!!
HUH?

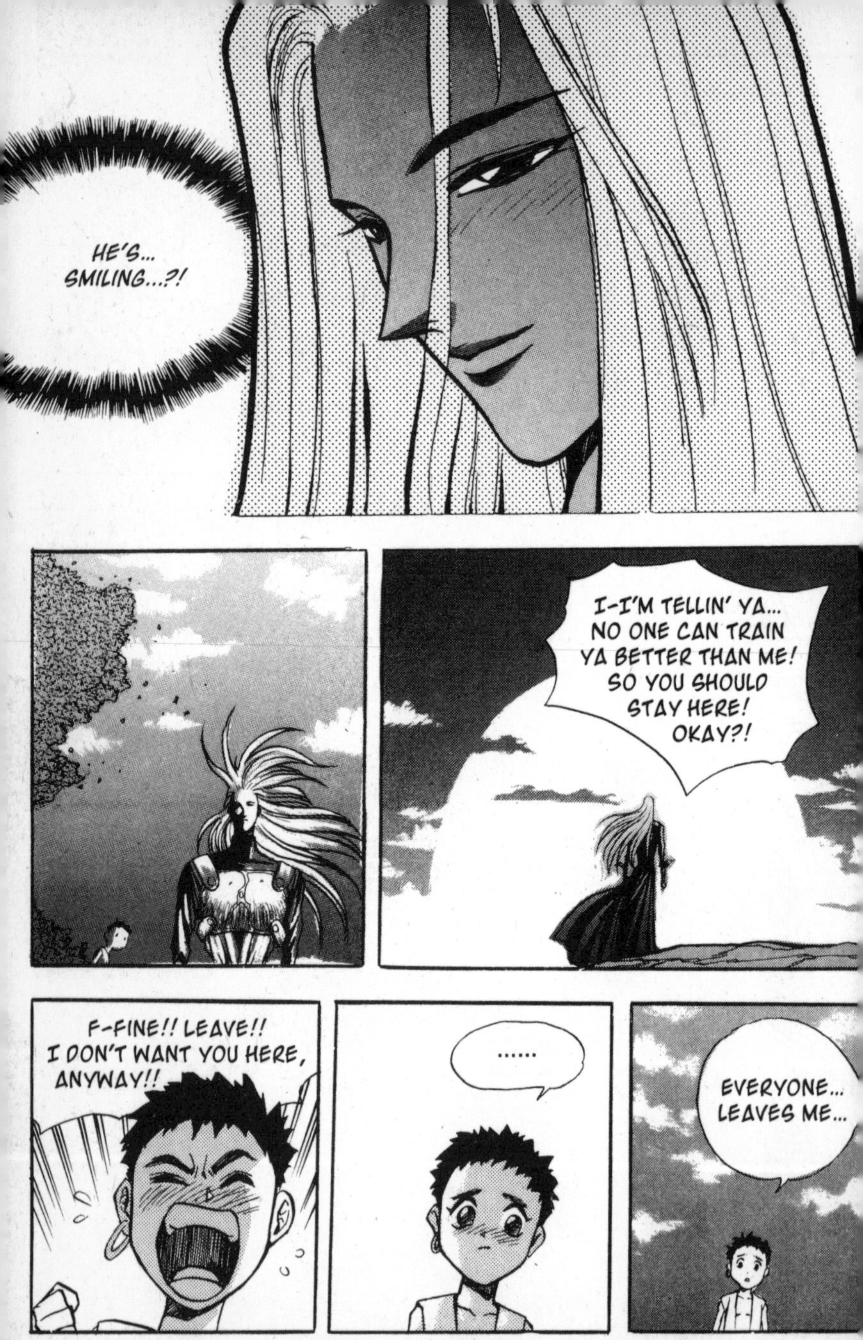
HE'S... SMILING...?!
I-I'M TELLIN' YA... NO ONE CAN TRAIN YA BETTER THAN ME! SO YOU SHOULD STAY HERE! OKAY?!
F-FINE!! LEAVE!! I DON'T WANT YOU HERE, ANYWAY!!
......
EVERYONE... LEAVES ME...

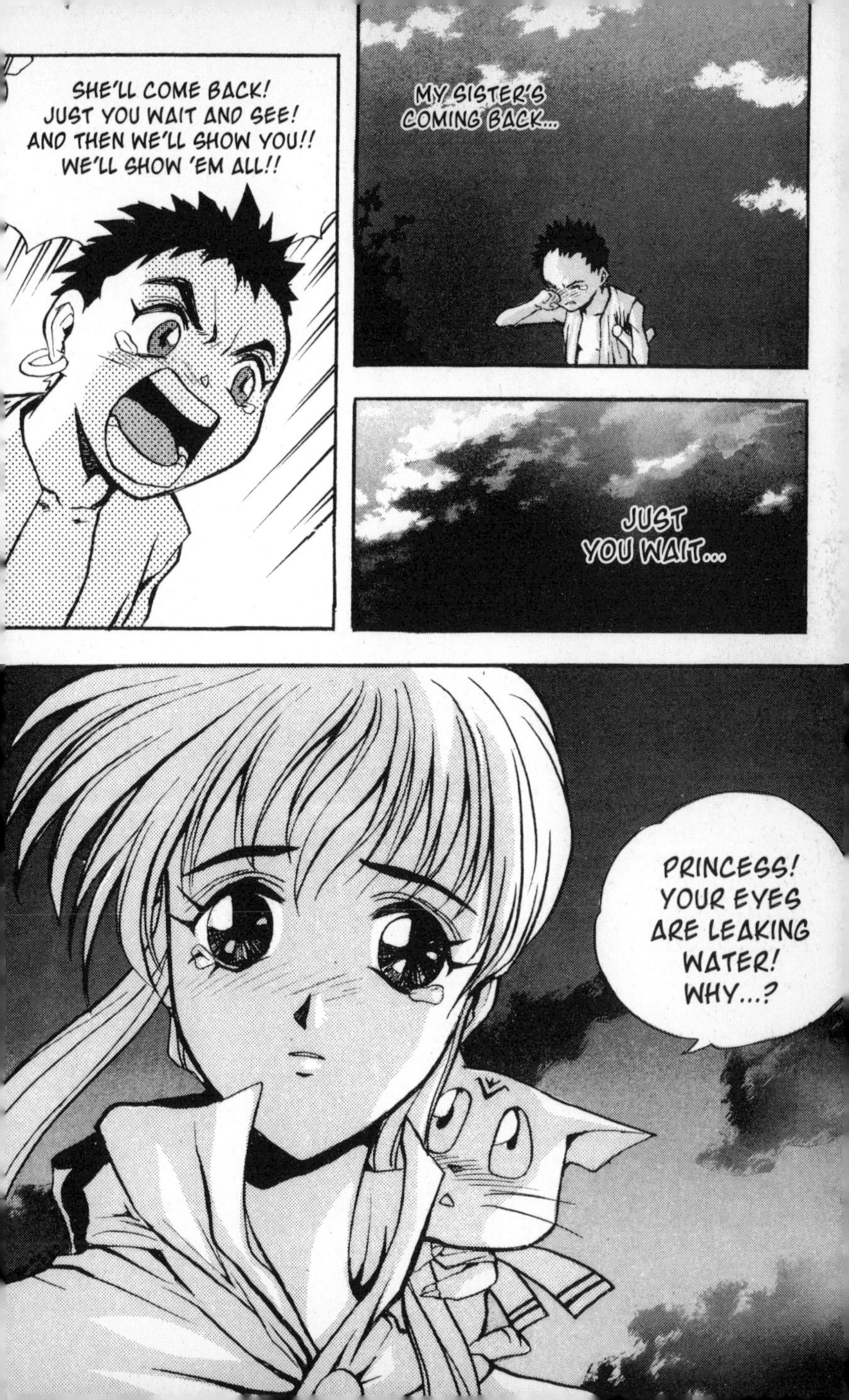
SHE'LL COME BACK! JUST YOU WAIT AND SEE! AND THEN WE'LL SHOW YOU!! WE'LL SHOW 'EM ALL!!
MY SISTER'S COMING BACK...
JUST YOU WAIT...
PRINCESS! YOUR EYES ARE LEAKING WATER! WHY...?

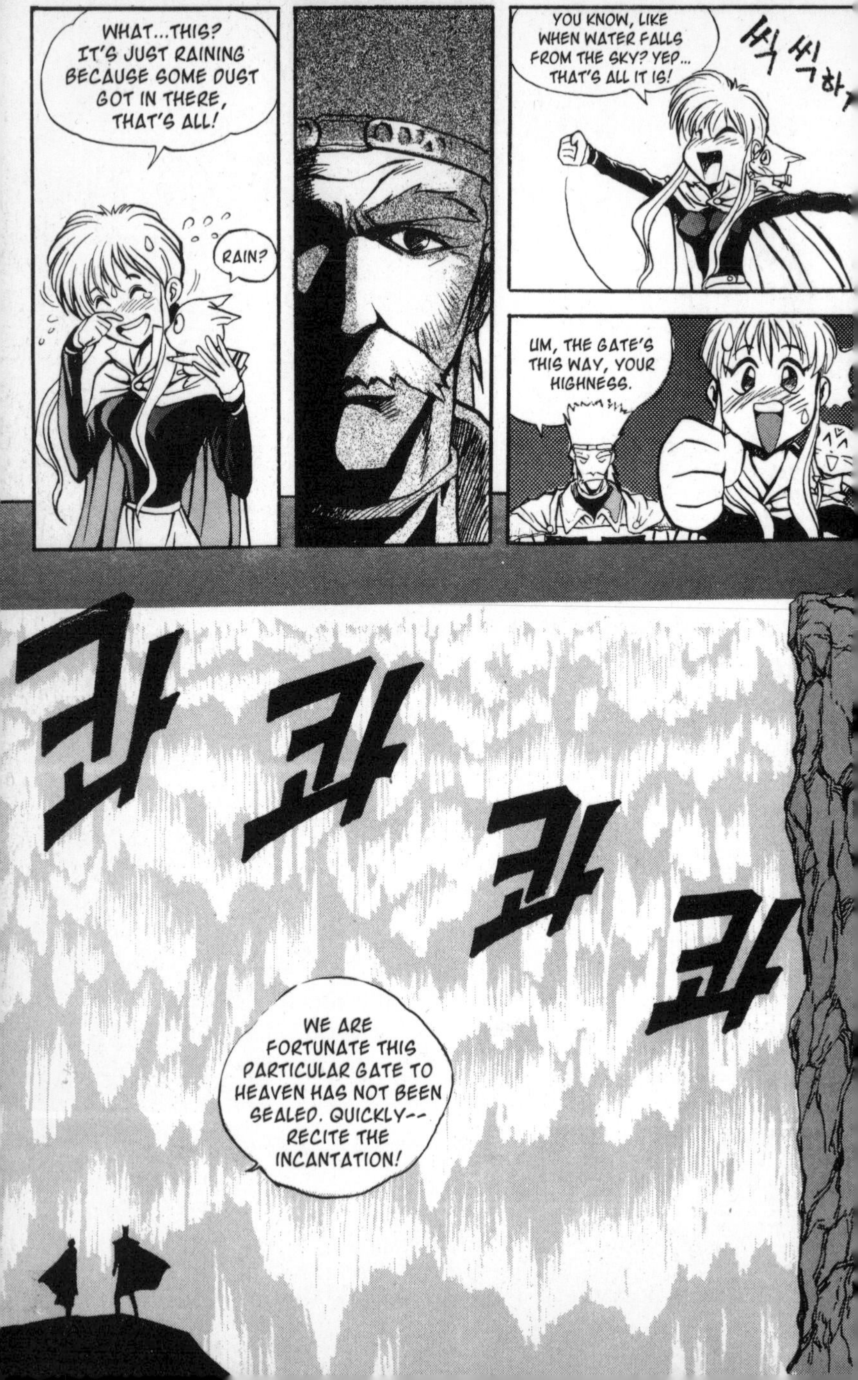
WHAT...THIS? IT'S JUST RAINING BECAUSE SOME DUST GOT IN THERE, THAT'S ALL!
RAIN?
YOU KNOW, LIKE WHEN WATER FALLS FROM THE SKY? YEP... THAT'S ALL IT IS!
씩 씩 하
UM, THE GATE'S THIS WAY, YOUR HIGHNESS.
콰 콰 콰 콰
WE ARE FORTUNATE THIS PARTICULAR GATE TO HEAVEN HAS NOT BEEN SEALED. QUICKLY-- RECITE THE INCANTATION!

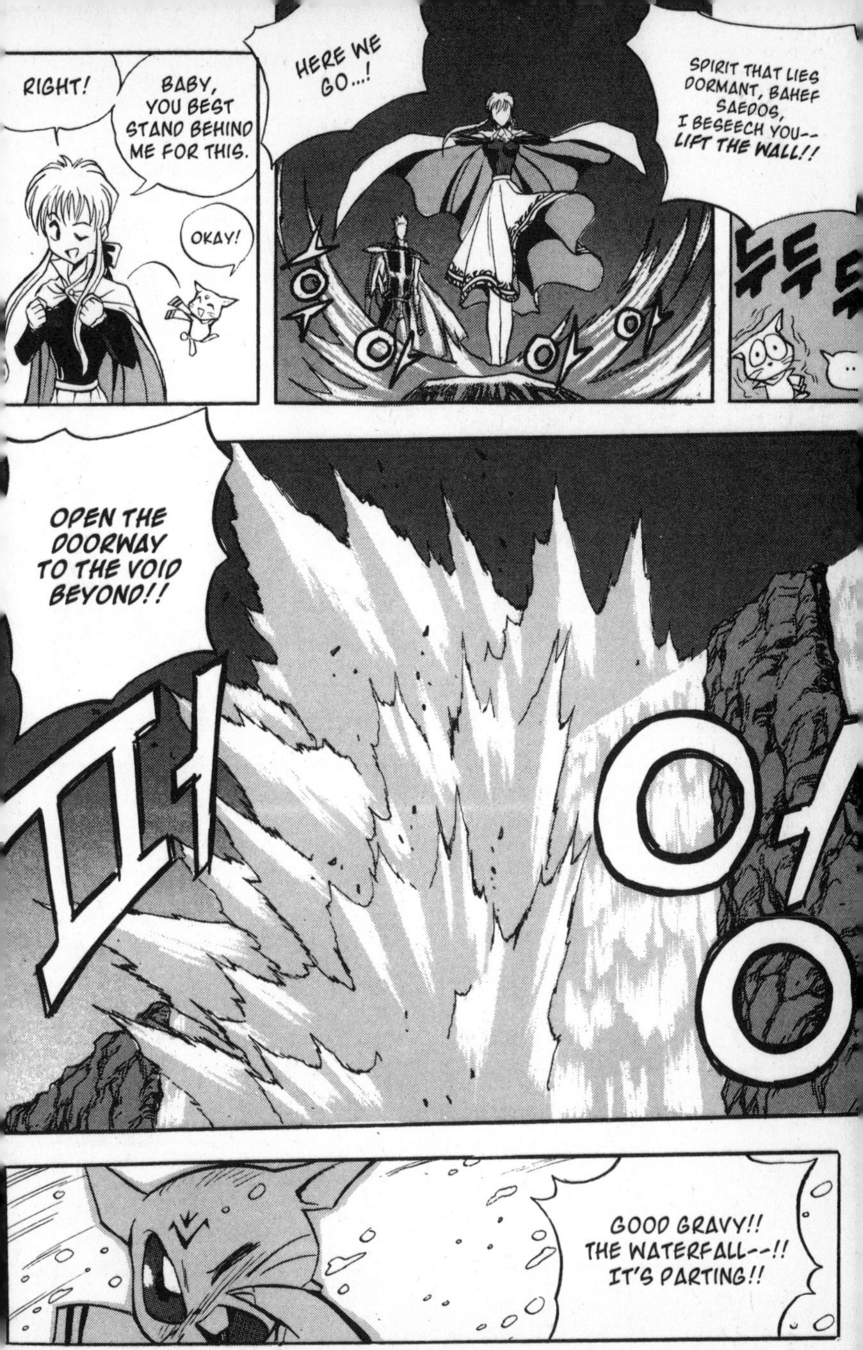
RIGHT!
BABY, YOU BEST STAND BEHIND ME FOR THIS.
OKAY!
HERE WE GO...!
SPIRIT THAT LIES DORMANT, BAHEF SAEDOS, I BESEECH YOU-- LIFT THE WALL!!
OPEN THE DOORWAY TO THE VOID BEYOND!!
GOOD GRAVY!! THE WATERFALL--!! IT'S PARTING!!

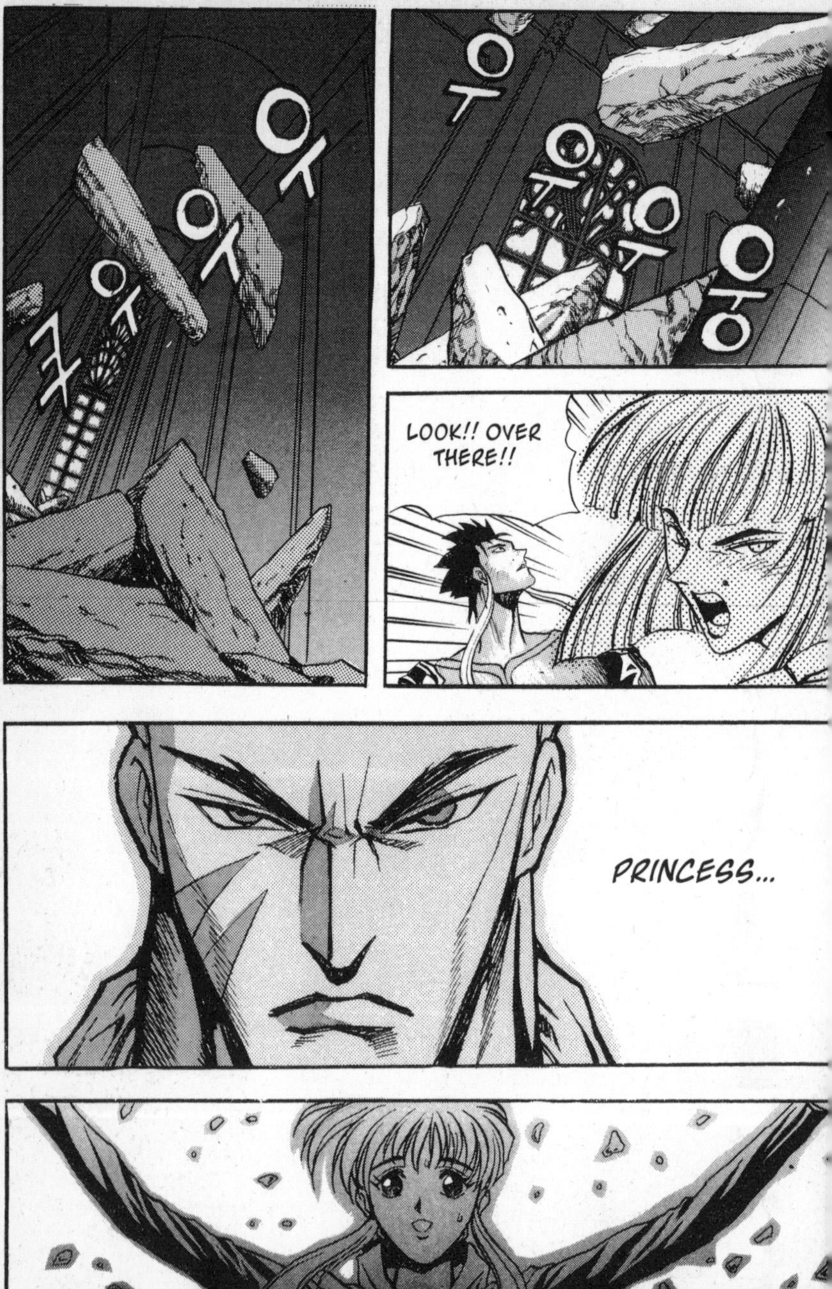
LOOK!! OVER THERE!!
PRINCESS...

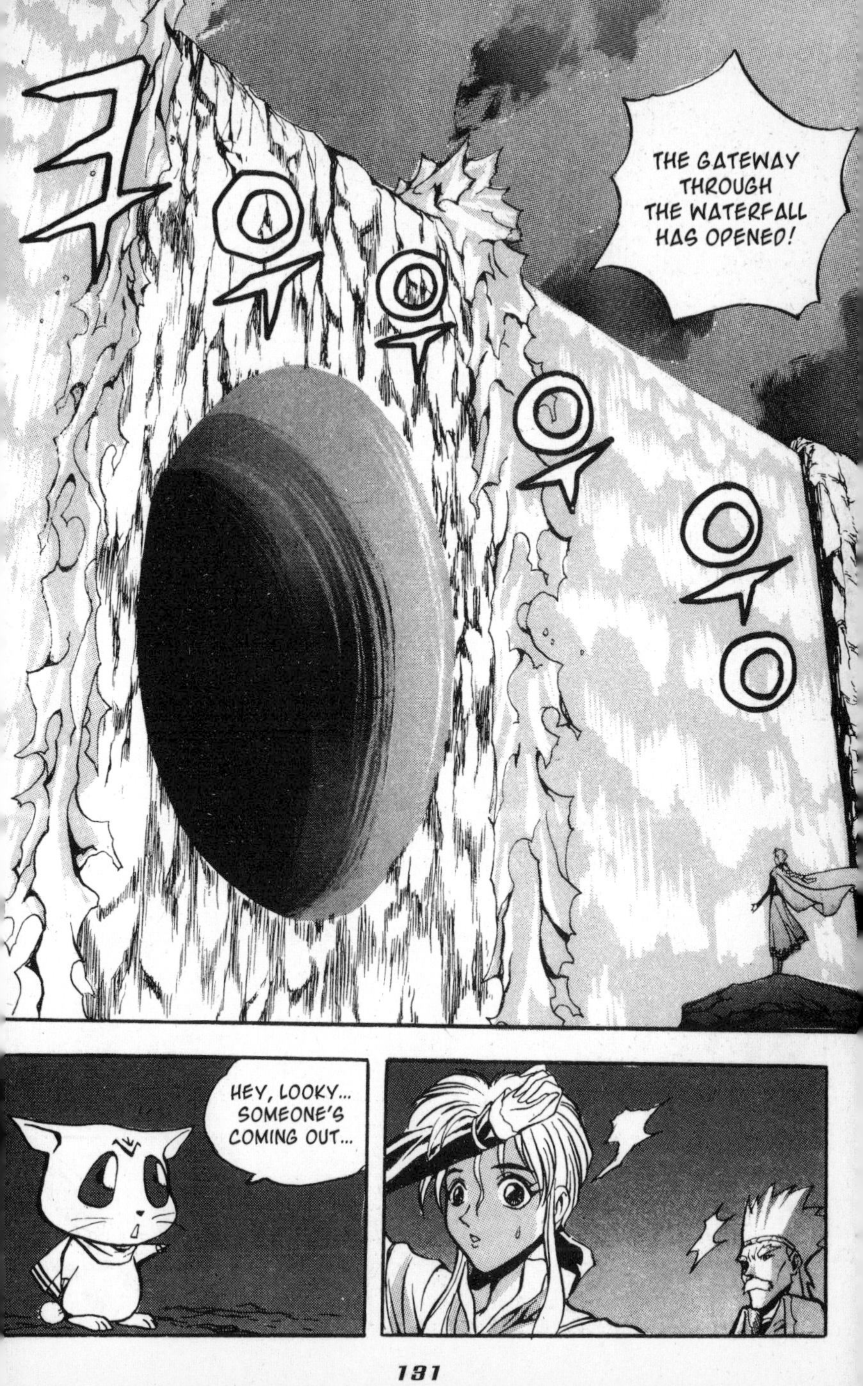
THE GATEWAY THROUGH THE WATERFALL HAS OPENED!
HEY, LOOKY... SOMEONE'S COMING OUT...

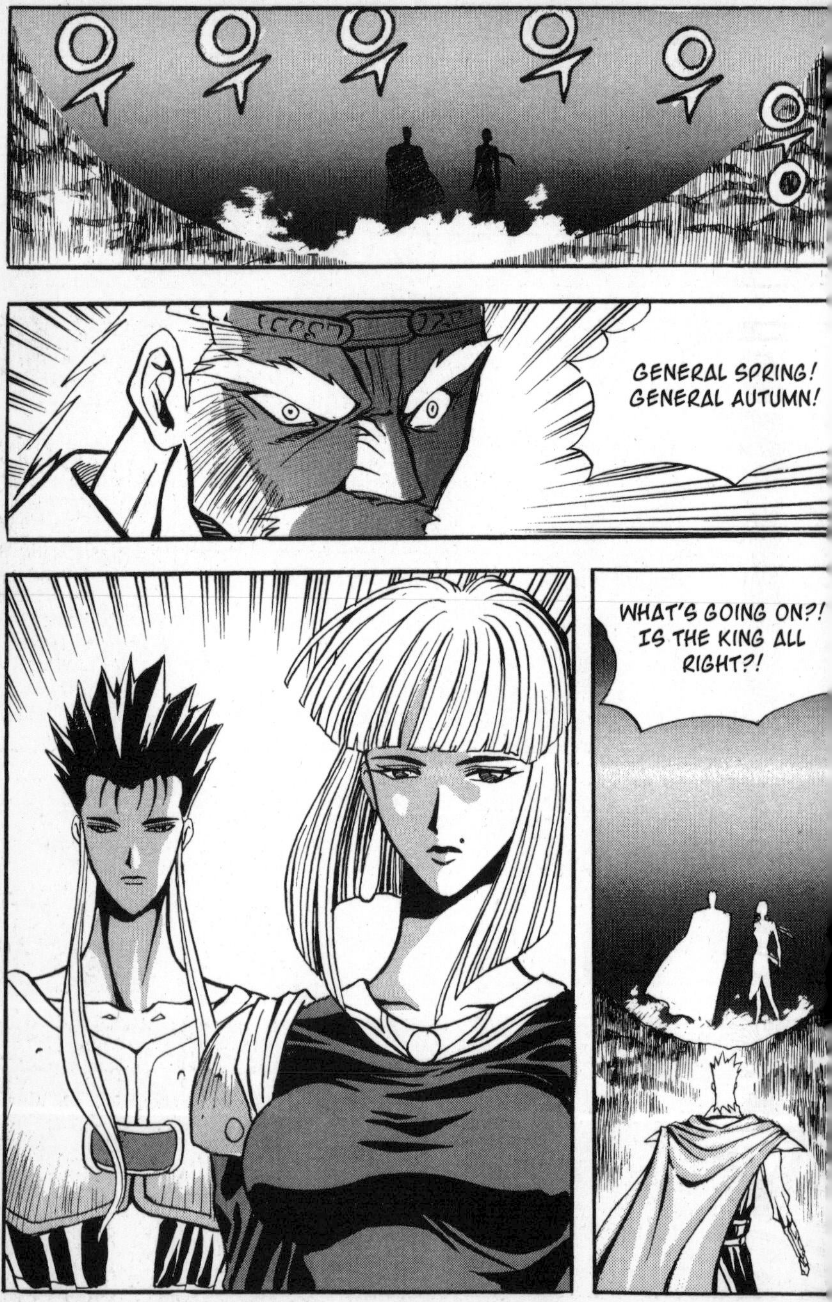

GENERAL SPRING! GENERAL AUTUMN!
WHAT'S GOING ON?! IS THE KING ALL RIGHT?!

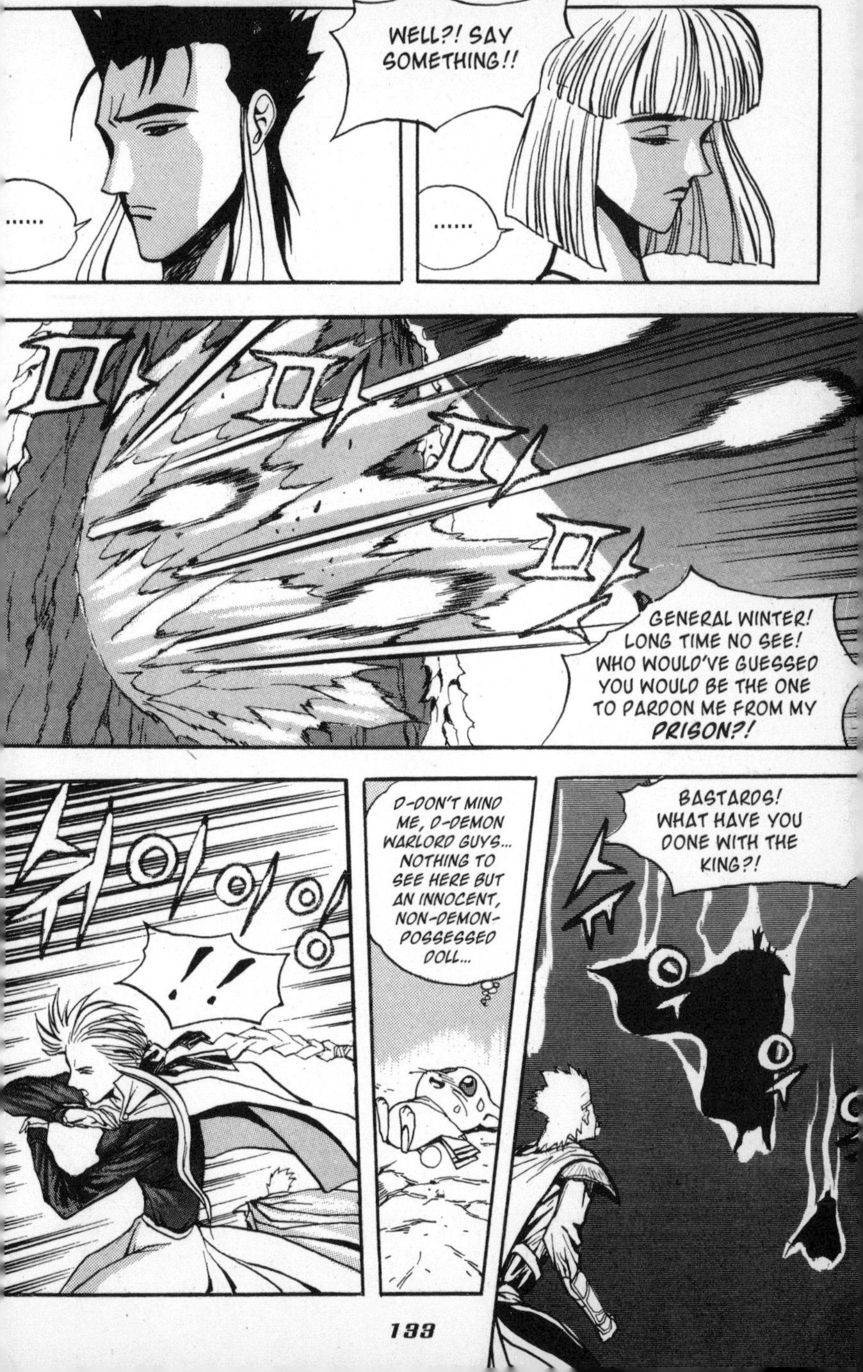

......
WELL?! SAY SOMETHING!!
......
GENERAL WINTER! LONG TIME NO SEE! WHO WOULD'VE GUESSED YOU WOULD BE THE ONE TO PARDON ME FROM MY PRISON?!
!!
D-DON'T MIND ME, D-DEMON WARLORD GUYS... NOTHING TO SEE HERE BUT AN INNOCENT, NON-DEMON-POSSESSED DOLL...
BASTARDS! WHAT HAVE YOU DONE WITH THE KING?!

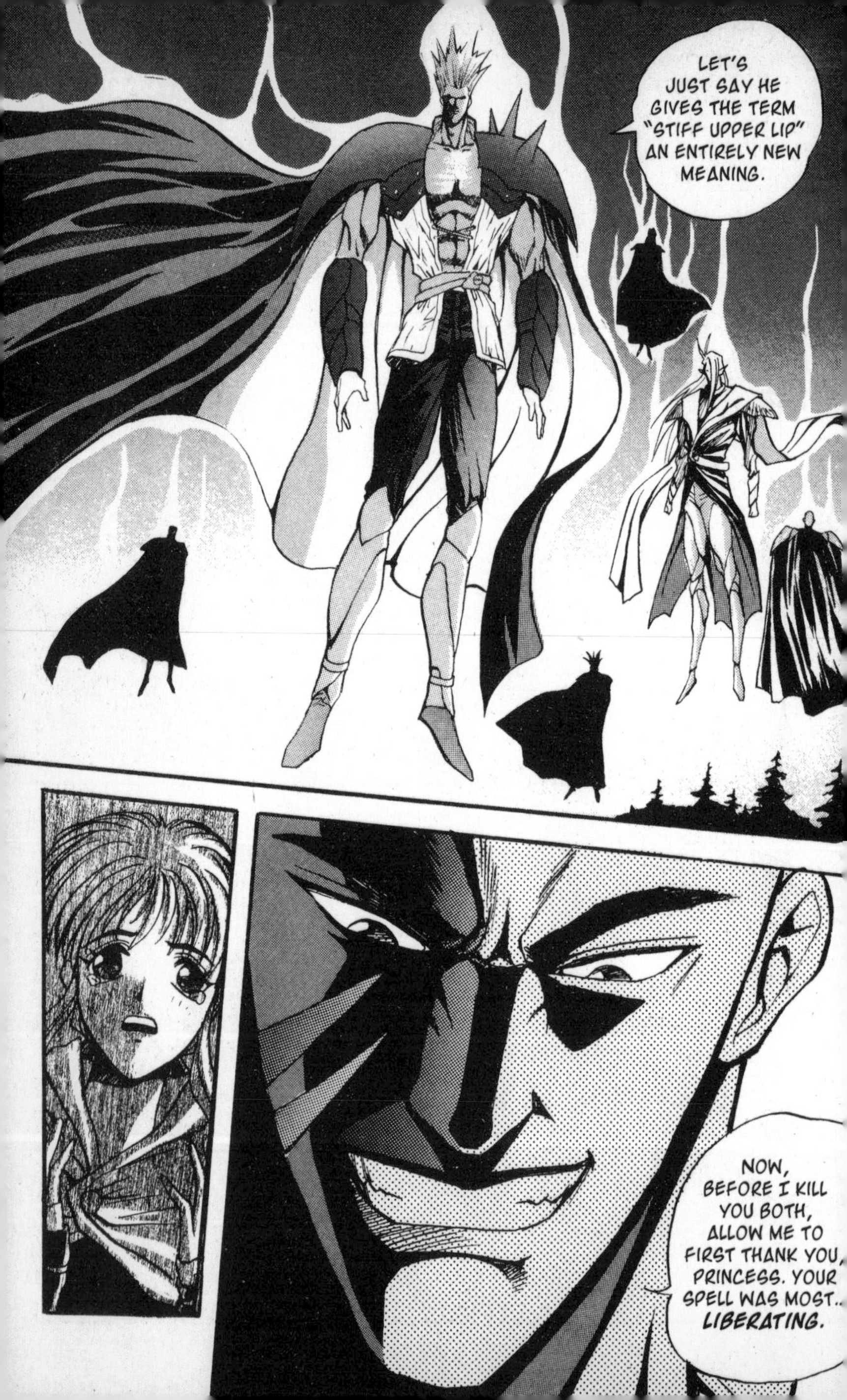
LET'S JUST SAY HE GIVES THE TERM "STIFF UPPER LIP" AN ENTIRELY NEW MEANING.
NOW, BEFORE I KILL YOU BOTH, ALLOW ME TO FIRST THANK YOU, PRINCESS. YOUR SPELL WAS MOST.. LIBERATING.

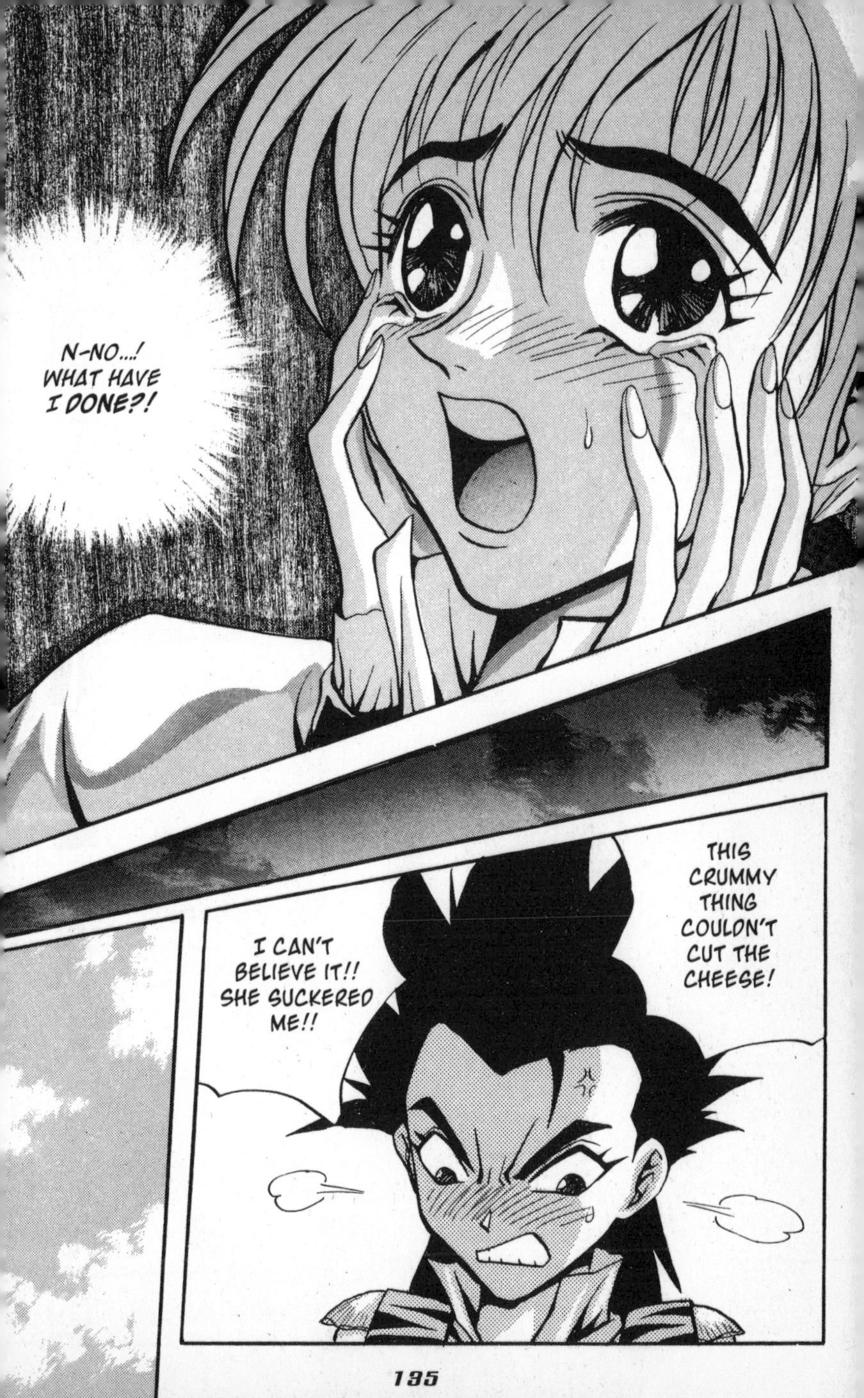
N-NO...! WHAT HAVE I DONE?!
I CAN'T BELIEVE IT!! SHE SUCKERED ME!!
THIS CRUMMY THING COULDN'T CUT THE CHEESE!

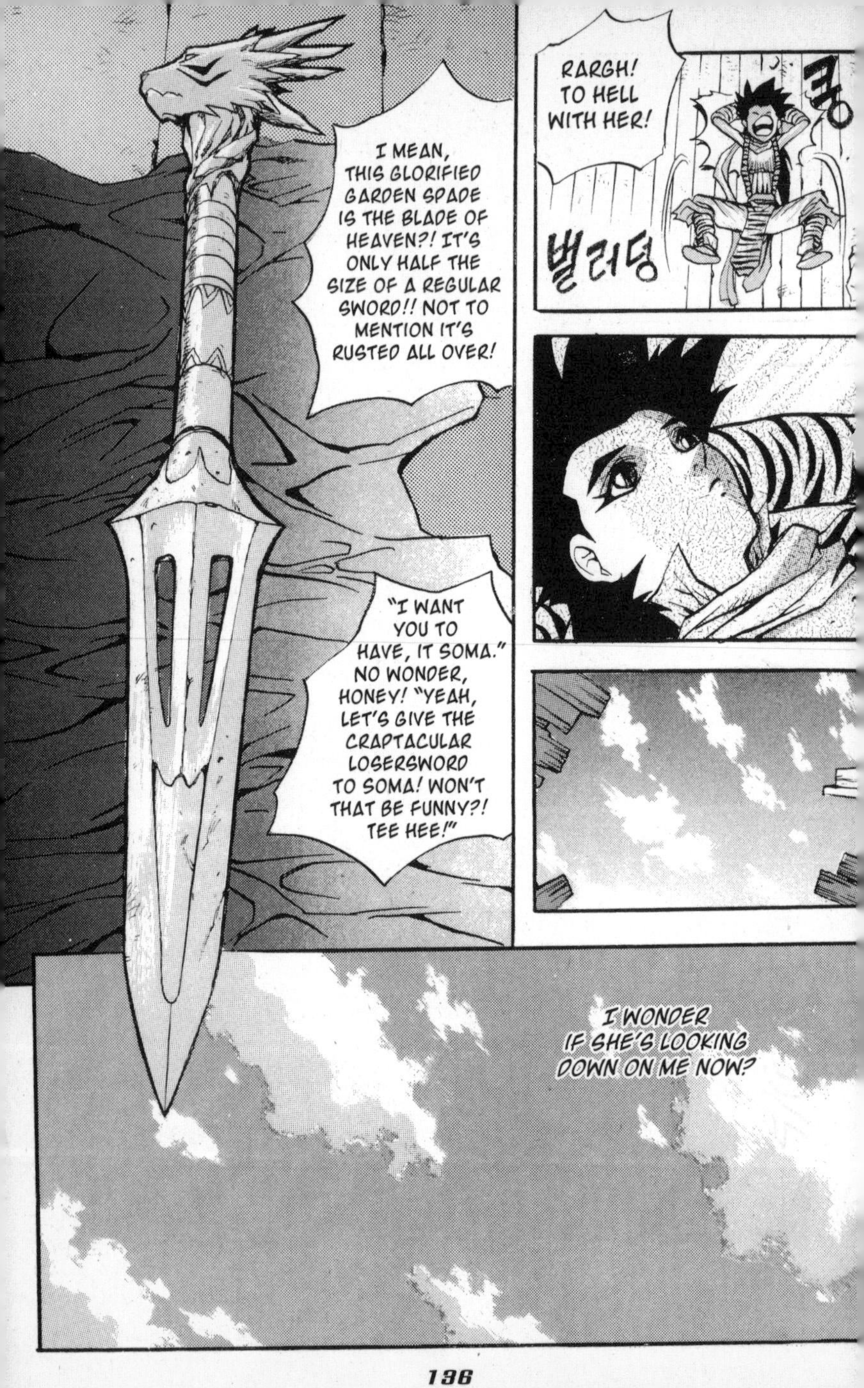
I MEAN, THIS GLORIFIED GARDEN SPADE IS THE BLADE OF HEAVEN?! IT'S ONLY HALF THE SIZE OF A REGULAR SWORD!! NOT TO MENTION IT'S RUSTED ALL OVER!
"I WANT YOU TO HAVE, IT SOMA." NO WONDER, HONEY! "YEAH, LET'S GIVE THE CRAPTACULAR LOSERSWORD TO SOMA! WON'T THAT BE FUNNY?! TEE HEE!"
RARGH! TO HELL WITH HER!
쿵
벌러덩
I WONDER IF SHE'S LOOKING DOWN ON ME NOW?

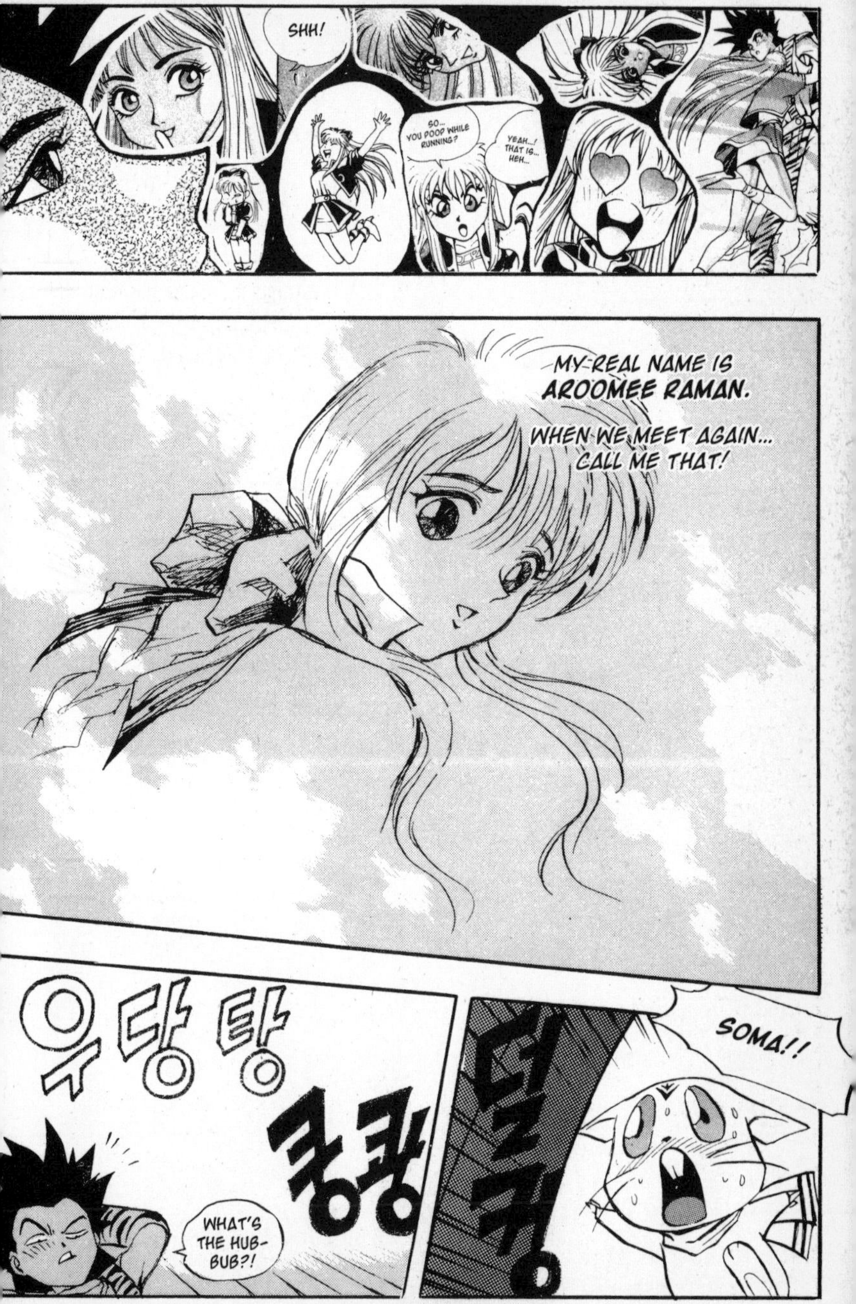
SHH!
SO... YOU POOP WHILE RUNNING?
YEAH...! THAT IS... HEH...
MY REAL NAME IS AROOMEE RAMAN.
WHEN WE MEET AGAIN... CALL ME THAT!
우당탕
쿵쾅
WHAT'S THE HUB-BUB?!
SOMA!!

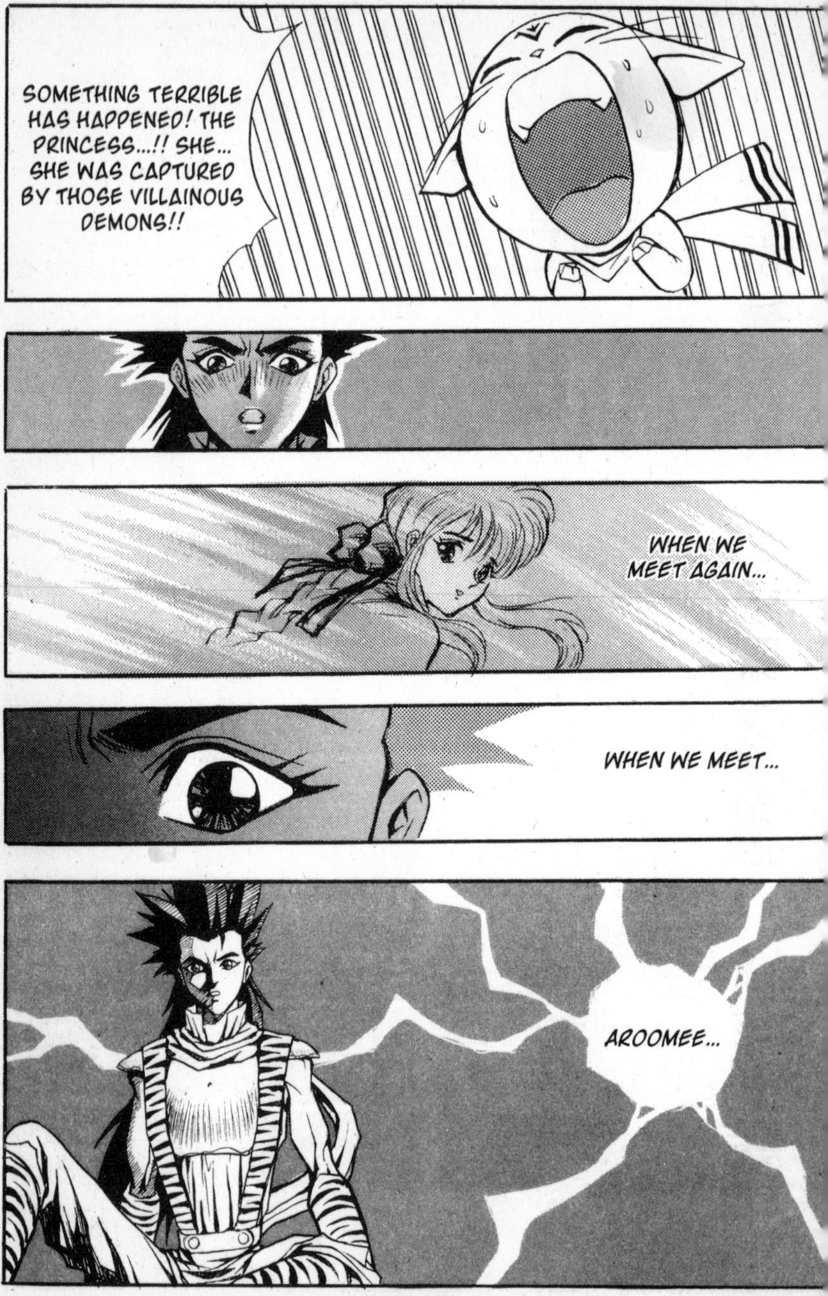
SOMETHING TERRIBLE HAS HAPPENED! THE PRINCESS...!! SHE... SHE WAS CAPTURED BY THOSE VILLAINOUS DEMONS!!
WHEN WE MEET AGAIN...
WHEN WE MEET...
AROOMEE...

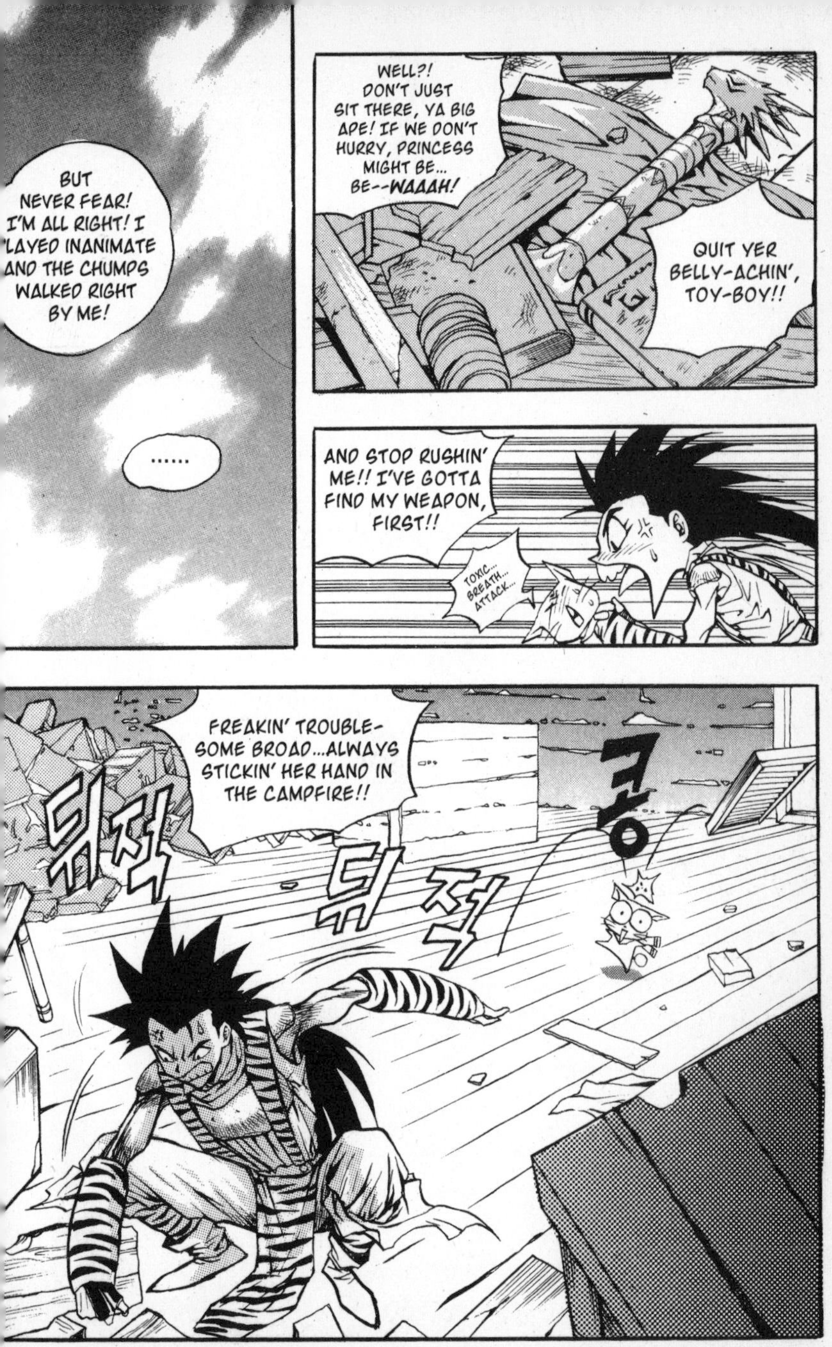
BUT NEVER FEAR! I'M ALL RIGHT! I 'LAYED INANIMATE AND THE CHUMPS WALKED RIGHT BY ME!
......
WELL?! DON'T JUST SIT THERE, YA BIG APE! IF WE DON'T HURRY, PRINCESS MIGHT BE... BE--WAAAH!
QUIT YER BELLY-ACHIN', TOY-BOY!!
AND STOP RUSHIN' ME!! I'VE GOTTA FIND MY WEAPON, FIRST!!
TOXIC... BREATH... ATTACK...
FREAKIN' TROUBLE-SOME BROAD...ALWAYS STICKIN' HER HAND IN THE CAMPFIRE!!
뒤적
콩
뒤적

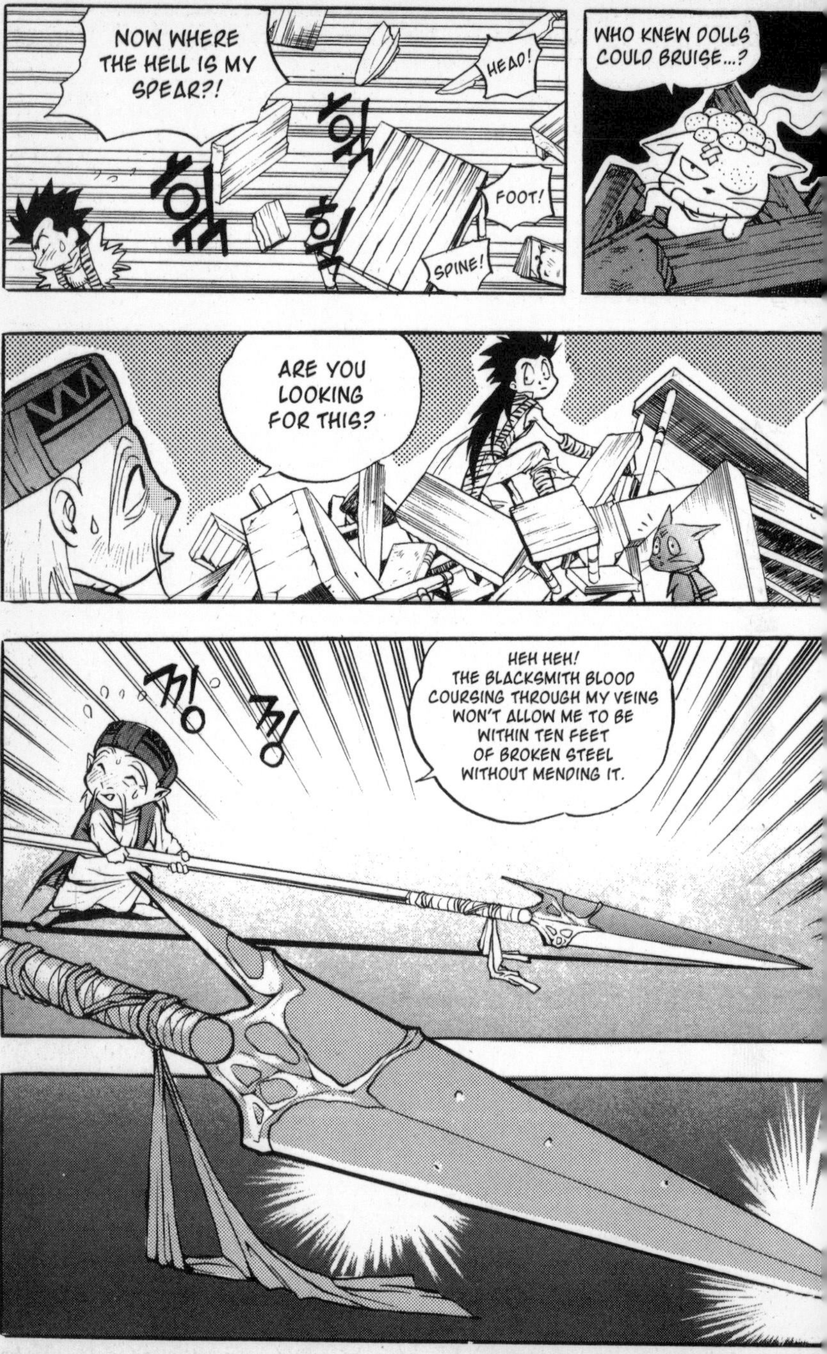
NOW WHERE THE HELL IS MY SPEAR?!
HEAD!
FOOT!
SPINE!
WHO KNEW DOLLS COULD BRUISE...?
ARE YOU LOOKING FOR THIS?
HEH HEH! THE BLACKSMITH BLOOD COURSING THROUGH MY VEINS WON'T ALLOW ME TO BE WITHIN TEN FEET OF BROKEN STEEL WITHOUT MENDING IT.

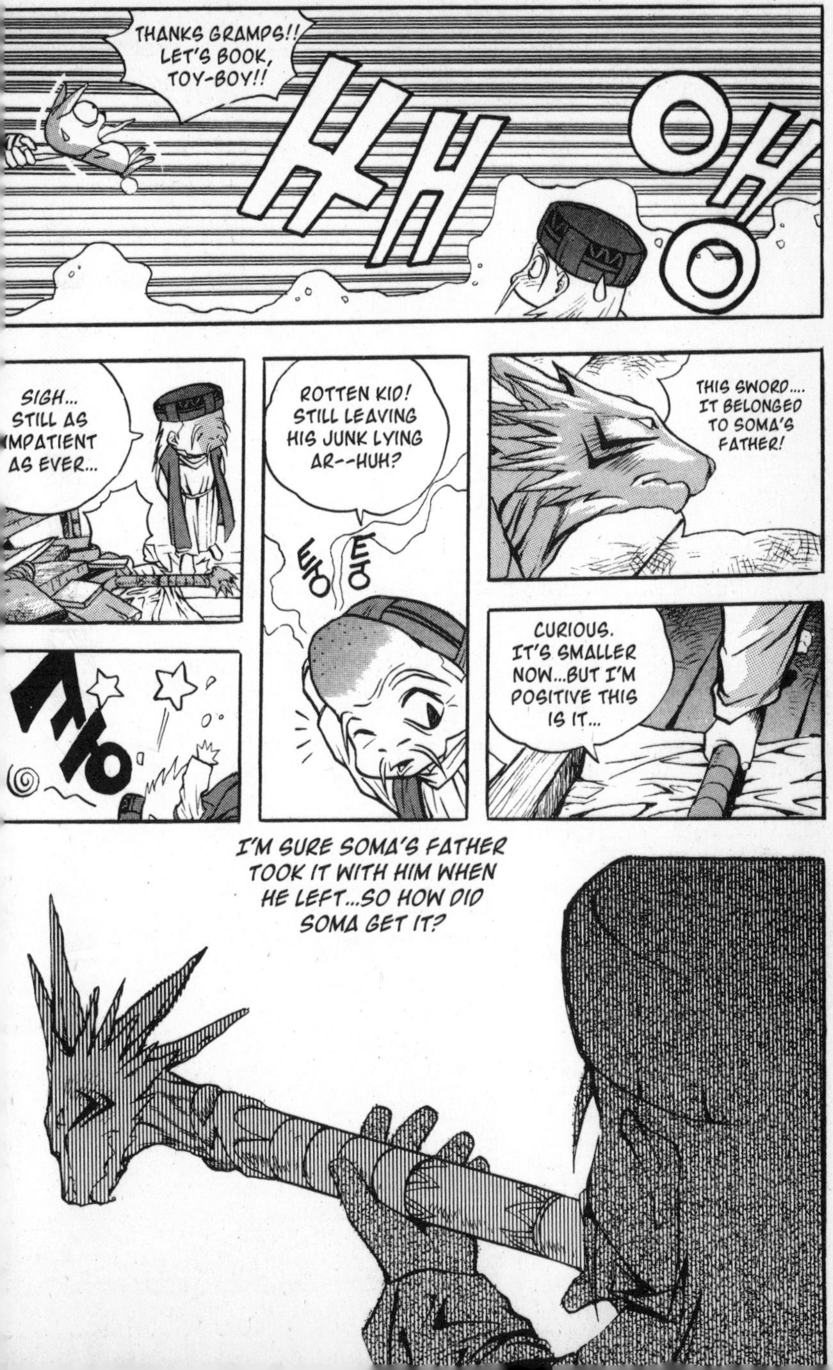

THANKS GRAMPS!! LET'S BOOK, TOY-BOY!!
SIGH... STILL AS MPATIENT AS EVER...
ROTTEN KID! STILL LEAVING HIS JUNK LYING AR--HUH?
THIS SWORD.... IT BELONGED TO SOMA'S FATHER!
CURIOUS. IT'S SMALLER NOW...BUT I'M POSITIVE THIS IS IT...
I'M SURE SOMA'S FATHER TOOK IT WITH HIM WHEN HE LEFT...SO HOW DID SOMA GET IT?

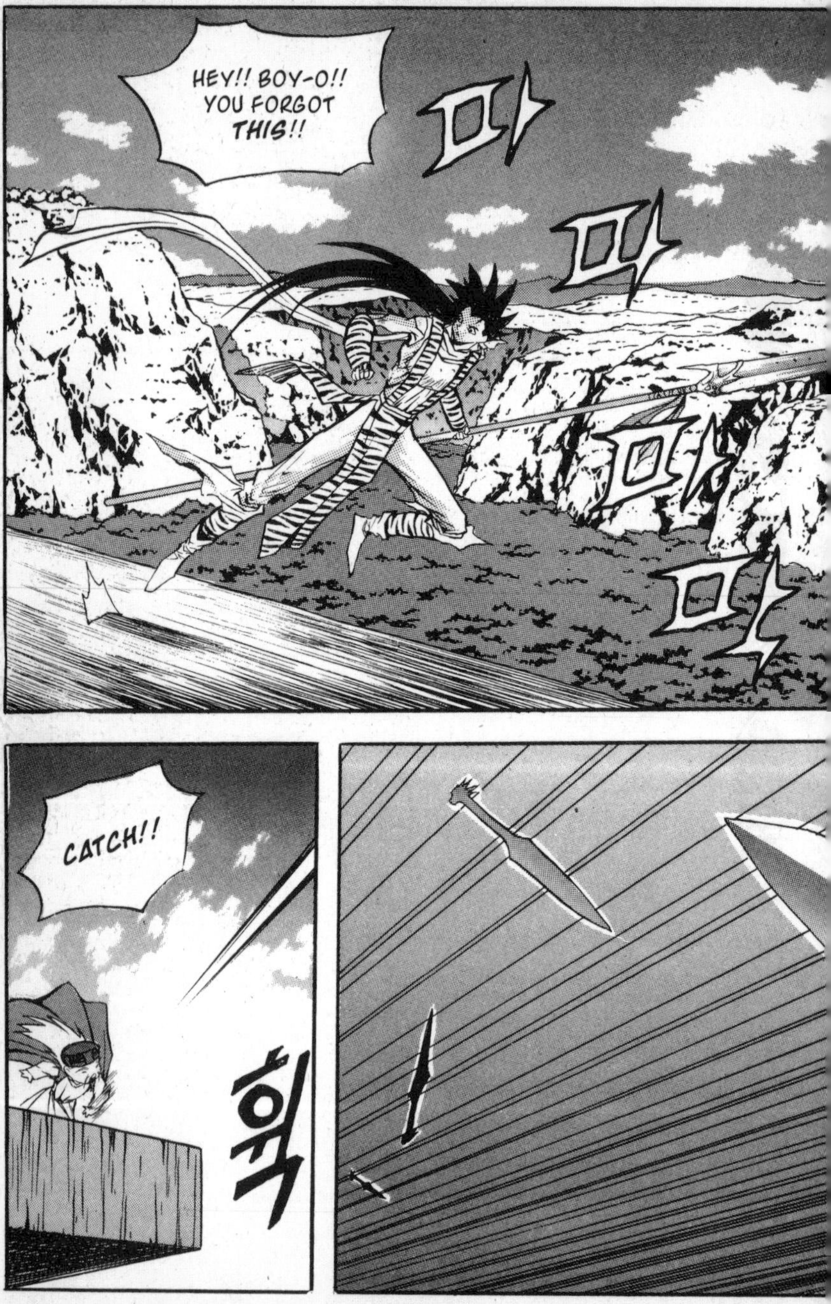
HEY!! BOY-O!! YOU FORGOT THIS!!
파
파
파
파
CATCH!!
휙

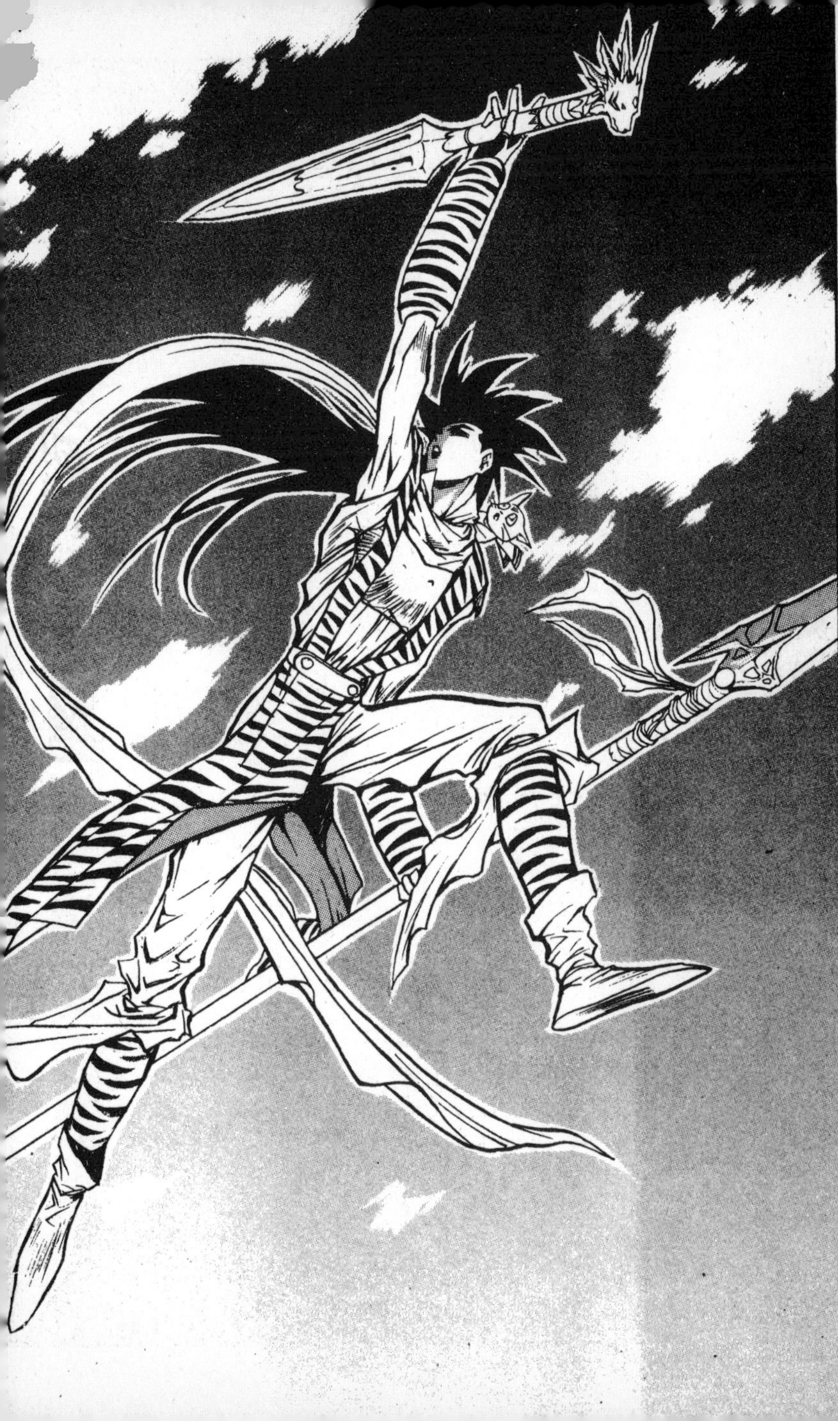

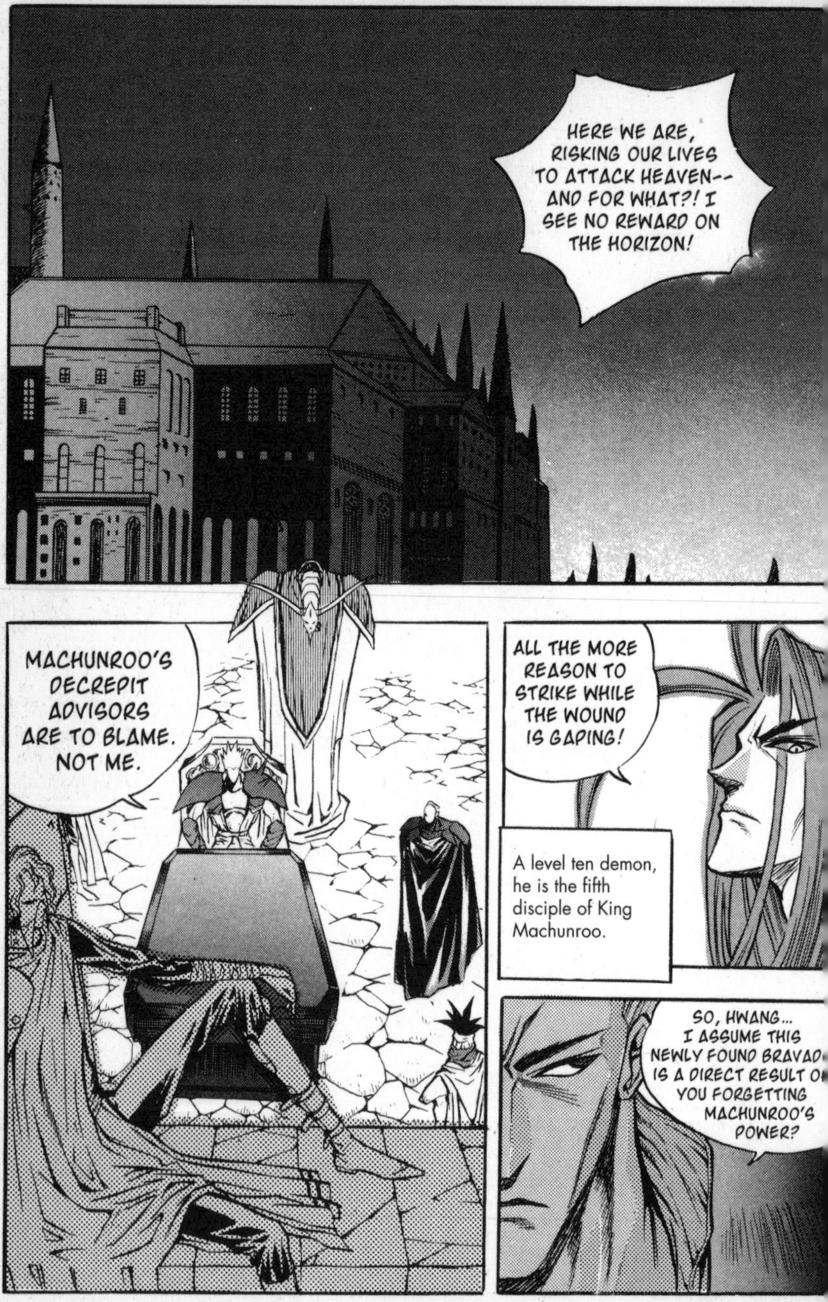

HERE WE ARE, RISKING OUR LIVES TO ATTACK HEAVEN-- AND FOR WHAT?! I SEE NO REWARD ON THE HORIZON!
MACHUNROO'S DECREPIT ADVISORS ARE TO BLAME. NOT ME.
ALL THE MORE REASON TO STRIKE WHILE THE WOUND IS GAPING!
A level ten demon, he is the fifth disciple of King Machunroo.
SO, HWANG... I ASSUME THIS NEWLY FOUND BRAVAD IS A DIRECT RESULT O YOU FORGETTING MACHUNROO'S POWER?

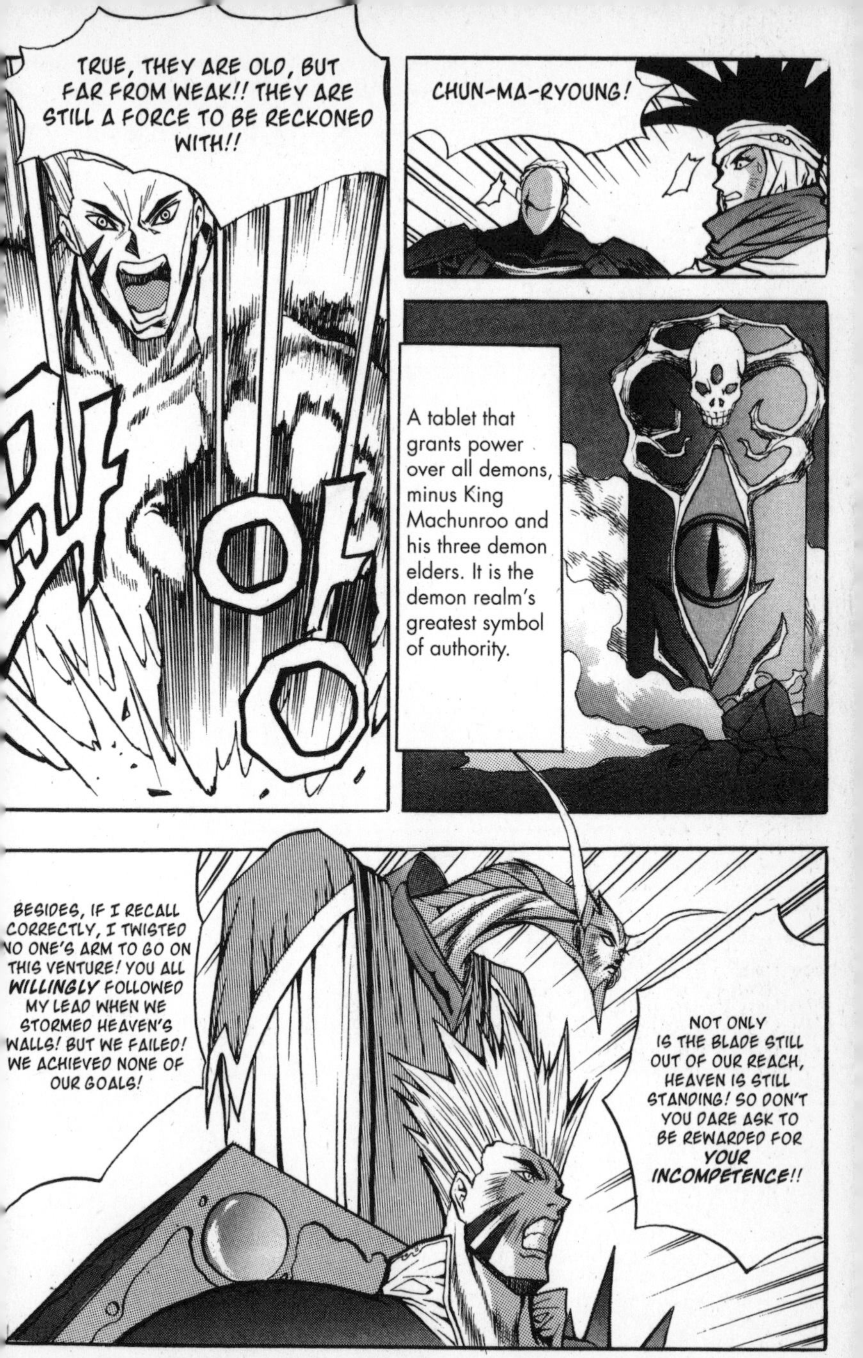
TRUE, THEY ARE OLD, BUT FAR FROM WEAK!! THEY ARE STILL A FORCE TO BE RECKONED WITH!!
CHUN-MA-RYOUNG!
A tablet that grants power over all demons, minus King Machunroo and his three demon elders. It is the demon realm's greatest symbol of authority.
BESIDES, IF I RECALL CORRECTLY, I TWISTED NO ONE'S ARM TO GO ON THIS VENTURE! YOU ALL ***WILLINGLY*** FOLLOWED MY LEAD WHEN WE STORMED HEAVEN'S WALLS! BUT WE FAILED! WE ACHIEVED NONE OF OUR GOALS!
NOT ONLY IS THE BLADE STILL OUT OF OUR REACH, HEAVEN IS STILL STANDING! SO DON'T YOU DARE ASK TO BE REWARDED FOR ***YOUR INCOMPETENCE***!!

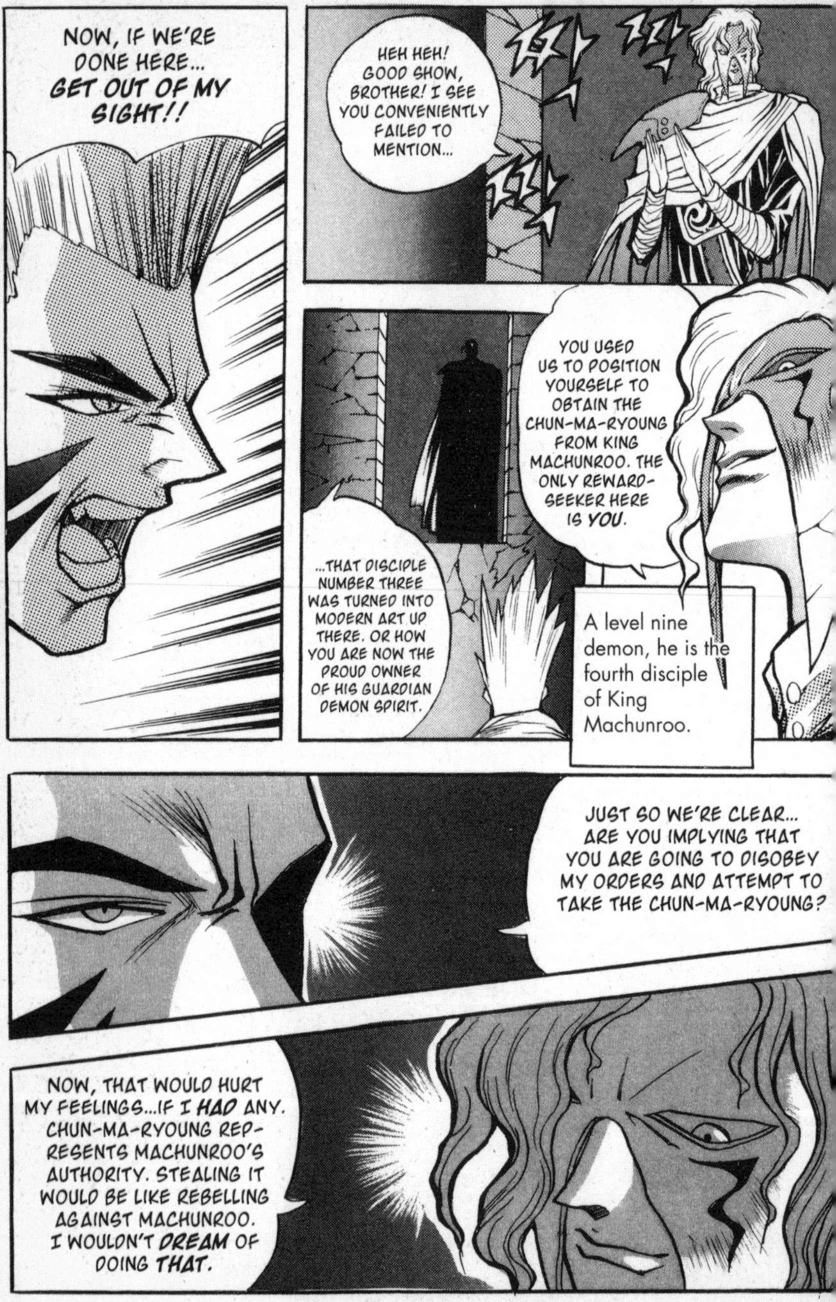
NOW, IF WE'RE DONE HERE... GET OUT OF MY SIGHT!!
HEH HEH! GOOD SHOW, BROTHER! I SEE YOU CONVENIENTLY FAILED TO MENTION...
...THAT DISCIPLE NUMBER THREE WAS TURNED INTO MODERN ART UP THERE. OR HOW YOU ARE NOW THE PROUD OWNER OF HIS GUARDIAN DEMON SPIRIT.
YOU USED US TO POSITION YOURSELF TO OBTAIN THE CHUN-MA-RYOUNG FROM KING MACHUNROO. THE ONLY REWARD-SEEKER HERE IS YOU.
A level nine demon, he is the fourth disciple of King Machunroo.
JUST SO WE'RE CLEAR... ARE YOU IMPLYING THAT YOU ARE GOING TO DISOBEY MY ORDERS AND ATTEMPT TO TAKE THE CHUN-MA-RYOUNG?
NOW, THAT WOULD HURT MY FEELINGS...IF I HAD ANY. CHUN-MA-RYOUNG REPRESENTS MACHUNROO'S AUTHORITY. STEALING IT WOULD BE LIKE REBELLING AGAINST MACHUNROO. I WOULDN'T DREAM OF DOING THAT.

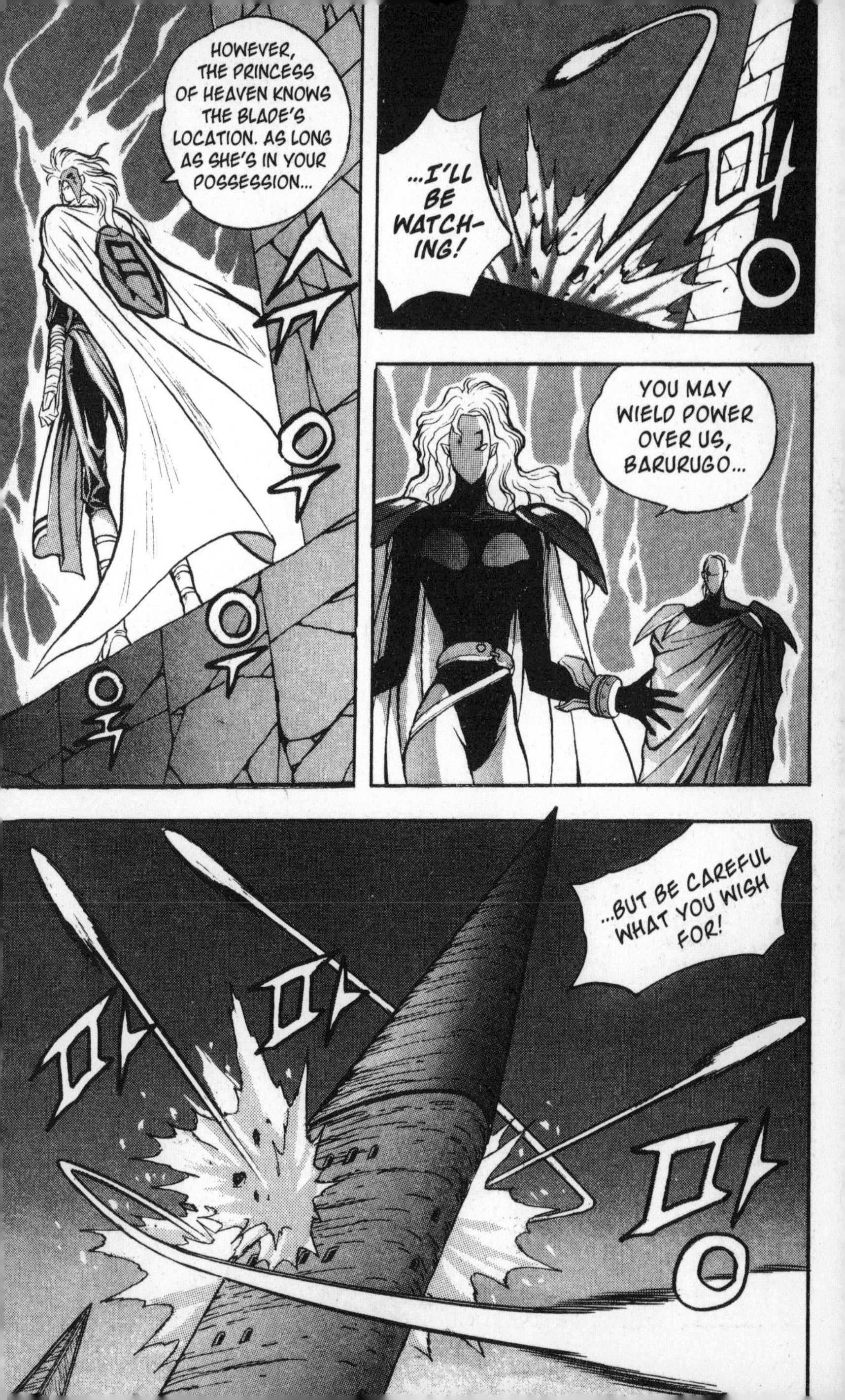
HOWEVER, THE PRINCESS OF HEAVEN KNOWS THE BLADE'S LOCATION. AS LONG AS SHE'S IN YOUR POSSESSION...
...I'LL BE WATCHING!
YOU MAY WIELD POWER OVER US, BARURUGO...
...BUT BE CAREFUL WHAT YOU WISH FOR!

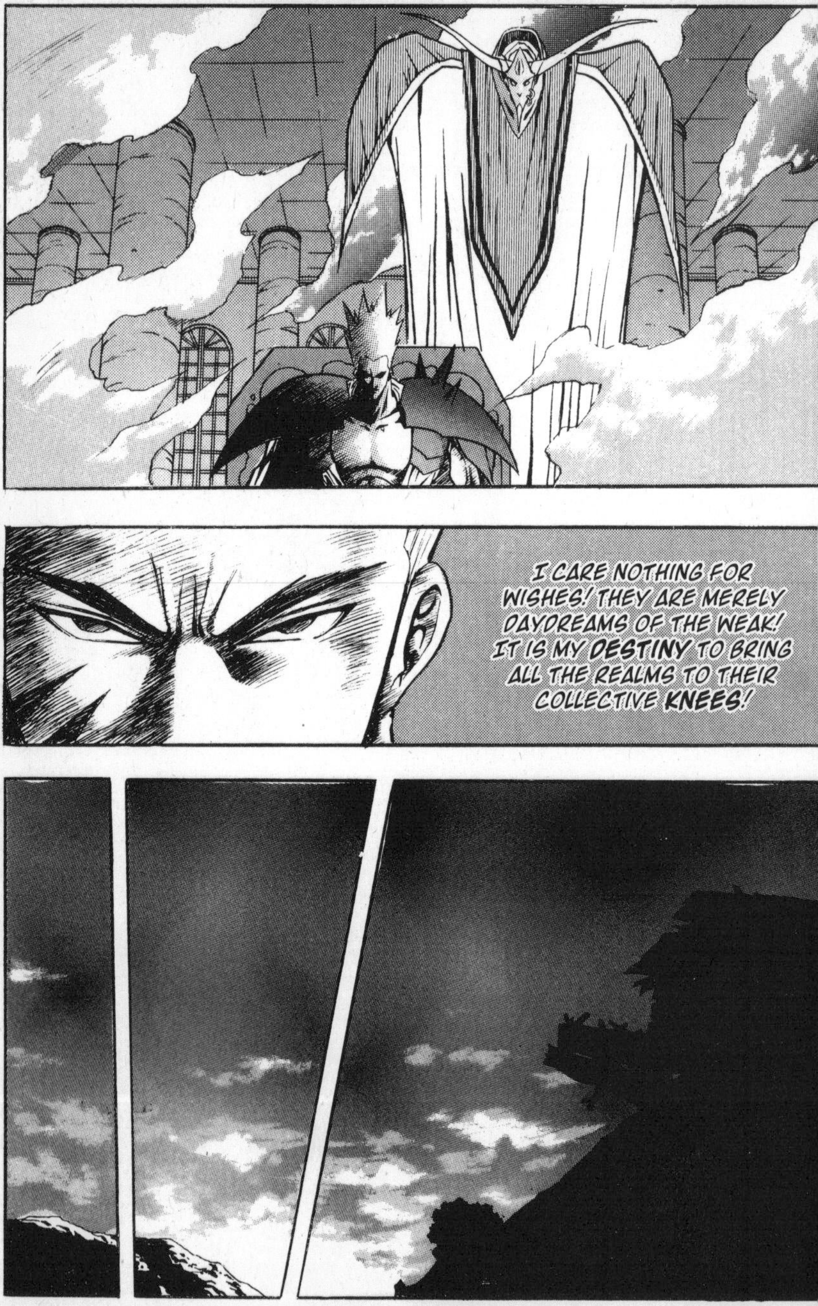
I CARE NOTHING FOR WISHES! THEY ARE MERELY DAYDREAMS OF THE WEAK! IT IS MY DESTINY TO BRING ALL THE REALMS TO THEIR COLLECTIVE KNEES!

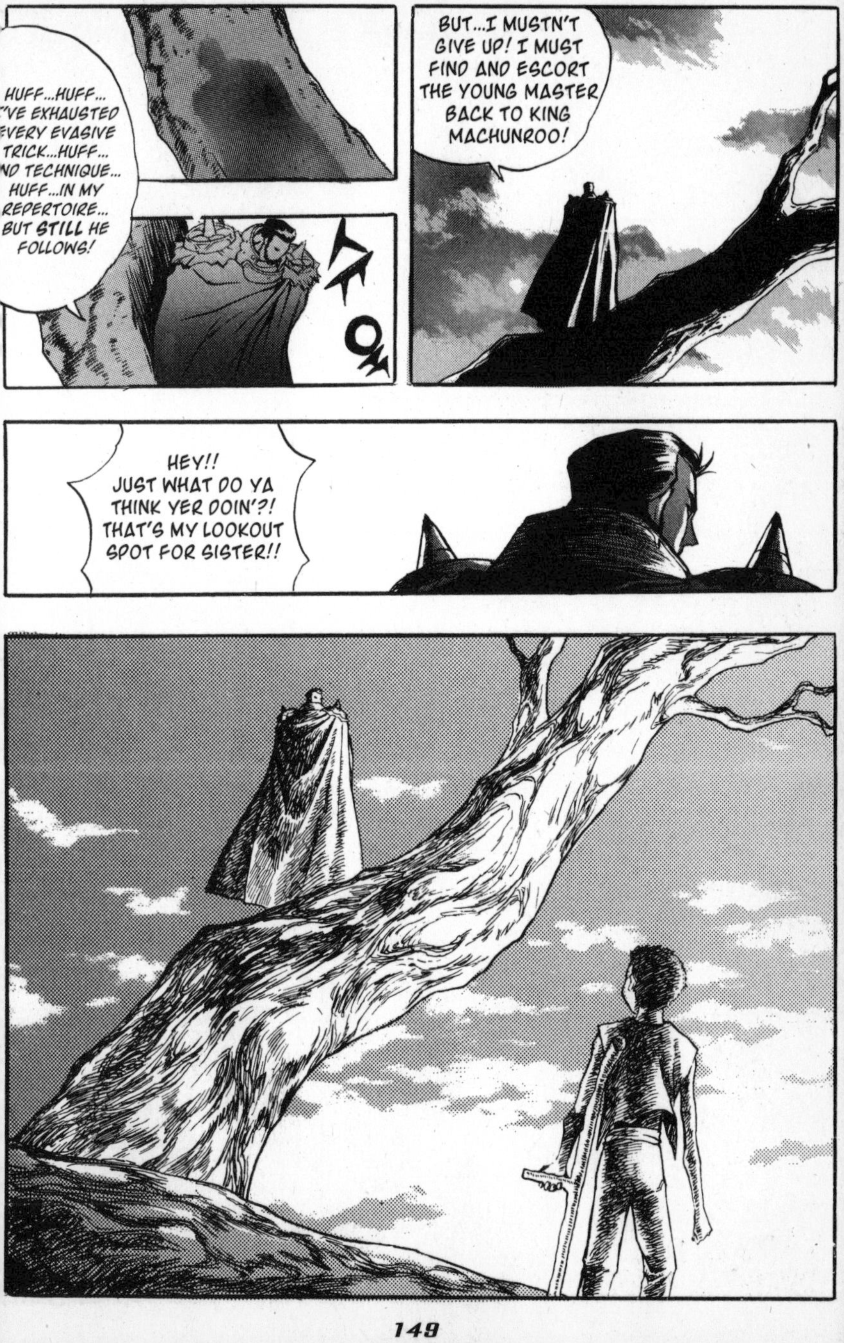
HUFF...HUFF... 'VE EXHAUSTED EVERY EVASIVE TRICK...HUFF... ND TECHNIQUE... HUFF...IN MY REPERTOIRE... BUT **STILL** HE FOLLOWS!
BUT...I MUSTN'T GIVE UP! I MUST FIND AND ESCORT THE YOUNG MASTER BACK TO KING MACHUNROO!
HEY!! JUST WHAT DO YA THINK YER DOIN'?! THAT'S MY LOOKOUT SPOT FOR SISTER!!

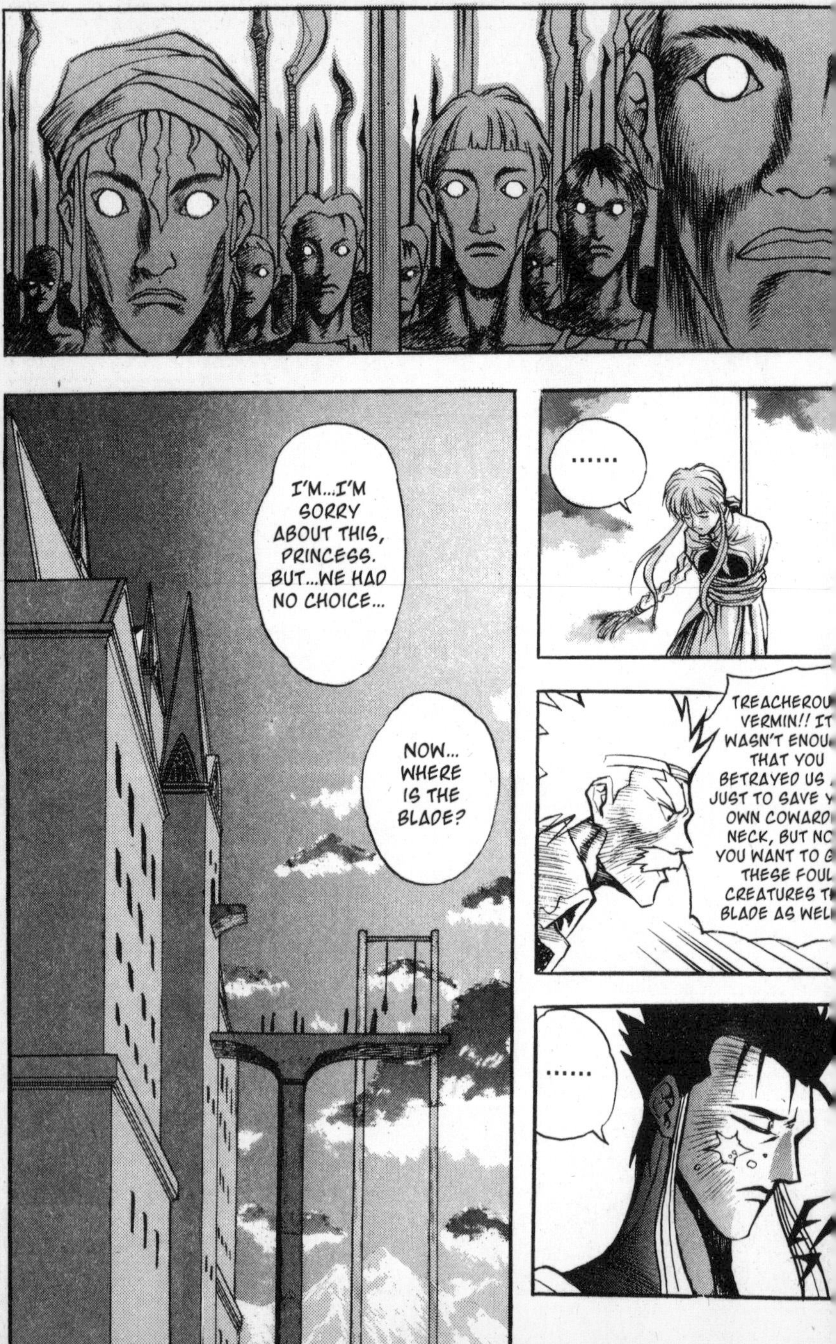
I'M...I'M SORRY ABOUT THIS, PRINCESS. BUT...WE HAD NO CHOICE...
NOW... WHERE IS THE BLADE?
......
TREACHEROU VERMIN!! IT WASN'T ENOU THAT YOU BETRAYED US JUST TO SAVE Y OWN COWARD NECK, BUT NO YOU WANT TO G THESE FOUL CREATURES T BLADE AS WEL
......

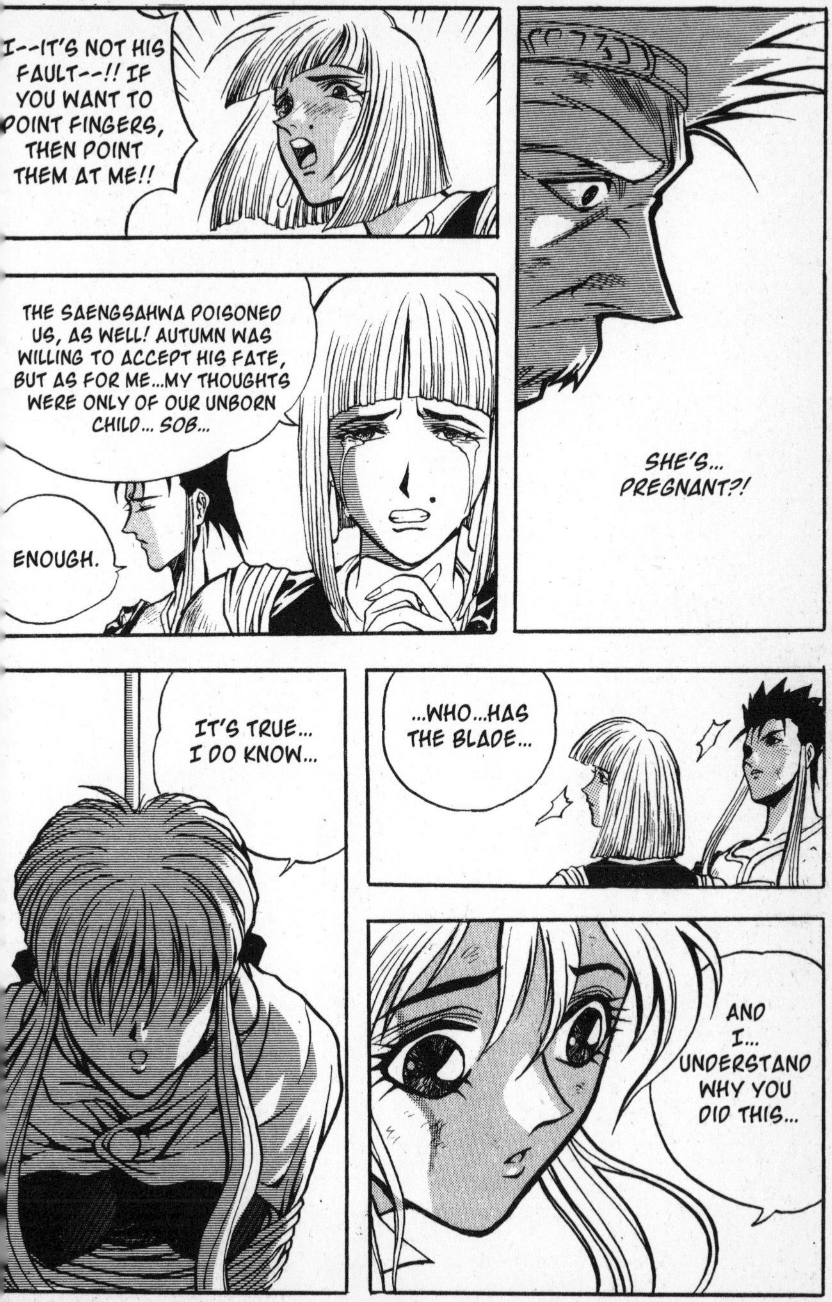
I--IT'S NOT HIS FAULT--!! IF YOU WANT TO POINT FINGERS, THEN POINT THEM AT ME!!
THE SAENGSAHWA POISONED US, AS WELL! AUTUMN WAS WILLING TO ACCEPT HIS FATE, BUT AS FOR ME...MY THOUGHTS WERE ONLY OF OUR UNBORN CHILD... SOB...
ENOUGH.
SHE'S... PREGNANT?!
IT'S TRUE... I DO KNOW...
...WHO...HAS THE BLADE...
AND I... UNDERSTAND WHY YOU DID THIS...

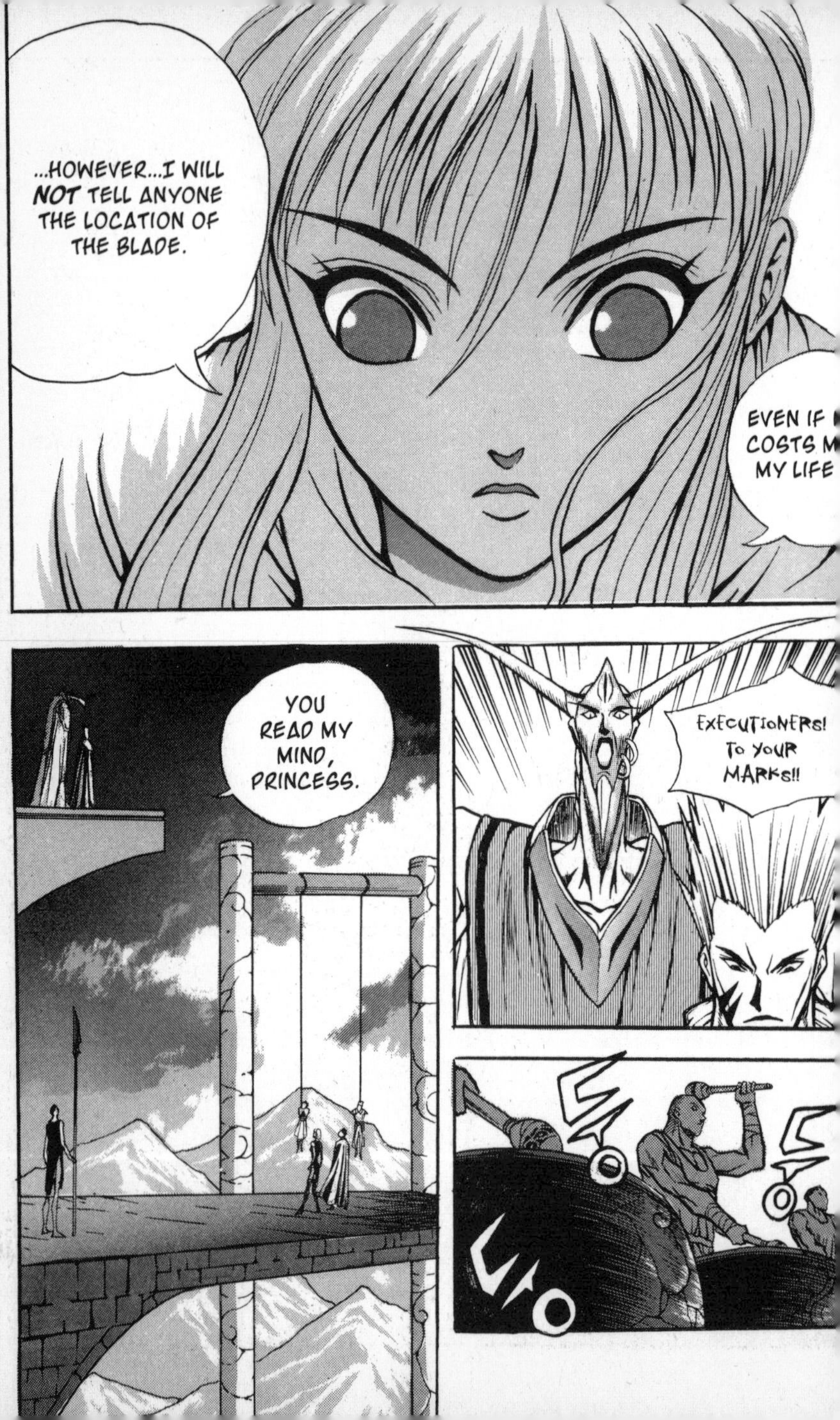
...HOWEVER...I WILL ***NOT*** TELL ANYONE THE LOCATION OF THE BLADE.
EVEN IF COSTS M MY LIFE
YOU READ MY MIND, PRINCESS.
EXECUTIONERS! TO YOUR MARKS!!

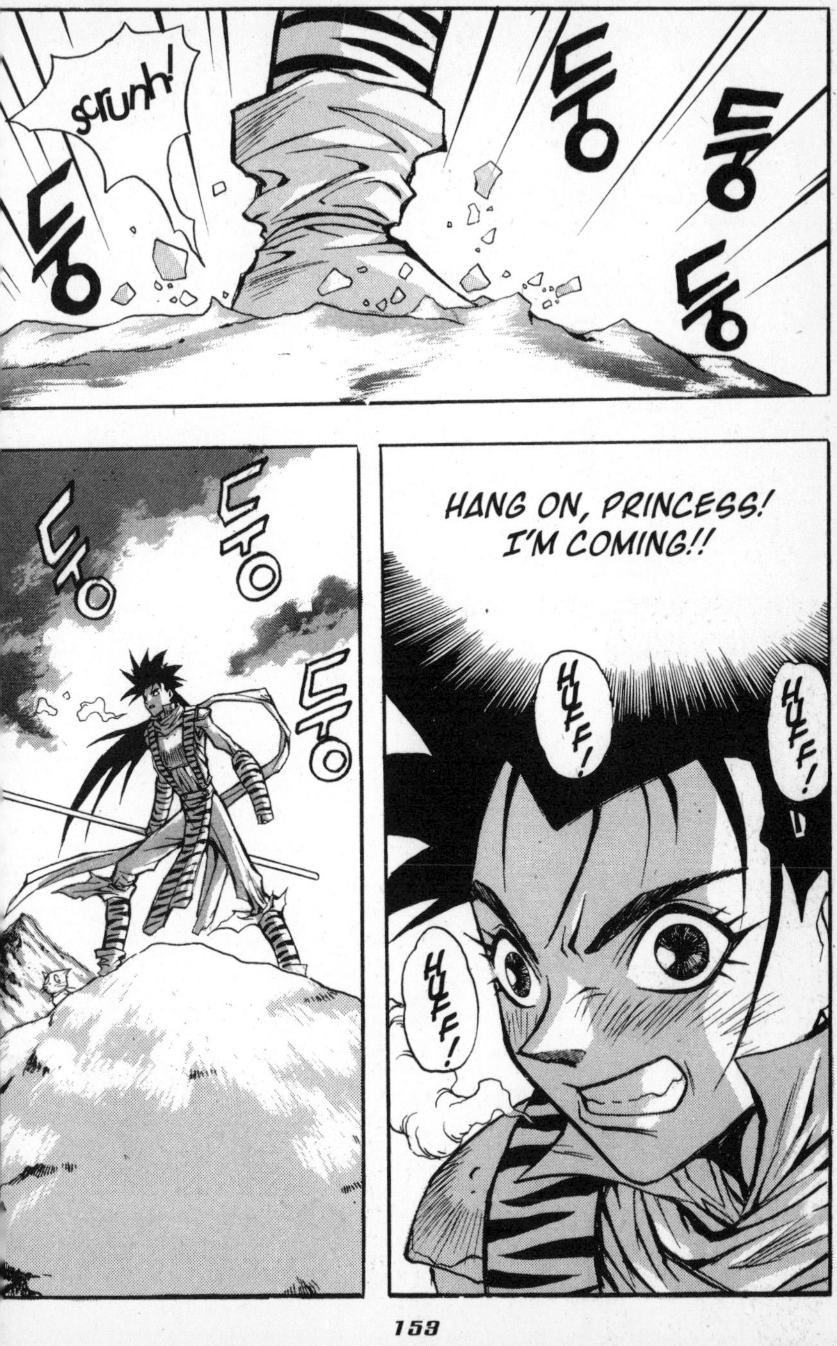
scrunh!
둥
둥
둥
둥
HANG ON, PRINCESS! I'M COMING!!
HUFF!
HUFF!
HUFF!

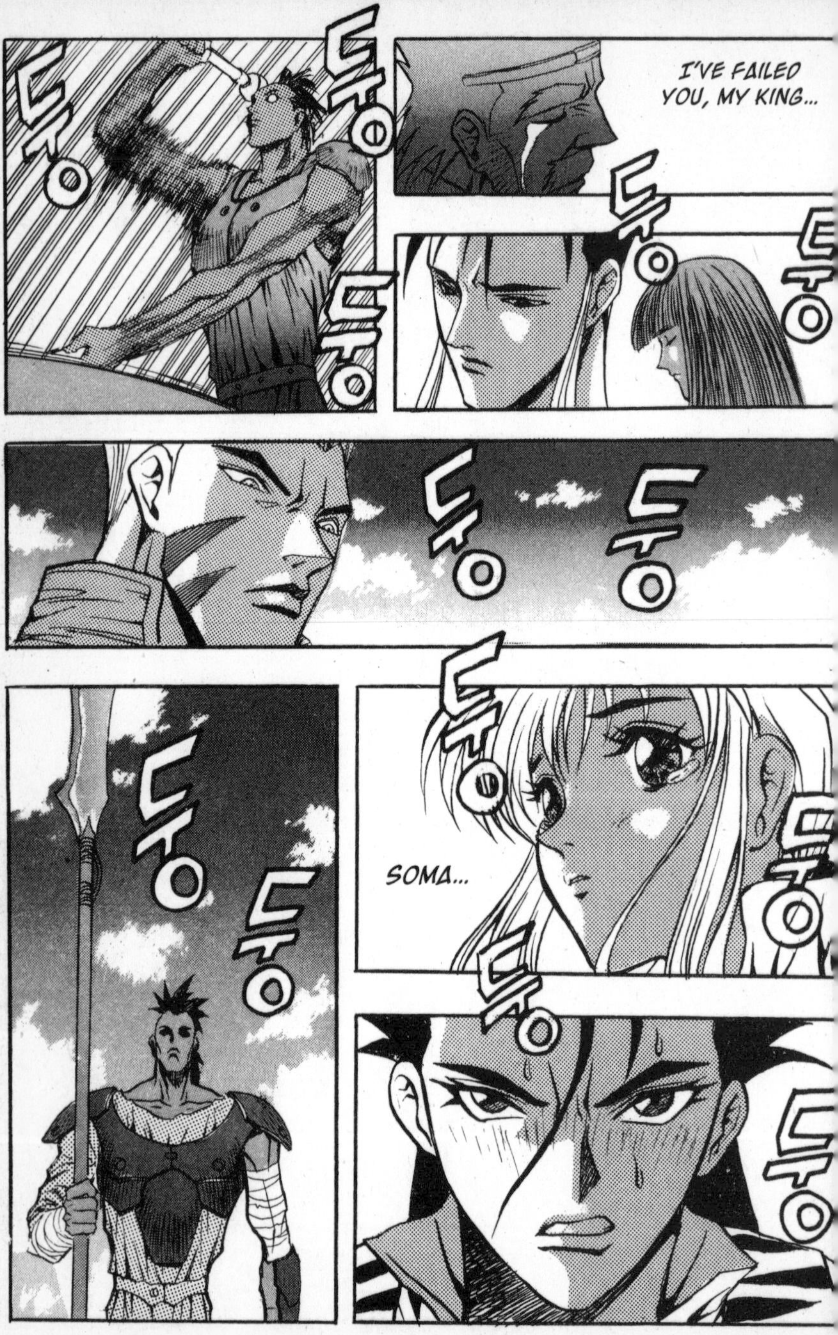
I'VE FAILED YOU, MY KING...
SOMA...

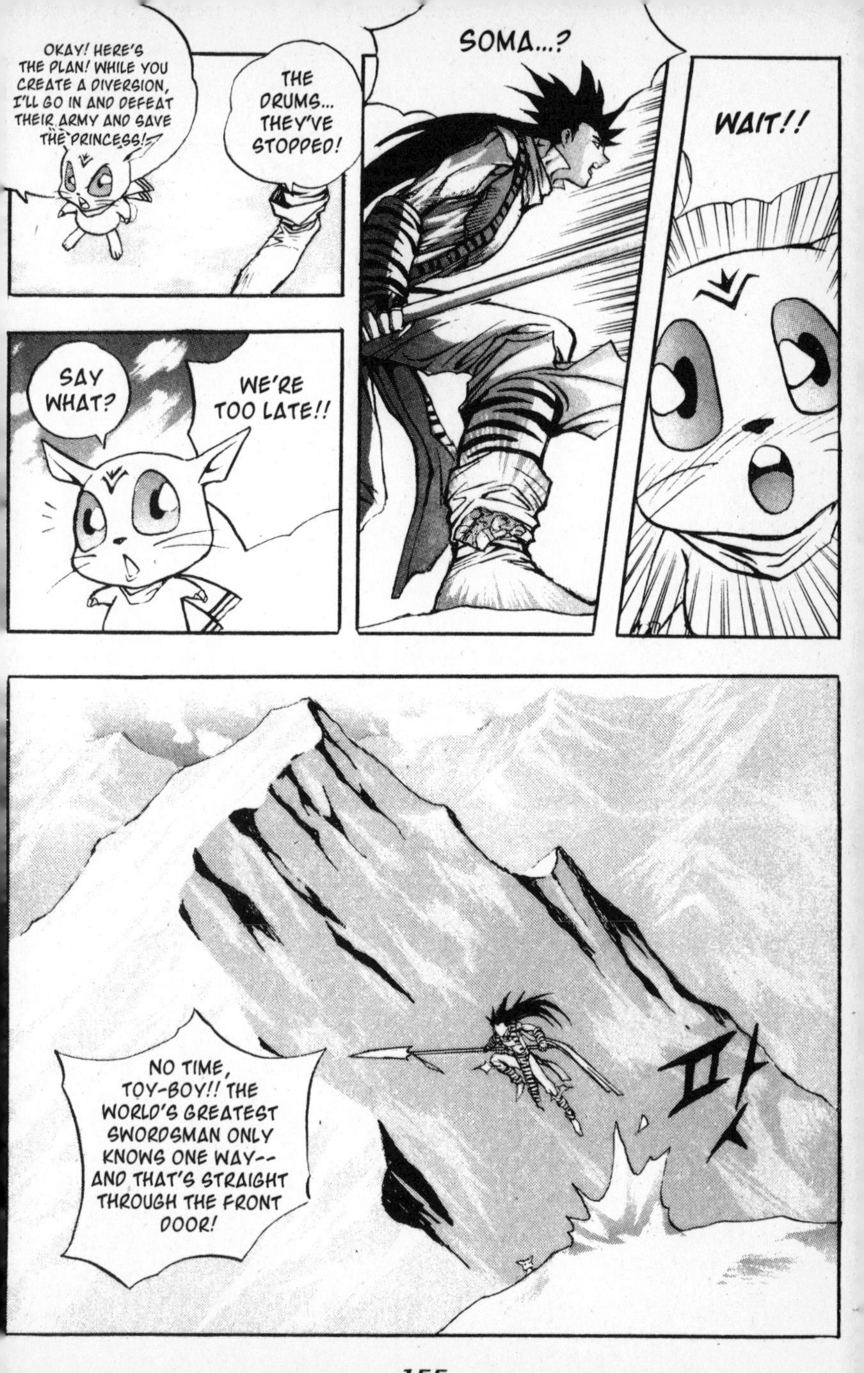

OKAY! HERE'S THE PLAN! WHILE YOU CREATE A DIVERSION, I'LL GO IN AND DEFEAT THEIR ARMY AND SAVE THE PRINCESS!
THE DRUMS... THEY'VE STOPPED!
SOMA...?
WAIT!!
SAY WHAT?
WE'RE TOO LATE!!
NO TIME, TOY-BOY!! THE WORLD'S GREATEST SWORDSMAN ONLY KNOWS ONE WAY-- AND THAT'S STRAIGHT THROUGH THE FRONT DOOR!

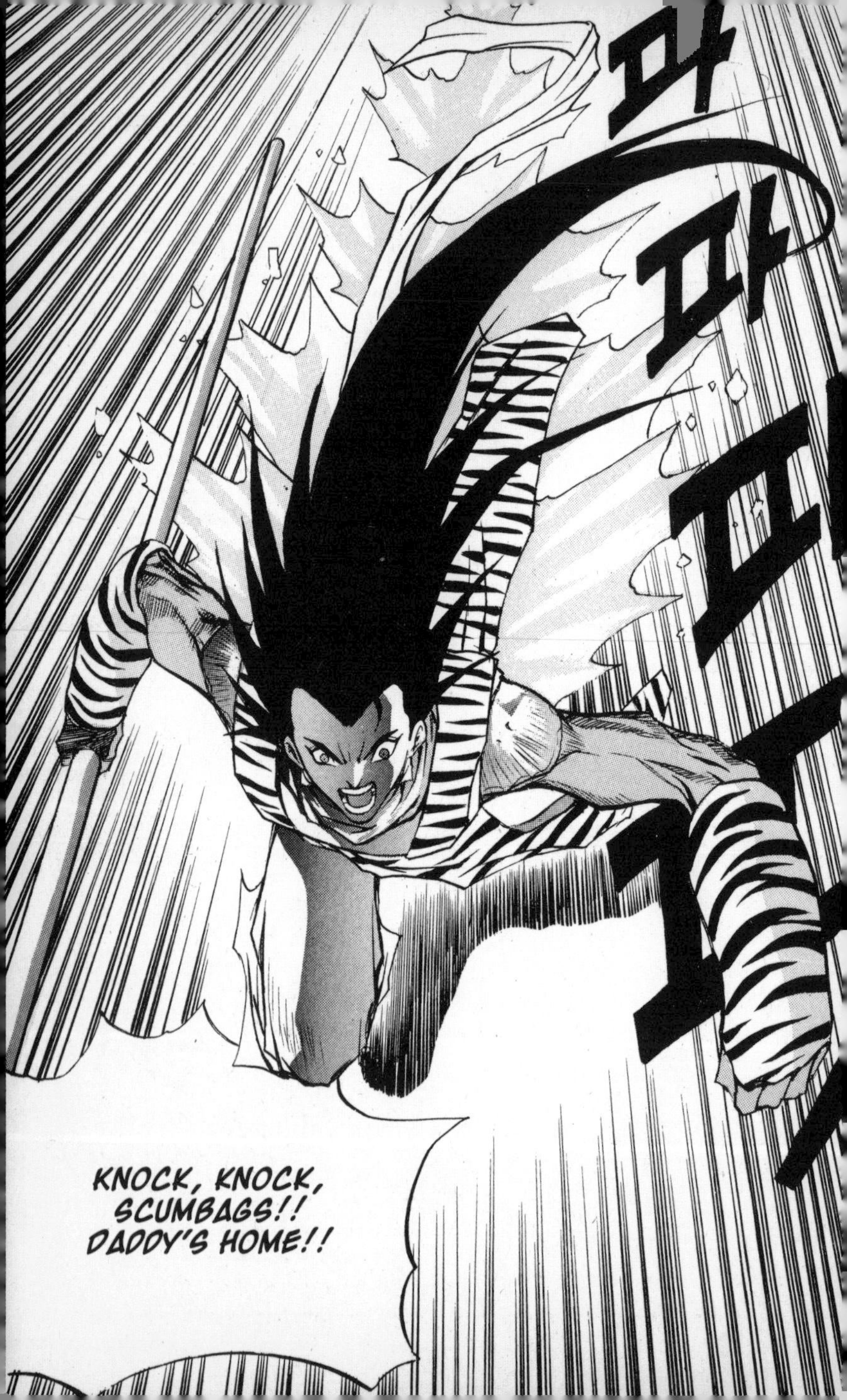
KNOCK, KNOCK, SCUMBAGS!! DADDY'S HOME!!

BLADE OF HEAVEN

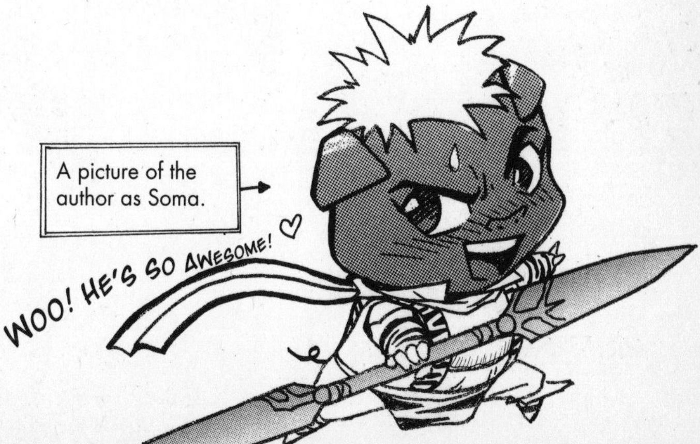
A picture of the author as Soma.
WOO! HE'S SO AWESOME!

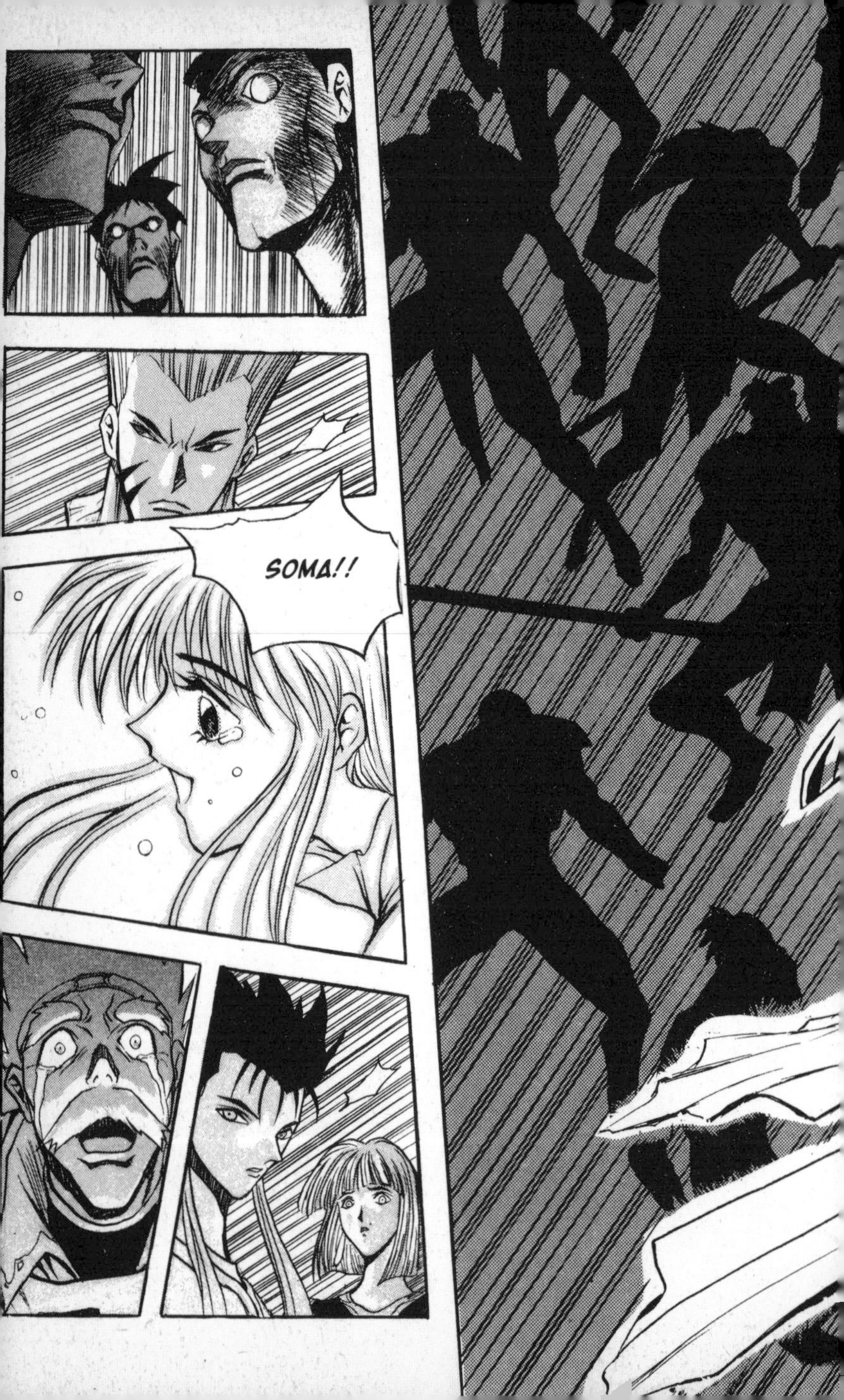
SOMA!!

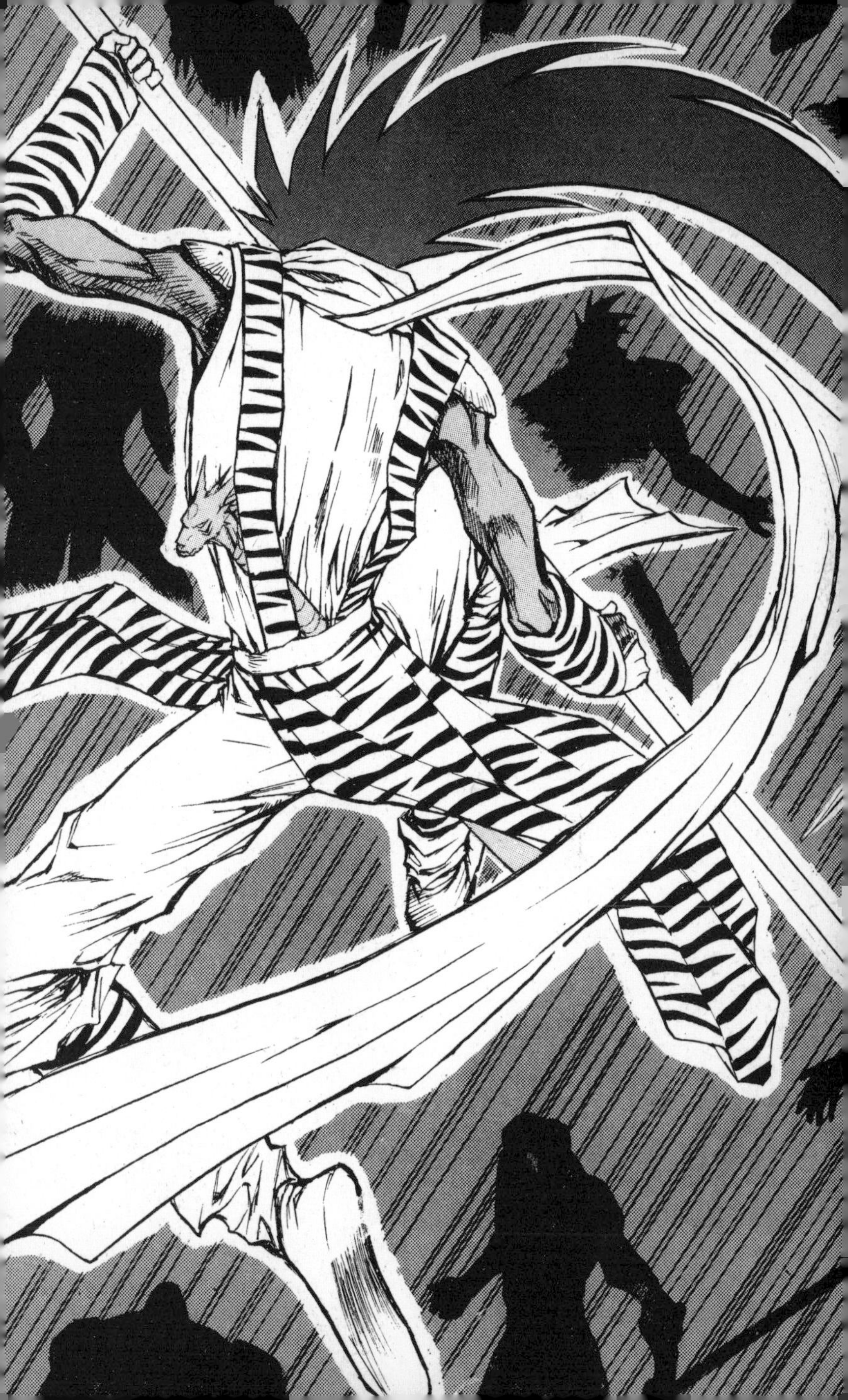

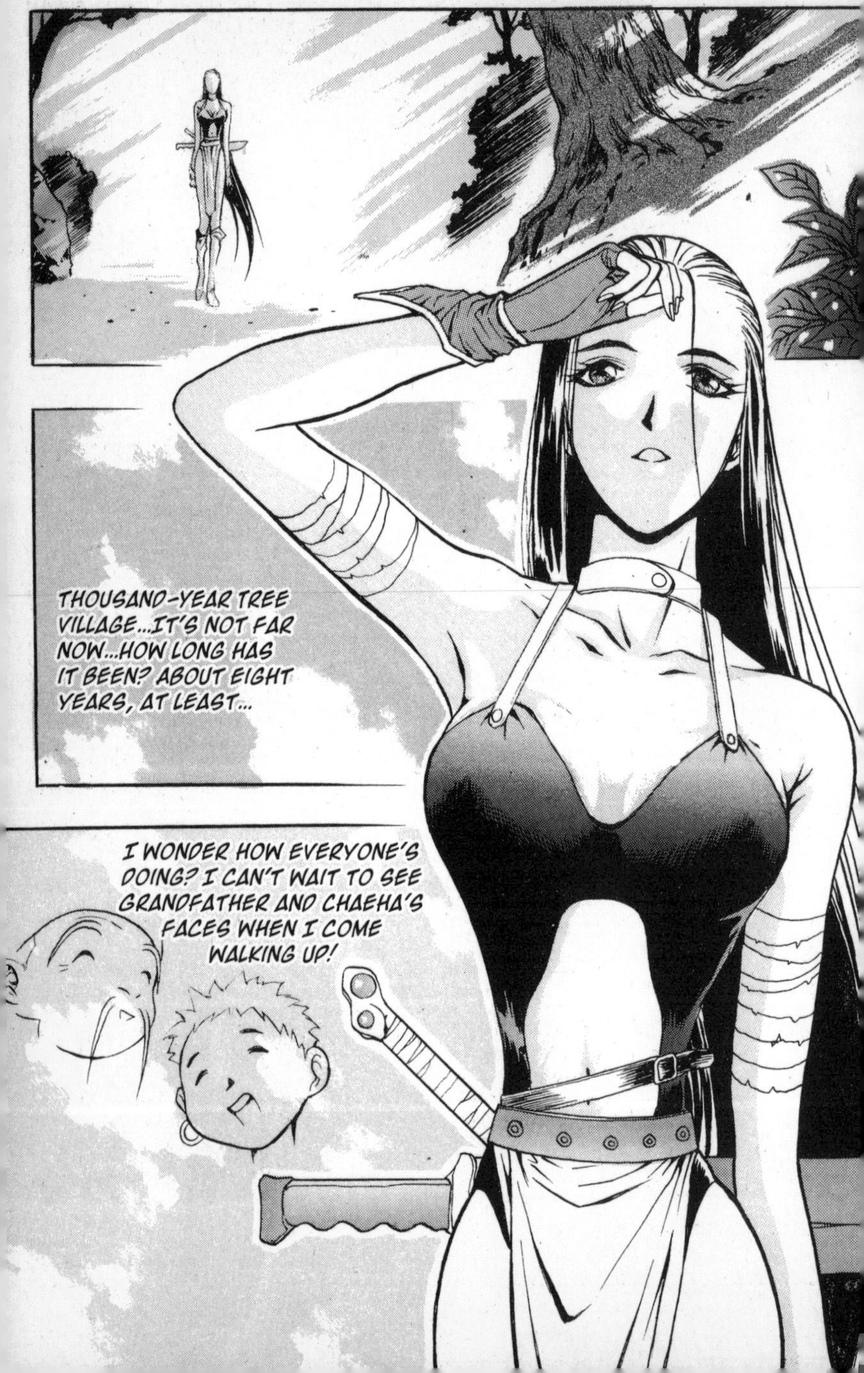
THOUSAND-YEAR TREE VILLAGE...IT'S NOT FAR NOW...HOW LONG HAS IT BEEN? ABOUT EIGHT YEARS, AT LEAST...
I WONDER HOW EVERYONE'S DOING? I CAN'T WAIT TO SEE GRANDFATHER AND CHAEHA'S FACES WHEN I COME WALKING UP!

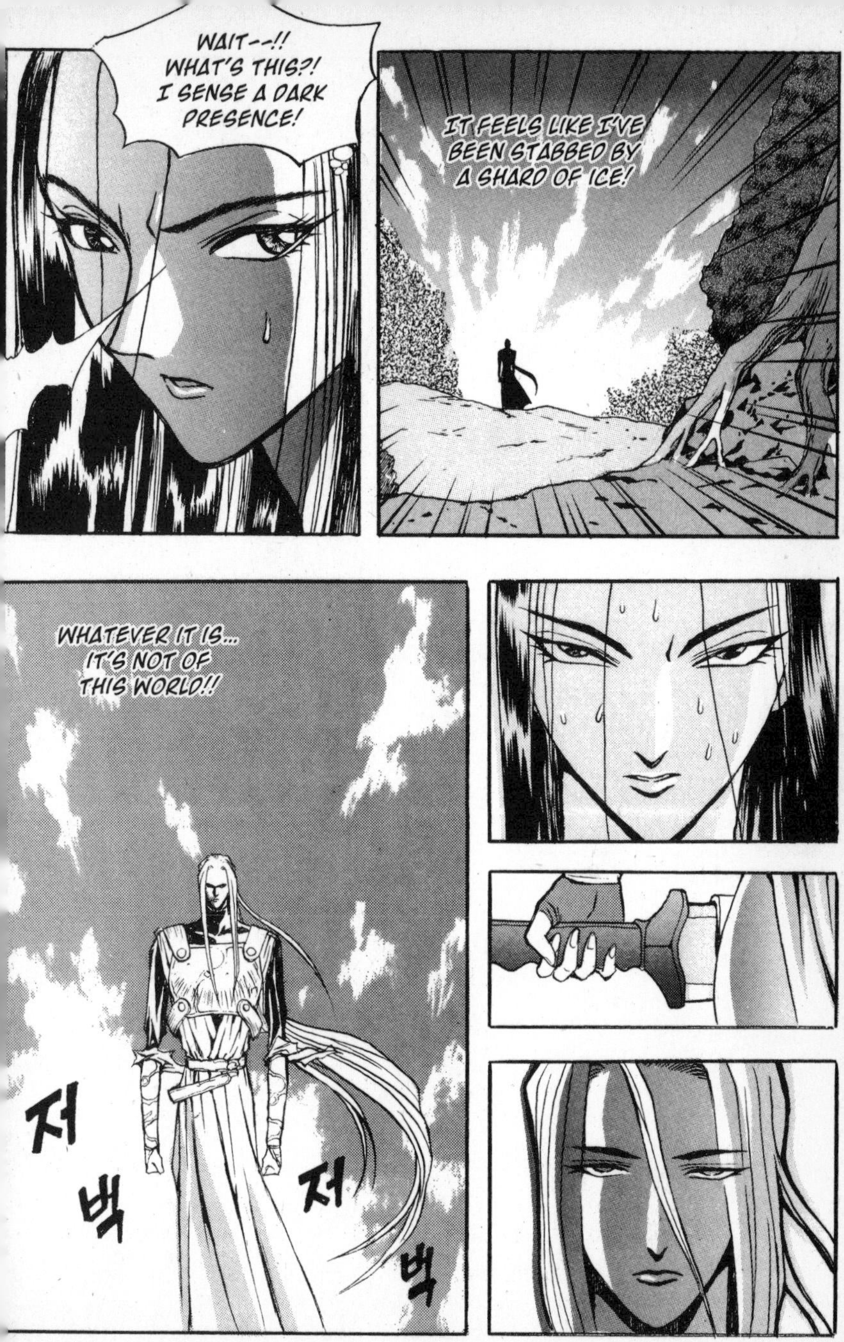
WAIT--!! WHAT'S THIS?! I SENSE A DARK PRESENCE!
IT FEELS LIKE I'VE BEEN STABBED BY A SHARD OF ICE!
WHATEVER IT IS... IT'S NOT OF THIS WORLD!!
저벅
저벅

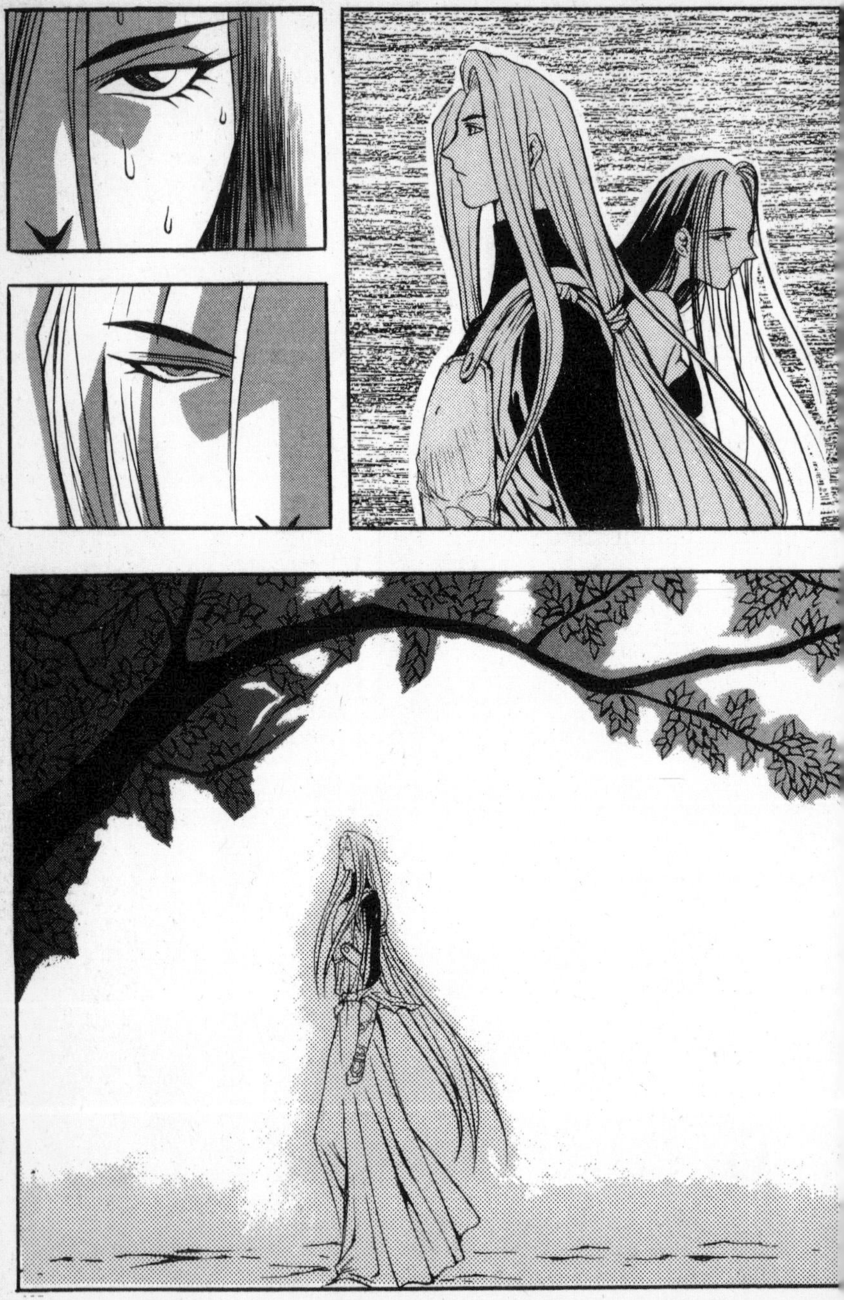

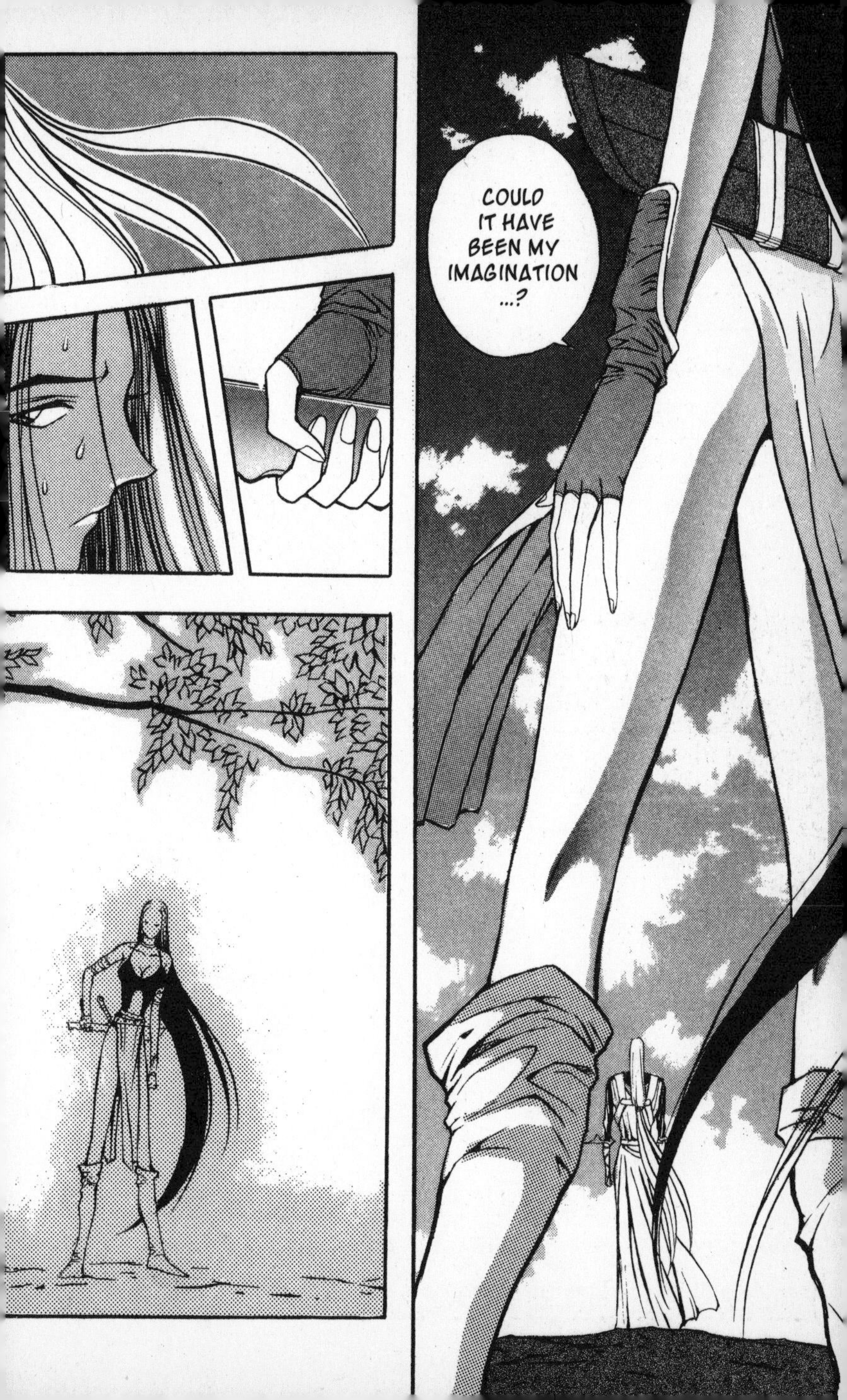
COULD IT HAVE BEEN MY IMAGINATION ...?

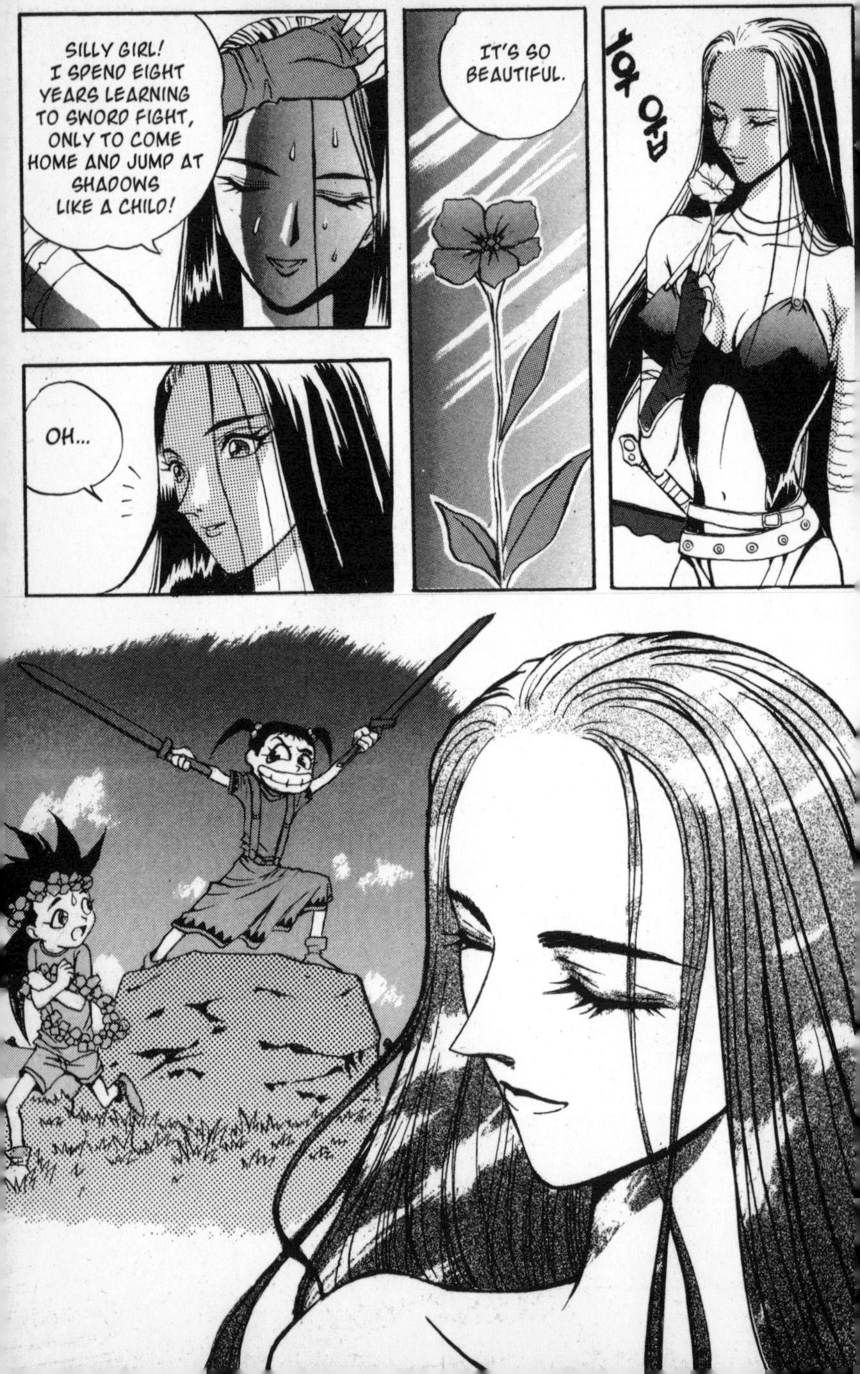
SILLY GIRL! I SPEND EIGHT YEARS LEARNING TO SWORD FIGHT, ONLY TO COME HOME AND JUMP AT SHADOWS LIKE A CHILD!
OH...
IT'S SO BEAUTIFUL.

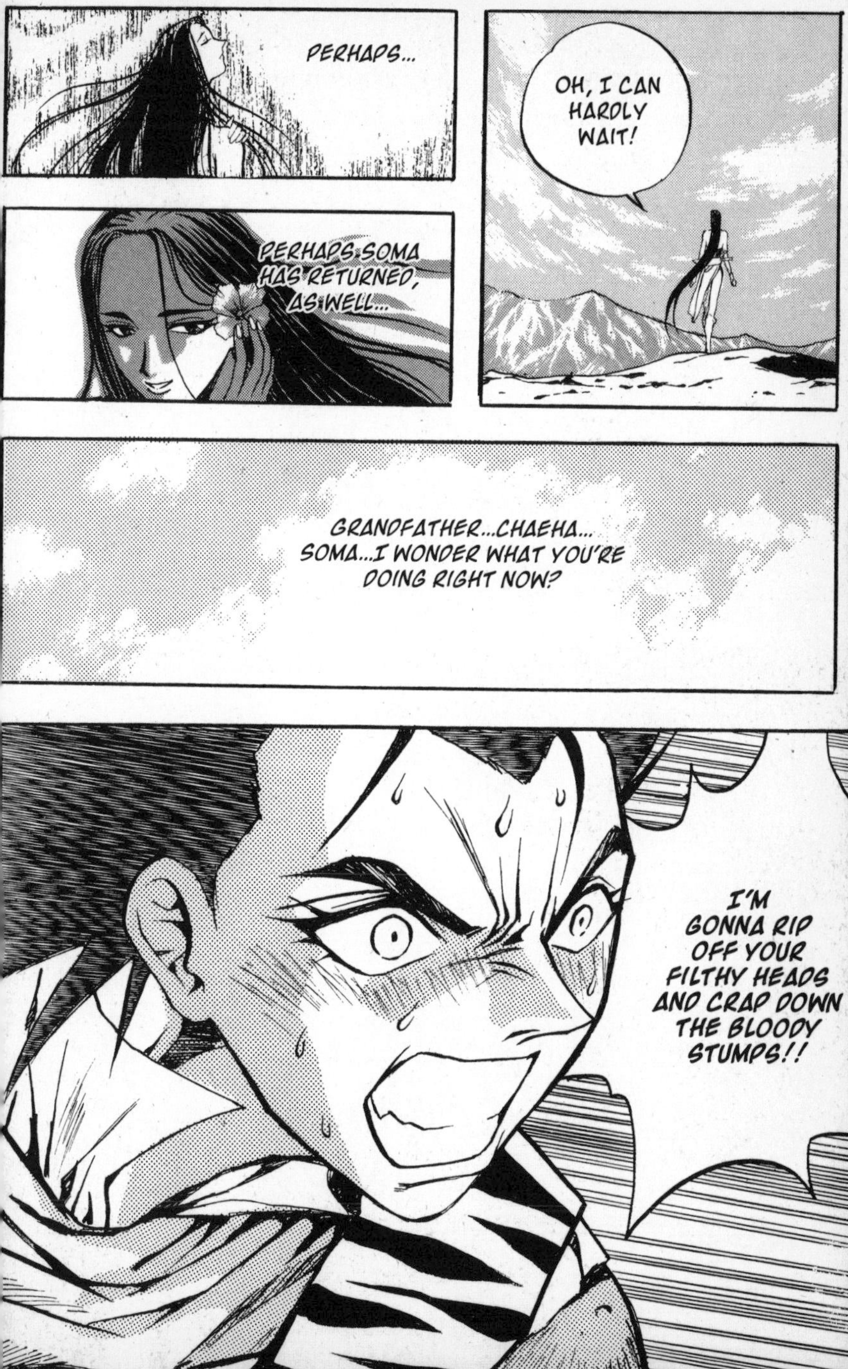
PERHAPS...
PERHAPS SOMA HAS RETURNED, AS WELL...
OH, I CAN HARDLY WAIT!
GRANDFATHER...CHAEHA... SOMA...I WONDER WHAT YOU'RE DOING RIGHT NOW?
I'M GONNA RIP OFF YOUR FILTHY HEADS AND CRAP DOWN THE BLOODY STUMPS!!

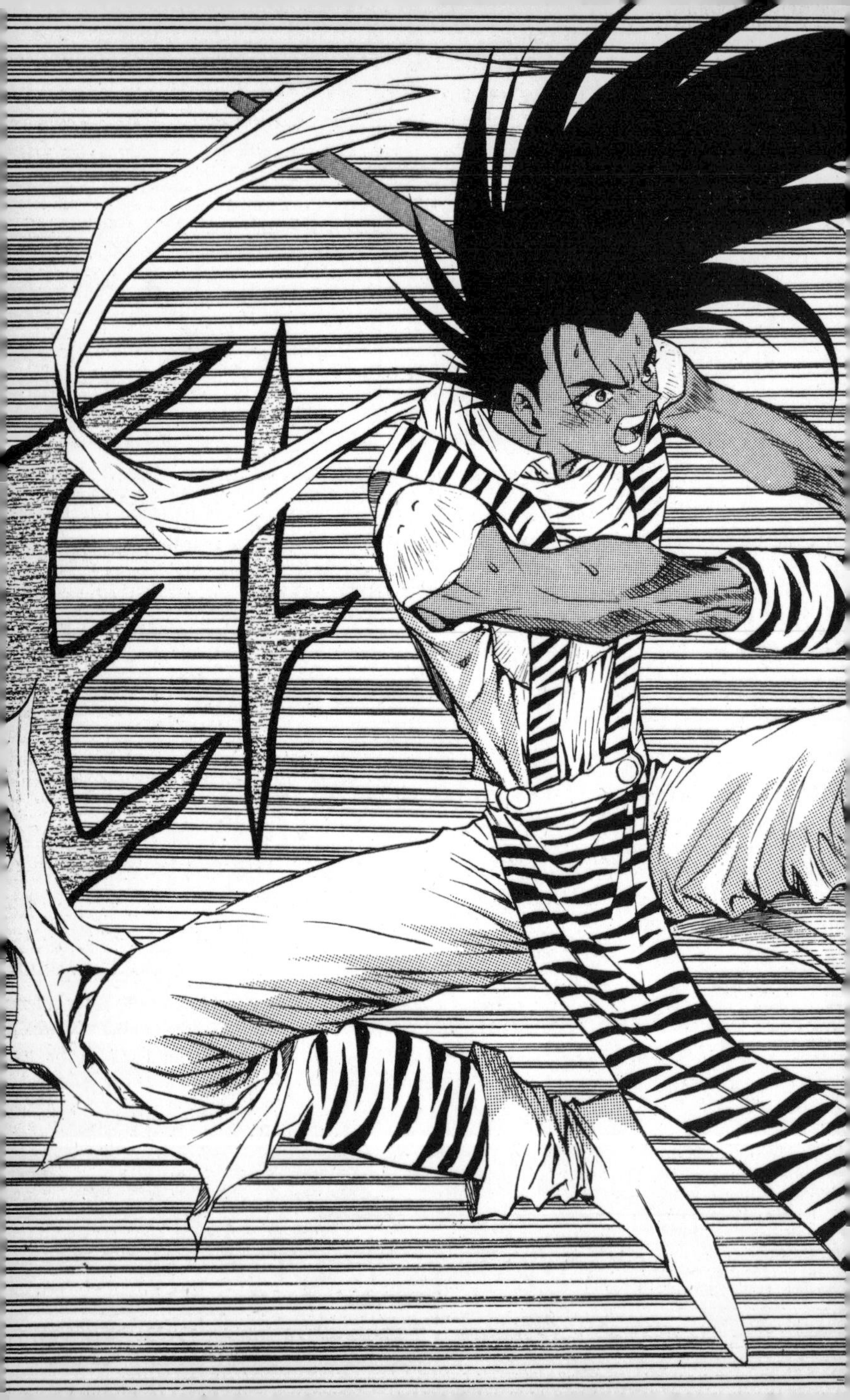

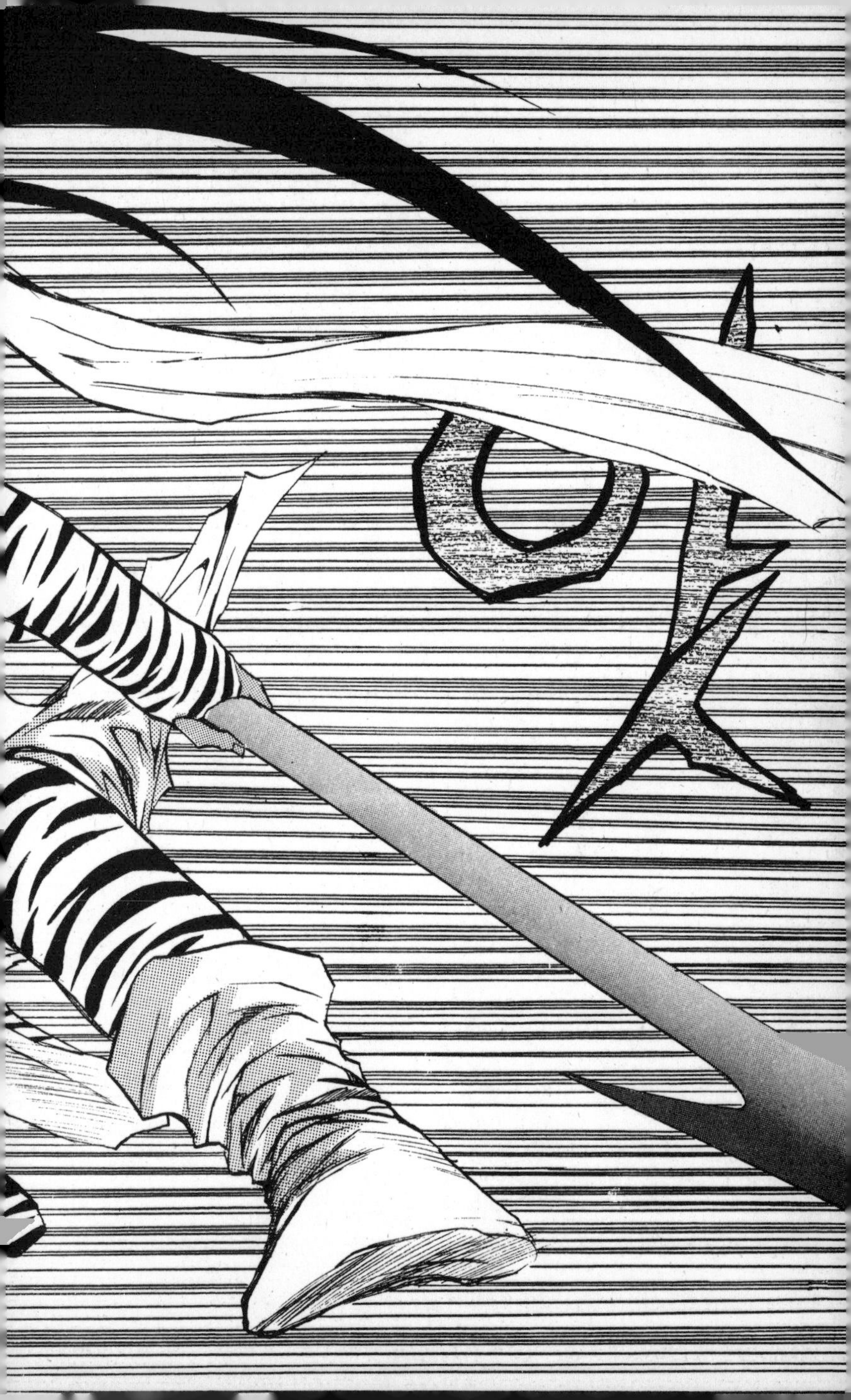

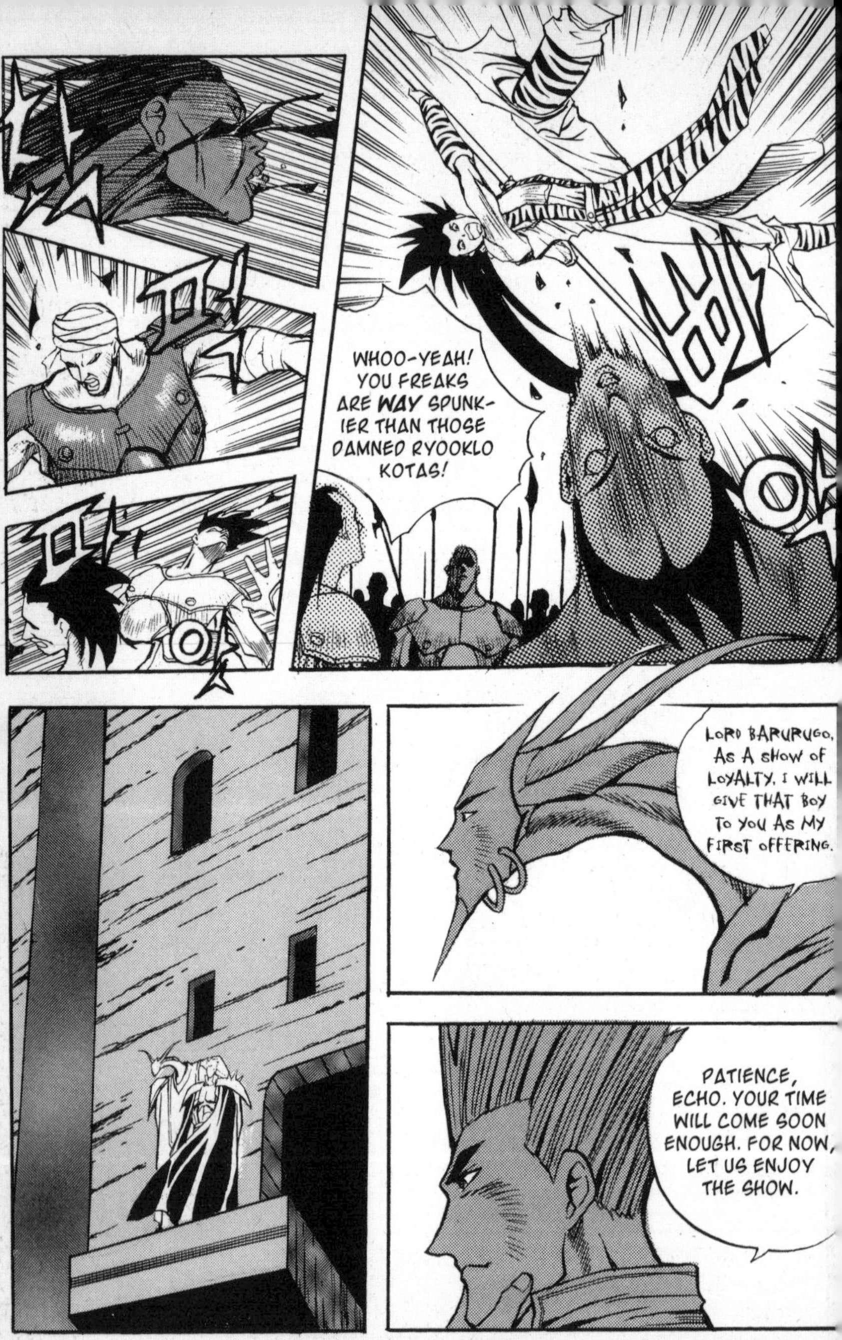
WHOO-YEAH! YOU FREAKS ARE **WAY** SPUNKIER THAN THOSE DAMNED RYOOKLO KOTAS!
LORD BARURUGO, AS A SHOW OF LOYALTY, I WILL GIVE THAT BOY TO YOU AS MY FIRST OFFERING.
PATIENCE, ECHO. YOUR TIME WILL COME SOON ENOUGH. FOR NOW, LET US ENJOY THE SHOW.

BOY...*HUFF*... YOU CREEPS ARE LIKE ROACHES...*HUFF*... YA KILL ONE, AND THREE MORE TAKE ITS PLACE! YEP...DEFINITELY SOME CRACKS IN THE WHOLE "CHARGING IN WITHOUT THINKING" PLAN!

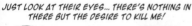

JUST LOOK AT THEIR EYES... THERE'S NOTHING IN THERE BUT THE DESIRE TO KILL ME!

THEY'RE BEING MANIPULATED BY BARURUGO'S MIND CONTROL MAGIC, BOY! THEY'RE JUST DEAD SHELLS OF MEN! Y'KNOW, ZOMBIES!

ZOMBIES?! YOU GOTTA BE KIDDIN' ME!

Zombies:
When average human beings fall under the control of a demon's spell, they lose their will and become mindless killing drones with augmented strength and an insatiable bloodlust.

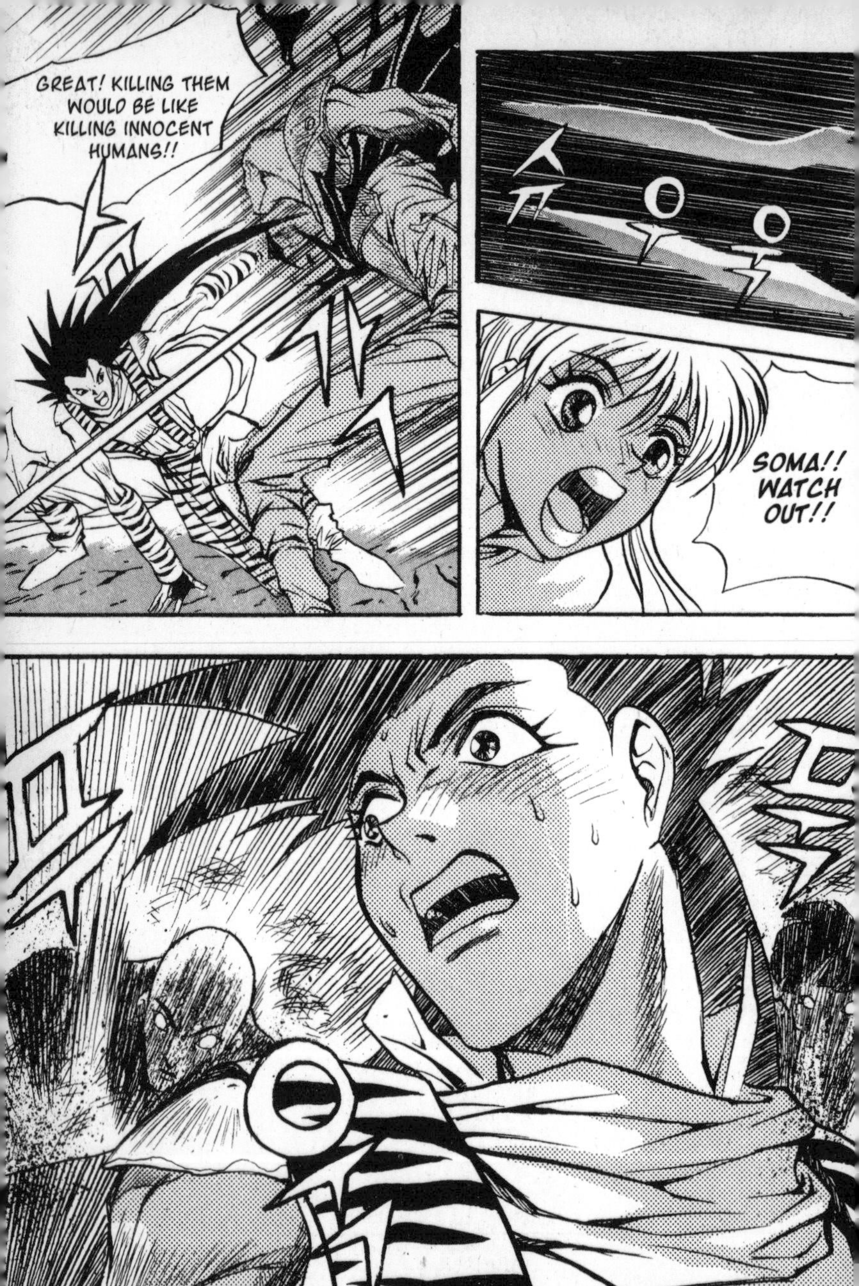
GREAT! KILLING THEM WOULD BE LIKE KILLING INNOCENT HUMANS!!
SOMA!! WATCH OUT!!

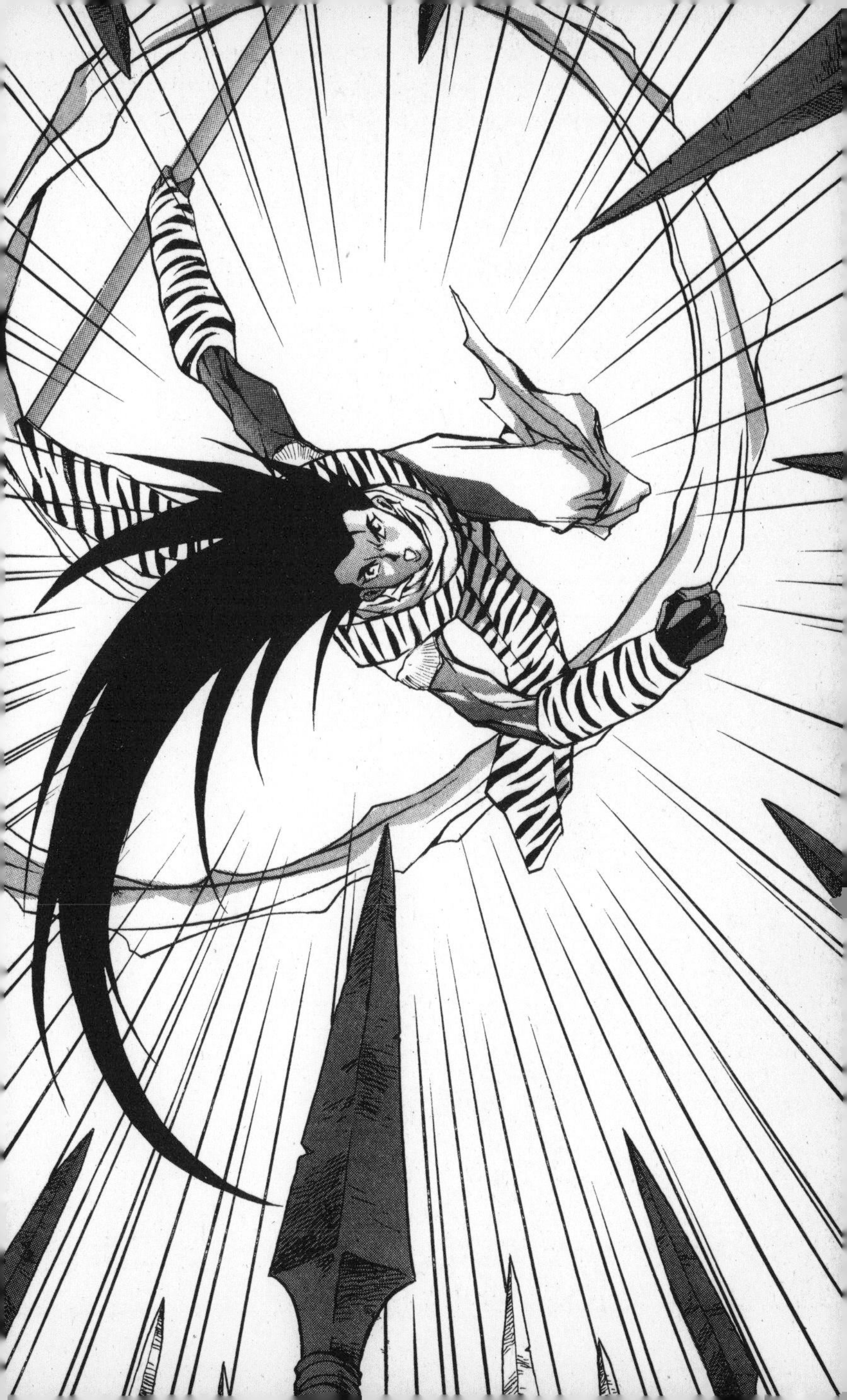

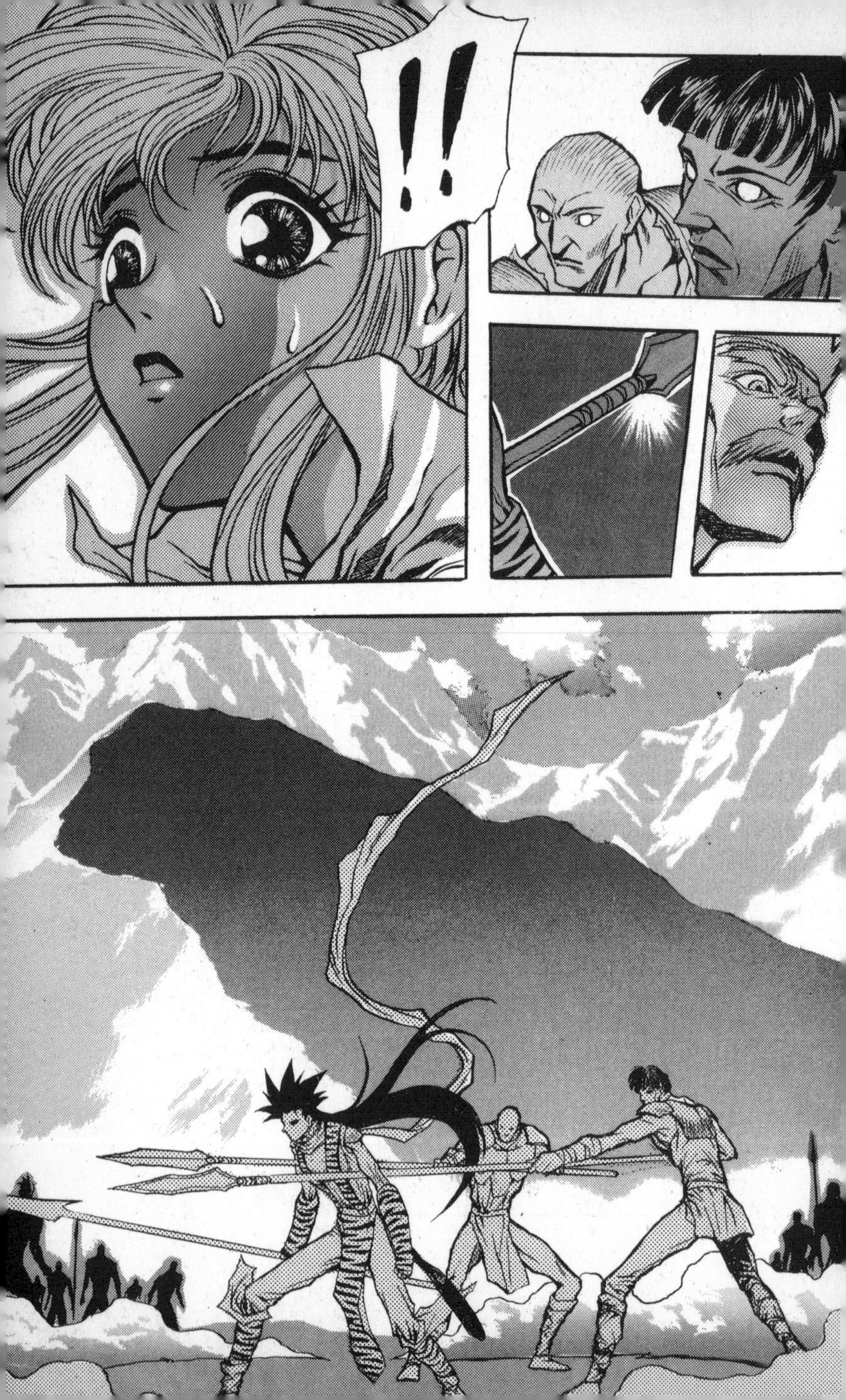
!!

THAT'S IT!!
INNOCENT OR NOT--
GLOVES ARE NOW
OFFICIALLY *OFF*!!

WELL...
AREN'T
I THE
POPULAR
ONE.

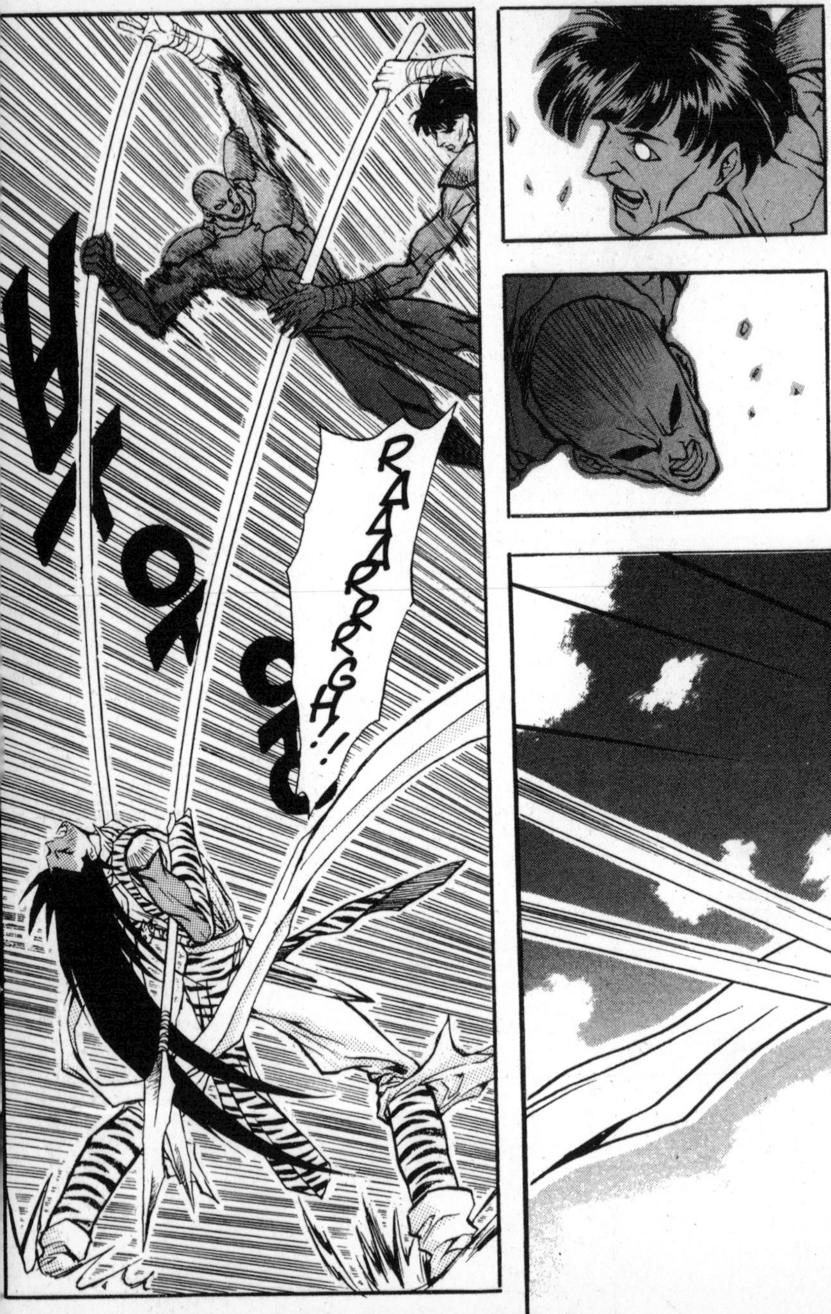
RAAARRRGH!!

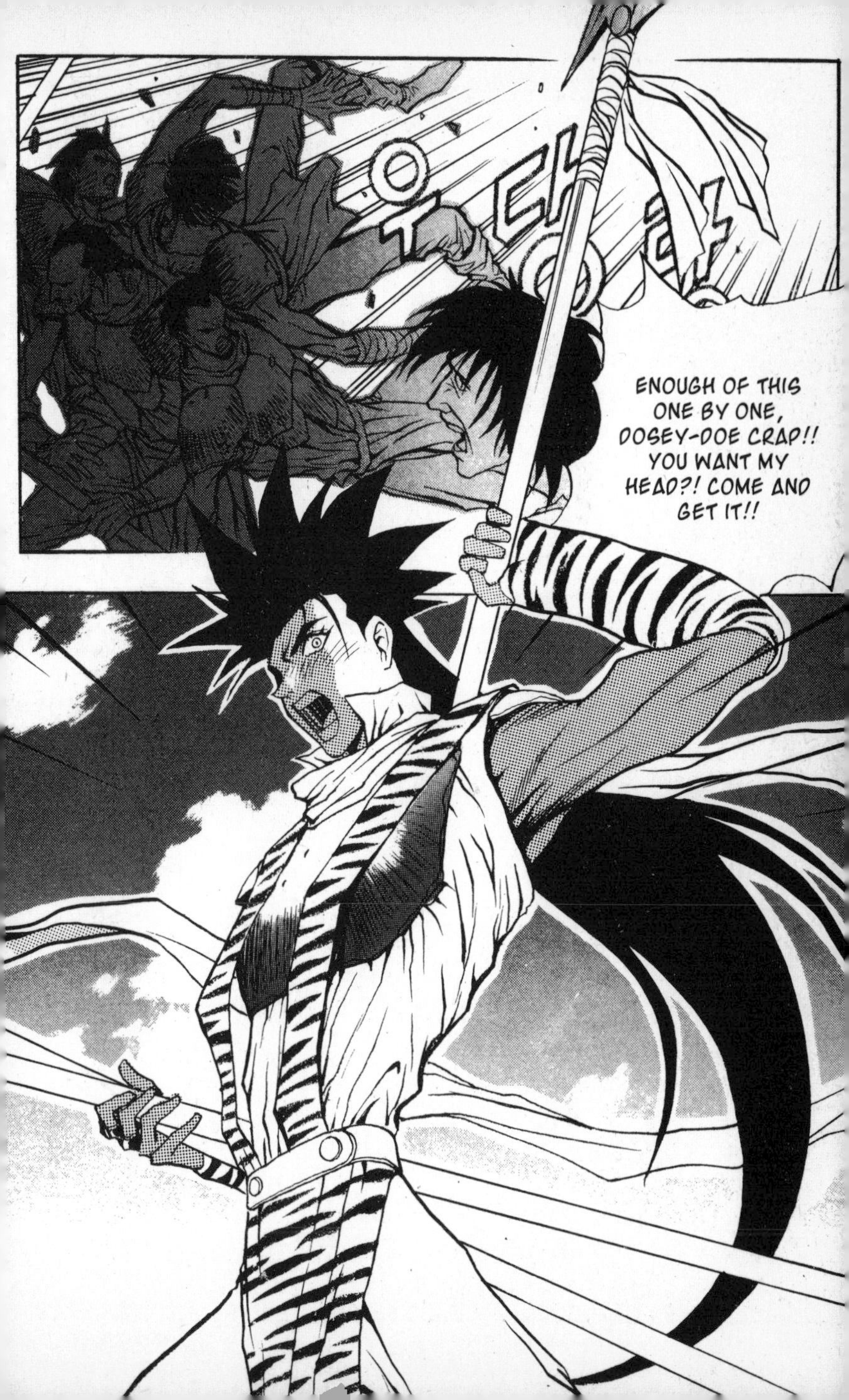

CHOCK
ENOUGH OF THIS ONE BY ONE, DOSEY-DOE CRAP!! YOU WANT MY HEAD?! COME AND GET IT!!

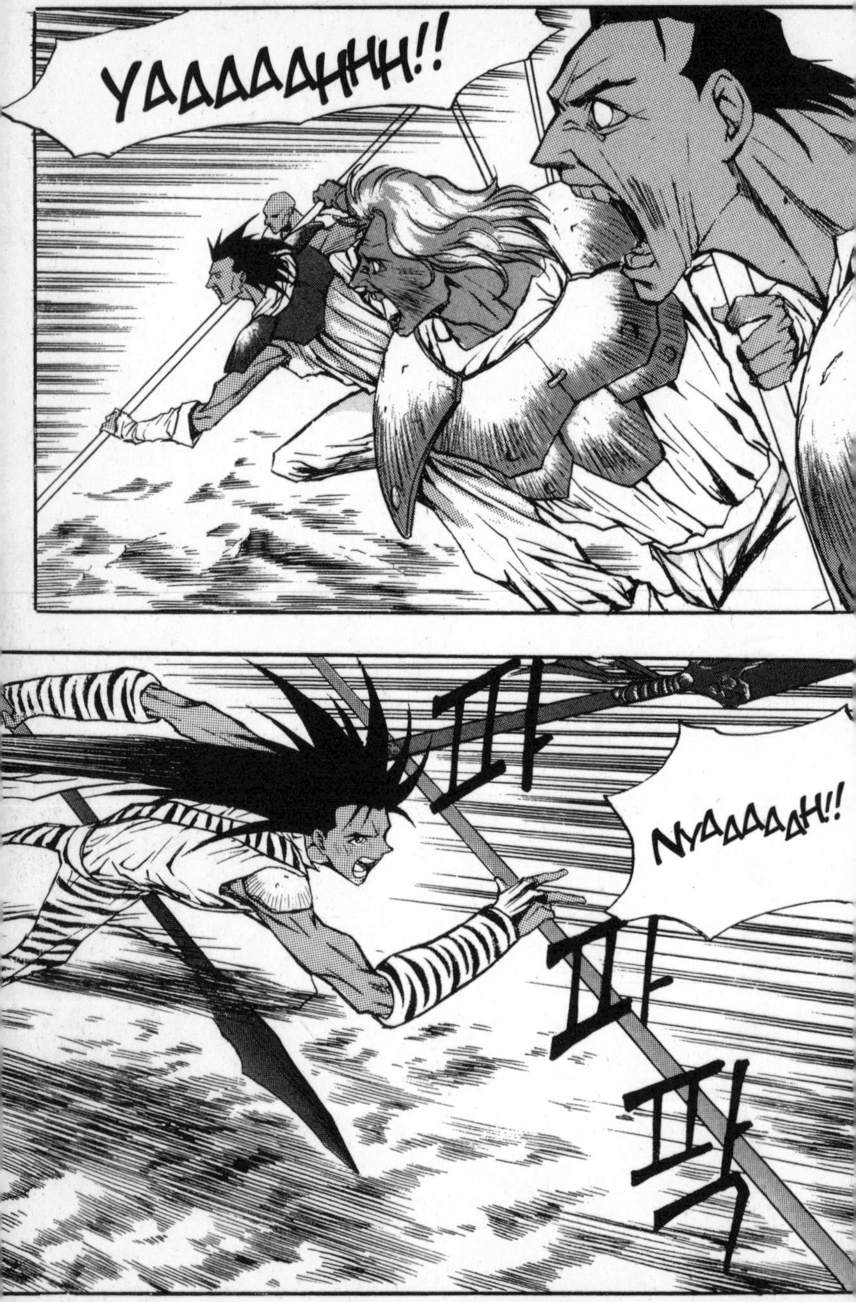
YAAAAAHHH!!
NYAAAAAH!!
파
파
팍

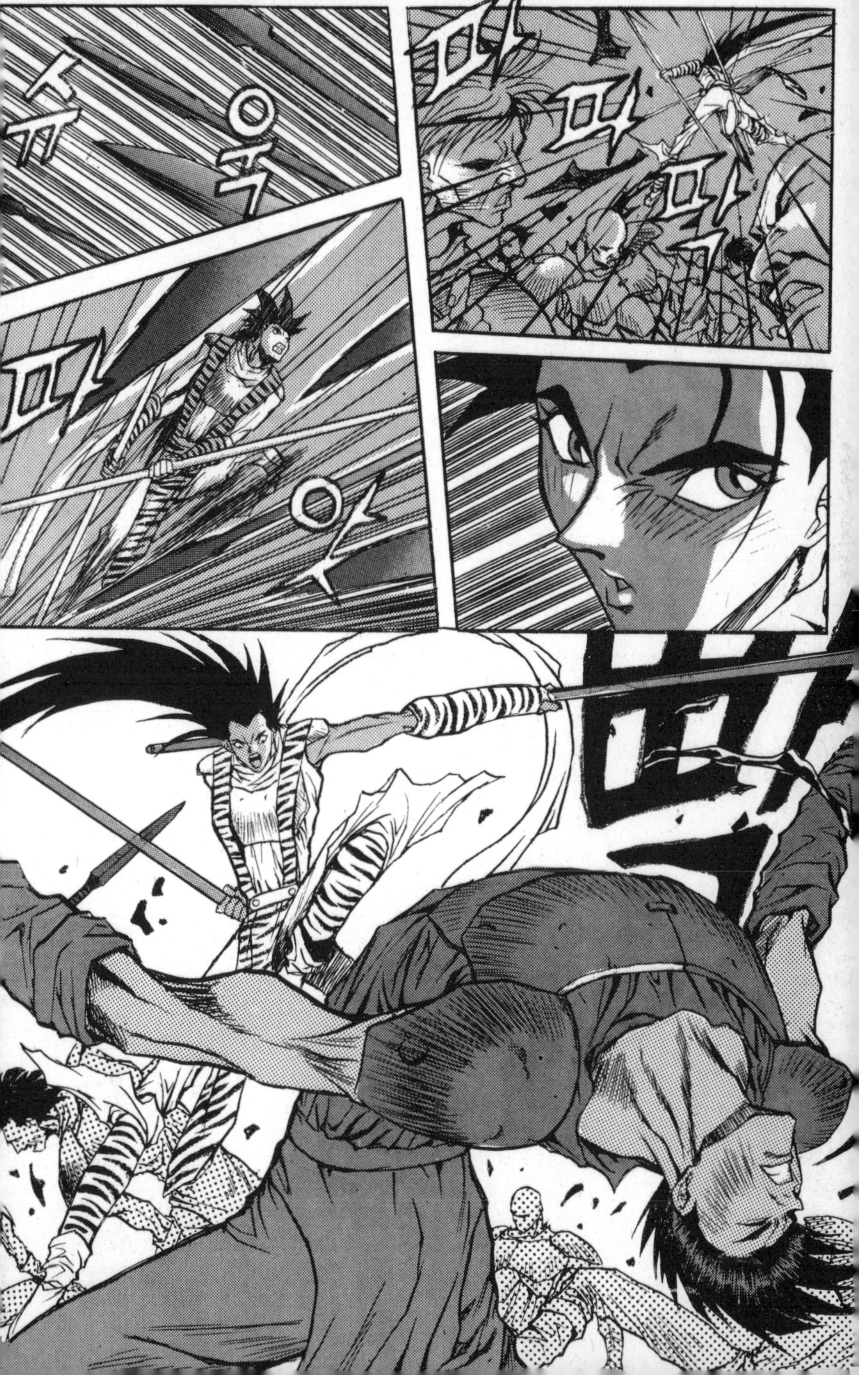

퍽
퍽

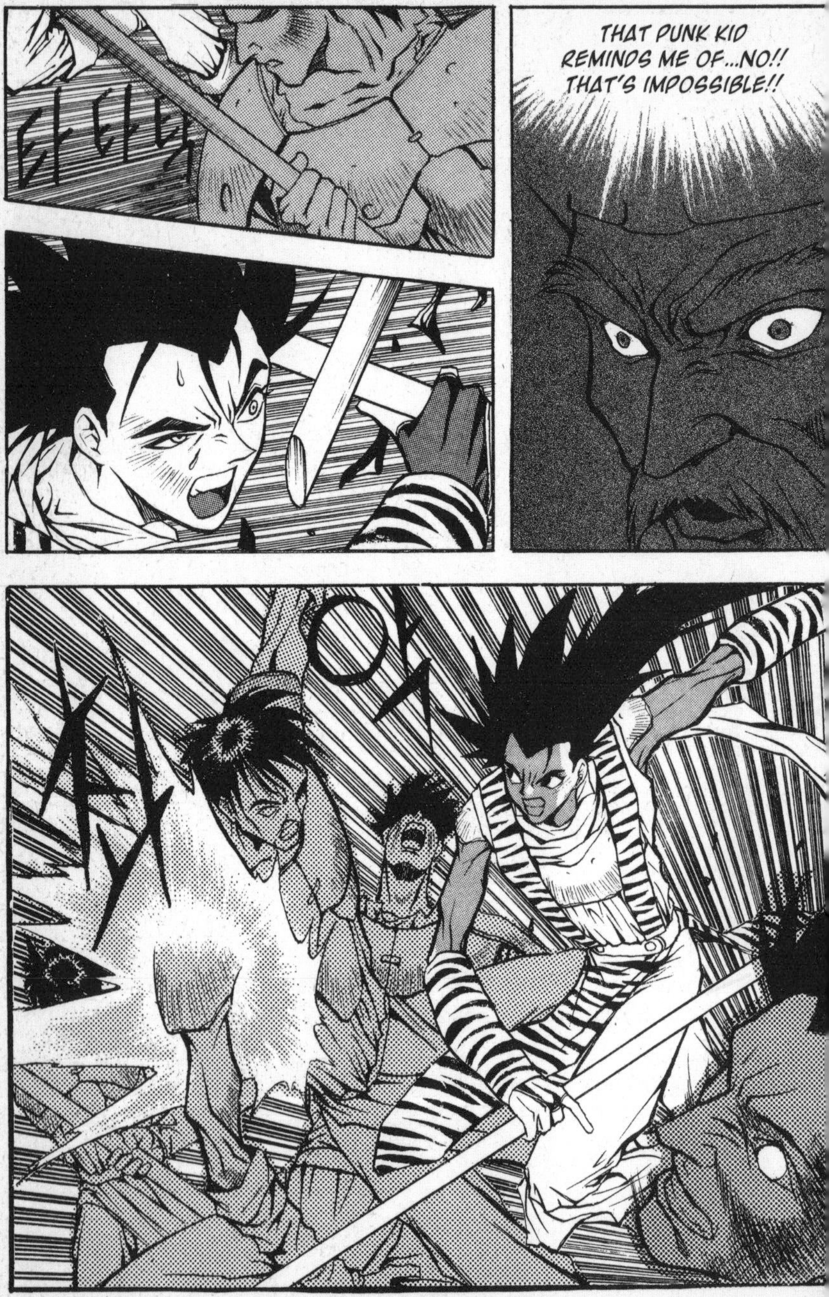
THAT PUNK KID REMINDS ME OF...NO!! THAT'S IMPOSSIBLE!!

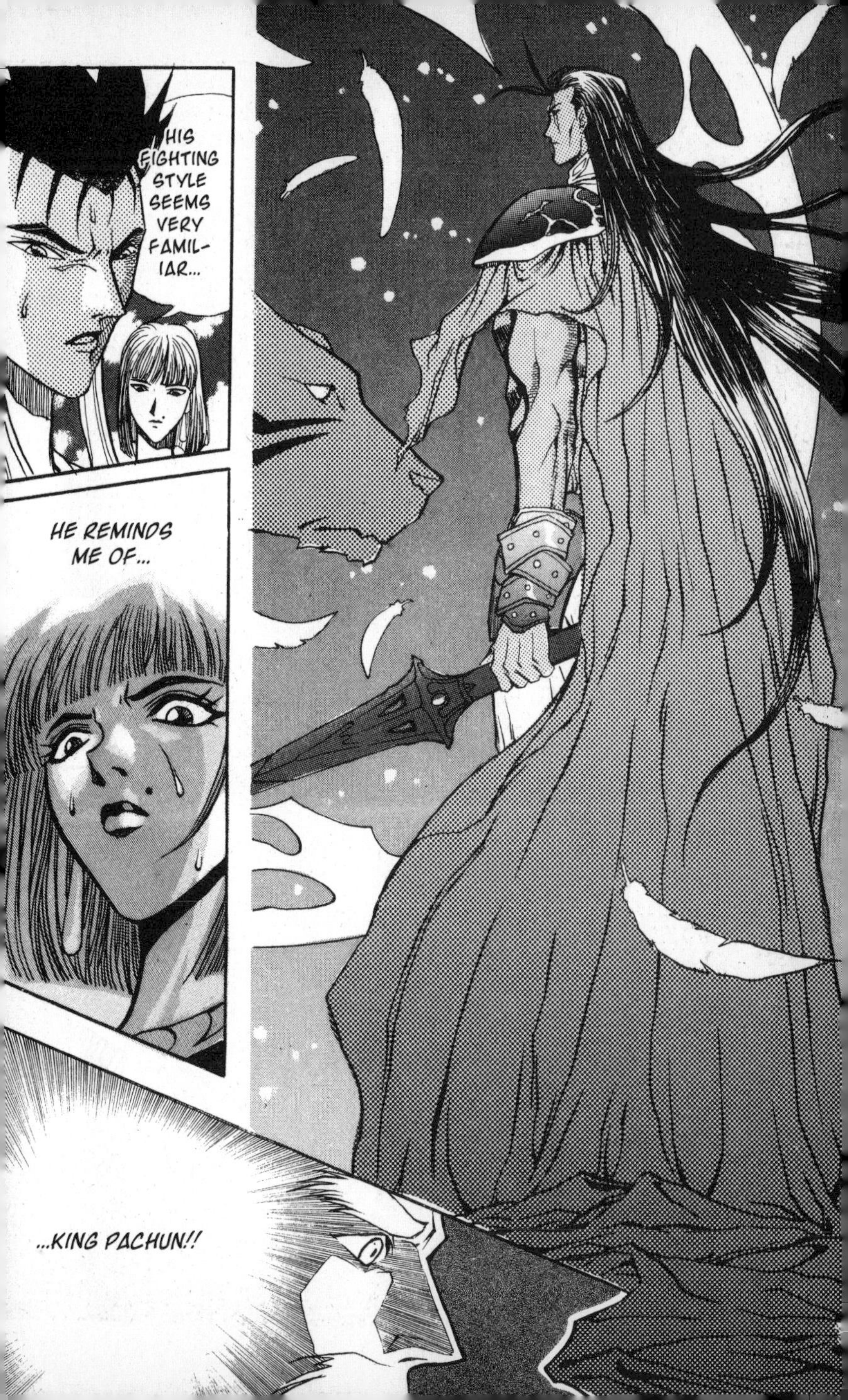
HIS FIGHTING STYLE SEEMS VERY FAMIL-IAR...
HE REMINDS ME OF...
...KING PACHUN!!

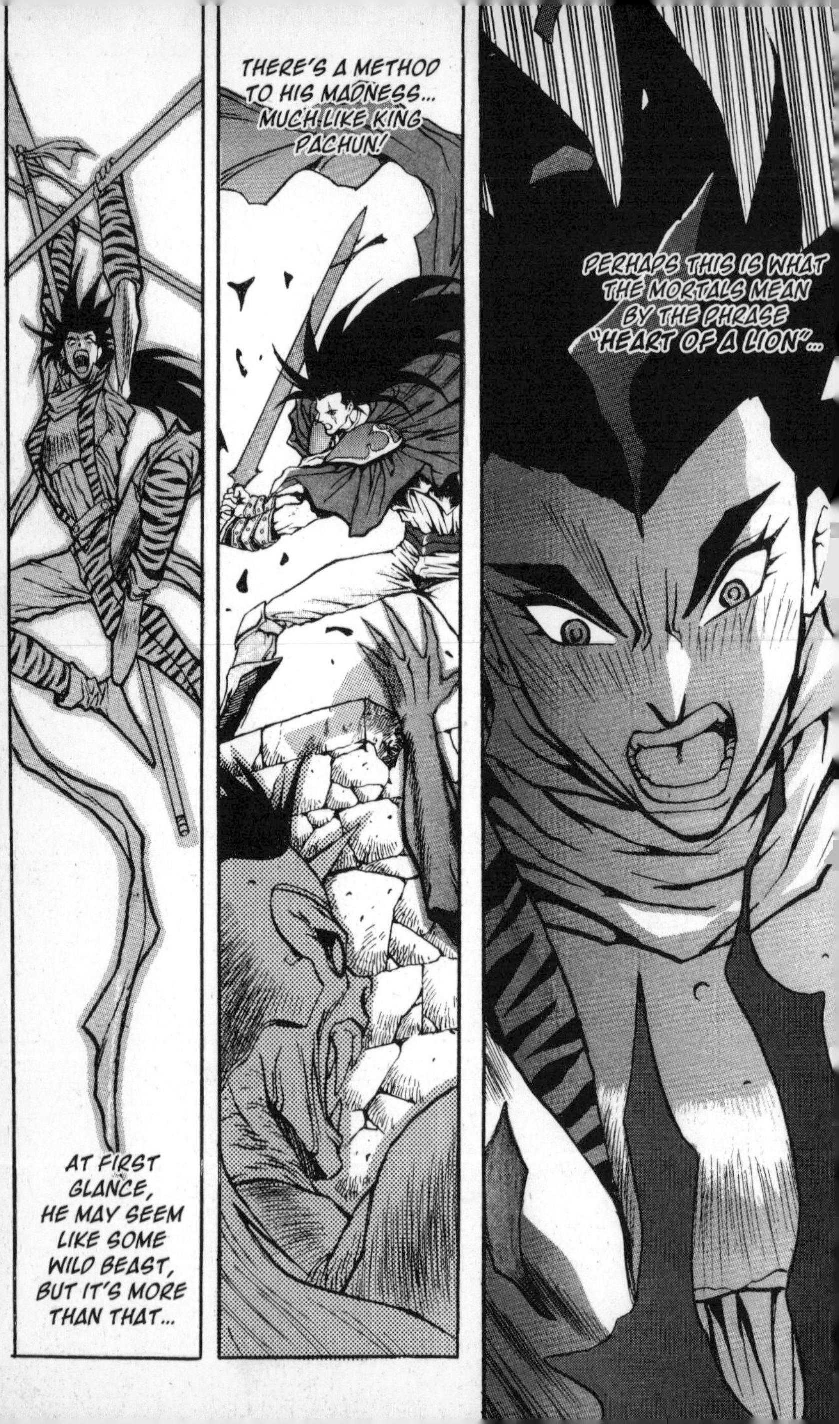
AT FIRST GLANCE, HE MAY SEEM LIKE SOME WILD BEAST, BUT IT'S MORE THAN THAT...
THERE'S A METHOD TO HIS MADNESS... MUCH LIKE KING PACHUN!
PERHAPS THIS IS WHAT THE MORTALS MEAN BY THE PHRASE "HEART OF A LION"...

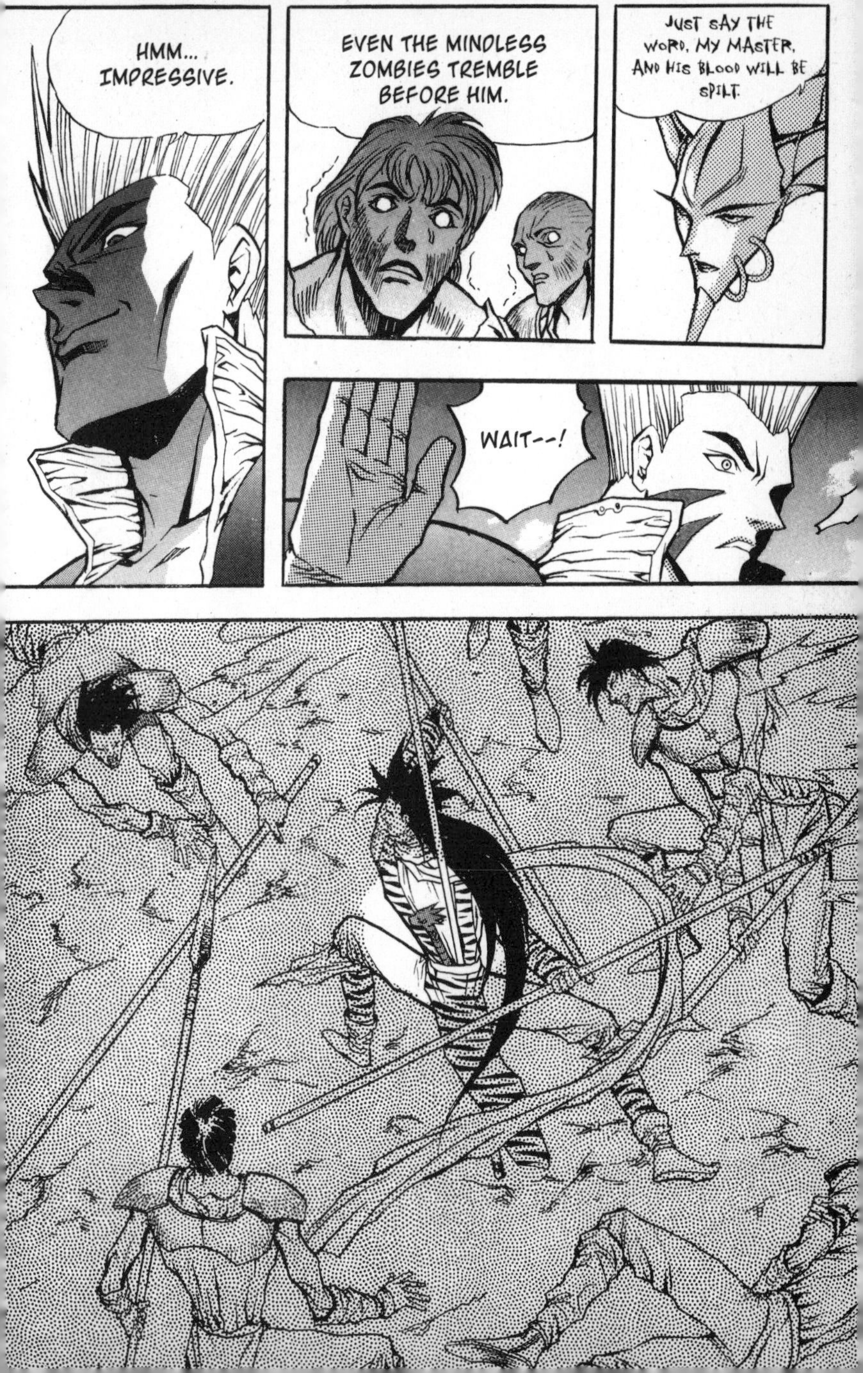
HMM... IMPRESSIVE.
EVEN THE MINDLESS ZOMBIES TREMBLE BEFORE HIM.
JUST SAY THE WORD, MY MASTER, AND HIS BLOOD WILL BE SPILT.
WAIT--!

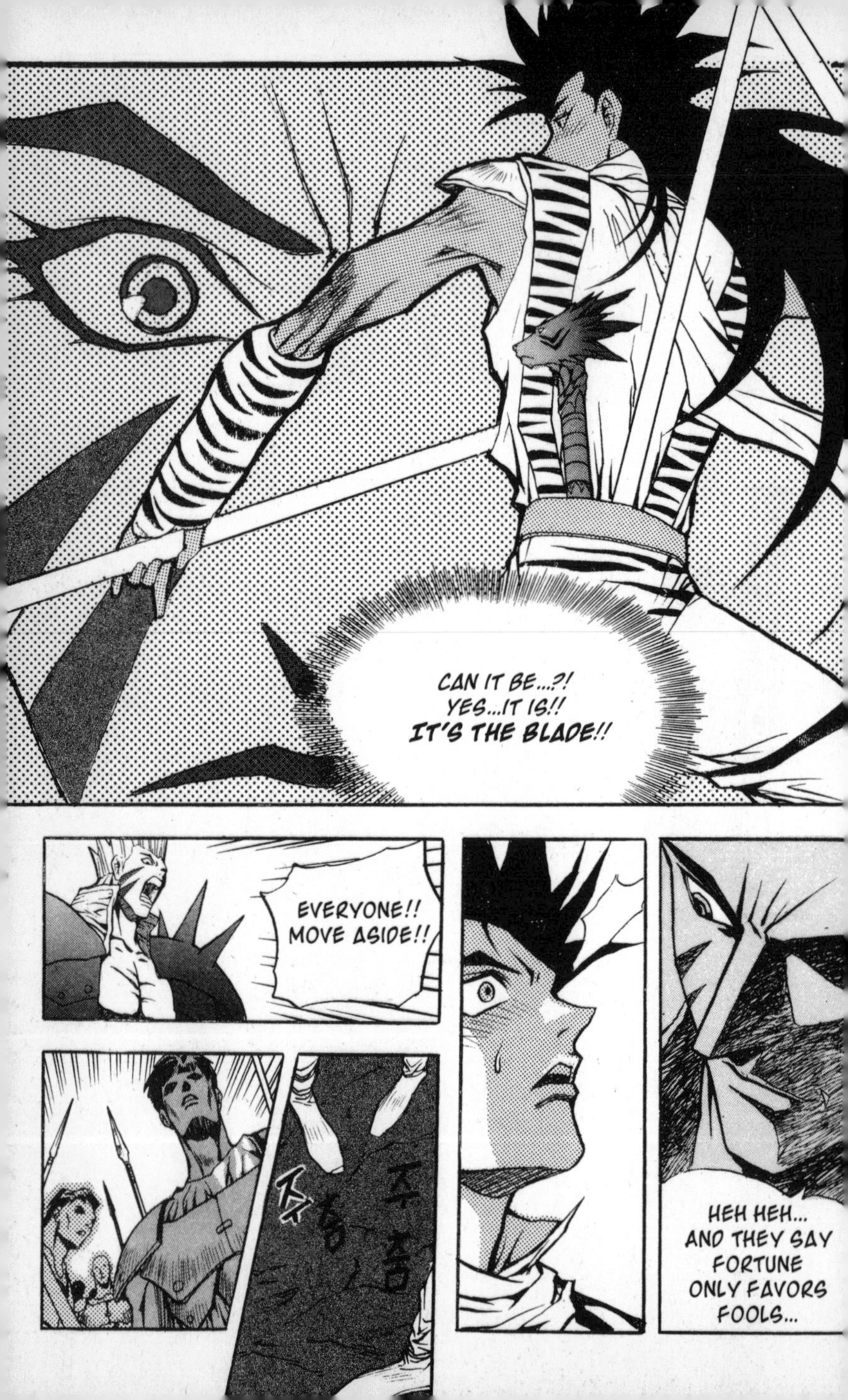
CAN IT BE...?!
YES...IT IS!!
IT'S THE BLADE!!
EVERYONE!!
MOVE ASIDE!!
주춤
HEH HEH...
AND THEY SAY
FORTUNE
ONLY FAVORS
FOOLS...

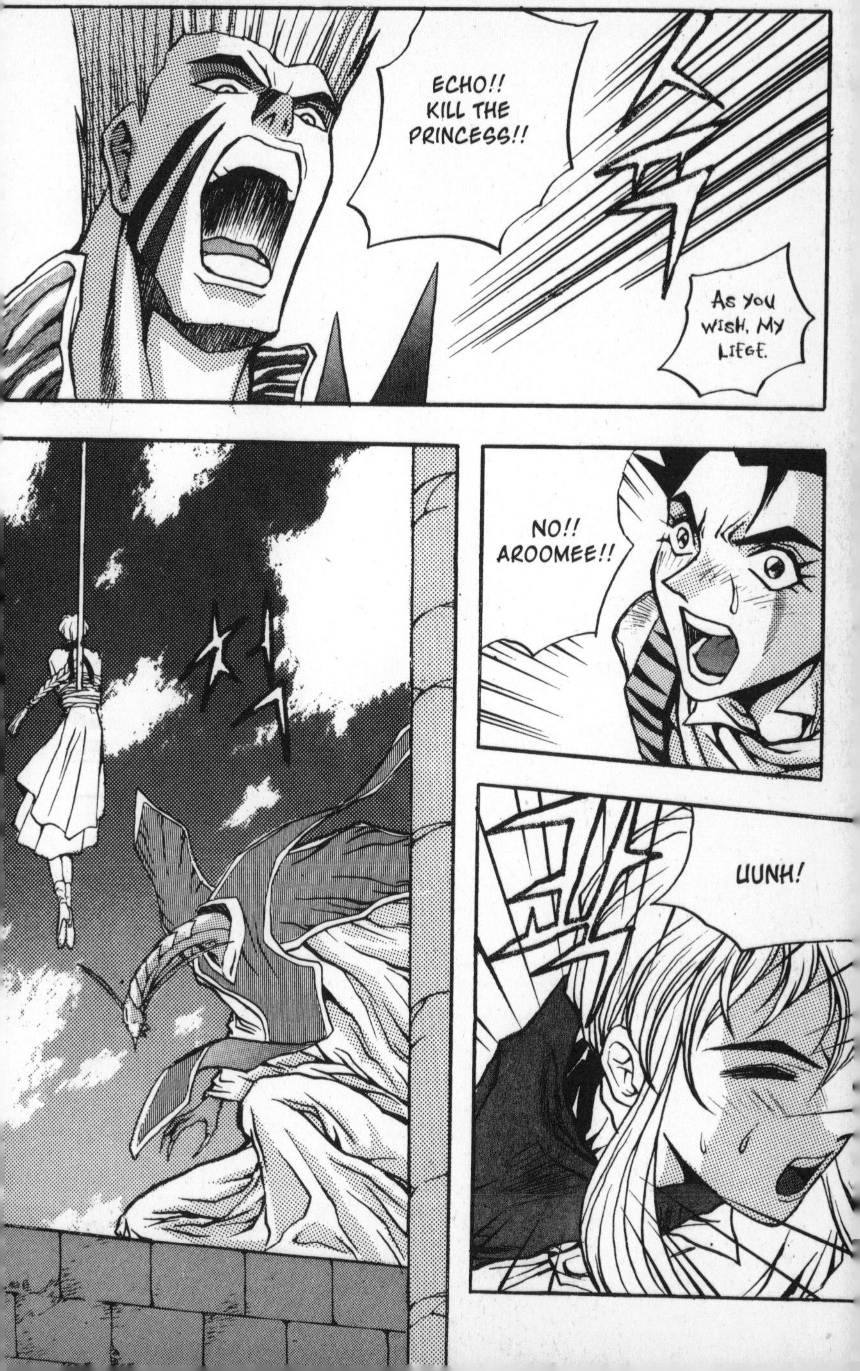
ECHO!! KILL THE PRINCESS!!
As you wish, My Liege.
NO!! AROOMEE!!
UUNH!

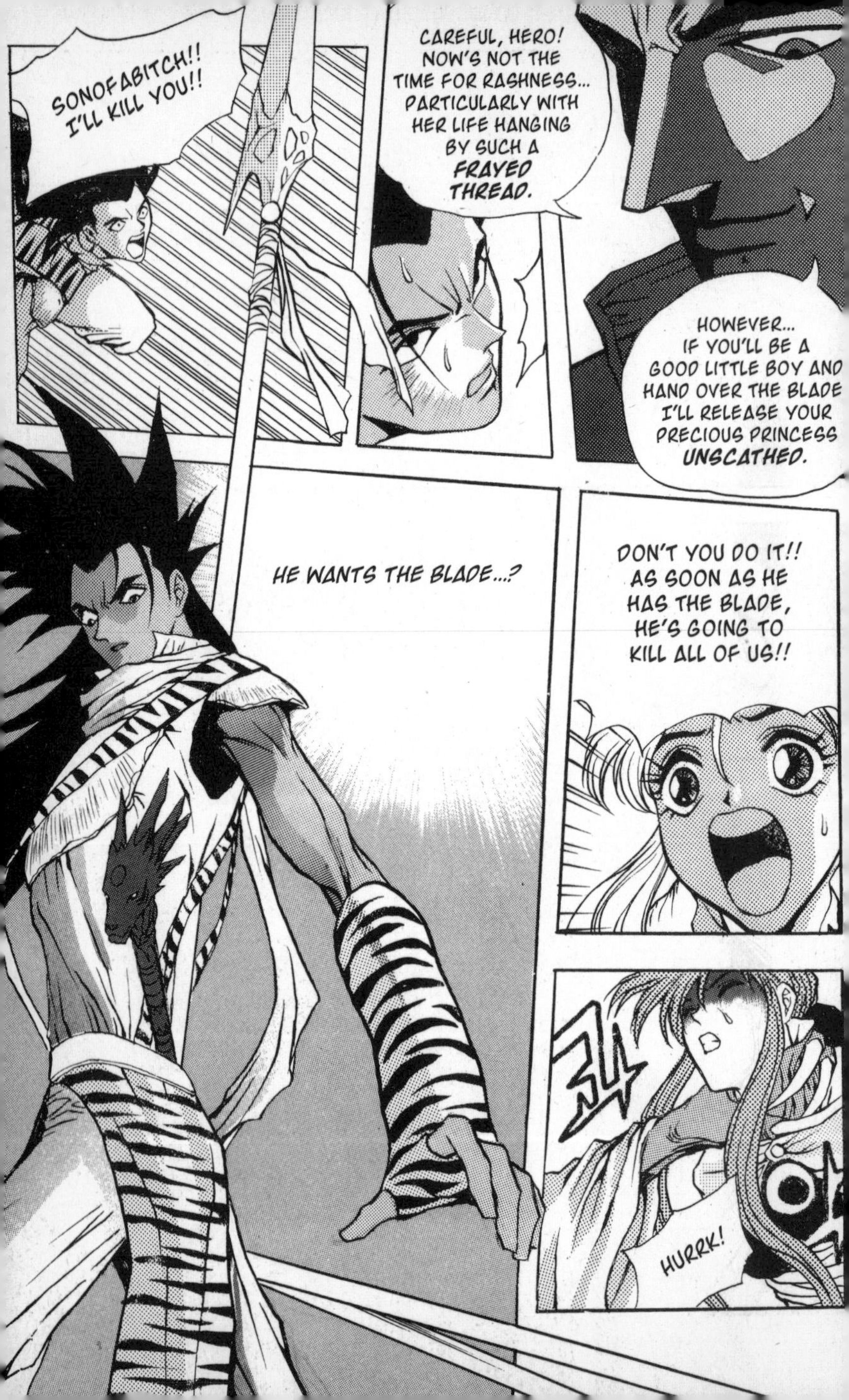
SONOFABITCH!! I'LL KILL YOU!!
CAREFUL, HERO! NOW'S NOT THE TIME FOR RASHNESS... PARTICULARLY WITH HER LIFE HANGING BY SUCH A *FRAYED THREAD.*
HOWEVER... IF YOU'LL BE A GOOD LITTLE BOY AND HAND OVER THE BLADE I'LL RELEASE YOUR PRECIOUS PRINCESS *UNSCATHED.*
HE WANTS THE BLADE...?
DON'T YOU DO IT!! AS SOON AS HE HAS THE BLADE, HE'S GOING TO KILL ALL OF US!!
HURRK!

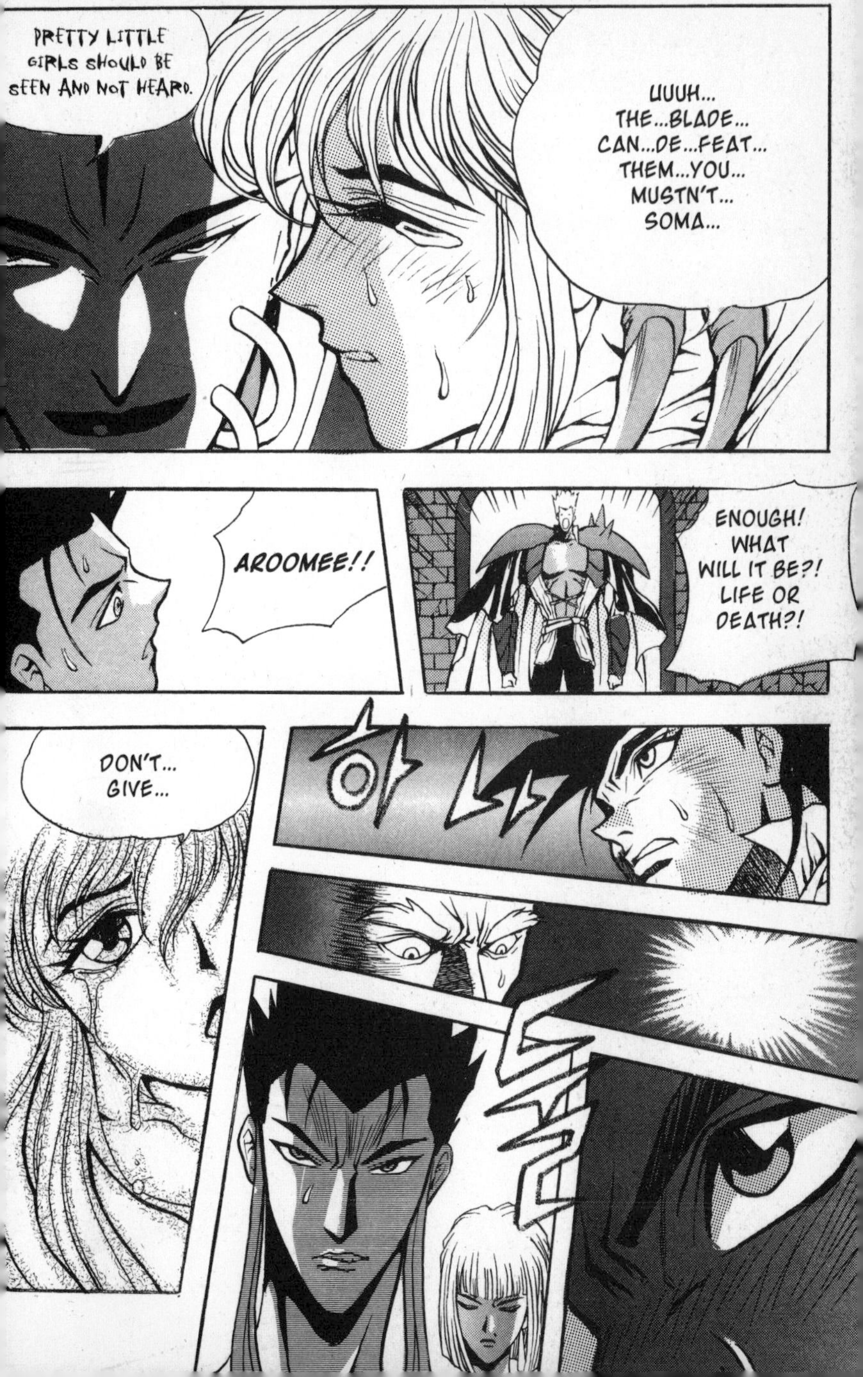
PRETTY LITTLE GIRLS SHOULD BE SEEN AND NOT HEARD.
UUUH... THE...BLADE... CAN...DE...FEAT... THEM...YOU... MUSTN'T... SOMA...
AROOMEE!!
ENOUGH! WHAT WILL IT BE?! LIFE OR DEATH?!
DON'T... GIVE...

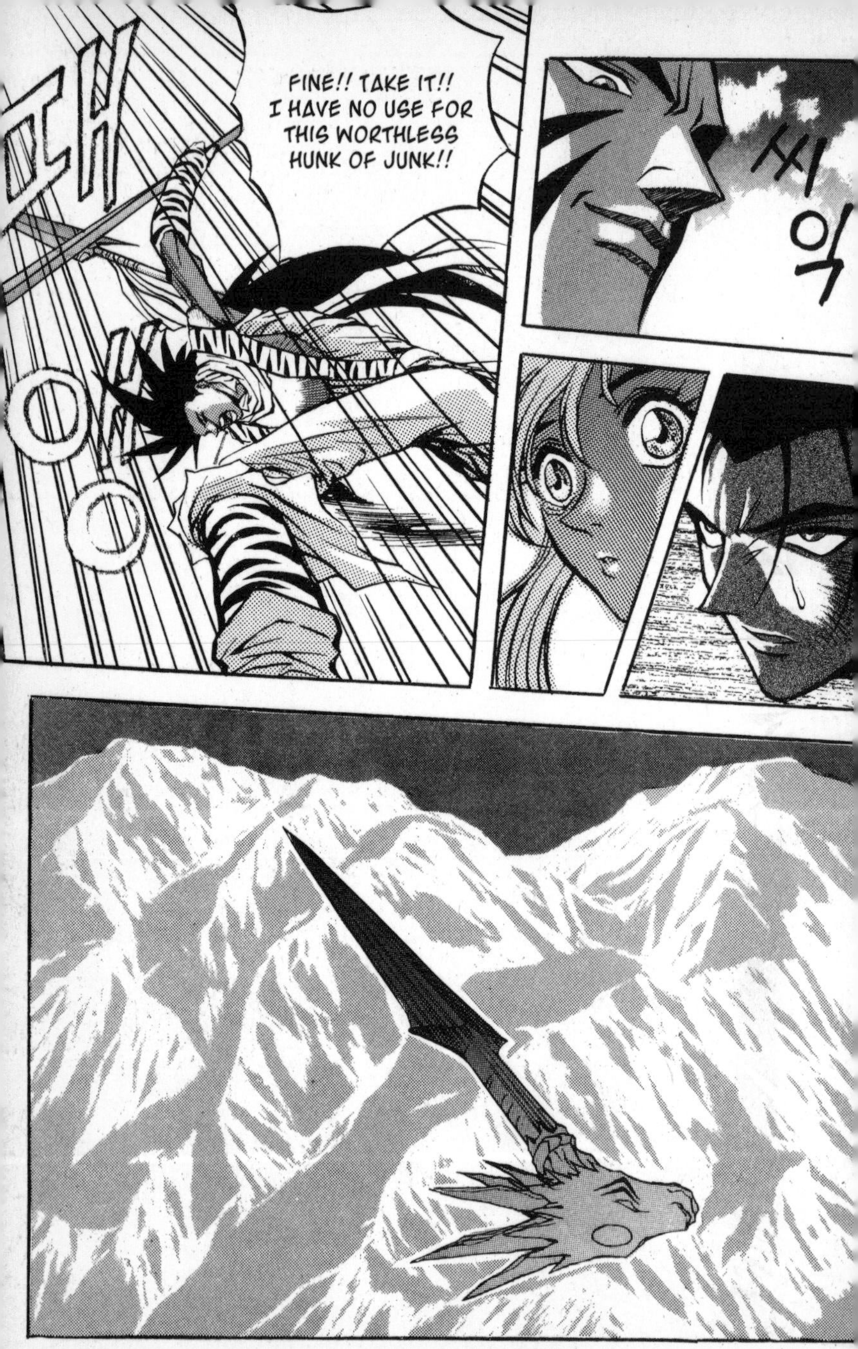
FINE!! TAKE IT!! I HAVE NO USE FOR THIS WORTHLESS HUNK OF JUNK!!

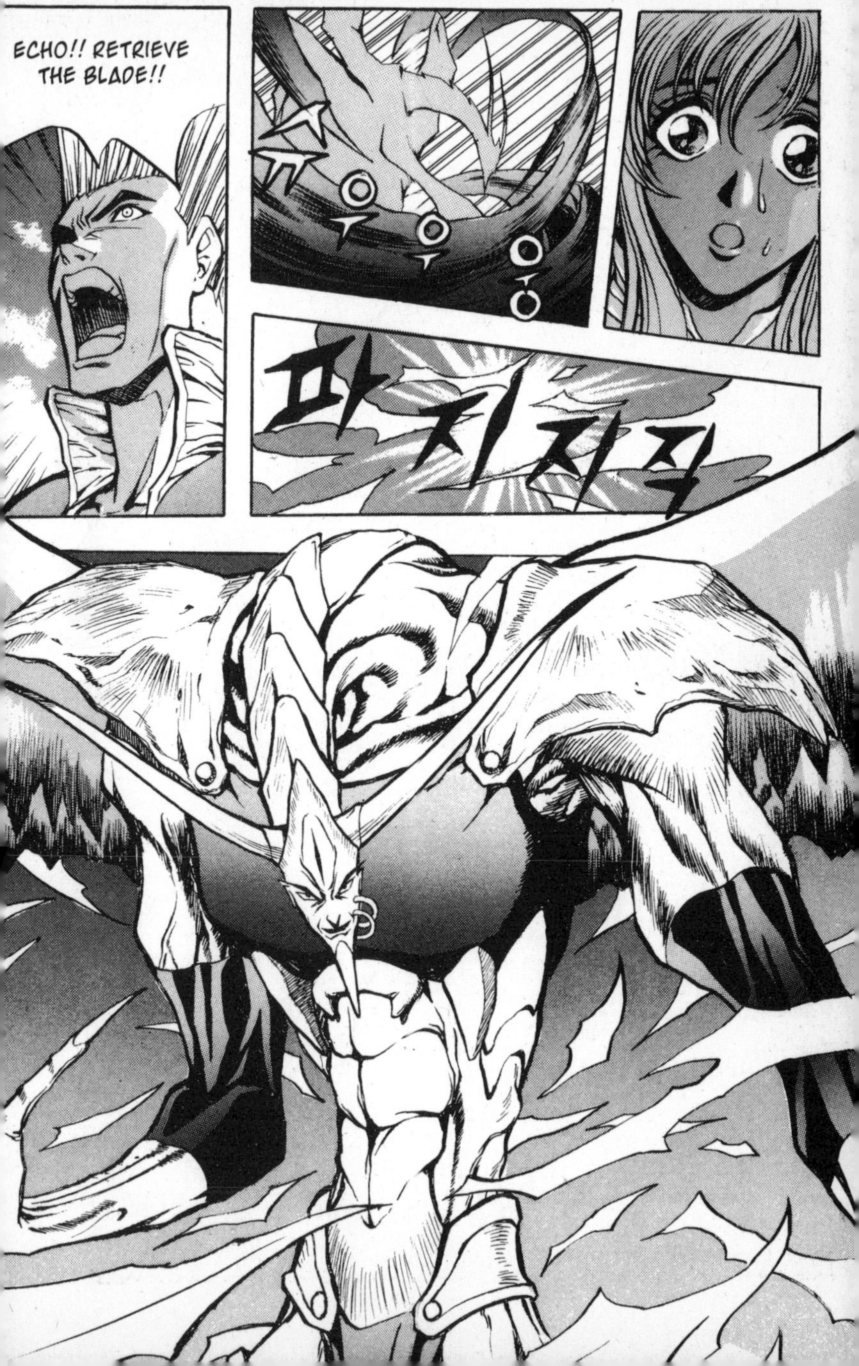
ECHO!! RETRIEVE THE BLADE!!

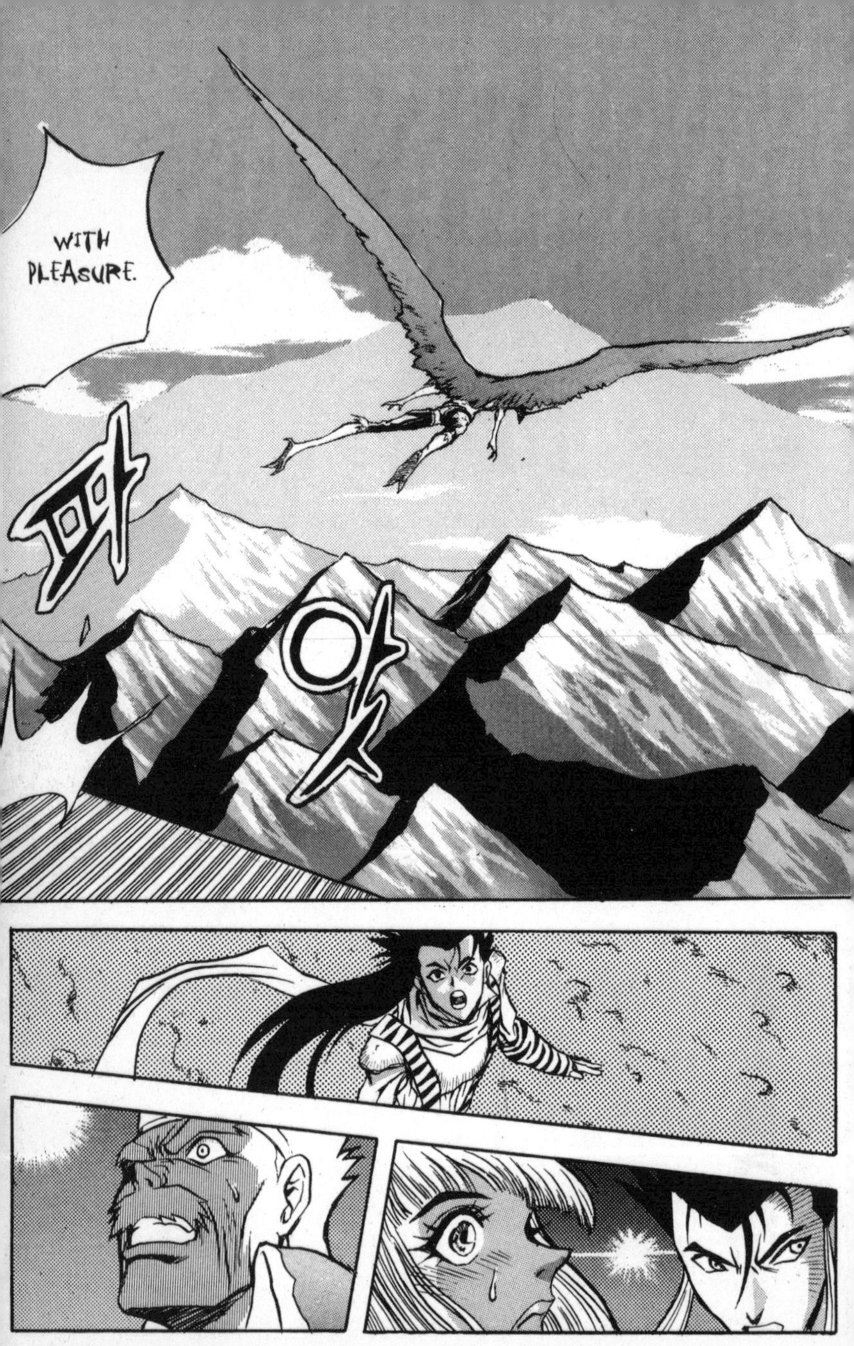
WITH PLEASURE.

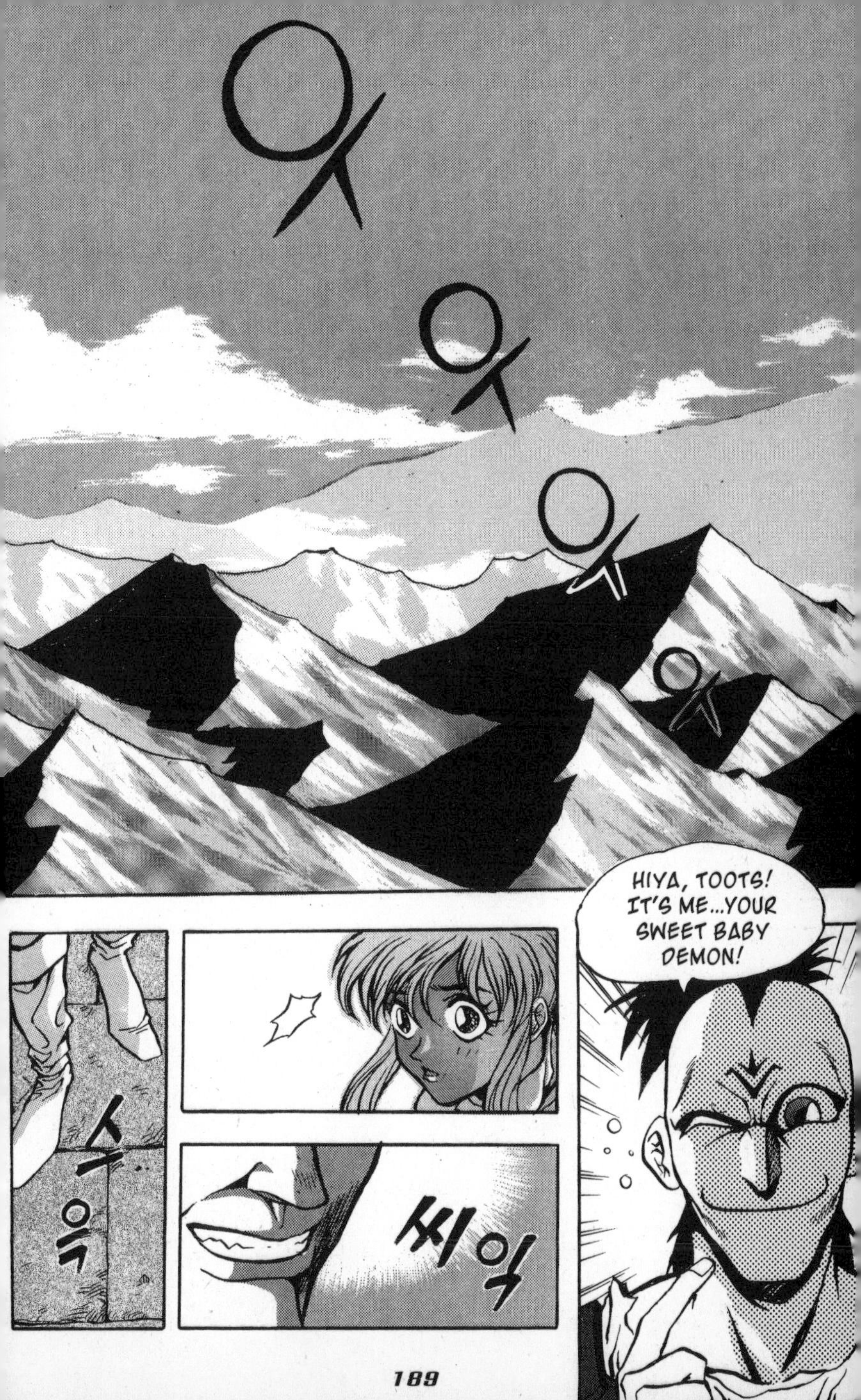
HIYA, TOOTS! IT'S ME...YOUR SWEET BABY DEMON!

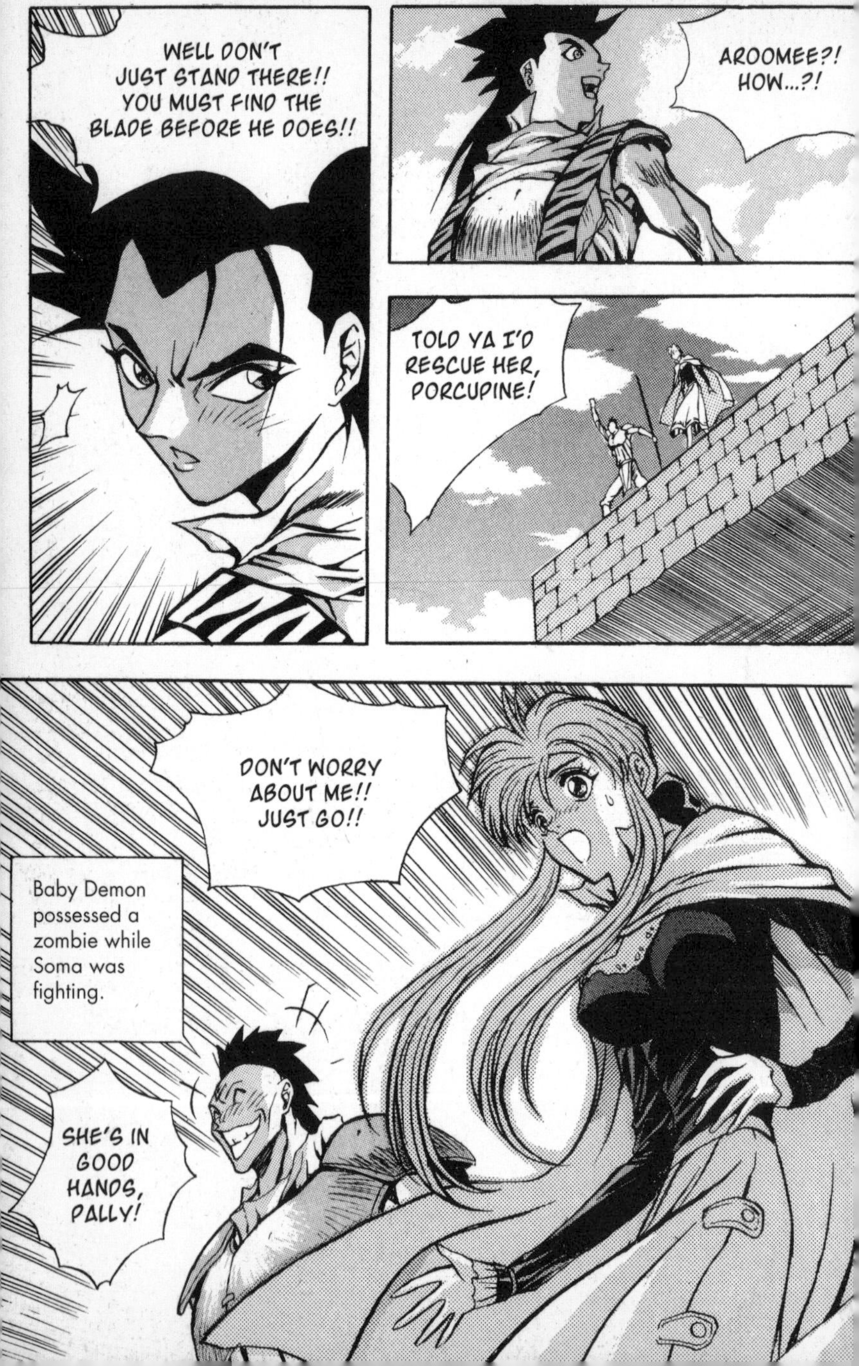
WELL DON'T JUST STAND THERE!! YOU MUST FIND THE BLADE BEFORE HE DOES!!
AROOMEE?! HOW...?!
TOLD YA I'D RESCUE HER, PORCUPINE!
DON'T WORRY ABOUT ME!! JUST GO!!
Baby Demon possessed a zombie while Soma was fighting.
SHE'S IN GOOD HANDS, PALLY!

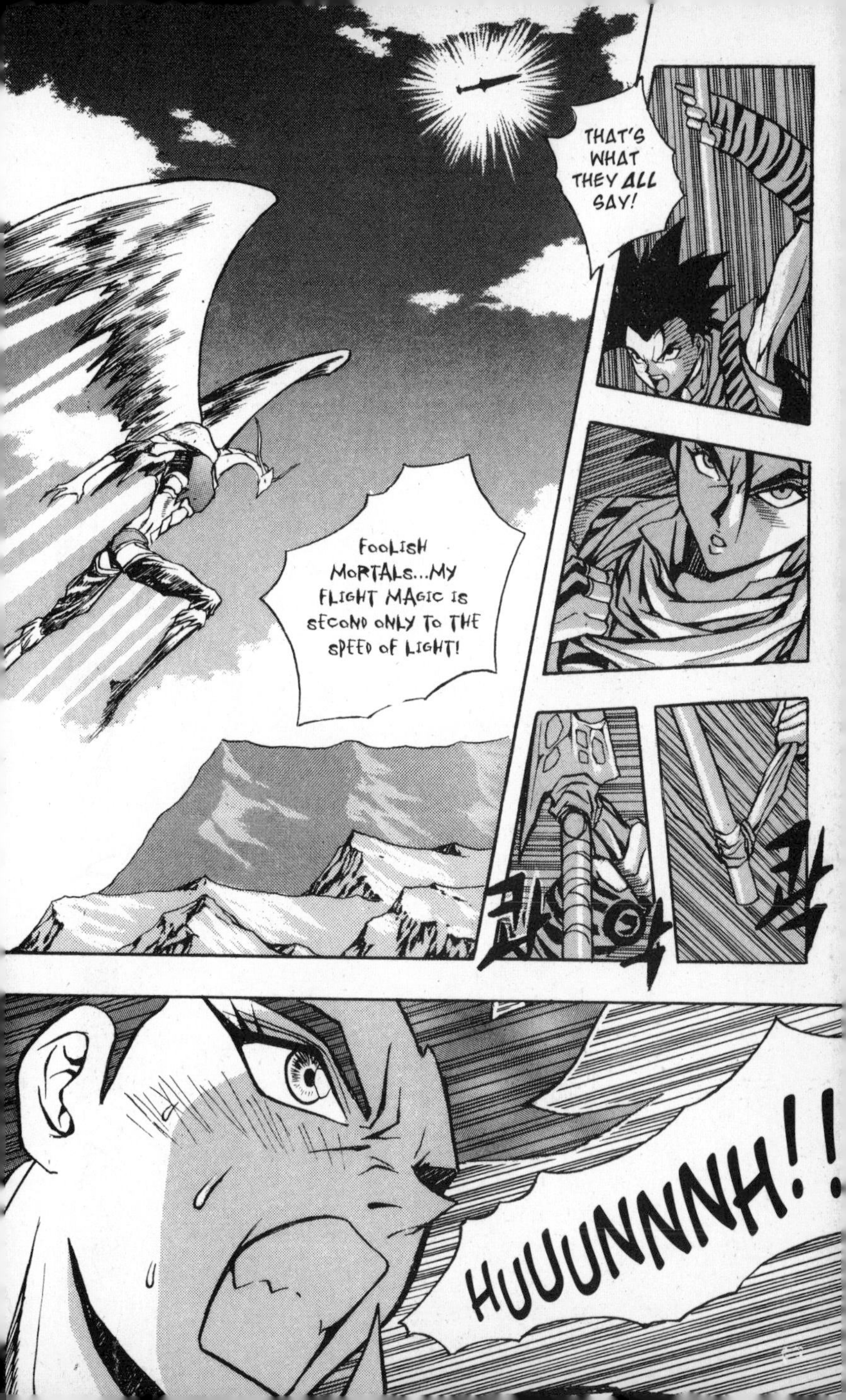
FOOLISH MORTALS...MY FLIGHT MAGIC IS SECOND ONLY TO THE SPEED OF LIGHT!
THAT'S WHAT THEY ALL SAY!
HUUUNNNH!!

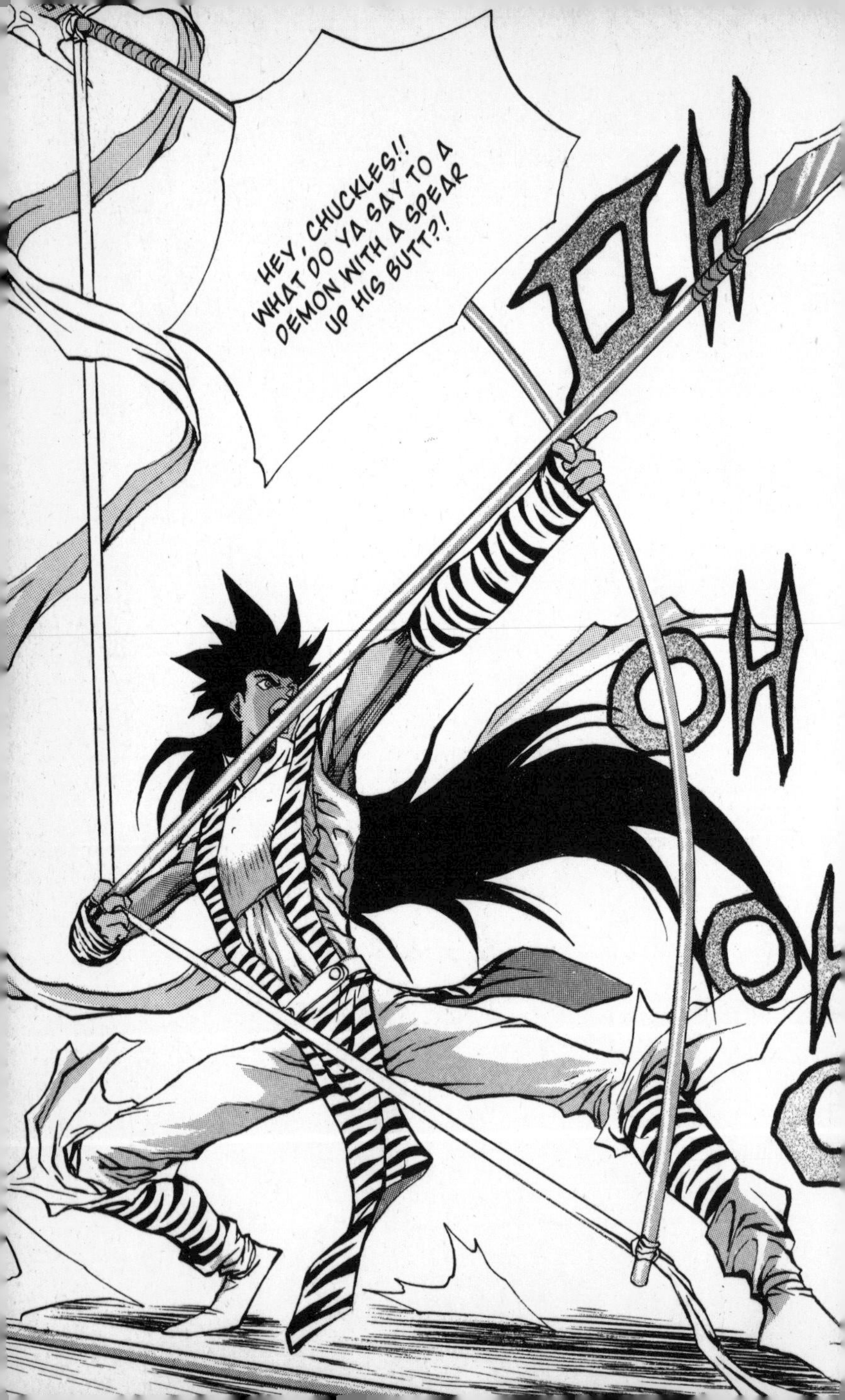
HEY, CHUCKLES!! WHAT DO YA SAY TO A DEMON WITH A SPEAR UP HIS BUTT?!
HOOOO

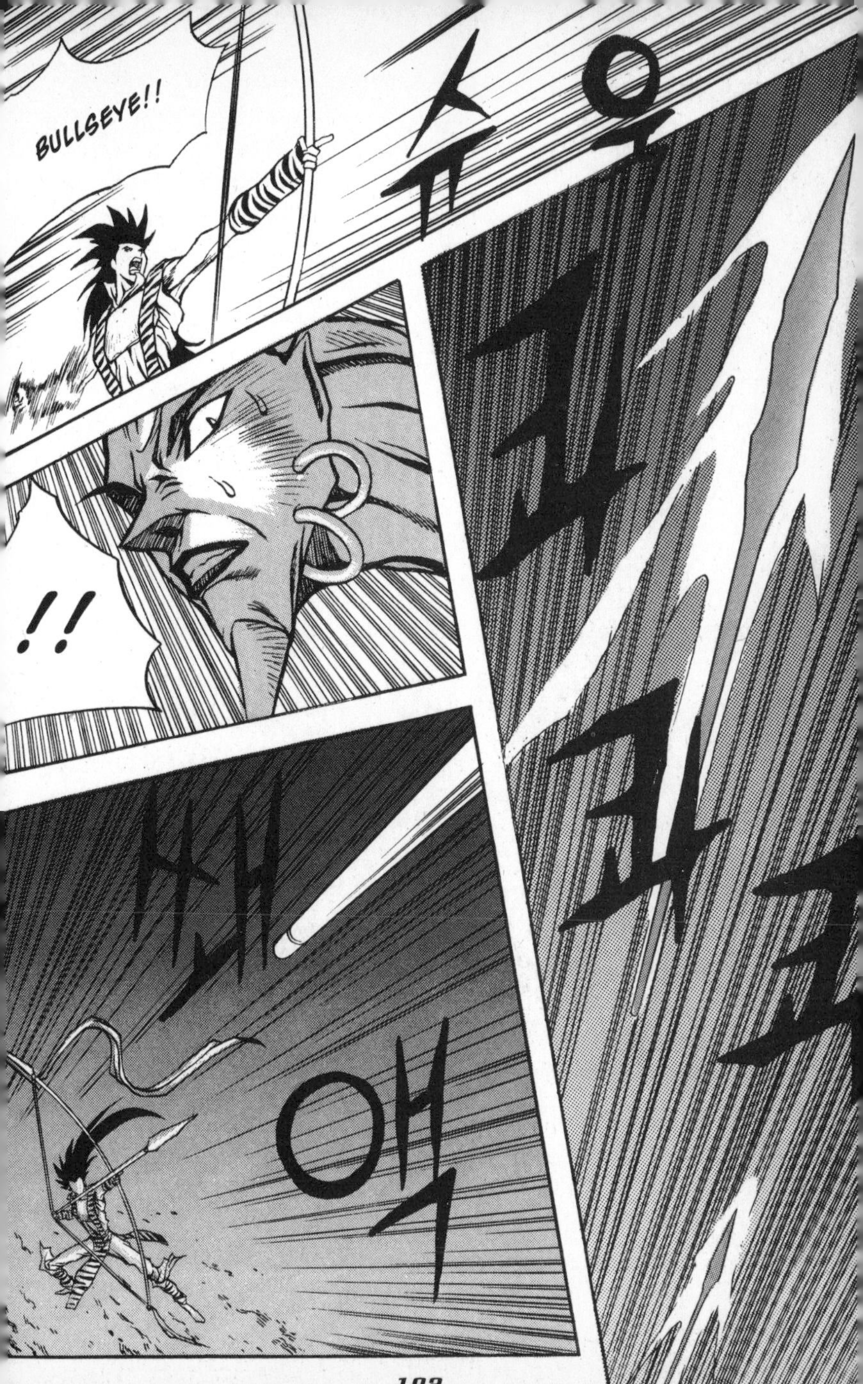
BULLSEYE!!
!!

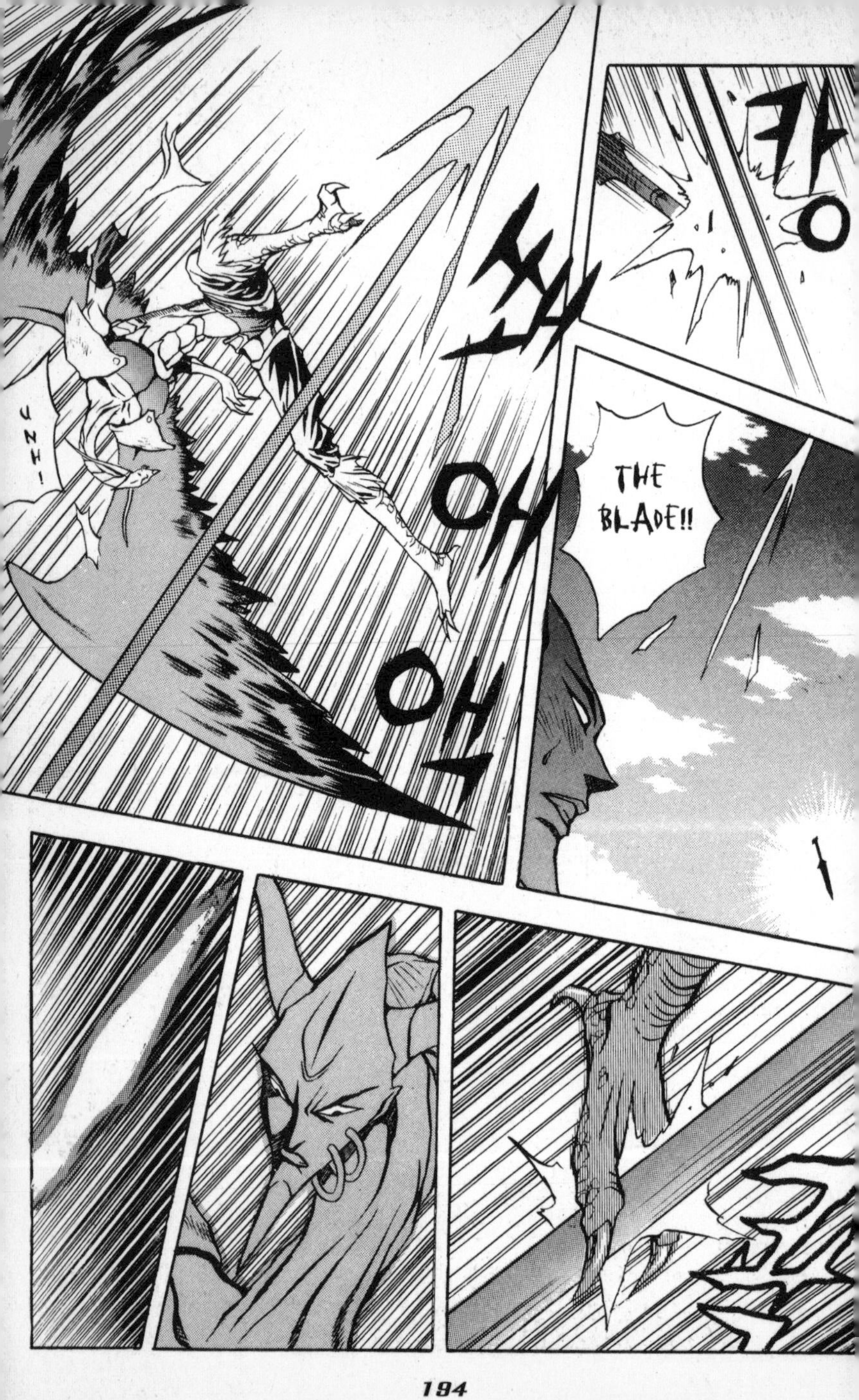
UNH!
THE BLADE!!

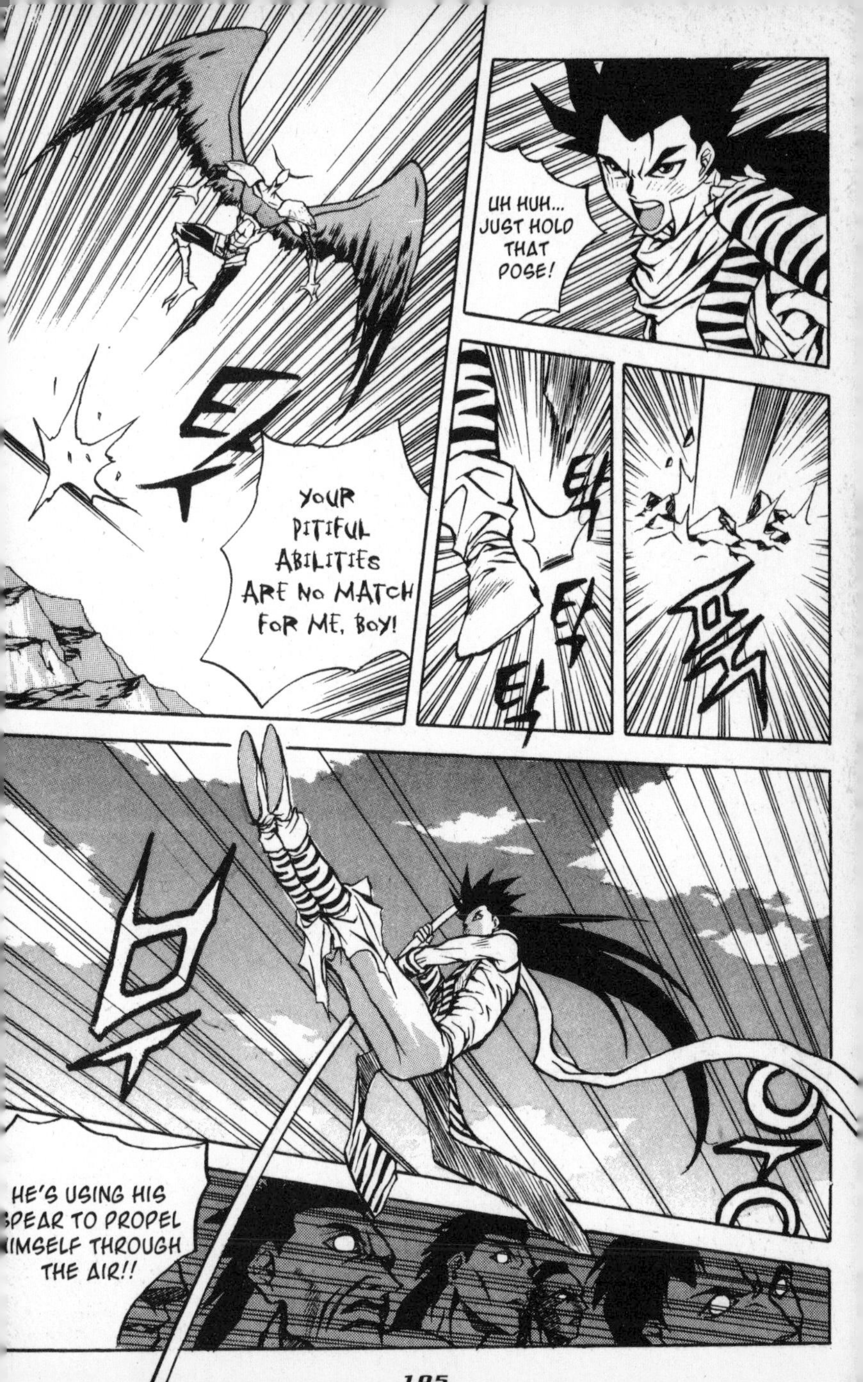
YOUR PITIFUL ABILITIES ARE NO MATCH FOR ME, BOY!
UH HUH... JUST HOLD THAT POSE!
HE'S USING HIS SPEAR TO PROPEL HIMSELF THROUGH THE AIR!!

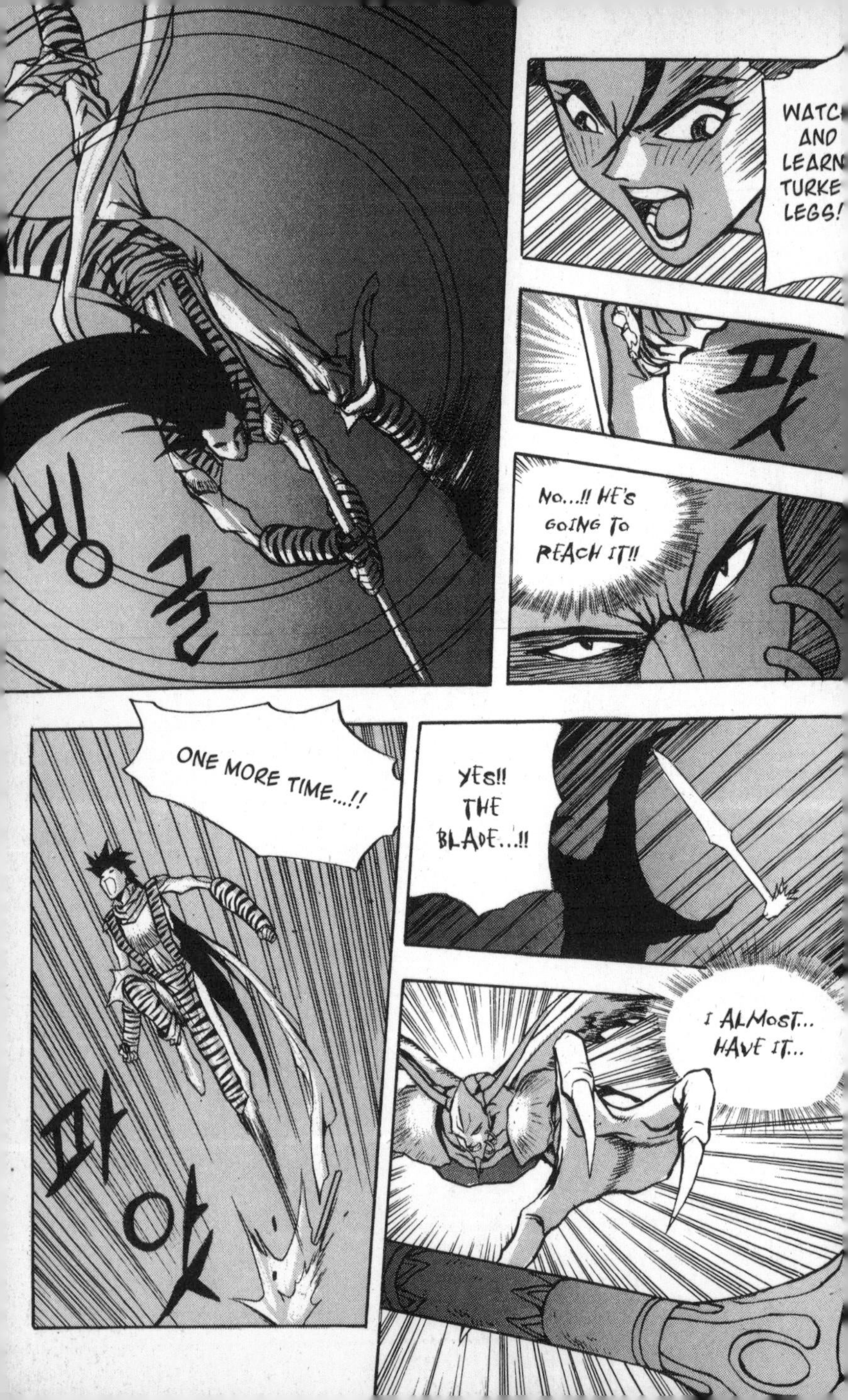

WATC AND LEARN TURKE LEGS!
NO...!! HE'S GOING TO REACH IT!!
ONE MORE TIME...!!
YES!! THE BLADE...!!
I ALMOST... HAVE IT...

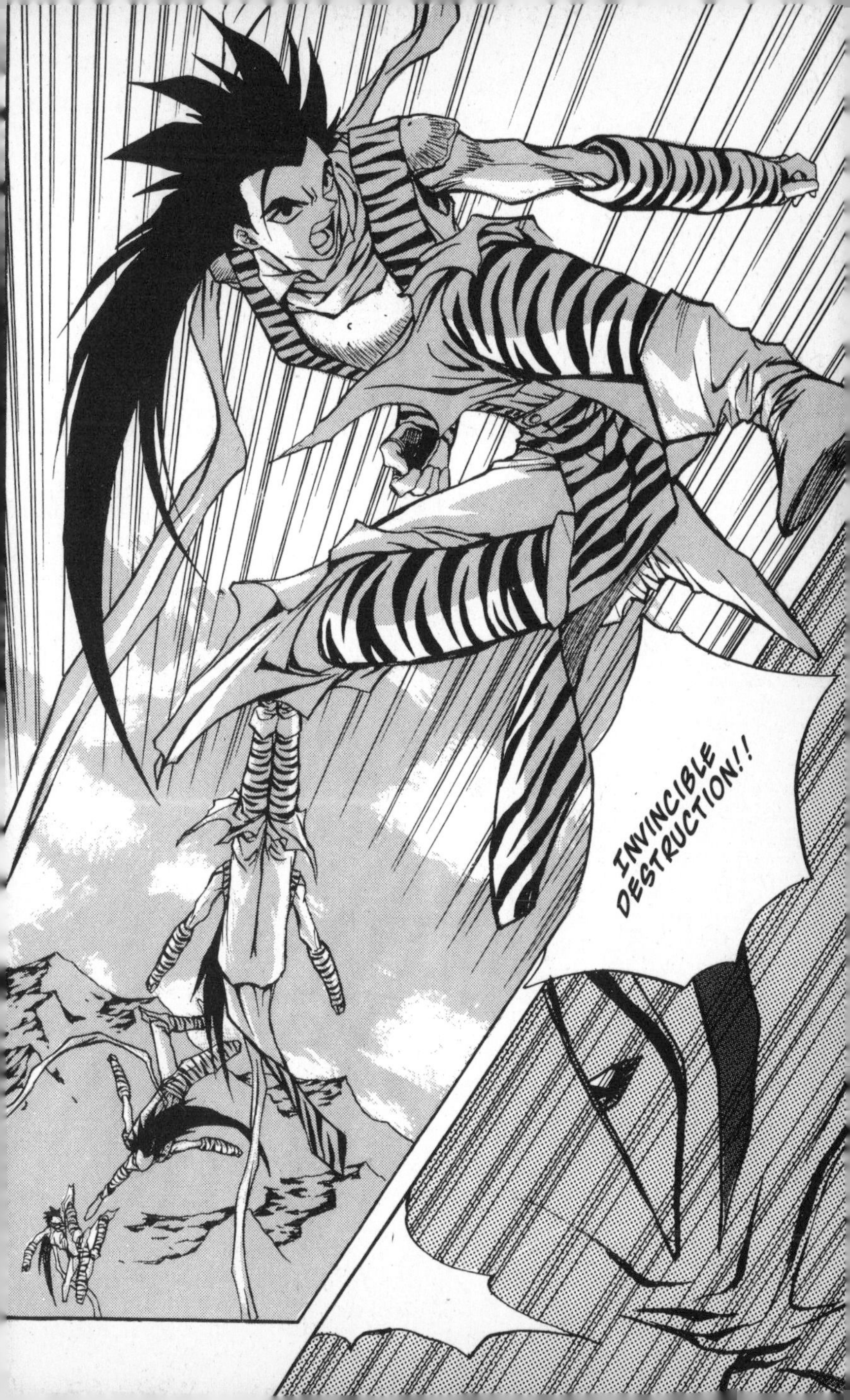
INVINCIBLE DESTRUCTION!!

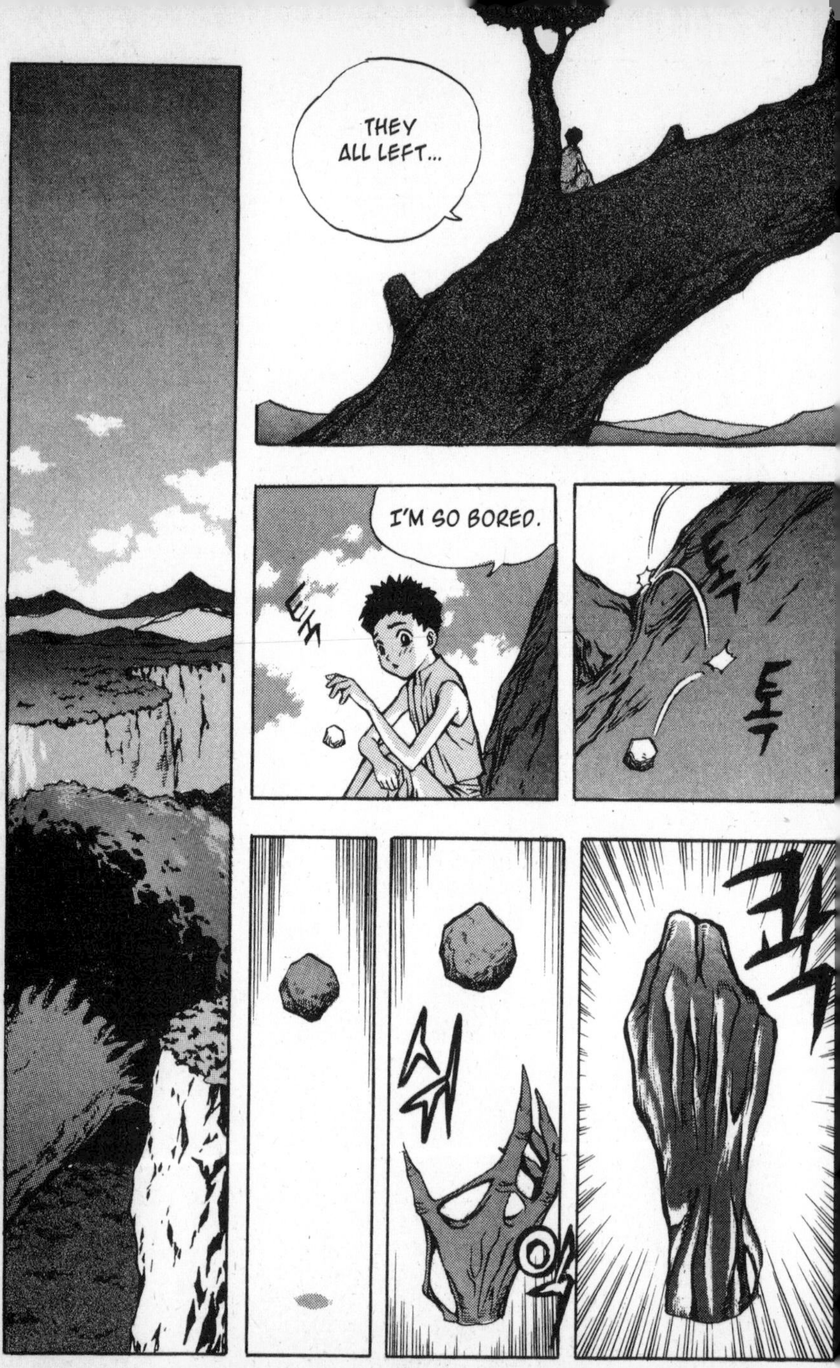
THEY ALL LEFT...
I'M SO BORED.

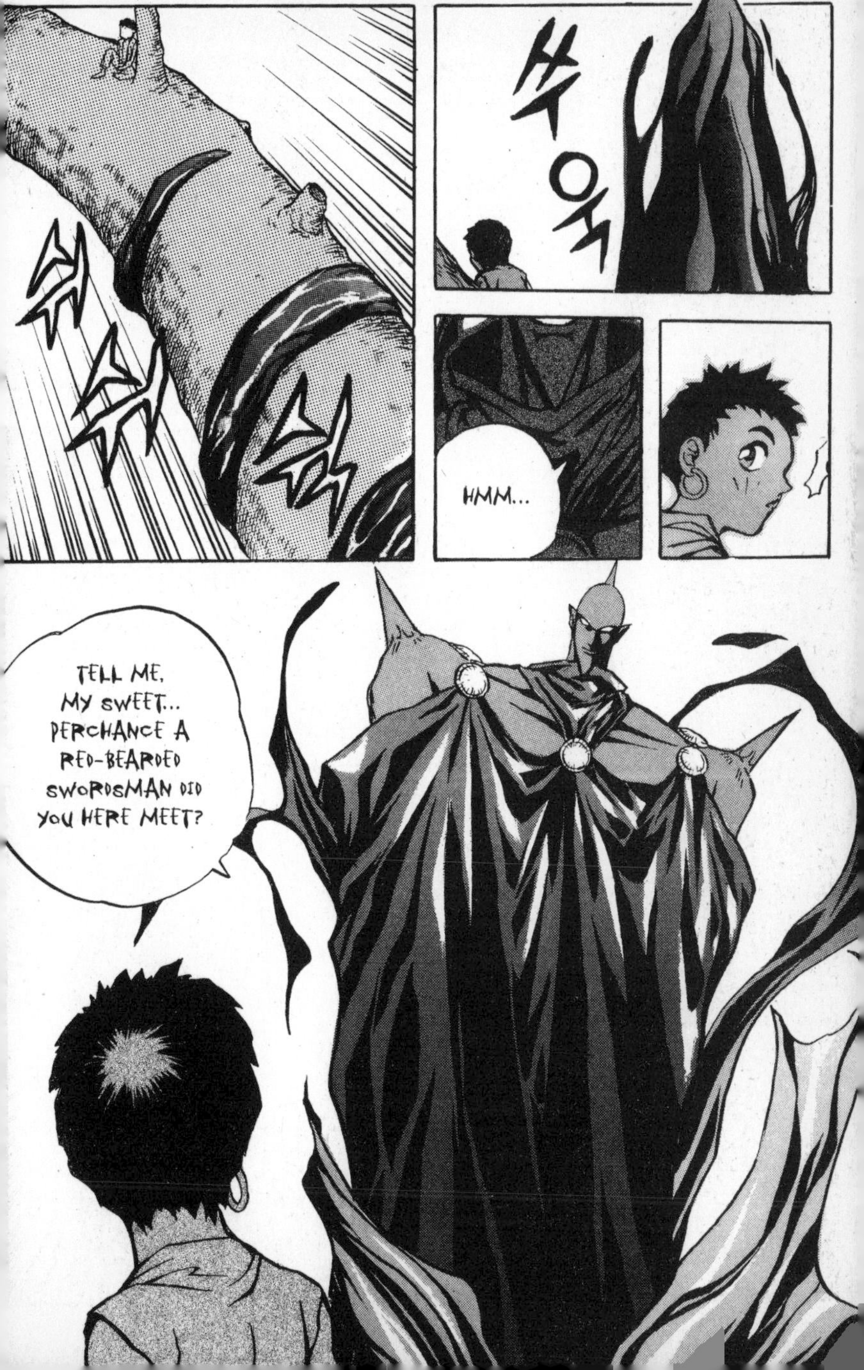
HMM...
TELL ME, MY SWEET... PERCHANCE A RED-BEARDED SWORDSMAN DID YOU HERE MEET?

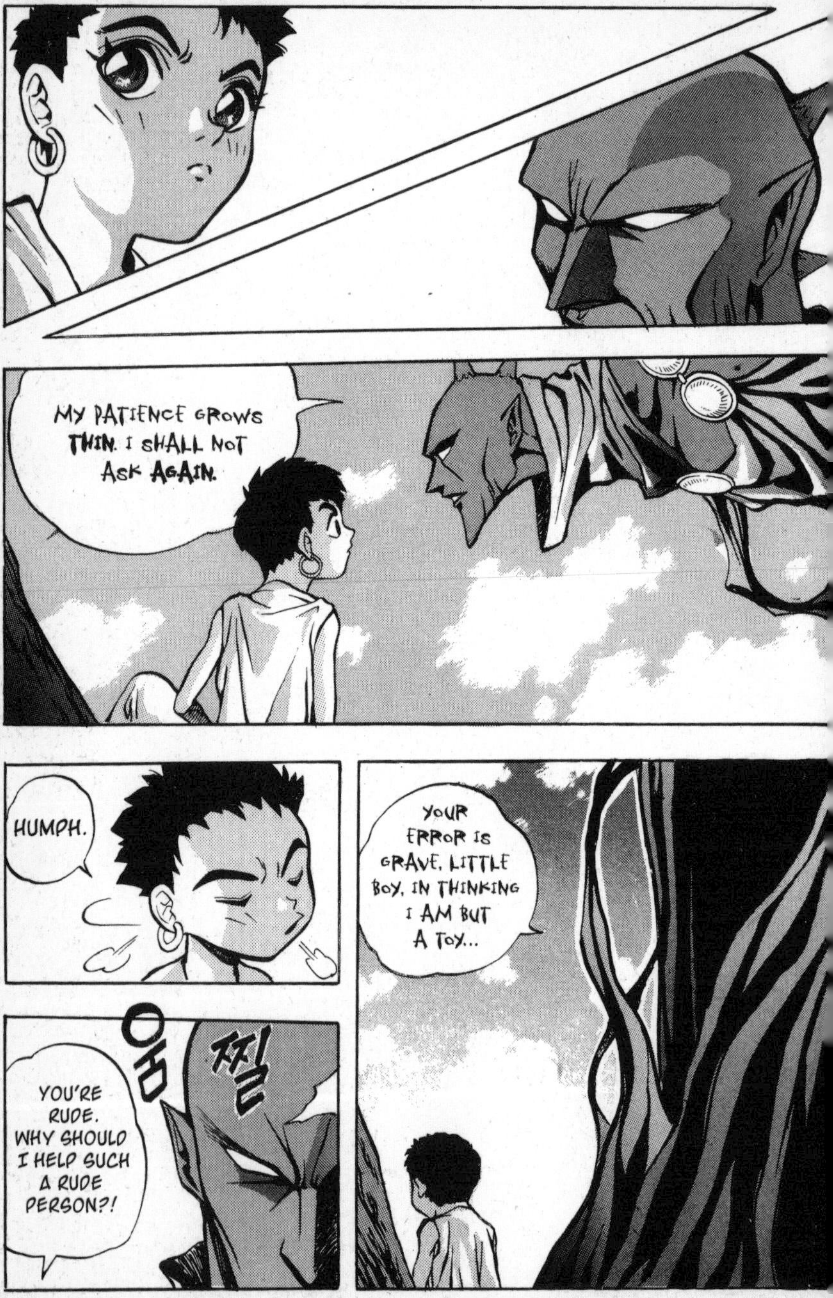
MY PATIENCE GROWS THIN. I SHALL NOT ASK AGAIN.
HUMPH.
YOUR ERROR IS GRAVE, LITTLE BOY, IN THINKING I AM BUT A TOY...
욱
찔
YOU'RE RUDE. WHY SHOULD I HELP SUCH A RUDE PERSON?!

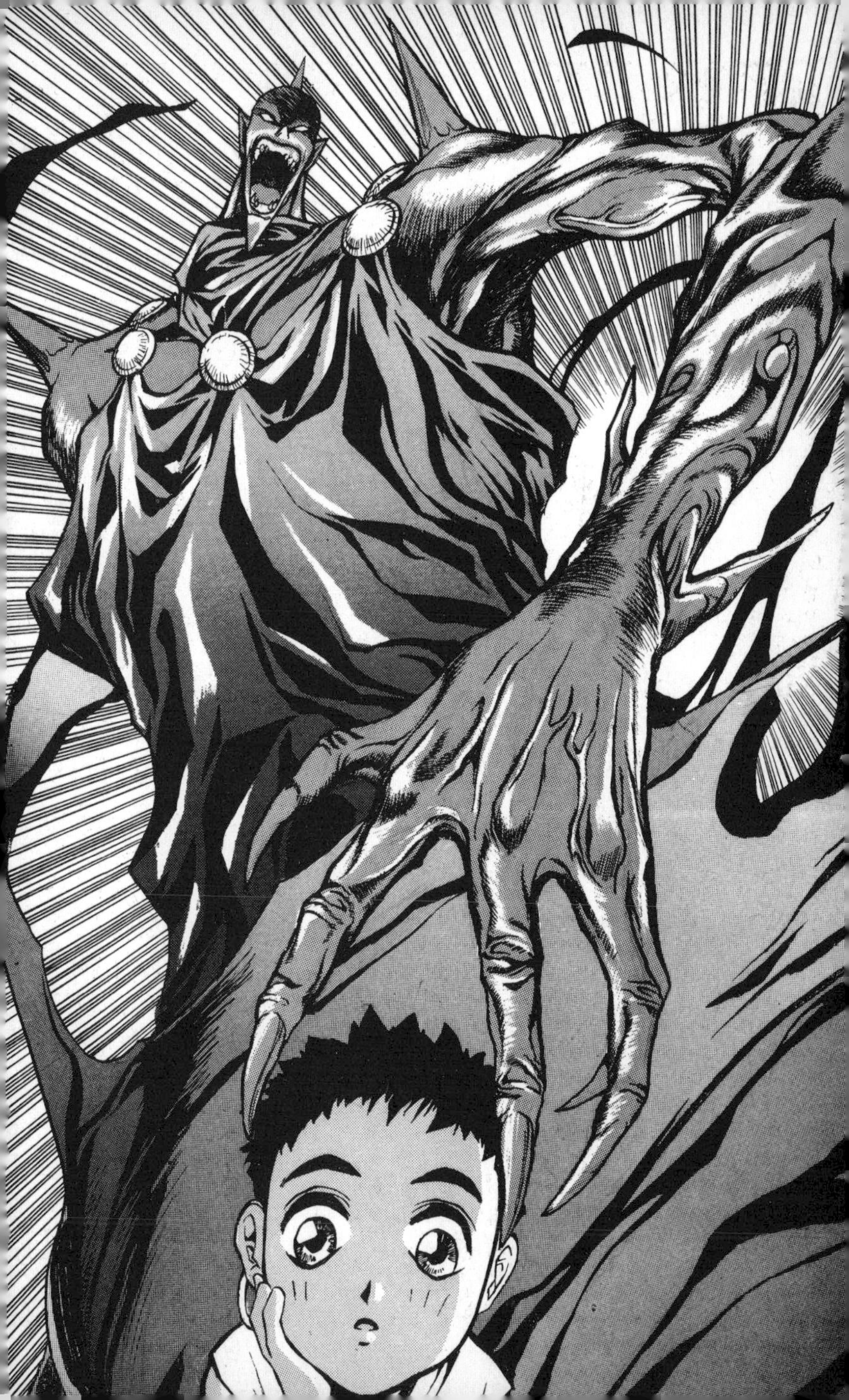

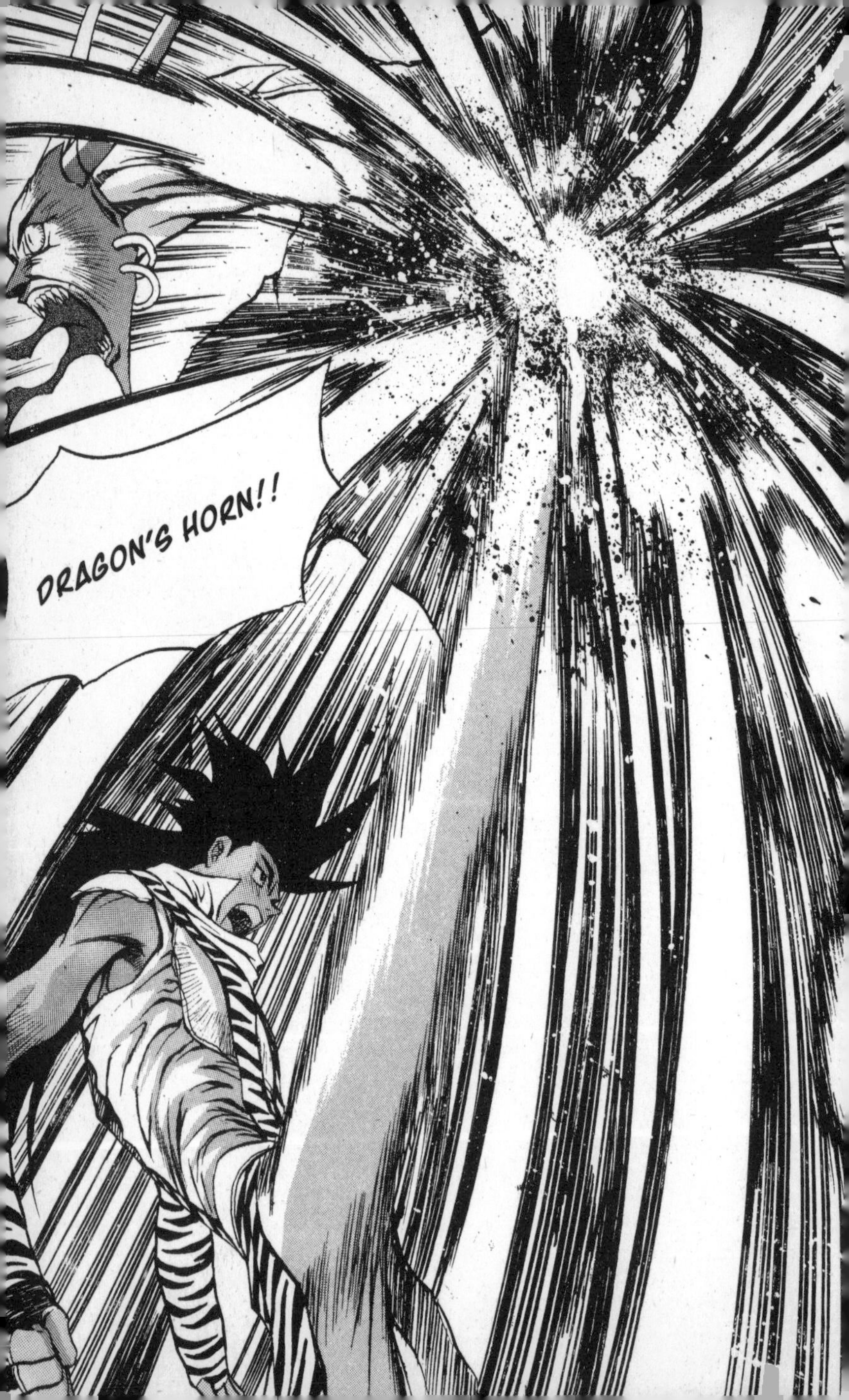
DRAGON'S HORN!!

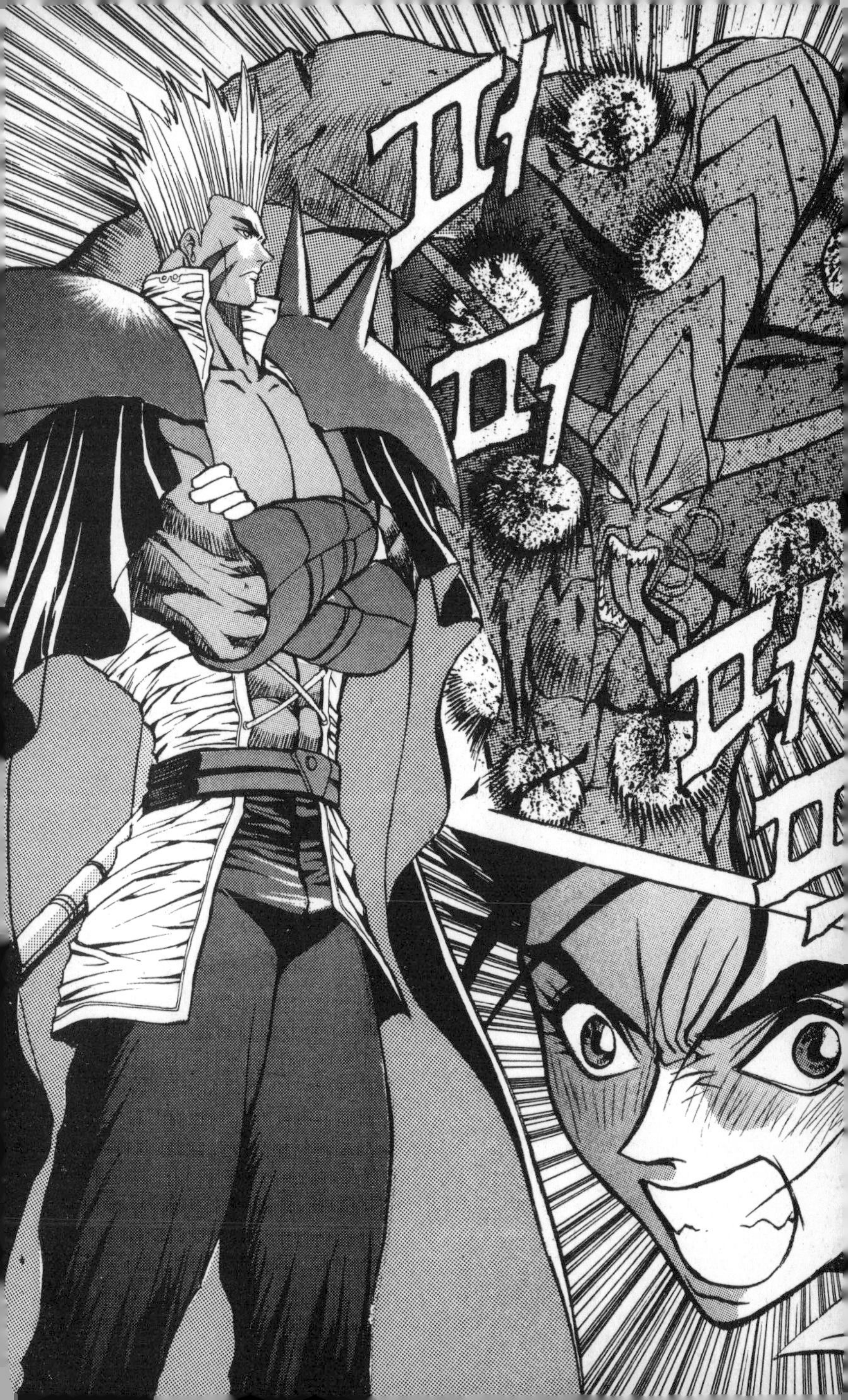

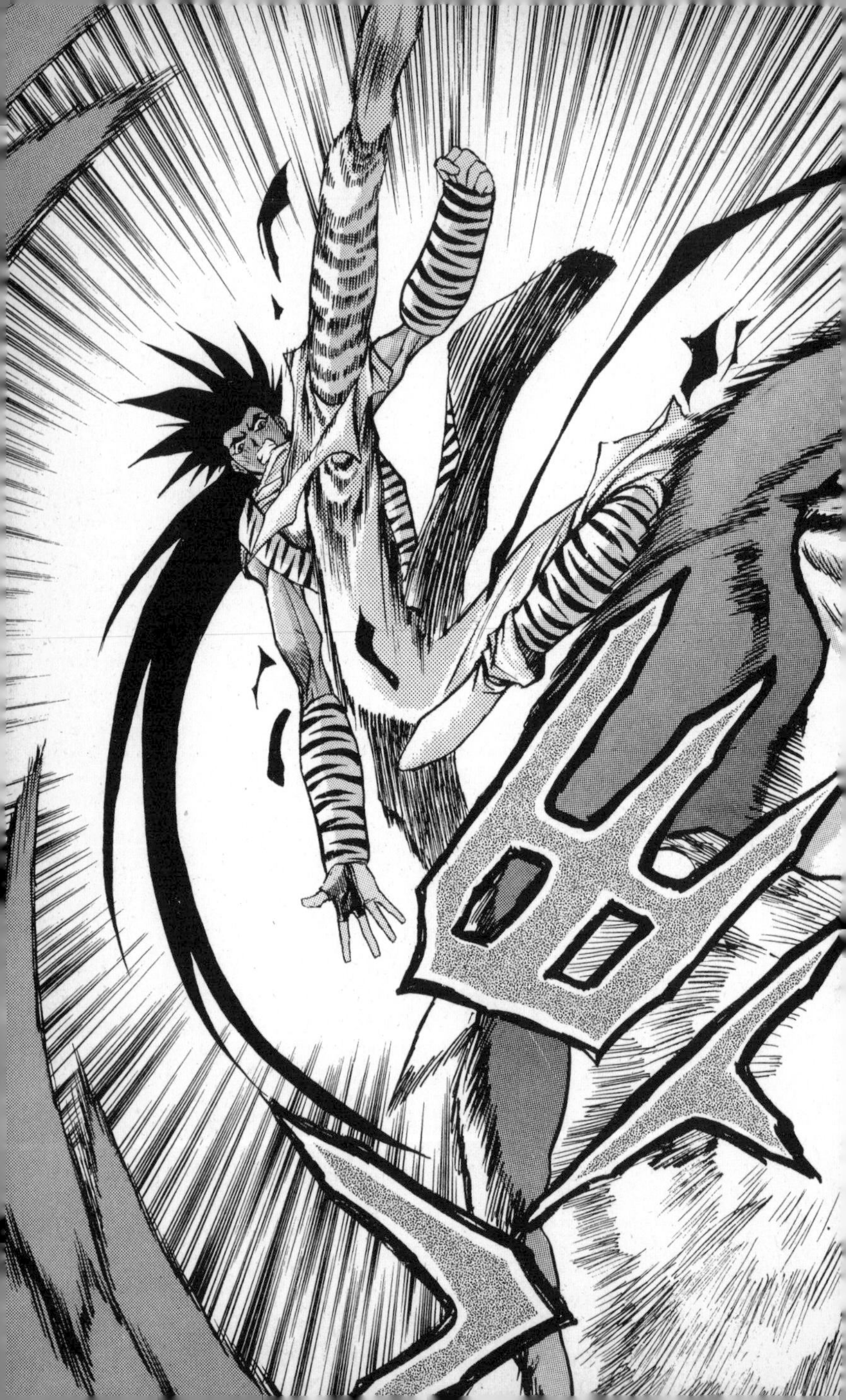

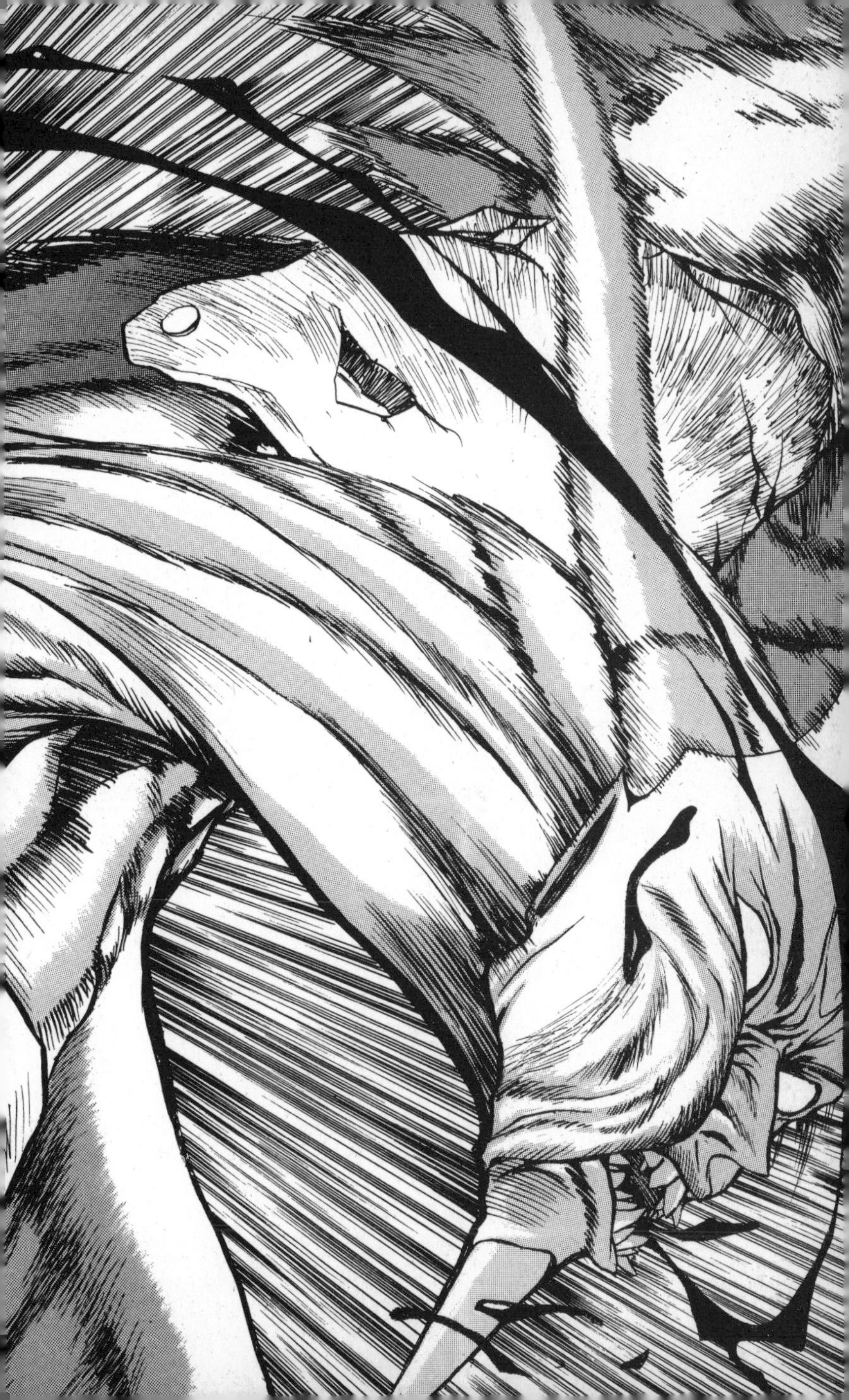

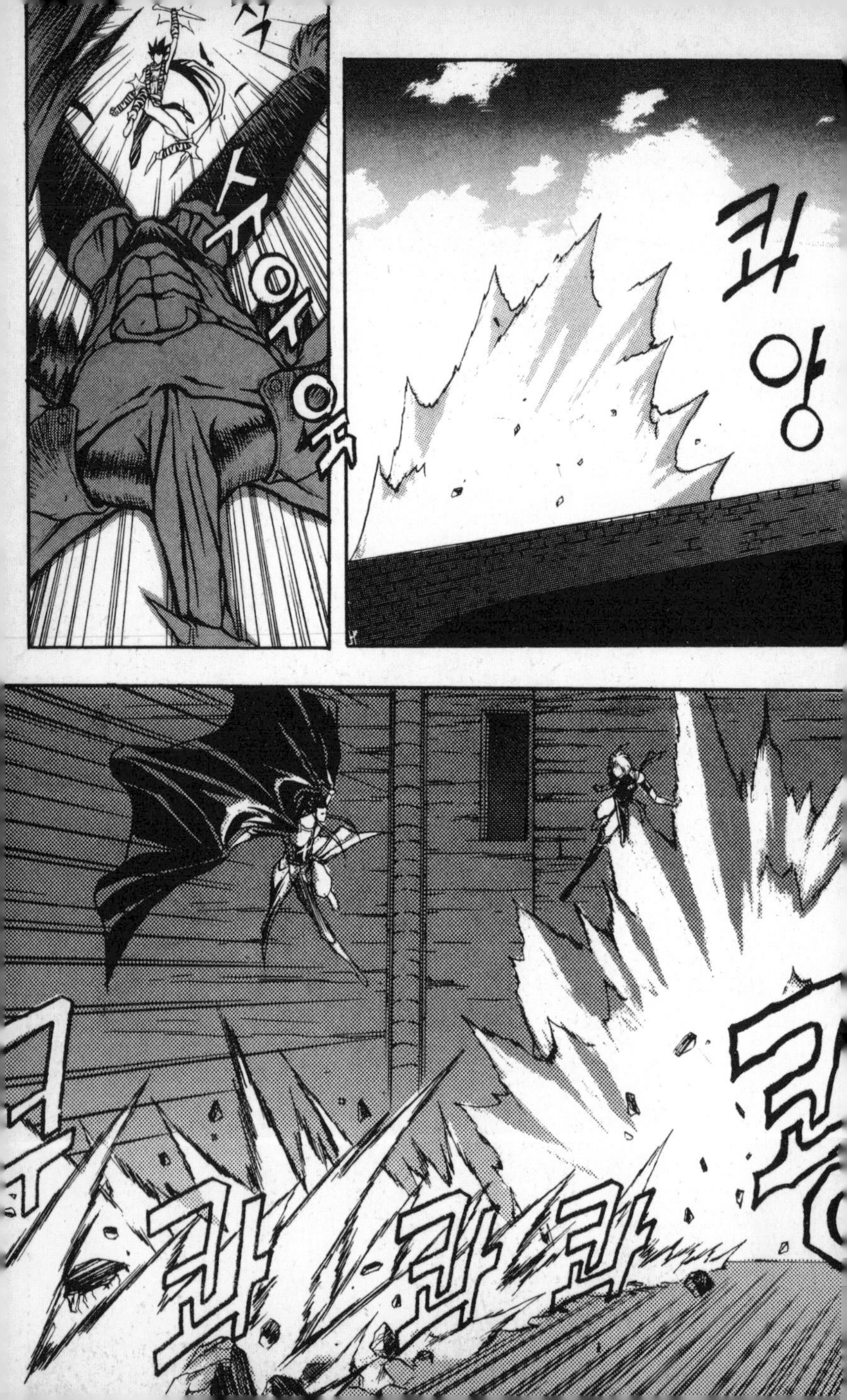
콰앙

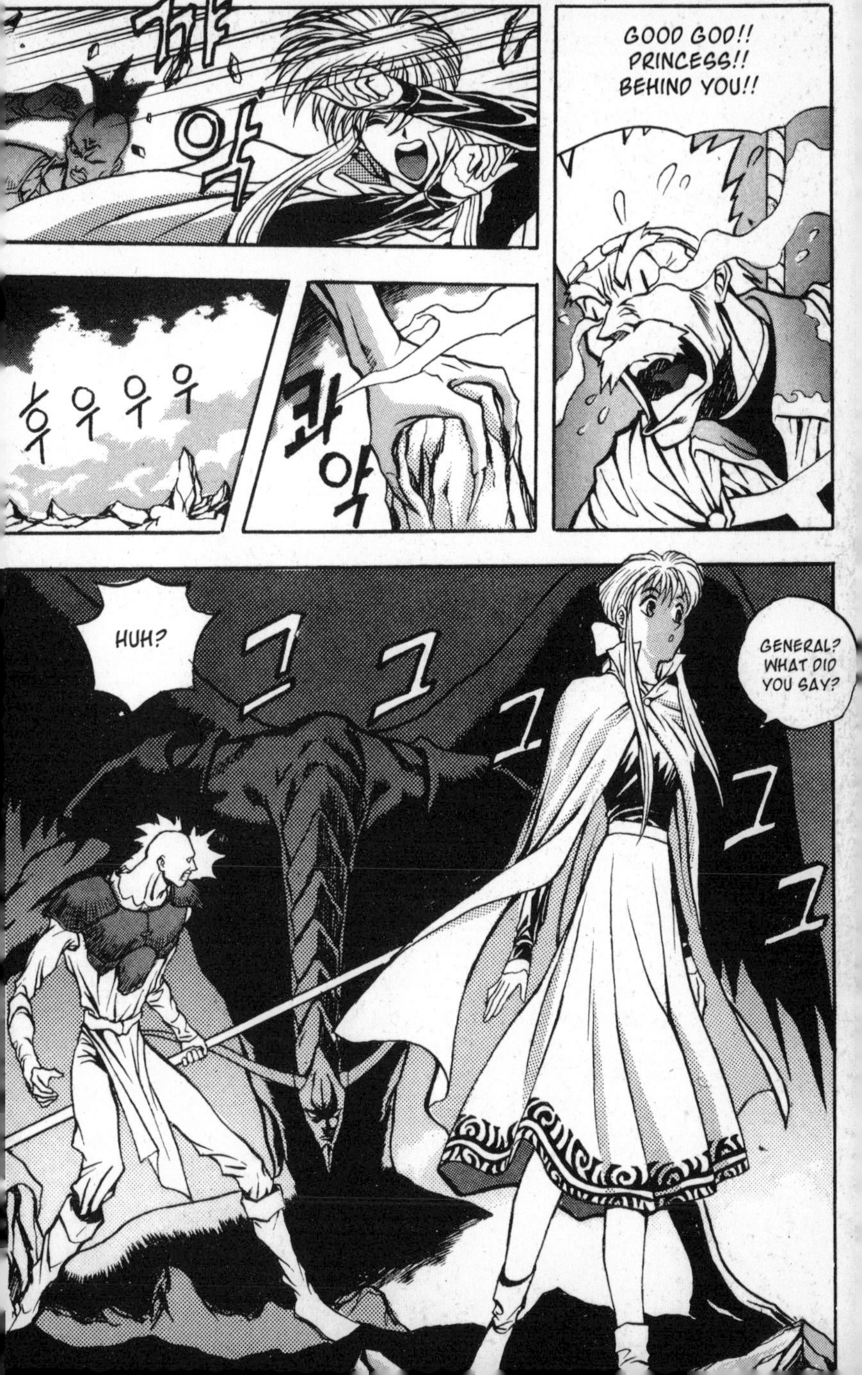

꽈악
후우우우
콰악
GOOD GOD!! PRINCESS!! BEHIND YOU!!
HUH?
GENERAL? WHAT DID YOU SAY?

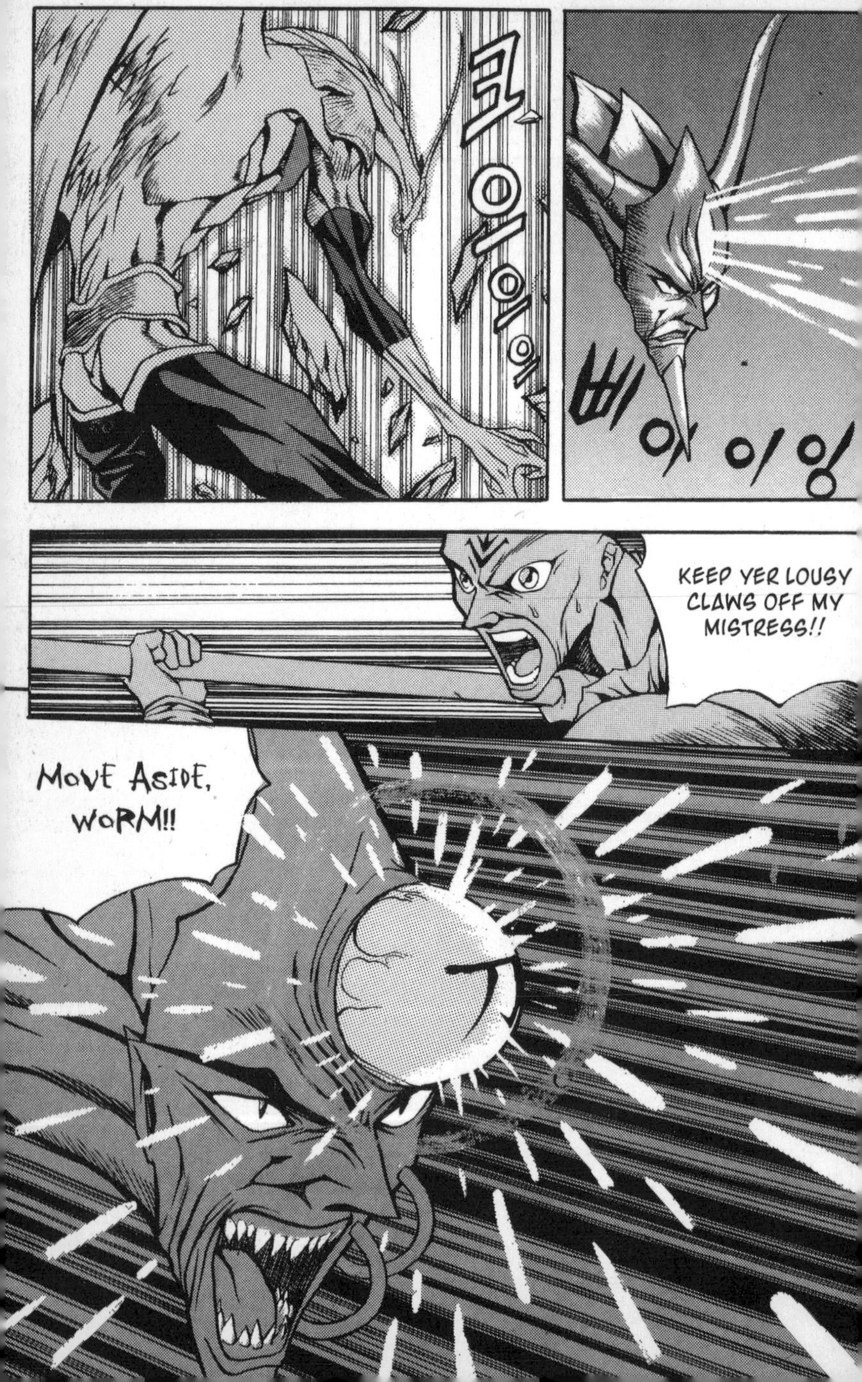
크아아아아
삐이이잉
KEEP YER LOUSY CLAWS OFF MY MISTRESS!!
MOVE ASIDE, WORM!!

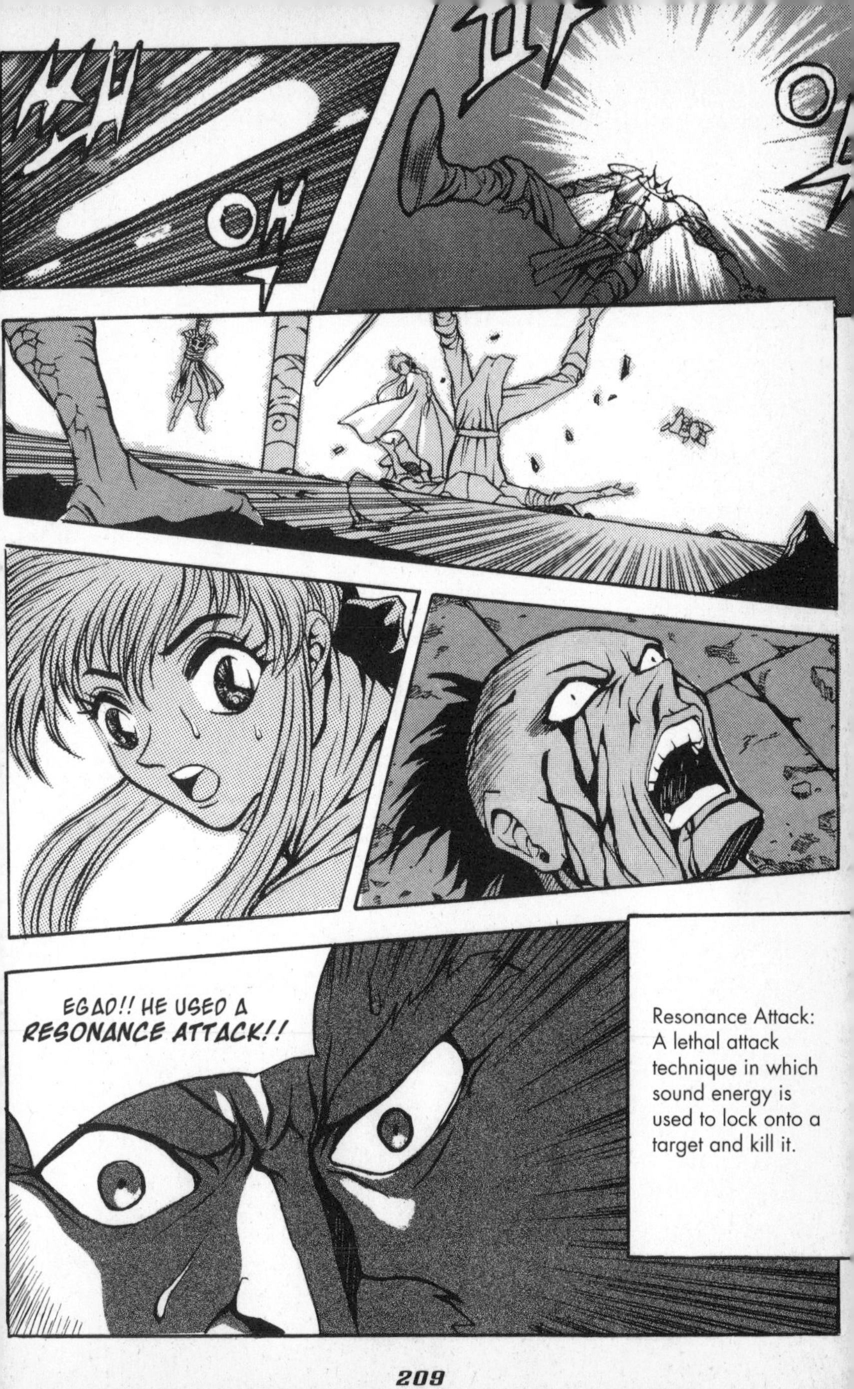
EGAD!! HE USED A RESONANCE ATTACK!!
Resonance Attack: A lethal attack technique in which sound energy is used to lock onto a target and kill it.

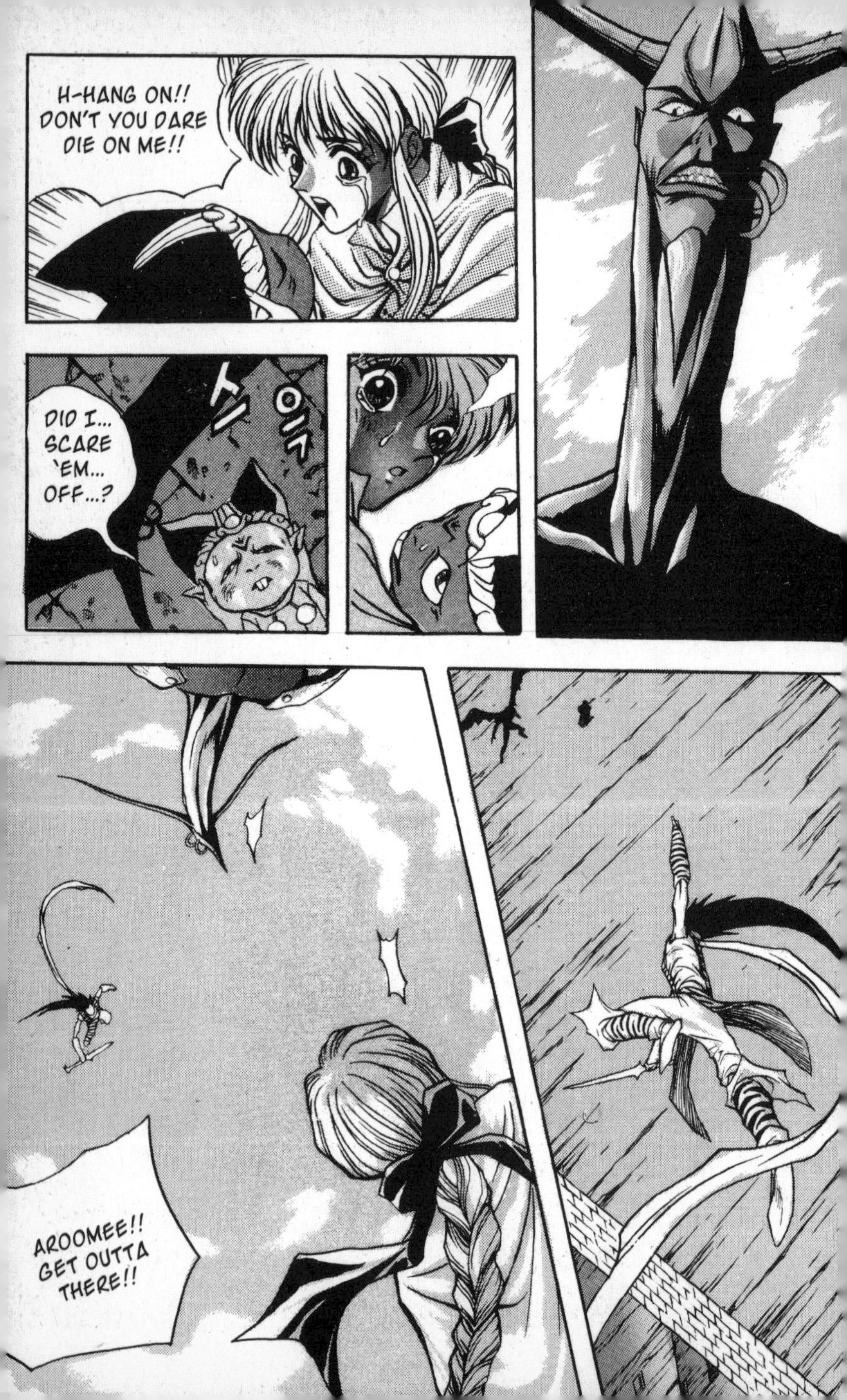
H-HANG ON!! DON'T YOU DARE DIE ON ME!!
DID I... SCARE 'EM... OFF...?
AROOMEE!! GET OUTTA THERE!!

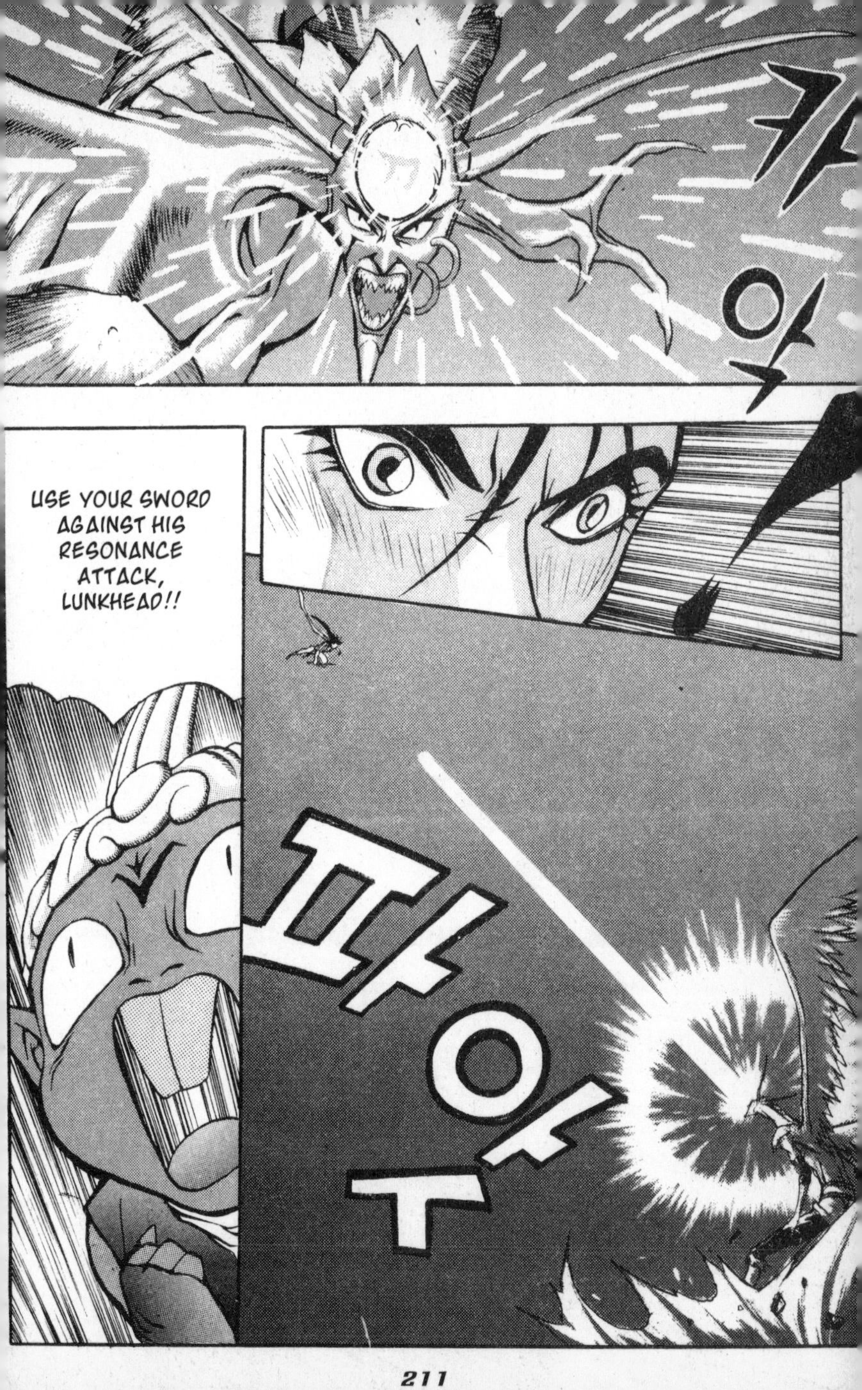
카악
USE YOUR SWORD AGAINST HIS RESONANCE ATTACK, LUNKHEAD!!
파악

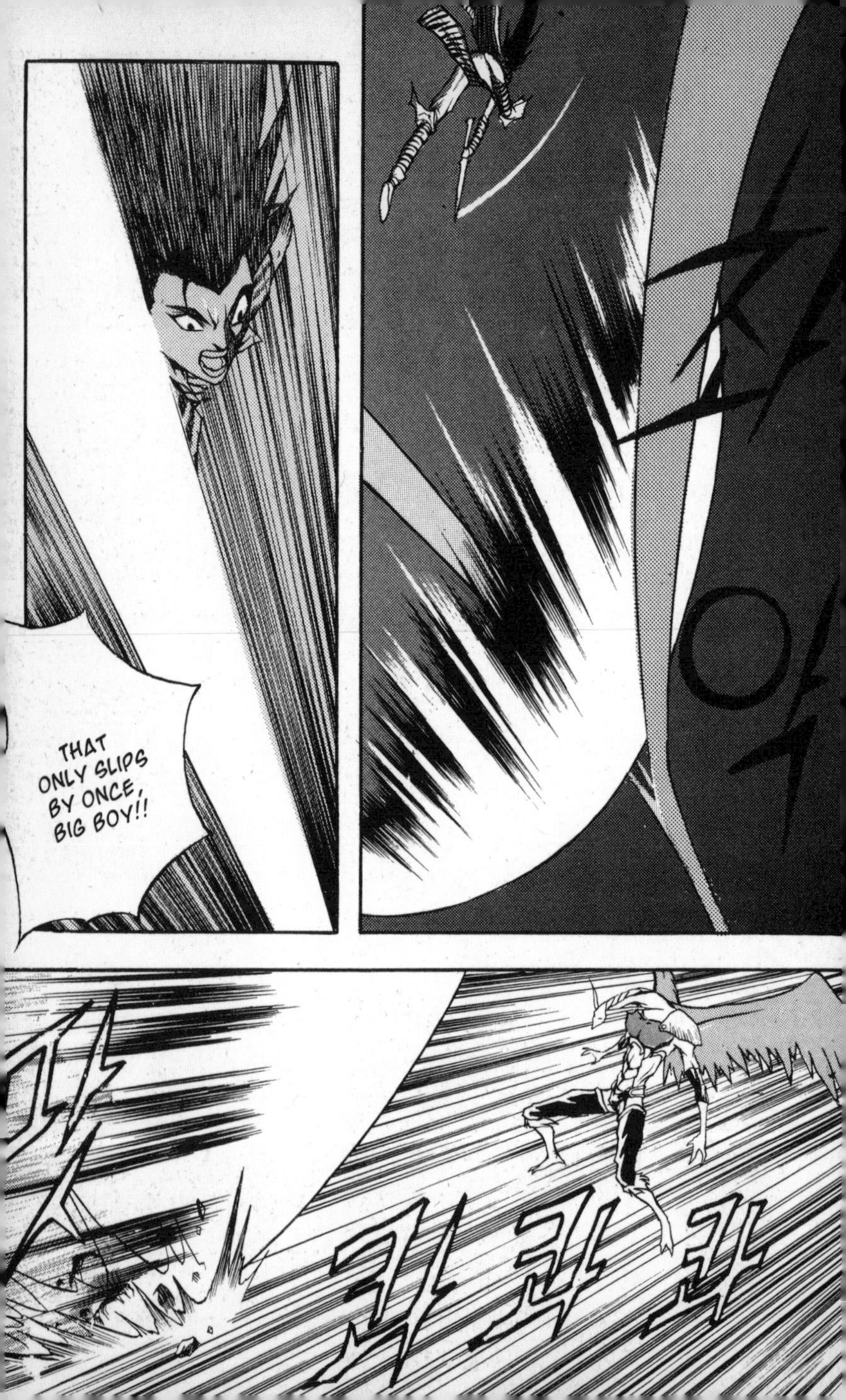
THAT ONLY SLIPS BY ONCE, BIG BOY!!

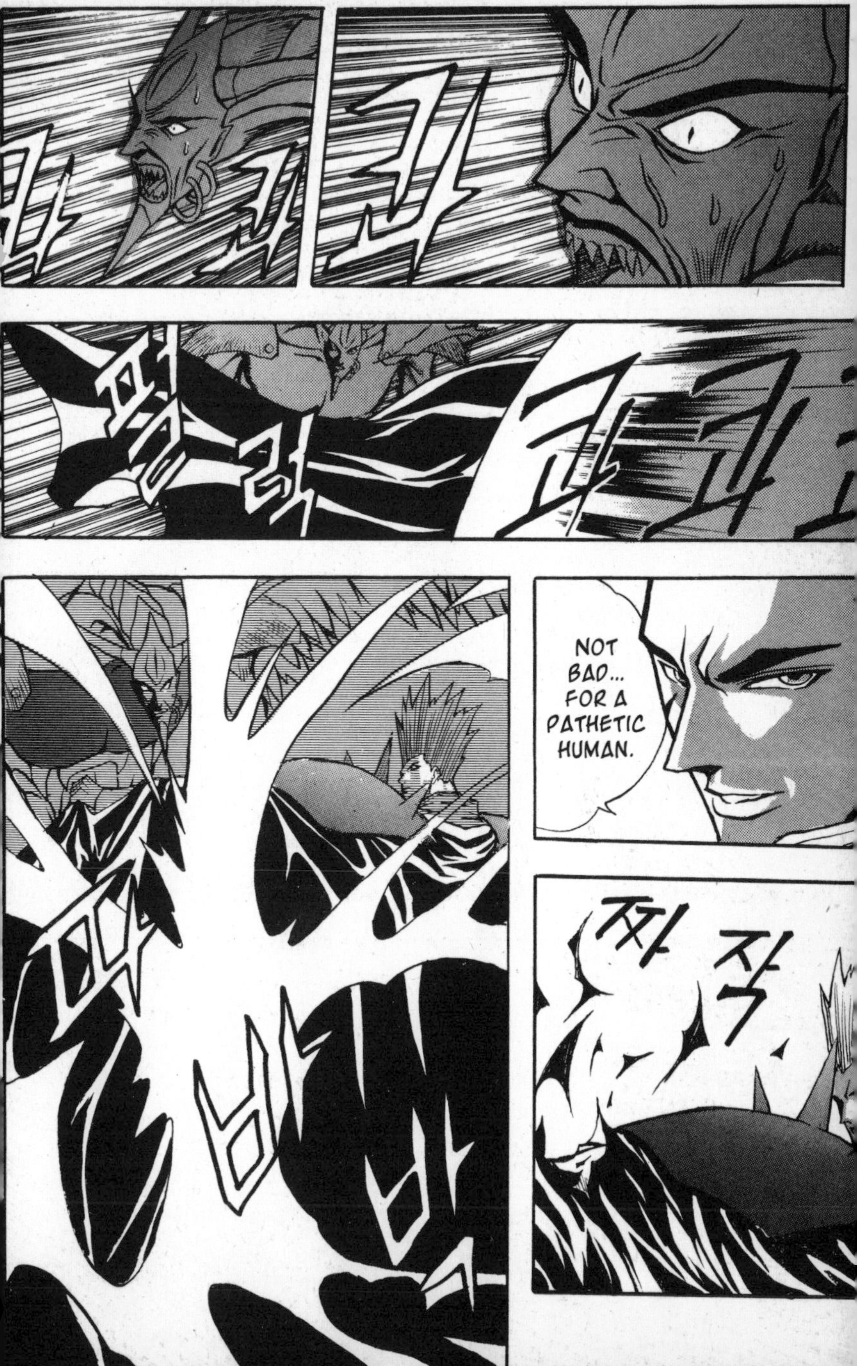
NOT BAD... FOR A PATHETIC HUMAN.

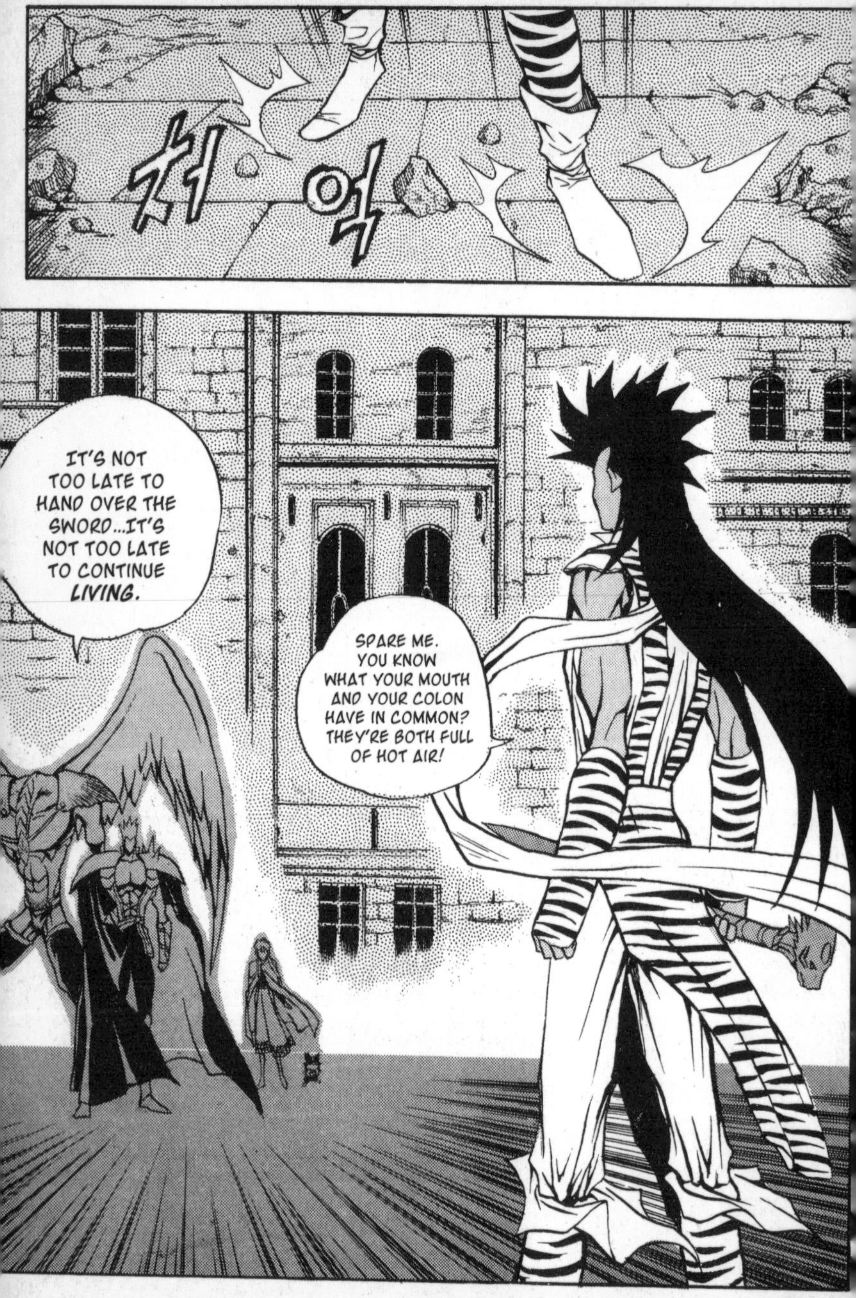
처 억
IT'S NOT TOO LATE TO HAND OVER THE SWORD...IT'S NOT TOO LATE TO CONTINUE ***LIVING.***
SPARE ME. YOU KNOW WHAT YOUR MOUTH AND YOUR COLON HAVE IN COMMON? THEY'RE BOTH FULL OF HOT AIR!

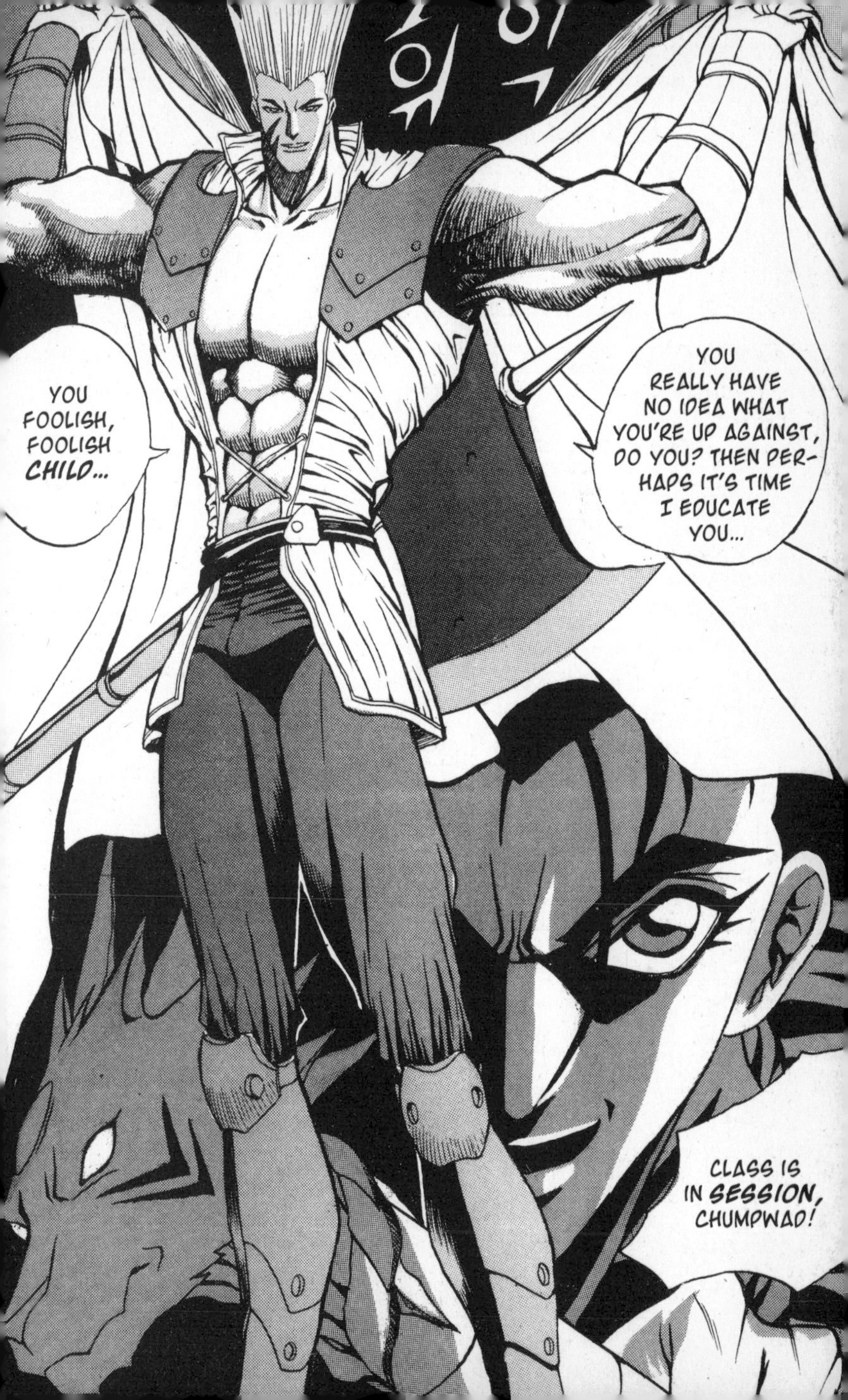
YOU FOOLISH, FOOLISH CHILD...
YOU REALLY HAVE NO IDEA WHAT YOU'RE UP AGAINST, DO YOU? THEN PER-HAPS IT'S TIME I EDUCATE YOU...
CLASS IS IN SESSION, CHUMPWAD!

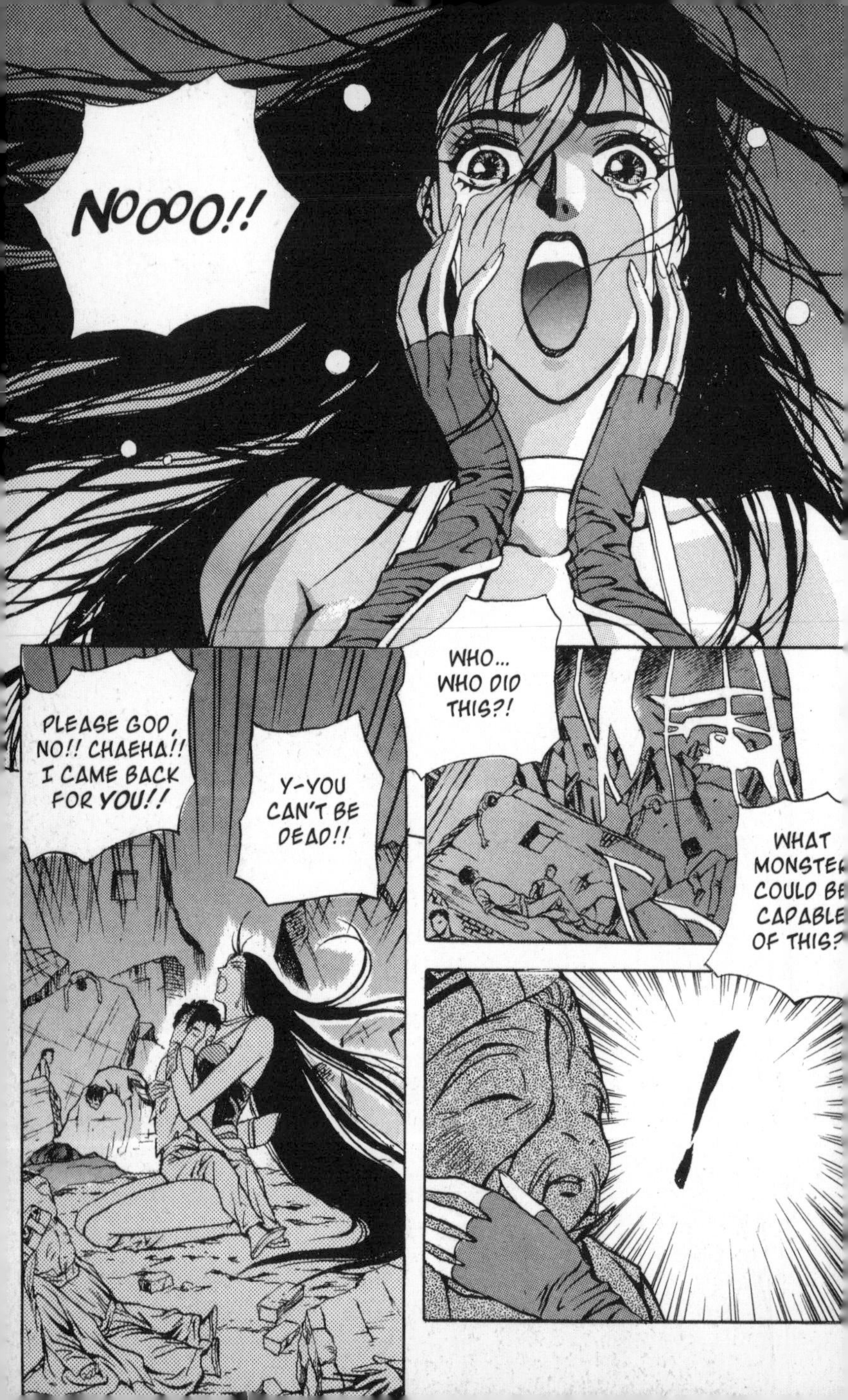
NOOOO!!
PLEASE GOD, NO!! CHAEHA!! I CAME BACK FOR YOU!!
Y-YOU CAN'T BE DEAD!!
WHO... WHO DID THIS?!
WHAT MONSTER COULD BE CAPABLE OF THIS?
!

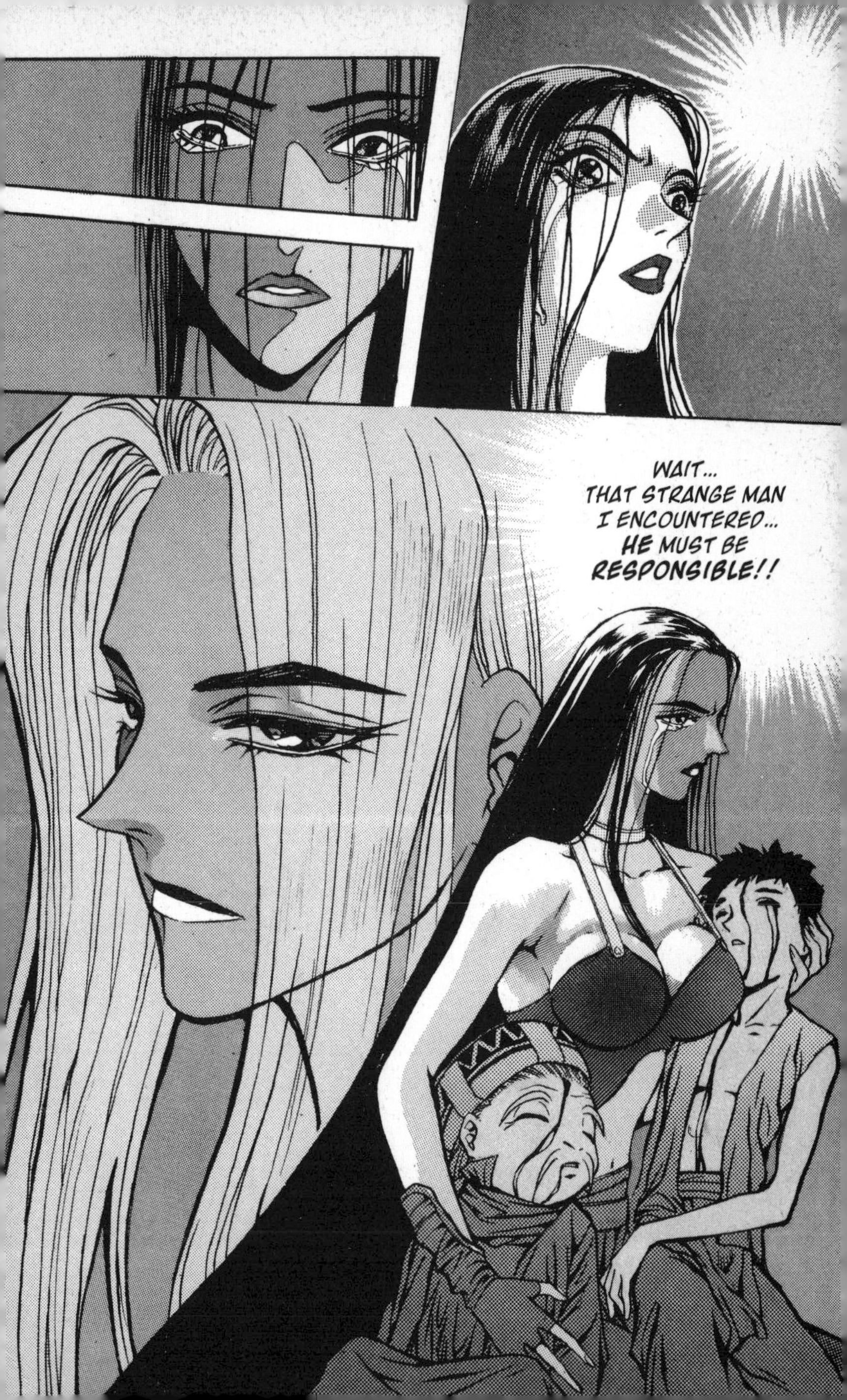
WAIT... THAT STRANGE MAN I ENCOUNTERED... HE MUST BE RESPONSIBLE!!

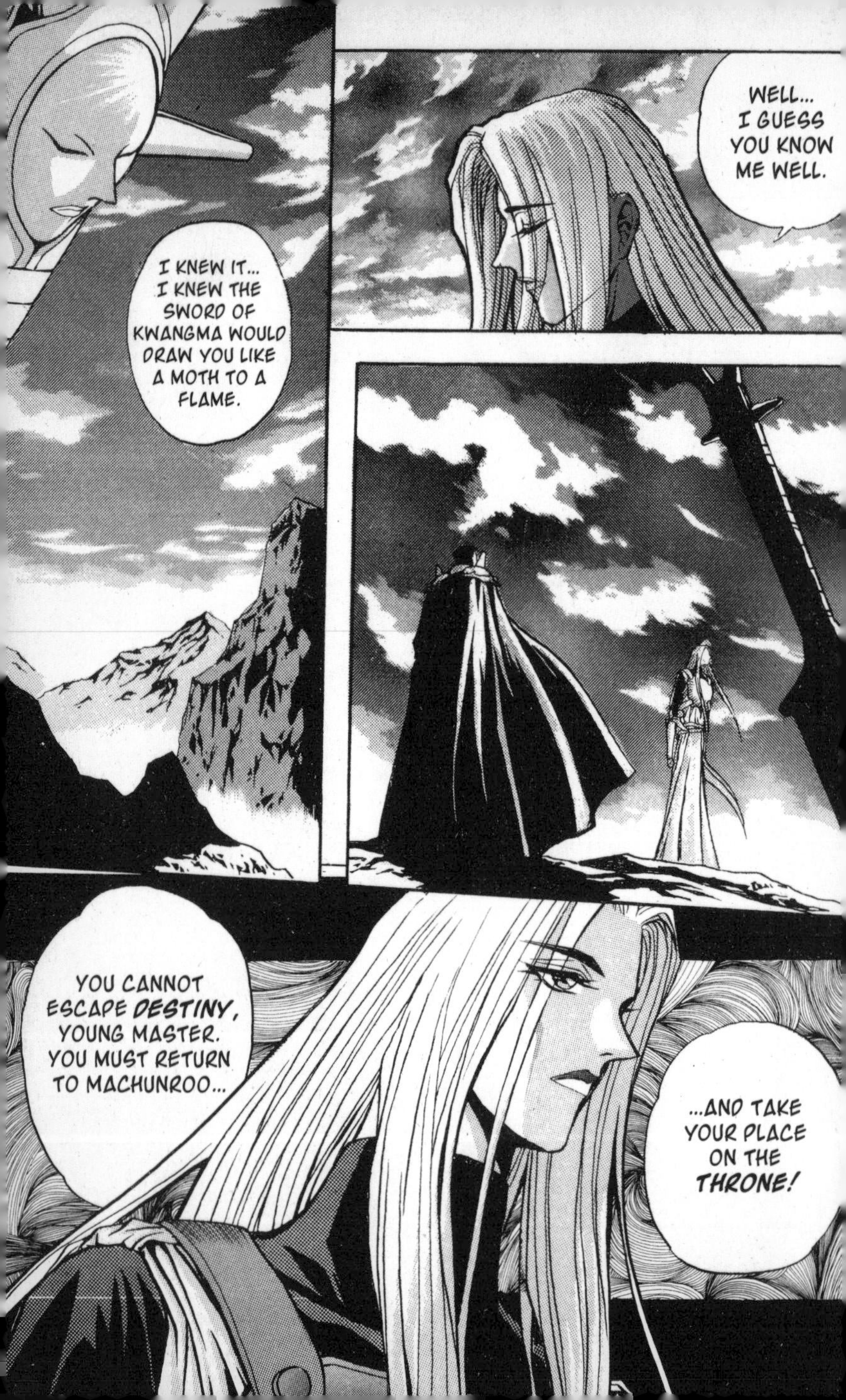
I KNEW IT... I KNEW THE SWORD OF KWANGMA WOULD DRAW YOU LIKE A MOTH TO A FLAME.
WELL... I GUESS YOU KNOW ME WELL.
YOU CANNOT ESCAPE DESTINY, YOUNG MASTER. YOU MUST RETURN TO MACHUNROO...
...AND TAKE YOUR PLACE ON THE THRONE!

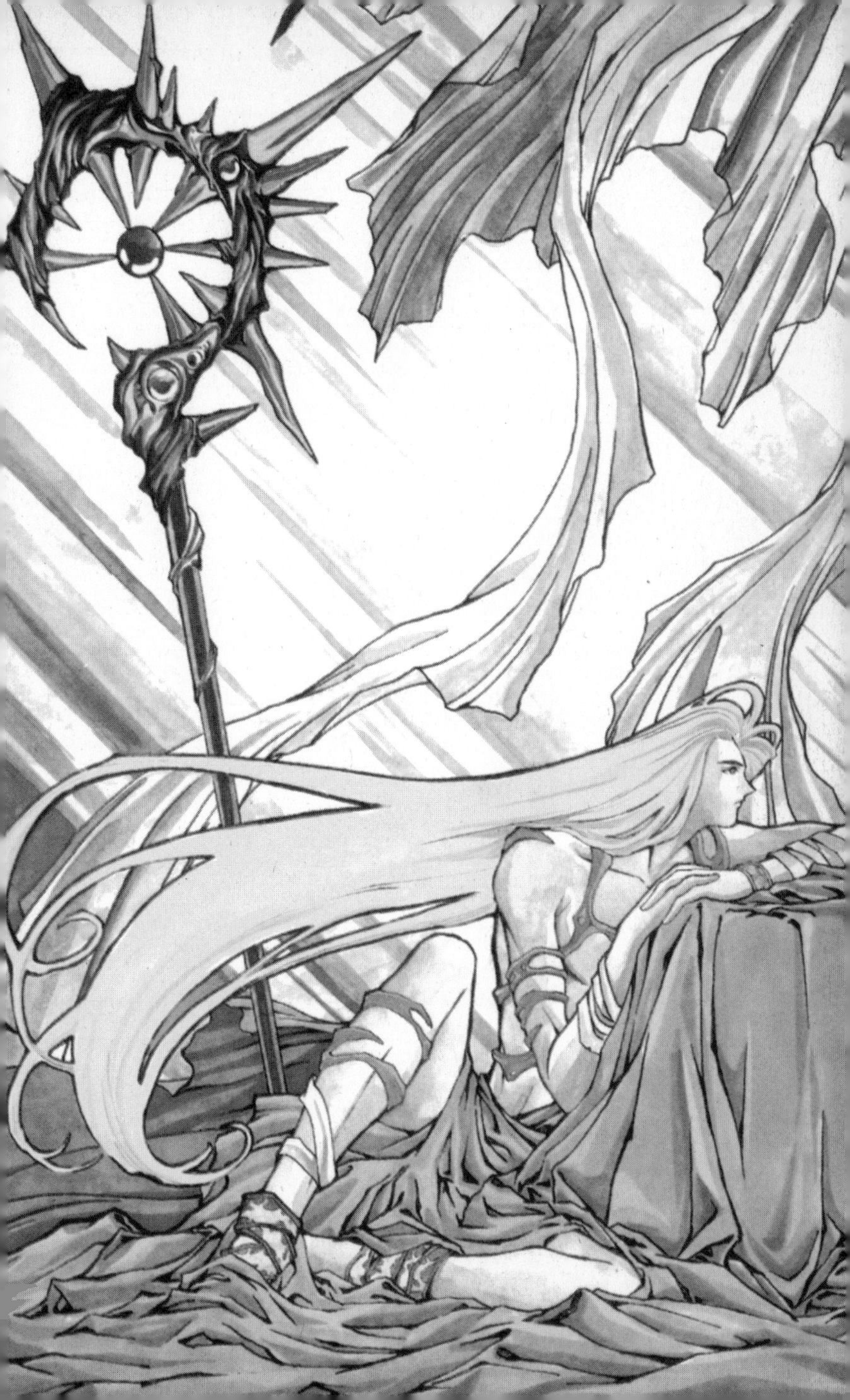

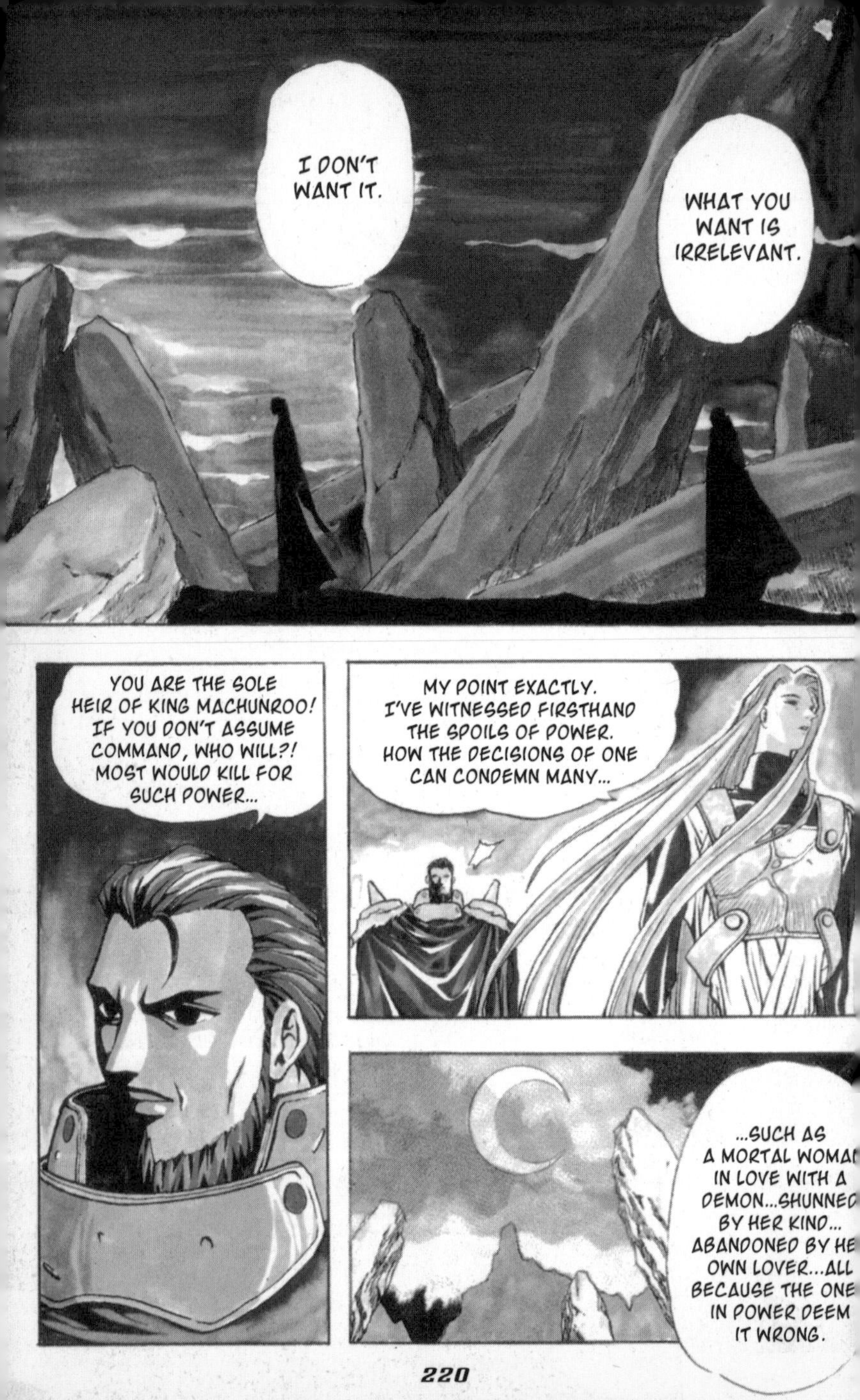
I DON'T WANT IT.
WHAT YOU WANT IS IRRELEVANT.
YOU ARE THE SOLE HEIR OF KING MACHUNROO! IF YOU DON'T ASSUME COMMAND, WHO WILL?! MOST WOULD KILL FOR SUCH POWER...
MY POINT EXACTLY. I'VE WITNESSED FIRSTHAND THE SPOILS OF POWER. HOW THE DECISIONS OF ONE CAN CONDEMN MANY...
...SUCH AS A MORTAL WOMA IN LOVE WITH A DEMON...SHUNNE BY HER KIND... ABANDONED BY HE OWN LOVER...ALL BECAUSE THE ONE IN POWER DEEM IT WRONG.

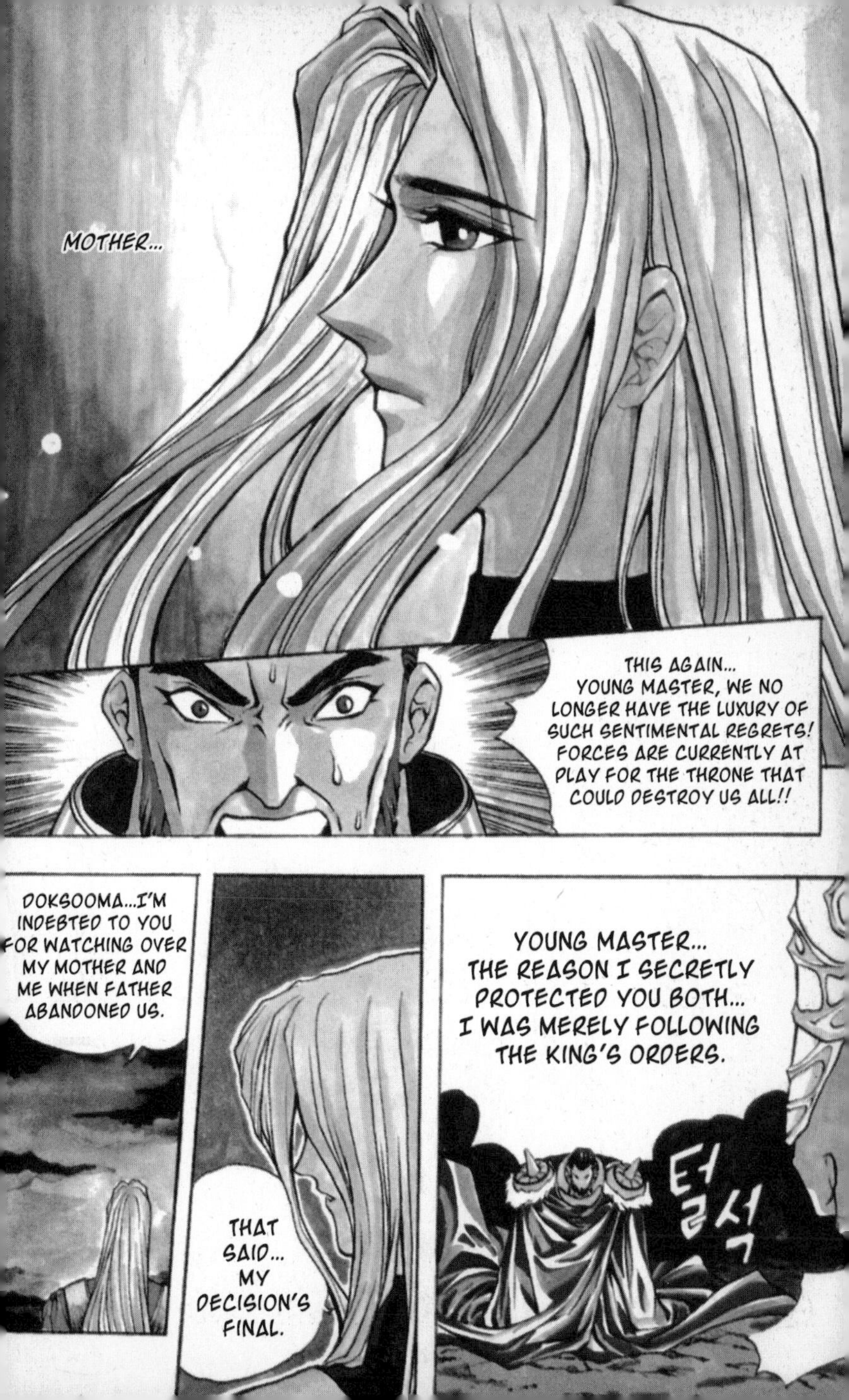
MOTHER...
THIS AGAIN... YOUNG MASTER, WE NO LONGER HAVE THE LUXURY OF SUCH SENTIMENTAL REGRETS! FORCES ARE CURRENTLY AT PLAY FOR THE THRONE THAT COULD DESTROY US ALL!!
DOKSOOMA...I'M INDEBTED TO YOU FOR WATCHING OVER MY MOTHER AND ME WHEN FATHER ABANDONED US.
THAT SAID... MY DECISION'S FINAL.
YOUNG MASTER... THE REASON I SECRETLY PROTECTED YOU BOTH... I WAS MERELY FOLLOWING THE KING'S ORDERS.
털석

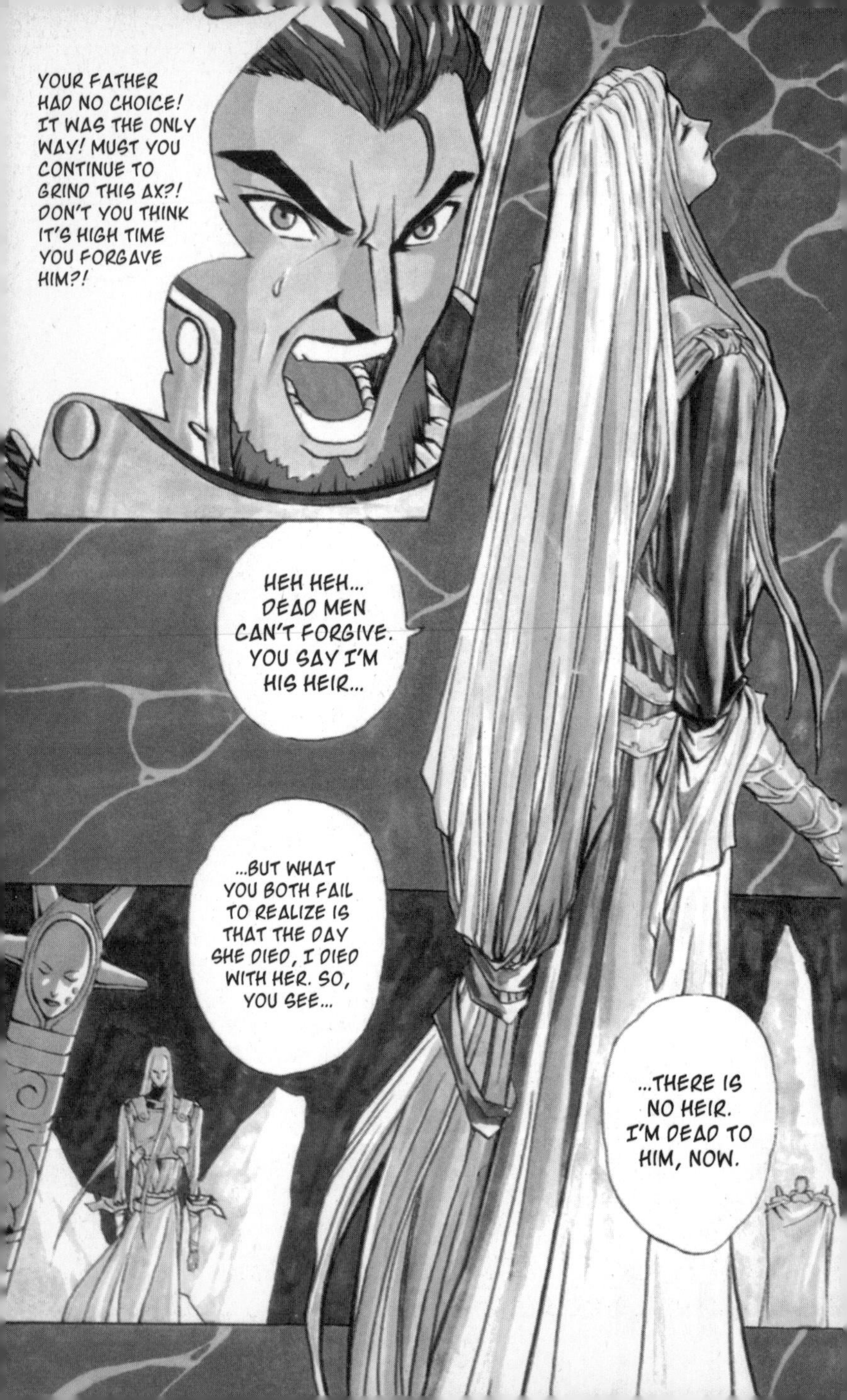
YOUR FATHER HAD NO CHOICE! IT WAS THE ONLY WAY! MUST YOU CONTINUE TO GRIND THIS AX?! DON'T YOU THINK IT'S HIGH TIME YOU FORGAVE HIM?!
HEH HEH... DEAD MEN CAN'T FORGIVE. YOU SAY I'M HIS HEIR...
...BUT WHAT YOU BOTH FAIL TO REALIZE IS THAT THE DAY SHE DIED, I DIED WITH HER. SO, YOU SEE...
...THERE IS NO HEIR. I'M DEAD TO HIM, NOW.

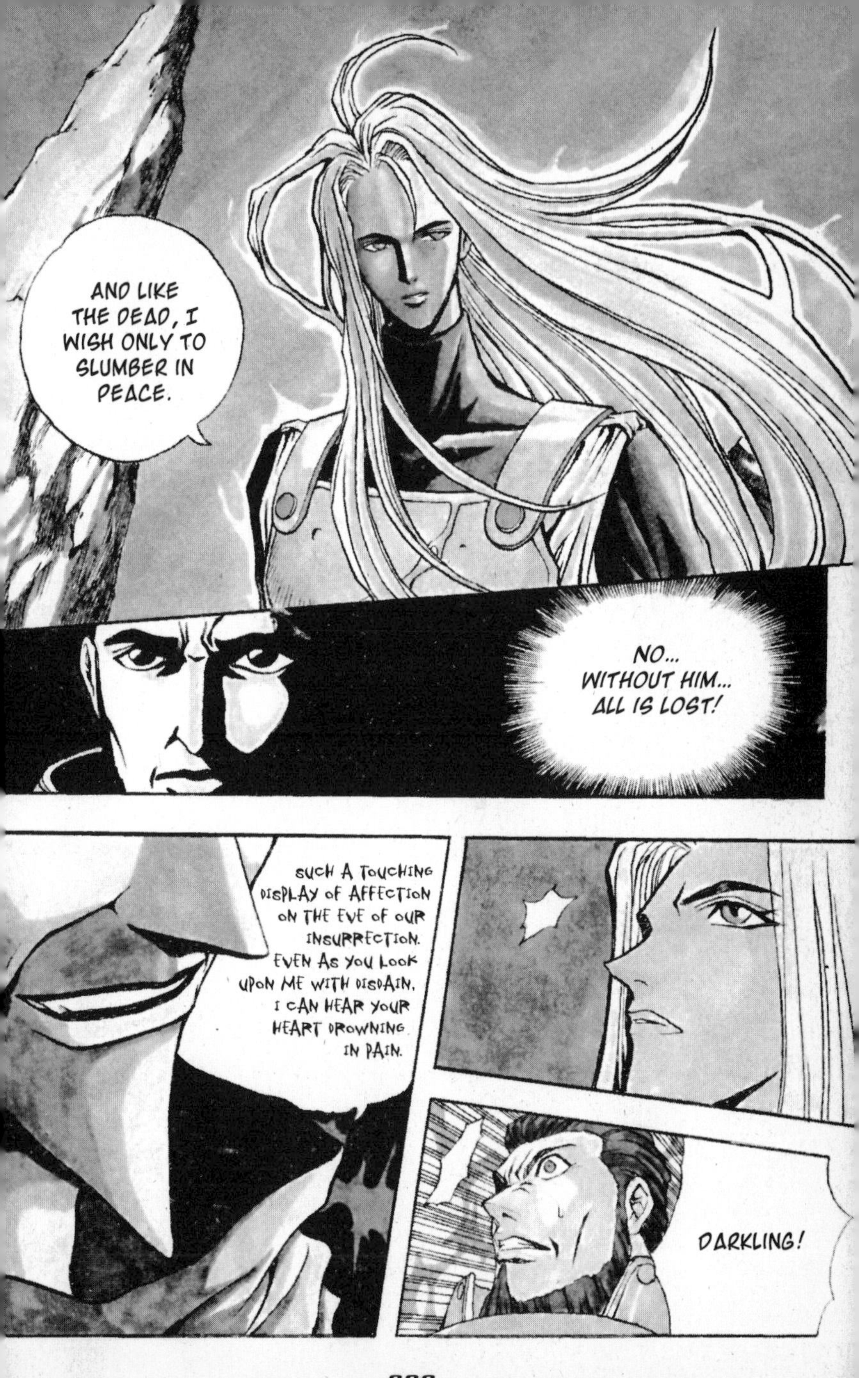
AND LIKE THE DEAD, I WISH ONLY TO SLUMBER IN PEACE.
NO... WITHOUT HIM... ALL IS LOST!
SUCH A TOUCHING DISPLAY OF AFFECTION ON THE EVE OF OUR INSURRECTION. EVEN AS YOU LOOK UPON ME WITH DISDAIN, I CAN HEAR YOUR HEART DROWNING IN PAIN.
DARKLING!

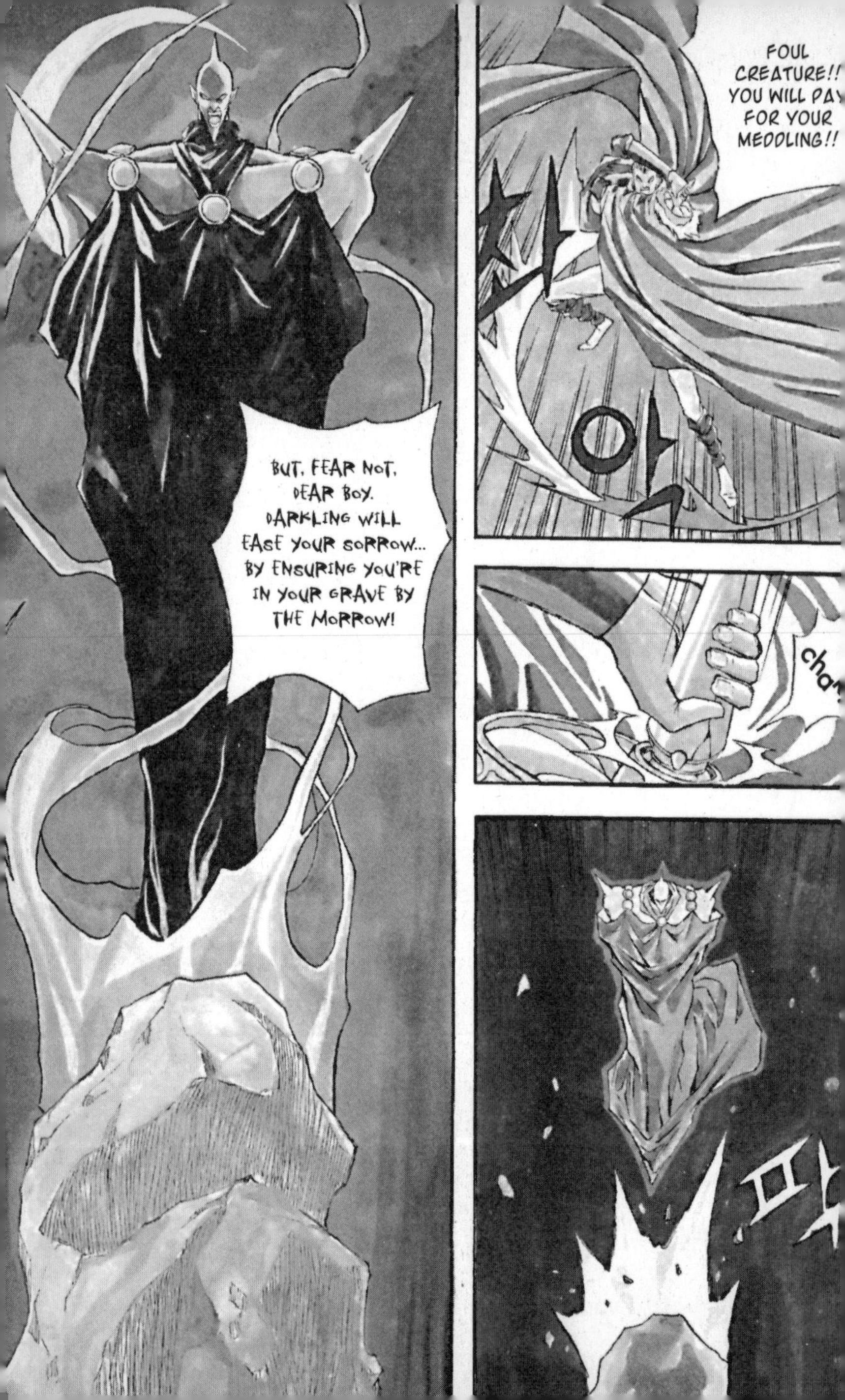
BUT, FEAR NOT, DEAR BOY. DARKLING WILL EASE YOUR SORROW... BY ENSURING YOU'RE IN YOUR GRAVE BY THE MORROW!
FOUL CREATURE!! YOU WILL PAY FOR YOUR MEDDLING!!
cha

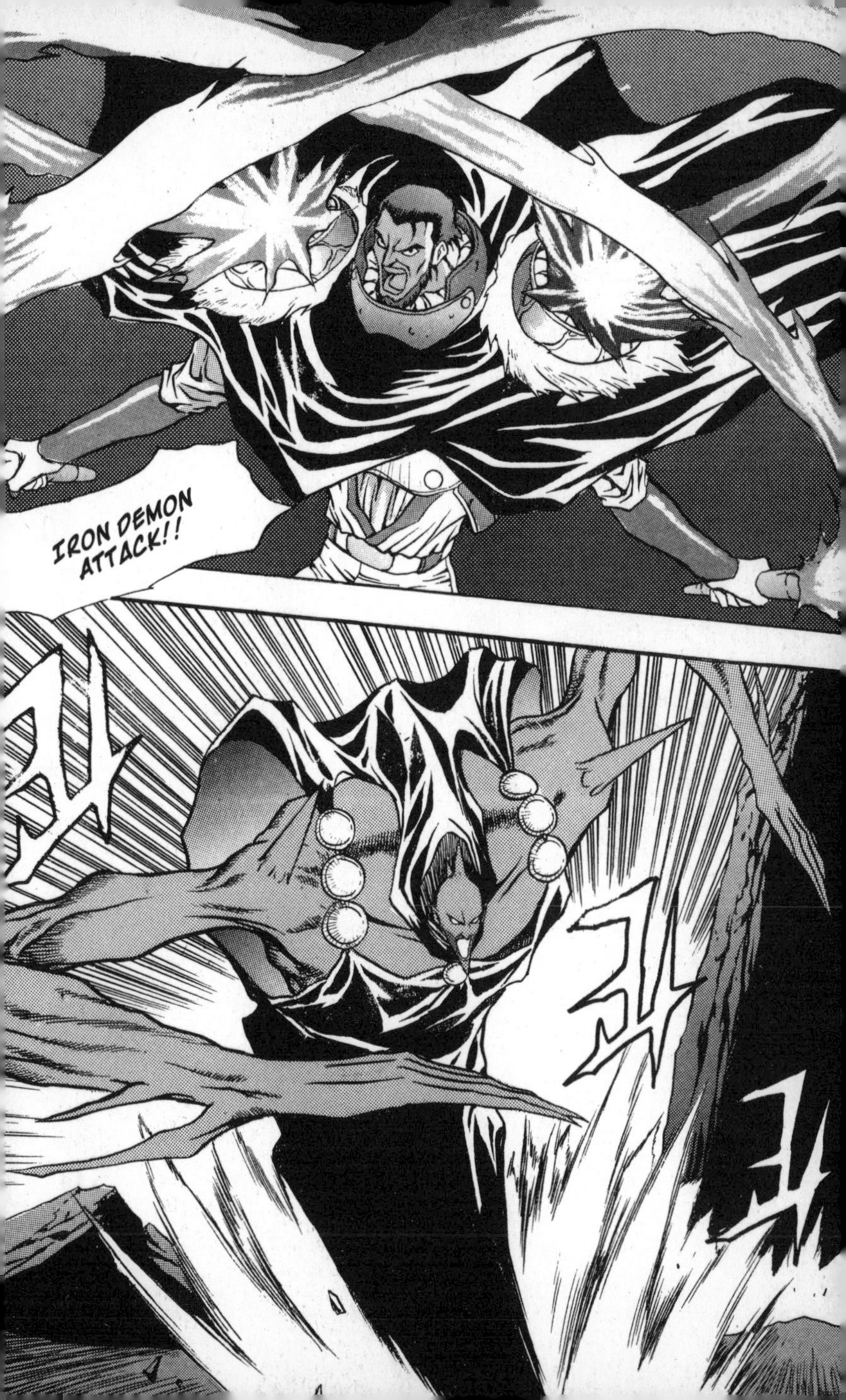
IRON DEMON
ATTACK!!

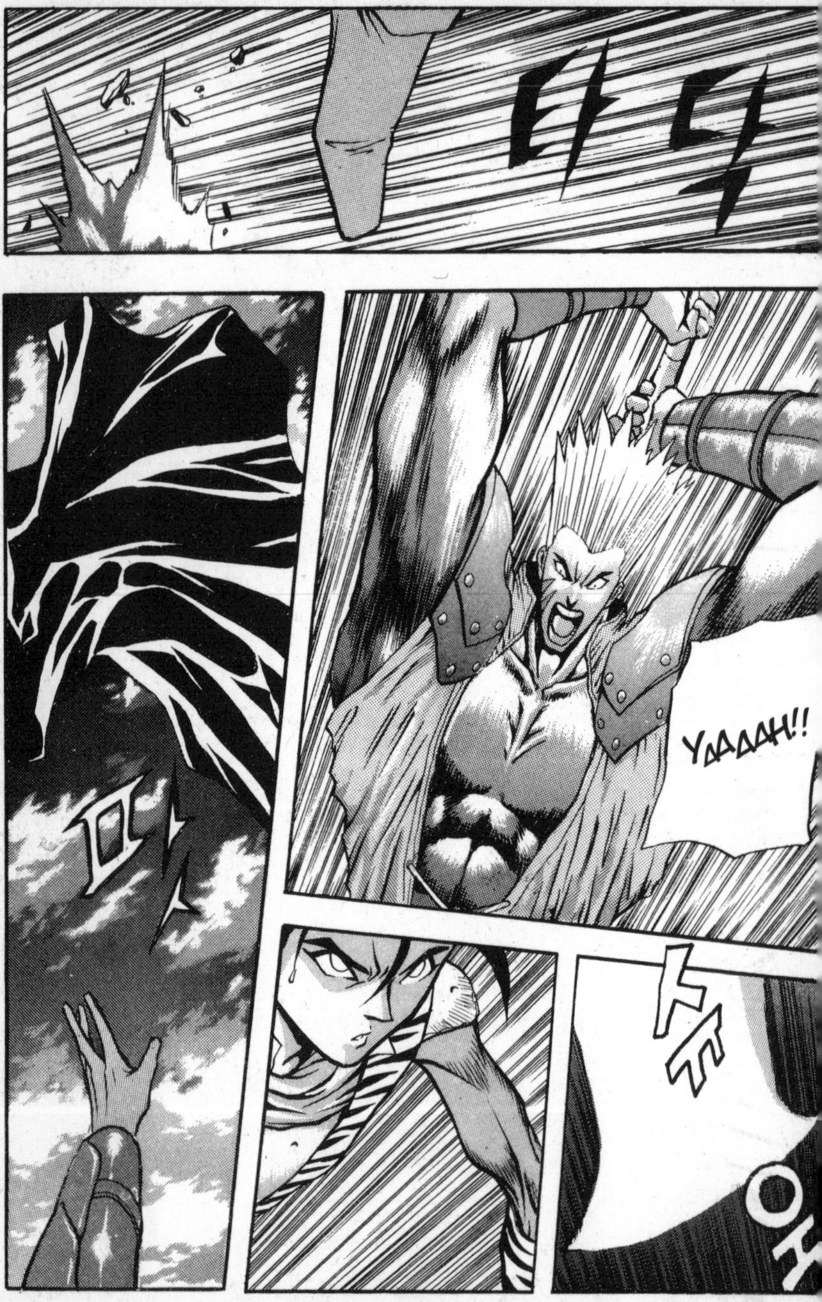
타닥
피
YAAAH!!
탁

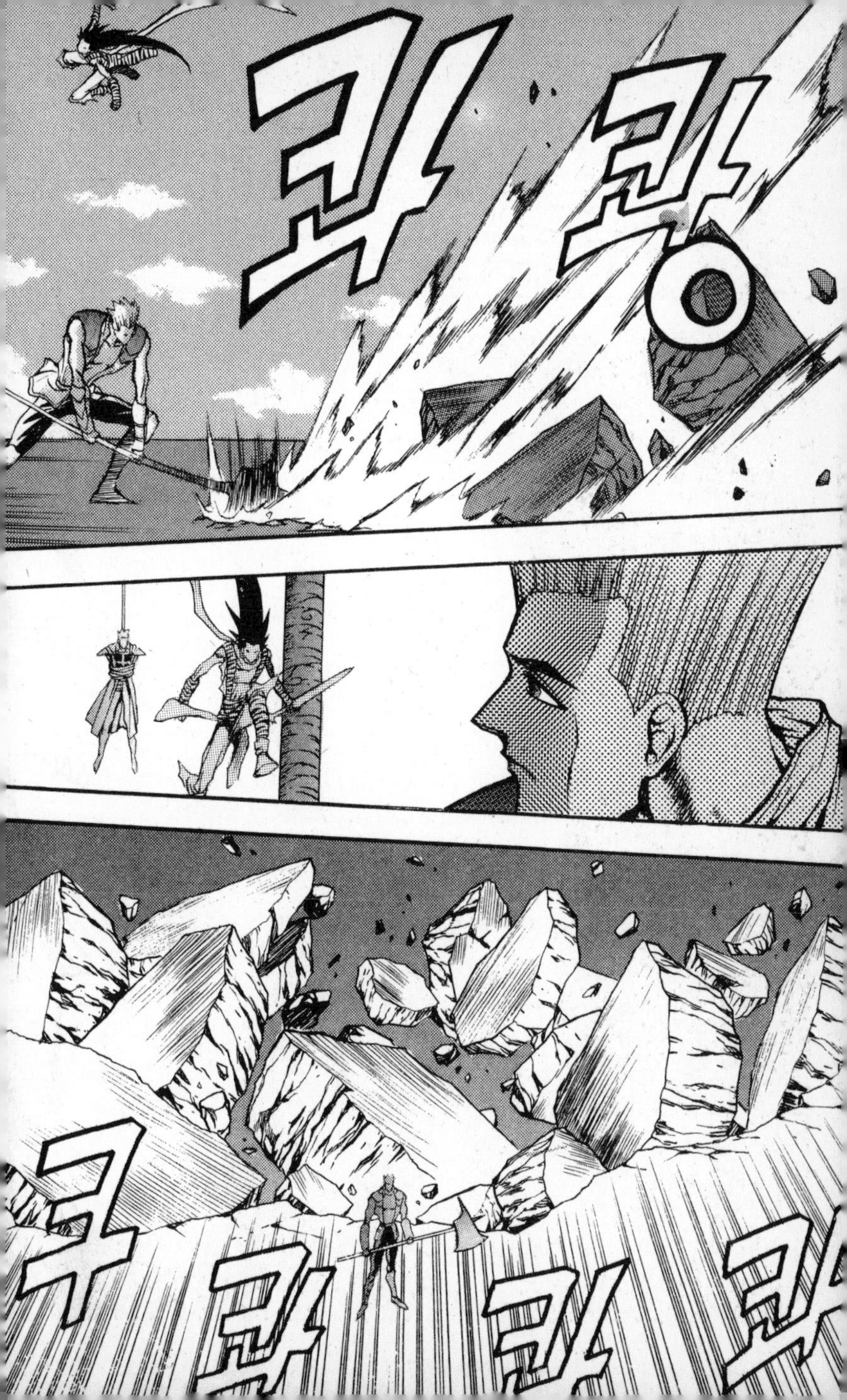

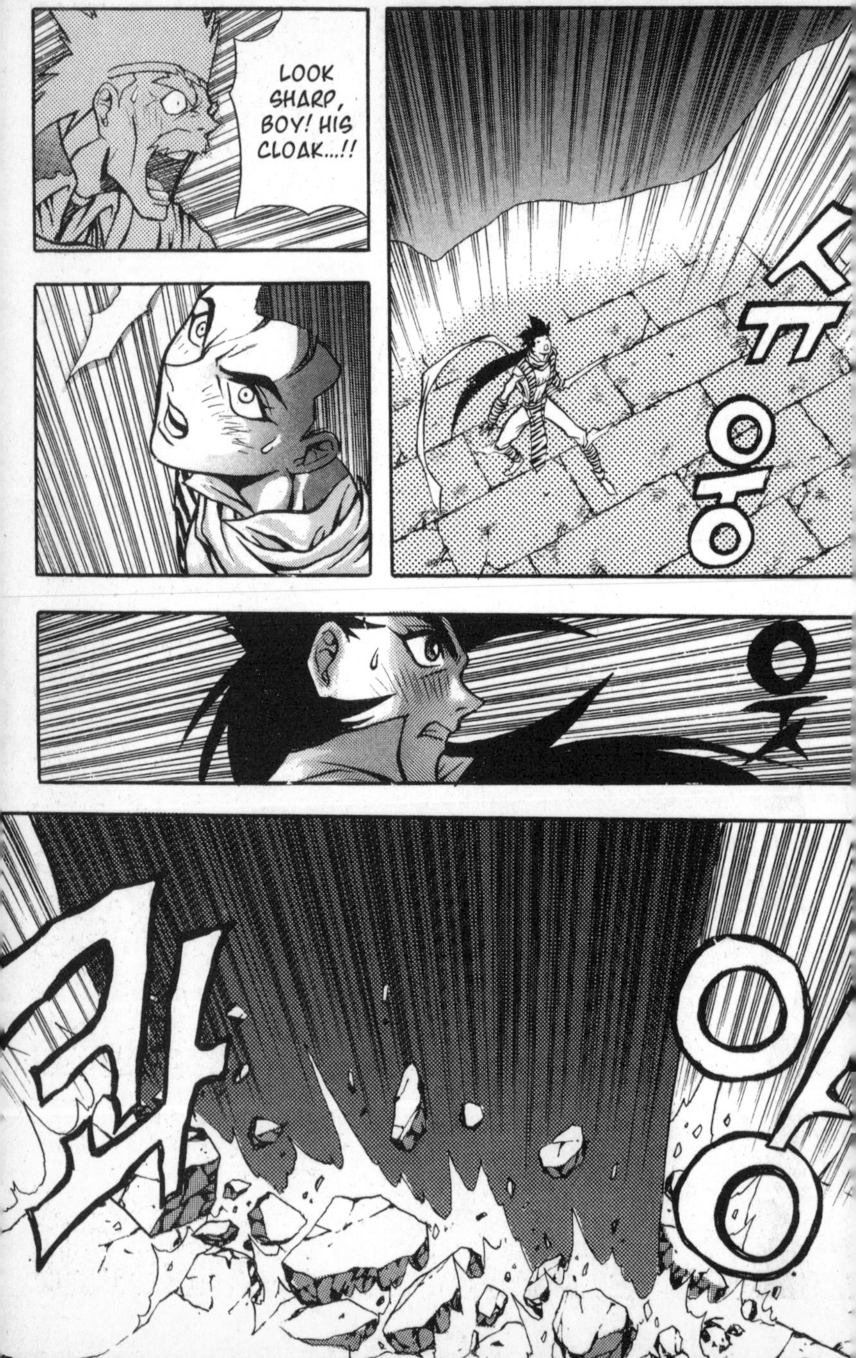
LOOK SHARP, BOY! HIS CLOAK...!!

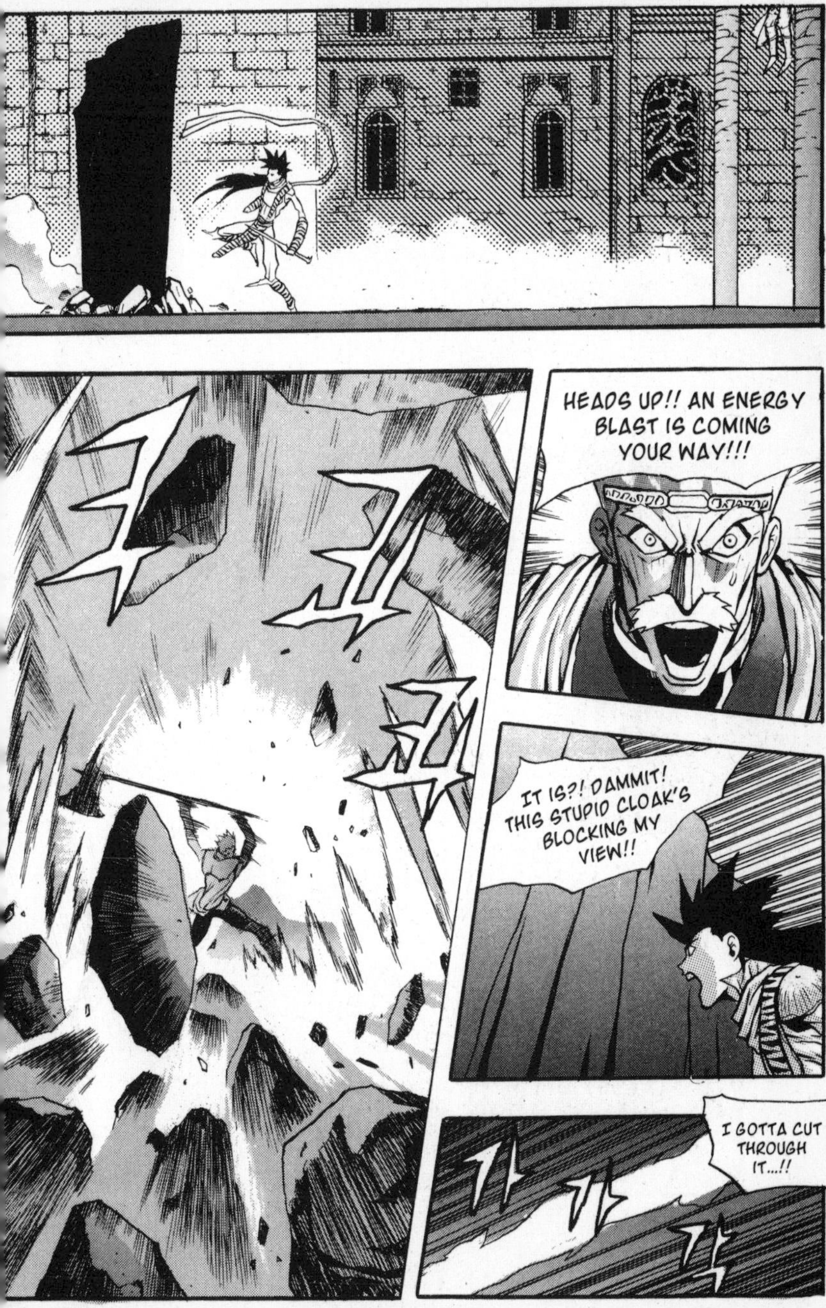
HEADS UP!! AN ENERGY BLAST IS COMING YOUR WAY!!!
IT IS?! DAMMIT! THIS STUPID CLOAK'S BLOCKING MY VIEW!!
I GOTTA CUT THROUGH IT...!!

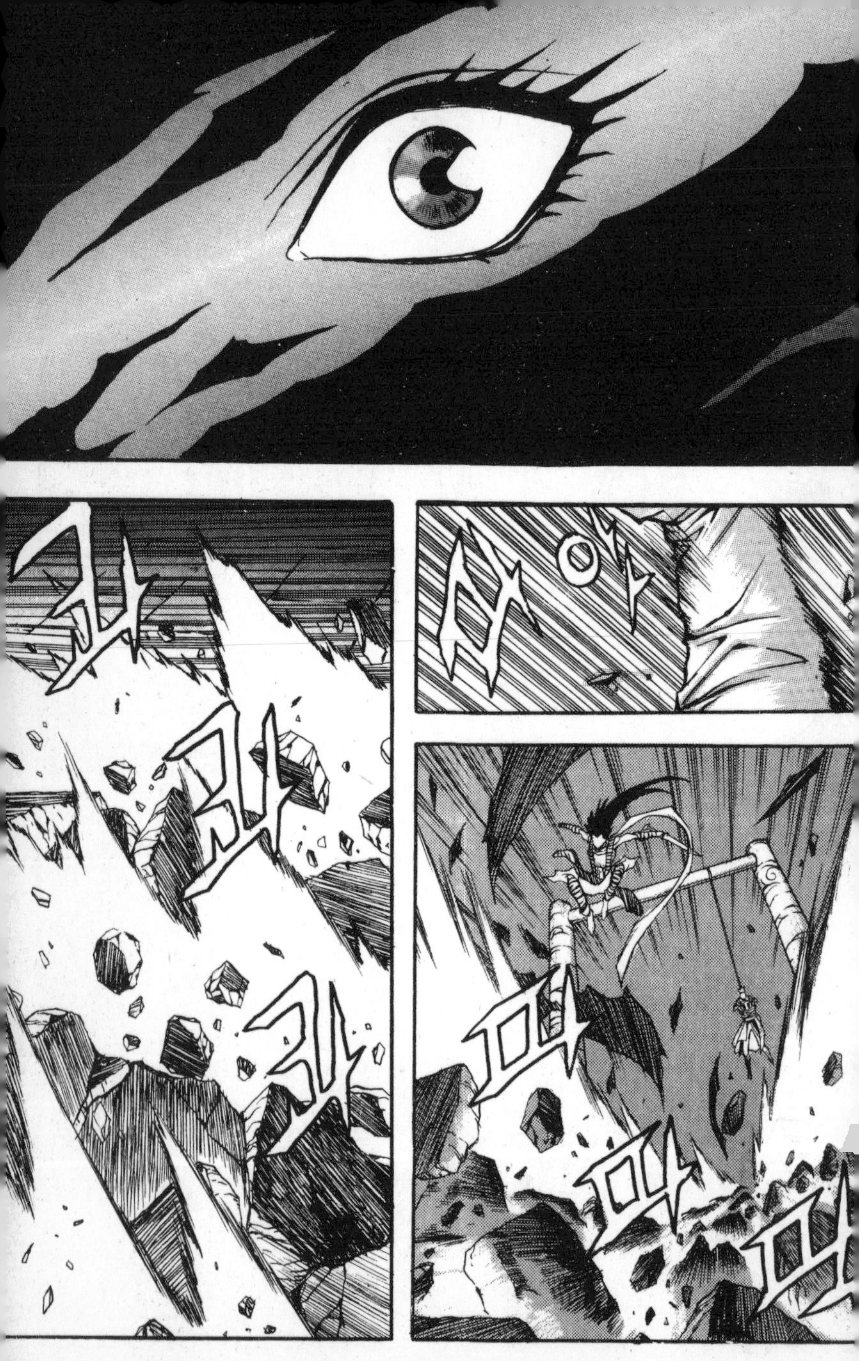
콰
콰
콰
타앗
파
파
파

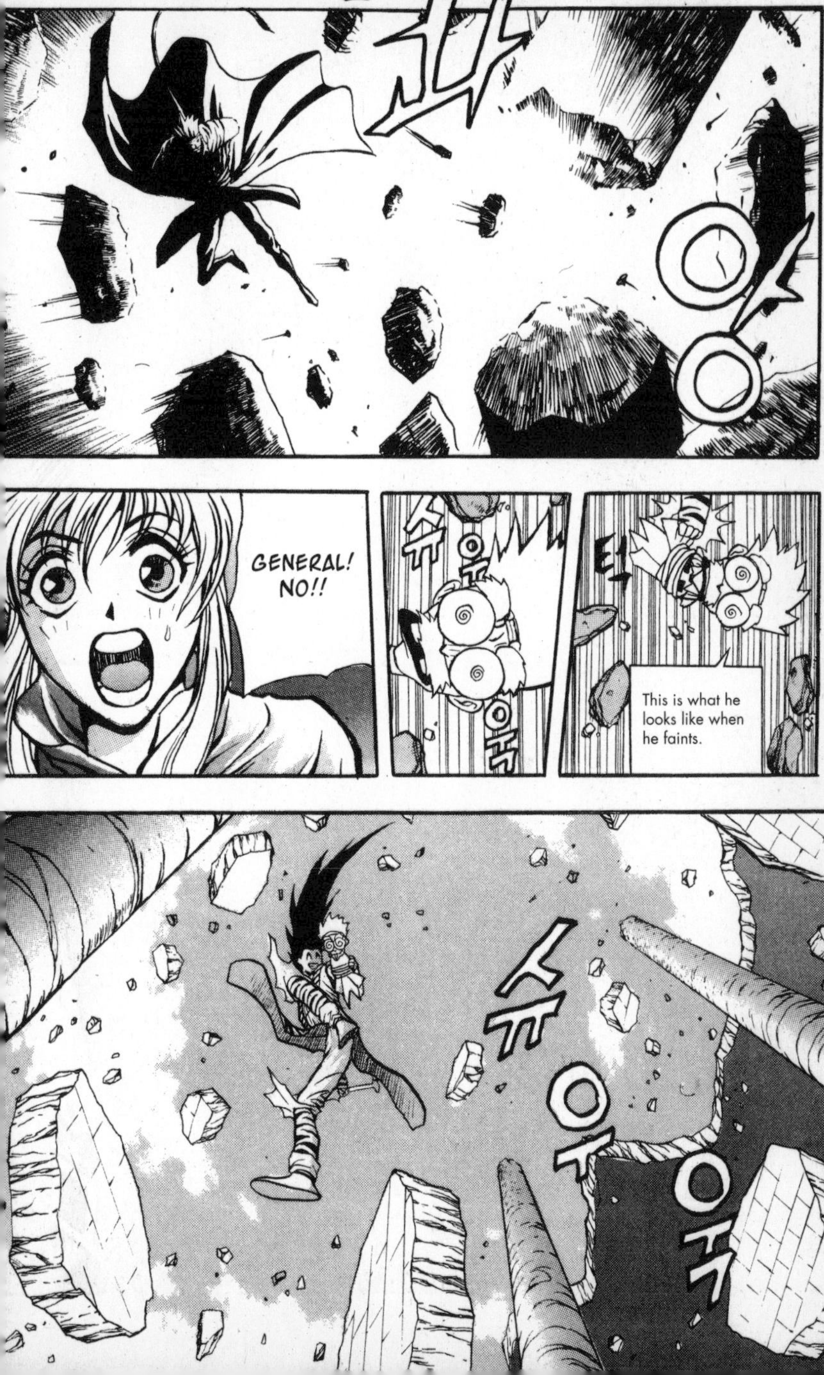
GENERAL! NO!!
This is what he looks like when he faints.

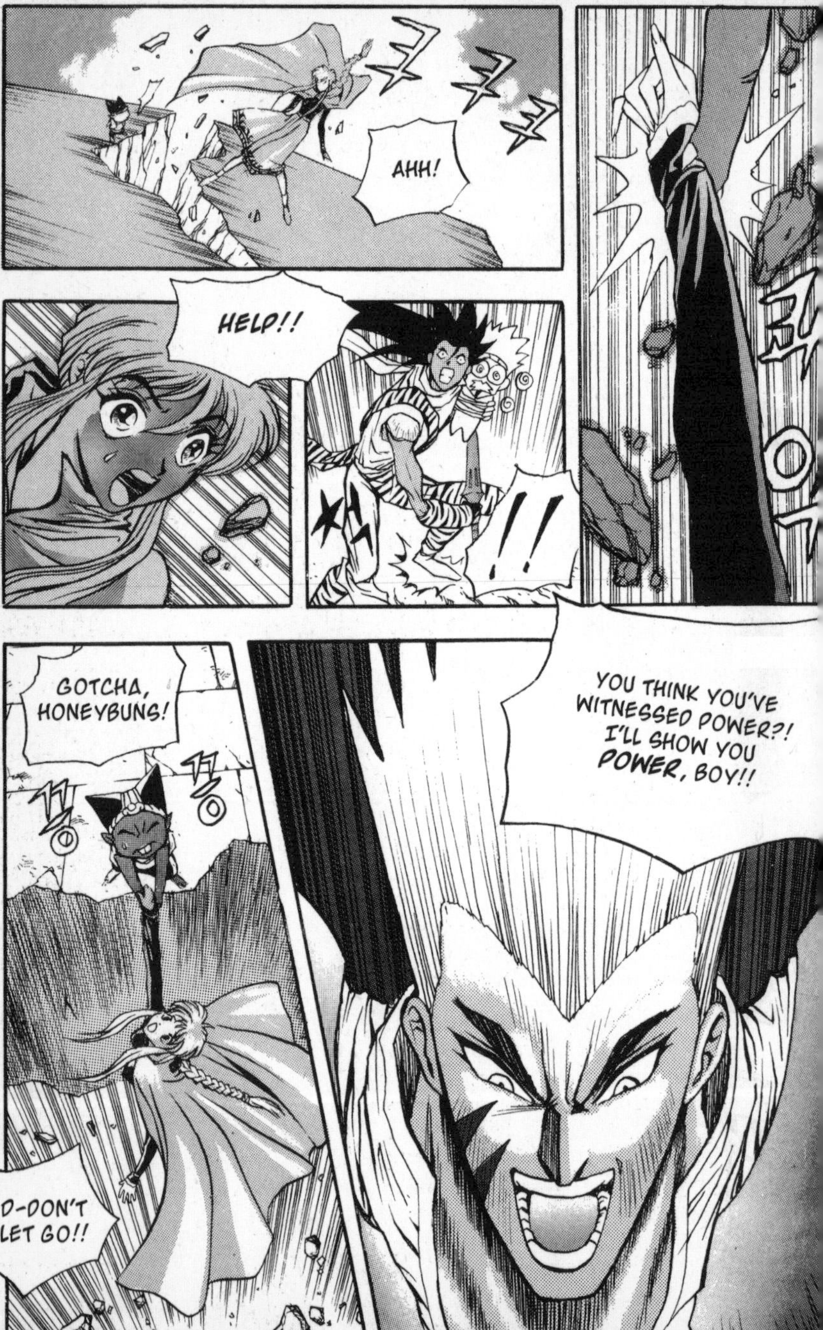
AHH!
HELP!!
!!
GOTCHA, HONEYBUNS!
D-DON'T LET GO!!
YOU THINK YOU'VE WITNESSED POWER?! I'LL SHOW YOU POWER, BOY!!

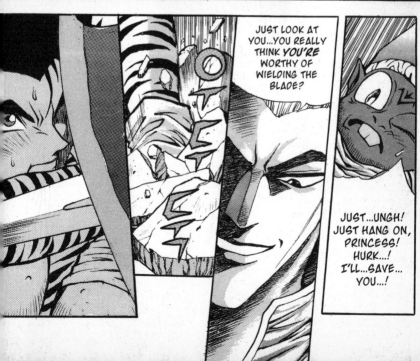

JUST LOOK AT YOU...YOU REALLY **THINK YOU'RE** WORTHY OF WIELDING THE BLADE?

JUST...UNGH! JUST HANG ON, PRINCESS! HURK...! I'LL...SAVE... YOU...!

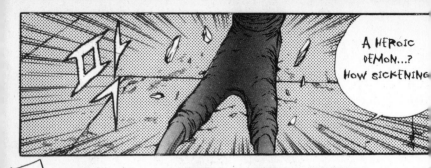

A HEROIC DEMON...? HOW SICKENING

AW, CRAP.

YOU CAN'T FIGHT DESTINY, BOY! I AM THE TRUE OWNER OF THE BLADE!!

I CAN'T... I CAN'T HOLD 'EM BACK MUCH LONGER...

BLADE OF HEAVEN

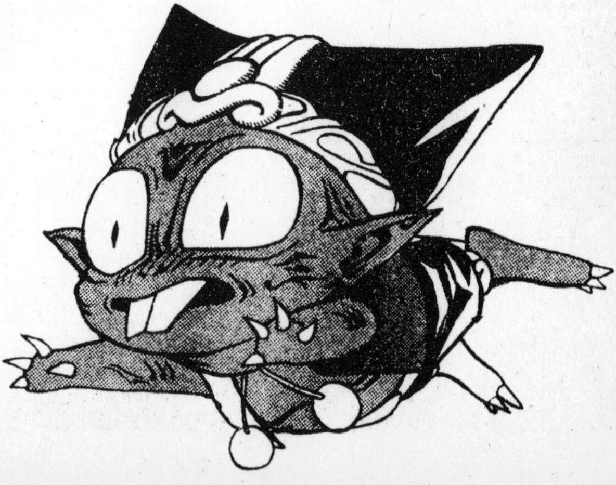

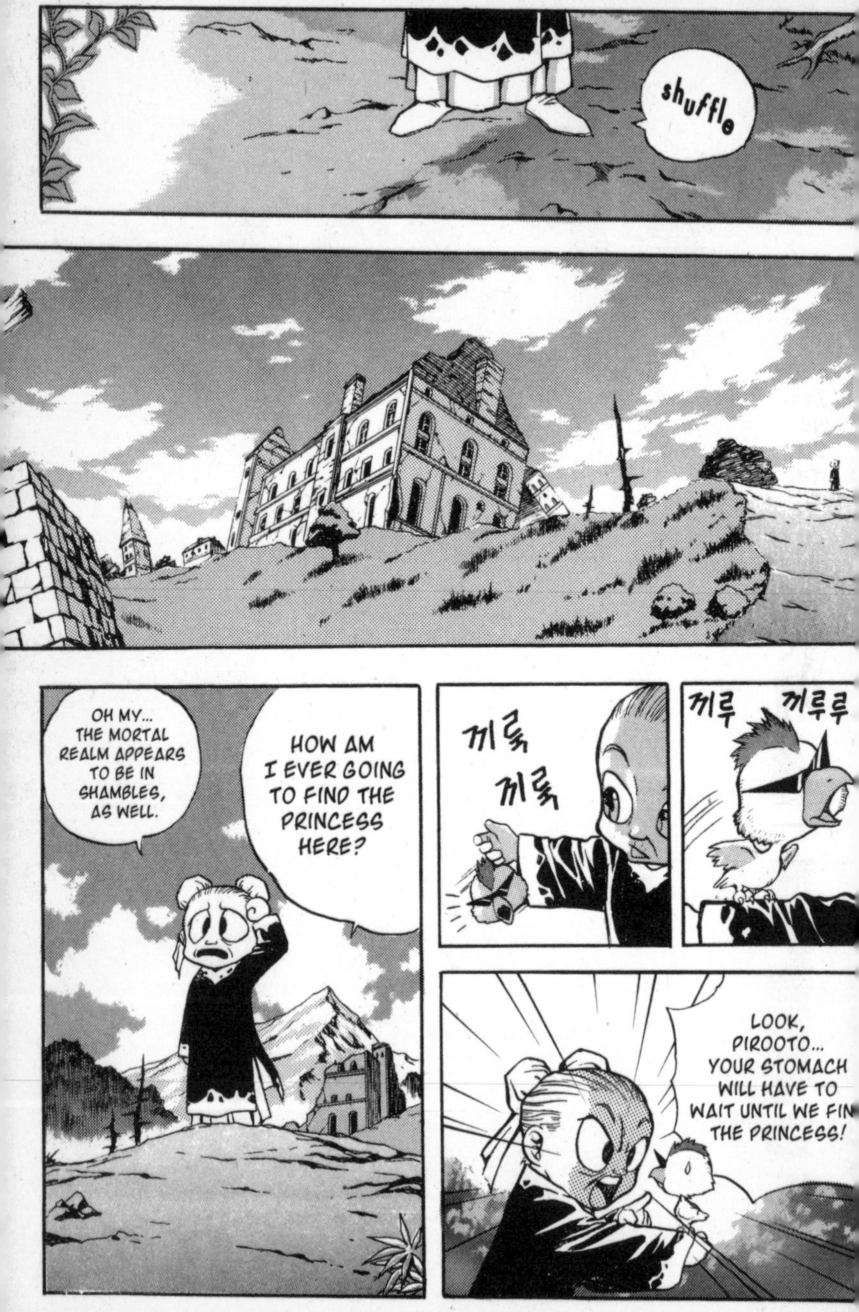
shuffle
OH MY... THE MORTAL REALM APPEARS TO BE IN SHAMBLES, AS WELL.
HOW AM I EVER GOING TO FIND THE PRINCESS HERE?
끼룩
끼룩
끼루
끼루루
LOOK, PIROOTO... YOUR STOMACH WILL HAVE TO WAIT UNTIL WE FIN THE PRINCESS!

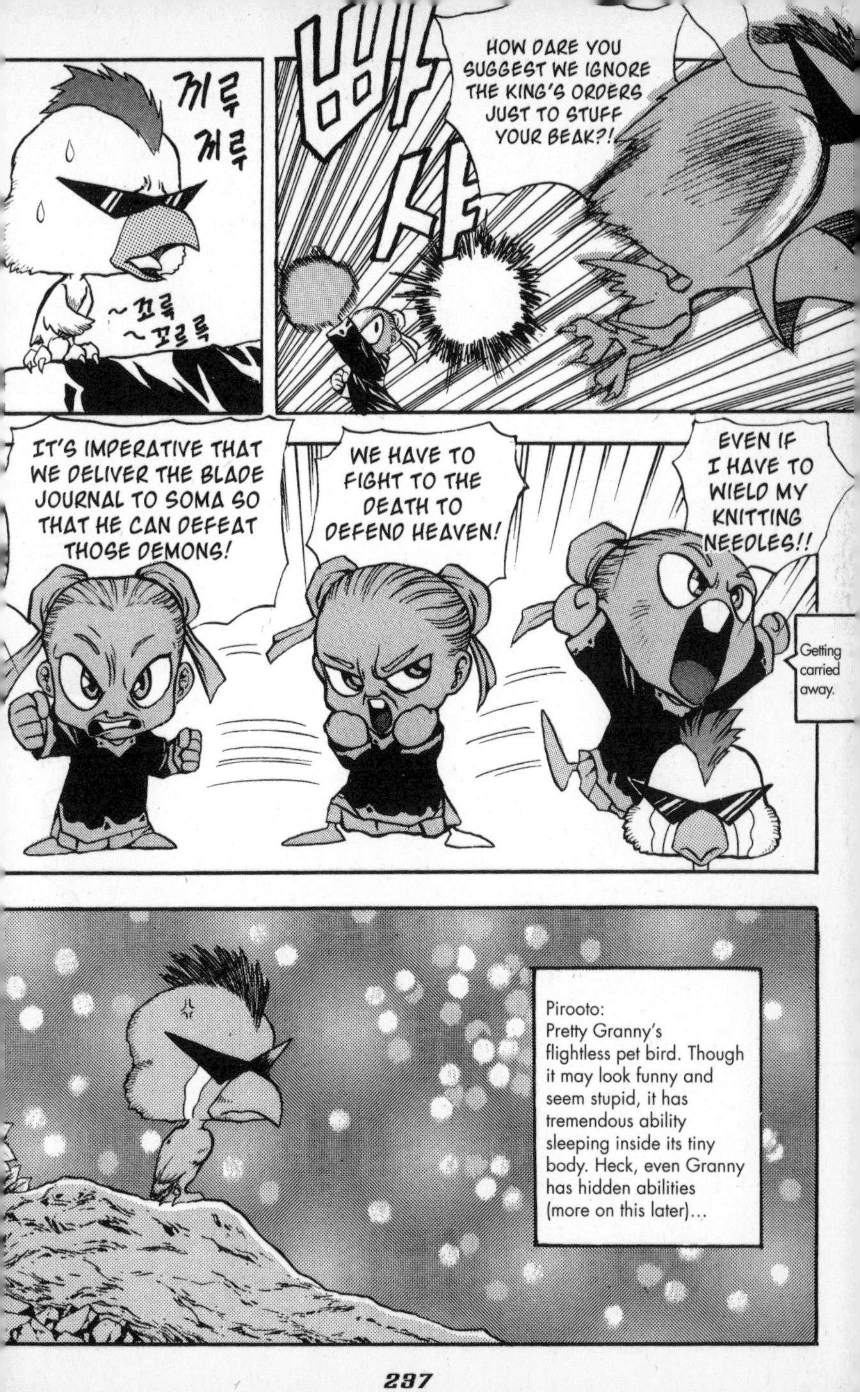
HOW DARE YOU SUGGEST WE IGNORE THE KING'S ORDERS JUST TO STUFF YOUR BEAK?!
IT'S IMPERATIVE THAT WE DELIVER THE BLADE JOURNAL TO SOMA SO THAT HE CAN DEFEAT THOSE DEMONS!
WE HAVE TO FIGHT TO THE DEATH TO DEFEND HEAVEN!
EVEN IF I HAVE TO WIELD MY KNITTING NEEDLES!!
Getting carried away.
Pirooto: Pretty Granny's flightless pet bird. Though it may look funny and seem stupid, it has tremendous ability sleeping inside its tiny body. Heck, even Granny has hidden abilities (more on this later)...

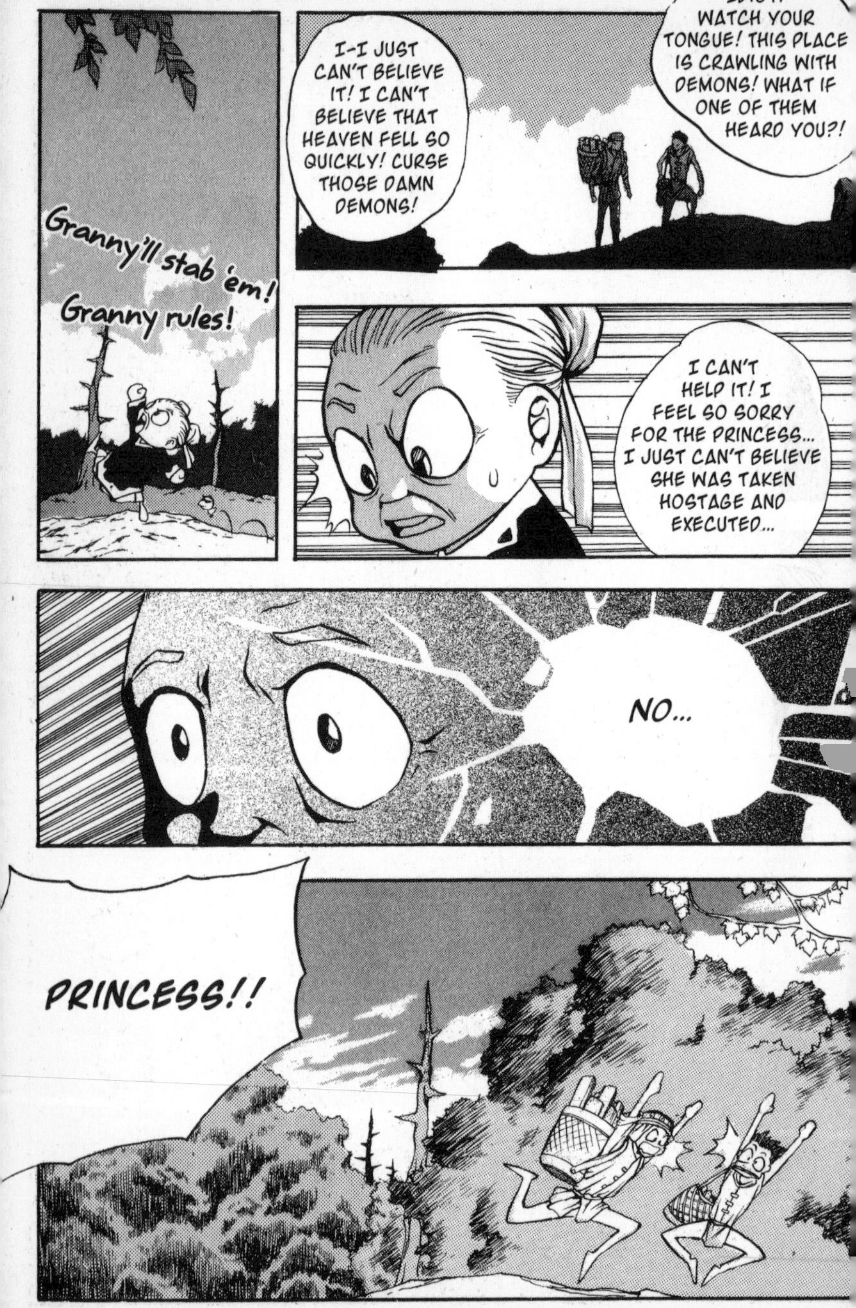
Granny'll stab 'em! Granny rules!
I-I JUST CAN'T BELIEVE IT! I CAN'T BELIEVE THAT HEAVEN FELL SO QUICKLY! CURSE THOSE DAMN DEMONS!
IDIOT! WATCH YOUR TONGUE! THIS PLACE IS CRAWLING WITH DEMONS! WHAT IF ONE OF THEM HEARD YOU?!
I CAN'T HELP IT! I FEEL SO SORRY FOR THE PRINCESS... I JUST CAN'T BELIEVE SHE WAS TAKEN HOSTAGE AND EXECUTED...
NO...
PRINCESS!!

WHERE DID
THEY TAKE
HER?!

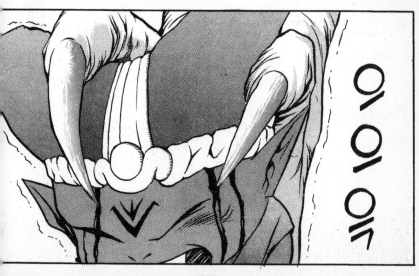

239

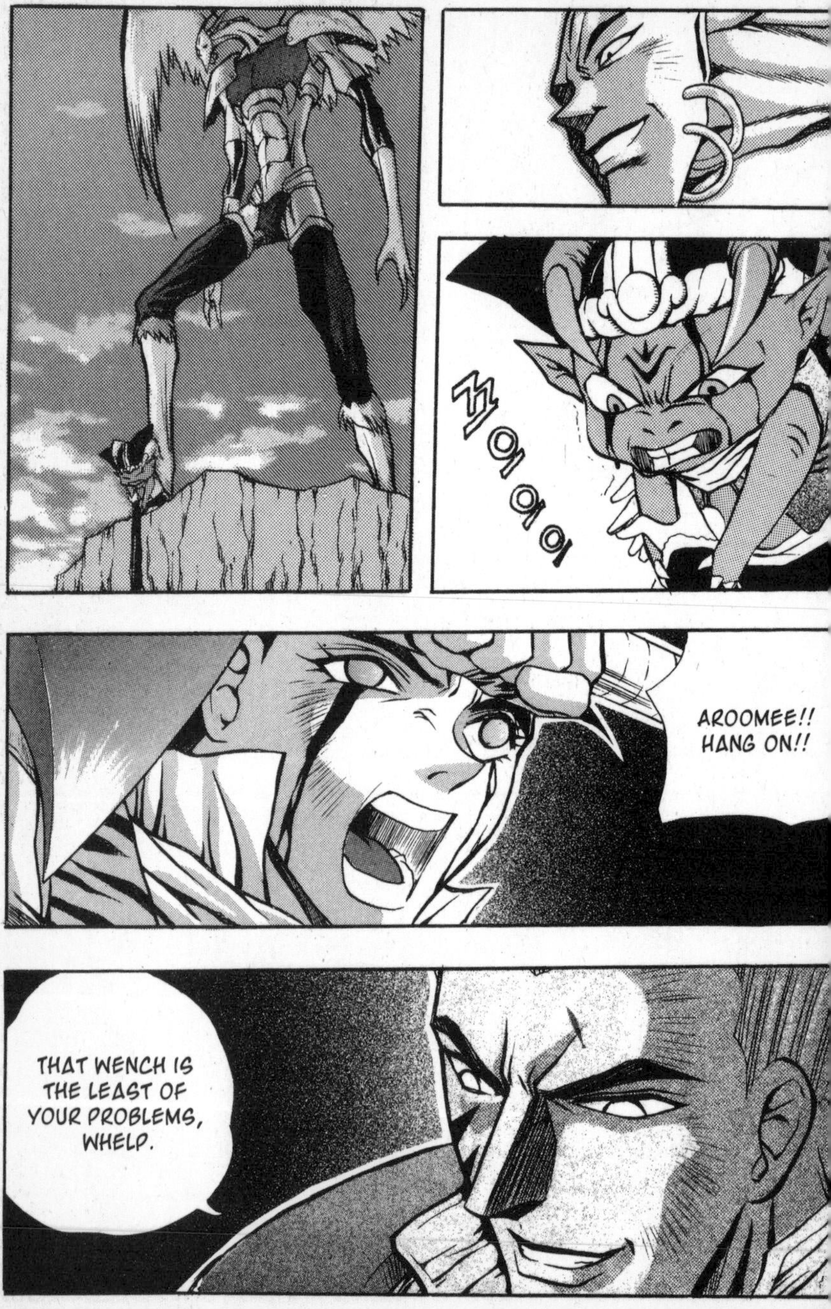
AROOMEE!! HANG ON!!
THAT WENCH IS THE LEAST OF YOUR PROBLEMS, WHELP.

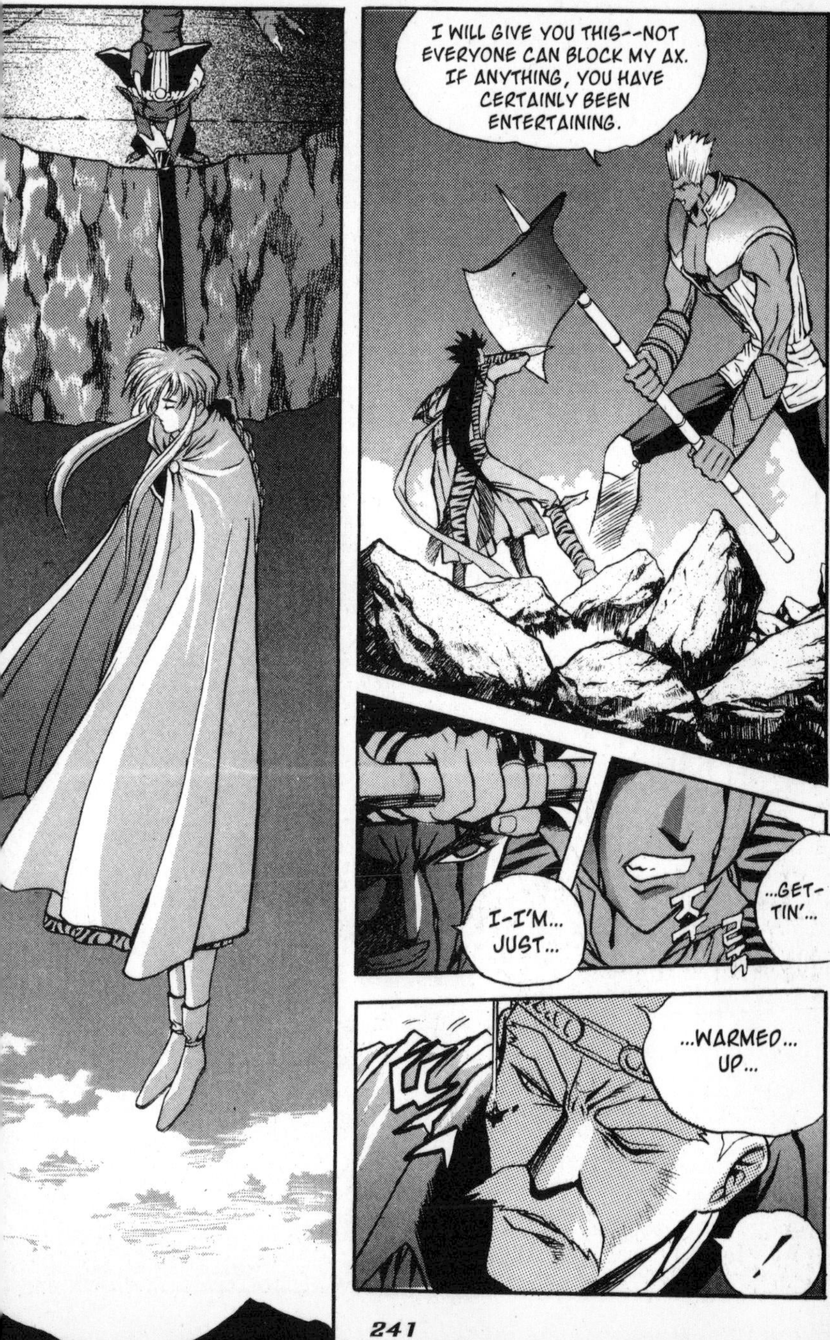
I WILL GIVE YOU THIS--NOT EVERYONE CAN BLOCK MY AX. IF ANYTHING, YOU HAVE CERTAINLY BEEN ENTERTAINING.
I-I'M... JUST...
...GET-TIN'...
...WARMED... UP...
!

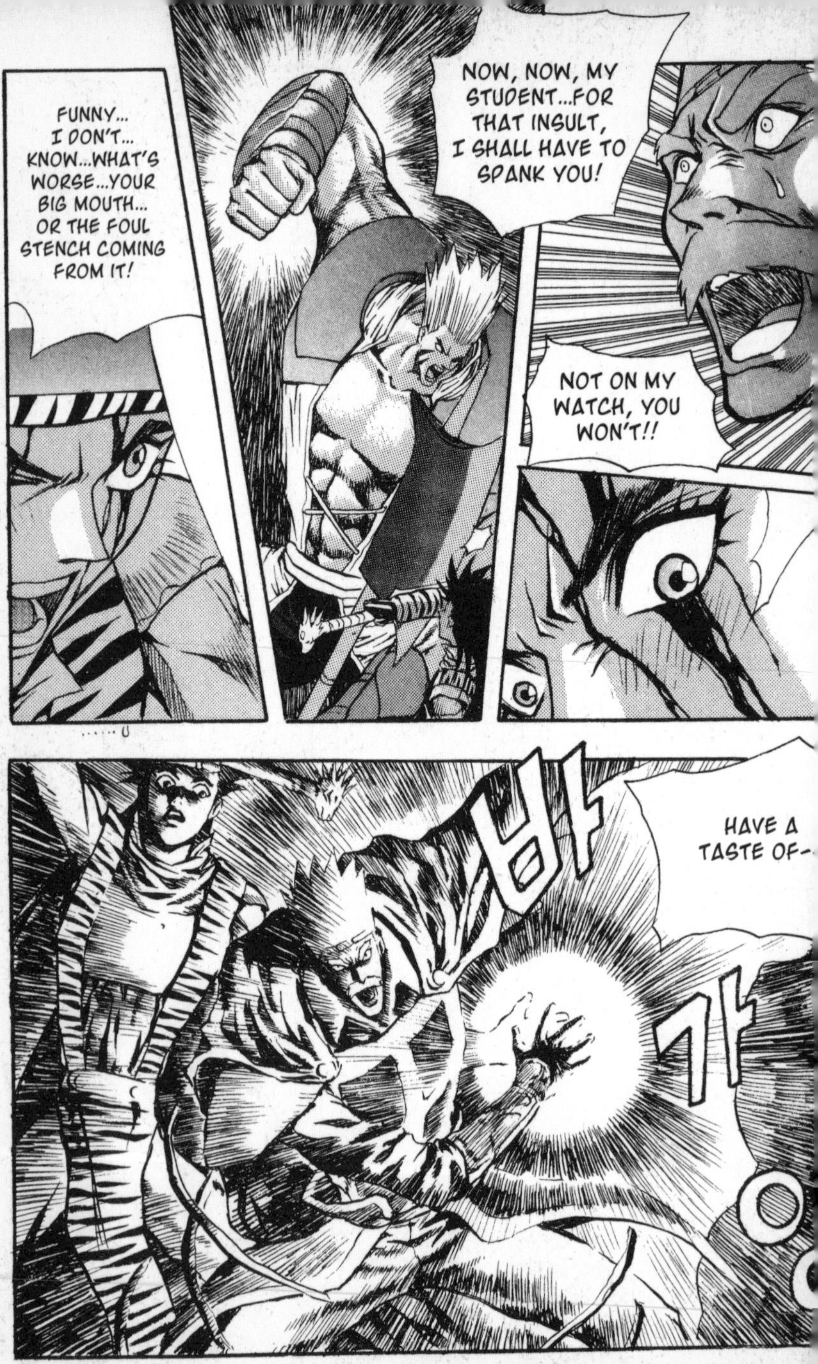

FUNNY... I DON'T... KNOW...WHAT'S WORSE...YOUR BIG MOUTH... OR THE FOUL STENCH COMING FROM IT!
NOW, NOW, MY STUDENT...FOR THAT INSULT, I SHALL HAVE TO SPANK YOU!
NOT ON MY WATCH, YOU WON'T!!
......
HAVE A TASTE OF--

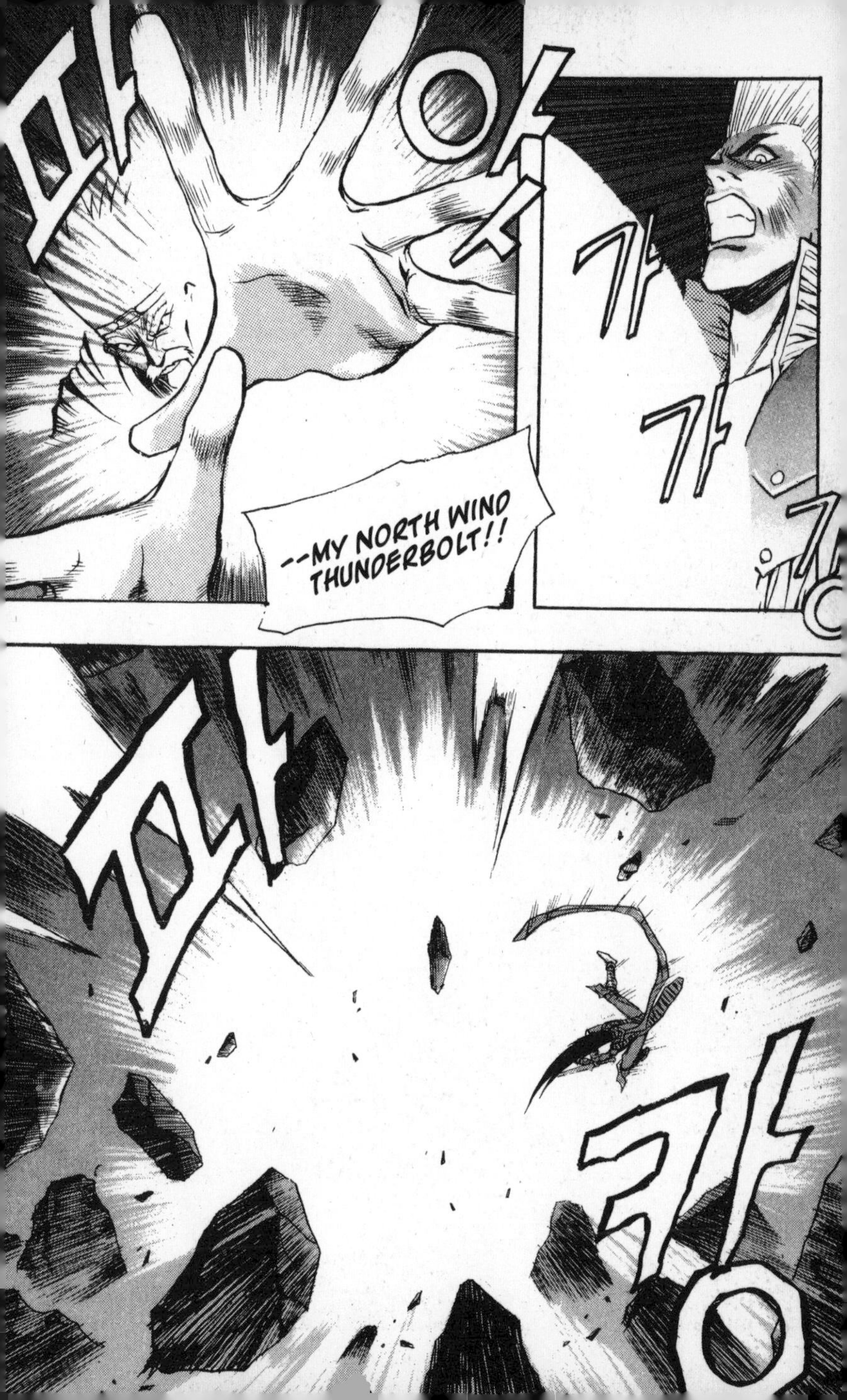
--MY NORTH WIND THUNDERBOLT!!

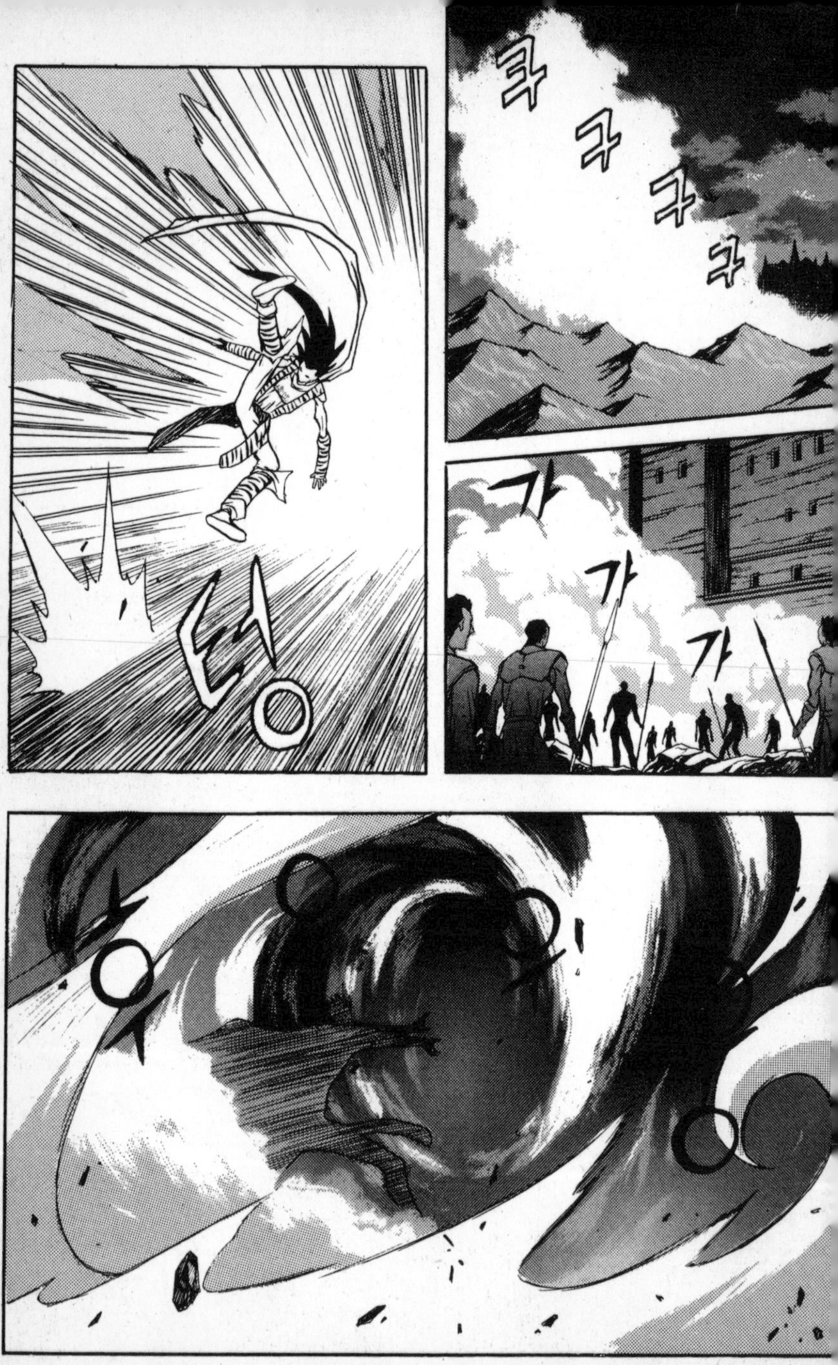
텅
쿠구구구
가가가

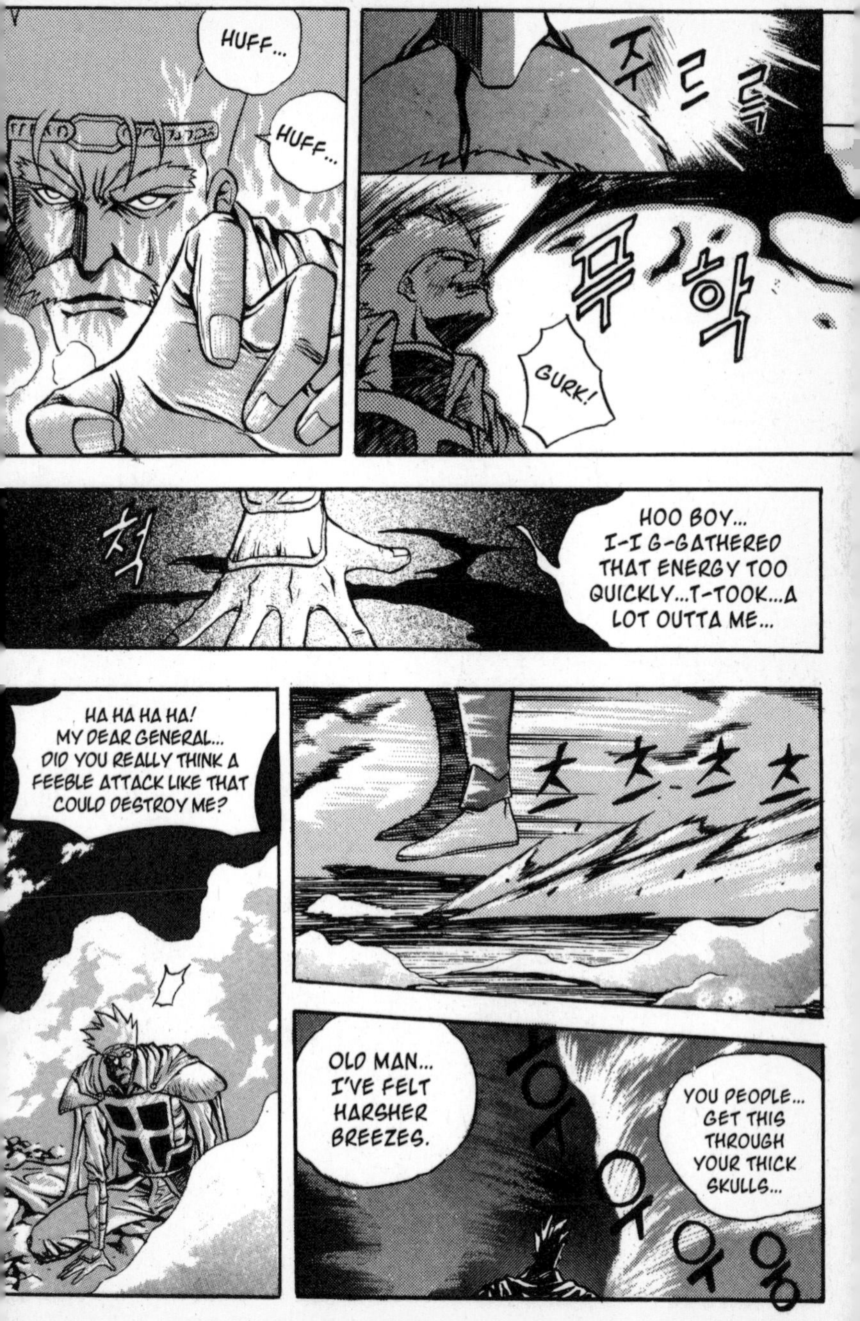
HUFF...
HUFF...
GURK!
HOO BOY... I-I G-GATHERED THAT ENERGY TOO QUICKLY...T-TOOK...A LOT OUTTA ME...
HA HA HA HA! MY DEAR GENERAL... DID YOU REALLY THINK A FEEBLE ATTACK LIKE THAT COULD DESTROY ME?
OLD MAN... I'VE FELT HARSHER BREEZES.
YOU PEOPLE... GET THIS THROUGH YOUR THICK SKULLS...

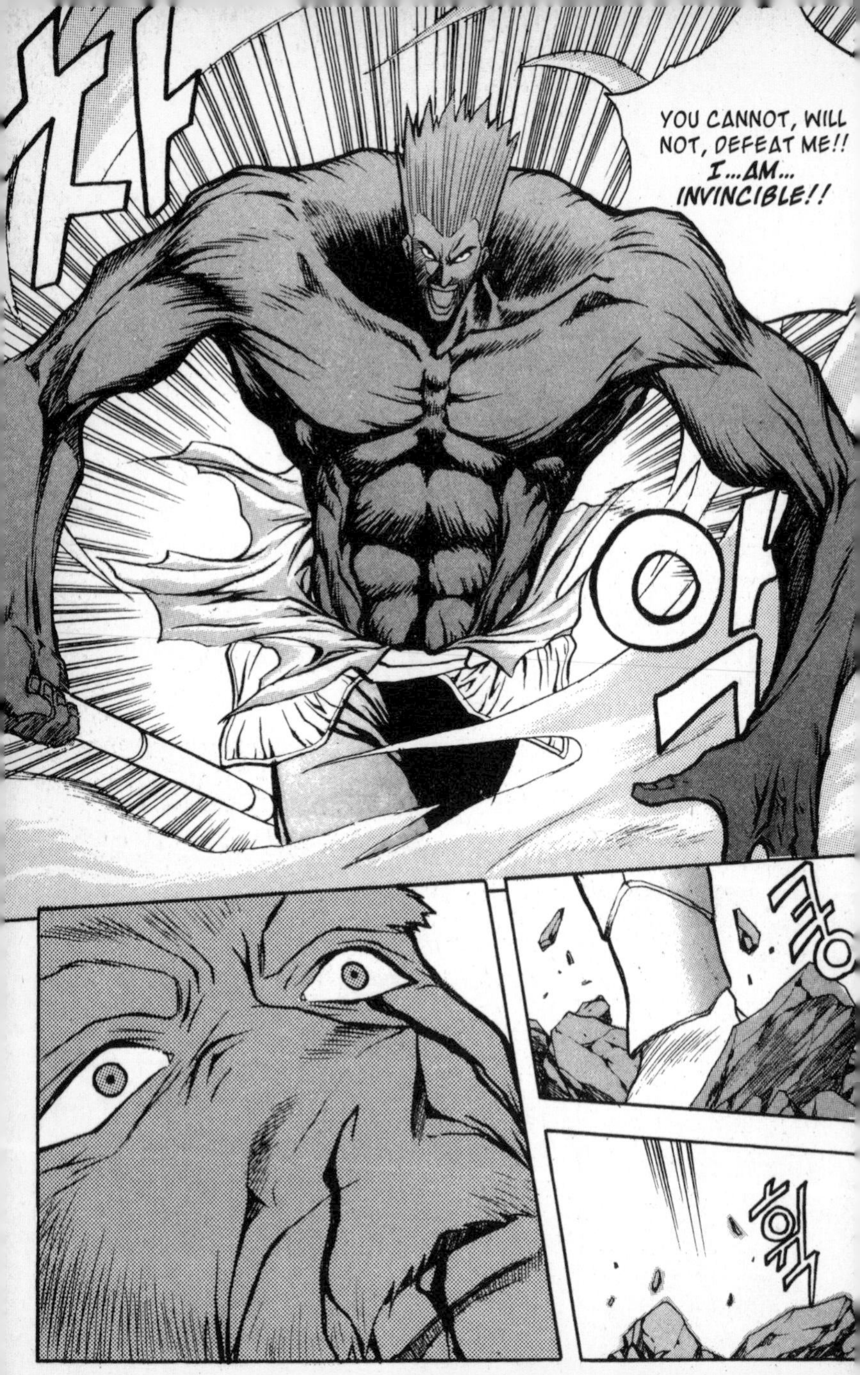
YOU CANNOT, WILL NOT, DEFEAT ME!!
I...AM... INVINCIBLE!!

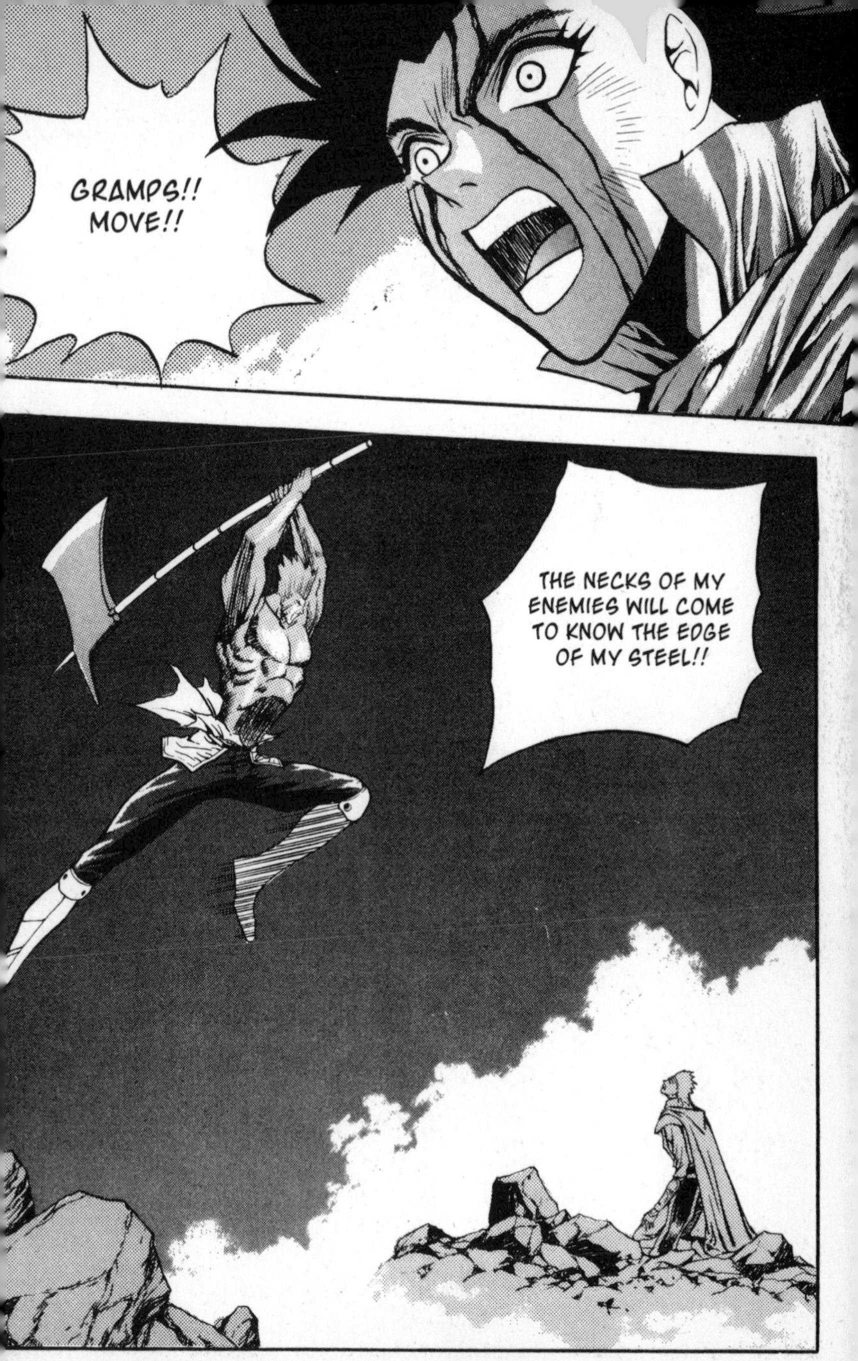
GRAMPS!! MOVE!!
THE NECKS OF MY ENEMIES WILL COME TO KNOW THE EDGE OF MY STEEL!!

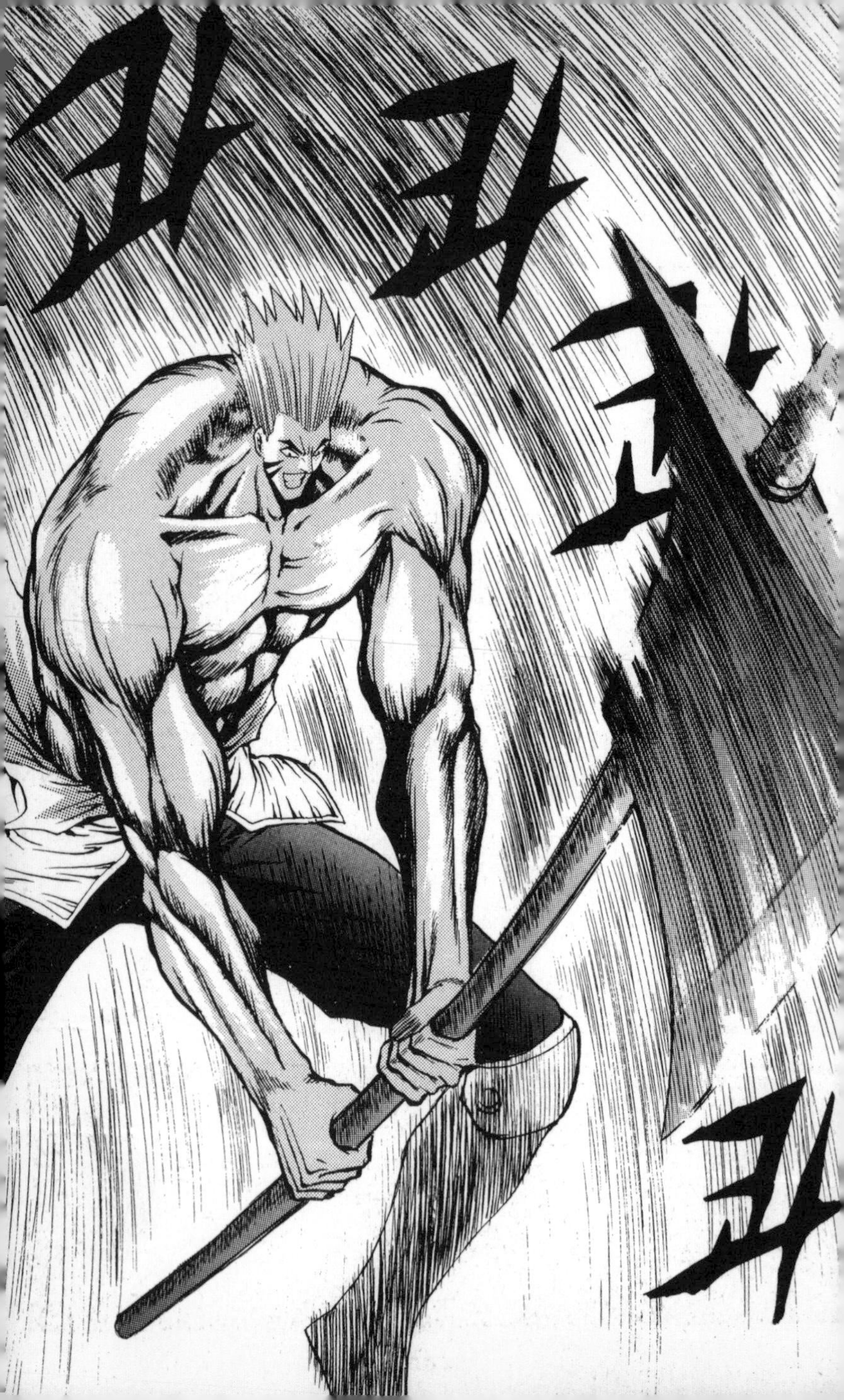
콰 콰 콰 콰

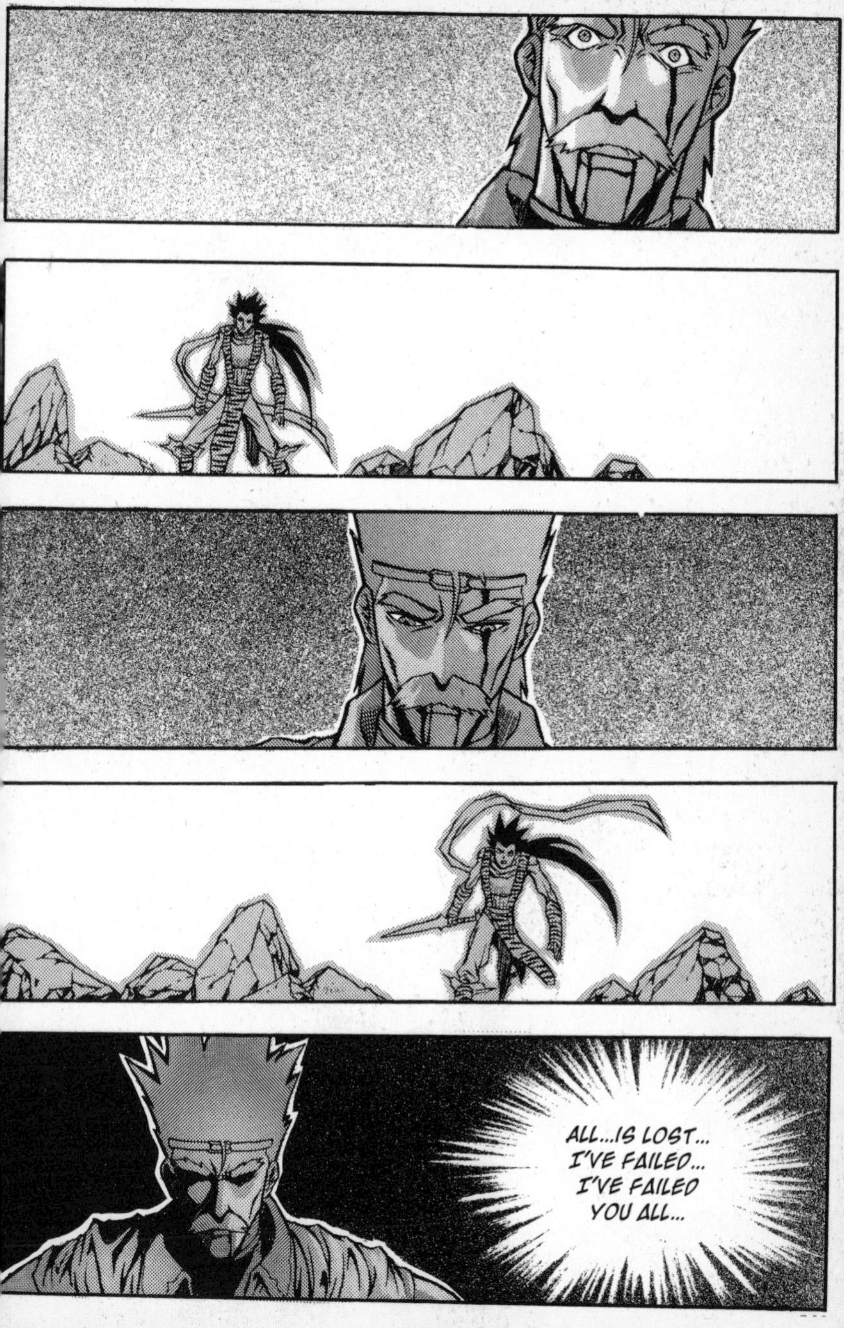
ALL...IS LOST...
I'VE FAILED...
I'VE FAILED
YOU ALL...

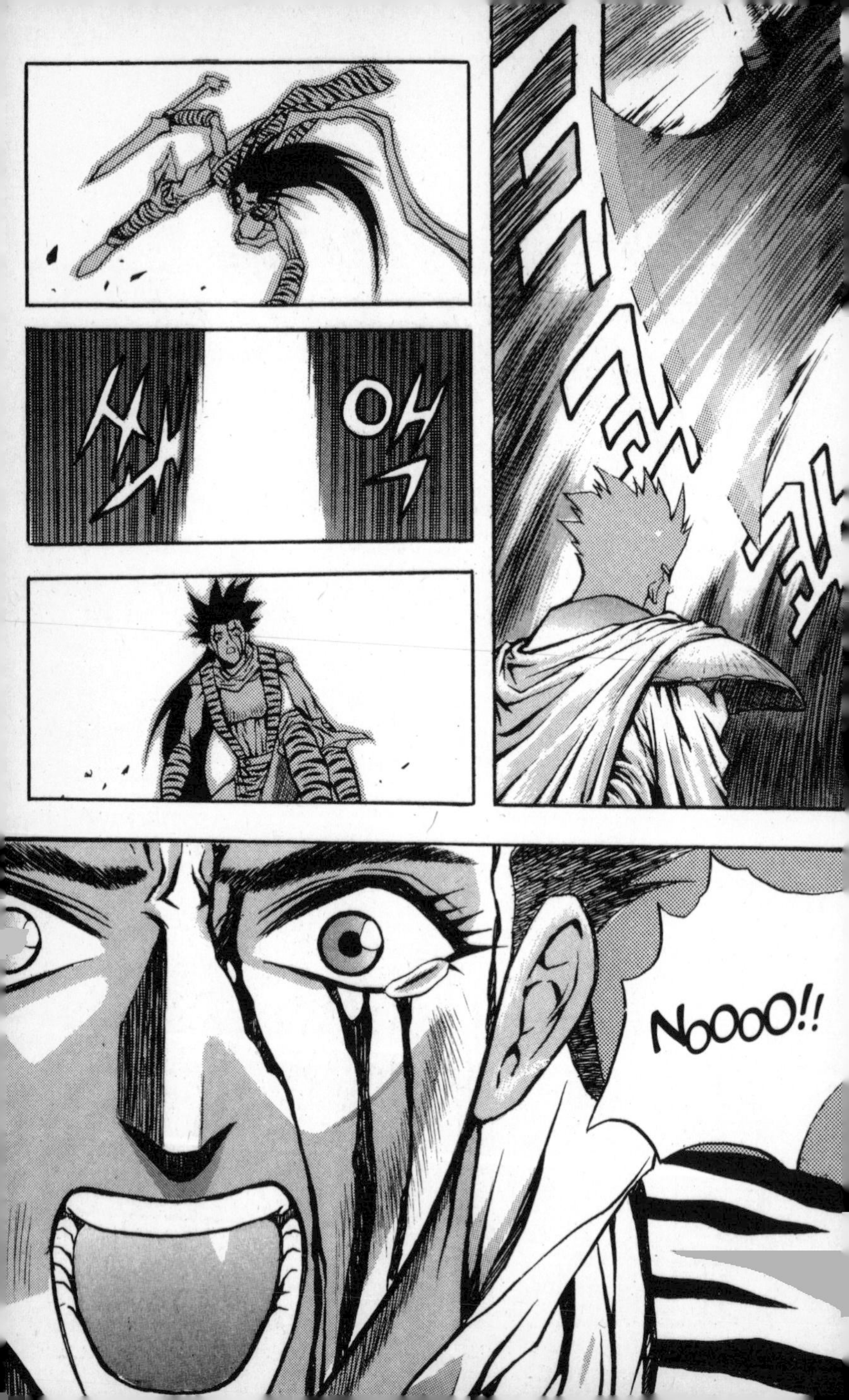
NOOOO!!

BLADE OF HEAVEN

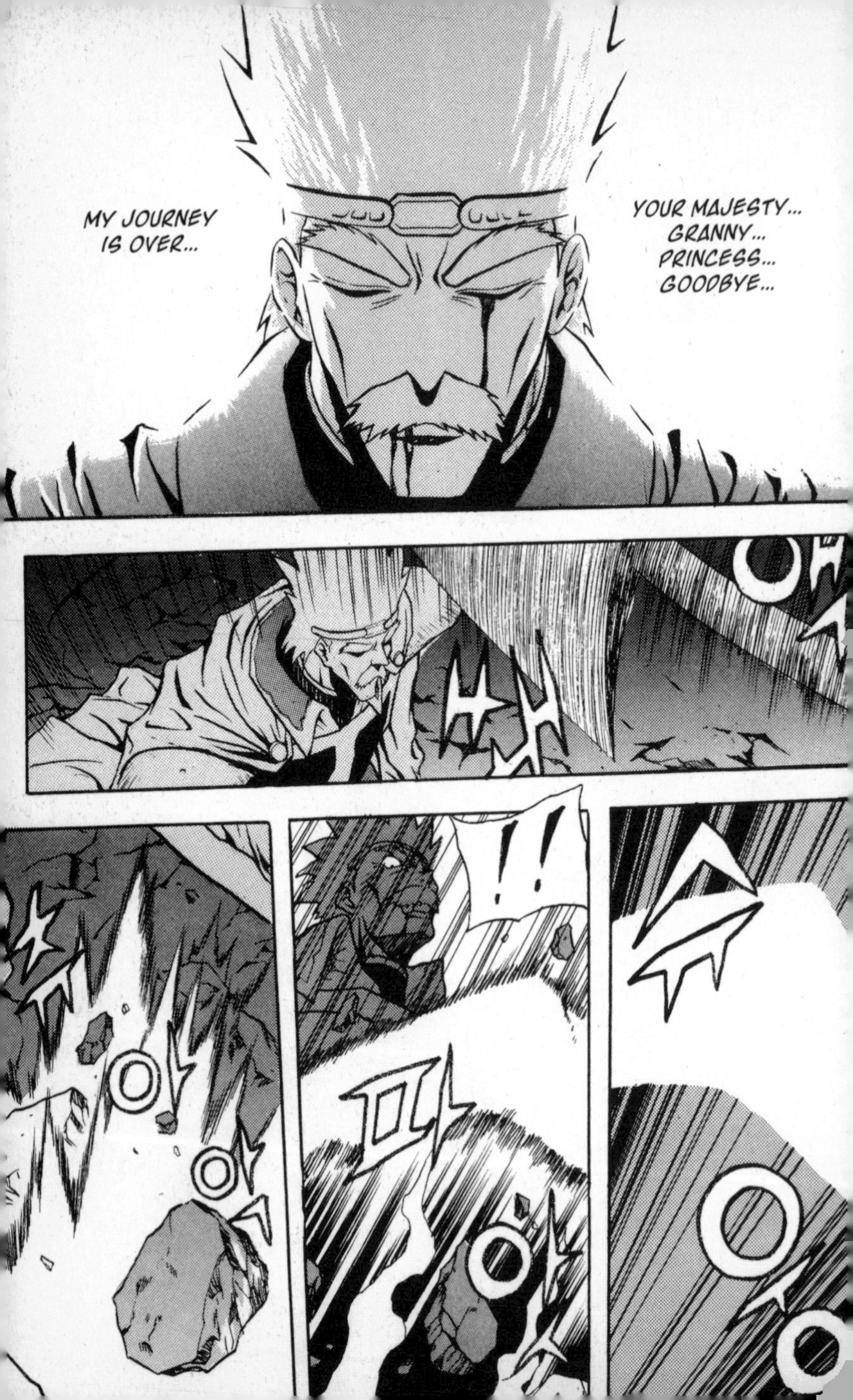
MY JOURNEY IS OVER...
YOUR MAJESTY... GRANNY... PRINCESS... GOODBYE...
!!

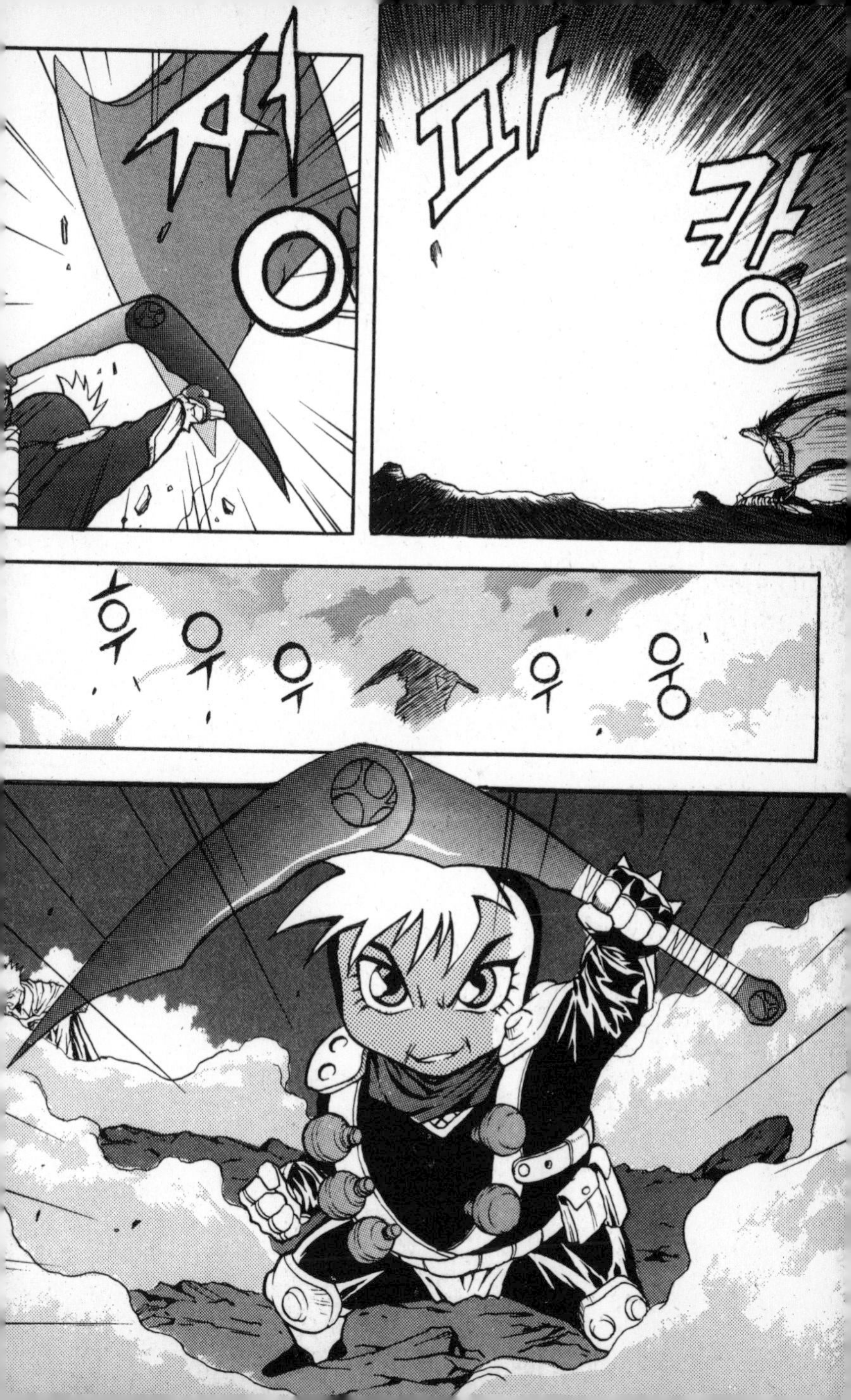

쩡
파캉
후우우
우웅

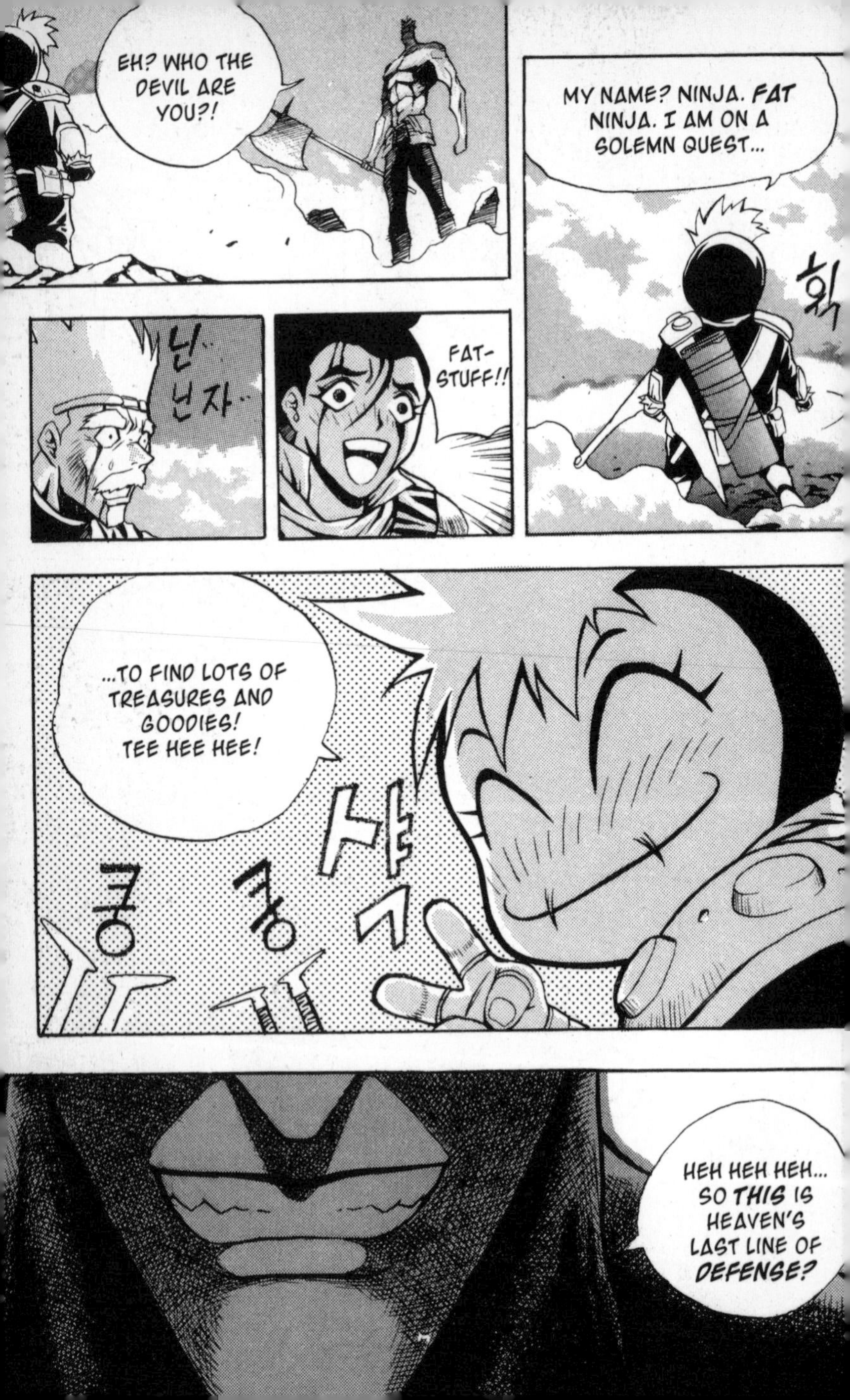
EH? WHO THE DEVIL ARE YOU?!
넌.. 넌자..
FAT-STUFF!!
MY NAME? NINJA. FAT NINJA. I AM ON A SOLEMN QUEST...
휙
...TO FIND LOTS OF TREASURES AND GOODIES! TEE HEE HEE!
쿵
쿵
HEH HEH HEH... SO THIS IS HEAVEN'S LAST LINE OF DEFENSE?

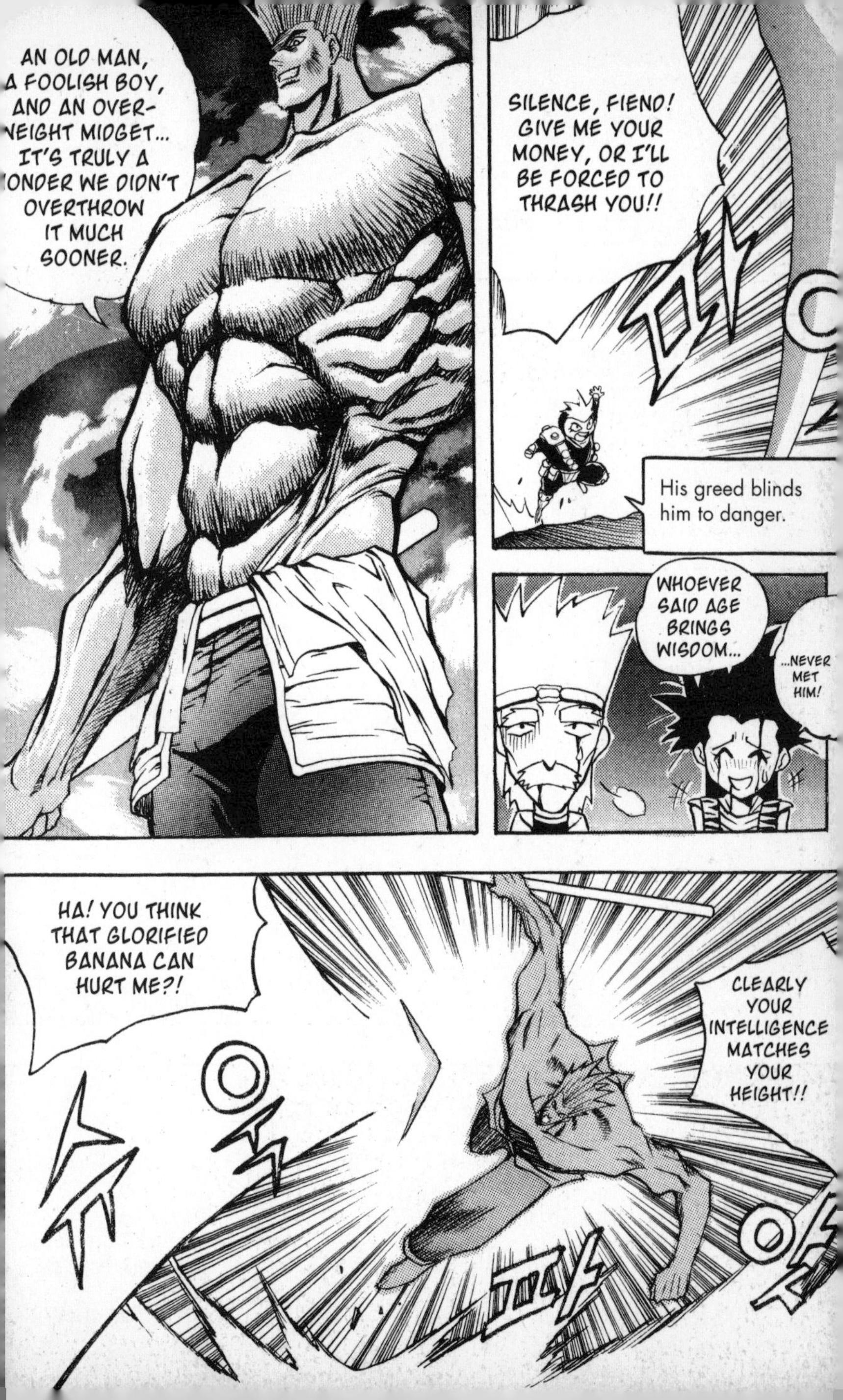
AN OLD MAN, A FOOLISH BOY, AND AN OVER-WEIGHT MIDGET... IT'S TRULY A WONDER WE DIDN'T OVERTHROW IT MUCH SOONER.
SILENCE, FIEND! GIVE ME YOUR MONEY, OR I'LL BE FORCED TO THRASH YOU!!
His greed blinds him to danger.
WHOEVER SAID AGE BRINGS WISDOM...
...NEVER MET HIM!
HA! YOU THINK THAT GLORIFIED BANANA CAN HURT ME?!
CLEARLY YOUR INTELLIGENCE MATCHES YOUR HEIGHT!!

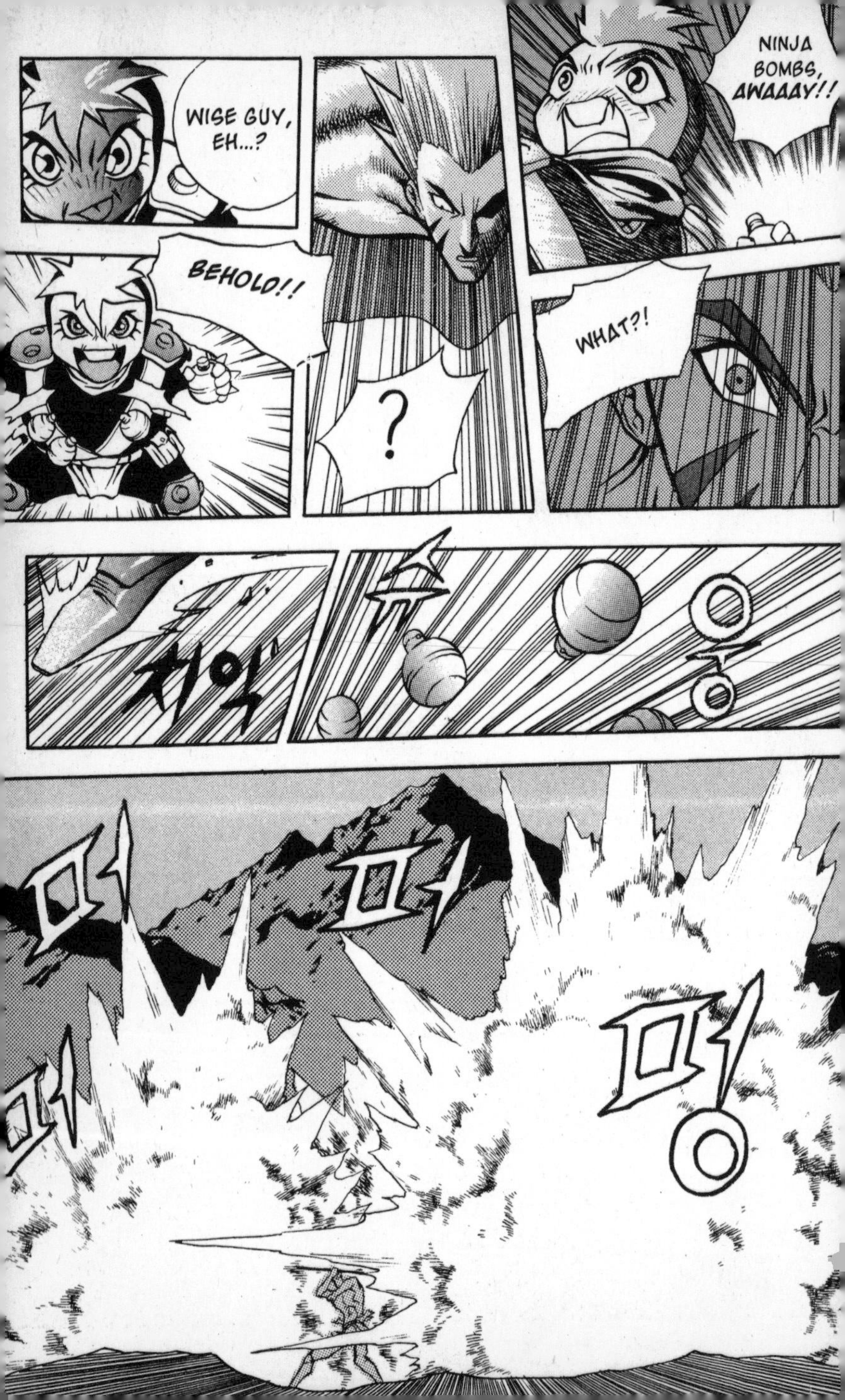
WISE GUY, EH...?
BEHOLD!!
?
NINJA BOMBS, AWAAAY!!
WHAT?!

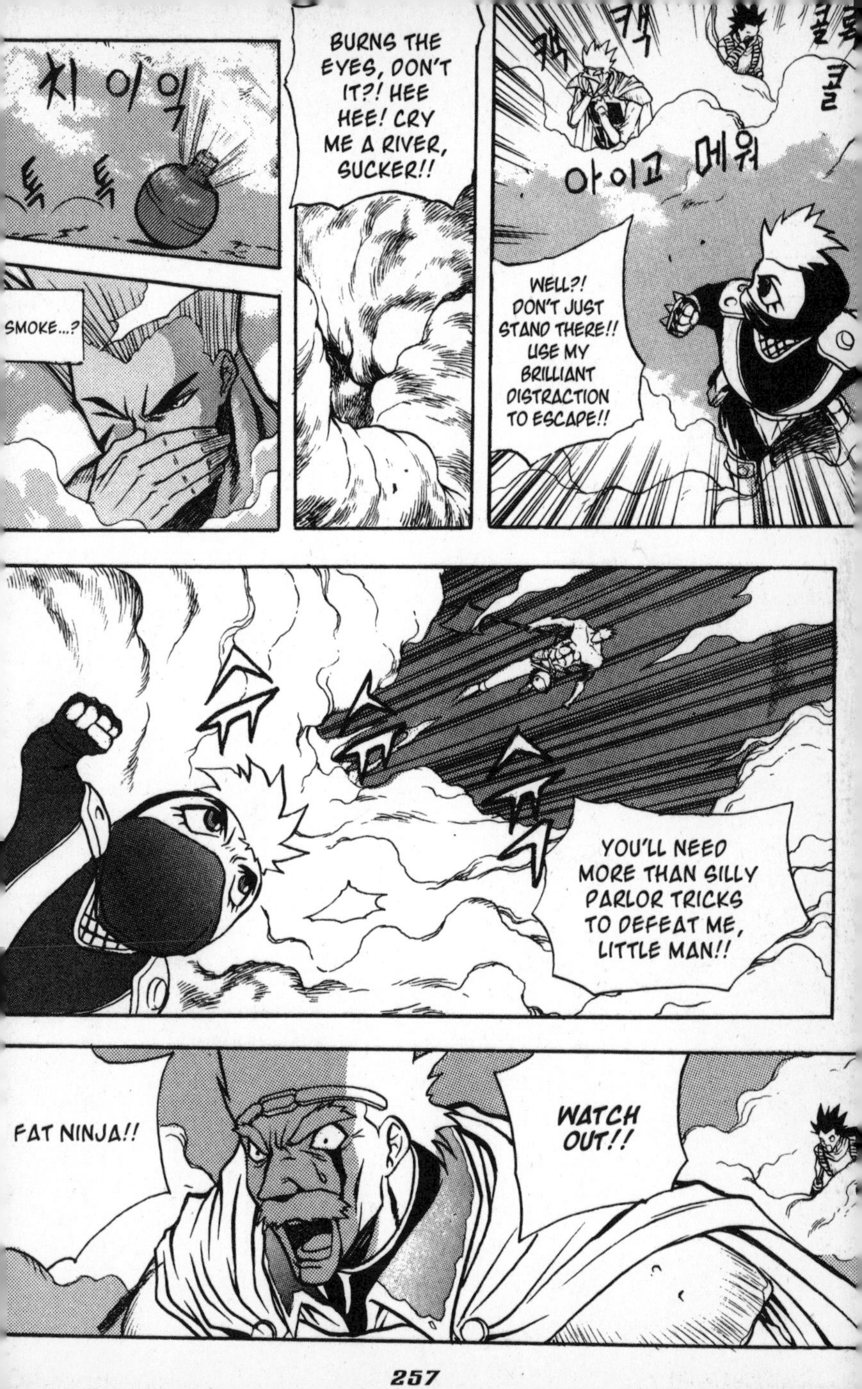

치이익
톡 톡
SMOKE...?
BURNS THE EYES, DON'T IT?! HEE HEE! CRY ME A RIVER, SUCKER!!
캑 캑
콜록 콜
아이고 매워
WELL?! DON'T JUST STAND THERE!! USE MY BRILLIANT DISTRACTION TO ESCAPE!!
YOU'LL NEED MORE THAN SILLY PARLOR TRICKS TO DEFEAT ME, LITTLE MAN!!
FAT NINJA!!
WATCH OUT!!

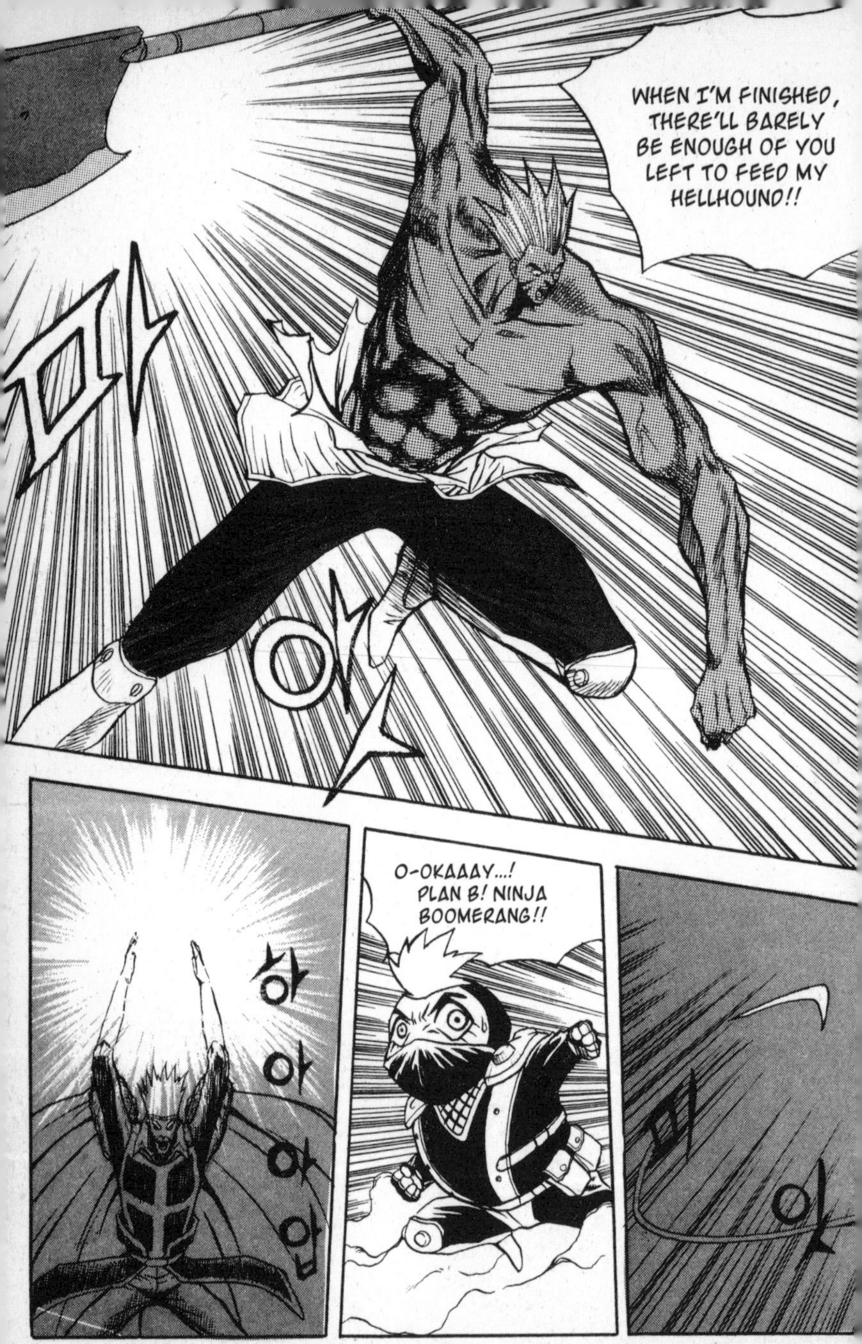
WHEN I'M FINISHED, THERE'LL BARELY BE ENOUGH OF YOU LEFT TO FEED MY HELLHOUND!!
O-OKAAAY...! PLAN B! NINJA BOOMERANG!!

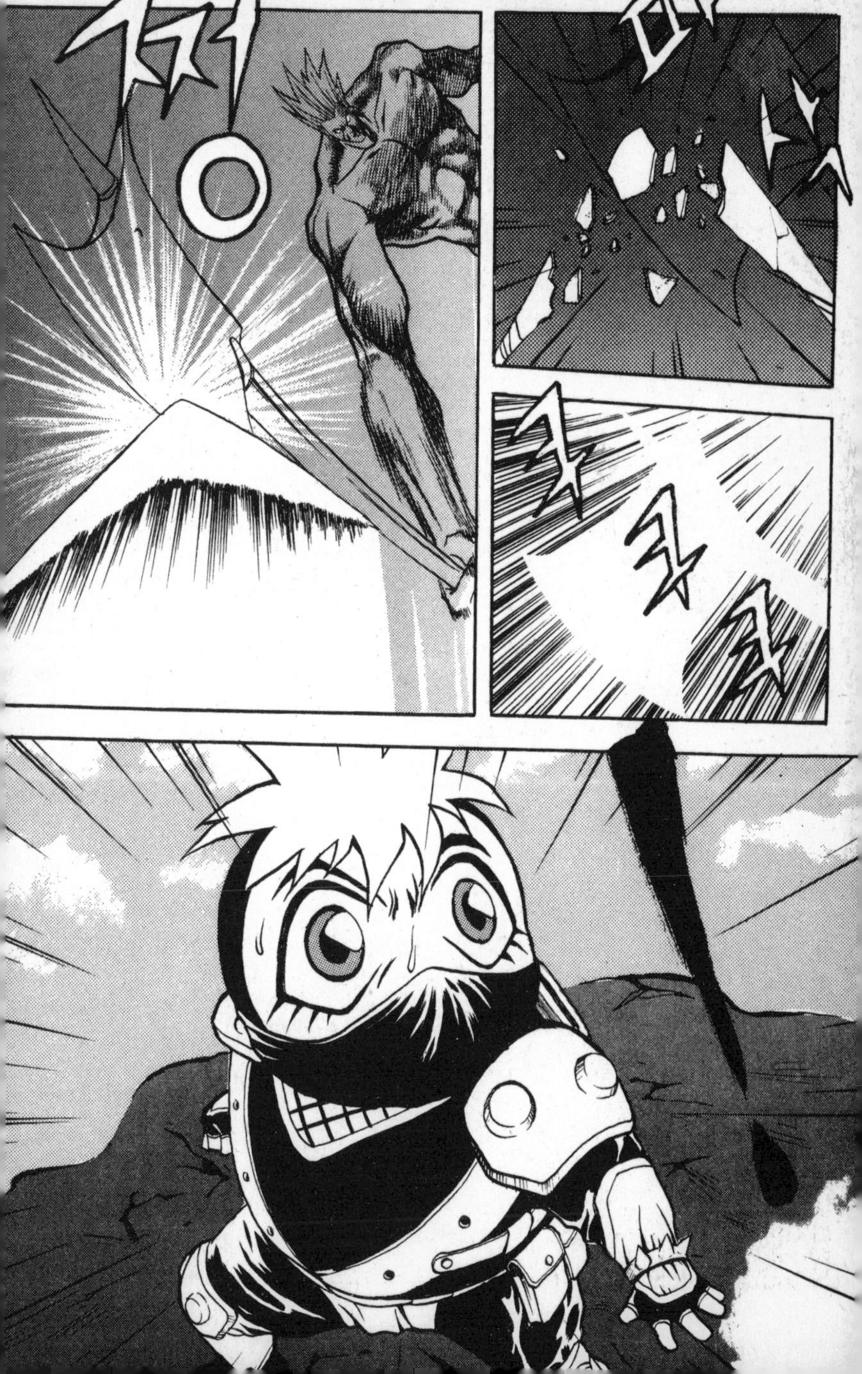

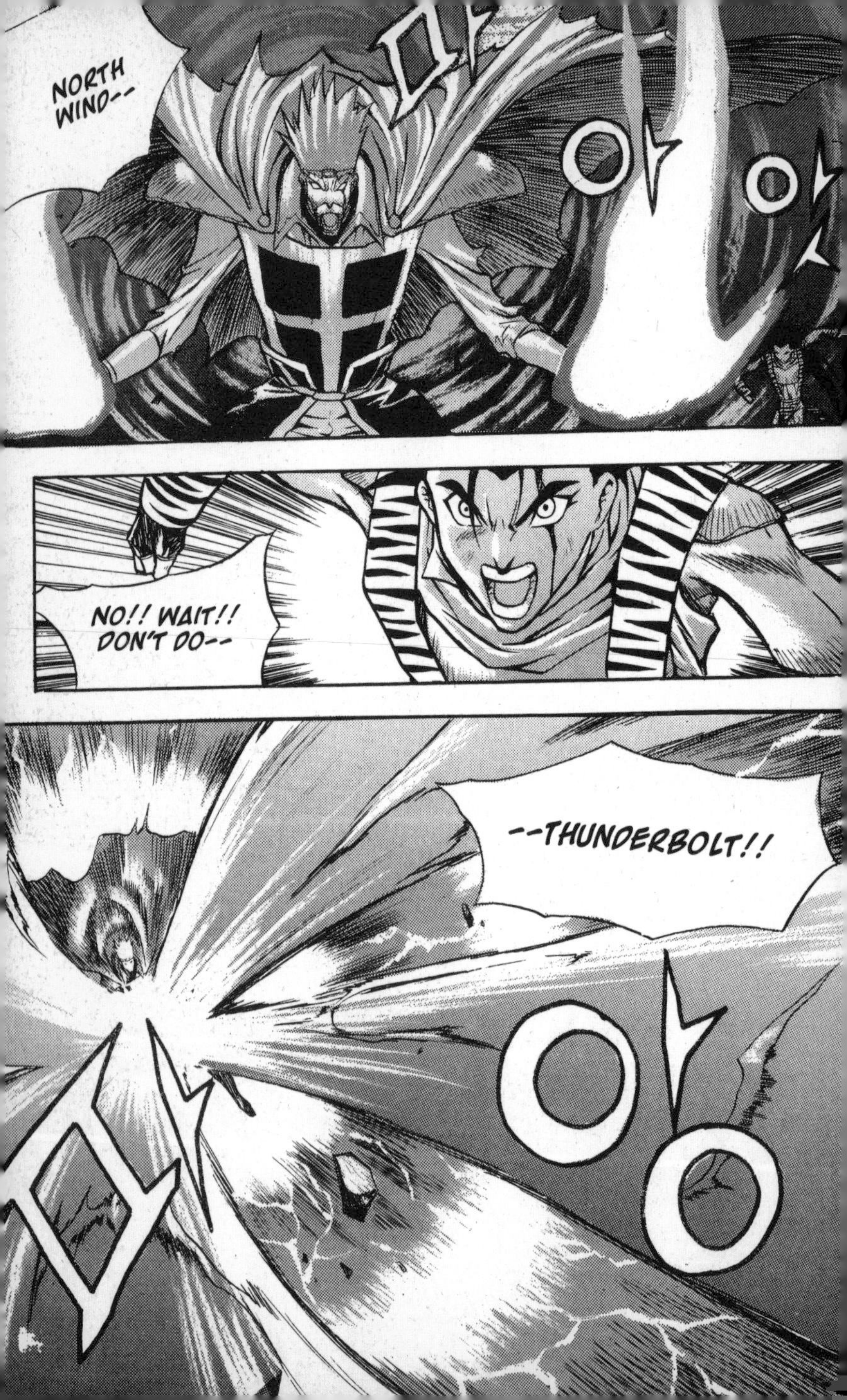
NORTH WIND--
NO!! WAIT!! DON'T DO--
--THUNDERBOLT!!

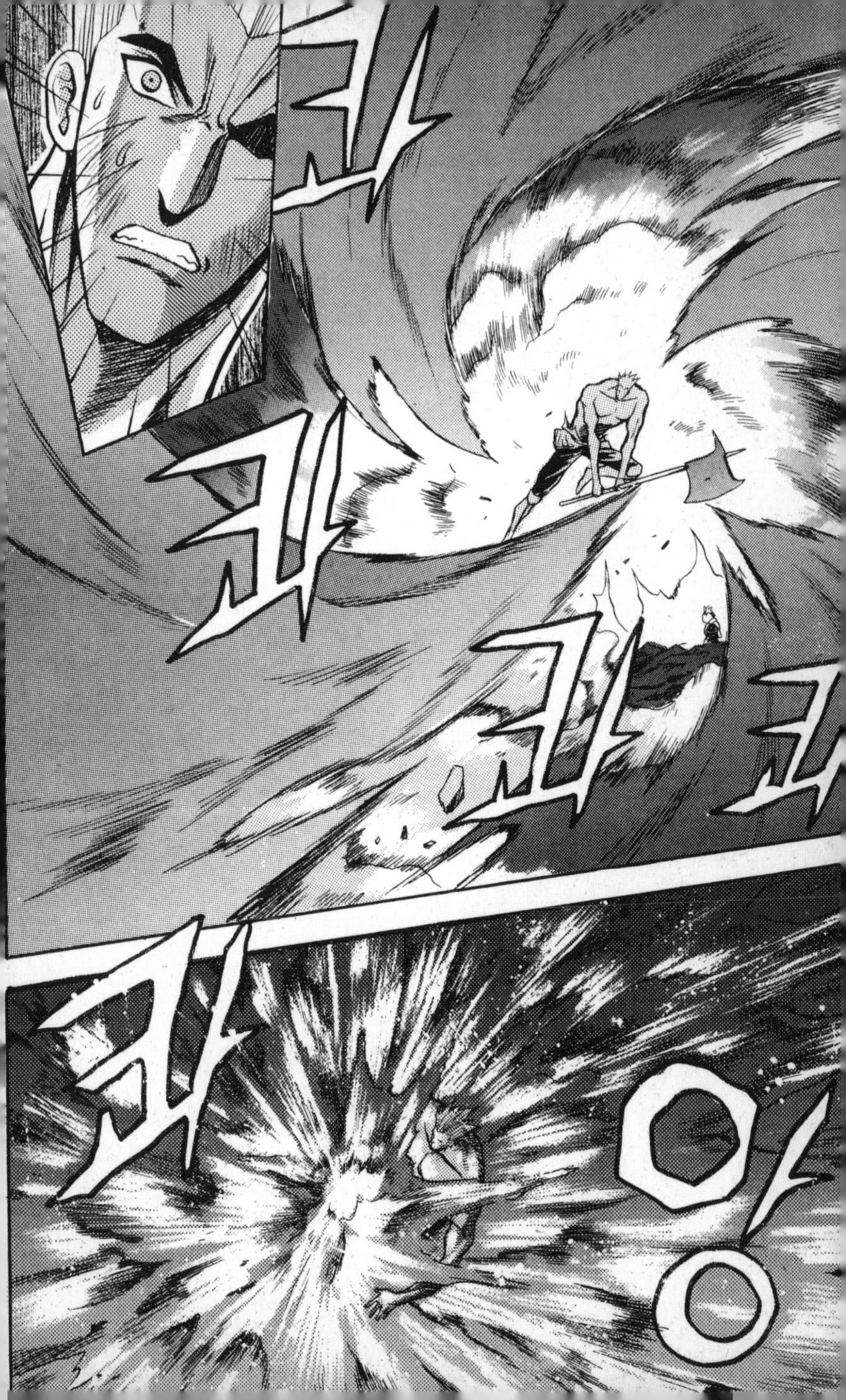
콰
콰
콰
콰
콰앙

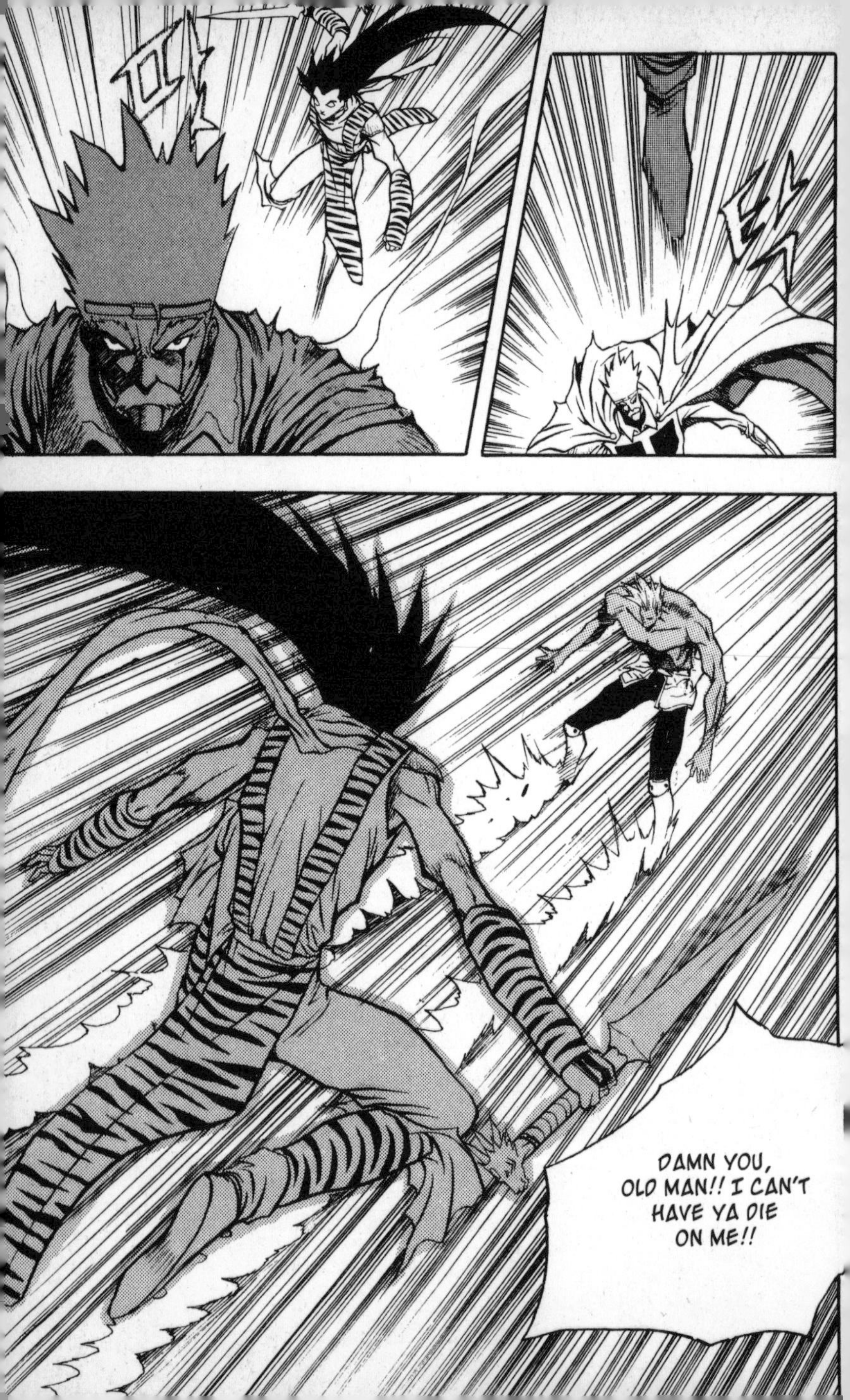
DAMN YOU, OLD MAN!! I CAN'T HAVE YA DIE ON ME!!

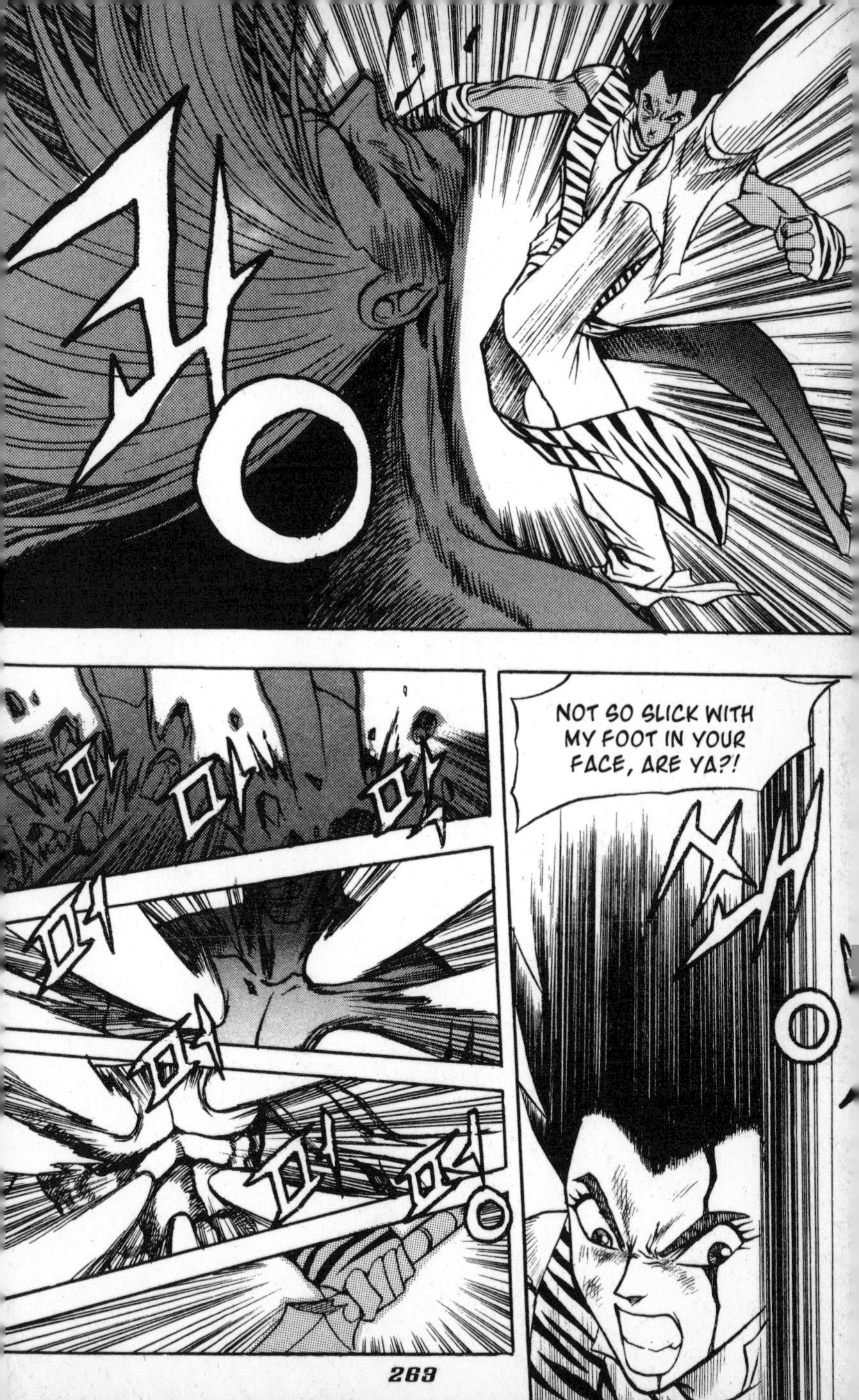
NOT SO SLICK WITH MY FOOT IN YOUR FACE, ARE YA?!

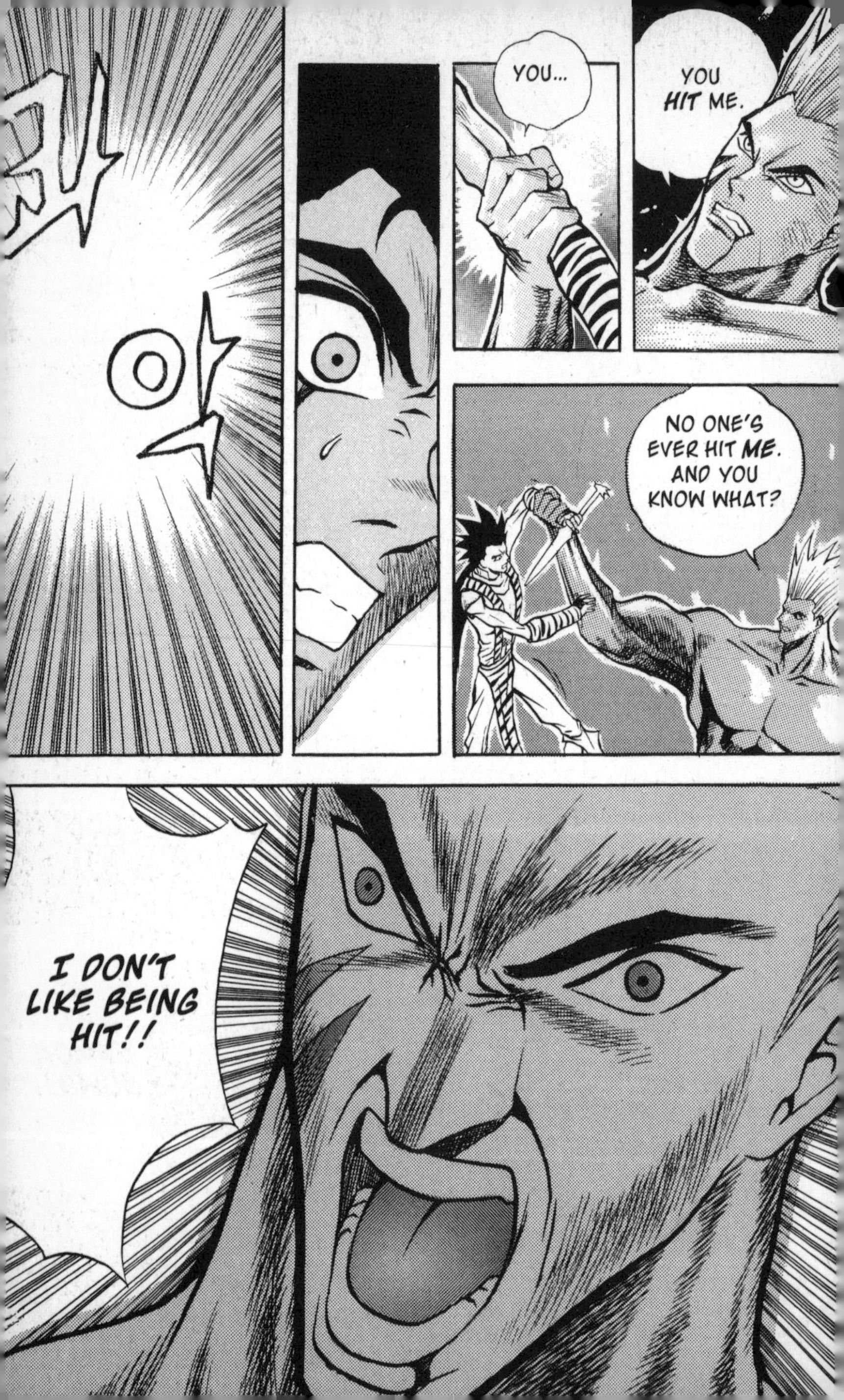
YOU...
YOU HIT ME.
NO ONE'S EVER HIT ME. AND YOU KNOW WHAT?
I DON'T LIKE BEING HIT!!

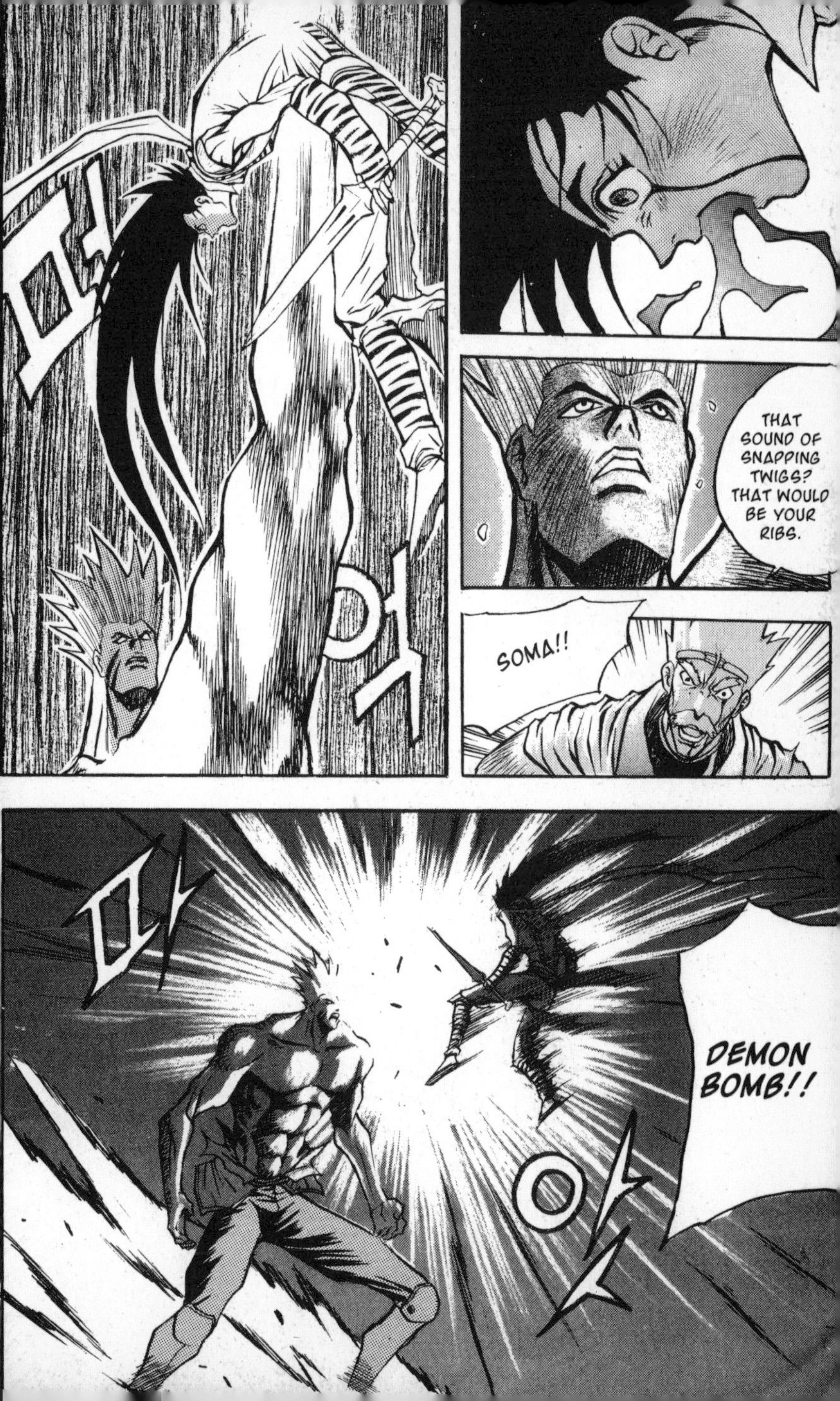
THAT SOUND OF SNAPPING TWIGS? THAT WOULD BE YOUR RIBS.
SOMA!!
DEMON BOMB!!

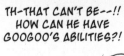

TH-THAT CAN'T BE--!! HOW CAN HE HAVE GOOGOO'S ABILITIES?!

CLASS DISMISSED.

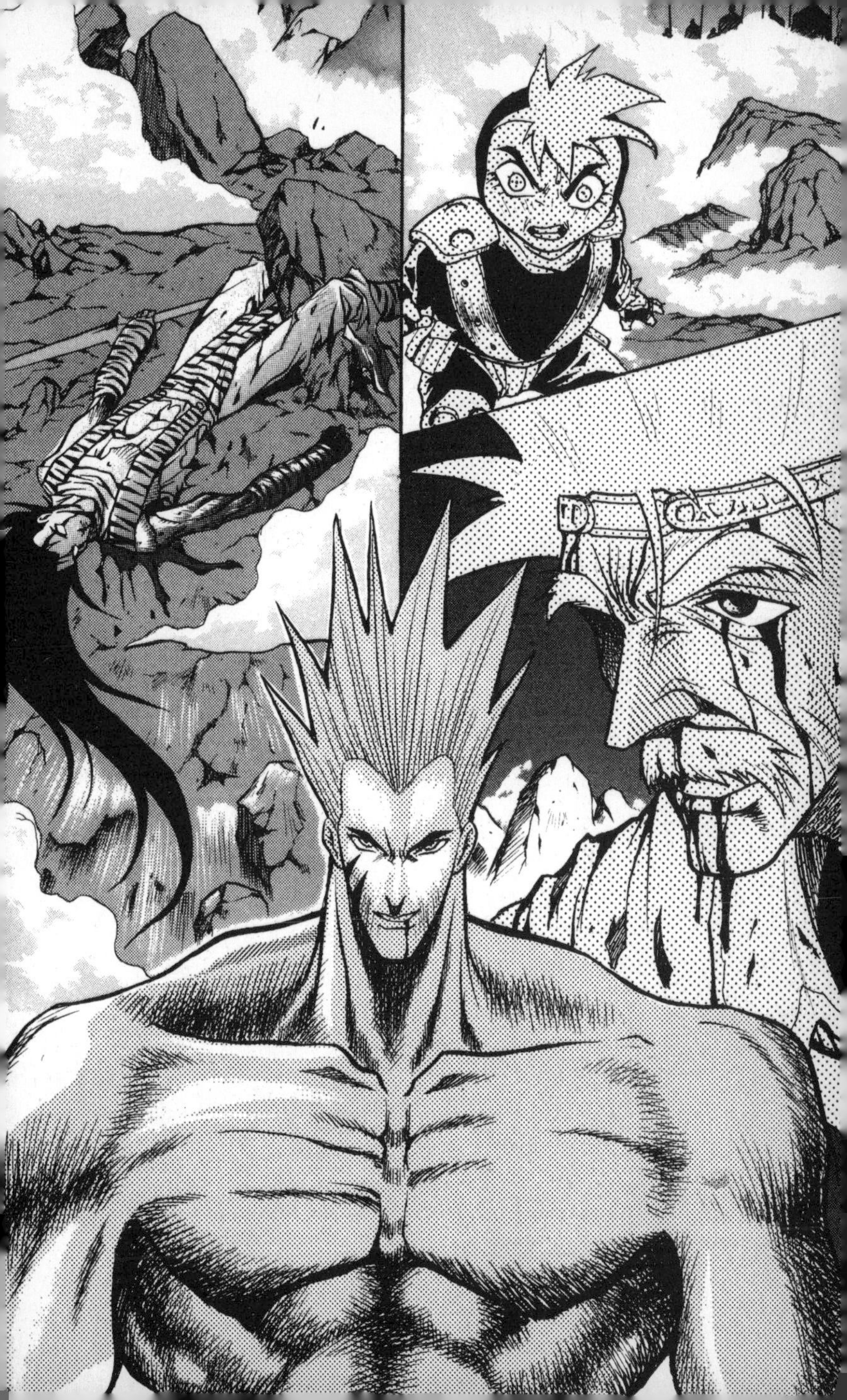

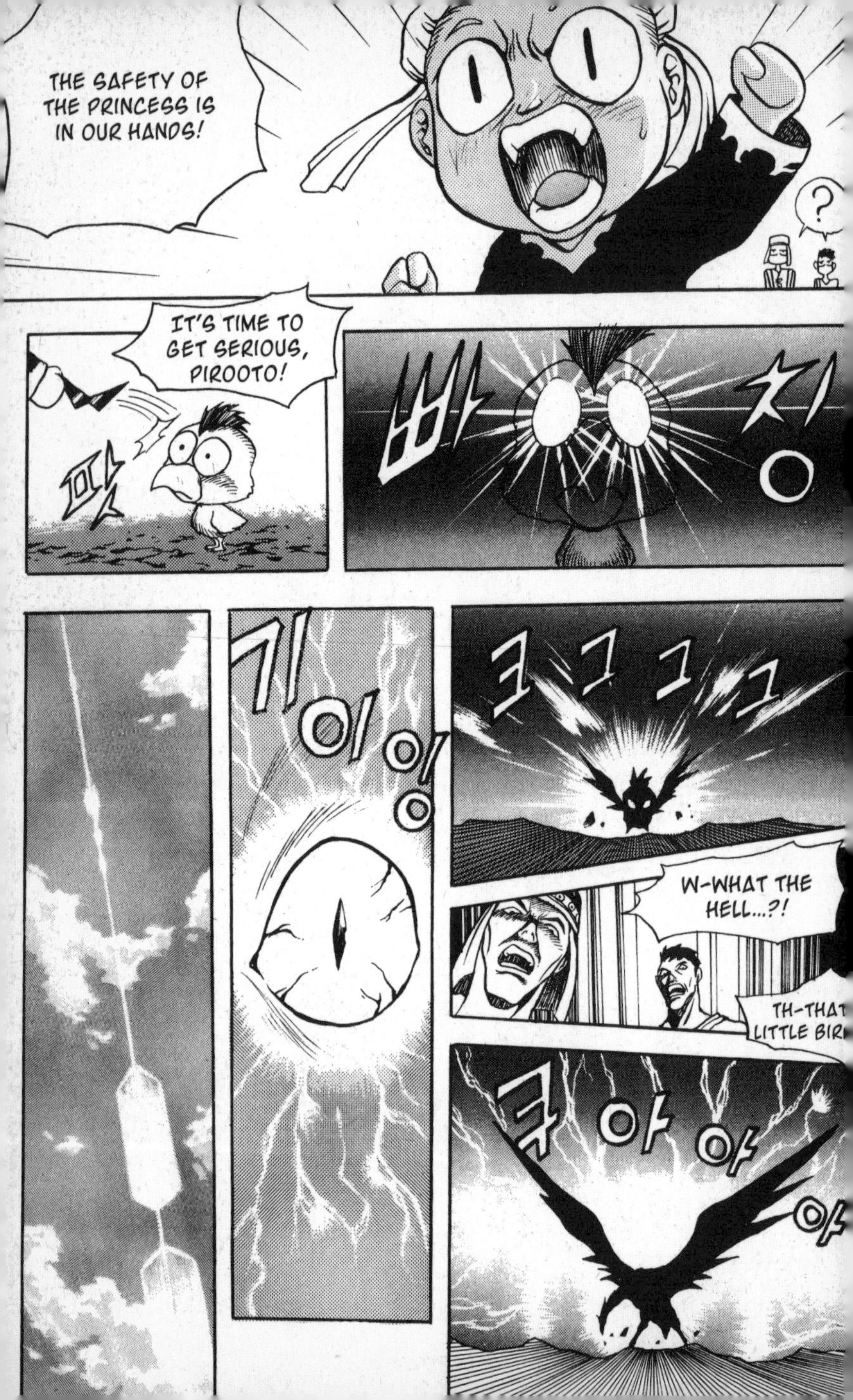
THE SAFETY OF THE PRINCESS IS IN OUR HANDS!
?
IT'S TIME TO GET SERIOUS, PIROOTO!
W-WHAT THE HELL...?!
TH-THAT LITTLE BIR

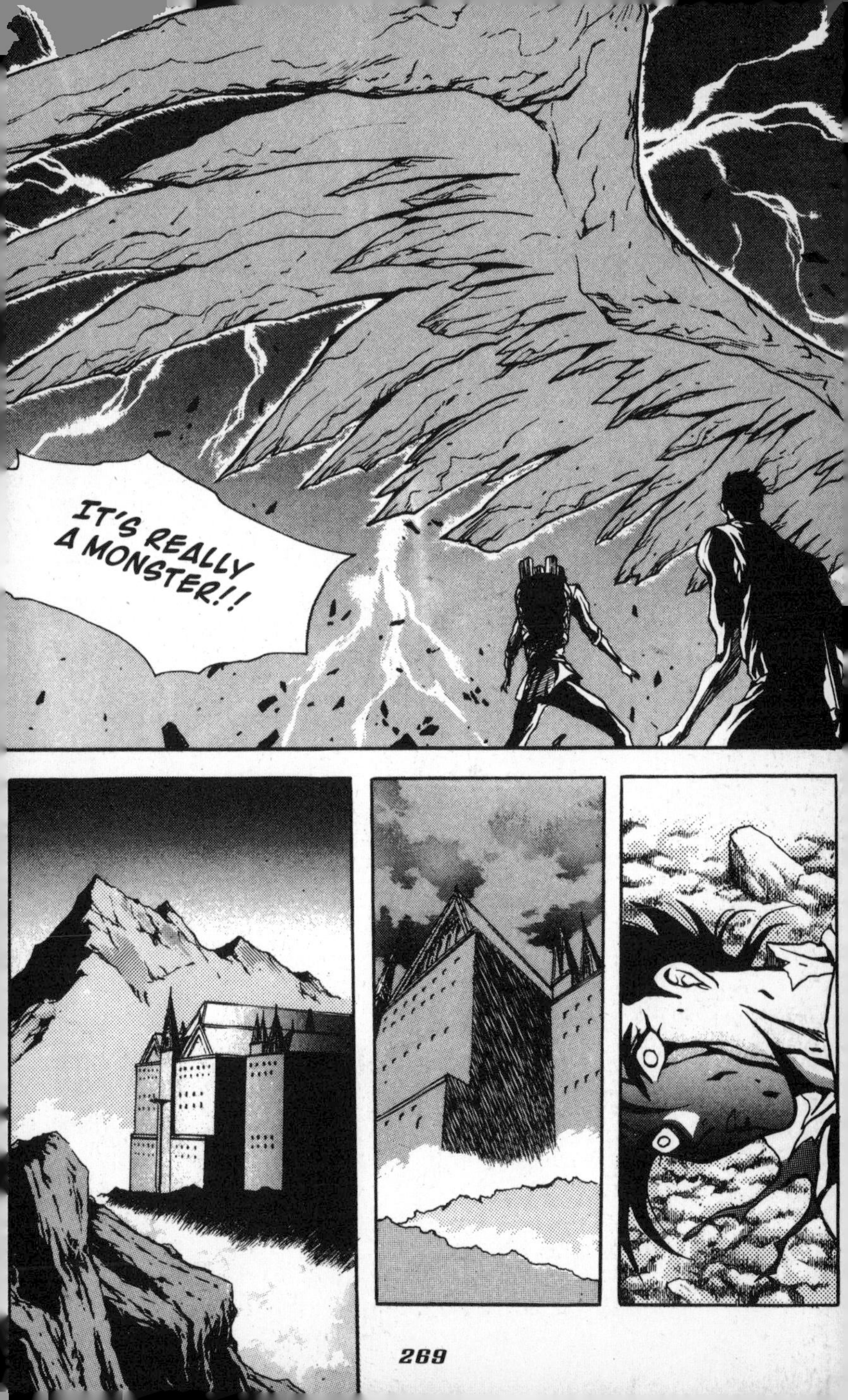
IT'S REALLY A MONSTER!!

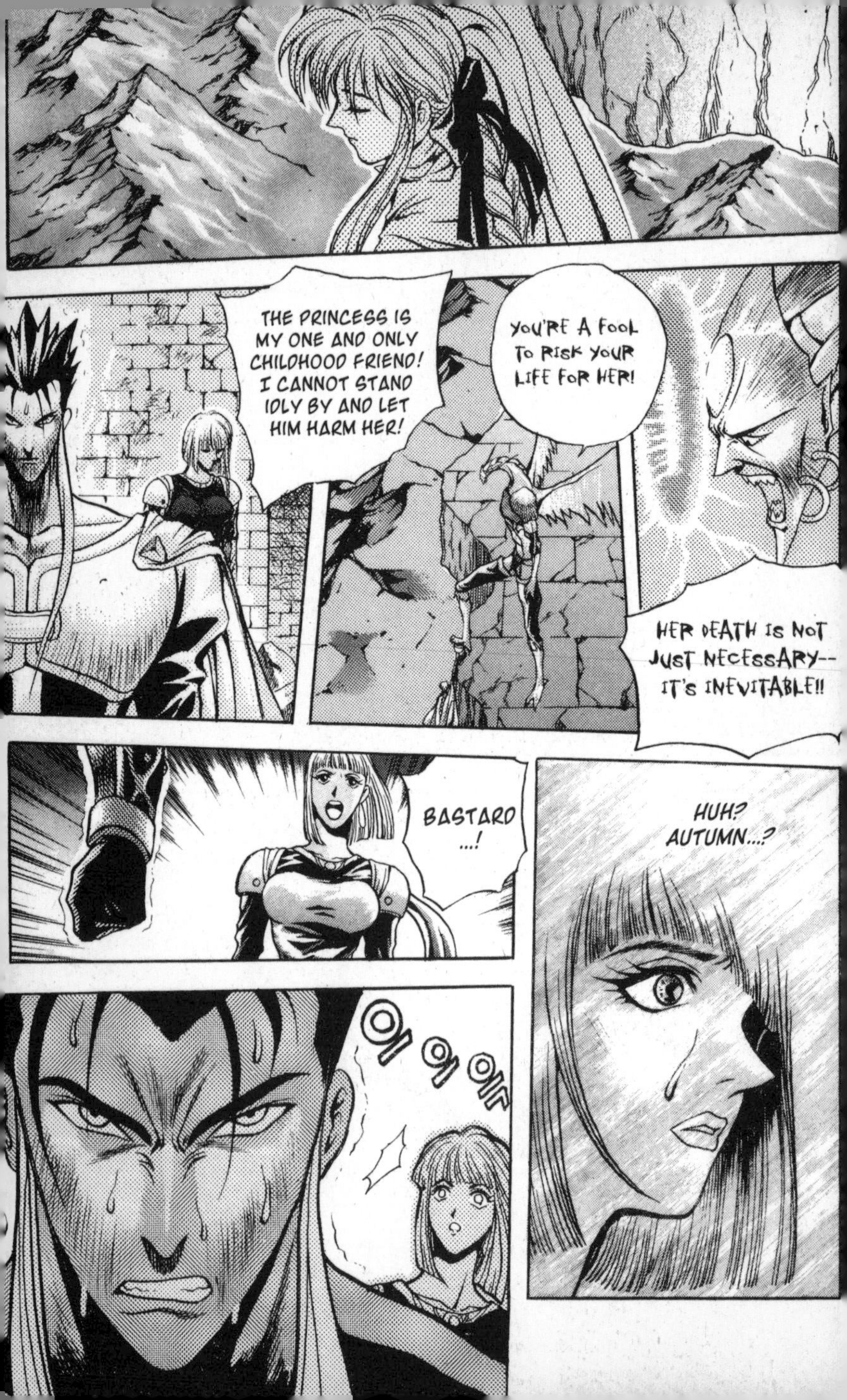
THE PRINCESS IS MY ONE AND ONLY CHILDHOOD FRIEND! I CANNOT STAND IDLY BY AND LET HIM HARM HER!
YOU'RE A FOOL TO RISK YOUR LIFE FOR HER!
HER DEATH IS NOT JUST NECESSARY-- IT'S INEVITABLE!!
BASTARD ...!
HUH? AUTUMN...?

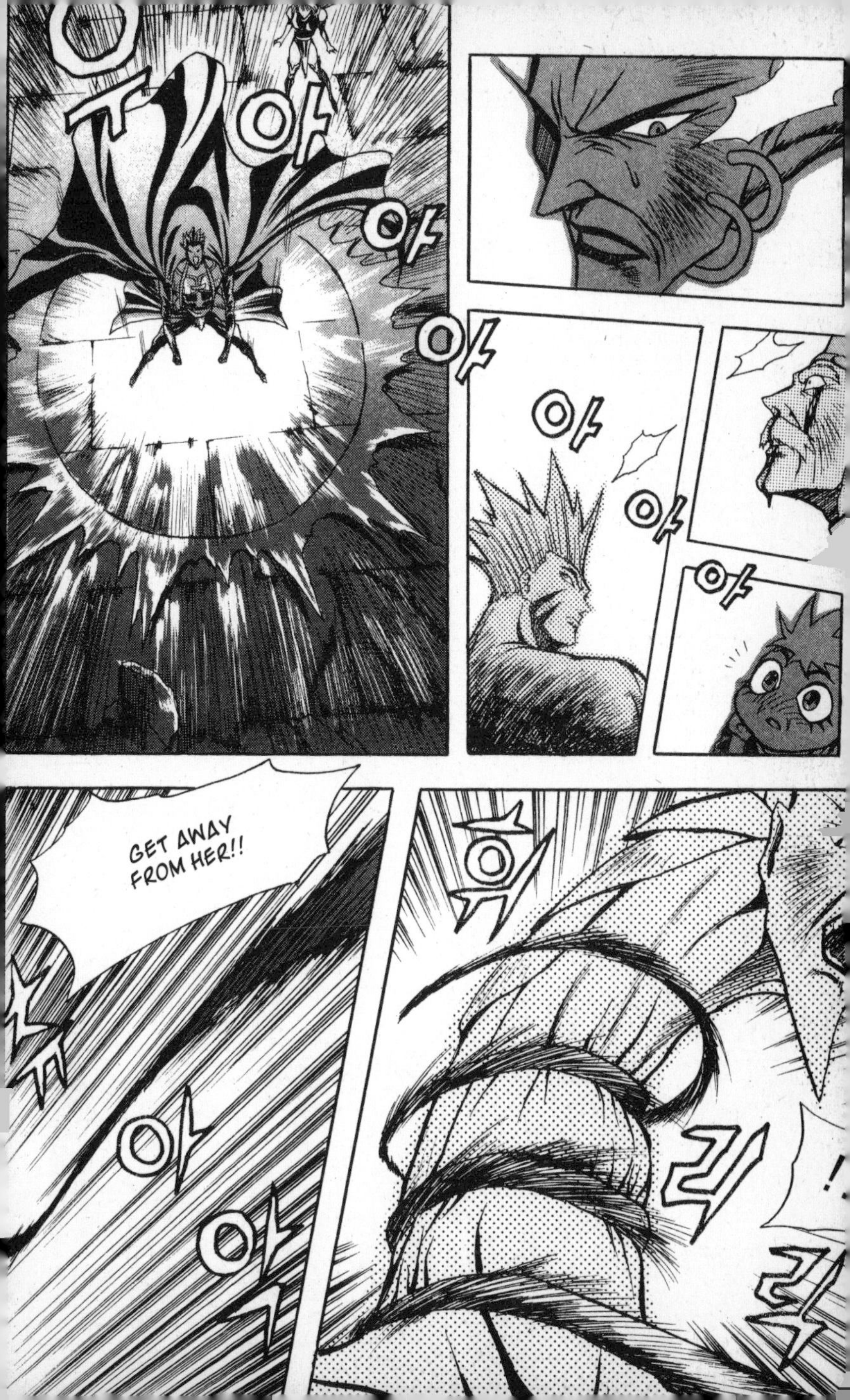
GET AWAY FROM HER!!

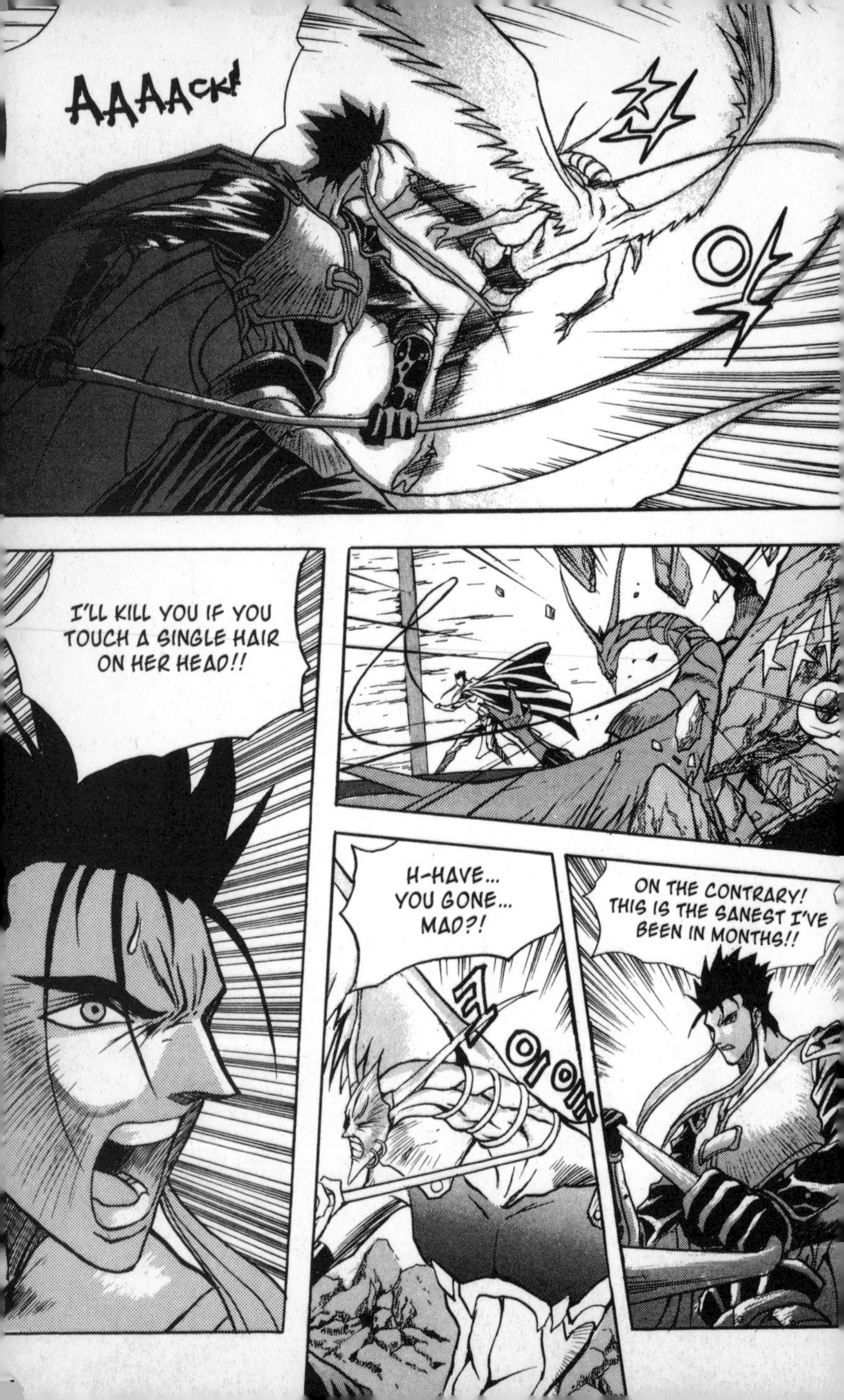
AAAACK!
I'LL KILL YOU IF YOU TOUCH A SINGLE HAIR ON HER HEAD!!
H-HAVE... YOU GONE... MAD?!
ON THE CONTRARY! THIS IS THE SANEST I'VE BEEN IN MONTHS!!

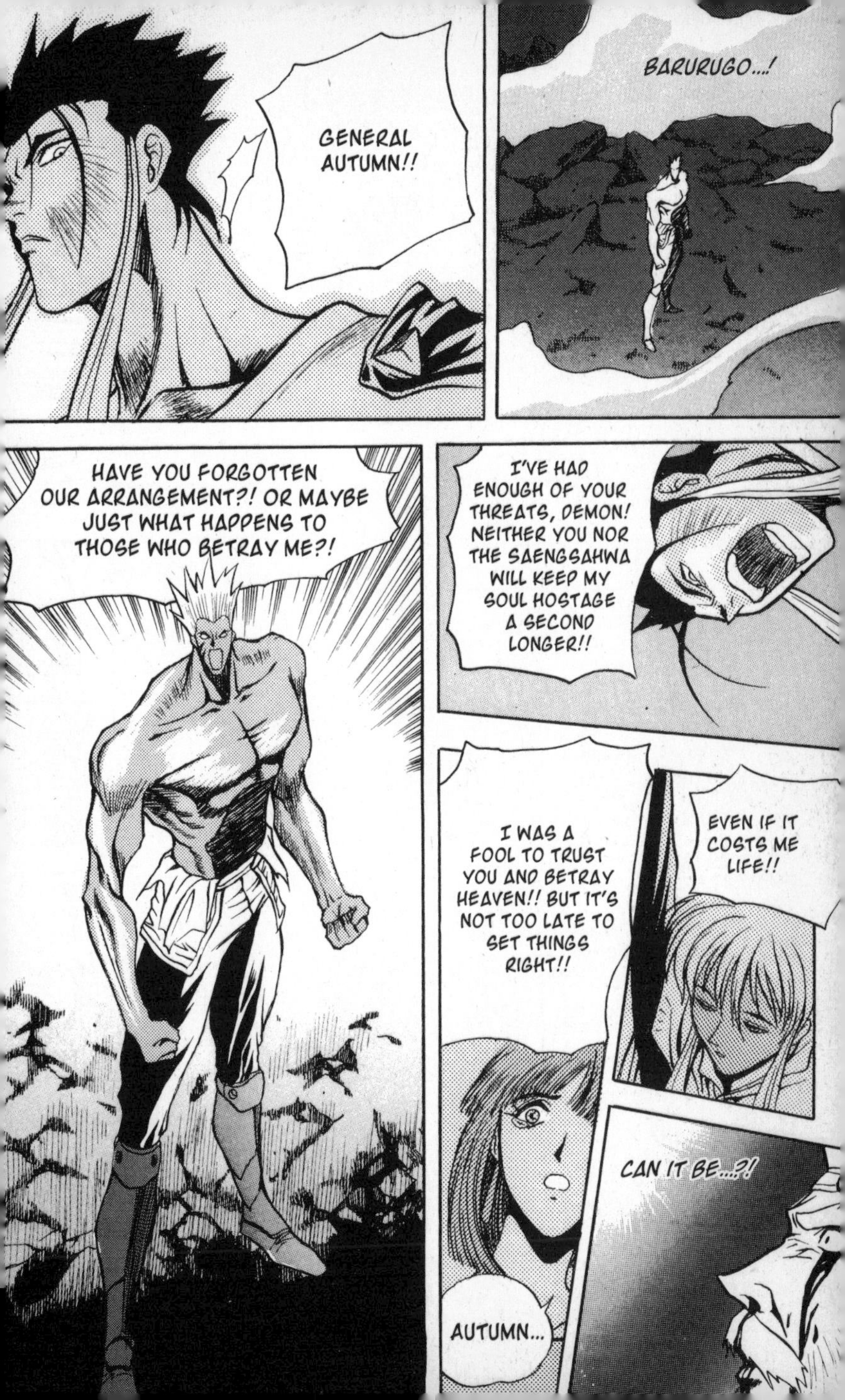
GENERAL AUTUMN!!
BARURUGO...!
HAVE YOU FORGOTTEN OUR ARRANGEMENT?! OR MAYBE JUST WHAT HAPPENS TO THOSE WHO BETRAY ME?!
I'VE HAD ENOUGH OF YOUR THREATS, DEMON! NEITHER YOU NOR THE SAENGSAHWA WILL KEEP MY SOUL HOSTAGE A SECOND LONGER!!
I WAS A FOOL TO TRUST YOU AND BETRAY HEAVEN!! BUT IT'S NOT TOO LATE TO SET THINGS RIGHT!!
EVEN IF IT COSTS ME LIFE!!
AUTUMN...
CAN IT BE...?!

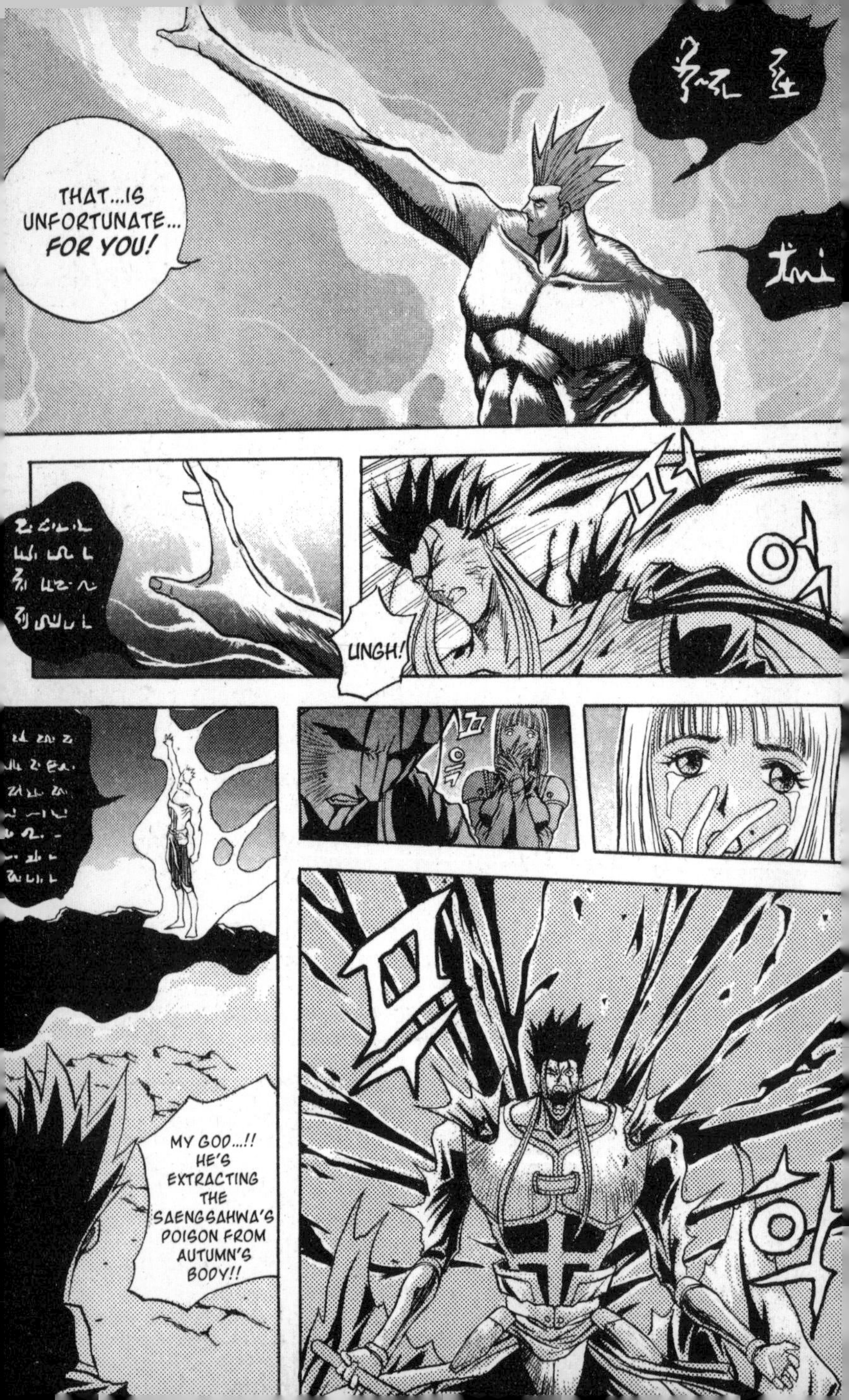
THAT...IS UNFORTUNATE... FOR YOU!
UNGH!
MY GOD...!! HE'S EXTRACTING THE SAENGSAHWA'S POISON FROM AUTUMN'S BODY!!

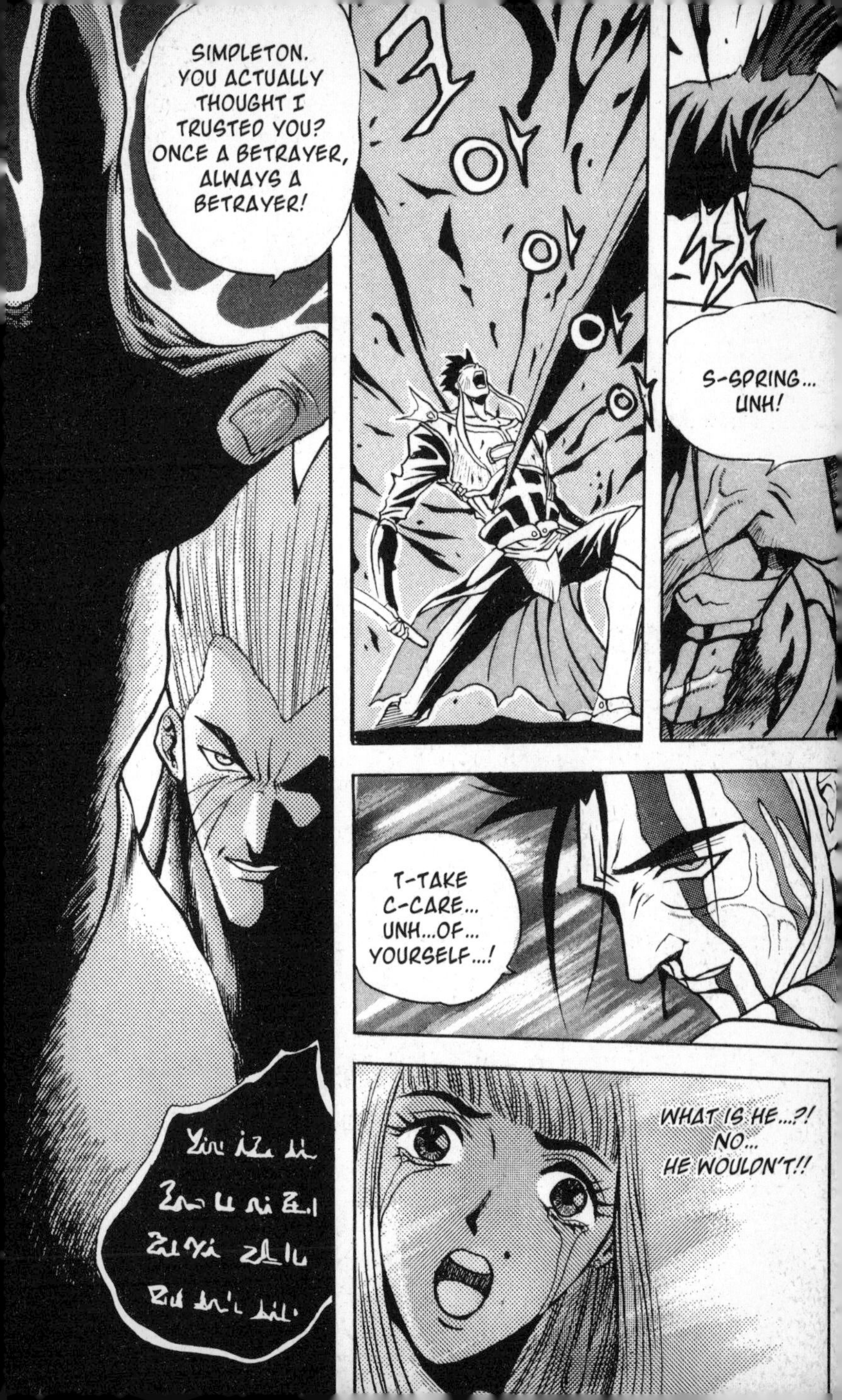
SIMPLETON. YOU ACTUALLY THOUGHT I TRUSTED YOU? ONCE A BETRAYER, ALWAYS A BETRAYER!
S-SPRING... UNH!
T-TAKE C-CARE... UNH...OF... YOURSELF...!
WHAT IS HE...?! NO... HE WOULDN'T!!

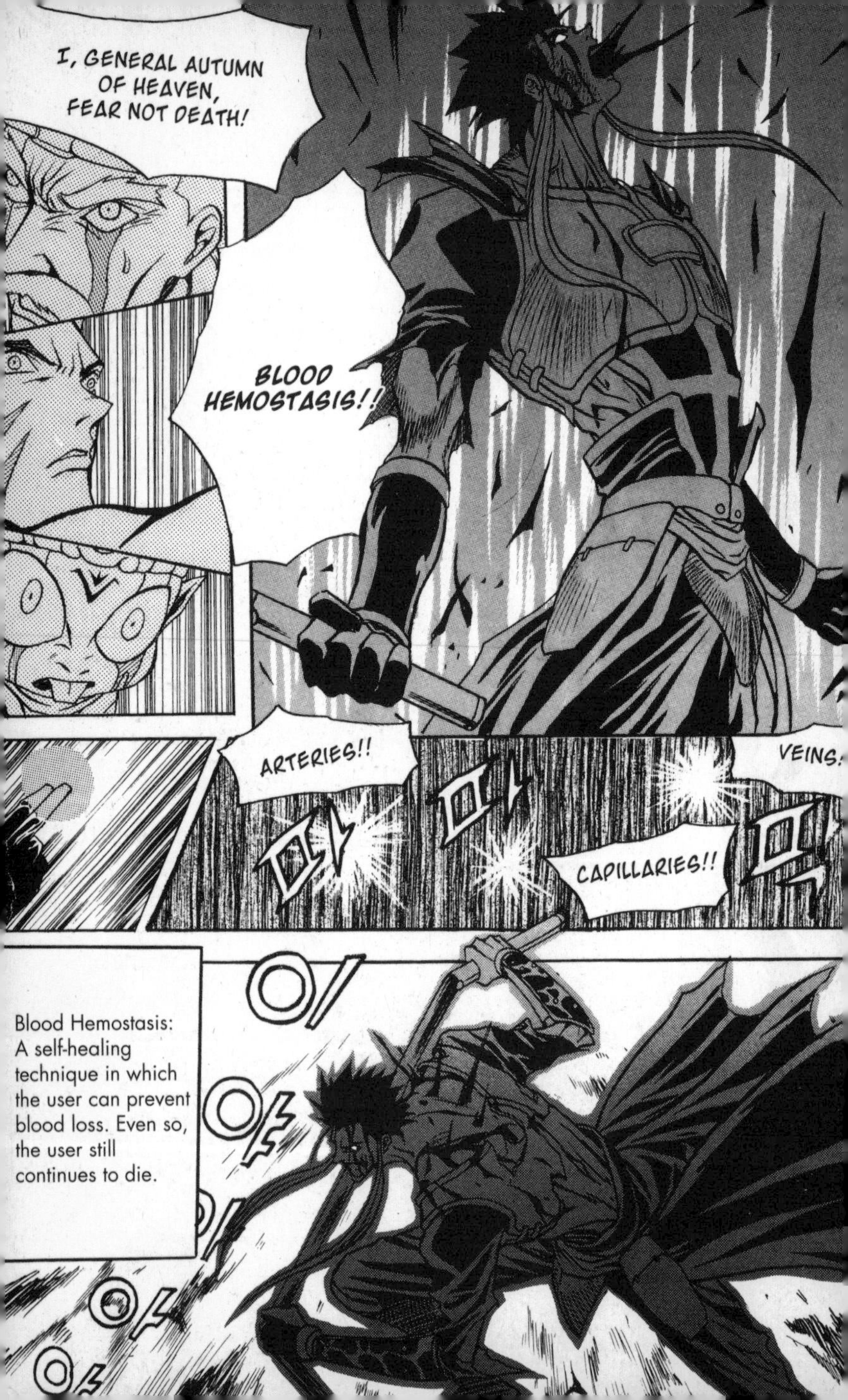
I, GENERAL AUTUMN OF HEAVEN, FEAR NOT DEATH!
BLOOD HEMOSTASIS!!
ARTERIES!!
VEINS!
CAPILLARIES!!
Blood Hemostasis: A self-healing technique in which the user can prevent blood loss. Even so, the user still continues to die.

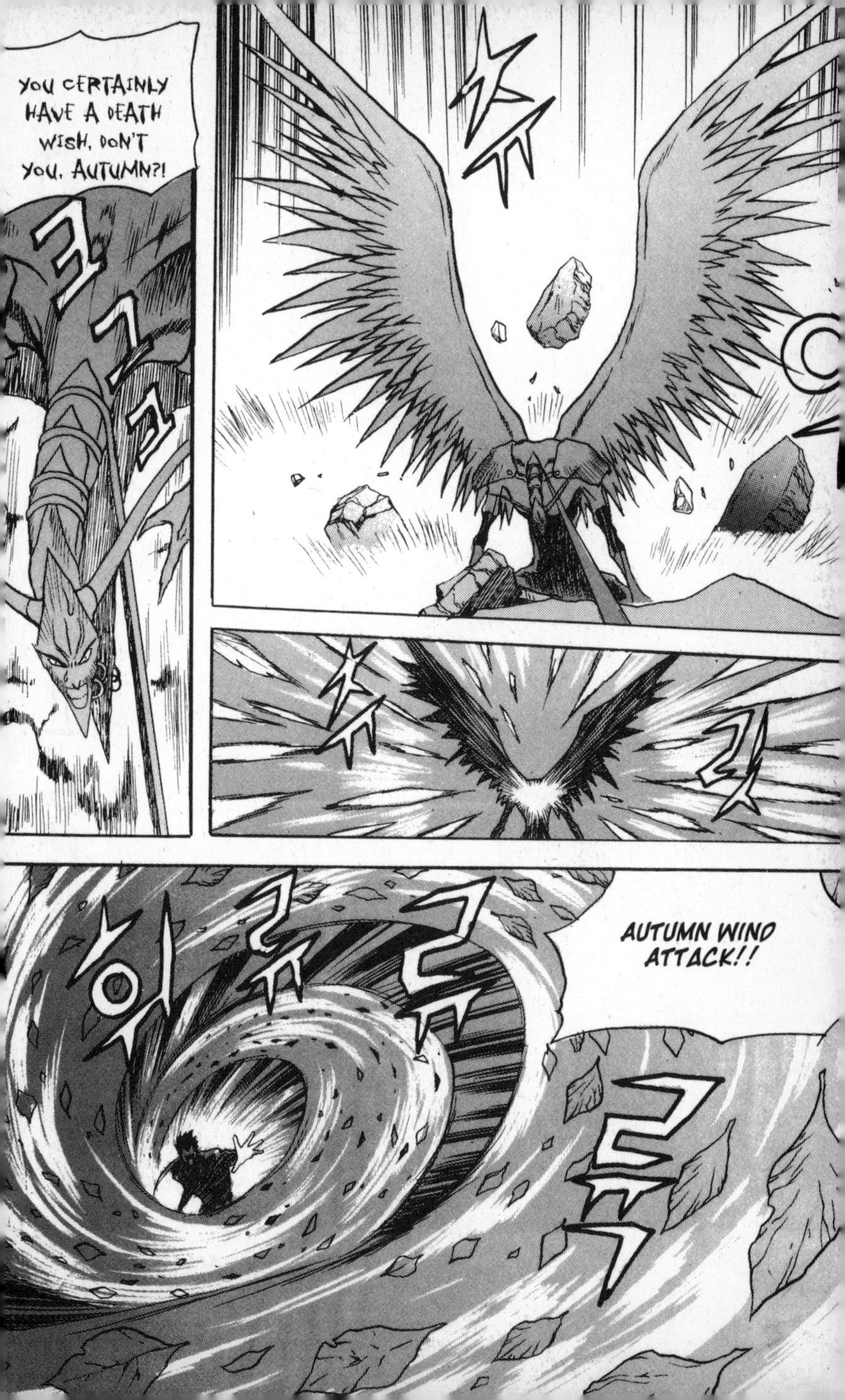
YOU CERTAINLY HAVE A DEATH WISH, DON'T YOU, AUTUMN?!
AUTUMN WIND ATTACK!!

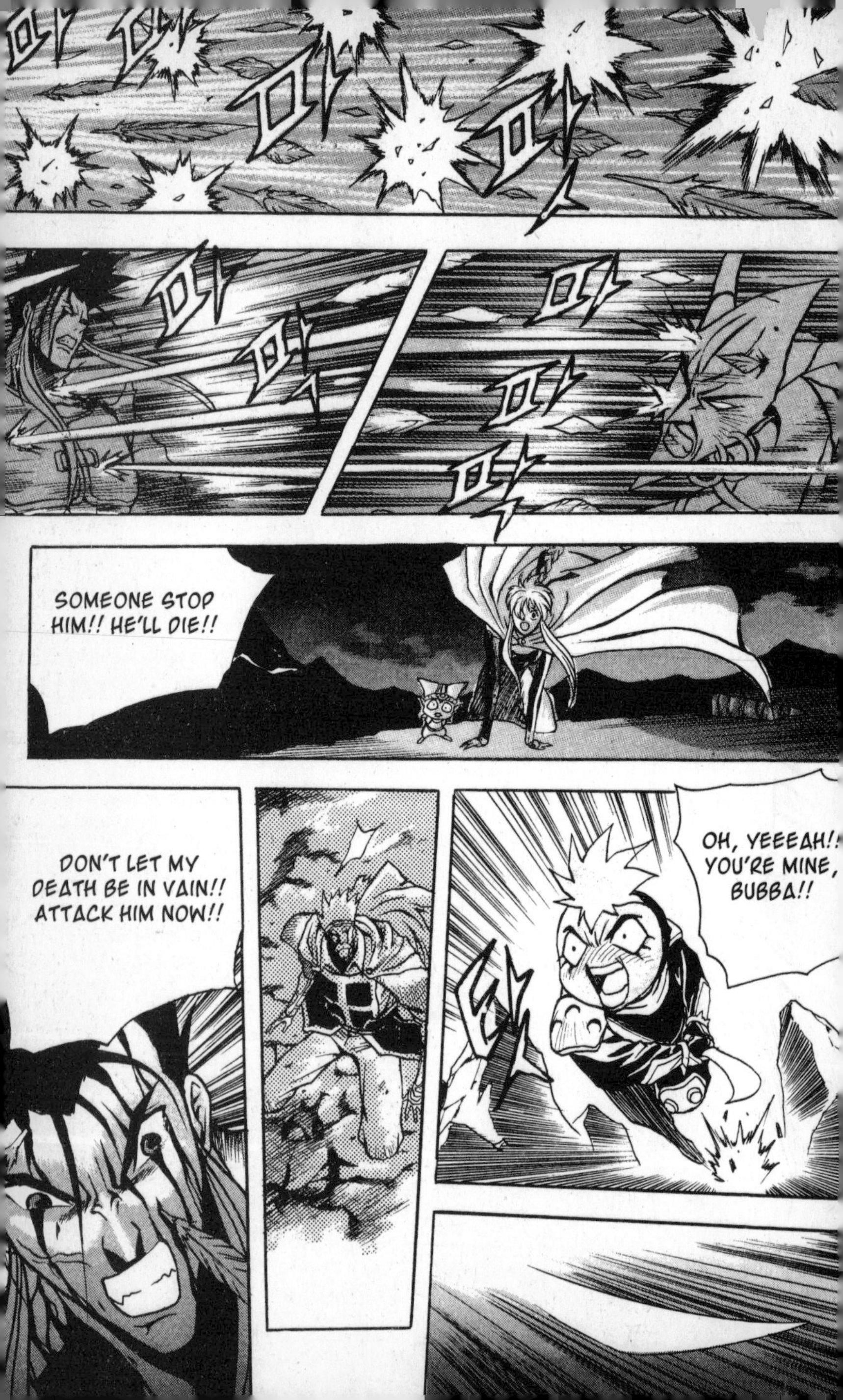
SOMEONE STOP HIM!! HE'LL DIE!!
DON'T LET MY DEATH BE IN VAIN!! ATTACK HIM NOW!!
OH, YEEEAH!! YOU'RE MINE, BUBBA!!

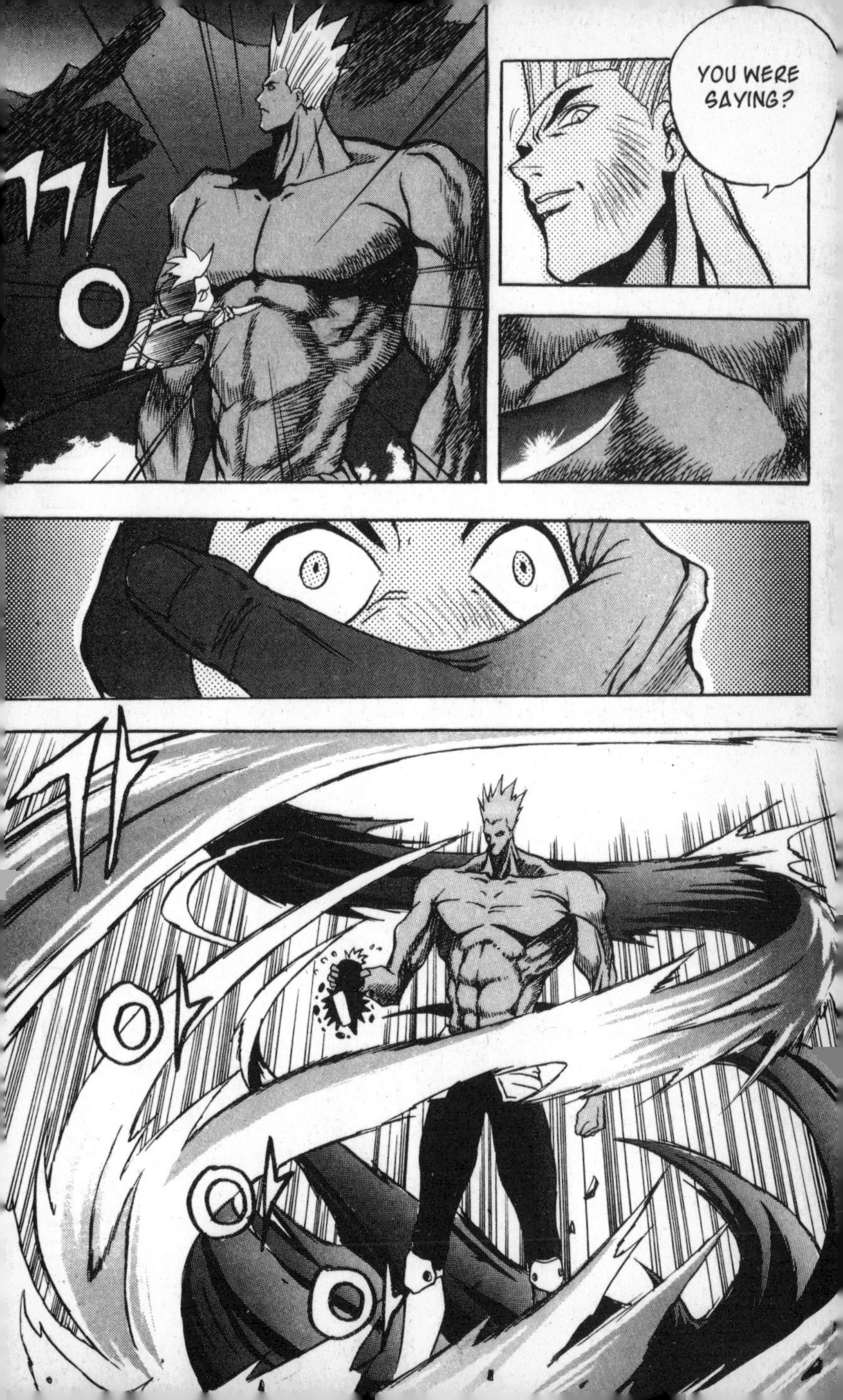
YOU WERE SAYING?

CAREFUL! THIS ISN'T THE SAME BARURUGO FROM THE GREAT WAR!!

HE'S SOMEHOW MANAGED TO AMPLIFY HIS STRENGTH TENFOLD!!

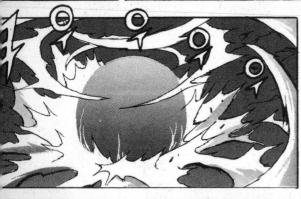

THERE'S ONLY ONE WAY TO GET THE KIDS OUT OF HERE ALIVE...

...BLOOD HEMOSTASIS!!

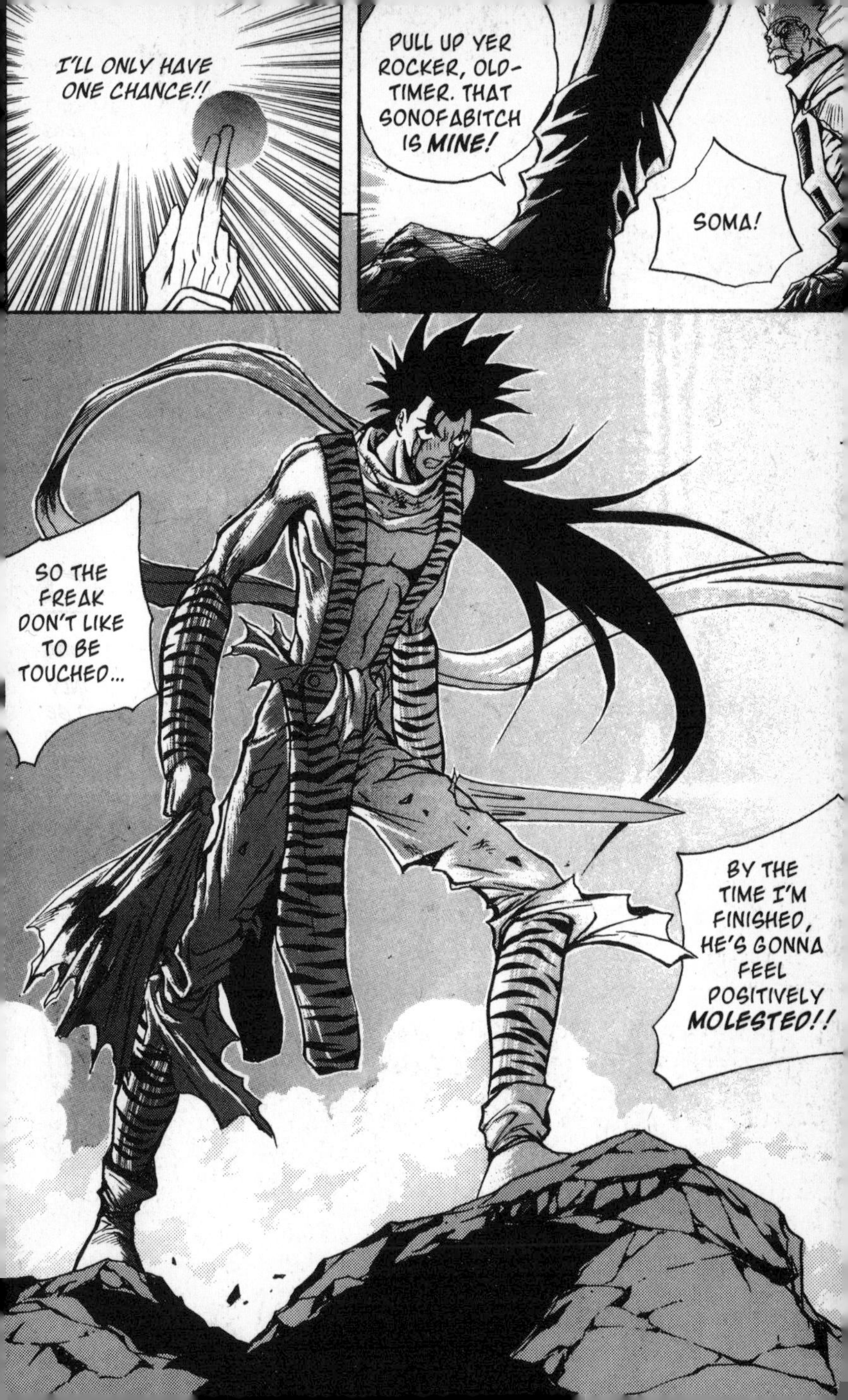
I'LL ONLY HAVE ONE CHANCE!!
PULL UP YER ROCKER, OLD-TIMER. THAT SONOFABITCH IS MINE!
SOMA!
SO THE FREAK DON'T LIKE TO BE TOUCHED...
BY THE TIME I'M FINISHED, HE'S GONNA FEEL POSITIVELY MOLESTED!!

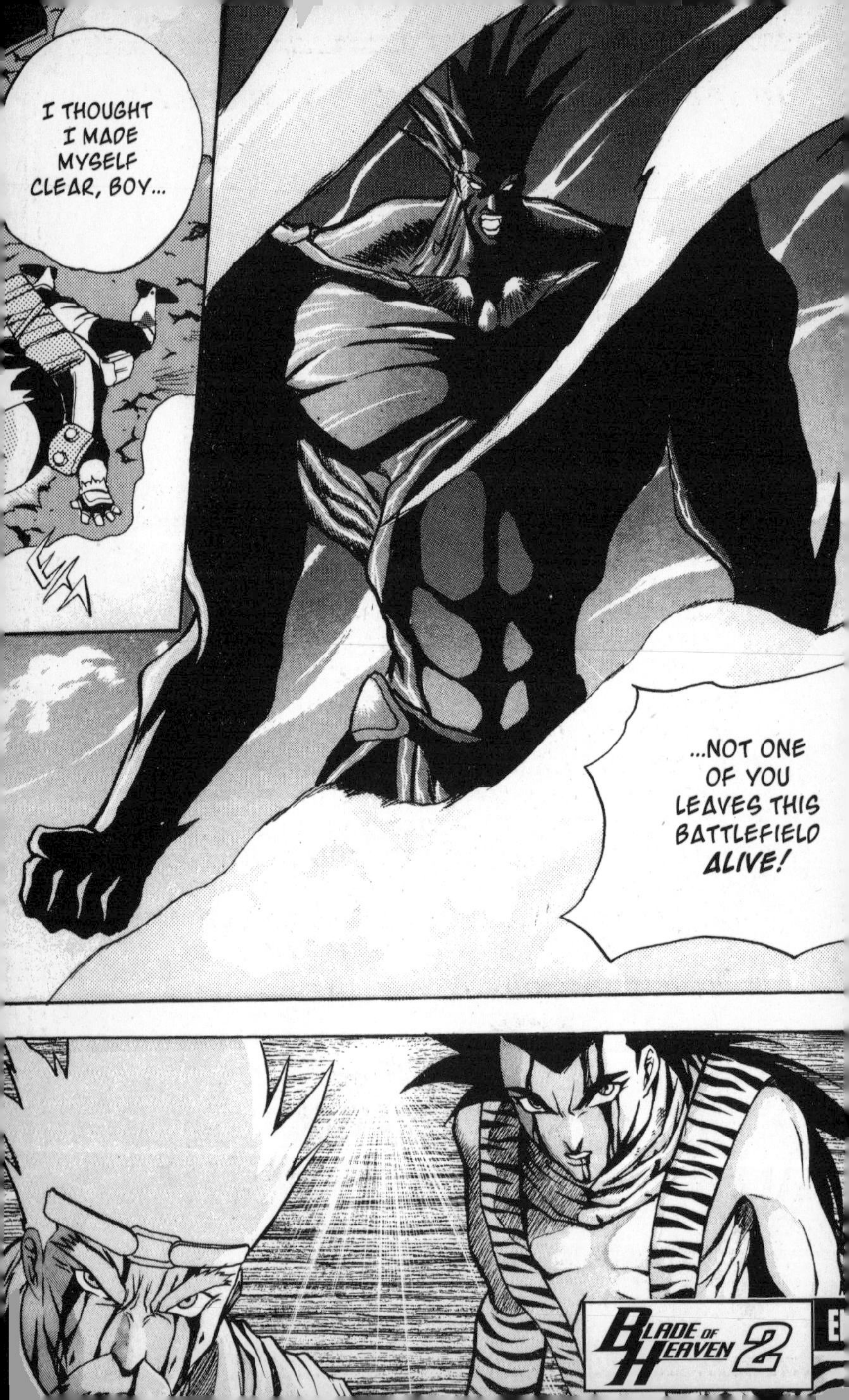
I THOUGHT I MADE MYSELF CLEAR, BOY...
...NOT ONE OF YOU LEAVES THIS BATTLEFIELD ALIVE!

IN THE NEXT BONE-CRUNCHING VOLUME OF

BLADE OF HEAVEN

THE BATTLE AGAINST THE EVIL BARURUGO AND HIS TWISTED LACKEY, DARKLING, REACHES ITS BLOODY ZENITH! DOKSOOMA AND THE VALIANT MAKUMRANG DO THEIR BEST AGAINST THE GROTESQUE DARKLING IN A PITCHED FIGHT TO THE DEATH! SIMULTANEOUSLY, GEN. WINTER, FAT NINJA AND SOMA DESPERATELY STRUGGLE TO BRING DOWN THE SEEMINGLY UNSTOPPABLE BARURUGO. AND JUST AT THE MOMENT WHEN ALL SEEMS LOST FOR OUR HEROES, GEN. SUMMER (A.K.A. GRANNY) SWOOPS IN WITH THE JOURNAL OF THE BLADE OF HEAVEN! WILL SOMA BE CONNECTED WITH THE MYSTICAL BLADE IN TIME? AND WHEN HE IS, WILL ANYONE SURVIVE THE SUBSEQUENT FURY HE WILL UNLEASH?

GET READY TO RUMBLE IN

BLADE OF HEAVEN VOLUME 3!

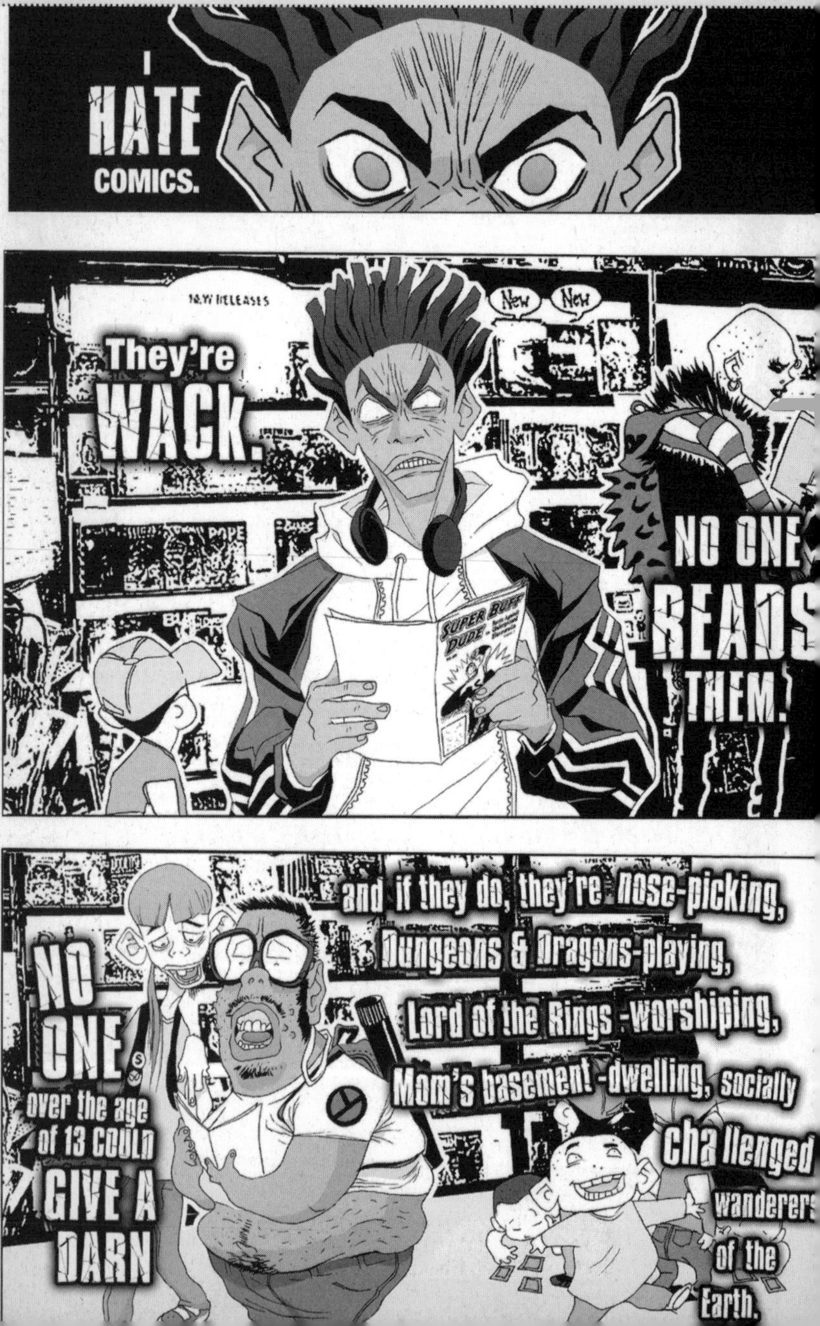
I HATE COMICS.
They're WACK.
New
New
SUPER BUFF DUDE
NO ONE READS THEM.
NO ONE over the age of 13 COULD GIVE A DARN
and if they do, they're nose-picking, Dungeons & Dragons-playing, Lord of the Rings -worshiping, Mom's basement -dwelling, socially challenged wanderers of the Earth.

TOKYOPOP SHOP

WWW.TOKYOPOP.COM/SHOP

HOT NEWS!
Check out the
TOKYOPOP SHOP!
The world's best
collection of manga in
English is now available
online in one place!

RG VEDA

VISITOR

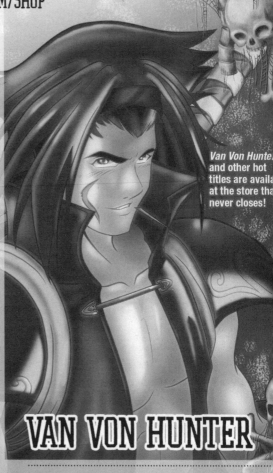

Van Von Hunter
and other hot
titles are availa
at the store tha
never closes!

VAN VON HUNTER

- LOOK FOR SPECIAL OFFERS
- PRE-ORDER UPCOMING RELEASES!
- COMPLETE YOUR COLLECTIONS